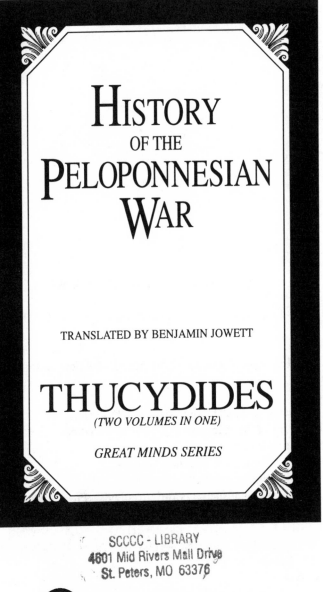

HISTORY
OF THE
PELOPONNESIAN WAR

TRANSLATED BY BENJAMIN JOWETT

THUCYDIDES
(TWO VOLUMES IN ONE)

GREAT MINDS SERIES

Prometheus Books
59 John Glenn Drive
Amherst, New York 14228-2197

Published 1998 by Prometheus Books

59 John Glenn Drive, Amherst, New York 14228–2197,
716–691–0133. FAX: 716–691–0137.

Library of Congress Cataloging-in-Publication Data

Thucydides.
[History of the Peloponnesian War. English]
History of the Peloponnesian War / Thucydides ; translated by
Benjamin Jowett.
    p.   cm. — (Great minds series)
"Two volumes in one."
Originally published: Oxford : Clarendon Press, 1900.
Includes index.
ISBN 1–57392–216–1 (alk. paper)
    I. Jowett, Benjamin, 1817–1893. II. Title. III. Series.
DF229.T4J6   1998
938′.05—dc21
                                                98–17507
                                                CIP

Printed in the United States of America on acid-free paper.

Also Available in Prometheus's Great Minds Paperback Series

Nicolaus Copernicus
On the Revolutions of Heavenly Spheres

Charles Darwin
The Descent of Man

Charles Darwin
The Origin of Species

Albert Einstein
Relativity

Desiderius Erasmus
The Praise of Folly

Michael Faraday
The Forces of Matter

Galileo Galilei
Dialogues Concerning Two New Sciences

Edward Gibbon
On Christianity

Charlotte Perkins Gilman
Women and Economics

Ernst Haeckel
The Riddle of the Universe

William Harvey
*On the Motion of the
Heart and Blood in Animals*

Herodotus
The History

Julian Huxley
Evolutionary Humanism

Thomas Henry Huxley
*Agnosticism and Christianity
and Other Essays*

Edward Jenner
Vaccination against Smallpox

Johannes Kepler
Epitome of Copernican Astronomy and
Harmonies of the World

John Maynard Keynes
*The General Theory of Employment,
Interest, and Money*

Alfred Marshall
Principles of Economics

Isaac Newton
The Principia

Louis Pasteur and Joseph Lister
*Germ Theory and Its Application to
Medicine* and *On the Antiseptic Principle
of the Practice of Surgery*

Ernest Renan
The Life of Jesus

David Ricardo
*Principles of Political Economy
and Taxation*

Adam Smith
Wealth of Nations

Jonathan Swift
A Modest Proposal and Other Satires

Thorstein Veblen
The Theory of the Leisure Class

Voltaire
*A Treatise on Toleration
and Other Essays*

Alfred Russel Wallace
Island Life

H. G. Wells
The Conquest of Time

Andrew D. White
*A History of the Warfare of Science with
Theology in Christendom*

See the back of this volume for a complete list of titles in
Prometheus's Great Books in Philosophy and Great Minds series.

THUCYDIDES was born between 460 and 455 B.C.E. External evidence for his life is scant and unreliable; the best information is that gleaned from Thucydides himself in his *History of the Peloponnesian War.*

He was the son of Olorus, a name which is significant, for it is that of the Thracian king whose daughter was married to Miltiades, the victor of Marathon and the father of the Athenian statesman Cimon (ca. 512–449 B.C.E.). Thucydides' family was therefore related to Cimon in some way, a connection also attested by Thucydides. A further link with Thrace is made by the fact that Thucydides owned property in the mining district there. He came, then, from a family of substance and distinction, and was a member of the leading conservative circle at Athens.

Thucydides tells us that he was a "young man" at the outbreak of hostilities between Athens and Sparta in 431 B.C.E. Between 430 and 427 he caught the plague (whose devastating impact on the Athenians is described in Book 2 of the *History*), but recovered. And in 424 he was serving as one of the city's ten *strategoi*, or generals, charged with safeguarding Athenian interests in the northern Aegean. But he could not save the coastal city of Amphipolis from the attack of the Spartan general Brasidas, as a result of which Thucydides was exiled from Athens for twenty years. Where Thucydides lived during this time is not known for certain, though it is likely that he spent at least part of it at his estate on the mainland opposite the island of Thasos. And he probably traveled, gathering material for his *History.* Thucydides returned to Athens in 404, and died a few years later, around 400.

Thucydides began to research and write his *History* shortly after the war started, and worked on it until his death; indeed, the work was left unfinished. A fanciful tradition recounts that Thucydides' daughter wrote Book 8; still, she may have had something to do with the work's preservation. Also, the present-day division into eight books is not original, but the work of a later editor.

But if the *History* remains unfinished and lacks revision in places, it is a coherent whole whose immediate purpose is clear: to recount the war between Athens and Sparta—its causes and how it brought in its wake a "convulsion" greater than anything yet known.

The first of the "scientific" historians, Thucydides strove for accuracy, which he achieved by having been present at the events he describes or by having interviewed reliable witnesses. He also consulted documentary material when possible. Where complete certainty was lacking, Thucydides recreated events and devised speeches to accord with probability, that is, with what is most likely to have happened, in order to arrive as near as possible to the truth. Thucydides' stress on etiology linked him with the medical and scientific writers. His carefully wrought speeches and vivid characterization put him with the dramatists. This antinomy, almost, between the detached observer and the impassioned poet would help explain the corresponding differences between Thucydides' manner of writing, which ranged from the plainly narrative to the highly oratorical.

Thus did Thucydides wed accuracy and historical probability with dramatic power. Part of the drama, the tragedy, really, of the *History* was to show how Athens' downfall resulted from a failure of leadership following the death of Pericles, Athens' "first citizen" and leader whom Thucydides greatly admired despite the fact that Pericles represented the "democratic" forces while Thucycides' background would link him with the oligarchs. The leaders after Pericles (who died of the plague) committed acts of barbarity and cruelty, e.g., the destruction of the neutral Melians in Book 5. The final disaster for Athens came with the failed Sicilian expedition, described in Books 7 and 8, which illustrates Athens' ruthless expansionism and overreaching ambition. But atrocities occurred among the Spartans as well (e.g., the Spartan siege of Plataea in Book 3). Such episodes on both sides gave Thucydides the clinician and the tragic poet the opportunity to assess the pathology of human behavior and how war unchains the most brutal passions.

Control of human passions, noble or otherwise, lay with the human agents themselves. Unlike Herodotus, who believed that humankind's destiny was governed by divine forces, Thucydides looked toward natural phenomena to find the underlying causes. But human intelligence has its limits, beyond which lies the unseen.

Thucydides realized that the loftiness and the severity of his ideals would prevent his work from becoming a mere showpiece or entertainment. Rather, his aim was to create a "possession for all time." Behind this vaunt lay Thucydides' deeper purpose: to impart a reliable picture of human behavior and motivations, and to display truly the causes of events.

CONTENTS

———◆———

VOLUME I

PAGE

On the Geography of Thucydides xi

Translation:

    Book   I 1

    ,,   Ii 102

    ,,   III 184

VOLUME II

Translation:

    Book   IV 2

    ,,   V 102

    ,,   VI 178

    ,,   VII 262

    ,,   VIII 335

Historical Index to Books I-VIII 421

NOTE ON THE

GEOGRAPHY OF THUCYDIDES

Various difficulties have been found in the geography of Thucydides: his accounts of places are at variance sometimes (1) with facts, sometimes (2) with the statements of later writers. It may be said of his descriptions generally, as of most early descriptions, that they are graphic rather than accurate. When we try to reproduce them in the mind something is wanting. For example, we do not gather from his narrative where the Euryelus was situated by which the Athenians, and also Gylippus, ascended the heights of Epipolae (vi. 97; vii. 2, 43), or how the Syracusan defences lay after the completion of the third counter-wall (vii. 7), or, without some consideration, how the dolphins were placed for the protection of the Athenian ships in the great Syracusan harbour (vii. 38). The topography of battles is often imperfect, and sometimes leads to a difficulty in the explanation of them. The narrative of the battle of Amphipolis leads to the inference (see Arnold's Appendix) that the city was not at the top but on the slope of the hill which Cleon ascended with his army, but this can only be inferred with some uncertainty and is not definitely expressed. Perhaps without maps and plans a better delineation was impossible. The narrative of the second sea-fight in the Crisaean gulf (ii. 90 ff.) is incoherent: for we are not told what happened to that portion of the Peloponnesian fleet which was originally victorious. The manner of the attack which ended in the capture of the first Syracusan counter-wall (vi. 100) is not fully described and can only be inferred; the 'Argive hoplites' who were killed in the Syracusan out-works after the capture of the stockade must have joined the attacking party from one of the two other divisions of the army. Once more, in the calculation of distances the eye or the information of the writer was frequently at fault. For examples see below.

There has been a good deal of controversy on this subject. Even into geography the spirit of party may find a way. Some commentators have been desirous of maintaining the credit of their author, like Dr. Arnold, who was of opinion that 'when Geographers who are also Scholars visit the places of which Thucydides speaks personally, most of the difficulties in his descriptions will vanish.' That remark of course supposes that Thucydides, rightly understood, is generally or always in the right. We may imagine the writer of it to feel what he does not say: 'The most accurate and trustworthy of historians can hardly be imagined to be ignorant as a schoolboy of geography.' And certainly, in his account of Pylos and Sphacteria, Dr. Arnold is ready, in a figure, to work a miracle in order to save the reputation of Thucydides. Changes in the formation of the coast are the 'Deus ex machina' to which he has recourse.

Yet it may very likely be true that Thucydides is far behind Strabo or Pausanias or Stephanus Byzantinus in geography, though his conception of history may be quite unattainable by them. Still greater would be the disparity of his knowledge when compared with that of a modern traveller, or resident in Greece, who has perhaps surveyed and explored places which the historian himself may not have visited. For the knowledge of geography is always growing with time, while history fades into the distance. The materials of the one are increasing, while those of the other are diminishing. The credibility of an author's geography is not therefore to be judged of by the credibility of his history, because in the one far more than in the other he is dependent on the conditions of his age.

In this short note it is not intended to enter into the discussion of particular passages, but rather to urge two general principles : (1) that geographical accuracy is not to be expected from a writer of the age of Thucydides : (2) that the number of his inaccuracies show them to be attributable rather to his ignorance, than to the ignorance of later writers, or of ourselves.

To attempt to reconcile the geography of Thucydides with facts may be the same error in kind, though not in degree, as to try and adapt the drive of Telemachus between Pylos and Sparta to the present condition of the country, or to seek on the sea-shore of Ithaca for the cave by which Odysseus was deposited. As the more familiar features of a scene are likely to be reproduced in the creations of the poet, so the ancient historian will roughly guess distances. But he may often make mistakes about a region with which he was unacquainted, and he will not always be able to judge what amount of description is required in order to place before his readers a just conception of a place or of a battle. There were no surveys of countries or measurements of distances in the age of Herodotus and Thucydides (except along the course of great roads such as the Persian highways), but only the proverbially uncertain measure of a day's journey or of a day's sail (see Thuc. ii. 97, and Arnold's note). There were no correct maps, but only rude delineations such as made Herodotus laugh (iv. 36). The eye was the judge of the distance across a strait or across the entrance of a harbour. Daily experience tells us how seldom the power of judging distances is found in any one who has not been trained by long habit.

Some of the errors or misleading expressions in Thucydides which have suggested the above remarks are the following :—

ii. 86 med. The distance of Rhium in Achaia from Rhium on the opposite coast is said by Thucydides to be less than a mile (7 stadia). According to Col. Leake (Morea, ii. 148) 'the distance is little, if at all, short of a mile and a half,' and would have been considerably greater in ancient times if we assume, as in this particular instance there is reason for thinking, that the sea, owing to the deposits of rivers, has retreated about 250 yards on the south, and somewhat less on the north coast.

iv. 8 med. The southern entrance of the harbour formed by the bay of Navarino is more than three-quarters of a mile in width, and the northern is 132 yards. But according to Thucydides the northern entrance admitted the passage of only two ships, the southern of not more than eight or nine, and the Lacedaemonians had intended to block up both passages by ships placed lengthways [1].

Thucydides also underrates considerably the length of the island, which he describes (iv. 8) as 15 stadia (about 3000 yards), whereas it is really $2\frac{3}{4}$ miles (4800 yards). [Mr. Grundy (see note) points out that the distance from the place where the Athenians must have landed on the bay side of the island to its N. point is about 15 stadia.]

---

[1] [It has been suggested that Thucydides fell into the error by combining the accounts of two informants, one of whom meant by 'the harbour' the lagoon of Osmyn Aga, behind Pylos, and the other the bay of Navarino : and mistook an intended blocking of the N. entrance to the bay of Navarino at both ends (by which a passage from the bay into the lagoon, which may have existed at the time, would also have been closed to the Athenians) for a blocking of the N. and S. entrances. See Mr. G. B. Grundy's admirable monograph on Pylos and Sphacteria. If this be so, the criticism, in the Essay, on Thucydides as a geographer would only be confirmed. It is clear from iv. 8 (τὴν δὲ νῆσον ταύτην φοβούμενοι μὴ ἐξ αὐτῆς τὸν πόλεμον σφίσι ποιῶνται, ὁπλίτας διεβίβασαν ἐς αὐτήν, καὶ παρὰ τὴν ἤπειρον ἄλλους ἔταξαν· οὕτω γὰρ τοῖς Ἀθηναίοις τήν τε νῆσον πολεμίαν ἔσεσθαι τήν τε ἤπειρον, ἀπόβασιν οὐκ ἐχουσαν· τὰ γὰρ αὐτῆς τῆς Πύλου ἔξω τοῦ ἔσπλου πρὸς τὸ πέλαγος ἀλίμενα ὄντα οὐχ ἕξειν ὅθεν ὁρμώμενοι ὠφελήσουσι τοὺς αὑτῶν) that Thucydides believed the Lacedaemonians to have intended to block both entrances of the bay of Navarino. —And it is after all hard to believe that as a fact they did not intend to keep out the Athenian ships by occupying (if not blocking) the S. entrance.]

iv. 57 init. According to Thucydides, Thyrea was situated about 10 stadia from the sea, or about $1\frac{1}{8}$ of a mile. According to Col. Leake (Morea, ii. 492) 'it is at least three times that distance.' Other writers suggest other sites. But there are no remains which agree with the distance mentioned in Thucydides (Bursian, Geographie von Griechenland, ii. p. 70).

vi. 104 med. Gylippus sailing from Tarentum to Sicily was caught by a storm in the Terinaean gulf. But the Terinaean gulf, called also the Sinus Hipponiates, is on the west coast of Italy (Pliny, iii. 72. 5, 10). Κατὰ τὸν Τεριναῖον κόλπον cannot mean 'opposite the Terinaean gulf.'

viii. 88 init. Alcibiades is described as sailing straight from Samos to Phaselis and Caunus on his way to Aspendus, and as returning to Samos from Caunus and Phaselis (108 init.). The inverse order in both cases is the true one. Dr. Arnold supposes the words to mean 'straight to Phaselis, having first touched at Caunus'; 'from Caunus, and before that from Phaselis.' But this explanation is forced in itself, and is rendered impossible by the repetition of the wrong order in the description of the return voyage.

viii. 101 fin. Similarly, Larissa and Hamaxitus are mentioned in a wrong order (see Strabo, xiii. 1. 47, 48, pp. 604, 605).

vi. 72 init. So Naxos and Catana.

iii. 29 med. So Icarus and Myconus.

vii. 19 init. Decelea is said to be distant about 120 stadia (i. e. about fourteen miles) from Athens, and about the same or a little more from Boeotia. In reality it was much nearer Boeotia. It has been suggested that Thucydides is here thinking of the far-off corner of Boeotia at Oropus, from which an important road ran through Decelea (vii. 28 init.) to Athens. Still this would only show how different his mode of expression is from that of a modern writer.

viii. 26 med. Λέρον τὴν πρὸ Μιλήτου νῆσον. But Leros

is forty miles from Miletus. All the MSS. except the Vatican read Ἔλεον, a place which is otherwise unknown. Λέρον is probably correct, and is confirmed by the close connexion which we find existing between Leros and Miletus in the tribute lists (C. I. A. 37, 226, 251, 262, 264). The expression is natural enough for a writer who had in his mind not maps of the Aegean, but the actual voyage past Leros to Miletus.

iii. 4 fin. ὥρμουν ἐν τῇ Μαλέᾳ, πρὸς βορέαν τῆς πόλεως (compare c. 6, περιορμισάμενοι τὸ πρὸς νότον). But, according to Strabo, Malea was at the southern extremity of the island. It is possible however to take πρὸς βορέαν τῆς πόλεως not with ὥρμουν but with ἀποστέλλουσι πρέσβεις τριήρει, referring to the Mytilenaeans, above.

i. 61 med. ἀφικόμενοι ἐς Βέροιαν κἀκεῖθεν ἐπιστρέψαντες. But Beroea was several days' march out of the road from Pydna to Potidaea ; nor could the Athenians possibly have reached Gigonus by slow marches three days after their departure from Beroea (κατ᾽ ὀλίγον δὲ προϊόντες τριταῖοι ἀφίκοντο ἐς Γίγωνον). The generally received correction ἐπὶ Στρέψαν for ἐπιστρέψαντες cannot be considered certain, and does not remove the difficulty about Beroea.

We may also notice that where Thucydides evidently wants to express geographical ideas with precision, as in ii. 9 fin., νῆσοι ὅσαι ἐντὸς Πελοποννήσου καὶ Κρήτης πρὸς ἥλιον ἀνίσχοντα, πᾶσαι αἱ ἄλλαι Κυκλάδες πλὴν Μήλου καὶ Θήρας, or in the description of the island of Cythera, iv. 53 fin., πᾶσα (i. e. either ἡ νῆσος or ἡ Λακωνικὴ) γὰρ ἀνέχει πρὸς τὸ Σικελικὸν καὶ Κρητικὸν πέλαγος, he has caused a great deal of trouble to his interpreters [1]. There is a lesser degree of obscurity in the description of the country about Chimerium (i. 46 fin.), especially the words ῥεῖ δὲ καὶ Θύαμις ποταμός, ὁρίζων τὴν Θεσπρωτίδα καὶ Κεστρίνην, ὧν ἐντὸς ἡ ἄκρα ἀνέχει τὸ Χειμέριον, where ὧν refers not to τὴν Θεσπρωτίδα καὶ Κεστρίνην, but to

---

[1] [In ii. 9 the variations in the text give good ground for suspecting a gloss.]

ποταμῶν, gathered from the previous sentence (scil. the Acheron and the Thyamis).

It is worth while also to compare the description of the kingdom of the Odrysae in ii. 97, which, though not obscure, is cumbrous and very unlike the manner of a modern geographer.

Considering the number of these errors and vague expressions, and the probability that Thucydides from his imperfect means of knowledge would have fallen into them, is it worth while, for the sake of vindicating his credit, either to alter the text, or to assume changes in the face of nature unless there is actual proof of them in each particular case? All that we can reasonably expect of him is that he should be a little in advance of his predecessors, not that he should vie with modern accuracy, or equally with a modern historian be alive to the value of topography, or realize the fulness and minuteness of detail which are required in a describer of places or of military movements.

THUCYDIDES

———•◦•———

BOOK I

THUCYDIDES, an Athenian, wrote the history of the war in which the Peloponnesians and the Athenians fought against one another. He began to write when they first took up arms, believing that it would be great and memorable above any previous war. For he argued that both states were then at the full height of their military power, and he *Greatness of the war.* saw the rest of the Hellenes either siding or intending to side with one or other of them. No movement ever stirred Hellas more deeply than this; it was shared by many of the Barbarians, and might be said even to affect the world at large. The character of the events which preceded, whether immediately or in more remote antiquity, owing to the lapse of time cannot be made out with certainty. ª But, judging from the evidence which I am able to trust after most careful enquiry ª, I should imagine that former ages were not great either in their wars or in anything else.

The country which is now called Hellas was not 2 regularly settled ᵇ in ancient times ᵇ. The people were

———

ª Or, connecting ὤν with μακρότατον: 'But after carrying the enquiry to the furthest point at which any trustworthy evidence can be obtained.' ᵇ Or, taking οὐ πάλαι closely together: 'until recent times.'

migratory, and readily left their homes whenever they were overpowered by numbers. There was no commerce,

Weakness of ancient Hellas: readiness of the early tribes to migrate: the richer districts the more unsettled; some of the poorer, like Attica, in reality the more prosperous.

and they could not safely hold intercourse with one another either by land or sea. The several tribes cultivated their own soil just enough to obtain a maintenance from it. But they had no accumulations of wealth, and did not plant the ground ; for, being without walls, they were never sure that an invader might not come and despoil them. Living in this manner and knowing that they could anywhere obtain a bare subsistence, they were always ready to migrate ; so that they had neither great cities nor any considerable resources. The richest districts were most constantly changing their inhabitants ; for example, the countries which are now called Thessaly and Boeotia, the greater part of the Peloponnesus with the exception of Arcadia, and all the best parts of Hellas. For the productiveness of the land [a] increased the power of individuals ; this in turn was a source of quarrels by which communities [a] were ruined, while at the same time they were more exposed to attacks from without. Certainly Attica, of which the soil was poor and thin, enjoyed a long freedom from civil strife, and therefore retained its original inhabitants. And a striking confirmation of my argument is afforded by the fact [b] that Attica through immigration increased in population more than any other region. For the leading men of Hellas [b], when driven

---

[a] Or, 'gave to some communities greater power; this was a source of quarrels, by which they' etc.   [b] Or, taking ἐς τὰ ἄλλα in another sense : 'that Attica through immigration increased in population quite out of proportion to her increase in other respects ;' or, supplying τὴν Ἑλλάδα and taking μετοικίας in another sense : 'And here is a striking confirmation of my argument that the constant migrations were the cause which prevented the rest of Hellas from increasing equally with Attica. The leading men of Hellas,' etc.

out of their own country by war or revolution, sought an
asylum at Athens; and from the very earliest times, being
admitted to rights of citizenship, so greatly increased
the number of inhabitants that Attica became incapable
of containing them, and was at last obliged to send out
colonies to Ionia.

The feebleness of antiquity is further proved to me by **3**
the circumstance that there appears to
have been no common action in Hellas
before the Trojan War. And I am
inclined to think that the very name
was not as yet given to the whole
country, and in fact did not exist at all

*No unity among the
early inhabitants: no
common name of Hel-
lenes or Barbarians;
or common action in
Hellas before the Trojan
War.*

before the time of Hellen, the son of Deucalion; the
different tribes, of which the Pelasgian was the most
widely spread, gave their own names to different districts.
But when Hellen and his sons became powerful in
Phthiotis, their aid was invoked by other cities, and those
who associated with them gradually began to be called
Hellenes, though a long time elapsed before the name
prevailed over the whole country. Of this Homer affords
the best evidence; for he, although he lived long after the
Trojan War, nowhere uses this name collectively, but
confines it to the followers of Achilles from Phthiotis, who
were the original Hellenes; when speaking of the entire
host he calls them Danaäns, or Argives, or Achaeans.
Neither is there any mention of Barbarians in his poems,
clearly because there were as yet no Hellenes opposed to
them by a common distinctive name. Thus [a] the several
Hellenic tribes (and I mean by the term Hellenes those
who, while forming separate communities, had a common
language, and were afterwards called by a common name)[a],
owing to their weakness and isolation, were never united

---

[a] Or, supplying κληθέντες with both clauses: 'those who successively
acquired the Hellenic name, which first spread among the several tribes
speaking the same language, and afterwards became universal.'

in any great enterprise before the Trojan War. And they only made the expedition against Troy after they had gained considerable experience of the sea.

4　　Minos is the first to whom tradition ascribes the
Beginnings of civilis- possession of a navy. He made him-
ation: Minos conquers self master of a great part of what is
the islands and clears now termed the Hellenic sea; he con-
the sea of pirates.
quered the Cyclades, and was the first coloniser of most of them, expelling the Carians and appointing his own sons to govern in them. Lastly, it was he who, from a natural desire to protect his growing revenues, sought, as far as he was able, to clear the sea of pirates.

5　　For in ancient times both the Hellenes, and those Barbarians, whose homes were on the coast of the mainland or in islands, when they began to find their way to one another by sea had recourse to piracy. They were commanded by powerful chiefs, who took this means of increasing their wealth and providing for their poorer followers. They would fall upon the unwalled and straggling towns, or rather villages, which they plundered, and maintained themselves chiefly by the plunder of them; for, as yet, such an occupation was held to be honourable and not disgraceful. This is proved by the practice of certain tribes on the mainland who, to the present day, glory in piratical exploits, and by the witness of the ancient poets, in whose verses the question is invariably asked of newly-arrived voyagers, whether they are pirates[a]; which implies that neither those who are questioned disclaim, nor those who are interested in knowing censure the occupation. On land also neighbouring communities plundered each other; and there are many parts of Hellas in which the old practices still continue, as for example among the Ozolian Locrians, Aetolians, Acarnanians, and the adjacent regions of the continent. The fashion of wearing arms among these continental tribes is a

---

[a] Od. iii. 73 ff.; ix. 252; Hymn to Apoll. 452 ff.

relic of their old predatory habits. For in ancient times
all Hellenes carried weapons because   *Old customs which*
their homes were undefended and inter-   *are still existing in*
course was unsafe ; like the Barbarians *some parts of the coun-*
                                         try: dress of Athenians
they went armed in their every-day life. *and Spartans.*
And the continuance of the custom in certain parts of the
country indicates that it once prevailed everywhere.

The Athenians were the first who laid aside arms and 6
adopted an easier and more luxurious way of life. Quite
recently the old-fashioned refinement of dress still lingered
among the elder men of their richer class, who wore
under-garments of linen, and bound back their hair in
a knot with golden clasps in the form of grasshoppers ;
and the same customs long survived among the elders of
Ionia, having been derived from their Athenian ancestors.
On the other hand, the simple dress which is now common
was first worn at Sparta ; and there, more than anywhere
else, the life of the rich was assimilated to that of the
people. The Lacedaemonians too were the first who in
their athletic exercises stripped naked and rubbed themselves over with oil. But this was not the ancient custom ;
athletes formerly, even when they were contending at
Olympia, wore girdles about their loins, a practice which
lasted until quite lately, and still prevails among Barbarians, especially those of Asia, where the combatants
in boxing and wrestling matches wear girdles. And many
other customs which are now confined to the Barbarians
might be shown to have existed formerly in Hellas.

In later times, when navigation had become general and 7
wealth was beginning to accumulate,   *Fortified towns begin*
cities were built upon the sea-shore and *to be built; at first in-*
fortified ; peninsulas too were occupied *land, afterwards on the*
                                         sea-shore.
and walled-off with a view to commerce
and defence against the neighbouring tribes. But the
older towns both in the islands and on the continent, in
order to protect themselves against the piracy which so
long prevailed, were built inland ; and there they remain

to this day. For the piratical tribes plundered, not only one another, but all those who, without being seamen, lived on the sea-coast.

8   The islanders were even more addicted to piracy than *The pirates in the* the inhabitants of the mainland. They *islands of Carian or* were mostly Carian or Phoenician *Phoenician origin.* settlers. This is proved by the fact that when the Athenians purified Delos [a] during the Peloponnesian War and the tombs of the dead were opened, more than half of them were found to be Carians. They were known by the fashion of their arms which were buried with them, and by their mode of burial, the same which is still practised among them.

After Minos had established his navy, communication by sea became more general. For, he having expelled the marauders [b] when he colonised the greater part of the islands, the dwellers on the sea-coast began to grow richer and to live in a more settled manner; and some of them, finding their wealth increase beyond their expectations, surrounded their towns with walls. The love of gain made the weaker willing to serve the stronger, [c] and the command of wealth enabled the more powerful to subjugate the lesser cities [c]. This was the state of society which was beginning to prevail at the time of the Trojan War.

9   I am inclined to think that Agamemnon succeeded in *Rise of the Pelo-* collecting the expedition, not because *pidae: the wealth and* the suitors of Helen had bound them-*power which Agamem-* selves by oath to Tyndareus, but *non inherited from At-* because he was the most powerful king *reus and Eurystheus* of his time. [d] Those Peloponnesians *enabled him to assemble* who possess the most accurate traditions *the chiefs who fought at* say that [d] originally Pelops gained his *Troy.* power by the great wealth which he brought with him

---

[a] Cp. iii. 104 init.   [b] Cp. i. 4.   [c] Or, 'and incited the more powerful, who now had wealth at their command, to subjugate the lesser cities.'   [d] Or, 'Those who possess the most accurate traditions respecting the history of Peloponnesus say that' etc.

from Asia into a poor country, whereby he was enabled, although a stranger, to give his name to the Peloponnesus; and that still greater fortune attended his descendants after the death of Eurystheus, king of Mycenae, who was slain in Attica by the Heraclidae. For Atreus the son of Pelops was the maternal uncle of Eurystheus, who, when he went on the expedition, naturally committed to his charge the kingdom of Mycenae. Now Atreus had been banished by his father on account of the murder of Chrysippus. But Eurystheus never returned; and the Mycenaeans, dreading the Heraclidae, were ready to welcome Atreus, who was considered a powerful man and had ingratiated himself with the multitude. So he suc-ceeded to the throne of Mycenae and the other dominions of Eurystheus. Thus the house of Pelops prevailed over that of Perseus.

And it was, as I believe, because Agamemnon inherited this power and also because he was the greatest naval potentate of his time that he was able to assemble the expedition; and the other princes followed him, not from good-will, but from fear. Of the chiefs who came to Troy, he, if the witness of Homer be accepted, brought the greatest number of ships himself, besides supplying the Arcadians with them. In the ' Handing down of the Sceptre ' he is described as ' The king of many islands, and of all Argos [a].' But, living on the mainland, he could not have ruled over any except the adjacent islands (which would not be 'many') unless he had possessed a con-siderable navy. From this expedition we must form our conjectures about the character of still earlier times.

When it is said that Mycenae was but a small place, 10 or that any other city which existed in those days is inconsiderable in our own, this argument will hardly prove that the expedition was not as great as the poets relate and as is commonly imagined. Suppose the city

---

[a] Il. ii. 108.

of Sparta to be deserted, and nothing left but the temples

That the ancient greatness of Mycenae, or of any other city, is not to be estimated by present appearances, proved from a comparison of Athens and Sparta. and the ground-plan, distant ages would be very unwilling to believe that the power of the Lacedaemonians was at all equal to their fame. And yet they own two-fifths of the Peloponnesus, and are acknowledged leaders of the whole, as well as of numerous allies in the rest of Hellas. But their city is not built continuously, and has no splendid temples or other edifices; it rather resembles a group of villages like the ancient towns of Hellas, and would therefore make a poor show. Whereas, if the same fate befell the Athenians, the ruins of Athens would strike the eye, and we should infer their power to have been twice as great as it really is. We ought not then to be unduly sceptical. The greatness of cities should be estimated by their real power and not by appearances. And we may

Homer's account of the number of the forces. fairly suppose the Trojan expedition to have been greater than any which preceded it, although according to Homer, if we may once more appeal to his testimony, not equal to those of our own day. He was a poet, and may therefore be expected to exaggerate; yet, even upon his showing, the expedition was comparatively small. For it numbered, as he tells us, twelve hundred ships, those of the Boeotians [a] carrying one hundred and twenty men each, those of Philoctetes [b] fifty; and by these numbers he may be presumed to indicate the largest and the smallest ships; else why in the catalogue is nothing said about the size of any others? That the crews were all fighting men as well as rowers he clearly implies when speaking of the ships of Philoctetes; for he tells us that all the oarsmen were likewise archers. And it is not to be supposed that many who were not sailors would accompany the expedition, except the kings and principal officers; for the troops had to cross the sea,

---

[a] Il. ii. 509, 510.   [b] Il. ii. 719, 720.

bringing with them the materials of war, in vessels without decks, built after the old piratical fashion. Now if we take a mean between the crews, the invading forces will appear not to have been very numerous when we remember that they were drawn from the whole of Hellas.

The cause of the inferiority was not so much the want 11 of men as the want of money ; the invading army was limited, by the difficulty of obtaining supplies, to such *Considerations respecting the Trojan War.* a number as might be expected to live on the country in which they were to fight. After their arrival at Troy, when they had won a battle (as they clearly did, for otherwise they could not have fortified their camp), even then they appear not to have used the whole of their force, but to have been driven by want of provisions to the cultivation of the Chersonese and to pillage. And in consequence of this dispersion of their forces, the Trojans were enabled to hold out against them during the whole ten years, being always a match for those who remained on the spot. Whereas if the besieging army had brought abundant supplies, and, instead of betaking themselves to agriculture or pillage, had carried on the war persistently with all their forces, they would easily have been masters of the field and have taken the city ; since, even divided as they were, and with only a part of their army available at any one time, they held their ground. Or, again, they might have regularly invested Troy, and the place would have been captured in less time and with less trouble. Poverty was the real reason why the achievements of former ages were insignificant, and why the Trojan War, the most celebrated of them all, when brought to the test of facts, falls short of its fame and of the prevailing traditions to which the poets have given authority.

Even in the age which followed the Trojan War, Hellas 12 was still in process of ferment and settlement, and had no time for peaceful growth. The return of the Hellenes from Troy after their long absence led to many changes :

quarrels too arose in nearly every city, and those who
Southward move- were expelled by them went and
ment in Hellas after founded other cities.   Thus in the
the Trojan War; Boeo- sixtieth year after the fall of Troy, the
tians descend out of Boeotian people, having been expelled
Thessalia; Dorian oc-
cupation of the Pelo- from Arnè by the Thessalians, settled
ponnesus; Ionian and in the country formerly called Cadmeis,
Dorian colonies. but now Boeotia: a portion of the
tribe already dwelt there, and some of these had joined
in the Trojan expedition.   In the eightieth year after
the war, the Dorians led by the Heraclidae conquered the
Peloponnesus.   A considerable time elapsed before Hellas
became finally settled; after a while, however, she recovered tranquillity and began to send out colonies.   The
Athenians colonised Ionia and most of the islands; the
Peloponnesians the greater part of Italy and Sicily, and
various places in Hellas.   These colonies were all founded
after the Trojan War.

13   As Hellas grew more powerful and the acquisition of
Rise of navies in Hel- wealth became more and more rapid,
las: Corinth, Corcyra, the revenues of her cities increased,
Ionia, Samos, Phocaea. and in most of them tyrannies were
established; they had hitherto been ruled by hereditary
kings, having fixed prerogatives.   The Hellenes likewise
began to build navies and to make the sea their element.
The Corinthians are said to have first adopted some-
thing like the modern style of marine, and the oldest
Hellenic triremes to have been constructed at Corinth.
A Corinthian ship-builder, Ameinocles, appears to have
built four ships for the Samians; he went to Samos
B.C. 704. about three hundred years before the end of the Pelo-
Ol. 19. ponnesian War.   And the earliest naval engagement on
record is that between the Corinthians and Corcyraeans
B.C. 664. which occurred about forty years later.   Corinth, being
Ol. 29. seated on an isthmus, was naturally from the first a centre
of commerce; for the Hellenes within and without the
Peloponnese in the old days, when they communicated

chiefly by land, had to pass through her territory in order to reach one another. Her wealth too was a source of power, as the ancient poets testify, who speak of 'Corinth the rich [a].' When navigation grew more common, the Corinthians, having already acquired a fleet, were able to put down piracy; they offered a market both by sea and land, and with the increase of riches the power of their city increased yet more. Later, in the time of Cyrus, the first Persian king, and of Cambyses his son, the Ionians had a large navy; they fought with Cyrus, and were for a time masters of the sea around their own coasts. Polycrates, too, who was a tyrant of Samos in the reign of Cambyses, had a powerful navy and subdued several of the islands, among them Rhenea, which he dedicated to the Delian Apollo [b]. And the Phocaeans, when they were colonising Massalia, defeated the Carthaginians on the sea.

B.C. 559–529.
Ol. 55, 2 – 624.

B.C. 529–522.
Ol. 62, 4 – 64, 4.

B.C. 600.
Ol. 45.

These were the most powerful navies, and even these, which came into existence many generations after the Trojan War, appear to have consisted chiefly of fifty-oared vessels and galleys of war, as in the days of Troy; as yet triremes were not common. But a little before the Persian War and the death of Darius, who succeeded Cambyses, the Sicilian tyrants and the Corcyraeans had them in considerable numbers. No other maritime powers of any consequence arose in Hellas before the expedition of Xerxes. The Aeginetans, Athenians, and a few more had small fleets, and these mostly consisted of fifty-oared vessels. [c] Even the ships which the Athenians built quite recently at the instigation of Themistocles, when they were at war with the Aeginetans

14

Scarcity of triremes. Smallness of the Athenian and Aeginetan fleets.

B.C. 485.
Ol. 73, 4.

---

[a] Il. ii. 570.   [b] Cp. iii. 104 init.   [c] Or, 'It was quite at a recent period, when the Athenians were at war with the Aeginetans and in expectation of the Barbarian, that Themistocles persuaded them to build the ships with which they fought at Salamis; and even these were not completely decked.'

and in expectation of the Barbarian, even these ships with which they fought at Salamis were not completely decked [c].

15   So inconsiderable were the Hellenic navies in recent as *The chief power of* well as in more ancient times. And *Hellas maritime. Wars* yet those who applied their energies to *by land inconsiderable.* the sea obtained a great accession of strength by the increase of their revenues and the extension of their dominion. For they attacked and subjugated the islands, especially when the pressure of population was felt by them. Whereas by land, no conflict of any kind which brought increase of power ever occurred; what wars they had were mere border feuds. Foreign and distant expeditions of conquest the Hellenes never undertook; for they were not as yet ranged under the command of the great states, nor did they form voluntary leagues or make expeditions on an equal footing. Their wars were only the wars of the several neighbouring tribes with one another. The conflict in which the rest of Hellas was most divided, allying itself with one side or the other, was the ancient war between the Chalcidians and Eretrians [a].

16   There were different impediments to the progress of the *Impediments to pro-* different states. The Ionians had at- *gress:* tained great prosperity when Cyrus and B.C. 546. the Persians, having overthrown Croesus and subdued the Ol. 58, 3.   (1) *The rising power* countries between the river Halys and *of the Persians.* the sea, made war against them and en- B.C. 493. slaved the cities on the mainland. Some time afterwards, Ol. 71, 4. Darius, strong in the possession of the Phoenician fleet, conquered the islands also.

17   Nor again did the tyrants of the Hellenic cities extend *(2) The petty aims* their thoughts beyond their own in- *and cautious natures* terest, that is, the security of their per- *of the tyrants.* sons, and the aggrandisement of themselves and their families. They were extremely cautious in the administration of their government, and nothing

---

[a] Herod. v. 99.

considerable was ever effected by them; except in wars with their neighbours, as in Sicily, where their power attained its greatest height. Thus for a long time everything conspired to prevent Hellas from uniting in any great action and to paralyse enterprise in the individual states.

At length the tyrants both at Athens and in the rest of Hellas (which had been under their dominion long before Athens), at least the greater number of them, and with the exception of the Sicilian the last who *They were at length overthrown by Sparta, which for four hundred years has been well governed.* ever ruled, were put down by the Lacedaemonians. For although Lacedaemon, after the conquest[a] of the country by the Dorians who now inhabit it, remained long unsettled, and indeed longer than any country which we know, nevertheless she obtained good laws at an earlier period than any other, and has never been subject to tyrants; she has preserved the same form of government for rather more than four hundred years, reckoning to the end of the Peloponnesian War. It was the excellence of her constitution which gave her power, and thus enabled her to regulate the affairs of other states. Not long after the overthrow of the tyrants by the Lacedaemonians, the battle of Marathon was fought between the Athenians and the Persians; ten years later, the Barbarian returned with the vast armament which was to enslave Hellas. In the greatness of the impending danger, the Lacedaemonians, who were the most powerful state in Hellas, assumed the lead of the confederates, while the Athenians, as the Persian host advanced, resolved to forsake their city, broke up their homes, and, taking to their ships, became seamen. The *The Hellenes, who had been united in resisting the Persian, soon broke up into two confederacies.* Barbarian was repelled by a common effort; but soon the Hellenes, [b]as well those who had

18

B.C. 510.
Ol. 67, 3.

B.C. 804–404.
Ol. 95.

B.C. 490.
Ol. 72, 3.
B.C. 480.
Ol. 75.

---

[a] Reading κτῆσιν, not κτίσιν.   [b] Or, 'as well those who had revolted from the King, as those who had joined with him.'

revolted from the King as those who formed the original confederacy [b], took different sides and became the allies either of the Athenians or of the Lacedaemonians; for these were now the two leading powers, the one strong by land and the other by sea. The league between them was of short duration; they speedily quarrelled and, with their respective allies, went to war. Any of the other Hellenes who had differences of their own now resorted to one or other of them. So that from the Persian to the Peloponnesian War, the Lacedaemonians and the Athenians were perpetually fighting or making peace, either with one another or with their own revolted allies; thus they attained military efficiency, and learned experience in the school of danger.

19   The Lacedaemonians did not make tributaries of those

Different character of the Athenian and Spartan league.

who acknowledged their leadership, but took care that they should be governed by oligarchies in the exclusive interest of Sparta. The Athenians, on the other hand, after a time deprived the subject cities of their ships and made all of them pay a fixed tribute, except Chios and Lesbos [a]. And the single power [b] of Athens [b] at the beginning of this war was greater than that of Athens and Sparta together at their greatest, while the confederacy remained intact.

20   Such are the results of my enquiries, [c] though the

Vulgar errors.

early history of Hellas is of a kind which forbids implicit reliance on every particular of the evidence [c]. Men do not discriminate, and are too ready to receive ancient traditions about their own as well as about other countries. For example, most

---

[a] Cp. i. 96, 99; iii. 39 init.; vi. 85 med.; vii. 57 init.   [b] Or, 'either of Athens or Sparta.'   [c] Or (1), 'Though they may not obtain entire credit, even when the proofs of them are all set down in order.' Or (2), 'Though they will not readily be believed upon a bare recital of all the proofs of them.' Or (3), 'Though it is difficult to set down all the proofs in order, so as to make the account credible.'

Athenians think that Hipparchus was actually tyrant when B.C. 514.
he was slain by Harmodius and Aristogeiton; they are Ol. 66, 3.
not aware that Hippias was the eldest of the sons of Peisi-
stratus, and succeeded him, and that Hipparchus and
Thessalus were only his brothers [n].   At the last moment,
Harmodius and Aristogeiton suddenly suspected that Hippias had been forewarned by some of their accomplices.
They therefore abstained from attacking him, but, wishing
to do something before they were seized, and not to risk
their lives in vain, they slew Hipparchus, with whom they
fell in near the temple called Leocorium as he was
marshalling the Panathenaic procession.   There are many
other matters, not obscured by time, but contemporary,
about which the other Hellenes are equally mistaken.   For
example, they imagine that the kings of Lacedaemon in
their council have not one but two votes each [b], and that
in the army of the Lacedaemonians there is a division
called the Pitanate division [c]; whereas they never had
anything of the sort.   So little trouble do men take in the
search after truth; so readily do they accept whatever
comes first to hand.

Yet any one who upon the grounds which I have given 21
arrives at some such conclusion as my   *Uncertainty of early*
own about those ancient times, would   *history. If estimated by*
not be far wrong.   He must not be   *facts the Peloponnesian*
misled by the exaggerated fancies of   *greater than any pre-*
                                         ceding war.
the poets, or by the tales of chroniclers who seek to
please the ear rather than to speak the truth.   Their
accounts cannot be tested by him; and most of the facts in
the lapse of ages have passed into the region of romance.
At such a distance of time he must make up his mind to be
satisfied with conclusions resting upon the clearest evidence
which can be had.   And, though men will always judge
any war in which they are actually fighting to be the
greatest at the time, but, after it is over, revert to their

---

[a] Cp. vi. 54 seqq.   [b] Herod. vi. 57.   [c] Herod. ix. 53.

admiration of some other which has preceded, still the Peloponnesian, if estimated by the actual facts, will certainly prove to have been the greatest ever known.

22   As to the speeches which were made either before or

The speeches could not be exactly reported. Great pains taken to ascertain the truth about events.

during the war, it was hard for me, and for others who reported them to me, to recollect the exact words. I have therefore put into the mouth of each speaker the sentiments proper to the occasion, expressed as I thought he would be likely to express them, while at the same time I endeavoured, as nearly as I could, to give the general purport of what was actually said. ✗Of the events of the war I have not ventured to speak from any chance information, nor according to any notion of my own ; I have described nothing but what I either saw myself, or learned from others of whom I made the most careful and particular enquiry. The task was a laborious one, because eye-witnesses of the same occurrences gave different accounts of them, as they remembered or were interested in the actions of one side or the other. And very likely the strictly historical character of my narrative may be disappointing to the ear. But if he who desires to have before his eyes a true picture of the events which have happened, and of the like events which may be expected to happen hereafter in the order of human things, shall pronounce what I have written to be useful, then I shall be satisfied. My history is an everlasting possession, not a prize composition which is heard and forgotten.

23   The greatest achievement of former times was the

Length of the war, which was attended by all sorts of calamities, ordinary and extraordinary. Among the latter might be enumerated earthquakes, eclipses, droughts, and lastly, the plague.

Persian War ; yet even this was speedily decided in two battles by sea and two by land. But the Peloponnesian War was a protracted struggle, and attended by calamities such as Hellas had never known within a like period of time. ✗Never were so many cities captured and depopulated—some by Barbarians, others by Hellenes themselves fighting against one another; and several of them after their capture were repeopled by strangers. Never were exile and slaughter more frequent, whether in the war or brought about by civil strife. And traditions which had often been current before, but rarely verified by fact, were now no longer doubted. For there were earthquakes unparalleled in their extent and fury, and eclipses of the sun more numerous than are recorded to have happened in any former age; there were also in some places great droughts causing famines, and lastly the plague which did immense harm and destroyed numbers of the people. All these calamities fell upon Hellas simultaneously with the war, which began when the Athenians and Peloponnesians violated the thirty years' truce concluded by them after the recapture of Euboea[a]. Why they broke it and what were the grounds of quarrel I will first set forth, that in time to come no man may be at a loss to know what was the origin of this great war. The real though unavowed cause I believe to have been the growth of the Athenian power, which terrified the Lacedaemonians and forced them into war; but the reasons publicly alleged on either side were as follows.

The city of Epidamnus is situated on the right hand as you sail up the Ionian Gulf. The neighbouring inhabitants are the Tau- lantians, a barbarian tribe of the Illyrian race. The place was colonised by the Corcyraeans, but under the leadership of a Corinthian, Phalius, son of Eratocleides, who was of the lineage of Heracles; he was invited, according to ancient custom, from the mother city, and Corinthians and other Dorians joined in the colony. In process of time Epidamnus became great and populous, but there followed a long period of civil commotion, and the city is said to have been brought low in a war against the neighbouring

24.

The story of Epi- damnus. Civil strife and war with the bar- barians.

---

[a] Cp. i. 115, 146.

barbarians, and to have lost her ancient power. At last, shortly before the Peloponnesian War, the notables were overthrown and driven out by the people ; the exiles went over to the barbarians, and, uniting with them, plundered the remaining inhabitants both by sea and land. These,

B.C. 435 or 434. Ol. 86, 2 or 3.

The prayer of the Epidamnians for help is rejected by their mother-city Corcyra.

finding themselves hard pressed, sent an embassy to the mother-city Corcyra, begging the Corcyraeans not to leave them to their fate, but to reconcile them to the exiles and settle the war with the barbarians. The ambassadors came, and sitting as suppliants in the temple of Herè preferred their request ; but the Corcyraeans would not listen to them, and they returned without

25 success. The Epidamnians, finding that they had no hope of assistance from Corcyra, knew not what to do, and sending to Delphi enquired of the God whether they should deliver up the city to their original founders, the Corinthians, and endeavour to obtain aid from them. The God replied that they should, and bade them place them-

They place them-selves under the pro-tection of Corinth.

selves under the leadership of the Corinthians. So the Epidamnians went to Corinth, and informing the Corinthians of the answer which the oracle had given, delivered up the city to them. They reminded them that the original leader of the colony was a citizen of Corinth ; and implored the Corinthians to come and help them, and not leave them to their fate. The Corinthians took up their cause, partly in vindication of their own rights (for they considered that Epidamnus belonged to them quite as much as to the Corcyraeans), partly too because they hated the Corcyraeans, who were their own colony but slighted them. In their common festivals they would not allow them the customary privileges of founders, and at their sacrifices denied to a Corinthian the right of receiving first the lock of hair cut from the head of the victim, an honour usually granted by colonies to a representative of the mother-country. In fact they despised the Corinthians, for they were more than a match for them in military strength, and as rich as any state then existing in Hellas. They would often boast that on the sea they were very far superior to them, and would appropriate to themselves the naval renown of the Phaeacians, who were the ancient inhabitants of the island. Such feelings led them more and more to strengthen their navy, which was by no means despicable ; for they had a hundred and twenty triremes when the war broke out.

Irritated by these causes of offence, the Corinthians 26 were too happy to assist Epidamnus ; accordingly they invited any one who was willing to settle there, and for the protection of the colonists despatched with them Ambracian and Leucadian troops and a force of their own. All these they sent by land as far as Apollonia, which is a colony of theirs, fearing that if they went by sea the Corcyraeans might oppose their passage. Great was the rage of the Corcyraeans when they discovered that the settlers and the troops had entered Epidamnus and that the colony had been given up to the Corinthians. They immediately set sail with five and twenty ships, followed by a second fleet, and in insulting terms bade the Epidamnians receive the exiled oligarchs, who had gone to Corcyra and implored the Corcyraeans to restore them, appealing to the tie of kindred and pointing to the sepulchres of their common ancestors[a]. They also bade them send away the troops and the new settlers. But the Epidamnians would not listen to their demands. Whereupon the Corcyraeans attacked them with forty ships. They were accompanied by the exiles whom they were to restore, and had the assistance of the native Illyrian troops. They sat down before the city, and made proclamation that any Epidamnian who chose, and the foreigners, might depart in

The Corinthians send troops and colonists to Epidamnus. The Corcyraeans demand their dismissal ; on being refused they besiege the city.

------

[a] Cp. iii. 58 med., 59 init.

safety, but that all who remained would be treated as
enemies. This had no effect, and the Corcyraeans proceeded to invest the city, which is built upon an isthmus.

27   When the news reached the Corinthians that Epidamnus

The Corinthians pre- was besieged, they equipped an army
pare for war and pro- and proclaimed that a colony was to be
claim a colony to Epi-
damnus. Megara and sent thither; all who wished might go
other friendly cities fur- and enjoy equal rights of citizenship;
nish ships. but any one who was unwilling to sail
at once might remain at Corinth, and, if he made a deposit
of fifty Corinthian drachmae, might still have a share in
the colony[a]. Many sailed, and many deposited the money.
The Corinthians also sent and requested the Megarians to
assist them with a convoy in case the Corcyraeans should
intercept the colonists on their voyage. The Megarians
accordingly provided eight ships, and the Cephallenians
of Palè four; the Epidaurians, of whom they made a similar
request, five; the Hermionians one; the Troezenians two;
the Leucadians ten; and the Ambraciots eight. Of the
Thebans and Phliasians they begged money, and of the
Eleans money, and ships without crews. On their own
account they equipped thirty ships and three thousand
hoplites.

28   When the Corcyraeans heard of their preparations they

The Corcyraeans pro- came to Corinth, taking with them Lace-
pose arbitration, offering daemonian and Sicyonian envoys, and
until a decision be given
to withdraw their troops summoned the Corinthians to withdraw
if the Corinthians with- the troops and the colonists, telling
draw theirs, or to allow them that they had nothing to do with
both to remain at Epi- Epidamnus. If they made any claim
damnus by agreement.
to it, the Corcyraeans expressed them-
selves willing to refer the cause for arbitration to such
Peloponnesian states as both parties should agree upon,
and their decision was to be final; or, they were willing

---

[a] The sum would amount to £2 15s. 4d., or to £1 2s. 6d., according
to the two systems of reckoning discussed in the note on iii. 70, q. v.

to leave the matter in the hands of the Delphian oracle. But they deprecated war, and declared that, if war there must be, they would be compelled by the Corinthians in self-defence to discard their present friends and seek others whom they would rather not, for help they must have. The Corinthians replied that if the Corcyraeans would withdraw the ships and the barbarian troops they would consider the matter, but that it would not do for them to be litigating while Epidamnus and the colonists were in a state of siege. The Corcyraeans rejoined that they would consent to this proposal if the Corinthians on their part would withdraw their forces from Epidamnus: [a] or again, they were willing that both parties should remain[a] on the spot, and that a truce should be made until the decision was given.

The Corinthians turned a deaf ear to all these overtures, 29 and, when their vessels were manned and their allies had arrived, they sent a herald before them to declare war, and set sail for Epidamnus with seventy-five ships and two thousand hoplites, intending to give battle to the Corcyraeans. Their fleet was commanded *The Corinthians refuse, and declare war. Sailing towards Epidamnus they are met and attacked by the Corcyraeans and completely defeated. On the same day Epidamnus surrenders.* by Aristeus the son of Pellichus, Callicrates the son of Callias, and Timanor the son of Timanthes; the land forces by Archetimus the son of Eurytimus, and Isarchidas the son of Isarchus. When they arrived at Actium in the territory of Anactorium, at the mouth of the Ambracian gulf, where the temple of Apollo stands, the Corcyraeans sent a herald to meet them in a small boat forbidding them to come on. Meanwhile their crews got on board; they had previously put their fleet in repair, and strengthened the old ships with cross-timbers, so as to make them serviceable. The herald brought back no message of peace

---

[a] Or, 'or again, they would agree to arbitration on the condition that both parties should remain ' etc.

from the Corinthians. The Corcyraean ships, numbering
eighty (for forty out of the hundred and twenty were
engaged in the blockade of Epidamnus), were now fully
manned ; these sailed out against the Corinthians and,
forming line, fought and won a complete victory over
them, and destroyed fifteen of their ships. On the very
same day the forces besieging Epidamnus succeeded in
compelling the city to capitulate, the terms being that the
Corinthians until their fate was determined should be
imprisoned and the strangers sold.

30   After the sea-fight the Corcyraeans raised a trophy on
The   Corcyraeans,   Leucimnè, a promontory of Corcyra,
having command of   and put to death all their prisoners with
the sea, plunder the   the exception of the Corinthians, whom
allies of Corinth.   they kept in chains. The defeated
Corinthians and their allies then returned home, and the
Corcyraeans (who were now masters of the Ionian sea),
sailing to Leucas, a Corinthian colony, devastated the
country. They also burnt Cyllenè, where the Eleans had
their docks, because they had supplied the Corinthians
with money and ships. And, during the greater part of
the summer after the battle, they retained the command of
the sea and sailed about plundering the allies of the
Corinthians. But, before the season was over, the Corinthians, perceiving that their allies were suffering, sent
At length the Corin- out a fleet and took up a position at
thians form a camp to Actium and near the promontory of
protect them.   Cheimerium in Thesprotia, that they
might protect Leucas and other friendly places. The
Corcyraeans with their fleet and army stationed themselves on the opposite coast at Leucimnè. Neither party
attacked the other, but during the remainder of the summer
they maintained their respective stations, and at the approach of winter returned home.

31   For the whole year after the battle and for a year after
B.C. 435, that, the Corinthians, exasperated by the war with Corcyra,
434.
Ol. 86, 2, 3. were busy in building ships. They took the utmost pains

to create a great navy: rowers were collected from the
Peloponnesus and from the rest of
Hellas by the attraction of pay. The
Corcyraeans were alarmed at the report of their preparations. They reflected that they had not enrolled
themselves in the league either of the
Athenians or of the Lacedaemonians, and that allies in
Hellas they had none. They determined to go to Athens,
join the Athenian alliance, and get what help they could
from them. The Corinthians, hearing of their intentions,
also sent ambassadors to Athens, fearing, lest the combination of the Athenian and Corcyraean navies might prevent
them from bringing the war to a satisfactory termination.
Accordingly an assembly was held at which both parties
came forward to plead their respective causes ; and first
the Corcyraeans spoke as follows :—

The Corinthians pre-
pare to renew the war,
and the Corcyraeans in
alarm send an embassy
to Athens, whither they
are followed by Corin-
thian envoys.

B.C. 433.
Ol. 86, 4.

'Men of Athens, those who, like ourselves, come to
others who are not their allies and to
whom they have never rendered any
considerable service and ask help of them, are bound to
show, in the first place, that the granting of their request
is expedient, or at any rate not inexpedient, and, secondly,
that their gratitude will be lasting. If they fulfil neither
requirement they have no right to complain of a refusal.
Now the Corcyraeans, when they sent us hither to ask for
an alliance, were confident that they could establish to
your satisfaction both these points. But, unfortunately,
we have had a practice alike inconsistent with the request
which we are about to make and contrary to our own
interest at the present moment :— Inconsistent; for hitherto
we have never, if we could avoid it, been the allies of
others, and now we come and ask you to enter into an
alliance with us :— Contrary to our interest; for through
this practice we find ourselves isolated in our war with the
Corinthians. The policy of not making alliances lest they
should endanger us at another's bidding, instead of being

32

Speech of the Corcy-
raeans.

wisdom, as we once fancied, has now unmistakably proved

Our neutrality was a mistake, and has left us isolated at the mercy of the Corinthians and their allies. to be weakness and folly. True, in the last naval engagement we repelled the Corinthians single-handed. But now they are on the point of attacking us with a much greater force which they have drawn together from the Peloponnesus and from all Hellas. We know that we are too weak to resist them unaided, and may expect the worst if we fall into their hands. We are therefore compelled to ask assistance of you and of all the world; and you must not be hard upon us if now, renouncing our indolent neutrality which was an error but not a crime, we dare to be inconsistent.

33   'To you at this moment the request which we are making

We ask the aid of Athens, who will thus assist the oppressed, and gain our undying affection. She should not reject the offer of the Corcyraean navy. offers a glorious opportunity. In the first place, you will assist the oppressed and not the oppressors; secondly, you will admit us to your alliance at a time when our dearest interests are at stake, and will lay up a treasure of gratitude in our memories which will have the most abiding of all records. Lastly, we have a navy greater than any but your own. Reflect; what good fortune can be more extraordinary, what more annoying to your enemies than the voluntary accession of a power for whose alliance you would have given any amount of money and could never have been too thankful? This power now places herself at your disposal; you are to incur no danger and no expense, and she brings you a good name in the world, gratitude from those who seek your aid, and an increase of your own strength. Few have ever had all these advantages offered them at once; equally few when they come asking an alliance are able to give in the way of security and honour as much as they hope to receive.

'And if any one thinks that the war in which our services may be needed will never arrive, he is mistaken. He does not see that the Lacedaemonians, fearing the growth

of your empire, are eager to take up arms, and that the
Corinthians, who are your enemies,
are all-powerful with them. They *For war is imminent.*
begin with us, but they will go on to you, that we may
not stand united against them in the bond of a common
enmity; they will not miss the chance of weakening us
or strengthening themselves. And it is our business to
strike first, we offering and you accepting our alliance,
and to forestall their designs instead of waiting to counteract them.

'If they say that we are their colony and that therefore 34
you have no right to receive us, they *True, we are a colony*
should be made to understand that all *of the Corinthians, but*
colonies honour their mother-city when *that is no reason why*
we should be wronged
she treats them well, but are estranged *by them.*
from her by injustice. For colonists are not meant to be
the servants but the equals of those who remain at home.
And the injustice of their conduct to us is manifest : for
we proposed an arbitration in the matter of Epidamnus,
but they insisted on prosecuting their quarrel by arms and
would not hear of a legal trial [a]. When you see how they
treat us who are their own kinsmen, take warning : if they
try deception, do not be misled by them ; and if they make
a direct request of you, refuse. For he passes through
life most securely who has least reason to reproach himself with complaisance to his enemies.

'But again, you will not break the treaty with the Lace-35
daemonians [b] by receiving us : for we *Reasons why the*
are not allies either of you or of *Athenians should re-*
ceive the Corcyraeans
them. What says the treaty ?—"Any *into alliance. They will*
Hellenic city which is the ally of no *not break the treaty.*
one may join whichever league it pleases." And how monstrous, that they should man their ships, not only from
their own confederacy, but from Hellas in general, nay,
even from your subjects, while they would debar us from

---

[a] Cp. i. 29 init. [b] Cp. i. 115 init.

the alliance which naturally offers and from every other,
and will denounce it as a crime if you accede to our
request. With far better reason shall we complain of you
if you refuse. For you will be thrusting away us who are
not your enemies and are in peril; and, far from restraining
the enemy and the aggressor, you will be allowing him to
gather fresh forces out of your own dominions. How
unjust is this! Surely if you would be impartial you
should either prevent the Corinthians from hiring soldiers
in your dominions, or send to us also such help as you can
be induced to send; but it would be best of all if you
would openly receive and assist us. Many, as we have
already intimated, are the advantages which we offer.
Above all, our enemies are your enemies, which is the best
guarantee of fidelity in an ally; and they are not weak but
well able to injure those who secede from them. Again,
when the proffered alliance is that of a maritime and not
of an inland power, it is a far more serious matter to refuse.
You should, if possible, allow no one to have a fleet but
yourselves; or, if this is impossible, whoever is strongest
at sea, make him your friend.

36   'Some one may think that the course which we recom-

They cannot afford
to be scrupulous; Cor-
cyra is on the way to
Sicily; and is one of
the three great maritime
powers of Hellas.

mend is expedient, but he may be
afraid that if he is convinced by our
arguments he will break the treaty.
To him we reply, that as long as he is
strong he may make a present of his
fears to the enemy, but that if he reject the alliance he will
be weak, and then his confidence, however reassuring to
himself, will be anything but terrifying to enemies who
are strong. It is Athens about which he is advising, and
not Corcyra: will he be providing for her best interests if,
when war is imminent and almost at the door, he is so
anxious about the chances of the hour that he hesitates to
attach to him a state which cannot be made a friend or
enemy without momentous consequences? Corcyra, besides offering many other advantages, is conveniently

situated for the coast voyage to Italy and Sicily; it stands
in the way of any fleet coming from thence to the Peloponnesus, and can also protect a fleet on its way to Sicily.
One word more, which is the sum of all and everything
we have to say, and should convince you that you must
not abandon us. Hellas has only three considerable
navies :—there is ours, and there is yours, and there is the
Corinthian. Now, if the Corinthians get hold of ours, and
you allow the two to become one, you will have to fight
against the united navies of Corcyra and the Peloponnesus. But, if you make us your allies, you will have our
navy in addition to your own ranged at your side in the
impending conflict.'

Thus spoke the Corcyraeans: the Corinthians replied
as follows :—

'Since these Corcyraeans have chosen to speak, not 37
only of their reception into your alliance, *The neutrality of the*
but of our misdoings and of the unjust *Corcyraeans a pretence*
war which has been forced upon them *by which they conceal*
by us, we too must touch on these two *their crimes.*
points before we proceed to our main argument, that you
may be better prepared to appreciate our claim upon you,
and may have a good reason for rejecting their petition.
They pretend that they have hitherto refused to make
alliances from a wise moderation, but they really adopted
this policy from a mean and not from a high motive. They
did not want to have an ally who might go and tell of their
crimes, and who would put them to the blush whenever
they called him in. Their insular position makes them
judges of their own offences against others, and they can
therefore afford to dispense with judges appointed under
treaties; for they hardly ever visit their neighbours, but
foreign ships are constantly driven to their shores by
stress of weather. And all the time they screen themselves under the specious name of neutrality, making
believe that they are unwilling to be the accomplices of
other men's crimes. But the truth is that they wish to

keep their own criminal courses to themselves: where they are strong, to oppress; where they cannot be found out, to defraud; and whatever they may contrive to appropriate, never to be ashamed. If they were really upright men, as they profess to be, the greater their immunity from attack the more clearly they might have made their honesty appear by a willingness to submit differences to arbitration.

38   'But such they have not shown themselves either to-

We go to war with them because they have wronged and insulted us.

wards us or towards others. Although they are our colony they have always stood aloof from us, and now they are fighting against us on the plea that they were not sent out to be ill used. To which we rejoin that we did not send them out to be insulted by them, but that we might be recognised as their leaders and receive proper respect. Our other colonies at any rate honour us; no city is more beloved by her colonies than Corinth. That we are popular with the majority proves that the Corcyraeans have no reason to dislike us; [a] and, if it seems extraordinary that we should go to war with them, our defence is that the injury which they are doing us is unexampled [a]. Even if we had been misled by passion, it would have been honourable in them to make allowance for us, and dishonourable in us to use violence when they showed moderation. But they have wronged us over and over again in their insolence and pride of wealth; and now there is our colony of Epidamnus which they would not acknowledge in her distress, but, when we came to her rescue, they seized and are now holding by force.

39   'They pretend that they first offered to have the matter decided by arbitration. The appeal to justice might have some meaning in the mouth of one [b] who before he had

---

[a] Or, 'and there is nothing extraordinary in our going to war with them, for they are doing us an unexampled injury.'

[b] Or, 'whose actions corresponded to his professions, before he entered on the struggle.'

recourse to arms acted honourably, as he now talks fairly [b],
but not when it is made from a position   *The Corcyraeans pro-*
of security and advantage. Whereas   *pose arbitration and*
these men began by laying siege to   *request your help only*
Epidamnus, and not until they feared   *when they are in danger.*
our vengeance did they put forward their specious offer
of arbitration. And as if the wrong which they have
themselves done at Epidamnus were not enough, they now
come hither and ask you to be, not their allies, but their
accomplices in crime, and would have you receive them
when they are at enmity with us. But they ought to have
come when they were out of all danger, not at a time
when we are smarting under an injury and they have
good reason to be afraid. You have never derived any
benefit from their power, but they will now be benefited
by yours, and, although innocent of their crimes, you will
equally be held responsible by us. If you were to have
shared the consequences with them, they ought long ago to
have shared the power with you [a].

   'We have proved that our complaints are justified and 40
that our adversaries are tyrannical   *You will break the*
and dishonest; we will now show you   *treaty by receiving them,*
that you have no right to receive   *and will compel us to*
them. Admitting that the treaty allows   *be your enemies.*
any unenrolled cities to join either league, this provision
does not apply to those who have in view the injury of
others, but only to him who is in need of protection,—
certainly not to one who forsakes his allegiance and who
will bring war instead of peace to those who receive him,
or rather, if they are wise, will not receive him on such
terms. And war the Corcyraeans will bring to you if you
listen to them and not to us. For if you become the allies

---

   [a] The last words of the chapter are omitted by Poppo on the authority
of several of the best MSS.; they may perhaps be a gloss. If they are
retained they may be translated: 'But you ought not to share all the
consequences of their crimes, while in the crimes, and in them alone,
you have no part.'

of the Corcyraeans you will be no longer at peace with us,
but will be converted into enemies; and we must, if you
take their part, in defending ourselves against them,
defend ourselves against you.   But you ought in common
justice to stand aloof from both; or, if you must join
either, you should join us and go to war with them; to
Corinth you are at all events bound by treaty, but with
Corcyra you never even entered into a temporary negotia-

We did not encourage   tion.   And do not set the precedent
your rebellious subjects,   of receiving the rebellious subjects of
and you should not re-   others.   At the revolt of Samos [a], when
ceive ours.   the other Peloponnesians were divided
B.C. 440.
Ol. 85.

upon the question of giving aid to the rebels, we voted in
your favour and expressly maintained "that every one
should be allowed to chastise his own allies."   If you mean
to receive and assist evil-doers, we shall assuredly gain as
many allies of yours as you will of ours; and you will
establish a principle which will tell against yourselves
more than against us.

41   'Such are the grounds of right which we urge; and
We lent you twenty   they are sufficient according to Hel-
ships in the Aeginetan   lenic law.   And may we venture to
war.   recall to your minds an obligation of
which we claim the repayment in our present need,
we and you being not enemies who seek one another's
hurt, nor yet friends who freely give and take?   There
was a time before the Persian invasion when you were in
want of ships for the Aeginetan war, and we Corinthians
lent you twenty: the service which we then rendered to
you gave you the victory over the Aeginetans [b], as the
other, which prevented the Peloponnesians from aiding
the Samians, enabled you to punish Samos.   Both benefits
were conferred on one of those critical occasions when
men in the act of attacking their enemies are utterly
regardless of everything but victory, and deem him who

B.C. 491.
Ol. 72. 2.

---

[a] Cp. i. 115.   [b] Cp. Herod. vi. 89.

assists them a friend though he may have previously
been a foe, him who opposes them a foe, even though
he may happen to be a friend; nay, they will often
neglect their own interests in the excitement of the
struggle.

'Think of these things; let the younger be informed 42
of them by their elders, and resolve all of you to render B.C. 433
like for like. Do not say to yourselves that this is just, Ol. 86, 4.
but that in the event of war something else is expedient;
for the true path of expediency is the path of right. The
war with which the Corcyraeans would frighten you into
doing wrong is distant, and may never come; is it worth
while to be so carried away by the prospect of it, that
you bring upon yourselves the hatred of the Corinthians
which is both near and certain? Would you not be wiser
in seeking to mitigate the ill-feeling which your treatment
of the Megarians has already inspired [a]? The later kindness done in season, though small in comparison, may
cancel a greater previous offence. And   *To do no wrong is*
do not be attracted by their offer of a *better than a great naval*
great naval alliance; for to do no wrong *alliance.*
to a neighbour is a surer source of strength than to gain
a perilous advantage under the influence of a momentary
illusion.

'We are now ourselves in the same situation in which 43
you were, when we declared at Sparta that every one so
placed should be allowed to chastise his own allies; and
we claim to receive the same measure at your hands. You
were profited by our vote, and we ought not to be injured
by yours. Pay what you owe, knowing that this is our
time of need, in which a man's best friend is he who does
him a service, he who opposes him, his worst enemy. Do
not receive these Corcyraeans into alliance in despite of
us, and do not support them in injustice. In acting thus you
will act rightly, and will consult your own true interests.'

---

[a] Cp. i. 67 fin.

Such were the words of the Corinthians.

44   The Athenians heard both sides, and they held two

The Athenians after some hesitation enter into a defensive alliance with Corcyra. .

assemblies ; in the first of them they were more influenced by the words of the Corinthians, but in the second they changed their minds and inclined towards the Corcyraeans.   They would not go so far as to make an alliance both offensive and defensive with them ;

B.C. 433.
Ol. 87.

for then, if the Corcyraeans had required them to join in an expedition against Corinth, the treaty with the Peloponnesians would have been broken.   But they concluded a defensive league, by which the two states promised to aid each other if an attack were made on the territory or on the allies of either.   For they knew that in any case the war with Peloponnesus was inevitable, and they had no mind to let Corcyra and her navy fall into the

Motives of the Athenians.

hands of the Corinthians.   Their plan was to embroil them more and more with one another, and then, when the war came, the Corinthians and the other naval powers would be weaker.   They also considered that Corcyra was conveniently situated for the coast voyage to Italy and Sicily.

45   Under the influence of these feelings, they received the

They send ten ships to Corcyra, giving them orders to act on the defensive.

Corcyraeans into alliance ; the Corinthians departed ; and the Athenians now despatched to Corcyra ten ships commanded by Lacedaemonius the son of Cimon, Diotimus the son of Strombichus, and Proteas the son of Epicles.   The commanders received orders not to engage with the Corinthians unless they sailed against Corcyra or to any place belonging to the Corcyraeans, and attempted to land there, in which case they were to resist them to the utmost.   These orders were intended to prevent a breach of the treaty[a].

---

[a] Cp. i. 40 init.

The Corinthians, when their preparations were com- 46
pleted, sailed against Corcyra with a   *The Corinthian fleet* B.C. 433.
hundred and fifty ships,—ten Elean,   *sails against Corcyra.* Ol. 86, 4.
twelve Megarian, ten Leucadian, twenty-seven Ambraciot,
one from Anactorium, and ninety of their own.   The
contingents of the several cities were commanded by their
own generals.   The Corinthian commander was Xenocleides the son of Euthycles, with four others.   The fleet
sailed from Leucas, and, arriving at the mainland opposite
Corcyra, came to anchor at Cheimerium in the country of
Thesprotia.   a Cheimerium is only a harbour a; above it,
at some distance from the sea, in that part of Thesprotia
called Eleatis, lies the city of Ephyrè, near which the
Acherusian lake finds a way out to the sea; the river
Acheron, whence the name is derived, flows through
Thesprotia and falls into the lake.   Another river, the
Thyamis, forms the boundary of Thesprotia and Cestrinè,
and the promontory of Cheimerium runs out between
these two rivers.   Here the Corinthians anchored and
formed a camp.

The Corcyraeans, observing their approach, manned 47
a hundred and ten ships.   These, which   *Disposition of the*
were placed under the command of   *forces.*
Meiciades, Aesimides, and Eurybatus, took up a position
off one of the islands called Sybota; the ten Athenian
ships accompanied them.   The land forces occupied the
promontory of Leucimnè, whither a thousand Zacynthians
had come to the aid of Corcyra.   The Corinthians on
their part were supported by a large force of barbarians,
which collected on the mainland; for the inhabitants of
this region have always been well disposed towards them.

The Corinthians had now made their preparations, and, 48
taking with them three days' provisions, put off by night
from Cheimerium, intending to give battle: at break of
day they descried the Corcyraean fleet, which had also

---

a Or, 'Here there is a harbour.'

put out to sea and was sailing to meet them. As soon
as they saw one another, they ranged themselves in order
of battle. On the right Corcyraean wing were the Athenian ships. The Corcyraeans themselves occupied the
centre and the left wing, and were drawn up in three
divisions, each under the command of one of the generals.
On the right wing of the Corinthians were the Megarian
and Ambraciot ships, in the centre the contingents of their
other allies; they themselves with their swiftest vessels
formed the left wing, which was opposed to the Athenians
and to the right division of the Corcyraeans.

49   The standards were now raised on both sides, and the
Character of the en- two fleets met and fought. The decks
gagement.   of both were crowded with heavy infantry, with archers and with javelin-men; for their naval
arrangements were still of the old clumsy sort. The
engagement was obstinate, but more courage than skill
was displayed, and it had almost the appearance of a battle
by land. When two ships once charged one another it
was hardly possible to part company, for the throng of
vessels was dense, and the hopes of victory lay chiefly in
the heavy-armed, who maintained a steady fight upon the
decks, the ships meanwhile remaining motionless. There
were no attempts to break the enemy's line. Brute force
and rage made up for the want of tactics. Everywhere
the battle was a scene of tumult and confusion. At any
point where they saw the Corcyraeans distressed, the Athenians appeared and kept the enemy in check; but the
generals, who were afraid of disobeying their instructions,
would not begin the attack themselves. The Corinthians
Partial success of the suffered most on their right wing. For
Corcyraeans on the left the Corcyraeans with twenty ships
wing and their com- routed them, drove them in disorder to
plete defeat on the right. the shore, and sailed right up to their
encampment; there landing, they plundered and burnt
the deserted tents. So in this part of the battle the Corinthians and their allies were worsted, and the Corcyraeans

prevailed.   But the left wing of the Corinthians, where
their own ships were stationed, had greatly the advantage, because the Corcyraeans, whose numbers were
originally inferior, had now twenty vessels detached in
the pursuit.   When the Athenians saw   *The Athenians share*
the distress of the Corcyraeans, they *in the engagement.*
began to assist them more openly.   At first they had
abstained from actual collision, but when the Corcyraeans
fled outright and the Corinthians pressed them hard, then
every man fell to work ; all distinctions were forgotten ;—
the time had arrived when Corinthian and Athenian were
driven to attack one another.

The Corinthians, having put to flight their enemies, 50
never stopped to take in tow the hulls of the vessels
which they had disabled, but fell upon the men ; they
rowed up and down and slew them, giving no quarter,
and unintentionally killing their own friends ; for they
were not aware that their right wing had been defeated.
There were so many ships on one side and on the other,
and they covered so great an extent of water, that, when
the engagement had once begun, it was hard among
conquerors and conquered to distinguish friend from foe.
For never before had two Hellenic navies so numerous
met in battle.

When the Corinthians had chased the Corcyraeans to
the shore, they turned their attention to their own wrecks
and the bodies of their dead.   Most of these were recovered by them and conveyed to Sybota, a desert harbour
of Thesprotia, whither their barbarian allies had come to
support them.   They then formed afresh and once more
made a movement towards the Corcyraeans, who, taking
such vessels as had not been disabled, and any others
which they had in their docks, together with the Athenian
ships, put out to meet them, dreading a descent upon
Corcyra.   It was now late in the day and the Paean had
been already sounded for the onset, when the Corinthians
suddenly began to row astern.   They had descried sailing

towards them twenty vessels which the Athenians had
Sudden appearance sent to reinforce the former ten, fear-
of twenty Athenian ing what had actually happened, that
ships. the Corcyraeans would be defeated, and
that the original squadron would be insufficient to protect
them.

51   The Corinthians, who had the first view of these vessels,
The two fleets sepa- suspecting that they were Athenian
rate. and that there were more of them than
they saw, were beginning to retreat. The Corcyraeans,
owing to their position, could not see them, and they
wondered why the Corinthians rowed astern. At length
some of them who spied the advancing fleet exclaimed,
' Yonder are ships coming up ; ' and then the Corcyraeans,
as it was getting dark, likewise retired, and the Corinthians turned about and sailed away. Thus the two fleets
separated after a battle which lasted until nightfall. The
twenty ships which came from Athens under the command
of Glaucon the son of Leagrus, and Andocides the son of
Leogoras, made their way through the wrecks and corpses
and sailed into the Corcyraean station at Leucimnè
almost as soon as they were sighted. At first in the darkness the Corcyraeans feared that they were enemies, but
they soon recognised them and the Athenian vessels came
to anchor.

52   On the next day the thirty Athenian and all the
The Corinthians want Corcyraean ships which were fit for
to return home. service, wanting to ascertain whether
the Corinthians would fight, sailed to the harbour at
Sybota where their fleet lay. The Corinthians, putting
out into deep water, drew up their ships in line and so
remained, but they did not intend to begin the battle.
For they saw that fresh ships, which had received no
damage in the action, had arrived from Athens, and their
own position was one of great difficulty. They had to
guard the prisoners in their vessels, and there were no
means of refitting in such a desert place. They were

more disposed to consider how they should get home
than to fight.   For they feared that the Athenians, deeming the peace, now that blows had been exchanged, to be
already broken, would intercept their return.

They therefore determined to send a few men in a boat 53
without a flag of truce to the Athenians,   *They hold a parley*
and so test their intentions.   The men   *with the Athenians.*
were to deliver the following message : 'You do wrong,
Athenians, to begin war and violate the treaty.   We were
only chastising our enemies, and you come with a hostile
force and place yourselves between us and them.   If it is
your intention to hinder us from sailing to Corcyra, or
whithersoever we choose, and you are going to break the
treaty, take us first and deal with us as enemies.'   Whereupon all the Corcyraeans who were within hearing cried
out 'Take and kill them.'   But the Athenians replied :
'Men of Peloponnesus, we are not beginning war, and we
are not violating the treaty ; we are only aiding the Corcyraeans here, who are our allies.   If you mean to sail
against Corcyra or any place belonging to the Corcyraeans,
we will do our utmost to prevent you, but, if you want to
go anywhere else, you may.'

Reassured by this reply, the Corinthians prepared to 54
sail home, first setting up a trophy at   *The Corinthians re-*
the Sybota which is on the mainland.   *turn home, capturing*
The Corcyraeans took up the wrecks   *Anactorium on the*
and dead bodies which were carried   *voyage.*
towards them, the current and the wind which had risen
during the night having scattered them in all directions.
They then set up a rival trophy on the island of Sybota.
Both parties claimed the victory, but on different grounds.
The Corinthians had retained the advantage in the sea-
fight until nightfall, and had thus secured a greater number
of wrecks and dead bodies ; they had taken not less than
a thousand prisoners and had disabled about seventy ships.
The Corcyraeans, on the other hand, had destroyed some
thirty sail, and when reinforced by the Athenians had

taken up the wrecks and dead bodies which had drifted in
their direction; whereas the enemy on the evening of the
battle had rowed astern at sight of the Athenian ships,
and after their arrival had not come out against them from
Sybota.   Upon these grounds both sides raised trophies
55 and claimed the victory.   On their homeward voyage the
Corinthians took by stratagem Anactorium, a town
situated at the mouth of the Ambracian Gulf, which they
and the Corcyraeans held in common; there they settled
colonists of their own, and returned to Corinth.   Of their
Corcyraean captives eight hundred who were slaves they
sold, but two hundred and fifty they detained in prison,
treating them with much consideration, in the hope that,
when they returned, they would win over Corcyra to the
Corinthian interest[a] : it so happened that the majority of
them were among the most influential men of the state.
Thus the war ended to the advantage of Corcyra, and the
Athenian fleet returned home.   This was the first among
the causes of the Peloponnesian War, the Corinthians
alleging that the Athenian fleet had taken part with the
Corcyraeans and had fought against them in a time of
truce.

56   There soon arose another cause of quarrel between the
Quarrel with Poti-   Athenians and Peloponnesians.   Poti-
daea. The Athenians   daea, which is situated on the isthmus
command the Potidae-
ans to raze their walls   of Pallenè, was originally a Corinthian
and to give hostages.   colony, although at this time the tribu-
B.C. 433 or tary and ally of Athens.   Now the Corinthians were
432.   forming plans of vengeance, and the Athenians, who
Ol. 86, 4 ;
or 87, 1. suspected their intentions, commanded the Potidaeans to
raze their walls on the side of Pallenè and give hostages;
also to send away and not to receive for the future the
magistrates whom the Corinthians annually sent to them.
For they were afraid lest the Potidaeans might be persuaded by the Corinthians and Perdiccas to revolt,

---

[a] Cp. iii. 70.

and might induce the rest of Chalcidicè to follow their example.

These measures of precaution were taken by the 57 Athenians immediately after the sea- *Perdiccas who had* fight off Corcyra. The hostility of the *quarrelled with the* Corinthians was no longer doubtful, and *up war between Pelo-* Perdiccas, king of Macedon, the son of *ponnesus and Athens.* Alexander, hitherto the friend and ally of Athens, had now become an enemy. He had quarrelled with the Athenians because they had made an alliance with his brother Philip and with Derdas, who were leagued against him. Alarmed by their attitude, he sent envoys to Sparta and did all he could to stir up a war between Athens and the Peloponnese. He also sought the alliance of Corinth, for he had an eye to the revolt of Potidaea ; and he proposed to the Chalcidians and to the Bottiaeans that they should join in the revolt, thinking, that if he had the assistance of the neighbouring peoples, the difficulties of the war would be diminished. The Athenians became aware of his designs and resolved to forestall the revolt of the cities. They were already intending to send against Perdiccas thirty ships and a thousand hoplites under the command of Archestratus the son of Lycomedes, and [a] ten others, and they told their admirals to take hostages from the Potidaeans and to demolish their wall. They were also to keep a watch over the towns in the neighbourhood and prevent any attempt at rebellion.

Meanwhile the Potidaeans sent envoys to the Athenians 58 in the hope of persuading them to take *The Potidaeans send* no strong measures; but at the same *envoys to Athens and* time other envoys of theirs accompanied *Sparta.* a Corinthian embassy to Lacedaemon and exerted themselves to procure assistance in case of need. A long negotiation was carried on at Athens which came to no satisfactory result ; the ships destined for Macedonia were

---

[a] Or *e conj.* 'four.'

also sent against Potidaea.   But at Lacedaemon they were

They receive promises promised by the magistrates that if
of assistance from the Athenians attacked Potidaea they
Sparta, and revolt. would invade Attica.   So they seized

B.C. 432.   the opportunity and revolted: the Chalcidians and Bot-
Ol. 87, 1.   tiaeans swore alliance with them and joined in the revolt.
Perdiccas persuaded the Chalcidians to abandon and pull
down their towns on the sea-coast, and settling at Olynthus
inland, there to form one strong city.   On their removal
he gave them part of his own territory of Mygdonia about
the lake Bolbè to cultivate while the contest lasted.   So,
dismantling their cities, they settled up the country and
made preparation for war.

59   The Athenians, when the thirty ships arrived in Chal-

The Athenians under cidicè, found that Potidaea and the
Archestratus arrive in other cities had already revolted.
Chalcidicè.   They first Whereupon the generals, thinking that
attack Macedonia. they were not able without a stronger
force to act against all the rebels as well as against Perdiccas, directed their attention to Macedonia, which was
their original destination, and there carried on a regular
campaign in concert with Philip and the brothers of Derdas,
who had invaded the country from the interior.

60   Now that Potidaea had revolted and the Athenian ships

The Corinthians send were on the coast of Macedonia, the
troops to the aid of Corinthians grew anxious about the
Potidaea under the town; they felt that the danger came
command of Aristeus. home to them, and despatched thither
volunteers of their own and other troops whom they
attracted by pay from various parts of the Peloponnese,
numbering in all sixteen hundred hoplites and four hundred
light-armed.   Their commander was Aristeus the son of
Adeimantus, who had always been a great friend of the
Potidaeans; it was mainly out of regard for him that most
of the Corinthian soldiers volunteered on the expedition.
They arrived in Chalcidicè forty days after the revolt of
Potidaea.

The news of the revolt in Chalcidicè quickly reached 61
Athens, and the Athenians, when they   *Athenian reinforce-*
heard that Aristeus had come with re-   *ments under Callias*
inforcements, sent against the revolted   *arrive in Macedonia;*
towns forty ships and two thousand of   *the Athenians make a*
                                          temporary peace with
their own hoplites under the command   *Perdiccas and move on*
of Callias the son of Calliades, and four *to Potidaea.*
others.   The expedition, sailing first of all to Macedonia,
found that the former thousand had just taken Thermè and
were blockading Pydna; they joined in the siege themselves; but before long the Athenian army were constrained
to come to an understanding and make an alliance with
Perdiccas.   For Potidaea, now that Aristeus had arrived,
urgently demanded their presence; so they prepared to
quit Macedonia.   They first marched out of their way to
Beroea, which they attempted to take without success.
Returning to their route, they moved on by land towards
Potidaea with three thousand hoplites of their own and
a large force of allies; they had also six hundred Macedonian horse, who fought under Philip and Pausanias;
meanwhile their ships, in number seventy, sailed along the
coast.   Proceeding by slow marches, they arrived on the
third day at Gigonus and there encamped.

The Potidaeans and the Peloponnesian force under 62
Aristeus had now taken up a position   *Engagement at the*
at the isthmus on the side towards   *isthmus of Pallenè.*
Olynthus[a], where they awaited the coming of the Athenians;
they held their market outside the walls of Potidaea.   The
allies had chosen Aristeus general of all the infantry, and
of the cavalry Perdiccas, for he had no sooner joined than
he again deserted the Athenians and was now fighting on
the side of the Potidaeans, having appointed Iolaus [b] to be
his lieutenant at home [b].   The plan of Aristeus was as
follows:—His own army was to remain on the isthmus

---

[a] Reading πρὸς Ὀλύνθου.

[b] Or, 'to take his place with the expedition:' cp. *infra*, τὴν παρὰ
Περδίκκου διακοσίαν ἵππον.

and watch for the approach of the Athenians, while the
Chalcidians, their allies from beyond the isthmus, and the
two hundred horse furnished by Perdiccas were stationed
at Olynthus; and as soon as the Athenians attacked
Aristeus himself and his army, they were to fall upon them
in the rear; thus the enemy would be assailed on both
sides. But Callias the Athenian general and his colleagues
sent the Macedonian horse and a few of the allied troops
towards Olynthus that they might check any movement in
that quarter, while they themselves, quitting their position,
marched against Potidaea. When they had reached the
isthmus and saw the enemy preparing for battle, they did
the same. The two armies soon closed. The wing led by
Aristeus, which was composed of his Corinthian followers
and other picked troops, routed their opponents and chased
them far away; but the rest of the army, both Potidaeans
and Peloponnesians, were defeated by the Athenians and
fled into the city.

63   Aristeus, when he returned from the pursuit and per-
The army of Aristeus ceived that the other wing of his army
is partially defeated; was defeated, hesitated whether he
he succeeds in making should make for Olynthus or return to
his way back to Poti-
daea. Potidaea. Both courses were hazard-
ous; but at last he determined to contract his troops into
the smallest compass and force his way at full speed into
Potidaea. Harassed by the missiles of the enemy he
pushed forward through the water[a] along the bank in
front of the sea-wall, not without loss; but he contrived to
save the greater part of his men. When the battle began,
the allies of the Potidaeans in Olynthus, which is only
about seven miles[b] distant, and is visible from Potidaea,
seeing the signals raised, came out a little way to support
their friends; and the Macedonian horse drew up in order
of battle to oppose them. But victory quickly declared for

---

[a] Cp. Herod. viii. 129.

[b] Sixty stadia, the stadium being reckoned at two hundred and two yards.

the Athenians; and when the signals were torn down the Olynthian auxiliaries retired within the walls, and the Macedonians rejoined the Athenians: thus on neither side did the cavalry take any part in the action. The Athenians raised a trophy and granted the Potidaeans a truce for the burial of their dead. Of the Potidaeans and their allies, there fell somewhat less than three hundred; of the Athenians, a hundred and fifty, and their general Callias.

The Athenians instantly blockaded the town on the side 64 towards the isthmus, raising a wall, which they guarded; but the side towards Pallenè was left open. They were conscious that they were too weak both to guard the isthmus and, crossing over to Pallenè, there to build another wall; they feared that their forces if divided would be attacked by the Potidaeans and their allies.

The Athenians blockade Potidaea: at first only on the side towards the isthmus; afterwards, by the help of reinforcements under Phormio, on the side towards Pallenè.

Afterwards, when the Athenians at home heard that on the side towards Pallenè Potidaea was not invested, they sent out sixteen hundred hoplites of their own under the command of Phormio the son of Asopius. On his arrival in Pallenè he made Aphytis his head-quarters, and brought his army by slow marches up to Potidaea, wasting the country as he went along. No one came out to meet him, and so he built a wall towards Pallenè. Potidaea was now closely invested on both sides, while the Athenian ships, lying off the city, cut off all communication from the sea.

Aristeus despaired of saving the place unless aid came 65 from Peloponnesus or he was relieved in some unforeseen manner. Being anxious to husband provisions, he proposed to the garrison that they should avail themselves of the first favourable wind and sail away, leaving behind five hundred men, of whom he offered to be one. But they would not listen to him; so, wanting to do the best he could, and to further the Peloponnesian interests beyond the walls, he sailed out undiscovered by

Aristeus leaves Potidaea and carries on the war outside the walls.

the Athenian guard-ships. He did not leave the country, but assisted the Chalcidians in carrying on the war. He succeeded in cutting off a large force of Sermylians by an ambuscade which he laid near their city ; he also exerted himself to obtain aid from Peloponnesus. Phormio with his sixteen hundred hoplites, now that Potidaea was invested, ravaged Chalcidicè and Botticè, and captured several places.

66   Such were the causes of ill-feeling which at this time existed between the Athenians and Peloponnesians : the Corinthians complaining that the Athenians were blockading their colony of Potidaea, and a Corinthian and Peloponnesian garrison in it ; the Athenians rejoining that a member of the Peloponnesian confederacy had excited to revolt a state which was an ally and tributary of theirs, and that they had now openly joined the Potidaeans, and were fighting on their side. The Peloponnesian war, however, had not yet broken out ; the peace still continued ; for thus far the Corinthians had acted alone.

67   But now, seeing Potidaea besieged, they bestirred them-
Excitement of the selves in earnest. Corinthian troops
Corinthians. Assembly were shut up within the walls, and
at Sparta. Grievances
of the Aeginetans and they were afraid of losing the town ;
Megarians. so without delay they invited the allies
to meet at Sparta. There they inveighed against the Athenians, whom they affirmed to have broken the treaty and to be wronging the Peloponnese. The Aeginetans did not venture to send envoys openly, but secretly they acted with the Corinthians, and were among the chief instigators of the war, declaring that they had been robbed of the independence which the treaty guaranteed them. The Lacedaemonians themselves then [a]proceeded to summon any of the allies who had similar charges[a]

---

[a] Or, adopting the inferior reading τῶν ξυμμάχων τε καὶ εἴ τις : 'proceeded to summon any of their own allies, and any one else, who had similar charges,' etc.

to bring against the Athenians, and calling their own ordinary assembly told them to speak. Several of them came forward and stated their wrongs. The Megarians alleged, among other grounds of complaint, that they were excluded from all harbours within the Athenian dominion and from the Athenian market, contrary to the treaty. The Corinthians waited until the other allies had stirred up the Lacedaemonians; at length they came forward, and, last of all, spoke as follows:—

'The spirit of trust, Lacedaemonians, which animates **68** your own political and social life, *The Corinthians com-* ᵃ makes you distrust others who, like *plain of the delays of* ourselves, have something unpleasant *the Lacedaemonians,* to say ᵃ, and this temper of mind, though favourable to moderation, too often leaves you in ignorance of what is going on outside your own country. Time after time we have warned you of the mischief which the Athenians would do to us, but instead of taking our words to heart, you chose to suspect that we only spoke from interested motives. And this is the reason why you have brought the allies to Sparta too late, not before but after the injury has been inflicted, and when they are smarting under the sense of it. Which of them all has a better right to speak than ourselves, who have the heaviest accusations to make, outraged as we are by the Athenians, and neglected by you? If the crimes which they are committing against Hellas were being done in a corner, then you might be ignorant, and we should have to inform you of them: but now, what need of many words? Some of us, as you see, have been already enslaved; they are at this moment intriguing against others, notably against allies of ours; and long ago they had made all their preparations in the prospect of war. Else why did they seduce from her allegiance Corcyra, which they still hold in defiance of

---

ᵃ Or, 'makes you distrustful of us when we bring a charge against others.'

us, and why are they blockading Potidaea, the latter a
most advantageous post for the command of the Thracian
peninsula, the former a great naval power which might
have assisted the Peloponnesians?

69   'And the blame of all this rests on you; for you
who have enslaved originally allowed them to fortify their
Hellas by not prevent- city after the Persian War[a], and after-
ing her enslavement. wards to build their Long Walls[b]; and
to this hour you have gone on defrauding of liberty their
unfortunate subjects, and are now beginning to take it
away from your own allies. For the true enslaver of
a people is he who can put an end to their slavery but
has no care about it; and all the more, if he be reputed
the champion of liberty in Hellas.—And so we have met
at last, but with what difficulty! and even now we have
no definite object. By this time we ought to have been
considering, not whether we are wronged, but how we are
to be revenged. The aggressor is not now threatening,
but advancing; he has made up his mind, while we are
resolved about nothing. And we know too well how by
slow degrees and with stealthy steps the Athenians encroach upon their neighbours. While they think that you
are too dull to observe them, they are more careful, but,
when they know that you wilfully overlook their aggressions, they will strike and not spare. Of all Hellenes,
Lacedaemonians, you are the only people who never do
anything: on the approach of an enemy you are content
to defend yourselves against him, not by acts, but by
intentions, and seek to overthrow him, not in the infancy
but in the fulness of his strength. How came you to be
considered safe? That reputation of yours was never
justified by facts. We all know that the Persian made
his way from the ends of the earth against Peloponnesus
before you encountered him in a worthy manner; and
now you are blind to the doings of the Athenians, who

------

[a] Cp. i. 90-92.   [b] Cp. i. 107.

are not at a distance as he was, but close at hand. Instead
of attacking your enemy, you wait to be attacked, and take
the chances of a struggle which has been deferred until
his power is doubled. And you know that the Barbarian
miscarried chiefly through his own errors; and that we
have oftener been delivered from these very Athenians
by blunders of their own, than by any aid from you.
Some have already been ruined by the hopes which you
inspired in them; for so entirely did they trust you that
they took no precautions themselves. These things we
say in no accusing or hostile spirit—let that be understood—but by way of expostulation. For men expostulate
with erring friends, they bring accusation against enemies
who have done them a wrong.

'And surely we have a right to find fault with our 70
neighbours, if any one ever had. There *Contrast of the Athe-*
are important interests at stake to *nian and Spartan*
which, as far as we can see, you are *characters.*
insensible. And you have never considered what manner
of men are these Athenians[a] with whom you will have
to fight, and how utterly unlike yourselves. They are
revolutionary, equally quick in the conception and in the
execution of every new plan; while you are conservative—
careful only to keep what you have, originating nothing,
and not acting even when action is most urgent. They
are bold beyond their strength; they run risks which
prudence would condemn; and in the midst of misfortune
they are full of hope. Whereas it is your nature, though
strong, to act feebly; when your plans are most prudent,
to distrust them; and when calamities come upon you, to
think that you will never be delivered from them. They
are impetuous, and you are dilatory; they are always
abroad, and you are always at home. For they hope to
gain something by leaving their homes; but you are afraid

---

[a] For descriptions of Athenian character, cp. ii. 37 ff.; iii. 38; 42, 43;
vi. 76; 87.

that any new enterprise may imperil what you have already. When conquerors, they pursue their victory to the utmost; when defeated, they fall back the least. Their bodies they devote to their country as though they belonged to other men; their true self is their mind, which is most truly their own when employed in her service. When they do not carry out an intention which they have formed, they seem to themselves to have sustained a personal bereavement; when an enterprise succeeds, they have gained a mere instalment of what is to come; but if they fail, they at once conceive new hopes and so fill up the void. With them alone to hope is to have, for they lose not a moment in the execution of an idea. This is the lifelong task, full of danger and toil, which they are always imposing upon themselves. None enjoy their good things less, because they are always seeking for more. To do their duty is their only holiday, and they deem the quiet of inaction to be as disagreeable as the most tiresome business. If a man should say of them, in a word, that they were born neither to have peace themselves nor to allow peace to other men, he would simply speak the truth.

71　　'In the face of such an enemy, Lacedaemonians, you

The Lacedaemonians must lay aside their policy of inaction.
persist in doing nothing. You do not see that peace is best secured by those who use their strength justly, but whose attitude shows that they have no intention of submitting to wrong. Justice with you seems to consist in giving no annoyance to others and ^a in defending yourselves only against positive injury ^a. But this policy would hardly be successful, even if your neighbours were like yourselves; and in the present case, as we pointed out just now, your ways compared with theirs are old-fashioned. And, as in the arts, so also in politics, the new must always prevail over the old. In settled times the traditions of govern-

---

^a Or, 'in running no risk even in self-defence.'

ment should be observed : but when circumstances are
changing and men are compelled to meet them, much
originality is required. The Athenians have had a wider
experience, and therefore the administration of their state
unlike yours has been greatly reformed. But here let
your procrastination end ; send an army at once into
Attica and assist your allies, especially the Potidaeans,
to whom your word is pledged [a]. Do not betray friends
and kindred into the hands of their worst enemies ; or
drive us in despair to seek the alliance of others ; in
taking such a course we should be doing nothing wrong
either before the Gods who are the witnesses of our oaths,
or before men whose eyes are upon us. For the true
breakers of treaties [b] are not those who, when forsaken,
turn to others, but those who forsake allies whom they
have sworn to defend. We will remain your friends if
you choose to bestir yourselves ; for we should be guilty
of an impiety if we deserted you without cause ; and we
shall not easily find allies equally congenial to us. Take
heed then : you have inherited from your fathers the
leadership of Peloponnesus; see that her greatness suffers
no diminution at your hands.'

Thus spoke the Corinthians. Now there happened to 72
be staying at Lacedaemon an Athenian   *Some Athenian en-*
embassy which had come on other   *voys who happen to be*
business, and when the envoys heard   *at Sparta desire to ad-*
what the Corinthians had said, they   *dress the assembly.*
felt bound to go before the Lacedaemonian assembly, not
with the view of answering the accusations brought against
them by the cities, but they wanted to put the whole
question before the Lacedaemonians, and make them
understand that they should take time to deliberate and
not be rash. They also desired to set forth the greatness
of their city, reminding the elder men of what they knew,
and informing the younger of what lay beyond their

---

[a] Cp. i. 58 med.   [b] Cp. i. 123 fin.

experience. They thought that their words would sway
the Lacedaemonians in the direction of peace. So they
came and said that, if they might be allowed, they too
would like to address the people. The Lacedaemonians
invited them to come forward, and they spoke as follows:—

73   'We were not sent here to argue with your allies, but
on a special mission; observing, however, that no small
outcry has arisen against us, we have come forward, not
to answer the accusations which they bring (for you are
not judges before whom either we or they have to plead),
but to prevent you from lending too ready an ear to their
bad advice and so deciding wrongly about a very serious
question. We propose also, in reply to the wider charges
which are raised against us, to show that what we have
acquired we hold rightfully and that our city is not to be
despised.

'Of the ancient deeds handed down by tradition and
They   recall   the   which no eye of any one who hears us
memory of their ser- ever saw, why should we speak?   But
vices in the Persian of the Persian War, and other events
War.   which you yourselves remember, speak
we must, ª although we have brought them forward so
often that the repetition of them is disagreeable to us ª.
When we faced those perils we did so for the common
benefit: in the solid good you shared, and of the glory,
whatever good there may be in that, we would not be
wholly deprived. Our words are not designed to deprecate
hostility, but to set forth in evidence the character of the
city with which, unless you are very careful, you will soon
be involved in war. We tell you that we, first and alone,
dared to engage with the Barbarian at Marathon, and that
when he came again, being too weak to defend ourselves
by land, we and our whole people embarked on shipboard
and shared with the other Hellenes in the victory of

ª Or, 'although it may be disagreeable to you to hear what we are
always bringing forward.'

Salamis. Thereby he was prevented from sailing to the
Peloponnesus and ravaging city after city; for against so
mighty a fleet how could you have helped one another?
He himself is the best witness of our words; for when he
was once defeated at sea, he felt that his power was gone
and quickly retreated with the greater part of his army.

'The event proved undeniably that the fate of Hellas 74
depended on her navy. And the three chief elements of
success were contributed by us; namely, the greatest
number of ships, the ablest general, the most devoted
patriotism. The ships in all numbered four hundred[a],
and of these, our own contingent amounted to nearly
two-thirds. To the influence of Themistocles our general
it was chiefly due that we fought in the strait, which was
confessedly our salvation; and for this service you yourselves honoured him above any stranger who ever visited
you. Thirdly, we displayed the most extraordinary courage
and devotion; there was no one to help us by land; for
up to our frontier those who lay in the enemy's path were
already slaves; so we determined to leave our city and
sacrifice our homes. Even in that extremity we did not
choose to desert the cause of the allies who still resisted,
or by dispersing ourselves to become useless to them;
but we embarked and fought, taking no offence at your
failure to assist us sooner. We maintain then that we
rendered you a service at least as great as you rendered
us. The cities from which you came to help us were still
inhabited and you might hope to return to them; your
concern was for yourselves and not for us; at any rate
you remained at a distance while we had anything to lose.
But we went forth from a city which was no more, and
fought for one of which there was small hope; and yet we
saved ourselves, and bore our part in saving you. If, in
order to preserve our land, like other states, we had gone
over to the Persians at first, or afterwards had not ventured

---

[a] Reading with the great majority of MSS. τετρακοσίας.

to embark because our ruin was already complete, it would have been useless for you with your weak navy to fight at sea, but everything would have gone quietly just as the Persian desired.

75   'Considering, Lacedaemonians, the energy and sagacity

Why should they be hated for having saved Hellas? Their empire was not a usurpation, but the growth of circumstances.
which we then displayed, do we deserve to be so bitterly hated by the other Hellenes merely because we have an empire? That empire was not acquired by force; but you would not stay and make an end of the Barbarian, and the allies came of their own accord and asked us to be their leaders. The subsequent development of our power was originally forced upon us by circumstances; fear was our first motive; afterwards honour, and then interest stepped in. And when we had incurred the hatred of most of our allies; when some of them had already revolted and been subjugated, and you were no longer the friends to us which you once had been, but suspicious and ill-disposed, how could we without great risk relax our hold? For the cities as fast as they fell away from us would have gone over to you. And no man is to be reproached who seizes every possible advantage when the danger is so great.

76   'At all events, Lacedaemonians, we may retort that you,

The Lacedaemonians would have been worse than they were.
in the exercise of your supremacy, manage the cities of Peloponnesus to suit your own views; and that if you, and not we, had persevered in the command of the allies long enough to be hated, you would have been quite as intolerable to them as we are, and would have been compelled, for the sake of your own safety, to rule with a strong hand. An empire was offered to us: can you wonder that, acting as human nature always will, we accepted it and refused to give it up again, constrained by three all-powerful motives, honour, fear, interest? We are not the first who have aspired to rule; the world has ever held that the weaker must be kept down by the stronger. And

B.C. 432.
Ol. 87.

we think that we are worthy of power; and there was
a time when you thought so too; but now, when you mean
expediency you talk about justice. Did justice ever deter
any one from taking by force whatever he could? Men
who indulge the natural ambition of empire deserve credit
if they are in any degree more careful of justice than they
need be. How moderate we are would speedily appear if
others took our place; indeed our very moderation, which
should be our glory, has been unjustly converted into
a reproach.

'For because in our suits with our allies, regulated by 77
treaty, we do not even stand upon our
rights, but have instituted the practice
of deciding them at Athens and by
Athenian [a] law, we are supposed to be
litigious. None of our opponents ob-
serve why others, who exercise dominion elsewhere and
are less moderate than we are in their dealings with their
subjects, escape this reproach. Why is it? Because men
who practise violence have no longer any need of law.
But we are in the habit of meeting our allies on terms of
equality, and, therefore, if through some legal decision of
ours, or exercise of our imperial power, contrary to their
own ideas of right, they suffer ever so little, they are not
grateful for our moderation in leaving them so much, but
are far more offended at their trifling loss than if we had
from the first plundered them in the face of day, laying
aside all thought of law. For then they would themselves
have admitted that the weaker must give way to the
stronger. Mankind resent injustice more than violence,
because the one seems to be an unfair advantage taken by
an equal, the other is the irresistible force of a superior.
They were patient under the yoke of the Persian, who
inflicted on them far more grievous
wrongs; but now our dominion is
odious in their eyes. And no wonder:
the ruler of the day is always detested by his subjects. And

*They were thought to
be litigious, because they
allowed their subjects a
law other than the law
of the stronger.*

*The ruler of the day
is always unpopular.*

---

[a] (?) by impartial law.

should your empire supplant ours, may not you lose the good-will which you owe to the fear of us? Lose it you certainly will, if you mean again to exhibit the temper of which you gave a specimen when, for a short time, you led the confederacy against the Persian. For the institutions under which you live are incompatible with those of foreign states; and further, when any of you goes abroad, he respects neither these nor any other Hellenic customs [a].

78　'Do not then be hasty in deciding a question which is serious; and do not, by listening to representations and complaints which concern others, bring trouble upon yourselves. Realise, while there is time, the inscrutable nature of war;

The Lacedaemonians should not go to war at the instigation of others, but submit to arbitration.

and how when protracted it generally ends in becoming a mere matter of chance, over which neither of us can have any control, the event being equally unknown and equally hazardous to both. The misfortune is that in their hurry to go to war, men begin with blows, and when a reverse comes upon them, then have recourse to words. But neither you, nor we, have as yet committed this mistake; and therefore while both of us can still choose the prudent part, we tell you not to break the peace or violate your oaths. Let our differences be determined by arbitration, according to the treaty. If you refuse we call to witness the Gods, by whom your oaths were sworn, that you are the authors of the war; and we will do our best to strike in return.'

79　When the Lacedaemonians had heard the charges brought by the allies against the Athenians, and their rejoinder, they ordered everybody but themselves to withdraw, and deliberated alone. The majority were agreed that there was now a clear case against the Athenians, and that they must fight at once. But Archidamus their

---

[a] For the misconduct of Spartan officers abroad, cp. i. 95; 130; iii. 32; 93 fin.; viii. 84 init.　Contrast Brasidas, iv. 81.

king, who was held to be both an able and a prudent man, came forward and spoke as follows :—

'At my age, Lacedaemonians, I have had experience of **80** many wars, and I see several of you who are as old as I am, and who will *We are no match for* not, as men too often do, desire war *the Athenians.* because they have never known it, or in the belief that it is either a good or a safe thing. Any one who calmly reflects will find that the war about which you are now deliberating is likely to be a very great one. When we encounter our neighbours in the Peloponnese, their mode of fighting is like ours, and they are all within a short march. But when we have to do with men whose country is a long way off, and who are most skilful seamen and thoroughly provided with the means of war,—having wealth, private and public, ships, horses, infantry, and a population larger than is to be found in any single Hellenic territory, not to speak of the numerous allies who pay them tribute,—is this a people against whom we can lightly take up arms or plunge into a contest unprepared? To what do we trust? To our navy? There we are inferior; and to exercise and train ourselves until we are a match for them, will take time. To our money? Nay, but in that we are weaker still; we have none in a common treasury, and we are never willing to contribute out of our private means.

'Perhaps some one may be encouraged by the superior **81** equipment and numbers of our infantry, *We have more hop-* which will enable us regularly to in- *lites, but their empire* vade and ravage their lands. But their *extends to distant coun-* empire extends to distant countries, *tries, by which their navy* and they will be able to introduce *ravage their land is use-* supplies by sea. Or, again, we may *less.* try to stir up revolts among their allies. But these are mostly islanders, and we shall have to employ a fleet in their defence, as well as in our own. How then shall we carry on the war? For if we can neither defeat them at sea, nor deprive them of the revenues by which their navy is maintained, we shall get the worst of it. And having gone so far, we shall no longer be able even to make peace with honour, especially if we are believed to have begun the quarrel. We must not for one moment flatter ourselves that if we do but ravage their country the war will be at an end. Nay, I fear that we shall bequeath it to our children; for the Athenians with their high spirit will never barter their liberty to save their land, or be terrified like novices at the sight of war.

82 'Not that I would have you shut your eyes to their designs and abstain from unmasking

Do not take up arms yet.

them, or tamely suffer them to injure our allies. But do not take up arms yet. Let us first send and remonstrate with them: we need not let them know positively whether we intend to go to war or not. In the meantime our own preparations may be going forward; we may seek for allies wherever we can find them, whether in Hellas or among the Barbarians, who will supply our deficiencies in ships and money. Those who, like ourselves, are exposed to Athenian intrigue cannot be blamed if in self-defence they seek the aid not of Hellenes only, but of Barbarians. And we must develope our own resources to the utmost. If they listen to our ambassadors, well and good; but, if not, in two or three years' time we shall be in a stronger position, should we then determine to attack them. Perhaps too when they begin to see that we are getting ready, [a]and that our words are to be interpreted by our actions[a], they may be more likely to yield; for their fields will be still untouched and their goods undespoiled, and it will be in their power to save them by their decision. Think of their land simply in the light of a hostage, all the more valuable in proportion as it is better cultivated; you should spare it as long as you can, and not by reducing them to despair

---

[a] Or, 'and that our words too sound a note of war.'

make their resistance more obstinate. For if we allow
ourselves to be stung into premature action by the reproaches of our allies, and waste their country before we
are ready, we shall only involve Peloponnesus in more
and more difficulty and disgrace. Charges brought by
cities or persons against one another can be satisfactorily
arranged; but when a great confederacy, in order to satisfy
private grudges, undertakes a war of which no man can
foresee the issue, it is not easy to terminate it with honour.

And let no one think that there is any want of courage 83
in cities so numerous hesitating to
attack a single one. The allies of the
Athenians are not less numerous; they
pay them tribute too; and war is not
an affair of arms, but of money which
There is no cowardice in hesitation; we are fighting not against Athens, but against the great Athenian empire.
gives to arms their use, and which is needed above all
things when a continental is fighting against a maritime
power: let us find money first, and then we may safely
allow our minds to be excited by the speeches of our allies.
We, on whom the future responsibility, whether for good
or evil, will chiefly fall, should calmly reflect on the consequences which may follow.

'Do not be ashamed of the slowness and procrastination 84
with which they are so fond of charging
you; if you begin the war in haste,
you will end it at your leisure, because
you took up arms without sufficient
preparation. Remember that we have
always been citizens of a free and most
illustrious state, and that for us the
Too much haste, too little speed. Our dis-cretion and discipline are the secret of our greatness. We must not undervalue our enemies, and we must not rely on fortune.
policy which they condemn may well be the truest good
sense and discretion. It is a policy which has saved us from
growing insolent in prosperity or giving way under adversity, like other men. We are not stimulated by the allure-
ments of flattery into dangerous courses of which we
disapprove; nor are we goaded by offensive charges into
compliance with any man's wishes. Our habits of discipline

make us both brave and wise; brave, because the spirit
of loyalty quickens the sense of honour, and the sense of
honour inspires courage ; wise, because we are not so highly
educated that we have learned to despise the laws, and are
too severely trained and of too loyal a spirit to disobey
them.   We have not acquired that useless over-intelligence
which makes a man an excellent critic of an enemy's plans,
but paralyses him in the moment of action.   We think that
the wits of our enemies are as good as our own, and that
the element of fortune cannot be forecast in words.   Let
us assume that they have common prudence, and let our
preparations be, not words, but deeds ᵃ.   Our hopes ought
not to rest on the probability of their making mistakes, but
on our own caution and foresight.   We should remember
that one man is much the same as another, and that he is
best who is trained in the severest school.

85   ' These are principles which our fathers have handed
We can afford to wait, down to us, and we maintain to our
and should try arbitra- lasting benefit ; we must not lose sight
tion first. of them, and when many lives and
much wealth, many cities and a great name are at stake,
we must not be hasty, or make up our minds in a few short
hours; we must take time.   We can afford to wait, when
others cannot, because we are strong.   And now, send to
the Athenians and remonstrate with them about Potidaea
first, and also about the other wrongs of which your allies
complain.   They say that they are willing to have the
matter tried ; and against one who offers to submit to
justice you must not proceed as against a criminal until his
cause has been heard.   In the meantime prepare for war.
This decision will be the best for yourselves and the most
formidable to your enemies.'

Thus spoke Archidamus.   Last of all, Sthenelaidas, at
that time one of the Ephors, came forward and addressed
the Lacedaemonians as follows :—

ᵃ Reading παρασκευαζώμεθα.

'I do not know what the long speeches of the Athenians 86
mean.   They have been loud in their   *We must stand by*
own praise, but they do not pretend to   *our allies.*
say that they are dealing honestly with our allies and with
the Peloponnesus.   If they behaved well in the Persian
War and are now behaving badly to us they ought to be
punished twice over, because they were once good men
and have become bad.   But we are the same now as we
were then, and we shall not do our duty if we allow our
allies to be ill-used, and put off helping them, for they
cannot put off their troubles.   Others may have money and
ships and horses, but we have brave allies and we must
not betray them to the Athenians.   If they were suffering
in word only, by words and legal processes their wrongs
might be redressed ; but now there is not a moment to be
lost, and we must help them with all our might.   Let no
one tell us that we should take time to think when we are
suffering injustice.   Nay, we reply, those who mean to do
injustice should take a long time to think.   Wherefore,
Lacedaemonians, prepare for war as the honour of Sparta
demands.   Withstand the advancing power of Athens.
Do not let us betray our allies, but, with the Gods on our
side, let us attack the evil-doer.'

When Sthenelaidas had thus spoken he, being Ephor, 87
himself put the question to the Lace-   *The Lacedaemonians,*
daemonian assembly.   Their custom is   *influenced chiefly by the*
to signify their decision by cries and not   *fear of the Athenians,*
by voting.   But he professed himself   *resolve to go to war.*
unable to tell on which side was the louder cry, and wishing to call forth a demonstration which might encourage the
warlike spirit, he said, 'Whoever of you, Lacedaemonians,
thinks that the treaty has been broken and that the Athenians are in the wrong, let him rise and go yonder' (pointing
to a particular spot), 'and those who think otherwise to the
other side.'   So the assembly rose and divided, and it was
determined by a large majority that the treaty had been
broken.   The Lacedaemonians then recalled the allies and

told them that in their judgment the Athenians were guilty,
but that they wished to hold a general assembly of the
allies and take a vote from them all ; then the war, if they
approved of it, might be undertaken by common consent.
Having accomplished their purpose, the allies returned
home ; and the Athenian envoys, when their errand was
done, returned likewise. Thirteen years of the thirty
years' peace which was concluded after the recovery of
Euboea had elapsed and the fourteenth year had begun
when the Lacedaemonian assembly decided that the treaty
had been broken.

B.C. 445.
Ol. 83, 4.

88   In arriving at this decision and resolving to go to war,
the Lacedaemonians were influenced, not so much by the
speeches of their allies, as by the fear of the Athenians
and of their increasing power[a]. For they saw the greater
part of Hellas already subject to them.

89   How the Athenians attained the position in which they
rose to greatness I will now proceed
to describe. When the Persians, defeated by the Hellenes on sea and land,
had retreated from Europe, and the remnant of the fleet,
which had taken refuge at Mycalè, had there perished,
Leotychides, the Lacedaemonian king, who had commanded the Hellenes in the battle, returned home with the
allies from Peloponnesus. But the Athenians and their
allies from Ionia and the Hellespont, who had now revolted
from the king, persevered and besieged Sestos, at that time
still in the hands of the Persians. Remaining there through
the winter they took the place, which the Barbarians
deserted. The allies then sailed back from the Hellespont
to their respective homes. Meanwhile the Athenian people,
now quit of the Barbarians, fetched their wives, their
children, and the remains of their property from the places
in which they had been deposited, and set to work, rebuilding the city and the walls. Of the old line of wall but

B.C. 479.
Ol. 75, 2.

*The Athenians after
the retreat of the Per-
sians continue the war.*

------

[a] Cp. i. 23 fin.

a small part was left standing. Most of the houses were in ruins, a few only remaining in which the chief men of the Persians had lodged.

The Lacedaemonians knew what would happen and sent 90 an embassy to Athens. They would rather themselves have seen neither the Athenians nor any one else protected by a wall ; but their main motive was the importunity of their allies, who dreaded *The Lacedaemonians at the instigation of their allies try to prevent the Athenians from rebuilding their walls.* not only the Athenian navy, which had until lately been quite small, but also the spirit which had animated them in the Persian War. So the Lacedaemonians requested them not to restore their walls [a], but on the contrary to join with them in razing the fortifications of other towns outside the Peloponnesus which had them standing. They did not reveal their real wishes or the suspicion which they entertained of the Athenians, but argued that the Barbarian, if he again attacked them, would then have no strong place B.C. 479– which he could make his head-quarters as he had lately 478. Ol. 75, 2, 3. made Thebes. Peloponnesus would be a sufficient retreat for all Hellas and a good base of operations. To this the Athenians, by the advice of Themistocles, replied, that they would send an embassy of their own to discuss the matter, and so got rid of the Spartan envoys. He then proposed that he should himself start at once for Sparta, and that they should give him colleagues who were not to go immediately, but were to wait until the wall reached the lowest height which could possibly be defended. The whole people, who were in the city, men, women, and children, should join in the work, and they must spare no building, private or public, which could be of use, but demolish them all. Having given these instructions and intimated that he would manage affairs at Sparta, he departed. On his arrival he did not at once present himself officially to the magistrates, but delayed and made

---

[a] Cp. i. 69 init.

excuses; and when any of them asked him 'why he did
not appear before the assembly,' he said 'that he was
waiting for his colleagues, who had been detained by
some engagement; he was daily expecting them, and
wondered that they had not appeared.'

91   The friendship of the Lacedaemonian magistrates for

The Lacedaemonians Themistocles induced them to believe
are outwitted by Themis- him; but when everybody who came
tocles. from Athens declared positively that
the wall was building and had already reached a considerable height, they knew not what to think.   He, aware of
their suspicions, desired them not to be misled by reports,
but to send to Athens men whom they could trust out of
their own number who would see for themselves and bring
back word.   They agreed; and he at the same time privately instructed the Athenians to detain the envoys as
quietly as they could, and not let them go until he and
his colleagues had got safely home.   For by this time
Habronichus the son of Lysicles, and Aristides the son of
Lysimachus, who were joined with him in the embassy,
had arrived, bringing the news that the wall was of sufficient height; and he was afraid that the Lacedaemonians,
when they heard the truth, might not allow them to return.
So the Athenians detained the envoys, and Themistocles,
coming before the Lacedaemonians, at length declared in
so many words that Athens was now provided with walls
and could protect her citizens; henceforward, if the Lacedaemonians or their allies wished at any time to negotiate,
they must deal with the Athenians as with men who knew
quite well what was for their own and the common good.
When they boldly resolved to leave their city and go on
board ship, they did not first ask the advice of the Lacedaemonians, and, when the two states met in council, their own
judgment had been as good as that of any one.   And now
they had arrived at an independent opinion that it was
better far, and would be more advantageous both for themselves and for the whole body of the allies, that their city

should have a wall; when any member of a confederacy
had not equal military advantages, his counsel could not
be of equal weight or worth.   Either all the allies should
pull down their walls, or they should acknowledge that the
Athenians were in the right.

On hearing these words the Lacedaemonians did not **92**
openly quarrel with the Athenians ; for   *But appearances are*
they professed that the embassy had   *maintained, and there*
been designed, not to interfere with   *is no open quarrel.*
them, but to offer a suggestion for the public good ; besides
at that time the patriotism which the Athenians had displayed in the Persian War had created a warm feeling of
friendliness between the two cities.   They were annoyed
at the failure of their purpose, but they did not show it.
And the envoys on either side returned home without any
formal complaint.

In such hurried fashion did the Athenians build the **93**
walls of their city.   To this day the structure shows evidence of haste.   The foundations are made up of all sorts
of stones, in some places unwrought, and laid just as each
worker brought them ; there were many columns too, taken
from sepulchres, and many old stones already cut, inserted
in the work.   The circuit of the city was extended in B.C. 478.
every direction, and the citizens, in their ardour to com-   Ol. 75, 3.
plete the design, spared nothing.

Themistocles also persuaded the Athenians to finish the B.C. 482.
Piraeus, of which he had made a begin-   Ol. 74, 3.
ning in his year of office as Archon.   The   *Construction of the*
situation of the place, which had three   *Piraeus, and founda-*
natural havens, was excellent ; and now   *tion of the maritime*
that the Athenians had become seamen, he thought that   *empire of Athens.*
they had great advantage for the attainment of empire.
For he first dared to say that 'they must make the sea
their domain,' and he lost no time in laying the foundations
of their empire.   By his advice, they built the wall of such
a width that two waggons carrying the stones could meet
and pass on the top ; this width may still be traced at the

Piraeus; inside there was no rubble or mortar, but the whole wall was made up of large stones hewn square, which were clamped on the outer face with iron and lead. The height was not more than half what he had originally intended; he had hoped by the very dimensions of the wall to paralyse the designs of an enemy, and he thought that a handful of the least efficient citizens would suffice for its defence, while the rest might man the fleet. His mind was turned in this direction, as I conceive, from observing that the King's armament had met with fewer obstacles by sea than by land. The Piraeus appeared to him to be of more real consequence than the upper city. He was fond of telling the Athenians that if ever they were hard pressed on land they should go down to the Piraeus and fight the world at sea.

Thus the Athenians built their walls and restored their city immediately after the retreat of the Persians.

94   Pausanias the son of Cleombrotus was now sent from
Cyprus and Byzan- Peloponnesus with twenty ships in
tium taken. Tyranny command of the Hellenic forces; thirty
and unpopularity of Athenian ships and a number of the
Pausanias. allies sailed with him. They first made
an expedition against Cyprus, of which they subdued the greater part; and afterwards against Byzantium, which was in the hands of the Persians, and was taken while he was still in command.

95   He had already begun to be oppressive[a], and the allies
B.C. 477 or   *The allies transfer* were offended with him, especially the
476.   *themselves to the Athe-* Ionians and others who had been re-
Ol. 75, 4 or   *nians.* cently emancipated from the King. So
76.
they had recourse to their kinsmen the Athenians and begged them to be their leaders, and to protect them against Pausanias, if he attempted to oppress them. The Athenians took the matter up and prepared to interfere, being fully resolved to manage the confederacy in their

------

[a] Cp. c. 130.

own way.   In the meantime the Lacedaemonians summoned Pausanias to Sparta, intending to investigate
certain reports which had reached them ; for he was
accused of numerous crimes by Hellenes returning from
the Hellespont, and appeared to exercise his command
more after the fashion of a tyrant than of a general.   His
recall occurred at the very time when the hatred which he
inspired had induced the allies, with the exception of the
Peloponnesians, to transfer themselves to the Athenians.
On arriving at Lacedaemon he was punished for the
wrongs which he had done to particular persons, but he
had been also accused of conspiring with the Persians, and
of this, which was the principal charge and was generally
believed to be proven, he was acquitted.   The government
however did not continue him in his command, but sent in
his place Dorcis and certain others with a small force.   To
these the allies refused allegiance, and Dorcis, seeing the
state of affairs, returned home.   Henceforth the Lacedaemonians sent out no more commanders, for they were
afraid that those whom they appointed would be corrupted,
as they had found to be the case with Pausanias ; they had
had enough of the Persian War; and they thought that
the Athenians were fully able to lead, and at that time
believed them to be their friends.

Thus the Athenians by the good-will of the allies, who **96**
detested Pausanias, obtained the leader-
ship.   They immediately fixed which of *Confederacy of Delos.*
the cities should supply money and which of them ships
for the war against the Barbarians, the avowed object being
to compensate themselves and the allies for their losses by
devastating the King's country.   Then was first instituted B.C. 478–
at Athens the office of Hellenic treasurers (Helleno- 477.
tamiae), who received the tribute, for so the contributions Ol.75, 3, 4.
were termed.   The amount was originally fixed at 460
talents [a].   The island of Delos was the treasury, and the
meetings of the allies were held in the temple.

---

[a] About £92,000.

97   At first the allies were independent and deliberated in

The interval between the Persian and Peloponnesian Wars omitted in most histories.

a common assembly under the leadership of Athens. But in the interval between the Persian and the Peloponnesian Wars, by their military success and by policy in dealing with the Barbarian, with their own rebellious allies and with the Peloponnesians who came across their path from time to time, the Athenians made immense strides in power. I have gone out of my way to speak of this period because the writers who have preceded me treat either of Hellenic affairs previous to the Persian invasion or of that invasion itself; the intervening portion of history has been omitted by all of them, with the exception of Hellanicus; and he, where he has touched upon it in his Attic history, is very brief, and inaccurate in his chronology. The narrative will also serve to explain how the Athenian empire grew up.

98   First of all under the leadership of Cimon, the son of

B.C. 476–466.
Ol. 76–78, 3.

The Athenians subject Eion, Scyros, Carystus, Naxos.

Miltiades, the Athenians besieged and took Eion upon the Strymon, then in the hands of the Persians, and sold the inhabitants into slavery. The same fate befell Scyros, an island in the Aegean inhabited by Dolopes; this they colonised themselves. They also made war on the Carystians of Euboea, who, after a time, capitulated; the other

B.C. 466.
Ol. 78, 3.

Euboeans took no part in the war. Then the Naxians revolted, and the Athenians made war against them and reduced them by blockade. This was the first of the allied cities which was enslaved contrary to Hellenic right; the turn of the others came later.

99   The causes which led to the defections of the allies

Most of the allies contribute money instead of ships. As they grow weaker the Athenians become more oppressive.

were of different kinds, the principal being their neglect to pay the tribute or to furnish ships, and, in some cases, failure of military service. For the Athenians were exacting and oppressive, using coercive measures towards men who were neither willing nor

accustomed to work hard. And for various reasons they
soon began to prove less agreeable leaders than at first.
They no longer fought upon an equality with the rest of
the confederates, and they had no difficulty in reducing
them when they revolted. Now the allies brought all this
upon themselves ; for the majority of them disliked military
service and absence from home, and so they agreed to
contribute their share of the expense instead of ships.
Whereby the Athenian navy was proportionally increased,
while they themselves were always untrained and unprepared for war when they revolted.

A little later the Athenians and their allies fought two 100
battles, one by land and the other *The Athenians con-*
by sea, against the Persians, at the *quer in a sea and land*
river Eurymedon in Pamphylia. The *fight at the river Eury-*
medon. Revolt of Tha-
Athenians, under the command of *sos. Attempted colonis-*
Cimon the son of Miltiades, on the *ation of Amphipolis.*
same day conquered in both, and took and destroyed all
the Phoenician triremes numbering two hundred. After
a while the Thasians revolted; a quarrel had arisen B.C. 465.
between them and the Athenians about the Thracian Ol. 78, 4.
markets and the mine on the Thracian coast opposite, of
which the Thasians received the profits. The Athenians
sailed to Thasos and, gaining a victory at sea, landed upon
the island. About the same time they sent ten thousand
of their own people and of their allies to the Strymon,
intending to colonise the place then called the Nine Ways
and now Amphipolis. They gained possession of the Nine
Ways, which were inhabited by the Edoni, but, advancing
into the interior of Thrace, they [a] were destroyed at
Drabescus in Edonia by the united Thracians[a], whose
country was threatened by the new settlement.

The Thasians, now blockaded after several defeats, had 101
recourse to the Lacedaemonians and entreated them to

---

[a] Or, reading ξύμπαντες, as Poppo is inclined to do, 'were destroyed
to a man by the Thracians.'

B.C. 464.
Ol. 79.

invade Attica.   Unknown to the Athenians they agreed,

Revolt of the Helots, and were on the point of setting out
who seize Ithomè. when the great earthquake occurred
and was immediately followed by the revolt of the Helots
and with them the Perioeci of Thuria and Aethaea, who
seized Ithomè.   These Helots were mostly the descendants of the Messenians who had been enslaved in ancient
times, and hence all the insurgents were called Messenians.

B.C. 463.
Ol. 79, 2.

While the Lacedaemonians were thus engaged, the
Thasians, who had now been block-
Surrender of Thasos. aded for more than two years, came to
terms with the Athenians ; they pulled down their walls
and surrendered their ships ; they also agreed to pay what
was required of them whether in the shape of immediate
indemnity or of tribute for the future ; and they gave up
their claim to the mainland and to the mine.

102
B.C. 463–
461.
Ol. 79, 2–4.

The siege of Ithomè proved tedious, and the Lacedae-
The Athenians come monians called in, among other allies,
to the assistance of the the Athenians, who sent to their aid
Lacedaemonians, but a considerable force under Cimon.
being suspected by them,
they are dismissed and The Athenians were specially invited
go away in a rage. because they were reputed to be skilful
in siege operations, and the length of the blockade proved
to the Lacedaemonians their own deficiency in that sort of
warfare ; else why had they not taken the place by assault ?
This expedition of the Athenians led to the first open
quarrel between them and the Lacedaemonians.   For the
Lacedaemonians, not succeeding in storming the place,
took alarm at the bold and original spirit of the Athenians.
They reflected that they were aliens in race, and fearing
that, if they were allowed to remain, they might be tempted
by the Helots in Ithomè to change sides, they dismissed
them, while they retained the other allies.   But they concealed their mistrust, and merely said that they no longer
needed their services.   Now the Athenians saw that their
dismissal was due to some suspicion which had arisen and
not to the less offensive reason which was openly avowed ;

they felt keenly that such a slight ought not to have been
offered them by the Lacedaemonians; and so, on their
return home, they forthwith abandoned the alliance which
they had made with them against the Persians and went
over to their Argive enemies.   At the same time both
Argos and Athens bound themselves to Thessaly by
a common oath of alliance.

B.C. 463–
461.
Ol. 79, 2–
79, 4.

In the [a]tenth year of the siege the defenders of Ithomè
were unable to hold out any longer,
and capitulated to the Lacedaemonians.
The terms were as follows: They were
to leave Peloponnesus under a safe-
conduct, and were never again to return; if any of them
were taken on Peloponnesian soil, he was to be the slave
of his captor.   Now an ancient oracle of Delphi was
current among the Lacedaemonians, bidding them let the
suppliant of Ithomaean Zeus go free.   So the Messenians
left Ithomè with their wives and children; and the
Athenians, who were now the avowed enemies of Sparta,
gave them a home at Naupactus, a place which they had
lately taken from the Ozolian Locrians.

103
B.C. 455.
Fall of Ithome. The Ol. 81, 2.
Athenians settle the [? B.C. 461.
exiled Messenians at Ol. 79, 4.]
Naupactus.

The Athenians obtained the alliance of the Megarians,
who revolted from the Lacedaemonians
because the Corinthians were pressing
them hard in a war arising out of
a question of frontiers.   Thus they
gained both Megara and Pegae; and they built for the
Megarians the long walls, extending from the city to the
port of Nisaea, which they garrisoned themselves.   This
was the original and the main cause of the intense hatred
which the Corinthians entertained towards the Athenians.

B.C. 461–
460.
Athens gains the al- Ol. 79, 4–
liance of Megara, as 80.
well as of Argos and
Thessaly.

Meanwhile Inaros the son of Psammetichus, king of the
Libyans who border on Egypt, had in-
duced the greater part of Egypt to
revolt from King Artaxerxes.   He began the rebellion

104
B.C. 460.
Egyptian revolt.   Ol. 80.

---

[a] Or, accepting τετάρτῳ (Krüger's conj.), 'the fourth year.'

at Mareia, a city opposite the island of Pharos, and, having made himself ruler of the country, called in the Athenians. They were just then engaged in an expedition against Cyprus with two hundred ships of their own and of their allies; and, quitting the island, they went to his aid. They sailed from the sea into the Nile, and, making themselves masters of the river and of two-thirds of Memphis, proceeded to attack the remaining part called the White Castle, in which some of the Persians and Medes had taken refuge, and with them such Egyptians as had not joined in the revolt.

B.C. 460–457. Ol. 80, 1–4.

105   An Athenian fleet made a descent upon Halieis, where

The Athenians defeat the Aeginetans, capture seventy ships, and besiege Aegina. The Corinthians invade Megara.

a battle took place against some Corinthian and Epidaurian troops; the Athenians gained the victory. Soon afterwards the Athenians fought at sea off Cecryphaleia with a Peloponnesian fleet, which they defeated. A war next broke out between the Aeginetans and the Athenians, and a great battle was fought off the coast of Aegina, in which the allies of both parties joined; the Athenians were victorious, and captured seventy of the enemy's ships; they then landed on Aegina and, under the command of Leocrates the son of Stroebus, besieged the town. Thereupon the Peloponnesians sent over to the assistance of the Aeginetans three hundred hoplites who had previously been assisting the Corinthians and Epidaurians. The Corinthians seized [a] on the heights of Geraneia, and thence made a descent with their allies into the Megarian territory, thinking that the Athenians, who had so large a force absent in Aegina and in Egypt, would be unable to assist the Megarians; or, if they did, would be obliged to raise the siege of Aegina. But the Athenians, without moving their army from Aegina, sent to Megara under the command of Myronides a force consisting of their oldest and youngest men, who had

---

[a] Omitting the stop after κατέλαβον.

remained at home. A battle was fought, which hung equally in the balance; and when the two armies separated, they both thought that they had gained the victory. The Athenians, who did however get rather the better, on the departure of the Corinthians erected a trophy. And then the Corinthians, irritated by the reproaches of the aged men in the city, after about twelve days' preparation came out again, and, claiming the victory, raised another trophy. Hereupon the Athenians sallied out of Megara, killed those who were erecting the trophy, and charged and defeated the rest of the army.

The Corinthians now retreated, but a considerable 106 number of them were hard pressed, *They suffer great loss* and missing their way got into an en- *in their retreat.* closure belonging to a private person, which was surrounded by a great ditch and had no exit. The Athenians, perceiving their situation, closed the entrance in front with heavy-armed troops, and, placing their light troops in a circle round, stoned all who had entered the enclosure. This was a great blow to the Corinthians. The main body of their army returned home.

About this time the Athenians began to build their 107 Long Walls extending to the sea, one *The Athenians build* to the harbour of Phalerum, and the *their long walls. Battle* other to the Piraeus. The Phocians *of Tanagra.* B.C. 457. made an expedition against the Dorians, who inhabit Ol. 80, 4. Boeum, Cytinium, and Erineum, and are the mother people of the Lacedaemonians; one of these towns they took. Thereupon the Lacedaemonians under the command of Nicomedes the son of Cleombrotus, who was general in the place of the king Pleistoanax the son of Pausanias (he being at that time a minor), came to the assistance of the Dorians with fifteen hundred hoplites of their own, and, of their allies, ten thousand, and compelled the Phocians to make terms and to restore the town. They then thought of returning; but there were difficulties. Either they might go by sea across the

Crisaean Gulf, in which case the Athenian fleet would be sure to sail round and intercept them, or they might march over Mount Geraneia; but this seemed dangerous when the Athenians were holding Megara and Pegae. The pass was not easy, and was always guarded by the Athenians, who were obviously intending to stop them by that route also. So they determined to remain in Boeotia and consider how they could best get home. They had another motive:—Certain Athenians were privately making overtures to them, in the hope that they would put an end to the democracy and the building of the Long Walls. But the Athenians were aware of their embarrassment, and they also suspected their design against the democracy. So they went out to meet them with their whole force, together with a thousand Argives and contingents from the other allies; they numbered in all fourteen thousand men. Among them were some Thessalian cavalry, who came to their aid in accordance with the treaty[a], but these deserted to the Lacedaemonians during the engagement.

108   The battle was fought at Tanagra in Boeotia, and the *Battle of Oenophyta.* Lacedaemonians and their allies, after *Surrender of Aegina.* great slaughter on both sides, gained the victory. They then marched into the Megarian territory, and, cutting down the fruit-trees, returned home by B.C. 456, way of Geraneia and the Isthmus. But on the sixty-Ol. 81. second day after the battle, the Athenians made another expedition into Boeotia under the command of Myronides, and there was a battle at Oenophyta, in which they defeated the Boeotians and became masters of Boeotia and Phocis. They pulled down the walls of Tanagra and took as hostages from the Opuntian Locrians a hundred of their richest citizens. They then completed their own Long Walls. Soon afterwards the Aeginetans came to terms with the Athenians, dismantling their walls, surrendering their ships, and agreeing to pay tribute for the future. The Athenians, under the command of Tolmides

------

[a] Cp. i. 102

the son of Tolmaeus, sailed round Peloponnesus and
burnt the Lacedaemonian dockyard[a]. They also took the
Corinthian town of Chalcis, and, making a descent upon
Sicyon, defeated a Sicyonian force.

B.C. 455.
Ol. 81, 2.

The Athenians and their allies were still in Egypt, 109
where they carried on the war with
varying fortune. At first they were
masters of the country.   The King
sent to Lacedaemon Megabazus a
Persian, who was well supplied with
money, in the hope that he might per-
suade the Peloponnesians to invade Attica, and so draw
off the Athenians from Egypt. He had no success ; the
money was being spent and nothing done ; so, with what
remained of it, he found his way back to Asia. The King
then sent into Egypt Megabyzus the son of Zopyrus,
a Persian, who marched overland with a large army and
defeated the Egyptians and their allies. He drove the
Hellenes out of Memphis, and finally shut them up in
the island of Prosopitis, where he blockaded them for
eighteen months. At length he drained the canal and
diverted the water, thus leaving their ships high and dry
and joining nearly the whole island to the mainland. He
then crossed over with a land force, and took the island.

After an ineffectual attempt to obtain assistance from Lacedaemon, the Persian King at length succeeds in driving the Athenians out of Memphis.

Thus, after six years' fighting, the cause of the Hellenes 110
in Egypt was lost. A few survivors
of their great army found their way
through Libya to Cyrenè ; by far the
larger number perished. Egypt again
became subject to the Persians, al-
though Amyrtaeus, the king in the fens, still held out.
He escaped capture owing to the extent of the fens and
the bravery of their inhabitants, who are the most warlike
of all the Egyptians. Inaros, the king of Libya, the chief
author of the revolt, was betrayed and impaled. Fifty
additional triremes, which had been sent by the Athenians

Nearly the whole of the expedition to Egypt, including a reinforcement of fifty triremes, is destroyed.

---

[a] i. e. Gythium.

and their allies to relieve their other forces, in ignorance
of what had happened, sailed into the Mendesian mouth
of the Nile. But they were at once attacked both from
the land and from the sea, and the greater part of them
destroyed by the Phoenician fleet, a few ships only
escaping. Thus ended the great Egyptian expedition of
the Athenians and their allies.

111　About this time Orestes, the exiled son of the Thes-
Attempted restora- salian king Echecratides, persuaded
tion of Orestes, the Thes- the Athenians to restore him. Taking
salian exile. with them a force of the Boeotians and
Phocians, who were now their allies, they marched against
Pharsalus in Thessaly. They made themselves masters of
the country in the neighbourhood of their camp, but the
Thessalian cavalry stopped any further advance. They
could not take the place, and none of their plans prospered;
so they returned unsuccessful and brought back Orestes.

B.C. 454.　A short time afterwards a thousand Athenians, under
Ol. 81, 3.　*The Athenians under* the command of Pericles the son of
Pericles defeat the Sicy- Xanthippus, embarking on board the
onians. fleet which they had at Pegae, now in
their possession, coasted along to Sicyon, and there landing, defeated the Sicyonians who came out to meet them.
With the least possible delay taking on board Achaean
troops and sailing to the opposite coast, they attacked and
besieged Oeniadae, a town of Acarnania; but failing to
reduce it, they returned home.

112　After an interval of three years a five years' truce was
B.C. 450.　*Truce for five years.* concluded between the Peloponnesians
Ol. 82, 3.　*Expedition to Cyprus.* and Athenians. The Athenians now
More ships sent to Egypt. abstained from war in Hellas itself, but
Death of Cimon. Bat-
tles at Salamis in Cy- made an expedition to Cyprus with
prus. two hundred ships of their own and of
their allies, under the command of Cimon. Sixty ships
were detached from the armament and sailed to Egypt,
at the request of Amyrtaeus the king in the fens; the
remainder proceeded to blockade Citium. Here Cimon

died, and a famine arose in the country; so the fleet quitted Citium. B.C. 449. Ol. 82, 4. Arriving off Salamis in Cyprus they fought at sea and also on land with Phoenician and Cilician forces. Gaining a victory in both engagements, they returned home, accompanied by the ships which had gone out with them and had now come back from Egypt. After this the Lacedaemonians engaged in the so-called Sacred War and gained possession of the temple of Delphi, which they handed over to the Delphians. But no sooner had they retired than the Athenians sent an expedition and recovered the temple, which they handed over to the Phocians.

Some time afterwards the Athenians, under the command of Tolmides the son of Tolmaeus, with a thousand hoplites of their own and contingents of their allies, made *Defeat of the Athenians at Coronea. Revolution in Boeotia.* 113 B.C. 447. Ol. 83, 2. an expedition against Orchomenus, Chaeronea, and certain other places in Boeotia which were in the hands of oligarchical exiles from different Boeotian towns, and so were hostile to them. They took Chaeronea, and leaving a garrison there, departed. But while they were on their march, the exiles who had occupied Orchomenus, some Locrians, some Euboean exiles and others of the same party, set upon them at Coronea and defeated them, killing many and taking many prisoners. The Athenians then agreed to evacuate the whole of Boeotia upon condition that the prisoners should be restored. And so the Boeotian exiles returned to their homes, and all the Boeotians regained their independence.

Not long afterwards Euboea revolted from Athens. Pericles had just arrived in the island with an Athenian army when the news came that Megara had likewise revolted, that the Peloponnesians were on the point of invading Attica, and that the Megarians had slaughtered the *Revolt of Euboea. Slaughter of the Athenian garrison at Megara. Invasion of Attica. Retirement of the Peloponnesians, and recovery of Euboea.* 114 B.C. 445. Ol. 83, 4. Athenian garrison, of whom a few only had escaped to

Nisaea. The Megarians had introduced a force of Corinthians, Sicyonians, and Epidaurians into the city, and by their help had effected the revolt. Pericles in haste withdrew his army from Euboea. The Peloponnesians then invaded Attica under the command of Pleistoanax son of Pausanias, the Lacedaemonian king. They advanced as far as Eleusis and Thria but no further, and after ravaging the country, returned home. Thereupon the Athenians under the command of Pericles again crossed over to Euboea and reduced the whole country; the Hestiaeans they ejected from their homes and appropriated their territory; the rest of the island they settled by agreement.

115   Soon after their return from Euboea they made a truce for thirty years with the Lacedaemonians and their allies, restoring Nisaea, Pegae, Troezen and Achaia, which were the places held by them in Peloponnesus. Six years later the Samians and Milesians went to war about the possession of Prienè, and the Milesians, who were getting worsted, came to Athens and complained loudly of the Samians. Some private citizens of Samos, who wanted to overthrow the government, supported their complaint. Whereupon the Athenians, sailing to Samos with forty ships, established a democracy, and taking as hostages fifty boys and fifty men whom they deposited at Lemnos, they returned leaving a garrison. But certain of the Samians who had quitted the island and fled to the mainland entered into an alliance with the principal oligarchs who remained in the city, and with Pissuthnes the son of Hystaspes, then governor of Sardis, and collecting troops to the number of seven hundred they crossed over by night to Samos. First of all they attacked the victorious populace and got most of them into their power; then they stole away their hostages from Lemnos, and finally revolted from Athens. The garrison of the Athenians and the officials who were

The Athenians agree to restore the places held by them in Peloponnesus. Revolt of the Samians, who are assisted by the Byzantians.

B.C. 440.
Ol. 85.

in their power were delivered by them into the hands of Pissuthnes. They at once prepared to make an expedition against Miletus. The Byzantians joined in their revolt.

When the Athenians heard of the insurrection they 116 sailed for Samos with sixty ships. But   *The Athenians defeat* of this number they sent away sixteen,   *the Samians at sea.* some towards Caria to keep a look out for the Phoenician fleet, others to summon aid from Chios and Lesbos. With the remaining forty-four ships they fought at sea under the command of Pericles and nine others, near the island of Tragia, against seventy Samian vessels, all sailing from Miletus, of which twenty were transports ; the Athenians gained the victory. After receiving a reinforcement of forty ships from Athens and of twenty-five from Chios and Lesbos they disembarked, and their infantry proving superior, invested the city with three walls ; they also blockaded it by sea. At the same time Pericles took sixty ships of the blockading force and sailed hastily towards Caunus in Caria, news having arrived that a Phoenician fleet was approaching ; Stesagoras and others had already gone with five ships from Samos to fetch it.

Meanwhile the Samians made a sudden sally, and at- 117 tacking the naval station of the Athe-   *Temporary success* nians which was unprotected, destroyed   *and final subjection of* the guard-ships and engaged and de-   *the Samians.* feated the other vessels which put out to meet them. During some fourteen days they were masters of the sea about their own coasts, and carried in and out whatever they pleased. But when Pericles returned, they were B.C. 439. again closely blockaded ; and there soon arrived from Ol. 85, 2. Athens forty additional ships under   *The Byzantians also* Thucydides, Hagnon, and Phormio,   *submit.* twenty more under Tlepolemus and Anticles, and thirty from Chios and Lesbos. The Samians made a feeble attempt at a sea-fight, but soon they were unable to resist, and after nine months were forced to surrender. The terms of capitulation were as follows :—They were to raze

their walls, give hostages, surrender their ships, and pay
a full indemnity by regular instalments. The Byzantians
too made terms and became subjects as before.

118   Not long afterwards occurred the affairs of Corcyra
The history is re- and Potidaea, which have been already
sumed from chap. 88. narrated, and the various other circum-
The Lacedaemonians, stances which led to the Peloponnesian
having decided to go to
war, obtain the sanction War. Fifty years elapsed between the
of the Delphian oracle. retreat of Xerxes and the beginning of
the war; during these years took place all those operations of the Hellenes against one another and against the
Barbarian which I have been describing. The Athenians
acquired a firmer hold over their empire and the city itself
became a great power. The Lacedaemonians saw what
was going on, but during most of the time they remained
inactive and hardly attempted to interfere. They had
never been of a temper prompt to take the field unless
they were compelled; and they were in some degree embarrassed by wars near home. But the Athenians were
growing too great to be ignored and were laying hands on
their allies. They could now bear it no longer: they
made up their minds that they must put out all their
strength and overthrow the Athenian power by force of
arms. And therefore they commenced the Peloponnesian
War. They had already voted in their own assembly that
the treaty had been broken and that the Athenians were
guilty[a]; they now sent to Delphi and asked the God if it
would be for their advantage to make war. He is reported
to have answered that, if they did their best, they would
be conquerors, and that he himself, invited or uninvited,
would take their part.

119   So they again summoned the allies, intending to put to
Activity of the Corin- them the question of war or peace.
thians in pressing on When their representatives arrived, an
the war. assembly was held; and the allies said
what they had to say, most of them complaining of the

---

[a] But cp. vii. 18 med.

Athenians and demanding that the war should proceed. B.C. 432.
The Corinthians had already gone the round of the Ol. 87.
cities and entreated them privately to vote for war; they
were afraid that they would be too late to save Potidaea.
At the assembly they came forward last of all and spoke
as follows :—

'Fellow allies, we can no longer find fault with the 120
Lacedaemonians; they have them-
selves resolved upon war and have
brought us hither to confirm their decision.   And they have done well; for
the leaders of a confederacy, while they
do not neglect the interests of their
own state, should look to the general
weal: as they are first in honour, they should be first in
the fulfilment of their duties.   Now those among us who
have ever had dealings with the Athenians, do not require
to be warned against them; but such as live inland and
not on any maritime highway should clearly understand
that, if they do not protect the sea-board, they will find it
more difficult to carry their produce to the sea, or to
receive in return the goods which the sea gives to the land.
They should not lend a careless ear to our words, for they
nearly concern them ; they should remember that, if they
desert the cities on the sea-shore, the danger may some
day reach them, and that they are consulting for their own
interests quite as much as for ours.   And therefore let no
one hesitate to accept war in exchange for peace.   Wise
men refuse to move until they are wronged, but brave men
as soon as they are wronged go to war, and when there is
a good opportunity make peace again.   They are not
intoxicated by military success; but neither will they
tolerate injustice from a love of peace and ease.   For he
whom pleasure makes a coward will quickly lose, if he
continues inactive, the delights of ease which he is so unwilling to renounce ; and he whose arrogance is stimulated
by victory does not see how hollow is the confidence which

No more fault to be found with the Lacedae-monians.   The Athenians are dangerous to all alike.   Men should be willing to fight, though they should be equally ready to cease from fighting.

elates him.   Many schemes which were ill-advised have
succeeded through the still greater folly which possessed
the enemy, and yet more, which seemed to be wisely contrived, have ended in foul disaster.   The execution of an
enterprise is never equal[a] to the conception of it in the
confident mind of its promoter; for men are safe while
they are forming plans, but, when the time of action comes,
then they lose their presence of mind and fail.

121   'We, however, do not make war upon the Athenians in
We are superior to a spirit of vain-glory, but from a sense
the Athenians in num- of wrong; there is ample justification,
bers, in military skill, and when we obtain redress, we will
in unanimity, and our put up the sword.   For every reason
fleet will soon be on a we are likely to succeed.   First, be-
level with theirs.
cause we are superior in numbers and in military skill;
secondly, because we all obey as one man the orders given
to us.   They are doubtless strong at sea, but we too will
provide a navy, for which the means can be supplied
partly by contributions from each state, partly out of the
funds at Delphi and Olympia.   A loan will be granted to
us, and by the offer of higher pay we can draw away
their foreign sailors.   The Athenian power consists of
mercenaries, and not of their own citizens; but our soldiers
are not mercenaries, and therefore cannot so be bought,
for we are strong in men if poor in money.   Let them be
beaten in a single naval engagement and they are probably
conquered at once; but suppose they hold out, we shall
then have more time in which to practise at sea.   As soon
as we have brought our skill up to the level of theirs our
courage will surely give us the victory.   For that is a natural
gift which they cannot learn, but their superior skill is a
thing acquired, [b] which we must attain by practice [b].

'And the money which is required for the war, we will
But we must find provide by a contribution.   What!
money.   shall their allies never fail in paying
the tribute which is to enslave them, and shall we refuse

---

[a] Reading ὅμοια.   [b] Or, 'which we must overcome by practice.'

to give freely in order to save ourselves and be avenged on
our enemies, or rather to prevent the money which we
refused to give from being taken from us by them and used
to our destruction ?

'These are some of the means by which the war may **122**
be carried on; but there are others. We   *By gaining over their*
may induce their allies to revolt,—a   *allies, we may cut off*
sure mode of cutting off the revenues   *their resources.*
in which the strength of Athens consists; or we may
plant a fort in their country; and there are many
expedients which will hereafter suggest themselves.
For war, least of all things, conforms to prescribed
rules; it strikes out a path for itself when the moment
comes. And therefore he who has his temper under
control in warfare is safer far, but he who gets into
a passion is, through his own fault, liable to the greater
fall.

'If this were merely a quarrel between one of us and
our neighbours about a boundary line   *If we quietly submit*
it would not matter; but reflect : the   *we shall deserve to be*
truth is that the Athenians are a match   *slaves.*
for us all, and much more than a match for any single city.
And if we allow ourselves to be divided or are not united
against them heart and soul—the whole confederacy and
every nation and city in it—they will easily overpower us.
It may seem a hard saying, but you may be sure that
defeat means nothing but downright slavery, and the bare
mention of such a possibility is a disgrace to the Peloponnese :—shall so many states suffer at the hands of one?
Men will say, some that we deserve our fate, others that
we are too cowardly to resist : and we shall seem
a degenerate race. For our fathers were the liberators
of Hellas, but we cannot secure even our own liberty; and
while we make a point of overthrowing the rule of
a single man in this or that city, we allow a city which
is a tyrant to be set up in the midst of us. Are we
not open to one of three most serious charges—folly,

cowardice, or carelessness? a For you certainly do not
escape such imputations by wrapping yourselves in that
contemptuous wisdom which has so often a brought men to
ruin, as in the end to be pronounced contemptible folly.

123   'But why should we dwell reproachfully upon the past,
except in the interest of the present?

*In going to war you
have the God and the
feeling of Hellas on your
side, and you will not
break the treaty.*

We should rather, looking to the future,
devote our energies to the task which
we have immediately in hand. By
labour to win virtue,—that is the lesson
which we b have learnt from our fathers, and which you
ought not to unlearn, because you chance to have some
trifling advantage over them in wealth and power; for
men should not lose in the time of their wealth what was
gained by them in their time of want.   There are many
reasons why you may advance with confidence. The God
has spoken and has promised to take our part himself. All
Hellas will fight at our side, from motives either of fear or
of interest.   And you will not break the treaty,—the God
in bidding you go to war pronounces it to have been
already broken,—but you will avenge the violation of it.
For those who attack others, not those who defend themselves, are the real violators of treaties c.

124   'On every ground you will be right in going to war:

*We cannot go on as
we are. War is the way
to peace; but peace may
be the way to war.*

it is our united advice; d and if you
believe community of interests to be
the surest ground of strength both to
states and individuals, send speedy aid d
to the Potidaeans, who are Dorians and now besieged
by Ionians (for times have changed), and recover the

---

a Or, 'For we cannot suppose that, having avoided these errors, you
have wrapped yourselves in that contemptuous wisdom, which has so
often' etc.

b Reading ἡμῖν.   c Cp. i. 71 fin.

d Reading ταὐτά: or, with all the MSS. retaining ταῦτα: 'And as
it is most certain that the policy which we recommend is for our
advantage both as states and individuals, send speedy aid' etc.

liberties which the rest of the allies have lost. We cannot go on as we are: for some of us are already suffering, and if it is known that we have met, but do not dare to defend ourselves, others will soon share their fate. Acknowledging then, allies, that there is no alternative, and that we are advising you for the best, vote for war; and be not afraid of the immediate danger, but fix your thoughts on the durable peace which will follow. For by war peace is assured, but to remain at peace when you should be going to war may be often very dangerous. The tyrant city which has been set up in Hellas is a standing menace to all alike; she rules over some of us already, and would fain rule over others. Let us attack and subdue her, that we may ourselves live safely for the future and deliver the Hellenes whom she has enslaved.'

Such were the words of the Corinthians.

The Lacedaemonians, having heard the opinions of all 125 the allies, put the question to them all, *Nearly a year is spent* one after the other, great and small *in preparation.* alike, and the majority voted for war. But, although they had come to this decision, they were not ready, and could not take up arms at once; so they determined to make the necessary preparations, each for themselves, with the least possible delay. Still nearly a whole year was passed in preparation before they invaded Attica and commenced open hostilities.

During this interval they sent embassies to Athens and 126 made various complaints that their *The story of Cylon* grounds for going to war might be all *told in explanation of* the stronger in case the Athenians *the curse of the Goddess.* refused to listen. The first ambassadors desired the Athenians to drive out 'the curse of the Goddess.' The B.C. 620? curse to which they referred was as follows:—In the days Ol. 40? of old there was an Athenian named Cylon, who had been an Olympic victor; he was powerful and of noble birth; and he had married the daughter of Theagenes, a Megarian who was at that time tyrant of Megara. In answer to an enquiry which Cylon made at Delphi, the God told him to seize the Acropolis of Athens at the greatest festival of Zeus. Thereupon he obtained forces from Theagenes, and, persuading his friends to join him, when the time of the Olympic festival in Peloponnesus came round, he took possession of the Acropolis, intending to make himself tyrant. He thought that this was the greatest festival of Zeus, and, having been an Olympic victor, he seemed to have a special interest in it. But whether the greatest festival spoken of was in Attica or in some other part of Hellas was a question which never entered into his mind, and the oracle said nothing about it. (For the Athenians also have a greatest festival of Zeus—the festival of Zeus the Gracious, or Diasia, as it is called [a]—this is held outside the city and the whole people sacrifice at it, some, ordinary victims, others, a kind of offering peculiar to the country.) However, Cylon thought that his interpretation was right, and made the attempt at the Olympic festival. The Athenians, when they saw what had happened, came in a body from the fields and invested the Acropolis. After a time they grew tired of the siege and most of them went away, committing the guard to the nine Archons, and giving them full powers to do what they thought best in the whole matter; for in those days public affairs were chiefly administered by the nine Archons [b]. Cylon and his companions were in great distress from want of food and water. So he and his brother made their escape; the rest, being hard pressed, and some of them ready to die of hunger, sat as suppliants at the altar which is in the Acropolis. When the Athenians, to whose charge the guard had been committed, saw them dying in the temple, they bade them rise, promising to do them no harm, and then led them away and put them to death. They even slew some of them in the very presence of the awful Goddesses at whose altars, in passing by, they had sought

---

[a] Placing the comma before instead of after Διάσια.
[b] Cp. Herod. v. 71.

refuge.   The murderers and their descendants are held to
be accursed, and offenders against the Goddess.   These
accursed persons were banished by the Athenians; and
Cleomenes, the Lacedaemonian king, again banished them
from Athens in a time of civil strife by the help of the
opposite faction, expelling the living and disinterring and
casting forth the bones of the dead[a].   Nevertheless they
afterwards returned, and to this day their race still survives
in the city.

The Lacedaemonians desired the Athenians to drive 127
away this curse, as if the honour of the   *This curse attached*
Gods were their first object, but in   *to Pericles.*
reality because they knew that the curse attached to
Pericles, the son of Xanthippus, by his mother's side, and
they thought that if he were banished they would find the
Athenians more manageable.   They did not really expect
that he would be driven into exile, but they hoped to
discredit him with the citizens and make them believe that
his misfortune was to a certain extent the cause of the war.
For he was the leader of the state and the most powerful
man of his day, and his policy was utterly opposed to the
Lacedaemonians.   He would not suffer the Athenians to
give way, but was always urging upon them the necessity
of war.

The Athenians retaliated by demanding that the Lace- 128
daemonians should drive away the   *The Athenians retali-*
curse of Taenarus.   They referred to   *ate by desiring the Lace-*
the murder of certain Helots who had   *daemonians to purge*
taken refuge in the temple of Poseidon   *away other curses. The*
at Taenarus; these the Lacedae-   *curse of the Goddess ex-*
monians, having first raised by the   *plained to be the murder*
hand, had then led away and slain.   *of certain suppliant He-*
The Lacedaemonians themselves be-   *lots; the curse of Athenè*
lieve this act of theirs to have been the   *of the Brazen House*
cause of the great earthquake which   *was caused by the death*
visited Sparta [b].   The Athenians also bade them drive out   *of Pausanias in the pre-*
                                                              cincts of her temple.

---

[a] Cp. Herod. v. 70, 72.   [b] Cp. i. 101, 102.

the curse of Athenè of the Brazen House. The story is
as follows:—When Pausanias the Lacedaemonian was
originally summoned by the Spartans to give an account
of his command at the Hellespont[a], and had been tried
and acquitted, he was no longer sent out in a public
capacity, but he hired a trireme of Hermionè on his own
account and sailed to the Hellespont, pretending that he
had gone thither to fight in the cause of the Hellenes.
In reality he wanted to prosecute an intrigue with the
King, by which he hoped to obtain the empire of Hellas.
He had already taken the first steps after the return from
Cyprus, when he captured Byzantium[b]. The city was at
that time held by the Persians and by certain relatives and
kinsmen of the King, who were taken prisoners. These
he restored to the King without the knowledge of the
allies, to whom he declared that they had made their
escape. This act was the beginning of the whole affair,
and thereby he originally placed the King under an obligation to him. His accomplice was Gongylus the Eretrian, to
whose care he had entrusted Byzantium and the captives.
To this same Gongylus he also gave a letter addressed to
the King, of which, as was afterwards discovered, the
terms were as follows:—

‘Pausanias, the Spartan commander, desiring to do you
a service, sends you back these captives of his spear.
And I propose, if you have no objection, to marry your
daughter, and to bring Sparta and the rest of Hellas
under your sway. I think that I can accomplish this if
you and I take counsel together. Should you approve of
my proposal, send a trusty person to the sea and through
him we will negotiate.’ Thus far the letter.

129   Xerxes was pleased, and sent Artabazus the son of
Intrigue of Pausa-   Pharnaces to the sea, commanding him
nias with Xerxes.   to assume the government of the satrapy
of Dascylium in the room of Megabates. An answer was

---

[a] Cp. i. 95.   [b] Cp. i. 94.

entrusted to him, which he was to send as quickly as possible to Pausanias at Byzantium; he was to show him at the same time the royal seal. If Pausanias gave him any order about his own affairs, he was to execute it with all diligence and fidelity. Artabazus came down to the sea, as he was desired, and transmitted the letter. The answer of the King was as follows:—

'Thus saith Xerxes, the King, to Pausanias. The benefit which thou hast done me in saving the captives who were taken at Byzantium beyond the sea is recorded in my house for ever, and thy words please me. Let neither day nor night hinder thee from fulfilling diligently the promise which thou hast made to me; spare not gold or silver, and take as large an army as thou wilt, wheresoever it may be required. I have sent to thee Artabazus, a good man; act with him for my honour and welfare, and for thine own, and be of good courage.'

B.C. 477 or 476 ff. Ol. 75, 4 or 76 ff.

Pausanias received the letter. He had already acquired 130 a high reputation among the Hellenes when in command at Plataea, and now he was so great that he could no longer contain himself or live like other men.

Pausanias, carried away by pride, manifests his ambitious designs.

Whenever he marched out of Byzantium he wore Persian apparel. On his way through Thrace he was always attended by a body-guard of Medes and Egyptians, and he had his table served after the Persian fashion. He could not conceal his ambition, but indicated by little things the greater designs which he was meditating. He made himself difficult of access, and displayed such a violent temper towards everybody that no one could come near him; and this was one of the chief reasons why the confederacy transferred themselves to the Athenians.

The news of his behaviour soon reached the Lacedae- 131 monians; who had recalled him in the first instance on this ground[a]. And now, when he had sailed away in the ship

---

[a] Cp. i. 93 init.

of Hermione without leave [a], and was evidently carrying

He is recalled a second time by the Lacedaemonians and thrown into prison, but soon comes out and offers himself for trial.

on the same practices; when he had been forced out of Byzantium and the gates had been shut against him by the Athenians; and when, instead of returning to Sparta, he settled at Colonae in Troas, and was reported to the Ephors to be negotiating with the Barbarians, and to be staying there for no good purpose, then at last they made up their minds to act. They sent a herald to him with a despatch rolled on a scytalè, commanding him to follow the officer home, and saying that, if he refused, Sparta would declare war against him. He, being desirous as far as he could to avoid suspicion and believing that he could dispose of the accusations by bribery, returned for the second time to Sparta. On his return he was at once thrown into prison by the Ephors, who have the power to imprison the king himself. But after a time he contrived to come out, and challenged any one who asserted his guilt to bring him to trial.

132   As yet however neither his enemies among the citizens

Sufficient evidence cannot be obtained. At last his confidential servant opens a letter which he was to carry to the Persian satrap, and finding an order for his own death, turns informer.

nor the Spartan government had any trustworthy evidence such as would have justified them in inflicting punishment upon a member of the royal family holding royal office at the time. For he was the guardian as well as cousin of the king, Pleistarchus son of Leonidas, who was still a minor. But his disregard of propriety and affectation of Barbarian fashions made them strongly suspect that he was dissatisfied with his position in the state. They examined into any violation of established usage which they could find in his previous life; and they remembered among other things how in past times he had presumed on his own authority to inscribe on the tripod at Delphi, which the Hellenes

---

[a] Cp. i. 128.

dedicated as the firstfruits of their victory over the Persians, this elegiac couplet:—

> 'Pausanias, captain of the Hellenes, having destroyed the Persian host,
> Made this offering to Phoebus for a memorial.'

The Lacedaemonians had at once effaced the lines and inscribed on the tripod the names of the cities which took part in the overthrow of the Barbarian and in the dedication of the offering. But still this act of Pausanias gave offence at the time, and, now that he had again fallen under suspicion, seemed to receive a new light from his present designs. They were also informed that he was intriguing with the Helots; and this was true, for he had promised them emancipation and citizenship if they would join him in an insurrection and help to carry out his whole design. Still the magistrates would not take decided measures; they even refused to believe the distinct testimony which certain Helots brought against him; their habit having always been to be slow in taking an irrevocable decision against a Spartan without incontestable proof. At last a certain man of Argilus, who had been a favourite and was still a confidential servant of Pausanias, turned informer. He had been commissioned by him to carry to Artabazus the last letters for the King, but the thought struck him that no previous messenger had ever returned; he took alarm, and so, having counterfeited the seal of Pausanias in order to avoid discovery if he were mistaken, or if Pausanias, wanting to make some alteration, should ask him for the letter, he opened it, and among the directions given in it found written, as he had partly suspected, an order for his own death.

He showed the letter to the Ephors, who were now **133** more inclined to believe, but still they wanted to hear something from Pausanias' own mouth , and so, according to a plan preconcerted with them, the man went to Taenarus as a suppliant and there put up a hut divided by a partition. In the inner part of the hut he placed some of the Ephors, and when Pausanias came to him and asked

His servant takes sanctuary at Taenarus, where he conceals some of the Ephors. Pausanias coming to enquire the reason reveals the whole.

him why he was a suppliant, the whole truth was at once revealed to them. There was the man reproaching Pausanias with the directions which he had found in the letter, and going into minute details about thé whole affair; he protested that never on any occasion had he brought him into any trouble when sent on his service in this matter to the King: why then should he share the fate of the other messengers, and be rewarded with death? And there was Pausanias, admitting the truth of his words, and telling him not to be angry at what had happened, offering to raise him by the hand that he might safely leave the temple, and bidding him start at once and not make difficulties.

134   The Ephors, who had heard every word, went away for

The Ephors attempt to arrest Pausanias. He flies to the temple of Athenè and is there shut in and starved to death.

the present, intending, now that they had certain knowledge, to take Pausanias in the city. It is said that he was on the point of being arrested in the street, when the face of one of them as they approached revealed to him their purpose, and another who was friendly warned him by a hardly perceptible nod. Whereupon he ran and fled to the temple of Athenè of the Brazen House and arrived before them, for the precinct was not far off. There, entering into a small chamber which belonged to the temple, that he might not suffer from exposure to the weather, he remained. His pursuers, failing to overtake him, afterwards unroofed the building, and watching when he was within, and preventing him from getting out, they built up the doors, and, investing the place, starved him to death. He was on the point of expiring in the chamber where he lay, when they, observing his condition, brought him out; he was still breathing, but as soon as he was brought out he died. The Spartans were going to cast his body into the Caeadas, a chasm into which they throw malefactors, but they changed their minds and buried him somewhere in the neighbourhood. The God of Delphi afterwards commanded them to transfer him to the place where he died, and he now lies in the entrance to the precinct, as the inscription on the column testifies. The oracle also told them that they had brought a curse upon themselves, and must offer two bodies for one to Athenè of the Brazen House. Whereupon they made two brazen statues, which they dedicated, intending them to be an expiation for Pausanias.

To this judgment of the God himself the Athenians 135 referred when they retorted on the Lacedaemonians, telling them to banish the curse.

Now the evidence which proved that Pausanias was in league with Persia implicated Themistocles; and the Lacedaemonians sent ambassadors to the Athenians charging him likewise with treason, and demanding that he should receive the same punishment. *Themistocles is implicated in the plot, and officers are sent to take him.* The Athenians agreed, but having been ostracised he was living at the time in Argos, whence he used to visit other parts of the Peloponnese. The Lacedaemonians were very ready to join in the pursuit; so they and the Athenians sent officers, who were told to arrest him wherever they should find him.

Themistocles received information of their purpose, and 136 fled from the Peloponnesus to the Corcyraeans, who were under an obligation to him. The Corcyraeans said that they were afraid to keep him, lest they should incur the enmity of Athens and Lacedaemon; so they conveyed him to the neighbouring continent, whither he was followed by the officers, who constantly enquired in which direction he had gone and pursued him everywhere. Owing to an accident he was compelled to stop at the house of Admetus, king of the Molossians, who was not his friend. *He seeks refuge among the Corcyraeans; they are afraid of Athens and Lacedaemon, and send him away to Epirus. Coming to the house of Admetus, king of the Molossians, he sits as a suppliant at the hearth.*

He chanced to be absent from home, but Themistocles presented himself as a suppliant to his wife, and was instructed by her to take their child and sit at the hearth. Admetus soon returned, and then Themistocles told him who he was, adding that if in past times he had opposed any request which Admetus had made to the Athenians, he ought not to retaliate on an exile. He was now in such extremity that a far weaker adversary than he could do him a mischief; but a noble nature should not be revenged by taking at a disadvantage one as good as himself. Themistocles further argued that he had opposed Admetus in some matter of business, and not when life was at stake; but that, if Admetus delivered him up, he would be consigning him to death. At the same time he told him who his pursuers were and what was the charge against him.

137   Admetus, hearing his words, raised him up, together *Admetus gives him* with his own son, from the place where *protection, and when* he sat holding the child in his arms, *the officers arrive in* which was the most solemn form of *pursuit, sends him to* *Pydna, whence he sails* supplication.   Not long afterwards the *to Ephesus.* Athenians and Lacedaemonians came and pressed him to give up the fugitive, but he refused; and as Themistocles wanted to go to the King, sent him on foot across the country to the sea at Pydna (which was in the kingdom of Alexander).   There he found a merchant B.C. 466. vessel sailing to Ionia, in which he embarked; it was Ol. 78, 3. driven, however, by a storm to the station of the Athenian fleet which was blockading Naxos.   He was unknown to his fellow passengers, but, fearing what might happen, he told the captain who he was and why he fled, threatening if he did not save his life to say that he had been bribed to take him on board.   The only hope was that no one should be allowed to leave the ship while they had to remain off Naxos; if he complied with his request, the obligation should be abundantly repaid.   The captain agreed, and after anchoring in a rough sea for a day and

a night off the Athenian station, he at length arrived at Ephesus. Themistocles rewarded him with a liberal present ; for he received soon afterwards from his friends the property which they had in their keeping at Athens, and which he had deposited at Argos. He then went up the country in the company of one of the Persians who dwelt on the coast, and sent a letter to Artaxerxes the son of B. C. 465. Xerxes, who had just succeeded to the throne. The letter Ol. 78, 4. was in the following words:—'I, Themistocles, have come to you, I who of all *His letter to the King.*
Hellenes did your house the greatest injuries so long as I was compelled to defend myself against your father ; but still greater benefits when I was in safety and he in danger during his retreat. And there is a debt of gratitude due to me' (here he noted how he had forewarned Xerxes at Salamis of the resolution of the Hellenes to withdraw [a], and how through his influence, as he pretended, they had refrained from breaking down the bridges) [b]. 'Now I am here, able to do you many other services, and persecuted by the Hellenes for your sake. Let me wait a year, and then I will myself explain why I have come.'

The King is said to have been astonished at the boldness 138 of his character, and told him to wait *Going to the Court* a year as he proposed. In the interval *of Persia, he acquires* he made himself acquainted, as far as *the favour of the King* he could, with the Persian language *and receives great hon-* and the manners of the country. When *our, but shortly after* the year was over, he arrived at the *dies.* court and became a greater man there than any Hellene had ever been before. This was due partly to his previous *The greatness of his* reputation, and partly to the hope *character. His natural* which he inspired in the King's mind *acuteness and foresight:* that he would enslave Hellas to him ; *his power of persuasion,* above all, his ability had been tried and *his readiness in an* not found wanting. For Themistocles *emergency.* was a man whose

---

[a] Cp. Herod. viii. 75.   [b] Cp. Herod. viii. 108.

natural force was unmistakeable; this was the quality for which he was distinguished above all other men; from his own native acuteness, and without any study either before or at the time, he was the ablest judge of the course to be pursued in a sudden emergency, and could best divine what was likely to happen in the remotest future. Whatever he had in hand he had the power of explaining to others, and even where he had no experience he was quite competent to form a sufficient judgment; no one could foresee with equal clearness the good or evil event which was hidden in the future. In a word, Themistocles, by natural power of mind and with the least preparation, was of all men the best able to extemporise the right thing to be done. A sickness put an end to his life, although some say that he poisoned himself because he felt that he could not accomplish what he had promised to the King. There is a monument of him in the agora of the Asiatic Magnesia, where he was governor—the King assigning to him, for bread, Magnesia, which produced a revenue of fifty talents [a] in the year; for wine, Lampsacus, which was considered to be the richest in wine of any district then known; and Myus for meat. His family say that his remains were carried home at his own request and buried in Attica, but secretly; for he had been accused of treason and had fled from his country, and he could not lawfully be interred there. Such was the end of Pausanias the Lacedaemonian, and Themistocles the Athenian, the two most famous Hellenes of their day.

139
B.C. 432.
Ol. 87.

The Lacedaemonians make a final demand for the restoration of independence to the Hellenes. Speech of Pericles.

Thus the demand for the banishment of the accursed made by the Lacedaemonians on the occasion of their first embassy was met by a counter demand on the part of Athens. They came again and again, and told the Athenians that they must raise the siege of Potidaea and restore Aegina to indepen-

---

[a] About £10,000

dence.   Above all, and in the plainest terms, they insisted   B.C. 432.
that if they wanted to avert war, they must rescind the   Ol. 87.
decree which excluded the Megarians from the market of
Athens and the harbours in the Athenian dominions.   But
the Athenians would not listen to them, nor rescind the
decree; alleging in reply that the Megarians had tilled
the holy ground and the neutral borderland, and had
received their runaway slaves.   Finally, there came from
Sparta an embassy, consisting of Rhamphias, Melesippus,
and Hegesander, who said nothing of all this, but only,
'The Lacedaemonians desire to maintain peace; and peace
there may be, if you will restore independence to the
Hellenes.'   Whereupon the Athenians called an assembly
and held a discussion; it seemed best to them to make up
their minds and to give a complete and final answer.   Many
came forward to speak, and much was said on both sides,
some affirming that they ought to go to war, and others
that this decree about the Megarians should be rescinded
and not stand in the way of peace.   At last Pericles the
son of Xanthippus, who was the first man of his day at
Athens, and the greatest orator and statesman, came
forward and advised as follows:—

'Athenians, I say, as I always have said, that we must 140
never yield to the Peloponnesians, *I still give you my*
although I know that men are per- *old advice,—Do not*
suaded to go to war in one temper of *yield to the Pelopon-*
mind, and act when the time comes in *nesians.*
another, and that their resolutions change with the
changes of fortune.   But I see that I must give you
the same or nearly the same advice which I gave
before, and I call upon those whom my words may
convince to maintain our united determination, even if
we should not escape disaster; or else, if our sagacity
be justified by success, to claim no share of the credit[a].

----

[a] Cp. ii. 64 init.

B.C. 432.
Ol. 87.

The movement of events is often as wayward and in-comprehensible as the course of human thought; and this is why we ascribe to chance whatever belies our calculation.

'For some time past the designs of the Lacedaemonians

The demands of the Lacedaemonians may seem trifling, but sub-mission to them will only provoke fresh de-mands and implies the loss of our indepen-dence.

have been clear enough, and they are still clearer now. Our agreement says that when differences arise, the two parties shall refer them to arbitration, and in the mean time both are to retain what they have. But for arbitration they never ask; and when it is offered by us, they refuse it[a]. They want to redress their grievances by arms and not by argument; and now they come to us, using the language, no longer of expostulation, but of command. They tell us to quit Potidaea, to leave Aegina independent, and to rescind the decree respecting the Megarians. These last ambassadors go further still, and announce that we must give the Hellenes independ-ence. I would have none of you imagine that he will be fighting for a small matter if we refuse to annul the Megarian decree, of which they make so much, telling us that its revocation would prevent the war. You should have no lingering uneasiness about this; you are not really going to war for a trifle. For in the seeming trifle is involved the trial and confirmation of your whole pur-pose. If you yield to them in a small matter, they will think that you are afraid, and will immediately dictate some more oppressive condition; but if you are firm, you will prove to them that they must treat you as their equals.

141 Wherefore make up your minds once for all, either to give way while you are still unharmed, or, if we are going to war, as in my judgment is best, then on no plea small or great to give way at all; we will not condescend to possess our own in fear. Any claim, the smallest as well

---

[a] Cp. i. 78.

as the greatest, imposed on a neighbour and an equal
when there has been no legal award,
can mean nothing but slavery.

'That our resources are equal to
theirs, and that we shall be as strong
in the war, I will now prove to you in
detail. The Peloponnesians cultivate
their own lands, and they have no
wealth either public or private. Nor
have they any experience of long
wars in countries beyond the sea;

Unless you mean to give way now, you must determine never to give way at all. Nor need you fear the result; for you have many advantages over the Peloponnesians; they are poor and till their own land, they are unaccustomed to great wars, and divided in race.

their poverty prevents them from fighting, except in
person against each other, and that for a short time only.
Such men cannot be often manning fleets or sending out
armies. They would be at a distance from their own
properties, upon which they must nevertheless draw, and
they will be kept off the sea by us. Now wars are supported out of accumulated wealth, and not out of forced
contributions. And men who cultivate their own lands
are more ready to serve with their persons than with their
property[a]; they do not despair of their lives, but they
soon grow anxious lest their money should all be spent,
especially if the war in which they are engaged is protracted beyond their calculation, as may well be the case.
In a single pitched battle the Peloponnesians and their
allies are a match for all Hellas, but they are not able to
maintain a war against a power different in kind from their
own[b]; they have no regular general assembly, and therefore cannot execute their plans with speed and decision.
The confederacy is made up of many races; all the representatives have equal votes, and press their several
interests. There follows the usual result, that nothing is
ever done properly. For some are all anxiety to be
revenged on an enemy, while others only want to get off
with as little loss as possible. The members of such

---

[a] Cp. i. 121 med.   [b] Cp. viii. 96 fin.

B.C. 432.
Ol. 87.
a confederacy are slow to meet, and when they do meet, they give little time to the consideration of any common interest, and a great deal to schemes which further the interest of their particular state. Every one fancies that his own neglect will do no harm, but that it is somebody else's business to keep a look-out for him, and this idea, cherished alike by each, is the secret ruin of all.

142 'Their greatest difficulty will be want of money, which

They cannot do you any real harm by building a rival city or fortified posts in Attica; nor can they, mere landsmen as they are, rival you at sea.

they can only provide slowly; delay will thus occur, and war waits for no man. Further, no fortified place which they can raise against us[a] is to be feared any more than their navy. As to the first, even in time of peace it would be hard for them to build a city able to compete with Athens; and how much more so when they are in an enemy's country, and our walls will be a menace to them quite as much as theirs to us! Or, again, if they simply raise a fort in our territory, they may do mischief to some part of our lands by sallies, and the slaves may desert to them; but that will not prevent us from sailing to the Peloponnese and there raising forts against them, and defending ourselves there by the help of our navy, which is our strong arm. For we have gained more experience of fighting on land from warfare at sea than they of naval affairs from warfare on land. And they will not easily acquire the art of seamanship[b]; even you yourselves, who have been practising ever since the Persian War, are not yet perfect. How can they, who are not sailors, but tillers of the soil, do much? They will not even be permitted to practise, because a large fleet will constantly be lying in wait for them. If they were watched by a few ships only, they might run the risk, trusting to their numbers and forgetting their inexperience; but if they are kept off the sea by our superior strength, their

---

[a] Cp. i. 122 init. [b] Cp. i. 121 med.

want of practice will make them unskilful, and their want B.C. 432.
of skill timid.   Maritime skill is like skill of other kinds, Ol. 87.
not a thing to be cultivated by the way or at chance times ;
it is jealous of any other pursuit which distracts the mind
for an instant from itself.

'Suppose, again, that they lay hands on the treasures 143
at Olympia and Delphi, and tempt our
mercenary sailors with the offer of   *Our foreign sailors*
higher pay[a], there might be serious   *will not be tempted by*
danger, if we and our metics [b] embark- *offers of high pay, and*
ing alone were not still a match for   *if they are, we can do*
                                            without them.
them.   But we are a match for them : and, best of all, our
pilots are taken from our own citizens, while no sailors
are to be found so good or so numerous as ours in all the
rest of Hellas.   None of our mercenaries will choose to
fight on their side for the sake of a few days' high pay,
when he will not only be an exile, but will incur greater
danger, and will have less hope of victory.

'Such I conceive to be the prospects of the Peloponnesians.   But we ourselves are free
from the defects which I have noted   *We must guard the*
in them ; and we have great advan-   *city and the sea, and*
tages.   If they attack our country by   *not mind about our*
                                          houses and lands in the
land, we shall attack theirs by sea ; and *country.*
the devastation, even of part of Peloponnesus, will be
a very different thing from that of all Attica.   For they, if
they want fresh territory, must take it by arms, whereas
we have abundance of land both in the islands and on the
continent ; such is the power which the empire of the sea
gives.   Reflect, if we were islanders, who would be more
invulnerable ?   Let us imagine that we are, and acting in
that spirit let us give up land and houses, but keep a watch
over the city and the sea.   We should not under any
irritation at the loss of our property give battle to the
Peloponnesians, who far outnumber us.   If we conquer,

---

a Cp. i. 121 init.   b Cp. iii. 16 init.

B.C. 432.
Ol. 87.
we shall have to fight over again with as many more ; and if we fail, besides the defeat, our confederacy, which is our strength, will be lost to us ; for our allies will rise in revolt when we are no longer capable of making war upon them. Mourn not for houses and lands, but for men ; men may gain these, but these will not gain men. If I thought that you would listen to me, I would say to you, "Go yourselves and destroy them, and thereby prove to the Peloponnesians that none of these things will move you."

144 'I have many other reasons for believing that you will
Let our answer be: conquer, but you must not be extending
We will grant inde- your empire while you are at war, or
pendence to our allies, run into unnecessary dangers. I am
if the Lacedaemonians more afraid of our own mistakes than of
will allow their subjects
to choose their own our enemies' designs. But of all this I
form of government. will speak again when the time of action
comes ; for the present, let us send the ambassadors away, giving them this answer : "That we will not exclude the Megarians from our markets and harbours, if the Lacedae-monians will cease to expel foreigners, whether ourselves or our allies, from Sparta ; for the treaty no more forbids the one than the other. That we will concede indepen-dence to the cities, if they were independent when we made the treaty, and as soon as the Lacedaemonians allow their allied states a true independence, not for the interest of Lacedaemon, but everywhere for their own. Also that
We do not want war, we are willing to offer arbitration ac-
but offer arbitration. cording to the treaty. And that we do
Still peace is hopeless;
and we must prepare not want to begin a war, but intend to
for war in a spirit defend ourselves if attacked." This
worthy of our fathers. answer will be just, and befits the dignity
of the city. We must be aware however that war will come ; and the more willing we are to accept the situation, the less ready will our enemies be to lay hands upon us. Remember that where dangers are greatest, there the greatest honours are to be won by men and states. Our

fathers, when they withstood the Persian, had no such B.C. 432. power as we have; what little they had they forsook: Ol. 87. not by good fortune but by wisdom, and not by power but by courage, they drove the Barbarian away and raised us to our present height of greatness. We must be worthy of them, and resist our enemies to the utmost, that we may hand down our empire unimpaired to posterity.'

Such were the words of Pericles. The Athenians, 145 approving, voted as he told them, and   *The Athenians adopt* on his motion answered the Lacedae-   *Pericles' advice.* monians in detail as he had suggested, and on the whole question to the effect 'that they would do nothing upon compulsion, but were ready to settle their differences by arbitration upon fair terms according to the treaty.' So the ambassadors went home and came no more.

These were the causes of offence alleged on either side 146 before the war began. The quarrel   *War, though not* arose immediately out of the affair of *formally proclaimed, is* Epidamnus and Corcyra. But, al-   *imminent.* though the contest was imminent, the contending parties still kept up intercourse and visited each other, without a herald, but not with entire confidence. For the situation was really an abrogation of the treaty, and might at any time lead to war.

BOOK II

1 AND now the war between the Athenians and Peloponnesians and the allies of both *Outbreak of the war.* actually began. Henceforward the struggle was uninterrupted, and they communicated with one another only by heralds. The narrative is arranged according to summers and winters and follows the order of events.

2 For fourteen years the thirty years' peace which was *The Thebans enter Plataea by night.* concluded after the recovery of Euboea remained unbroken. But in the fifteenth year, when Chrysis the high-priestess of Argos was in the forty-eighth year of her priesthood, Aenesias being Ephor at Sparta, and at Athens Pythodorus having two months of his archonship to run[a], in the sixth month after the engagement at Potidaea and at the beginning of spring, about the first watch of the night an armed force of somewhat more than three hundred Thebans entered Plataea, a city of Boeotia, which was an ally of Athens, under the command of two Boeotarchs, Pythangelus the son of Phyleides, and Diemporus the son of Onetorides. They were invited by Naucleides, a Plataean, and his partisans, who opened the gates to them. These men wanted to kill certain citizens of the opposite faction and to make over the city to the Thebans, in the hope of getting the power into their own hands. The intrigue had been conducted by Eurymachus the son of Leontiades,

---

[a] For the difficulties attending the chronology see note on the passage.

one of the chief citizens of Thebes.   There was an old B.C. 431.
quarrel between the two cities, and the Thebans, seeing Ol. 87, 2.
that war was inevitable, were anxious to surprise the
place while the peace lasted and before hostilities had
actually broken out.   No watch had been set; and so they
were enabled to enter the city unperceived.   They
grounded their arms in the Agora, but instead of going to
work at once and making their way into the houses of
their enemies, as those who invited them suggested, they
resolved to issue a conciliatory proclamation and try to
make friends with the citizens.   The herald announced
that if any one wished to become their ally and return to
the ancient constitution of Boeotia, he should join their
ranks.   In this way they thought that the inhabitants
would easily be induced to come over to them.

The Plataeans, when they found that the city had been 3
surprised and taken and that the *The Plataeans, ter-*
Thebans were within their walls, were *rified by the sudden*
panic-stricken.   In the darkness they *attack, come to terms.*
were unable to see them and greatly *But afterwards, dis-*
over-estimated their numbers.   So they *covering the weakness of*
came to terms, and accepting the pro- *the enemy, they gather*
posals which were made to them, *and fall upon the The-*
bans.
remained quiet, the more readily since the Thebans offered
violence to no one.   But in the course of the negotiations
they somehow discovered that their enemies were not so
numerous as they had supposed, and concluded that they
could easily attack and master them.   They determined to
make the attempt, for the commons at Plataea were strongly
attached to the Athenian alliance.   They began to collect
inside the houses, breaking through the party-walls that
they might not be seen going along the streets; they
likewise raised barricades of waggons (without the beasts
which drew them), and took other measures suitable to the
emergency.   When they had done all which could be done
under the circumstances, they sallied forth from their
houses, choosing the time of night just before daybreak,

B.C. 431.
Ol. 87, 2. lest, if they put off the attack until dawn, the enemy might be more confident and more a match for them. While darkness lasted they would be timid, and at a disadvantage, not knowing the streets so well as themselves. So they fell upon them at once hand to hand.

4   When the Thebans found that they had been deceived

The Thebans, after some resistance, turn and fly. Being ignorant of the way, many are slain in the streets; a few escape; the remainder surrender. they closed their ranks and resisted their assailants on every side. Two or three times they drove them back. But when at last the Plataeans charged them, and the women and slaves on the housetops screamed and yelled and pelted them with stones and tiles, the confusion, which was aggravated by the rain which had been falling heavily during the night, became too much for them, and they turned and fled in terror through the city. Hardly any of them knew the way out, and the streets were dark as well as muddy, for the affair happened at the end of the month when there was no moon; whereas their pursuers knew well enough how to prevent their escape; and thus many of them perished. The gates by which they entered were the only ones open, and these a Plataean fastened with the spike of a javelin, which he thrust into the bar instead of the pin. So this exit too was closed and they were chased up and down the city. Some of them mounted upon the wall and cast themselves down into the open. Most of these were killed. Others got out by a deserted gate, cutting through the bar unperceived with an axe which a woman gave them; but only a few, for they were soon found out. Others lost themselves in different parts of the city, and were put to death. But the greater number kept together and took refuge in a large building abutting upon the wall, of which the doors on the near side chanced to be open, they thinking them to be the gates of the city, and expecting to find a way through them into the country. The Plataeans, seeing that they were in a trap, began to consider whether they should not set the building on fire,

and burn them where they were. At last they and the
other Thebans who were still alive, and were wandering
about the city, agreed to surrender themselves and their
arms unconditionally. Thus fared the Thebans in Plataea.

B.C. 431.
Ol. 87, 2.

The main body of the Theban army, which should have 5
come during the night to the support
of the party entering the city in case of
a reverse, having on their march heard
of the disaster, were now hastening to
the rescue. Plataea is about eight
miles distant from Thebes, and the
heavy rain which had fallen in the
night delayed their arrival; for the river
Asopus had swollen, and was not
easily fordable. Marching in the rain,
and with difficulty crossing the river,
they came up too late, some of their friends being already
slain and others captives. When the Thebans became
aware of the state of affairs, they resolved to lay hands
on what was outside the walls; for there were men and
property left in the fields, as would naturally happen when
a sudden blow was struck in time of peace. They
meant to keep any one whom they caught as a hostage
and exchange him for one of their own men, if any of them
were still alive. But before they had executed their plan,
the Plataeans, suspecting their intentions, and fearing for
their friends outside, sent a herald to the Thebans protesting against the crime of which they had been guilty in
trying to seize their city during peace, and warning them
not to touch anything which was outside the walls. If
they persisted they threatened in return to kill the
prisoners; but if they retired, they would give them up.
This is the Theban account, and they add that the
Plataeans took an oath. The Plataeans do not admit that
they ever promised to restore the captives at once, but only
if they could agree after negotiations; and they deny that
they took an oath. However this may have been, the

Reinforcements come from Thebes. The Plataeans, suspecting that the Thebans intend to seize their citizens outside the walls, send a herald, promising with an oath (according to the Theban account) to restore the prisoners if the Thebans retired. The prisoners are put to death.

B.C. 431.
Ol. 87, 2.
Thebans withdrew, leaving the Plataean territory unhurt; but the Plataeans had no sooner got in their property from the country than they put the prisoners to death. Those who were taken were a hundred and eighty in number, and Eurymachus, with whom the betrayers of the city had negotiated, was one of them.

6   When they had killed their prisoners, they sent a

The Athenians, know-
ing only of the attempt
on the city, bid the
Plataeans spare their
prisoners.   Learning
the truth, they garri-
son Plataea and re-
move the women and
children.

messenger to Athens and gave back the dead to the Thebans under a flag of truce; they then took the necessary measures for the security of the city. The news had already reached Athens, and the Athenians had instantly seized any Boeotians who were in Attica, and sent a herald to Plataea bidding them do no violence to the Theban prisoners, but wait for instructions from Athens. The news of their death had not arrived. For the first messenger had gone out when the Thebans entered, and the second when they were just defeated and captured; but of what followed the Athenians knew nothing; they sent the message in ignorance, and the herald, when he arrived, found the prisoners dead. The Athenians next despatched an army to Plataea, and brought in supplies. Then leaving a small force in the place they conveyed away the least serviceable of the citizens, together with the women and children.

7   The affair of Plataea was a glaring violation of the thirty

Both sides now pre-
pare for the struggle.

years' truce, and the Athenians now made preparations for war. The Lacedaemonians and their allies made similar preparations. Both they and the Athenians meditated sending embassies to the King [a], and to the other Barbarian potentates [b] from whom either party might hope to obtain aid; they likewise sought the alliance of independent cities outside their own dominion. The Lacedaemonians ordered their friends in

---

[a] Cp. ii. 67 init.; iv. 50.   [b] Cp. ii. 29, 67.

Italy and Sicily to build others in number proportioned to the size of their cities, in addition to the ships which they had on the spot ; for they intended to raise the Peloponnesian navy to a total of five hundred. The cities were also required to furnish a fixed sum of money ; they were not to receive more than one ship of the Athenians at a time, but were to take no further measures until these preparations had been completed. The Athenians reviewed their confederacy, and sent ambassadors to the places immediately adjacent to Peloponnesus—Corcyra, Cephallenia, Acarnania, and Zacynthus. They perceived that if they could only rely upon the friendship of these states [a], they might completely encircle Peloponnesus with war.

On neither side were there any mean thoughts ; they 8 were both full of enthusiasm : and no *Excitement and en-* wonder, for all men are energetic when *thusiasm in Hellas.* they are making a beginning. At that time the youth of Peloponnesus and the youth of Athens were numerous ; they had never seen war, and were therefore very willing to take up arms. All Hellas was excited by the coming conflict between her two chief cities. Many were the prophecies circulated and many the oracles chanted by diviners, not only in the cities about to engage in the struggle, but throughout Hellas. Quite recently the island of Delos had been shaken by an earthquake for the first time within the memory of the Hellenes ; this was interpreted and generally believed to be a sign of coming events. And everything of the sort which occurred was curiously noted.

The feeling of mankind was strongly on the side of 9 the Lacedaemonians ; for they professed *Universal hatred and* to be the liberators of Hellas. Cities *fear of the Athenians.* and individuals were eager to assist them to the utmost, both by word and deed ; and where a man could not hope

---

[a] Taking βεβαίως with εἰ σφίσι φίλια ταῦτα εἴη.

B.C. 431.
Ol. 87, 2.
to be present, there it seemed to him that all things were at a stand. For the general indignation against the Athenians was intense ; some were longing to be delivered from them, others fearful of falling under their sway.

Such was the temper which animated the Hellenes, and *List of the allies on either side.* such were the preparations made by the two powers for the war. Their respective allies were as follows :—The Lacedaemonian confederacy included all the Peloponnesians with the exception of the Argives and the Achaeans—they were both neutral ; only the Achaeans of Pellene took part with the Lacedaemonians at first ; afterwards all the Achaeans joined them[a]. Beyond the borders of the Peloponnese, the Megarians, Phocians, Locrians, Boeotians, Ambraciots, Leucadians, and Anactorians were their allies. Of these the Corinthians, Megarians, Sicyonians, Pellenians, Eleans, Ambraciots, and Leucadians provided a navy, the Boeotians, Phocians, and Locrians furnished cavalry, the other states only infantry. The allies of the Athenians were Chios, Lesbos, Plataea, the Messenians of Naupactus, the greater part of Acarnania, Corcyra, Zacynthus, and cities in many other countries which were their tributaries. There was the maritime region of Caria, the adjacent Dorian peoples, Ionia, the Hellespont, the Thracian coast, the islands that lie to the east within the line of Peloponnesus and Crete, including all the Cyclades with the exception of Melos and Thera. Chios, Lesbos, and Corcyra furnished a navy ; the rest, land forces and money. Thus much concerning the two confederacies, and the character of their respective forces.

10   Immediately after the affair at Plataea the Lacedae-*The Lacedaemonians summon their allies to meet at the Isthmus.* monians sent round word to their Peloponnesian and other allies, bidding them equip troops and provide all things necessary for a foreign expedition, with the object

---

[a] Cp. v. 82 init.

of invading Attica. The various states made their preparations as fast as they could, and at the appointed time,
with contingents numbering two-thirds of the forces of
each, met at the Isthmus. When the whole army was
assembled, Archidamus, the king of the Lacedaemonians,
and the leader of the expedition, called together the
generals of the different states and their chief officers
and most distinguished men, and   *Speech of Archida-*
spoke as follows:—   *mus.*

B.C. 431.
Ol. 87, 2.

'Men of Peloponnesus, and you, allies, many are the
expeditions which our fathers made   *We have had great*
both within and without the Pelo-   *experience in war, and*
ponnese, and the veterans among our- *our army was never*
selves are experienced in war; and   *finer. But we must*
yet we never went forth with a greater *beware of haste, and*
army than this. But then we should   *not hold our enemy too*
                                      cheap.
remember that, whatever may be our numbers or our
valour, we are going against a most powerful city. And
we are bound to show ourselves worthy of our fathers,
and not wanting to our own reputation. For all Hellas
is stirred by our enterprise, and her eyes are fixed upon
us: she is friendly and would have us succeed because
she hates the Athenians. Now although some among
you, surveying this great host, may think that there is
very little risk of the enemy meeting us in the field, we
ought not on that account to advance heedlessly; but the
general and the soldier of every state should be always
expecting that his own division of the army will be the
one first in danger. War is carried on in the dark;
attacks are generally sudden and furious, and often the
smaller army, animated by a proper fear, has been more
than a match for a larger force which, disdaining their
opponent, were taken unprepared by him. When invading
an enemy's country, men should always be confident in
spirit, but they should fear too, and take measures of precaution; and thus they will be at once most valorous
in attack and impregnable in defence.

11

'And the city which we are attacking is not so utterly

For they are tho- powerless against an invader, but is in
roughly prepared, and the best possible state of preparation,
the least likely of all and for this reason our enemies may
men to sit idly by while be quite expected to meet us in the
we waste their lands. field. Even if they have no such intention beforehand,
yet as soon as they see us in Attica, wasting and de-
stroying their property, they will certainly change their
mind. For all men are angry when they not only suffer
but see, and some strange form of calamity strikes full
upon the eye; the less they reflect the more ready they
are to fight; above all men the Athenians, who claim
imperial power, and are more disposed to invade and
waste their neighbour's land than to look on while their
own is being wasted. Remembering how great this city
is which you are attacking, and what a fame you will bring
on your ancestors and yourselves for good or evil according
to the result, follow whithersoever you are led; maintain
discipline and caution above all things, and be on the
alert to obey the word of command. It is both the noblest
and the safest thing for a great army to be visibly animated
by one spirit.'

12   Having thus spoken, Archidamus dismissed the assembly.

Archidamus sends His first step was to send Melesippus,
Melesippus to Athens, the son of Diacritus, a Spartan,
but he is refused ad- to Athens in the hope that the
mission to the city, and Athenians might after all give way,
immediately sent across when they saw their enemies actually
the frontier. on the march. But they would not admit him to the
assembly, nor even into the city. For Pericles had already
carried a motion to the effect that they would have nothing
to do with herald or embassy while the Lacedaemonians
were in the field. So Melesippus was sent away without
a hearing and told that he must cross the frontier before
sunset; if the Lacedaemonians wanted to hold any parley
with the Athenians, they must go home first. He was
attended by an escort in order to prevent his communi-

cating with any one.   When he arrived at the Athenian B.C. 431.
frontier, and was about to leave them, he uttered these Ol. 87, 2.
words: 'This day will be to the Hellenes the beginning
of great sorrows.'   On the return of the herald to the
camp Archidamus learned that the Athenians were not as
yet at all in the mood to yield; so at last he moved
forward his army and prepared to enter Attica.   The
Boeotians who had sent their contingent of two-thirds, including their cavalry, to the Peloponnesian army, marched
to Plataea with the remainder of their forces and wasted
the country.

While the Peloponnesians were gathering at the Isthmus, 13
and were still on their way, but before *Pericles, suspecting*
they entered Attica, Pericles the son of *that Archidamus will*
Xanthippus, who was one of the ten *spare his lands, either*
Athenian generals, knowing that the *from friendship, or to*
invasion was inevitable, and suspecting *prejudice him with the*
that Archidamus in wasting the country *Athenians, promises to*
might very likely spare his lands, either *give them to the public*
out of courtesy and because he happened to be his friend, *if they are uninjured by*
the enemy.
or by the order of the Lacedaemonian authorities (who had
already attempted to raise a prejudice against him[a] when
they demanded the expulsion of the polluted family, and
might take this further means of injuring him in the eyes
of the Athenians), openly declared in the assembly that
Archidamus was his friend, but was not so to the injury of
the state, and that supposing the enemy did not destroy
his lands and buildings like the rest, he would make a
present of them to the public; and he desired that the
Athenians would have no suspicion of him on that account.
As to the general situation, he repeated his previous
advice; they must prepare for war and bring their property
from the country into the city; they must defend their
walls but not go out to battle; they should also equip for
service the fleet in which lay their strength.   Their allies

---

[a] Cp. i. 126 init. and 127.

should be kept well in hand, for their power depended on the revenues which they derived from them; military successes were generally gained by a wise policy and command of money. The state of their finances was encouraging; they had on an average six hundred talents [a] of tribute coming in annually from their allies, to say nothing of their other revenue; and there were still remaining in the Acropolis six thousand talents of coined silver. (The whole amount had once been as much as nine thousand seven hundred talents [b], but from this had to be deducted a sum of three thousand seven hundred expended on various buildings, such as the Propylaea of the Acropolis, and also on the siege of Potidaea.) Moreover there was uncoined gold and silver in the form of private and public offerings, sacred vessels used in processions and games, the Persian spoil and other things of the like nature, worth at least five hundred talents [c] more. There were also at their disposal, besides what they had in the Acropolis, considerable treasures in various temples. If they were reduced to the last extremity they could even take off the plates of gold with which the image of the goddess was overlaid; these, as he pointed out, weighed forty talents, and were of refined gold, which was all removeable. They might use this treasure in self-defence, but they were bound to replace all that they had taken. By this estimate of their wealth he strove to encourage them. He added that they had thirteen thousand hoplites, besides the sixteen thousand who occupied the fortresses or who manned the walls of the city. For this was the number engaged on garrison duty at the beginning of the war [d], whenever the enemy invaded Attica; they were made up of the elder and younger men, and of such metics as bore

He reminds the Athenians of their enormous wealth and military and naval resources, telling them that victory is certain if they act with prudence.

---

[a] About £120,000.   [b] About £1,940,000.   [c] About £100,000.
[d] Cp. what is said of the citizens on garrison duty, vii. 28 init.

heavy arms. The Phaleric wall extended four miles from Phalerum to the city walls: the portion of the city wall which was guarded was somewhat less than five miles; that between the Long Wall and the Phaleric requiring no guard. The Long Walls running down to the Piraeus were rather more than four and a half miles in length; the outer only was guarded. The whole circuit of the Piraeus and of Munychia was not quite seven miles, of which half required a guard. The Athenian cavalry, so Pericles pointed out, numbered twelve hundred, including mounted archers; the foot-archers, sixteen hundred; of triremes fit for service the city had three hundred.—The forces of various kinds which Athens possessed at the commencement of the war, when the first Peloponnesian invasion was impending, cannot be estimated at less.—To these Pericles added other arguments, such as he was fond of using, which were intended to prove to the Athenians that victory was certain.

The citizens were persuaded, and brought into the city 14 their children and wives, their house- *The citizens, following* hold goods, and even the wood-work of *his advice, gather into* their houses, which they took down. *the city;* Their flocks and beasts of burden they conveyed to Euboea and the adjacent islands.

The removal of the inhabitants was painful; for the Athenians had always been accustomed to reside in the country. Such a life had been characteristic of them, 15 more than of any other Hellenic people, from very early times. In the *but reluctantly, for they* days of Cecrops and the first kings, *had ever loved a country* down to the reign of Theseus, Attica *life. In old times they* was divided into communes, having *lived in separate com-* their own town halls and magistrates. *munes, until Theseus* Except in case of alarm the whole *united them into the* people did not assemble in council under the king, but administered their own affairs, and advised together in their several townships. Some of them at times even

went to war with him, as the Eleusinians under Eumolpus
with Erectheus. But when Theseus came to the throne,
he, being a powerful as well as a wise ruler, among
other improvements in the administration of the country,
dissolved the councils and separate governments, and
united all the inhabitants of Attica in the present city,
establishing one council and town hall. They continued
to live on their own lands, but he compelled them to
resort to Athens as their metropolis, and henceforward
they[a] were all inscribed in the roll of her citizens[a].
A great city thus arose which was handed down by
Theseus to his descendants, and from his day to this
the Athenians have regularly celebrated the national
festival of the Synoecia, or 'union of the communes' in
honour of the Goddess Athenè.

Before his time, what is now the Acropolis and the
Small extent of the ground lying under it to the south was
ancient city. the city. Many reasons may be urged
in proof of this statement :—The temples of Athenè and
of other divinities are situated in the Acropolis itself, and
those which are not lie chiefly thereabouts ; the temples
of Olympian Zeus, for example, and of the Pythian Apollo,
and the temple of Earth and of Dionysus in the Marshes,
in honour of whom the more ancient Dionysia are celebrated on the twelfth day of the month Anthesterion[b],
a festival which also continues to be observed by the
Ionian descendants of the Athenians. In the same quarter
are other ancient temples, and not far off is the fountain
now called Enneacrounos, or the Nine Conduits, from the
form given to it by the tyrants, but originally, before the
springs were covered in, Callirrhoè, or the Fair Stream.
The water of this fountain was used by the ancient
Athenians on great occasions, it being near the original
city; and at marriage rites and other ceremonies the
custom is still retained. To this day the Acropolis or

---

[a] Or, 'all paid taxes to Athens.'   [b] February–March.

Citadel is called by the Athenians *Polis*, or City, because
that neighbourhood was first inhabited.

Thus for a long time the ancient Athenians enjoyed 16
a country life in self-governing communities ; and although
they were now united in a single city, they and their descendants, down to the time of this war, from old habit
generally resided with their households in the country
where they had been born. For this reason, and also
because they had recently restored their country-houses
and estates after the Persian War, they had a disinclina-
tion to move. They were depressed at the thought of
forsaking their homes and the temples which had come
down to them from their fathers and were the abiding
memorials of their early constitution. They were going
to change their manner of life, and in leaving their villages
were in fact each of them going into exile.

When they came to Athens, only a few of them had 17
houses or could find homes among
friends or kindred. The majority took   *The new-comers, hav-
up their abode in the vacant spaces of   ing no homes of their
the city, and in the temples and shrines   own, occupy the temples
                                            and waste spaces in the*
of heroes, with the exception of those on   *city.*
the Acropolis, the Eleusinium, and any other precinct which
could be securely closed. The Pelasgian ground, as it
was called, which lay at the foot of the citadel, was under
a curse forbidding its occupation. There was also a half-
line of a Pythian oracle to the same effect :—

'Better the Pelasgian ground left waste.'

Yet even this was filled under the sudden pressure of
necessity. And to my mind the oracle came true in a sense
exactly contrary to the popular expectation ; for the unlaw-
ful occupation to which men were driven was not the cause
of the calamities which befell the city, but the war was the
cause of the occupation ; and the oracle without mentioning
the war foresaw that the place would be inhabited some
day for no good. Many also established themselves in

the turrets of the walls, or in any other place which they could find; for the city could not contain them when they first came in. But afterwards they divided among them the Long Walls and the greater part of the Piraeus. At the same time the Athenians applied themselves vigorously to the war, summoning their allies, and preparing an expedition of a hundred ships against the Peloponnese.

18   While they were thus engaged, the Peloponnesian army was advancing: it arrived first of all at

The Peloponnesians advance to Oenoè, which they attempt in vain to capture.

Oenoè, a fortress on the confines of Attica and Boeotia, which was garrisoned by the Athenians whenever war broke out, and was the point at which the Peloponnesians intended to enter the enemy's country. There they encamped and prepared to assault the walls by means of engines and siege works. But these and other measures took up time and detained them in the neighbourhood. Archidamus was severely blamed for the delay; he was also thought not to have been energetic enough in levying war, and to have done the Athenians good service by discouraging vigorous action. After the muster of the forces he had been accused of delay at the isthmus, and of loitering on the march. But his reputation was most affected by his halt at Oenoè. For the Athenians employed the interval in getting away their property; and the Peloponnesians fancied that, if they had advanced quickly and he had not lingered, they could have seized everything before it was conveyed within the walls. Such were the feelings entertained towards Archidamus by his troops during the halt. He is said to have held back in the belief that the Athenians, while their lands were still unravaged [a], would yield, and that the thought of allowing them to be devastated would be too much for them.

19   But when they had assaulted Oenoè, and after leaving no means untried were unable to take it, and no herald

_____

[a] Cp. i. 82 med.

came from the Athenians, at last they marched on, and about the eightieth day after the entry of the Thebans into Plataea, in the middle of the summer[a], *Leaving Oenoë, they* when the corn was in full ear, invaded *enter Attica and march* Attica, under the command of Archi- *to Acharnae,* damus the son of Zeuxidamus the Lacedaemonian king. They encamped and ravaged, first of all, Eleusis and the plain of Thria, where they put to flight some Athenian horse near the streams called Rheiti; they then advanced, keeping Mount Aegaleos on the right hand, through the district of Kropeia until they reached Acharnae, which is the largest of the Athenian townships or demes, as they are called; and at Acharnae they encamped, and remained there a considerable time ravaging the country.

In this first invasion Archidamus is said to have lingered 20 about Acharnae with his army ready *where they linger, in the* for battle, instead of descending into *hope that the Athenians* the plain[b], in the hope that the Athe- *will come out to fight.* nians, who were now flourishing in youth and numbers and provided for war as they had never been before, would perhaps meet them in the field rather than allow their lands to be ravaged. When therefore they did not appear at Eleusis or in the plain of Thria, he tried once more whether by encamping in the neighbourhood of Acharnae he could induce them to come out. The situation appeared to be convenient, and the Acharnians, being a considerable section of the city and furnishing three thousand hoplites, were likely to be impatient at the destruction of their property, and would communicate to the whole people a desire to fight. Or if the Athenians did not come out to meet him during this invasion, he could henceforward ravage the plain with more confidence, and march right up to the walls of the city. The Achar-nians, having lost their own possessions, would be less willing to hazard their lives on behalf of their neighbours,

---

[a] i.e. of the Attic summer, including spring, see note.

[b] i.e. the plain round Athens.

and so there would be a division in the Athenian counsels. Such was the motive of Archidamus in remaining at Acharnae.

21   The Athenians, so long as the Lacedaemonians were in *Rage and excitement* the neighbourhood of Eleusis and the *of the Athenians. Un-* plain of Thria, entertained a hope that *popularity of Pericles.* they would come no further. They remembered how, fourteen years before [a], the Lacedaemonian king, Pleistoanax the son of Pausanias, invaded Attica with a Peloponnesian army, and how after advancing as far as Eleusis and Thria he came no further, but retreated. And indeed this retreat was the cause of his exile; for he was thought to have been bribed. But when they saw the army in the neighbourhood of Acharnae, and barely seven miles from the city, they felt the presence of the invader to be intolerable. The devastation of their country before their eyes, which the younger men had never seen at all, nor the elder except in the Persian invasion, naturally appeared to them a horrible thing, and the whole people, the young men especially, were anxious to go forth and put a stop to it. Knots were formed in the streets, and there were loud disputes, some eager to go out, a minority resisting. Soothsayers were repeating oracles of the most different kinds, which all found in some one or other enthusiastic listeners. The Acharnians, who in their own estimation were no small part of the Athenian state, seeing their land ravaged, strongly insisted that they should go out and fight. The excitement in the city was universal; the people were furious with Pericles, and, forgetting all his previous warnings, they abused him for not leading them to battle, as their general should, and laid all their miseries to his charge.

22   But he, seeing that they were overcome by the irritation of the moment and inclined to evil counsels, and confident that he was right in refusing to go out, would not

---

[a] Cp. i. 114 fin.

summon an assembly or meeting of any kind, lest, coming
together more in anger than in pru-   *He refuses to comply*
dence, they might take some false step.   *with their wishes.*
He maintained a strict watch over the city, and sought to
calm the irritation as far as he could.   Meanwhile he sent
out horsemen from time to time to prevent flying parties
finding their way into the fields near the city and doing
mischief.   A skirmish took place at Phrygia between one
of the divisions of the Athenian horse   *Skirmish at Phrygia,*
assisted by their Thessalian allies on   *in which the Athenians*
the one hand, and the Boeotian cavalry   *are worsted.*
on the other, in which the Athenians and Thessalians were
at least a match for their opponents, until, the Boeotian
infantry coming up to support the horse, they were compelled to fly.   The Athenians and Thessalians lost a few
men, but recovered their bodies on the same day without
asking for a truce.   On the morrow the Peloponnesians
raised a trophy.   The forces which the Thessalians brought
to the aid of the Athenians, according to the terms of their
old alliance[a], consisted of Larissaeans, Pharsalians,
Cranonians, Pyrasians, Gyrtonians, and Pheraeans.   The
leaders of the Larissaeans were Polymedes and Aristonous,
one from each of the two leading factions of their city ; the
Pharsalians were commanded by Meno.   The forces of
the other cities had likewise generals of their own.

When the Peloponnesians found that the Athenians did **23**
not come out to meet them, they moved   *The Athenians send*
their army from Acharnae, and ravaged   *one hundred ships to*
some of the townships which lie be-   *cruise round Pelopon-*
tween Mount Parnes and Mount   *nesus. The enemy re-*
Brilessus.   While they were still in   *tire from Attica.*
the country, the Athenians sent the fleet of a hundred ships
which they had been equipping on an expedition round
the Peloponnese.   These ships carried on board a thousand
hoplites and four hundred archers ; they were under the

---

[a] Cp. i. 102 fin., 107 fin.; iv. 78 med.

command of Carcinus the son of Xenotimus, Proteas the
son of Epicles, and Socrates the son of Antigenes. After
the departure of the fleet the Peloponnesians remained in
Attica as long as their provisions lasted, and then, taking
a new route, retired through Boeotia. In passing by
Oropus they wasted the country called Peiraïkè[a], inhabited
by the Oropians, who are subjects of the Athenians. On
their return to Peloponnesus the troops dispersed to their
several cities.

24   When they had retreated, the Athenians posted guards
*The Athenians set
aside a thousand talents
and a hundred triremes
in case of an attack by
sea.*
to keep watch both by land and sea,
a precaution which they maintained
throughout the war. They then
passed a decree reserving of the
treasure in the Acropolis a thousand
talents[b]: this sum was set apart and was not to be
expended unless the enemy attacked the city with a fleet
and they had to defend it. In any other case, he who
brought forward or put to the vote a proposal to touch the
money was to be punished with death. They also resolved
to set apart yearly a hundred triremes, the finest of the
year, and to appoint trierarchs for them ; these they were
only to use at the same time with the money, and in the
same emergency.

25   The Athenian forces, which had lately been dispatched
*Proceedings of the
Athenian fleet.*
to Peloponnesus in the hundred vessels,
and were assisted by the Corcyraeans
with fifty ships and by some of the allies from the same
region, did considerable damage on the Peloponnesian
coast. They also disembarked and attacked Methonè,
a fortress in Laconia, which was weak and had no regular
garrison. Now Brasidas the son of Tellis, a Spartan,
happened to be in those parts in command of a force, and,
seeing the danger, he came to the aid of the inhabitants

---

[a] Reading with the MSS. τὴν γῆν τὴν Πειραϊκήν. Cp. iii. 91 med., ἐς
᾽Ωρωπὸν τῆς πέραν γῆς, i. e. the coast opposite Euboea.

[b] About £200,000.

with a hundred hoplites.   He dashed through the scattered
parties of Athenian troops, whose attention was occupied
with the fortress, and threw himself into Methonè, suffering
a slight loss; he thus saved the place.   The exploit was
publicly acknowledged at Sparta, Brasidas being the first
Spartan who obtained this distinction in the war.   The
Athenians, proceeding on their voyage, ravaged the
territory of Pheia in Elis for two days, and defeated three
hundred chosen men from the vale of Elis, as well as
some Elean perioeci from the neighbourhood of Pheia who
came to the rescue.   But a violent storm arose, and there
was no harbour in which the fleet could find shelter; so
the greater part of the army re-embarked and sailed round
the promontory called Ichthys towards the harbour of
Pheia.   Meanwhile the Messenians and others who were
unable to get on board marched by land and captured
Pheia.   The fleet soon sailed into the harbour and took
them up; they then evacuated Pheia and put to sea.   By
this time the main army of the Eleans had arrived; whereupon the Athenians proceeded on their way to other places,
which they ravaged.

About the same time the Athenians sent thirty ships to 26
cruise off Locris, having an eye also to   *Thirty ships are sent*
the safety of Euboea.   Cleopompus the   *to Locris.*
son of Cleinias was their commander.   He made descents
on the Locrian coast and ravaged various places.   He also
captured Thronium, taking hostages of the inhabitants, and
at Alopè defeated the Locrians who came to defend the
place.

In the same summer the Athenians   expelled the 27
Aeginetans and their families from   *The Athenians expel*
Aegina, alleging that they had been the   *the Aeginetans from*
main cause of the war.   The island lies   *their country. Some of*
close to Peloponnesus, and they thought   *the exiles are settled by*
it safer to send thither settlers of their   *the Lacedaemonians in*
own, an intention which they shortly   *Thyrea.*
afterwards carried
out.   The Lacedaemonians gave the Aeginetan exiles the

town of Thyrea to occupy and the adjoining country to cultivate, partly in order to annoy the Athenians, partly out of gratitude to the Aeginetans, who had done them good service at the time of the earthquake and the revolt of the Helots. The Thyrean territory is a strip of land coming down to the sea on the borders of Argolis and Laconia. There some of them found a home; others dispersed over Hellas.

28   During the same summer, at the beginning of the lunar

Eclipse of the sun.

month (apparently the only time when such an event is possible), and in the afternoon, there was an eclipse of the sun, which took the form of a crescent, and then became full again; during the eclipse a few stars were visible.

29   In the same summer, Nymphodorus the son of Pythes,

The Athenians make Nymphodorus their proxenus, hoping that he will gain over Sitalces, king of Thrace.

a native of Abdera and a man of great influence with Sitalces who had married his sister, was made by the Athenians their proxenus at that place and invited by them to Athens. He had formerly been considered their enemy, but now they hoped that he would gain over to their alliance Sitalces, who was the son of Teres and king of Thrace.

This Teres, the father of Sitalces, was the first founder

Sitalces was the son of Teres, the founder of the Odrysian empire. This Teres has no connexion with the Tereus of mythology.

of the great Odrysian empire, which he extended over a large part of Thrace, although many of the Thracian tribes are still independent. He has no connexion with Tereus who took to wife from Athens Procnè, the daughter of Pandion; they do not even belong to the same Thrace. For Tereus dwelt in Daulia, a part of the region which is now called Phocis but in those days was inhabited by Thracians, and in that country Itys suffered at the hands of the women Procnè and Philomela. Many of the poets when they make mention of the nightingale (Philomela) apply to the bird the epithet Daulian. Further, Pandion would surely have formed a marriage connexion for his daughter among his neighbours with a view to mutual protection, and not at a distance of so many days' journey, among the Odrysian Thracians. And the Teres of whom I am speaking, and who was the first powerful king of the Odrysae, has not even the same name [a].

Now Sitalces, whom the Athenians made their ally, was the son of this Teres; they wanted him to assist them in the conquest of Chalcidicè and of Perdiccas. So Nymphodorus came to Athens, nego- tiated the alliance with Sitalces, and *Sitalces becomes an ally of Athens, and his son is made an Athe- nian citizen: Perdiccas is also reconciled.*
got his son Sadocus enrolled an Athenian citizen. He also undertook to terminate the war in Chalcidicè, promising that he would persuade Sitalces to send the Athenians an army of Thracian horsemen and targeteers. He further reconciled Perdiccas with the Athenians, and persuaded them to restore Thermè to him [b]. Whereupon Perdiccas joined the Athenian army under Phormio [c], and with him fought against the Chalcidians. Thus Sitalces the son of Teres king of Thrace, and Perdiccas son of Alexander king of Macedonia, entered into the Athenian alliance.

The Athenians, in the hundred ships which were still 30 cruising about Peloponnesus, took Sollium, a town belonging to the Corinthians, which they handed over to the Palaereans of Acarnania, giving *The Athenians cap- ture Sollium and Asta- cus, and gain over Ce- phallenia.*
to them alone of the Acarnanians the right of occupying the city and country. They also stormed the town of Astacus, and driving out Evarchus who was tyrant there, added it to the Athenian confederacy. They next sailed to the island of Cephallenia, which they gained over with- out fighting. The island lies over against Acarnania and Leucas, and contains four cities inhabited by the Paleans,

---

[a] i.e. is called Teres, not Tereus.

[b] Cp. i. 61 init.   [c] Cp. i. 64 med.

Cranians, Samaeans, and Pronnaeans. Soon afterwards the fleet proceeded on its voyage homewards.

31   About the end of the summer the entire Athenian force,

The Athenians under the command of Pericles march into the Megarid and ravage the country. including the metics, invaded the territory of Megara, under the command of Pericles the son of Xanthippus. The Athenian fleet had reached Aegina on its way home, and when the commanders heard that the whole armed force of the city was in Megara, they sailed thither and joined them. This was the largest army which the Athenians ever had in one place; for the city was still in her full strength, and had not as yet suffered from the plague. The Athenians themselves numbered not less than ten thousand hoplites, exclusive of the remaining three thousand who were engaged at Potidaea. A force of metic hoplites amounting to at least three thousand took part in the invasion, and also a large number of light-armed troops. After ravaging the greater part of the country they retired. They repeated the invasion, sometimes with cavalry, sometimes with the whole Athenian army, every year during the war until Nisaea was taken [a].

32   At the end of this summer the island of Atalantè, which

The Athenians fortify the island of Atalantè. lies off the coast of the Opuntian Locrians and had hitherto been uninhabited, was fortified and made a guard-station by the Athenians. They wanted to prevent pirates sailing from Opus and other places in Locris and plundering Euboea. Such were the events which occurred during the remainder of the summer after the Peloponnesians had retired from Attica.

33   *The Corinthians restore the tyrant Evarchus to Astacus. On their return they attack Cephallenia, but are defeated.*   During the following winter, Evarchus the Acarnanian, desiring to be restored to Astacus, persuaded the Corinthians to sail with forty ships and fifteen hundred hoplites and reinstate him, he

---

[a] Cp. iv. 66 init., 69 fin.

himself hiring some mercenaries. Of this expedition Euphamidas the son of Aristonymus, Timoxenus the son of Timocrates, and Eumachus the son of Chrysis, were the commanders. They sailed to Astacus, and restored Evarchus; they then tried to gain over certain other towns on the coast of Acarnania; but, failing in their attempt, they proceeded homewards. Touching at Cephallenia on their voyage, they made a descent on the country of the Cranians, but being entrapped by means of a pretended agreement, and then unexpectedly attacked, they lost a part of their forces; at length, not without a severe struggle, they put to sea again and returned home.

During the same winter, in accordance with an old 34 national custom, the funeral of those who first fell in this war was celebrated by the Athenians at the public charge. The ceremony is as follows: Three *The Athenians celebrate the funeral of their citizens who had died in the war.* days before the celebration they erect a tent in which the bones of the dead are laid out, and every one brings to his own dead any offering which he pleases. At the time of the funeral the bones are placed in chests of cypress wood, which are conveyed on hearses; there is one chest for each tribe. They also carry a single empty litter decked with a pall for all whose bodies are missing, and cannot be recovered after the battle. The procession is accompanied by any one who chooses, whether citizen or stranger, and the female relatives of the deceased are present at the place of interment and make lamentation. The public sepulchre is situated in the most beautiful spot outside the walls; there they always bury those who fall in war; only after the battle of Marathon the dead, in recognition of their pre-eminent valour, were interred on the field. When the remains have been laid in the earth, some man of known ability and high reputation, chosen by the city, delivers a suitable oration over them; after which the people depart. Such is the manner of interment; and the ceremony was repeated from time to time throughout the war.   Over those who were the first buried Pericles was chosen to speak.   At the fitting moment he advanced from the sepulchre to a lofty stage, which had been erected in order that he might be heard as far as possible by the multitude, and spoke as follows:—

(FUNERAL SPEECH.)

35   'Most of those who have spoken here before me

The law which enjoins this oration has been often praised.   But I should prefer to praise the brave by deeds only, not to imperil their reputation on the skill of an orator.   Still, our ancestors approved the practice, and I must obey.

have commended the lawgiver who added this oration to our other funeral customs; it seemed to them a worthy thing that such an honour should be given at their burial to the dead who have fallen on the field of battle.   But I should have preferred that, when men's deeds have been brave, they should be honoured in deed only, and with such an honour as this public funeral, which you are now witnessing.   Then the reputation of many would not have been imperilled on the eloquence or want of eloquence of one, and their virtues believed or not as he spoke well or ill.   For it is difficult to say neither too little nor too much; and even moderation is apt not to give the impression of truthfulness.   The friend of the dead who knows the facts is likely to think that the words of the speaker fall short of his knowledge and of his wishes; another who is not so well informed, when he hears of anything which surpasses his own powers, will be envious and will suspect exaggeration.   Mankind are tolerant of the praises of others so long as each hearer thinks that he can do as well or nearly as well himself, but, when the speaker rises above him, jealousy is aroused and he begins to be incredulous.   However, since our ancestors have set the seal of their approval upon the practice, I must obey, and to the utmost of my power shall endeavour to satisfy the wishes and beliefs of all who hear me.

'I will speak first of our ancestors, for it is right and 36
seemly that now, when we are lament-
ing the dead, a tribute should be paid
to their memory.   There has never
been a time when they did not inhabit
this land, which by their valour they
have handed down from generation to
generation, and we have received from
them a free state.   But if they were worthy of praise, still
more were our fathers, who added to their inheritance,
and after many a struggle transmitted to us their sons this
great empire.   And we ourselves assembled here to-day,
who are still most of us in the vigour of life, have carried
the work of improvement further, and have richly endowed
our city with all things, so that she is sufficient for herself
both in peace and war.   Of the military exploits by which
our various possessions were acquired, or of the energy
with which we or our fathers drove back the tide of war,
Hellenic or Barbarian, I will not speak ; for the tale would
be long and is familiar to you.   But before I praise the
dead, I should like to point out by what principles of
action we rose [a] to power, and under what institutions and
through what manner of life our empire became great.
For I conceive that such thoughts are not unsuited to the
occasion, and that this numerous assembly of citizens and
strangers may profitably listen to them.

I will first commemorate our predecessors, who gave us freedom and empire.   And before praising the dead, I will describe how Athens has won her greatness.

'Our form of government does not enter into rivalry 37
with the institutions of others.   We
do not copy our neighbours, but are
an example to them.   It is true that
we are called a democracy, for the
administration is in the hands of the
many and not of the few.   But while
the law secures equal justice to all
alike in their private disputes, the
claim of excellence is also recognised ;   and when a

Our government is a democracy, but we honour men of merit, whether rich or poor.   Our public life is free from exclusiveness, our private from suspicion ; yet we revere alike the injunctions of law and custom.

---

[a] Reading ἤλθομεν.

citizen is in any way distinguished, he is preferred to the public service, not as a matter of privilege, but as the reward of merit. Neither is poverty a bar, but a man may benefit his country whatever be the obscurity of his condition. There is no exclusiveness in our public life, and in our private intercourse we are not suspicious of one another, nor angry with our neighbour if he does what he likes; we do not put on sour looks at him which, though harmless, are not pleasant. While we are thus unconstrained in our private intercourse, a spirit of reverence pervades our public acts; we are prevented from doing wrong by respect for the authorities and for the laws, having an especial regard to those which are ordained for the protection of the injured as well as to those unwritten laws which bring upon the transgressor of them the reprobation of the general sentiment.

38   'And we have not forgotten to provide for our weary spirits many relaxations from toil; we have regular games and sacrifices throughout the year; our homes are beautiful and elegant; and the delight which we daily feel in all these things helps to banish melancholy. Because of the greatness of our city the fruits of the whole earth flow in upon us; so that we enjoy the goods of other countries as freely as of our own.

We find relaxation in our amusements, and in our homes; and the whole world contributes to our enjoyment.

39   'Then, again, our military training is in many respects superior to that of our adversaries. Our city is thrown open to the world, and we never expel a foreigner or prevent him from seeing or learning anything of which the secret if revealed to an enemy might profit him. We rely not upon management or trickery, but upon our own hearts and hands. And in the matter of education, whereas they from early youth are always undergoing laborious exercises which are to make them brave, we live at ease, and yet are equally

In war we singly are a match for the Pelopon-nesians united; though we have no secrets and undergo no laborious training.

ready to face ᵃ the perils which they face ᵃ. And here is
the proof. The Lacedaemonians come into Attica not by
themselves, but with their whole confederacy following;
we go alone into a neighbour's country; and although our
opponents are fighting for their homes and we on a foreign
soil, we have seldom any difficulty in overcoming them.
Our enemies have never yet felt our united strength; the
care of a navy divides our attention, and on land we are
obliged to send our own citizens everywhere. But they, if
they meet and defeat a part of our army, are as proud as
if they had routed us all, and when defeated they pretend
to have been vanquished by us all.

'If then we prefer to meet danger with a light heart but
without laborious training, and with
a courage which is gained by habit and
not enforced by law, are we not greatly
the gainers? Since we do not anticipate the pain, although, when the hour
comes, we can be as brave as those
who never allow themselves to rest;
and thus too our city is equally admirable in peace and in war. For we
are lovers of the beautiful, yet simple in our tastes, and
we cultivate the mind without loss of manliness. Wealth
we employ, not for talk and ostentation, but when there is
a real use for it. To avow poverty with us is no disgrace;
the true disgrace is in doing nothing to avoid it. An
Athenian citizen does not neglect the state because he
takes care of his own household; and even those of us
who are engaged in business have a very fair idea of
politics. We alone regard a man who takes no interest
in public affairs, not as a harmless, but as a useless
character; and if few of us are originators, we are all
sound judges of a policy. The great impediment to action

We are not enervated by culture, or vulgarised by wealth. We are all interested in public affairs, believing that nothing is lost by free discussion. Our goodness to others springs not from interest, but from the generous confidence of freedom.   40

ᵃ Or, 'perils such as our strength can bear;' or 'perils which are
enough to daunt us.'

is, in our opinion, not discussion, but the want of that
knowledge which is gained by discussion preparatory to
action.   For we have a peculiar power of thinking before
we act and of acting too, whereas other men are courageous
from ignorance but hesitate upon reflection.   And they
are surely to be esteemed the bravest spirits who, having
the clearest sense both of the pains and pleasures of life,
do not on that account shrink from danger.   In doing
good, again, we are unlike others; we make our friends
by conferring, not by receiving favours.   Now he who
confers a favour is the firmer friend, because he would
fain by kindness keep alive the memory of an obligation ;
but the recipient is colder in his feelings, because he
knows that in requiting another's generosity he will not
be winning gratitude but only paying a debt.   We alone
do good to our neighbours not upon a calculation of
interest, but in the confidence of freedom and in a frank

41 *In fine, Athens is the*   and fearless spirit.   To sum up : I say
school of Hellas. She   that Athens is the school of Hellas,
alone in the hour of   and that the individual Athenian in
trial rises above her re-   his own person seems to have the
putation.   Her citizens
need no poet to sing   power of adapting himself to the most
their praises : for every   varied forms of action with the utmost
land bears witness to   versatility and grace.   This is no
their valour.
passing and idle word, but truth and
fact ; and the assertion is verified by the position to which
these qualities have raised the state.   For in the hour of
trial Athens alone among her contemporaries is superior
to the report of her.   No enemy who comes against her is
indignant at the reverses which he sustains at the hands
of such a city ; no subject complains that his masters are
unworthy of him.   And we shall assuredly not be without
witnesses ; there are mighty monuments of our power
which will make us the wonder of this and of succeeding
ages ; we shall not need the praises of Homer or of any
other panegyrist whose poetry may please for the moment [a],

---

[a] Cp. i. 10 med., and 21.

although his representation of the facts will not bear the light of day. For we have compelled every land and every sea to open a path for our valour, and have everywhere planted eternal memorials of our friendship and of our enmity. Such is the city for whose sake these men nobly fought and died ; they could not bear the thought that she might be taken from them; and every one of us who survive should gladly toil on her behalf.

'I have dwelt upon the greatness of Athens because 42 I want to show you that we are con-   *The praise of the city*
tending for a higher prize than those   *is the praise of these*
who enjoy none of these privileges, and   *men, for they made her*
to establish by manifest proof the merit   *great. Good and bad,*
of these men whom I am now com-   *rich and poor alike,*
memorating. Their loftiest praise has   *preferred death to dis-*
   honour.
been already spoken. For in magnifying the city I have magnified them, and men like them whose virtues made her glorious. And of how few Hellenes can it be said as of them, that their deeds when weighed in the balance have been found equal to their fame ! Methinks that a death such as theirs has been gives the true measure of a man's worth ; it may be the first revelation of his virtues, but is at any rate their final seal. For even those who come short in other ways may justly plead the valour with which they have fought for their country; they have blotted out the evil with the good, and have benefited the state more by their public services than they have injured her by their private actions. None of these men were enervated by wealth or hesitated to resign the pleasures of life ; none of them put off the evil day in the hope, natural to poverty, that a man, though poor, may one day become rich. But, deeming that the punishment of their enemies was sweeter than any of these things, and that they could fall in no nobler cause, they determined at the hazard of their lives to be honourably avenged, and to leave the rest. They resigned to hope their unknown chance of happiness ; but in the face of death they resolved to rely upon them-

selves alone. And when the moment came they were minded to resist and suffer, rather than to fly and save their lives; they ran away from the word of dishonour, but on the battle-field their feet stood fast, and [a] in an instant, at the height of their fortune, they passed away from the scene, not of their fear, but of their glory [a].

43   'Such was the end of these men; they were worthy of Athens, and the living need not desire to have a more heroic spirit, although they may pray for a less fatal issue. The value of such a spirit is not to be expressed in words. Any one can discourse to you for ever about the advantages of a brave defence, which you know already. But instead of listening to him I would have you day by day fix your eyes upon the greatness of Athens, until you become filled with the love of her; and when you are impressed by the spectacle of her glory, reflect that this empire has been acquired by men who knew their duty and had the courage to do it, who in the hour of conflict had the fear of dishonour always present to them, and who, if ever they failed in an enterprise, would not allow their virtues to be lost to their country, but freely gave their lives to her as the fairest offering which they could present at her feast. The sacrifice which they collectively made was individually repaid to them; for they received again each one for himself a praise which grows not old, and the noblest of all sepulchres—I speak not of that in which their remains are laid, but of that in which their glory survives, and is proclaimed always and on every

Contemplate and love Athens, and you will know how to value them. They were united in their deaths, but their glory is separate and single. Their sepulchre is the remembrance of them in the hearts of men. Follow their example without fear: it is the prosperous, not the unfortunate, who should be reckless.

---

[a] Or, taking τύχης with καιροῦ: 'while for a moment they were in the hands of fortune, at the height, not of terror but of glory, they passed away.'

fitting occasion both in word and deed. For the whole
earth is the sepulchre of famous men; not only are they
commemorated by columns and inscriptions in their own
country, but in foreign lands there dwells also an unwritten
memorial of them, graven not on stone but in the hearts of
men. Make them your examples, and, esteeming courage
to be freedom and freedom to be happiness, do not weigh
too nicely the perils of war. The unfortunate who has no
hope of a change for the better has less reason to throw
away his life than the prosperous who, if he survive, is
always liable to a change for the worse, and to whom any
accidental fall makes the most serious difference. To
a man of spirit, cowardice and disaster coming together
are far more bitter than death striking him unperceived at
a time when he is full of courage and animated by the
general hope.

'Wherefore I do not now commiserate the parents of the 44
dead who stand here; I would rather
comfort them. You know that your
life has been passed amid manifold
vicissitudes; and that they may be
deemed fortunate who have gained
most honour, whether an honourable
death like theirs, or an honourable
sorrow like yours, and whose days
have been so ordered that the term
of their happiness is likewise the term
of their life. I know how hard it is
*The parents of the
dead are to be com-
forted rather than pitied.
Some of them may
yet have children who
will lighten their sor-
row and serve the state;
while others should re-
member how large their
share of happiness has
been, and be consoled
by the glory of those who
are gone.*
to make you feel this, when the good fortune of others
will too often remind you of the gladness which once
lightened your hearts. And sorrow is felt at the want of
those blessings, not which a man never knew, but which
were a part of his life before they were taken from him.
Some of you are of an age at which they may hope to
have other children, and they ought to bear their sorrow
better; not only will the children who may hereafter be
born make them forget their own lost ones, but the city

will be doubly a gainer. She will not be left desolate, and she will be safer. For a man's counsel cannot have equal weight or worth, when he alone has no children to risk in the general danger. To those of you who have passed their prime, I say: "Congratulate yourselves that you have been happy during the greater part of your days; remember that your life of sorrow will not last long, and be comforted by the glory of those who are gone. For the love of honour alone is ever young, and not riches, as some say, but honour is the delight of men when they are old and useless."

45 'To you who are the sons and brothers of the departed, *Sons and brothers will find their example hard to imitate, for men are jealous of the living, but envy follows not the dead. Let the widows restrain their natural weakness, and avoid both praise and blame.* I see that the struggle to emulate them will be an arduous one. For all men praise the dead, and, however preeminent your virtue may be, hardly will you be thought, I do not say to equal, but even to approach them. The living have their rivals and detractors, but when a man is out of the way, the honour and good-will which he receives is unalloyed. And, if I am to speak of womanly virtues to those of you who will henceforth be widows, let me sum them up in one short admonition: To a woman not to show more weakness than is natural to her sex is a great glory, and not to be talked about for good or for evil among men.

46 'I have paid the required tribute, in obedience to the *So have I paid a due tribute of words to the dead. The city will pay them in deeds, as by this funeral, so too by the maintenance of their children.* law, making use of such fitting words as I had. The tribute of deeds has been paid in part; for the dead have been honourably interred, and it remains only that their children should be maintained at the public charge until they are grown up: this is the solid prize with which, as with a garland, Athens crowns her sons living and dead, after a struggle like theirs. For where the rewards of virtue are greatest, there the noblest citizens

are enlisted in the service of the state. And now, when
you have duly lamented, every one his own dead, you
may depart.'

Such was the order of the funeral celebrated in this *Second invasion of Attica; outbreak of the plague,* B.C. 430. Ol. 87, 3.
winter, with the end of which ended
the first year of the Peloponnesian
War. As soon as summer returned,
the Peloponnesian army, comprising as before two-thirds of
the force of each confederate state, under the command
of the Lacedaemonian king Archidamus, the son of Zeuxidamus, invaded Attica, where they established themselves
and ravaged the country. They had not been there many
days when the plague broke out at Athens for the first
time. A similar disorder is said to have previously smitten
many places, particularly Lemnos, but there is no record
of such a pestilence occurring elsewhere, or of so great
a destruction of human life. For a while physicians, in
ignorance of the nature of the disease, sought to apply
remedies ; but it was in vain, and they themselves were
among the first victims, because they oftenest came into
contact with it. No human art was of any avail, and as to
supplications in temples, enquiries of oracles, and the like,
they were utterly useless, and at last men were overpowered by the calamity and gave them all up.

The disease is said to have begun south of Egypt in *which commenced in Aethiopia. The origin and causes of it are un- known, but I shall con- fine myself to the facts. I was myself a sufferer.*
Aethiopia ; thence it descended into
Egypt and Libya, and after spreading
over the greater part of the Persian
empire, suddenly fell upon Athens. It
first attacked the inhabitants of the
Piraeus, and it was supposed that the Peloponnesians had
poisoned the cisterns, no conduits having as yet been
made there. It afterwards reached the upper city, and
then the mortality became far greater. As to its probable
origin or the causes which might or could have produced
such a disturbance of nature, every man, whether a
physician or not, will give his own opinion. But I shall

describe its actual course, and the symptoms by which
any one who knows them beforehand may recognise the
disorder should it ever reappear.   For I was myself
attacked, and witnessed the sufferings of others.

49   The season was admitted to have been remarkably free
The characteristics of from ordinary sickness; and if any-
the disease. body was already ill of any other
disease, it was absorbed in this.   Many who were in
perfect health, all in a moment, and without any apparent
reason, were seized with violent heats in the head and
with redness and inflammation of the eyes.   Internally
the throat and the tongue were quickly suffused with blood,
and the breath became unnatural and fetid.   There followed
sneezing and hoarseness; in a short time the disorder,
accompanied by a violent cough, reached the chest; then
fastening lower down, it would move the stomach and
bring on all the vomits of bile to which physicians have
ever given names; and they were very distressing.   An
ineffectual retching producing violent convulsions attacked
most of the sufferers; ᵃ some as soon as the previous
symptoms had abated, others not until long afterwards ᵃ.
The body externally was not so very hot to the touch, nor
yet pale; it was of a livid colour inclining to red, and
breaking out in pustules and ulcers.   But the internal fever
was intense; the sufferers could not bear to have on them
even the finest linen garment; they insisted on being naked,
and there was nothing which they longed for more eagerly
than to throw themselves into cold water.   And many of
those who had no one to look after them actually plunged
into the cisterns, for they were tormented by unceasing
thirst, which was not in the least assuaged whether they
drank little or much.   They could not sleep; a restlessness which was intolerable never left them.   While the
disease was at its height the body, instead of wasting away,

ᵃ Or, taking λωφήσαντα with σπασμόν : 'these convulsions in some
cases soon abated, in others not until long afterwards.'

held out amid these sufferings in a marvellous manner, and either they died on the seventh or ninth day, not of weakness, for their strength was not exhausted, but of internal fever, which was the end of most; or, if they survived, then the disease descended into the bowels and there produced violent ulceration; severe diarrhoea at the same time set in, and at a later stage caused exhaustion, which finally with few exceptions carried them off. For the disorder which had originally settled in the head passed gradually through the whole body, and, if a person got over the worst, would often seize the extremities and leave its mark, attacking the privy parts and the fingers and the toes; and some escaped with the loss of these, some with the loss of their eyes. Some again had no sooner recovered than they were seized with a forgetfulness of all things and knew neither themselves nor their friends.

The general character of the malady no words can *Even the animals and* describe, and the fury with which it *birds of prey refused to* fastened upon each sufferer was too *touch the corpses.* much for human nature to endure. There was one circumstance in particular which distinguished it from ordinary diseases. The birds and animals which feed on human flesh, although so many bodies were lying unburied, either never came near them, or died if they touched them. This was proved by a remarkable disappearance of the birds of prey, which were not to be seen either about the bodies or anywhere else; while in the case of the dogs the result was even more obvious, because they live with man.

Such was the general nature of the disease: I omit *Nothing availed a-* many strange peculiarities which char- *gainst the disease.* acterised individual cases. None of the ordinary sicknesses attacked any one while it lasted, or, if they did, they ended in the plague. Some of the sufferers died from want of care, others equally who were receiving the greatest attention. No single remedy could be deemed a specific ; for that which did good to one did harm to another. No constitution was of itself strong enough to resist or weak enough to escape the attacks ; the disease carried off all alike and defied every mode of treatment. Most appalling was the despondency which seized upon any one who felt himself sickening ; for he instantly abandoned his mind to despair and, instead of holding out, absolutely threw away his chance of life.

Rapidity with which the infection spread. None could visit the sick with impunity except those who had already been attacked and had recovered. Appalling too was the rapidity with which men caught the infection ; dying like sheep if they attended on one another ; and this was the principal cause of mortality. When they were afraid to visit one another, the sufferers died in their solitude, so that many houses were empty because there had been no one left to take care of the sick ; or if they ventured they perished, especially those who aspired to heroism. For they went to see their friends without thought of themselves and were ashamed to leave them, at a time when the very relations of the dying were at last growing weary and ceased even to make lamentations, overwhelmed by the vastness of the calamity. But whatever instances there may have been of such devotion, more often the sick and the dying were tended by the pitying care of those who had recovered, because they knew the course of the disease and were themselves free from apprehension. For no one was ever attacked a second time, or not with a fatal result. All men congratulated them, and they themselves, in the excess of their joy at the moment, had an innocent fancy that they could not die of any other sickness.

52   The crowding of the people out of the country into the *The misery aggra-vated by the overcrowd-ing of the city.* city aggravated the misery ; and the newly-arrived suffered most. For, having no houses of their own, but inhabiting in the height of summer stifling huts, the mortality among them was dreadful, and they perished

in wild disorder. ªThe dead lay as they had died, one upon another, while others hardly alive wallowed ª in the streets and crawled about every fountain craving for water. The temples in which they lodged were full of the corpses of those who died in them ; for the violence of the calamity was such that men, not knowing where to turn, grew reckless of all law, human and divine. The *General violation of* customs which had hitherto been ob- *ancient customs of* served at funerals were universally *burial.* violated, and they buried their dead each one as best he could. Many, having no proper appliances, because the deaths in their household had been so numerous already, lost all shame in the burial of the dead ᵇ. When one man had raised a funeral pile, others would come, and throwing on their dead first, set fire to it ; or when some other corpse was already burning, before they could be stopped, would throw their own dead upon it and depart.

There were other and worse forms of lawlessness 53 which the plague introduced at Athens. *All legal and religious* Men who had hitherto concealed what *restraint disappears in* they took pleasure in, now grew bolder. *the terror of the plague.* For, seeing the sudden change,—how the rich died in a moment, and those who had nothing immediately inherited their property,— they reflected that life and riches were alike transitory, and they resolved to enjoy themselves while they could, and to think only of pleasure. Who would be willing to sacrifice himself to the law of honour when he knew not whether he would ever live to be held in honour ? The pleasure of the moment and any sort of thing which conduced to it took the place both of honour and of expediency. No fear of Gods or law of man deterred a criminal. Those who saw all perishing alike, thought that the worship or neglect of the Gods

---

ª More literally : 'They, dying, lay dead one upon another, or wallowed hardly alive ' &c.

ᵇ See note *ad loc.*

made no difference.   For offences against human law no
punishment was to be feared; no one would live long
enough to be called to account.   Already a far heavier
sentence had been passed and was hanging over a man's
head; before that fell, why should he not take a little
pleasure?

54   Such was the grievous calamity which now afflicted the
Athenians; within the walls their people were dying, and
without, their country was being ravaged.   In their
troubles they naturally called to mind a verse which the
elder men among them declared to have been current
long ago:—

'A Dorian war will come and a plague with it.'

There was a dispute about the precise expression; some
saying that *limos*, a famine, and not
loimos, a plague, was the original word.
Nevertheless, as might have been expected, for men's memories reflected
their sufferings, the argument in favour of *loimos* prevailed
at the time.   But if ever in future years another Dorian
war arises which happens to be accompanied by a famine,
they will probably repeat the verse in the other form.
The answer of the oracle to the Lacedaemonians when the
God was asked 'whether they should go to war or not,'
and he replied 'that if they fought with all their might,
they would conquer, and that he himself would take their
part[a],' was not forgotten by those who had heard of it, and
they quite imagined that they were witnessing the fulfilment
of his words.   The disease certainly did set in immediately
after the invasion of the Peloponnesians, and did not
spread into Peloponnesus in any degree worth speaking
of, while Athens felt its ravages most severely, and next to
Athens the places which were most populous.   Such was
the history of the plague[b].

Dispute about an ancient oracle: whether limos *or* loimos *was the word.*

[a] Cp. i. 118 fin.   [b] Cp. iii. 87

After the Peloponnesians had wasted the plain they 55
entered what are called the coast lands   *The Peloponnesians*
(*Paralus*) and penetrated as far as   *at Laurium. Pericles*
Laurium, where are the silver mines   *still restrains the people*
belonging to the Athenians. First they   *from going out, but*
                                              sends a hundred ships
ravaged that part of the coast which   *to ravage Peloponnesus.*
looks towards Peloponnesus, and afterwards that situated
towards Euboea and Andros.   But Pericles, who was
still general, continued to insist, as in the former invasion,
that the Athenians should remain within their walls.

Before, however, the Peloponnesians had left the plain 56
and moved forward into the coast lands he had begun to
equip an expedition of a hundred ships against Peloponnesus. When all was ready he put to sea, having on
board four thousand Athenian hoplites and three hundred
cavalry conveyed in horse transports which the Athenians
then constructed for the first time out of their old ships.
The Chians and Lesbians joined them with fifty vessels.
The expedition did not actually put to sea until the
Peloponnesians had reached the coast lands. Arriving at
Epidaurus in Peloponnesus the Athenians devastated most
of the country and attacked the city, which at one time
they were in hopes of taking, but did not quite succeed.
Setting sail again they ravaged the territory of Troezen,
Halieis, and Hermionè, which are all places on the coast
of Peloponnesus. Again putting off they came to Prasiae,
a small town on the coast of Laconia, ravaged the country,
and took and plundered the place. They then returned
home and found that the Peloponnesians had also returned
and were no longer in Attica.

All the time during which the Peloponnesians remained 57
in the country and the armament of the   *The Peloponnesians*
Athenians continued at sea the plague   *leave Attica after a stay*
was raging both among the troops and   *of forty days.*
in the city.   The fear which it inspired was said to have
induced the enemy to leave Attica sooner than they
intended; for they heard from deserters that the disease

was in the city, and likewise saw the burning of the dead. Still in this invasion the whole country was ravaged by them, and they remained about forty days, which was the longest stay they ever made.

58   In the same summer, Hagnon the son of Nicias, and *Expedition against* Cleopompus the son of Cleinias, who *Potidaea. The plague* were colleagues of Pericles in his *breaks out among the* military command, took the fleet which *troops, and the rein-* *forcements return to* he had employed and sailed forthwith *Athens.* against the Thracian Chalcidians and against Potidaea, which still held out. On their arrival they brought engines up to the walls, and tried every means of taking the town. But they did not succeed ; nor did the result by any means correspond to the magnitude of their armament; for thither too the plague came and made dreadful havoc among the Athenian troops. Even the soldiers who were previously there and had been in good health caught the infection from the forces under Hagnon. But the army of Phormio [a] escaped ; for he and his sixteen hundred troops had left Chalcidicè. And so Hagnon returned with his fleet to Athens, having lost by the plague out of four thousand hoplites a thousand and fifty men in about forty days. But the original armament [b] remained and prosecuted the siege.

59   After the second Peloponnesian invasion, now that *The Athenians sue* Attica had been once more ravaged, *for peace and are re-* and the war and the plague together *jected. They turn upon* lay heavy upon the Athenians, a change *Pericles. His defence.* came over their spirit. They blamed Pericles because he had persuaded them to go to war, declaring that he was the author of their troubles ; and they were anxious to come to terms with the Lacedae-monians. Accordingly envoys were despatched to Sparta, but they met with no success. And now, being completely at their wits' end, they turned upon Pericles. He saw

---

[a] Cp. i. 64 med.   [b] Cp. i. 59, 61 init.

that they were exasperated by their misery and were behaving just as he had always anticipated that they would. And so, being still general, he called an assembly, wanting to encourage them and to convert their angry feelings into a gentler and more hopeful mood. At this assembly he came forward and spoke as follows :—

'I was expecting this outburst of indignation ; the causes of it are not unknown to me. And I have summoned an assembly that I may remind you of your resolutions and reprove you for your inconsiderate anger against me, and want of fortitude in misfortune. In my judgment it would be better for individuals themselves that the citizens should suffer and the state flourish *Your anger is inconsiderate and unmanly; you forget that the fortunes of the individual depend on those of the state. If you believed that I was wise, loyal, disinterested, when you consented to the war, why should you attack me now?* than that the citizens should flourish and the state suffer. A private man, however successful in his own dealings, if his country perish is involved in her destruction ; but if he be an unprosperous citizen of a prosperous city he is much more likely to recover. Seeing then that states can bear the misfortunes of individuals, but individuals cannot bear the misfortunes of the state, let us all stand by our country and not do what you are doing now, who because you are stunned by your private calamities are letting go the hope of saving the state, and condemning not only me who advised, but yourselves who consented to, the war. Yet I with whom you are so angry venture to say of myself, that I am as capable as any one of devising and explaining a sound policy ; and that I am a lover of my country, and incorruptible. Now a man may have a policy which he cannot clearly expound, and then he might as well have none at all ; or he may possess both ability and eloquence, but if he is disloyal to his country he cannot, like a true man, speak in her interest ; or again he may be unable to resist a bribe, and then all his other good qualities will be sold for money. If, when you determined to go to war, you believed me to have somewhat more of the statesman in me than others, it is not fair that I should now be charged with anything like crime.

61   'I allow that for men who are in prosperity and free to choose it is great folly to make war.

I am not changed, but you are changed by misfortune. Such a change is unbecoming the citizens of Athens: you should forget your sorrows, and think only of the public good.

But when they must either submit and at once surrender independence, or strike and be free, then he who shuns and not he who meets the danger is deserving of blame.   For my own part, I am the same man and stand where I did.   But you are changed; for you have been driven by misfortune to recall the consent which you gave when you were yet unhurt, and to think that my advice was wrong because your own characters are weak.   The pain is present and comes home to each of you, but the good is as yet unrealised by any one; and your minds have not the strength to persevere in your resolution, now that a great reverse has overtaken you unawares.   Anything which is sudden and unexpected and utterly beyond calculation, such a disaster for instance as this plague coming upon other misfortunes, enthralls the spirit of a man.   Nevertheless, being the citizens of a great city and educated in a temper of greatness, you should not succumb to calamities however overwhelming, or darken the lustre of your fame.   For if men hate the presumption of those who claim a reputation to which they have no right, they equally condemn the faint-heartedness of those who fall below the glory which is their own.   You should lose the sense of your private sorrows and cling to the deliverance of the state.

62   'As to your sufferings in the war, if you fear that they may be very great and after all fruitless, I have shown you already over and over again that such a fear is groundless. If you are still unsatisfied I will indicate [a] one element of

---

[a] Or, taking ὑπάρχον ὑμῖν absolutely: 'a consideration which, however obvious, appears to have escaped you.'   Or, again, taking μεγέθους

your superiority which appears to have escaped you[a],
although it nearly touches your imperial
greatness.   I too have never mentioned
it before, nor would I now, because the
claim may seem too arrogant, if I did
not see that you are unreasonably depressed.   You think that your empire
is confined to your allies, but I say that
of the two divisions of the world accessible to man, the land and the sea, there
is one of which you are absolute masters,
and have, or may have, the dominion to
any extent which you please.   Neither
the great King nor any nation on earth can hinder
a navy like yours from penetrating whithersoever you
choose to sail.   When we reflect on this great power,
houses and lands, of which the loss seems so dreadful
to you, are as nothing.   We ought not to be troubled
about them or to think much of them in comparison ;
they are only the garden of the house, the superfluous
ornament of wealth ; and you may be sure that if we
cling to our freedom and preserve that, we shall soon
enough recover all the rest.   But, if we are the servants
of others, we shall be sure to lose not only freedom, but
all that freedom gives.   And where your ancestors doubly
succeeded, you will doubly fail.   For their empire was
not inherited by them from others but won by the labour
of their hands, and by them preserved and bequeathed to
us.   And to be robbed of what you have is a greater
disgrace than to attempt a conquest and fail.   Meet your
enemies therefore not only with spirit but with disdain.
A coward or a fortunate fool may brag and vaunt, but he
only is capable of disdain whose conviction that he is

Do you fear that your sufferings will be fruitless?   I tell you that you are absolute masters of the sea, which is half the world.   What are your possessions in comparison with freedom?   Keep that, and you will soon regain the rest.   Meet your enemies with disdain, as having a rational conviction of your superiority.

πέρι with ἐνθυμηθῆναι: ' one element of your superiority which nearly
touches your empire, but of which you never seem to have considered
the importance.'

stronger than his enemy rests, like our own, on grounds of reason. Courage fighting in a fair field is fortified by the intelligence which looks down upon an enemy; an intelligence relying, not on hope, which is the strength of helplessness, but on that surer foresight which is given by reason and observation of facts.

63   'Once more, you are bound to maintain the imperial

Your empire is at stake, and it is too late to resign it; for you have already incurred the hatred of mankind.

dignity of your city in which you all take pride; for you should not covet the glory unless you will endure the toil. And do not imagine that you are fighting about a simple issue, freedom or slavery; you have an empire to lose, and there is the danger to which the hatred of your imperial rule has exposed you. Neither can you resign your power, if, at this crisis, any timorous or inactive spirit is for thus playing the honest man. For by this time your empire has become a tyranny which in the opinion of mankind may have been unjustly gained, but which cannot be safely surrendered. The men of whom I was speaking, if they could find followers, would soon ruin a city, and if they were to go and found a state of their own, would equally ruin that. For inaction is secure only when arrayed by the side of activity; nor is it expedient or safe for a sovereign, but only for a subject state, to be a servant.

64   'You must not be led away by the advice of such

Nothing has happened, except the plague, but what we all anticipated when we agreed on war. Do not lose the spirit which has made Athens great and, even though she fall, will render her glorious for all time.

citizens as these, nor be angry with me; for the resolution in favour of war was your own as much as mine. What if the enemy has come and done what he was certain to do when you refused to yield? What too if the plague followed? That was an unexpected blow, but we might have foreseen all the rest. I am well aware that your hatred of me is aggravated by it. But how unjustly, unless to me you also ascribe the credit of any extraordinary

success which may befall you [a] !   The visitations of heaven
should be borne with resignation, the sufferings inflicted
by an enemy with manliness.   This has always been the
spirit of Athens, and should not die out in you.   Know
that our city has the greatest name in all the world because
she has never yielded to misfortunes, but has sacrificed
more lives and endured severer hardships in war than any
other; wherefore also she has the greatest power of any
state up to this day; and the memory of her glory will
always survive.   Even if we should be compelled at last to
abate somewhat of our greatness (for all things have their
times of growth and decay), yet will the recollection live,
that, of all Hellenes, we ruled over the greatest number of
Hellenic subjects; that we withstood our enemies, whether
single or united, in the most terrible wars, and that we
were the inhabitants of a city endowed with every sort of
wealth and greatness.   The indolent may indeed find
fault, but [b] the man of action [b] will seek to rival us, and he
who is less fortunate will envy us.   To be hateful and
offensive has ever been at the time the fate of those who
have aspired to empire.   But he judges well who accepts
unpopularity in a great cause.   Hatred does not last long,
and, besides the immediate splendour of great actions, the
renown of them endures for ever in men's memories.
Looking forward to such future glory and present
avoidance of dishonour, make an effort now and secure
both.   Let no herald be sent to the Lacedaemonians, and
do not let them know that you are depressed by your
sufferings.   For those are the greatest states and the
greatest men, who, when misfortunes come, are the least
depressed in spirit and the most resolute in action.'

By these and similar words Pericles endeavoured to 65
appease the anger of the Athenians against himself, and

---

[a] Cp. i. 140 init.
[b] Or, taking καὶ αὐτὸς with βουλόμενος: 'he who is ambitious like ourselves.'

to divert their minds from their terrible situation.   In
the conduct of public affairs they took
his advice, and sent no more embassies
to Sparta; they were again eager to
prosecute the war.   Yet in private
they felt their sufferings keenly; the
common people had been deprived even
of the little which they possessed, while
the upper class had lost fair estates in
the country with all their houses and
rich furniture.   Worst of all, instead of
enjoying peace, they were now at war.
The popular indignation was not
pacified until they had fined Pericles;
but, soon afterwards, with the usual
fickleness of a multitude, they elected
him general and committed all their
affairs to his charge.   Their private sorrows were beginning to be less acutely
felt, and for a time of public need they thought that there
was no man like him.   During the peace while he was at
the head of affairs he ruled with prudence; under his
guidance Athens was safe, and reached the height of her
greatness in his time.   When the war began he showed
that here too he had formed a true estimate of the Athenian
power.   He survived the commencement of hostilities two
years and six months; and, after his death, his foresight
was even better appreciated than during his life.   For
he had told the Athenians that if they would be patient
and would attend to their navy, and not seek to enlarge
their dominion while the war was going on, nor imperil
the existence of the city, they would be victorious; but
they did all that he told them not to do, and in matters
which seemingly had nothing to do with the war, from
motives of private ambition and private interest they
adopted a policy which had disastrous effects in respect
both of themselves and of their allies; their measures,

The Athenians follow Pericles' advice, but are not appeased until they have fined him.   He soon regains their esteem, and takes the lead of affairs.   After his death his wisdom was even better appreciated than during his life.   His advice about the war was sound if the Athenians would only have followed it.   But they were continually em- barking on rash enter- prises, and the city was distracted by the strug- gles of rival dema- gogues, whereas Pericles had been their natural leader.

[a] had they been successful, would only have brought [a] honour and profit to individuals, and, when unsuccessful, crippled the city in the conduct of the war. The reason of the difference was that he, deriving authority from his capacity and acknowledged worth, being also a man of transparent integrity, was able to control the multitude in a free spirit; he led them rather than was led by them; for, not seeking power by dishonest arts, he had no need to say pleasant things, but, on the strength of his own high character, could venture to oppose and even to anger them. When he saw them unseasonably elated and arrogant, his words humbled and awed them; and, when they were depressed by groundless fears, he sought to reanimate their confidence. Thus Athens, though still in name a democracy, was in fact ruled by her greatest citizen. But his successors were more on an equality with one another, and, each one struggling to be first himself, they were ready to sacrifice the whole conduct of affairs to the whims of the people. Such weakness in a great and imperial city led to many errors, of which the greatest was the Sicilian expedition; not that the Athenians miscalculated their enemy's power, but they themselves, instead of consulting for the interests of the expedition which they had sent out, were occupied in intriguing against one another for the leadership of the democracy [b], and not only hampered the operations of the army, but became embroiled, for the first time, at home. And yet after they had lost in the Sicilian expedition the greater part of their fleet and army, and were now distracted by revolution, still they held out three years not only against their former enemies, but against the Sicilians who had combined with them, and against most of their own allies who had risen in revolt. Even when Cyrus the son of the King joined

Even after the Sicilian disaster they held out against their old enemies and many new ones, and were at last only ruined by themselves. So that Pericles was quite right after all.

---

[a] Or, 'while they continued to succeed, only brought.'   [b] Cp. vi. 28.

in the war and supplied the Peloponnesian fleet with money, they continued to resist, and were at last overthrown, not by their enemies, but by themselves and their own internal dissensions. So that at the time Pericles was more than justified in the conviction at which his foresight had arrived, that the Athenians would win an easy victory over the unaided forces of the Peloponnesians.

66   During the same summer the Lacedaemonians and their *The Lacedaemonians attack Zacynthus without result.* allies sent a fleet of a hundred ships against the island of Zacynthus, which lies opposite Elis. The Zacynthians are colonists of the Peloponnesian Achaeans, and were allies of the Athenians. There were on board the fleet a thousand Lacedaemonian hoplites, under the command of Cnemus the Spartan admiral. They disembarked and ravaged the greater part of the country; but as the inhabitants would not come to terms, they sailed away home.

67   At the end of the same summer, Aristeus the Corinthian, *Envoys sent from the Peloponnesian cities to the King are detained by Sitalces and given up to the Athenians. They are carried to Athens and put to death.* the Lacedaemonian ambassadors Aneristus, Nicolaus, and Stratodemus, Timagoras of Tegea, and Pollis of Argos who had no public mission, were on their way to Asia in the hope of persuading the King to give them money and join in the war. They went first of all to Sitalces son of Teres, in Thrace, wishing if possible to detach him from the Athenians, and induce him to lead an army to the relief of Potidaea, which was still blockaded by Athenian forces; they also wanted him to convey them across the Hellespont on their intended journey to Pharnaces, the son of Pharnabazus, who was to send them on to the King. At the time of their arrival two Athenian envoys, Learchus the son of Callimachus, and Ameiniades the son of Philemon, chanced to be at the court of Sitalces; and they entreated his son Sadocus, who had been made

an Athenian citizen [a], to deliver the envoys into their hands, that they might not find their way to the King and so injure a city which was in some degree his own. He consented, and, sending a body of men with Learchus and Ameiniades, before they embarked, as they were on their way through Thrace to the vessel in which they were going to cross the Hellespont, seized them; they were then, in accordance with the orders of Sadocus, handed over to the Athenian envoys, who conveyed them to Athens. On the very day of their arrival the Athenians, fearing that Aristeus, whom they considered to be the cause of all their troubles at Potidaea and in Chalcidicè, would do them still further mischief if he escaped, put them all to death without trial and without hearing what they wanted to say; they then threw their bodies down precipices. They considered that they had a right to retaliate on the Lacedaemonians, who had begun by treating in the same way the traders of the Athenians and their allies when they caught their vessels off the coast of Peloponnesus. For at the commencement of the war, all whom the Lacedaemonians captured at sea were treated by them as enemies and indiscriminately slaughtered, whether they were allies of the Athenians or neutrals.

About the end of the same summer the Ambraciots, with a large Barbarian force which they had called out, made war upon the Amphilochian Argos and upon Amphilochia. The original cause of their

68

The Ambraciots make war without success upon the Amphilochian Argives.

enmity against the Argives was as follows :—The Amphilochian territory had been occupied and the city founded by Amphilochus the son of Amphiaraus, who on returning home after the Trojan War was dissatisfied at the state of Argos. He fixed the site on the shore of the Ambracian Gulf, and called the new city by the name of his native place ; it was the greatest city in that region, and its

---

[a] Cp. ii. 29 fin.

inhabitants were the most powerful community. Many generations afterwards, these Amphilochians in a time of distress invited their neighbours the Ambraciots to join in the settlement, and from them they first learned the Hellenic language which they now speak; the other Amphilochians are Barbarians. After a while the Ambraciots drove out the Amphilochian Argives and themselves took possession of the city. The expelled Amphilochians placed themselves under the protection of the Acarnanians, and both together called in the Athenians, who sent them a fleet of thirty ships under the command of Phormio. When Phormio arrived, they stormed Argos, and sold the Ambraciots into slavery; and the Amphilochians and Acarnanians dwelt together in the place. The alliance between the Acarnanians and Athenians then first began. The hatred of the Ambraciots towards the Amphilochian Argives commenced with the enslavement of their countrymen; and now when the war offered an opportunity they invaded their territory, accompanied by the Chaonians and some others of the neighbouring Barbarians. They came as far as Argos and made themselves masters of the country; but not being able to take the city by assault they returned, and the several tribes dispersed to their own homes. Such were the events of the summer.

69   In the following winter the Athenians sent twenty ships on an expedition round Peloponnesus. *Phormio at Naupactus. Melesander sent to collect tribute in Lycia and Caria is defeated and slain.* These were placed under the command of Phormio, who, stationing himself at Naupactus, guarded the straits and prevented any one from sailing either out of or into Corinth and the Crisaean Gulf. Six other vessels were sent to collect tribute in Lycia and Caria; they were under the command of Melesander, who was to see that Peloponnesian privateers did not establish themselves in those parts, and damage merchant vessels coming from Phaselis and Phoenicia and all that region. But he, going up the country into Lycia with an army composed

of Athenians taken from the crews and of allied troops, was defeated, and himself and a part of his forces slain.

In the same winter the Potidaeans, who were still 70 blockaded, found themselves unable to   *The Potidaeans are* hold out; for the Peloponnesian in-   *compelled by hunger to* vasions of Attica did not make the   *surrender. The Athe-* Athenians withdraw; and they had no   *rals for giving easy* more food. When they had been re-   *terms.* duced to such straits as actually in some cases to feed on human flesh, they entered into communications with the Athenian generals, Xenophon the son of Euripides, Hestiodorus the son of Aristocleides, and Phanomachus the son of Callimachus, to whom the siege had been entrusted. They, seeing that the army was suffering from the exposed situation, and considering that the city had already spent two thousand talents ᵃ on the siege, accepted the terms proposed. The Potidaeans, with their wives and their children, and likewise the foreign troops ᵇ, were to come out of the city, the men with one garment, the women with two, and they were allowed a certain fixed sum of money for their journey. So they came out under a safe-conduct, and went into Chalcidicè, or wherever they could find a home. But the Athenians blamed the generals for coming to terms without their authority, thinking that they could have made the city surrender at discretion. Soon afterwards they sent thither colonists of their own. Such were the events of the winter. And so ended the second year in the Peloponnesian War of which Thucydides wrote the history.

In the following summer the Peloponnesians and their 71 allies under the command of Archida-   *Expedition of the* B.C. 429. mus the son of Zeuxidamus, the Lace-   *Peloponnesians under* Ol. 87, 4. daemonian king, instead of invading   *Archidamus against* Attica, made an expedition against   *Plataea.* Plataea. There he encamped and was about to ravage the

----

ᵃ £400,000.   ᵇ Cp. i. 60.

country, when the Plataeans sent envoys to him bearing
the following message :—

'Archidamus, and you Lacedaemonians, in making war

Protest of the Pla-
taeans.

You are violating the
promise of independence
which Pausanias made
us after the battle of
Plataea.

upon Plataea you are acting unjustly,
and in a manner unworthy of yourselves
and of your ancestors. Pausanias the
son of Cleombrotus, the Lacedaemonian, when he and such Hellenes as
were willing to share the danger with
him fought a battle in our land and liberated Hellas from
the Persian, offered up sacrifice in the Agora of Plataea to
Zeus the God of Freedom, and in the presence of all the
confederates then and there restored to the Plataeans their
country and city to be henceforth independent; no man
was to make unjust war upon them at any time or to seek
to enslave them; and if they were attacked, the allies who
were present promised that they would defend them to the
utmost of their power. These privileges your fathers
granted to us as a reward for the courage and devotion
which we displayed in that time of danger. But you are
acting in an opposite spirit; for you have joined the
Thebans, our worst enemies, and have come hither to
enslave us. Wherefore, calling to witness the Gods to
whom we all then swore, and also the Gods of your race
and the Gods who dwell in our country, we bid you do no
harm to the land of Plataea. Do not violate your oaths,
but allow the Plataeans to be independent, and to enjoy
the rights which Pausanias granted to them.'

72 To this appeal Archidamus rejoined :—

'What you say, Plataeans, is just, but your acts should

Archidamus offers
peace if they will either
join the Lacedaemonian
confederacy or remain
neutral.

correspond to your words. Enjoy the
independence which Pausanias granted
to you, but also assist us in freeing the
other Hellenes who were your sworn
confederates in that time of danger and
are now in subjection to the Athenians. With a view to
the emancipation of them and of the other subject states,

this great war has been undertaken and all these preparations made.   It would be best for you to join with us,
and observe the oaths yourselves which you would have
us observe.   But if you prefer to be neutral, a course
which we have already once proposed to you, retain
possession of your lands, and receive both sides in
peace, but neither for the purposes of war ; and we shall
be satisfied.'

The Plataean ambassadors then returned to the city and
reported these words of Archidamus to *The Plataeans reply*
the people, who made answer that they *that they cannot act*
could not do what they were asked *without the Athenians,*
without the sanction of the Athenians, *and also that they dis-*
in whose power they had left their *trust the Thebans.*
wives and children, and that they also feared for the very
existence of their state.   When the Lacedaemonians were
gone the Athenians might come and not allow them to
carry out the treaty; or the Thebans, who would be
included in the clause requiring them 'to receive both
sides,' might again attempt to seize their town.   To this
Archidamus, wanting to reassure them, made the following
answer :—

'Then deliver over your city and houses to the Lacedaemonians ; mark the boundaries of *Archidamus then asks*
your land, and number your fruit-trees *them to surrender the*
and anything else which can be counted. *city till the end of the*
Go yourselves whithersoever you *war.*
please, while the war lasts, and on the return of peace we
will give back to you all that we have received.   Until then
we will hold your property in trust, and will cultivate
your ground, paying you such a rent as will content you.'

Upon hearing these words the en- *The Plataeans, ob-* 73
voys again returned into the city, *taining permission to*
and, after holding a consultation with *consult the Athenians,*
the people, told Archidamus that *are encouraged by them*
they wished first to communicate his *to resist.*
proposals to the Athenians, and if they could get their

consent they would do as he advised ; in the meantime they desired him to make a truce with them, and not to ravage their land. So he made a truce which allowed sufficient time for their ambassadors to return from Athens ; and meanwhile he spared their land. The Plataean envoys came to Athens, and after advising with the Athenians they brought back the following message to their fellow-citizens :—
' Plataeans, the Athenians say that never at any time since you first became their allies [a] have they suffered any one to do you wrong, and that they will not forsake you now, but will assist you to the utmost of their power ; and they adjure you, by the oaths which your fathers swore, not to forsake the Athenian alliance.'

74   When the answer came, the Plataeans resolved not to
They reply that they desert the Athenians, but patiently to
cannot accept the Lace- look on, if they must, while the Lace-
daemonian proposals. daemonians wasted their country, and
to endure the worst. No one was henceforward to leave the town, but answer was to be made from the walls that they could not possibly consent to the Lacedaemonian proposal. King Archidamus, as soon as he received the reply, before proceeding to action, fell to calling upon the Gods and heroes of the country in the following words :—

' O ye Gods and heroes who possess the land of Plataea,
Archidamus appeals be our witnesses that our invasion of
to the Gods. this land in which our fathers prayed
to you when they conquered the Persians, and which you made a propitious battle-field to the Hellenes, has thus far been justified, for the Plataeans first deserted the alliance ; and that if we go further we shall be guilty of no crime, for we have again and again made them fair proposals and they have not listened to us. Be gracious to us and grant that the real authors of the iniquity may be punished, and that they may obtain revenge who lawfully seek it.'

---

[a] Herod. vi. 108.

After this appeal to the Gods he began military opera- 75
tions. In the first place, the soldiers
felled the fruit-trees and surrounded
the city with a stockade, that henceforth
no one might get out. They then
began to raise a mound against it,
thinking that with so large an army at
work this would be the speediest way
of taking the place. So they cut timber
from Cithaeron and built on either side of the intended
mound a frame of logs placed cross-wise in order that the
material might not scatter. Thither they carried wood,
stones, earth, and anything which would fill up the vacant
space. They continued raising the mound seventy days
and seventy nights without intermission; the army was
divided into relays, and one party worked while the other
slept and ate. The Lacedaemonian officers who commanded the contingents of the allies stood over them and
kept them at work. The Plataeans, seeing the mound
rising, constructed a wooden frame, which they set upon
the top of their own wall opposite the mound; in this they
inserted bricks, which they took from the neighbouring
houses; the wood served to strengthen and bind the
structure together as it increased in height; they also
hung curtains of skins and hides in front; these were
designed to protect the wood-work and the workers, and
shield them against blazing arrows. The wooden wall
rose high, but the mound rose quickly too. Then the
Plataeans had a new device;—they made a hole in that
part of the wall against which the mound pressed and
drew in the earth.

The siege operations begin: the Pelopon- nesians raise a mound, which the Plataeans counteract by raising the height of a part of their wall and by draw- ing away earth from the mound.

The Peloponnesians discovered what they were doing, 76
and threw into the gap clay packed in
wattles of reed, which could not scatter
and like the loose earth be carried away.
Whereupon the Plataeans, baffled in
one plan, resorted to another. Calcu-

This plan being de- feated, the Plataeans build a second line of defence within their old wall in the form of a crescent.

lating the direction, they dug a mine from the city to the mound and again drew the earth inward. For a long time their assailants did not find them out, and so what the Peloponnesians threw on was of little use, since the mound was always being drawn off below and settling into the vacant space. But in spite of all their efforts, the Plataeans were afraid that their numbers would never hold out against so great an army; and they devised yet another expedient. They left off working at the great building opposite the mound, and beginning at both ends, where the city wall returned to its original lower height, they built an inner wall projecting inwards in the shape of a crescent, that if the first wall were taken the other might still be defensible. The enemy would be obliged to begin again and carry the mound right up to it, and as they advanced inwards would have their trouble all over again, and be exposed to missiles on both flanks. While the mound was rising the Peloponnesians brought battering engines up to the wall; one which was moved forward on the mound itself shook a great part of the raised building, to the terror of the Plataeans. They brought up others

By ingenious devices too at other points of the wall. But *they disable the battering-* the Plataeans dropped nooses over the *rams of the enemy.* ends of these engines and drew them up; they also let down huge beams suspended at each end by long iron chains from two poles leaning on the wall and projecting over it. These beams they drew up at right angles to the advancing battering-ram, and whenever at any point it was about to attack them they slackened their hold of the chains and let go the beam, which fell with great force and snapped off the head of the ram.

77   At length the Peloponnesians, finding that their engines

The Peloponnesians were useless, and that the new wall *nearly succeed in setting* was rising opposite to the mound, and *the city on fire.* perceiving that they could not without more formidable means of attack hope to take the city, made preparations for a blockade. But first of all they resolved to try whether, the wind favouring, the place, which was but small, could not be set on fire; they were anxious not to incur the expense of a regular siege, and devised all sorts of plans in order to avoid it. So they brought faggots and threw them down from the mound along the space between it and the wall, which was soon filled up when so many hands were at work; then they threw more faggots one upon another into the city as far as they could reach from the top of the mound, and casting in lighted brands with brimstone and pitch, set them all on fire. A flame arose of which the like had never before been made by the hand of man; I am not speaking of fires in the mountains, when the forest has spontaneously blazed up from the action of the wind and mutual attrition. There was a great conflagration, and the Plataeans, who had thus far escaped, were all but destroyed; a considerable part of the town was unapproachable, and if a wind had come on and carried the flame that way, as the enemy hoped, they could not have been saved. It is said that there was also a violent storm of thunder and rain, which quenched the flames and put an end to the danger.

The Peloponnesians, having failed in this, as in their former attempts, sent away a part of their army but retained the rest [a], and dividing the task among the contingents of the several cities, surrounded Plataea with a wall. Trenches, out of which *Failing in their attempt, they draw a double wall round the city and retire, leaving a guard of themselves and the Boeotians.* they took clay for the bricks, were formed both on the inner and the outer side of the wall. About the rising of Arcturus [b] all was completed. They then drew off their army, leaving a guard on one half of the wall, while the other half was guarded by the Boeotians; the disbanded troops returned to their homes. The Plataeans had already conveyed to Athens [c] their wives, children, and old men,

---

[a] Retaining in the text τὸ δὲ λοιπὸν ἀφέντες.
[b] i. e. about the middle of September.   [c] ii. 6 fin.

with the rest of their unserviceable population. Those who remained during the siege were four hundred Plataeans, eighty Athenians, and a hundred and ten women to make bread. These were their exact numbers when the siege began. There was no one else, slave or freeman, within the walls. In such sort was the blockade of Plataea completed.

79   During the same summer, when the corn was in full ear, and about the time of the attack on

The Athenians attack Spartolus. An engagement takes place, in which they are at first victorious, but Chalcidian reinforcements arriving, the engagement is renewed and they are defeated with loss.

Plataea, the Athenians sent an expedition against the Chalcidians of Thrace and against the Bottiaeans, consisting of two thousand heavy-armed troops of their own and two hundred horsemen under the command of Xenophon the son of Euripides, and two others. They came close up to the Bottian Spartolus and destroyed the crops. They expected that the place would be induced to yield to them by a party within the walls. But the opposite party sent to Olynthus and obtained from thence a garrison, partly composed of hoplites, which sallied out of Spartolus and engaged with the Athenians under the walls of the town. The Chalcidian hoplites and with them certain auxiliaries were defeated and retreated into Spartolus, but their cavalry and light-armed troops had the advantage over those of the Athenians. They were assisted by a few targeteers, who came from the district called Crusis. The engagement was scarcely over when another body of targeteers from Olynthus came up to their aid. Encouraged by the reinforcement and their previous success, and supported by the Chalcidian horse and the newly-arrived troops, the light-armed again attacked the Athenians, who began to fall back upon the two companies which they had left with their baggage: as often as the Athenians charged, the enemy retired; but when the Athenians continued their retreat, they pressed upon them and hurled darts at them. The Chalcidian cavalry too rode up, and wherever they pleased charged the Athenians, who now fled utterly disconcerted and were pursued to a considerable distance. At length they escaped to Potidaea, and having recovered their dead under a flag of truce, returned to Athens with the survivors of their army, out of which they had lost four hundred and thirty men and all their generals. The Chalcidians and Botti- aeans, having set up a trophy and carried off their dead, disbanded and dispersed to their several cities.

In the same summer, not long afterwards, the Ambra- 80 ciots and Chaonians, designing to sub- jugate the whole of Acarnania and detach it from the Athenian alliance, persuaded the Lacedaemonians to equip a fleet out of the confederate forces, and to send into that region a thousand hoplites. They said that if the Lace- daemonians would join with them and attack the enemy both by sea and land,

The Ambraciots per- suade the Lacedaemo- nians to send a land and sea force under Cnemus against Acar- nania. Disembarking his troops, he is joined by a number of barbar- ous tribes and marches towards Stratus.

the Acarnanians on the sea-coast would be unable to assist the inland tribes, and they might easily conquer Acarnania. Zacynthus and Cephallenia would then fall into their hands, and the Athenian fleet would not so easily sail round Peloponnesus. They might even hope to take Naupactus. The Lacedaemonians agreed, and at once despatched Cnemus, who was still admiral[a], with the thousand hoplites in a few ships; they ordered the rest of the allied navy to get ready and at once sail to Leucas. The interests of the Ambraciots were zealously supported by Corinth, their mother city. The fleet which was to come from Corinth, Sicyon, and the adjacent places was long in preparation; but the contingent from Leucas, Anactorium, and Ambracia was soon equipped, and waited at Leucas. Undiscovered by Phormio, the commander of the twenty Athenian ships which were keeping guard at

---

[a] Cp. ii. 66.

Naupactus, Cnemus and his thousand hoplites crossed the sea and began to make preparations for the land expedition. Of Hellenes he had in his army Ambraciots, Leucadians, Anactorians, and the thousand Peloponnesians whom he brought with him,—of Barbarians a thousand Chaonians, who, having no king, were led by Photyus and Nicanor, both of the governing family and holding the presidency for a year. With the Chaonians came the Thesprotians, who, like them, have no king. A Molossian and Atintanian force was led by Sabylinthus, the guardian of Tharypas the king, who was still a minor; the Paravaeans were led by their king Oroedus, and were accompanied by a thousand Orestians placed at the disposal of Oroedus by their king Antiochus. Perdiccas also, unknown to the Athenians, sent a thousand Macedonians, who arrived too late. With this army Cnemus, not waiting for the ships from Corinth, began his march. They passed through the Argive territory and plundered Limnaea, an unwalled village. At length they approached Stratus, which is the largest city in Acarnania, thinking that, if they could take it, the other places would soon come over to them.

81   The Acarnanians, seeing that a great army had invaded their territory, and that the enemy was

The Acarnanians, being refused aid by Phormio, confine themselves to the defence of their cities. Cnemus marches on Stratus in three divisions. While the Hellenes encamp, the Chaonians, rushing forward, attempt to storm the place, but fall into an ambush and are routed.

threatening them by sea as well as by land, did not attempt any united action, but guarded their several districts, and sent to Phormio for aid. He replied that a fleet of the enemy was about to sail from Corinth, and that he could not leave Naupactus unguarded. Meanwhile the Peloponnesians and their allies marched in three divisions towards Stratus, intending to encamp near and try negotiations; if these failed, they would take stronger measures and assault the wall. The Chaonians and the other Barbarians advanced in the centre; on the

right wing were the Leucadians, Anactorians, and their
auxiliaries; on the left was Cnemus with the Peloponnesians and Ambraciots. The three divisions were
a long way apart, and at times not even in sight of one
another. The Hellenic troops maintained order on the
march and kept a look out, until at length they found
a suitable place in which to encamp; the Chaonians,
confident in themselves, and having a great military
reputation in that part of the country, would not stop to
encamp, but they and the other Barbarians rushed on at
full speed, hoping to take the place by storm and
appropriate to themselves the glory of the action. The
Stratians perceiving their approach in time, and thinking
that, if they could overcome them before the others
arrived, the Hellenic forces would not be so ready to
attack them, set ambuscades near the city. When they
were quite close, the troops came out of the city and from
the ambuscades and fell upon them hand to hand. Whereupon the Chaonians were seized with a panic and many of
them perished; the other Barbarians, seeing them give
way, no longer stood their ground, but took to flight.
Neither of the Hellenic divisions knew of the battle;
the Chaonians were far in advance of them, and were
thought to have hurried on because they wanted to
choose a place for their camp. At length the Barbarians
in their flight broke in upon their lines; they received
them, and the two divisions uniting during that day
remained where they were, the men of Stratus not coming
to close quarters with them, because the other Acarnanians
had not as yet arrived, but slinging at them from a distance
and distressing them greatly. For they could not move
a step without their armour. Now the Acarnanians are
famous for their skill in slinging.

When night came on, Cnemus withdrew his army in 82
haste to the river Anapus, which is rather more than nine
miles from Stratus, and on the following day carried off
his dead under a flag of truce. The people of Oeniadae

were friendly and had joined him; to their city therefore
Cnemus withdraws he retreated before the Acarnanians
his troops to Oeniadae, had collected their forces. From
whence they are con- Oeniadae all the Peloponnesian troops
veyed home. returned home. The Stratians erected
a trophy of the battle in which they had defeated the
Barbarians.

83   The fleet from Corinth and the other allied cities on the
The fleet of the Pelo- Crisaean Gulf, which was intended to
ponnesians which was support Cnemus and to prevent the
intended to support Acarnanians on the sea-coast from
Cnemus is compelled to assisting their friends in the interior of
engage by Phormio. the country, never arrived, but was
compelled, almost on the day of the battle of Stratus, to
fight with Phormio and the twenty Athenian ships which
were stationed at Naupactus. As they sailed by into the
open sea, Phormio was watching them, preferring to make
his attack outside the gulf. Now the Corinthians and
their allies were not equipped for a naval engagement, but
for the conveyance of troops into Acarnania, and they
never imagined that the Athenians with twenty ships
would venture to engage their own forty-seven. But, as
they were coasting along the southern shore, they saw the
Athenian fleet following their movements on the northern;
they then attempted to cross the sea from Patrae in Achaea
to the opposite continent in the direction of Acarnania,
when they again observed the enemy bearing down upon
them from Chalcis and the mouth of the river Evenus.
They had previously endeavoured to anchor under cover
of night [a], but had been detected. So at last they were
compelled to fight in the middle of the channel. The ships
were commanded by generals of the cities which had
furnished them; the Corinthian squadron by Machaon,
Isocrates, and Agatharchidas. The Peloponnesians

---

[a] Or, reading ἀφορμισάμενοι, 'they had weighed anchor before it was
light, but had been detected.'

arranged their ships in such a manner as to make the
largest possible circle without leaving   *Their ships form a*
space to break through, turning their   *circle.*
prows outwards and their sterns inwards; within the
circle they placed the smaller craft which accompanied
them, and five of their swiftest ships that they might be
close at hand and row out at whatever point the enemy
charged them.

The Athenians ranged their ships in a single line and 84
sailed round and round the Pelopon-   *The Athenians sail*
nesian fleet, which they drove into   *round and round till*
a narrower and narrower space, almost   *the morning wind rises*
touching as they passed, and leading   *and throws the enemy's*
the crews to suppose that they were on   *vessels into confusion,*
the point of charging. But they had   *when they make their*
been warned by Phormio not to begin   *attack and win a com-*
    plete victory.
until he gave the signal, for he was hoping that the
enemy's ships, not having the steadiness of an army on
land, would soon fall into disorder and run foul of one
another; they would be embarrassed by the small craft,
and if the usual morning breeze, for which he continued
waiting as he sailed round them, came down from the gulf,
they would not be able to keep still for a moment. He
could attack whenever he pleased, because his ships were
better sailers; and he knew that this would be the right
time. When the breeze began to blow, the ships, which
were by this time crowded into a narrow space and were
distressed at once by the force of the wind and by the
small craft which were knocking up against them, fell into
confusion; ship dashed against ship, and they kept
pushing one another away with long poles; there were
cries of 'keep off' and noisy abuse, so that nothing could
be heard either of the word of command or of the cox-
swains' giving the time; and the difficulty which un-
practised rowers had in clearing the water in a heavy sea
made the vessels disobedient to the helm. At that moment
Phormio gave the signal; the Athenians, falling upon the

enemy, began by sinking one of the admirals' vessels, and then wherever they went made havoc of them; at last such was the disorder that no one any longer thought of resisting, but the whole fleet fled away to Patrae and Dymè in Achaea. The Athenians pursued them, captured twelve ships, and taking on board most of their crews, sailed away to Molycrium. They set up a trophy on Rhium, and having there dedicated a ship to Poseidon, retired to Naupactus. The Peloponnesians likewise, with the remainder of their fleet, proceeded quickly along the coast from Dymè and Patrae to Cyllenè, where the Eleans have their docks. Cnemus with the ships from Leucas, which should have been joined by these, arrived after the battle of Stratus at Cyllenè.

85   The Lacedaemonians at home now sent to the fleet three *The Lacedaemonians* commissioners, Timocrates, Brasidas, *send Brasidas and two* and Lycophron, to advise Cnemus. *others to advise Cnemus.* He was told that he must contrive to fight again and be more successful; he should not allow a few ships to keep him off the sea. The recent sea-fight had been the first attempt of the Lacedaemonians, and they were quite amazed and could not imagine that their own fleet was so inferior to that of the enemy. They suspected that there had been cowardice, not considering that the Athenians were old sailors and that they were only beginners[a] So they despatched the commissioners in a rage. On their arrival they and Cnemus sent round to the allied cities for ships, and equipped for action those which were on the spot. Phormio likewise sent home *The Athenians send* messengers to announce the victory, *reinforcements to Phor-* and at the same time to inform the *mio, but order them to* Athenians of the preparations which *go to Crete first.* the enemy were making. He told them to send him immediately as large a reinforcement as possible, for he might have to fight any day. They sent

---

[a] Cp. i. 142.

him twenty ships, but ordered the commander of them to go to Crete first; for Nicias of Gortys in Crete, who was the proxenus of the Athenians, had induced them to send a fleet against Cydonia, a hostile town which he promised to reduce. But he really invited them to please the Polichnitae, who are neighbours of the Cydoniatae. So the Athenian commander took the ships, went to Crete, and joined the Polichnitae in ravaging the lands of the Cydoniatae; there, owing to contrary winds and bad weather, a considerable time was wasted.

While the Athenians were detained in Crete the Peloponnesians at Cyllene, equipped for a naval engagement, coasted along to Panormus in Achaia, whither the Peloponnesian army had gone to co-operate with them. Phormio also coasted along to the Molycrian Rhium and anchored outside the gulf with the twenty ships which had fought in the previous engagement. This Rhium was friendly to the Athenians; there is another Rhium on the opposite coast in Peloponnesus; the space between them, which is rather less than a mile, forms the mouth of the Crisaean Gulf. When the Peloponnesians saw that the Athenians had come to anchor, they likewise anchored with seventy-seven ships at the Rhium which is in Achaia, not far from Panormus where their land forces were stationed. For six or seven days the two fleets lay opposite one another, and were busy in practising and getting ready for the engagement—the one resolved not to sail into the open sea, fearing a recurrence of their disaster, the other not to sail into the strait, because the confined space was favourable to their enemies. At length Cnemus, Brasidas, and the other Peloponnesian generals determined to bring on an engagement at once, and not wait until the Athenians too received their reinforcements. So they assembled their soldiers and, seeing that they were generally dispirited at their former defeat

86 *The Peloponnesians and Phormio take up a position opposite to each other, outside the Crisaean Gulf.*

and reluctant to fight, encouraged them in the following words :—

87   'The late sea-fight, Peloponnesians, may have made

You are terrified by our late mishap. But you were then unprepared. Your superior courage outweighs their superior skill, for without courage skill is useless. We for our part will arrange the attack better. But you must all do your duty.

some of you anxious about the one which is impending, but it really affords no just ground for alarm.   In that battle we were, as you know, ill-prepared, and our whole expedition had a military and not a naval object.   Fortune was in many ways unpropitious to us, and this being our first sea-fight we may possibly have suffered a little from inexperience.   The defeat which ensued was not the result of cowardice ; nor should the unconquerable quality which is inherent in our minds, and refuses to acknowledge the victory of mere force, be depressed by the accident of the event.   For though fortune may sometimes bring disaster, yet the spirit of a brave man is always the same, and while he retains his courage he will never allow inexperience to be an excuse for misbehaviour.   And whatever be your own inexperience, it is more than compensated by your superiority in valour.   The skill of your enemies which you so greatly dread, if united with courage, may be able in the moment of danger to remember and execute the lesson which it has learned, but without courage no skill can do anything at such a time.   For fear makes men forget, and skill which cannot fight is useless.   And therefore against their greater skill set your own greater valour, and against the defeat which so alarms you set the fact that you were unprepared.   But now you have a larger fleet ; this turns the balance in your favour ; and you will fight close to a friendly shore under the protection of heavy-armed troops.   Victory is generally on the side of those who are more numerous and better equipped.   So that we have absolutely no reason for anticipating failure. Even our mistakes will be an additional advantage, because they will be a lesson to us.   Be of good courage, then, and let every one of you, pilot or sailor, do his own duty and maintain the post assigned to him. We will order the attack rather better than your old commanders, and so give nobody an excuse for cowardice. But, if any one should be inclined to waver, he shall be punished as he deserves, while the brave shall be honoured with the due rewards of their valour.'

Such were the words of encouragement addressed to 88 the Peloponnesians by their com- *Phormio, seeing his* manders. Phormio too, fearing that *sailors dispirited, as-* his sailors might be frightened, and *sembles and addresses* observing that they were gathering in *them.* knots and were evidently apprehensive of the enemy's numbers, resolved to call them together and inspirit them by a suitable admonition. He had always been in the habit of telling them and training their minds to believe that no superiority of hostile forces could justify them in retreating. And it had long been a received opinion among the sailors that, as Athenians, they were bound to face any quantity of Peloponnesian ships. When, however, he found them dispirited by the sight which met their eyes, he determined to revive their drooping courage, and, having assembled them together, he spoke as follows :—

' Soldiers, I have summoned you because I see that you 89 are alarmed at the numbers of the enemy, and I would not have you dismayed when there is nothing to fear. In the first place, the reason why they have provided a fleet so disproportionate is because we have defeated them already, and they can see themselves that they are no match for us ; next, ᵃ as to the courage which they suppose to be native to them and which is the ground of their confidence when they attack us ᵃ, that reliance is merely inspired by the success which their experience on land

---

ᵃ Or, taking the antecedent to ᾧ as supplied by the clause οὐ δι' ἄλλο τι θαρσοῦσιν . . . κατορθοῦντες : 'as to the ground of the confidence with which they attack us as if courage were native to them.'

usually gives them, and will, as they fancy, equally ensure
them by sea. But the superiority
which we allow to them on land we may
justly claim for ourselves at sea; for in
courage at least we are their equals, and
the superior confidence of either of us
is really based upon greater experience.
The Lacedaemonians lead the allies
for their own honour and glory; the
majority of them are dragged into
battle against their will; if they were
not compelled they would never have
ventured after so great a defeat to fight
again at sea. So that you need not fear
their valour; they are far more afraid
of you and with better reason, not
only because you have already defeated

I see that you fear the number of the enemy. Yet (1) their fleet is only so large because you defeated them before; (2) they boast of their courage, but it is only a courage on land; (3) they go unwillingly to battle, for (4) they believe that your very disproportion shows your superiority. I will not, if possible, sail into the gulf, where the confined space would baffle your skill. Do you keep your presence of mind, for the maritime supremacy of Athens is at stake.

them, but because they cannot believe that you would
oppose them at all if you did not mean to do something
worthy of that great victory. [a]For most men when, like
these Peloponnesians, they are a match for their enemies [a]
rely more upon their strength than upon their courage;
but those who go into battle against far superior numbers
and under no constraint must be inspired by some extraordinary force of resolution. Our enemies are well aware
of this, and are more afraid of our surprising boldness than
they would be if our forces were less out of proportion to
their own. Many an army before now has been overthrown by smaller numbers owing to want of experience;
some too through cowardice; and from both these faults
we are certainly free. If I can help I shall not give battle
in the gulf, or even sail into it. For I know that where
a few vessels which are skilfully handled and are better
sailers engage with a larger number which are badly

---

[a] Or, 'For men who, like these Peloponnesians, are numerically
superior to the enemy whom they face.'

managed the confined space is a disadvantage. Unless the captain of a ship see his enemy a good way off he cannot come on or strike properly; nor can he retreat when he is pressed hard. The manœuvres suited to fast-sailing vessels, such as breaking of the line or returning to the charge, cannot be practised in a narrow space. The sea-fight must of necessity be reduced to a land-fight [a] in which numbers tell. For all this I shall do my best to provide. Do you meanwhile keep order and remain close to your ships. Be prompt in taking your instructions, for the enemy is near at hand and watching us. In the moment of action remember the value of silence and order, which are always important in war, especially at sea. Repel the enemy in a spirit worthy of your former exploits. There is much at stake; for you will either destroy the rising hope of the Peloponnesian navy, or bring home to Athens the fear of losing the sea. Once more I remind you that you have beaten most of the enemy's fleet already; and, once defeated, men do not meet the same dangers with their old spirit.' Thus did Phormio encourage his sailors.

The Peloponnesians, when they found that the Athenians 90 would not enter the straits or the gulf, determined to draw them in against their will. So they weighed anchor early in the morning, and, ranging their ships four deep, stood in towards the gulf [b] along their own coast [b], keeping the order in which they were anchored. The right wing, consisting of twenty of their fastest vessels, took the lead. These were intended to close upon the Athenians and prevent them from eluding their attack and getting beyond the wing in case Phormio, apprehending an attack upon Naupactus, should sail along

The Peloponnesians by a feigned attack on Naupactus draw the Athenians into the gulf, and, suddenly turning upon them, drive most of their vessels upon shore. Bravery of the Messenians.

---

[a] Cp. vii. 62.   [b] Reading παρά for ἐπί with the Laurentian and three other MSS. Or, adopting the conjecture ἐκείνων for ἑαυτῶν : 'making for the enemy's shore, and' &c.

shore to its aid.　He, when he saw them weighing anchor, was alarmed, as they anticipated, for the safety of the town, which was undefended.　Against his will and in great haste he embarked and sailed along the shore ; the land forces of the Messenians followed.　The Peloponnesians, seeing that the enemy were in single file and were already within the gulf and close to land, which was exactly what they wanted, at a given signal suddenly brought their ships round, and the whole line faced the Athenians and bore down upon them, every ship rowing at the utmost speed, for they hoped to cut off all the Athenian fleet. Eleven vessels which were in advance evaded the sudden turn of the Peloponnesians, and rowed past their right wing into the open water ; but they caught the rest, forced them aground, and disabled them.　All the sailors who did not swim out of them were slain.　Some of the empty ships they fastened to their own and began to tow away ; one they had already taken with the crew, but others were saved by the Messenians, who came to the rescue, dashed armed as they were into the sea, boarded them, and, fighting from their decks when they were being already towed away, finally recovered them.

91　　While in this part of the engagement the Lacedae-

The Lacedaemonians chase the eleven Athenian ships, which had escaped, to Naupactus. One of these by a sudden turn sinks her pursuer.
monians had the victory and routed the Athenian ships, their twenty vessels on the right wing were pursuing the eleven of the Athenians which had escaped from their attack into the open water of the gulf.　These fled and, with the exception of one, arrived at Naupactus before their pursuers.　They stopped off the temple of Apollo, and, turning their beaks outward, prepared to defend themselves in case the enemy followed them to the land.　The Peloponnesians soon came up ; they were singing a paean of victory as they rowed, and one Leucadian ship far in advance of the rest was chasing the single Athenian ship which had been left behind. There chanced to be anchored in the deep water a merchant

vessel, round which the Athenian ship rowed just in time, struck the Leucadian amidships, and sank her. At this sudden and unexpected feat the Peloponnesians were dismayed; they had been carrying on the pursuit in disorder because of their success. And some of them, dropping the blades of their oars, halted, intending to await the rest, which was a foolish thing to do when the enemy were so near and ready to attack them. Others, not knowing the coast, ran aground.

When the Athenians saw what was going on their hopes 92 revived, and at a given signal they charged their enemies with a shout. The Lacedaemonians did not long resist, for they had made mistakes and were all in confusion, but fled to *The Athenians, taking advantage of the confusion, turn upon the enemy and gain a complete victory.* Panormus, whence they had put to sea. The Athenians pursued them, took six of their ships which were nearest to them, and recovered their own ships which the Peloponnesians had originally disabled and taken in tow near the shore. The crews of the captured vessels were either slain or made prisoners. Timocrates the Lacedaemonian [a] was on board the Leucadian ship which went down near the merchant vessel; when he saw the ship sinking he killed himself; the body was carried into the harbour of Naupactus. The Athenians then retired and raised a trophy on the place from which they had just sailed out to their victory. They took up the bodies and wrecks which were floating near their own shore, and gave back to the enemy, under a flag of truce, those which belonged to them. The Lacedaemonians also set up a trophy of the victory which they had gained over the ships destroyed by them near the shore; the single ship which they took they dedicated on the Achaean Rhium, close to the trophy. Then, fearing the arrival of the Athenian reinforcements, they sailed away at nightfall to the Crisaean Gulf and to

---

[a] Cp. ii. 85 init.

Corinth, all with the exception of the Leucadians. And not long after their retreat the twenty Athenian ships from Crete, which ought to have come to the assistance of Phormio before the battle, arrived at Naupactus. So the summer ended.

93   Before breaking up the fleet which had returned to

The Peloponnesians determine to make an attempt on the Piraeus; but losing heart, only sail to Salamis and ravage the island.

Corinth and the Crisaean Gulf, Cnemus, Brasidas, and the other Peloponnesian commanders, it being now the beginning of winter, wished to make an attempt, suggested by some Megarians, on Piraeus, the harbour of Athens. The entrance was unclosed and unguarded; as was natural, since the Athenians were complete masters of the sea. Each sailor was to carry his cushion and his oar with its thong, and cross on foot with all haste from Corinth to the Athenian side of the Isthmus; they were to go to Megara and from Nisaea, the harbour of Megara, to launch forty ships which happened to be lying in the docks; thence they were to sail straight for the Piraeus. No guard ships were stationed there, for no one ever expected [a] that the enemy would attempt a surprise of this kind. As to an open and deliberate attack, how was he likely to venture on that? and if he even entertained such a design, would he not have been found out in time [a]? The plan was immediately carried out. Arriving at night, they launched the ships from Nisaea and sailed away, but not to the Piraeus; the danger seemed too great, and also the wind is said to have been unfavourable. So they gave up their original idea and made for the projecting point of Salamis which looks towards Megara; here there was a fort, and three ships were stationed in order to prevent anything being conveyed by sea into or out of Megara. This fort they

---

[a] Or, taking ἐπεί differently, and καθ' ἡσυχίαν in the sense of 'without interference:' 'that the enemy would make a sudden attack of this kind. An attempt so bold and open was not likely to be unopposed, or the very design, if entertained, to escape detection.'

assailed, towed away the ships without their crews, and ravaged the rest of Salamis which was unprepared for their attack.

By this time fire-signals had carried the alarm to Athens. 94 Nothing which happened in the war caused a greater panic. The inhabi- *Temporary panic at Athens. Relief is im-* tants of the city thought that the enemy *mediately sent to Sala-* had already sailed into the Piraeus; *mis, and the Pelopon-* the belief in the Piraeus was that *nesians retire.* Salamis had been taken and that the enemy were on the point of sailing into the harbour, which, if they had been bolder, they might easily have done, and no wind would have prevented them. But as soon as day dawned, the Athenians, coming down with the whole strength of the city to the Piraeus, launched their ships and, embarking in tumultuous haste, sailed to Salamis, while their land-forces remained and guarded the Piraeus. When the Peloponnesians saw the fleet coming they sailed quickly back to Nisaea, but not until they had ravaged the greater part of Salamis and taken many prisoners and much spoil, as well as the three ships which lay off the fort of Budorum. There was some apprehension about their own ships; for they had long been lain up and were not sea-worthy. Arriving at Megara they marched back again to Corinth, and the Athenians, having failed to overtake them in Salamis, sailed back likewise. Henceforth they kept more careful watch over the Piraeus, among other precautions closing the entrance to the harbour.

About the same time, at the beginning of winter, Sitalces 95 the Odrysian, the son of Teres, king of *Sitalces king of Thrace,* Thrace, made war upon Perdiccas, the *in alliance with Athens,* son of Alexander, king of Macedon, *attacks Perdiccas and* and upon the Thracian Chalcidians. *the Thracian Chalcidi-* There were two promises, of which he *ans.* wished to perform one, and exact fulfilment of the other. The promise of which he claimed fulfilment had been made to him by Perdiccas, when, being hard pressed at the beginning of the war, he wanted Sitalces to reconcile him to the Athenians[a], and not to restore and place on the throne his brother Philip, who was his enemy; but Perdiccas did not keep his word. The other was a promise which Sitalces had himself made to the Athenians when he entered into alliance with them, that he would put an end to their war with the Chalcidians. For these two reasons he invaded the country, taking with him Amyntas the son of Philip, whom he intended to make king of Macedon, and also certain Athenian envoys who had just come to remind him of his engagement, and an Athenian commander Hagnon. For the Athenians on their part were bound to assist him against the Chalcidians with ships and with as large an army as they could provide.

96   Accordingly Sitalces, beginning with the Odrysae, made

The forces of Sitalces.   a levy of all his Thracian subjects dwelling between Mount Haemus and Mount Rhodope as far as the shores of the Euxine and of the Hellespont. Beyond the Haemus he made a levy of the Getae and of all the tribes lying more towards the Euxine on this side of the Ister. Now the Getae and their neighbours border on the Scythians, and are equipped like them, for they are all horse-archers. He also summoned to his standard many of the highland Thracians, who are independent and carry dirks; they are called Dii, and most of them inhabit Mount Rhodopè; of these some were attracted by pay, while others came as volunteers. He further called out the Agrianians, the Laeaeans, and the other Paeonian nations who were his subjects. These tribes were the last within his empire; they extended as far as the Graaean Paeonians and the river Strymon, which rises in Mount Scombrus and flows through the country of the Graaeans and Laeaeans; there his dominion ended and the independent Paeonians began. In the

---

[a] The reconciliation had been effected through the instrumentality of Nymphodorus; ii. 29.

direction of the Triballi, who are likewise independent, the Treres and the Tilataeans formed his boundary. These tribes dwell to the north of Mount Scombrus and reach westward as far as the Oscius. This river rises in the same mountains as the Nestus and the Hebrus, an uninhabited and extensive range which adjoins Rhodopè.

The empire of the Odrysae measured by the coast-line reaches from the city of Abdera to the mouth of the Ister in the Euxine. The voyage round can be made by a merchant vessel, if the wind is favourable the whole way, at the quickest in four days and as many nights. Or an expeditious traveller going by land from Abdera to the mouth of the Ister, if he takes the shortest route, will accomplish the journey in eleven days. Such was the extent of the Odrysian empire towards the sea: up the country the land journey from Byzantium to the Laeaeans and to the Strymon, this being the longest line which can be drawn from the sea into the interior, may be accomplished by an expeditious traveller in thirteen days. The tribute which was collected from the Hellenic cities and from all the barbarous nations in the reign of Seuthes, the successor of Sitalces, under whom the amount was greatest, was valued at about four hundred talents of coined money[a], reckoning only gold and silver. Presents of gold and silver equal in value to the tribute, besides stuffs embroidered or plain and other articles, were also brought, not only to the king himself, but to the inferior chiefs and nobles of the Odrysae. For their custom was the opposite of that which prevailed in the Persian kingdom; they were more ready to receive than to give; and he who asked and was refused was not so much discredited as he who refused when he was asked. The same custom prevailed among the other Thracians in a less degree, but among the Odrysae, who were richer, more extensively; nothing could be done without presents. By these means

Extent and wealth of the Odrysian empire.

97

---

[a] £80,000.

the kingdom became very powerful, and in revenue and general prosperity exceeded all the nations of Europe which lie between the Ionian Sea and the Euxine; in the size and strength of their army being second only, though far inferior, to the Scythians. For if the Scythians were united, there is no nation which could compare with them, or would be capable of resisting them [a]; I do not say in Europe, but even in Asia—not that they are at all on a level with other nations in sense, or in that intelligence which uses to advantage the ordinary means of life.

98   Such was the great country over which Sitalces ruled. *Sitalces and his army* When he had collected his army and *enter Macedonia.* his preparations were complete he marched into Macedonia, passing first of all through his own territory, and then through Cercinè, a desert mountain which lies between the Sinti and the Paeonians. He went by the road which he had himself constructed when he made his expedition against the Paeonians and cut down the forest. As he left the Odrysian territory in going through the mountain he had on the right hand the Paeonians and on the left hand the Sinti and Maedi; on quitting the mountain he arrived at Doberus in Paeonia. He lost no part of his army on the march, except by sickness, but rather increased it; for many of the independent Thracian tribes followed him of their own accord in hopes of plunder. The whole number of his forces was estimated at a hundred and fifty thousand, of which about two-thirds were infantry and the rest cavalry. The largest part of the cavalry was furnished by the Odrysae themselves, and the next largest by the Getae. Of the infantry, those armed with dirks who came from the independent tribes of Mount Rhodopè were the most warlike. The remainder of the army was a mixed multitude, chiefly formidable from its numbers.

99   Having mustered at Doberus, they made ready to

---

[a] Cp. Herod. iv. 46.

descend over the heights into the plains of Macedonia, which were the territory of Perdiccas.   *Early history of the* There is an upper Macedonia, which is   *Macedonian kingdom.* inhabited by Lyncestians, Elimiots, and other tribes; these are the allies and tributaries of the lower Macedonians, but have kings of their own.   The maritime country which we now call Macedonia was conquered and formed into a kingdom by Alexander the father of Perdiccas and his ancestors the Temenidae, who originally came from Argos [a]. They defeated and drove out of Pieria the Pierians, who afterwards settled in Phagres and other places at the foot of Mount Pangaeus, beyond the Strymon; the land which lies under Mount Pangaeus towards the sea is still called the Pierian vale.   They also drove out of Bottia, as it is called, the Bottiaeans, who are now the neighbours of the Chalcidians, and they acquired a narrow strip of Paeonia by the river Axius, reaching down to Pella and the sea. Beyond the Axius they possess the country called Mygdonia reaching to the Strymon, out of which they have driven the Edonians.   They expelled from the country still called Eordia the Eordians, of whom the greater part perished, but a small remnant of them settled in the neighbourhood of Physca; and from Almopia the Almopians.   They and their subjects further subdued and still hold various places belonging to other tribes, Anthemus, Grestonia, Bisaltia, and a great part of the original Macedonia.   But the whole of this country is now called Macedonia, and was under the rule of Perdiccas the son of Alexander at the time of the invasion of Sitalces.

The Macedonians were unable to defend themselves **100** against the onset of so vast a host; they therefore retired into their strongholds and forts, which at that time were few.   For those which now exist were built by Archelaus the son of Perdiccas, who, when he became king, made straight roads and in various ways improved the country.

---

[a] Herod. viii. 137-139.

In his force of cavalry and infantry and in his military
resources generally he surpassed all
the eight kings who preceded him.

The Macedonians retire into their strongholds. Their cavalry oppose the invaders, but are compelled by their inferiority of numbers to desist.

The Thracian army, leaving Doberus,
invaded first of all the country which
had formerly been the principality of
Philip, and took Eidomenè by storm.
Gortynia, Atalantè, and some other towns came to terms
out of regard for Amyntas the son of Philip, who accompanied the expedition.   They also besieged but failed to
take Europus; they next advanced into that part of
Macedonia which lay on the left of Pella and Cyrrhus.
Farther south into Bottiaea and Pieria they did not
penetrate, but were content to ravage the territory of
Mygdonia, Grestonia, and Anthemus.   The Macedonians
had no idea of facing them with infantry, but sent for
additional cavalry from their allies in the upper part
of the country, and, although a handful of men, dashed
in amongst the great Thracian host wherever they
pleased.   No one withstood their onset; for they were
excellent horsemen and well protected with coats of mail.
But hemmed in as they continually were by a multitude
many times their own number, they ran into great danger.
At last, feeling that they were not strong enough to
encounter such superiority of force, they desisted.

101   Sitalces now held a conference with Perdiccas touching the matters which gave occasion to the war.   The fleet which the
Athenians had promised never arrived;
for not believing that Sitalces would
come, they only sent gifts and envoys
to him.   After waiting for them in vain
he despatched a part of his army
against the Chalcidians and Bottiaeans,
and, driving them within their walls,
devastated the country.   While he was encamped in these
parts, the Thessalians, who lie towards the south, the

Sitalces holds a conference with Perdiccas, and after an unsuccessful campaign in Botticè and Chalcidicè, is persuaded by his nephew Seuthes (who had been gained over by Perdiccas) to return home. Alarm in Hellas.

Magnesians and other dependants of the Thessalians, and all the Hellenes as far as Thermopylae were afraid that his army would move on them, and took measures of precaution. Those independent Thracian tribes to the north beyond the Strymon who dwelt in the plains, namely the Panaeans, Odomantians, Droans, and Dersaeans, were also in great alarm. A belief arose, which spread far and wide among the enemies of Athens, that the Athenians meant to lead their Odrysian allies against the rest of Hellas. Meanwhile Sitalces overran and ravaged Chalcidicè, Botticè, and Macedonia, but could not effect his objects; and, his army being without food and suffering from the winter, he was persuaded by his nephew, who next to himself had the greatest authority, Seuthes the son of Spardacus[a], to return home at once. Now Perdiccas had secretly gained over Seuthes, promising to give him his sister in marriage, with a portion. And so Sitalces and his army, having remained thirty days in all, of which eight were passed among the Chalcidians, returned home in haste. Perdiccas in fulfilment of his promise gave his sister Stratonicè in marriage to Seuthes. Thus ended the expedition of Sitalces.

During the same winter the Athenian forces at Naupactus, after the Peloponnesian fleet had dispersed, made an expedition under the command of Phormio into the centre of Acarnania with four *The Athenians, under Phormio, make an expedition into Acarnania.* hundred hoplites of their own taken from the fleet[b] and four hundred Messenian hoplites. They first coasted along towards Astacus[c] and disembarked. From Stratus, Coronta, and other places they expelled those of the inhabitants whom they distrusted, and restoring Cynes the son of Theolytus to Coronta, they returned to their ships. Oeniadae, of which the inhabitants, unlike the rest of

---

[a] Cp. iv. 101 fin.　　　　　　　[b] Cp. ii. 83 init.; 92 fin.
　　　　　[c] Cp. ii. 30; 33.

the Acarnanians, were their persistent enemies, was unapproachable in winter. For the town

*Oeniadae was inac-
cessible, owing to the
flooding of the Ache-
lous. Opposite to the
town lie the Echinades,
islands formed by the
deposits of the river.
Here Alcmaeon, after
the murder of his mother,
is said to have found a
home which was indi-
cated to him by the
oracle of Apollo.*

is in the midst of a marsh formed by
the river Achelous, which, rising in
Mount Pindus and passing first through
the territory of the Dolopians, Agraeans, and Amphilochians, and then
through the Acarnanian plain, at some
distance from its mouth flows by the
city of Stratus and finds an exit into the
sea near Oeniadae: an expedition in
winter is thus rendered impossible by
the water. Most of the islands called Echinades are situated
opposite to Oeniadae and close to the mouth of the Achelous. The consequence is that the river, which is large,
is always silting up: some of the islands have been already
joined to the mainland, and very likely, at no distant period,
they may all be joined to it. The stream is wide and
strong and full of mud; and the islands are close together
and serve to connect the deposits made by the river, not
allowing them to dissolve in the water. For, lying irregularly and not one behind the other, they prevent the river
from finding a straight channel into the sea. These
islands are small and uninhabited. The story is that when
Alcmaeon the son of Amphiaraus was wandering over the
earth after the murder of his mother, he was told by Apollo
that here he should find a home, the oracle intimating that
he would never obtain deliverance from his terrors until
he discovered some country which was not yet in existence
and not seen by the sun at the time when he slew his
mother; there he might settle, but the rest of the earth
was accursed to him. He knew not what to do, until at
last, according to the story, he spied the deposit of earth
made by the Achelous, and he thought that a place sufficient
to support life must have accumulated in the long time
during which he had been wandering since his mother's
death. There, near Oeniadae, he settled, and, becoming

ruler, left to the country the name of his son Acarnan. Such is the tradition which has come down to us concerning Alcmaeon.

The Athenians under Phormio sailed back from Acar- 103 nania to Naupactus, and later at the *The Athenians return* beginning of spring returned to Athens, *to Naupactus, and in* bringing with them the ships which *the spring sail back to* they had captured, besides the prisoners *Athens.* of free birth whom they had taken in the naval engagements. These were exchanged man for man. And so the winter ended, and with it the third year in the Peloponnesian War of which Thucydides wrote the history.

BOOK III

1   In the following summer, when the corn was in full ear,
Third invasion of Attica by the Peloponnesians. the Peloponnesians and their allies, under the command of Archidamus, the son of Zeuxidamus, the Lacedaemonian king, invaded Attica, and encamping wasted the country. The Athenian cavalry as usual attacked them whenever an opportunity offered, and prevented the great body of the light-armed troops from going beyond their lines and injuring the lands near the city. The invaders remained until their supplies were exhausted; they were then disbanded, and returned to their several homes.

2   No sooner had the Peloponnesians quitted Attica than
The Lesbians, with the exception of the Methymnaeans, revolt, but sooner than they had intended, information of their plans having been sent to Athens from Tenedos, Methymna, and Mytilenè itself. the whole people of Lesbos, with the exception of the Methymnaeans, revolted from Athens. They had entertained the design before the war began, but the Lacedaemonians gave them no encouragement. And now they were not ready, and were compelled to revolt sooner than they had intended. For they were waiting until they had completed the work of closing their harbours, raising walls, and building ships, and they had not as yet received from Pontus the force of archers, the corn and the other supplies for which they had sent. But the inhabitants of Tenedos, who were not on good terms with them, and the Methymnaeans, and individual citizens who were of the opposite faction and

were proxeni of Athens, turned informers and told the Athenians that the Mytilenaeans were forcibly making Mytilenè the centre of government for the whole island; that the preparations which they were pressing forward had been throughout undertaken by them in concert with the Lacedaemonians and with their Boeotian kinsmen, and meant revolt; and that if something were not immediately done, Lesbos would be lost to Athens.

The Athenians, who were suffering severely from the plague and from the war, of which they had begun to feel the full effects, reflected that it was a serious matter to bring upon themselves a second war with a naval power like Lesbos, whose resources were unimpaired; and so, *The Athenians determine to surprise Mytilenè at a festival, and send Cleïppides thither with forty ships. The inhabitants are forewarned.* mainly because they wished that the charges might not be true, they at first refused to listen to them. But, when they had sent envoys to Mytilenè and found that the Mytilenaeans, in spite of remonstrances, continued their preparations and persisted in the attempt to concentrate the government in Mytilenè, they took alarm and determined to be beforehand with them. Without losing a moment, they sent to Lesbos, under the command of Cleïppides the son of Deinias, and two others, forty ships which had been intended to cruise about Peloponnesus. They had heard that there was a festival of Apollo Maloeis held outside the walls in which the whole population took part, and that if they made haste they might hope to surprise them. The attempt would very likely succeed; but, if not, they might bid the Mytilenaeans give up their fleet and dismantle their walls, and in case they refused they might go to war with them. So the ships sailed; and as there happened to be at Athens ten Mytilenaean triremes, serving in accordance with the terms of the alliance, the Athenians seized them and threw their crews into prison. But the Mytilenaeans were warned by a messenger from Athens, who crossed to Euboea and went on foot to Geraestus; there he found a merchant vessel just about to sail; he took ship, and arriving at Mytilenè on the third day after he left Athens, announced the coming of the Athenian fleet. Whereupon the Mytilenaeans abstained from going out to the temple of Apollo Maloeis. They also kept good watch about their walls and harbours, and barricaded the unfinished works.

4   Soon afterwards the Athenians arrived. The com-
The Mytilenaeans, after a slight resistance at sea, negotiate an armistice. They send envoys openly to Athens, secretly to Sparta. manders of the fleet, seeing that they were foiled, delivered the message entrusted to them; the city refused to yield and they commenced hostilities. Taken by surprise, and unprepared for the war which was forced upon them, the Mytilenaeans came out once and made a show of fighting a little in front of the harbour; but they were soon driven back by the Athenian ships, and then they began to parley with the generals, in the hope of obtaining tolerable terms of some kind, and getting rid of the fleet for the time. The Athenian generals accepted their proposals, they too fearing that they were not strong enough to make war against the whole island. Having got the armistice, the Mytilenaeans sent envoys to Athens; one of them was a person who had given information against his fellow-citizens, but was now repentant. They had a faint hope that the Athenians would be induced to withdraw their ships and believe in their good intentions. But as they did not really expect to succeed in their Athenian mission, they also sent an embassy to Lacedaemon, unperceived by the Athenian fleet, which was stationed at Malea [a] to the north of the city [a]. After a troublesome voyage through the open sea, the envoys arrived at Lacedaemon and solicited aid for their countrymen.

---

[a] Or, to avoid the geographical contradiction (see notes), we may take the words with ἀποστέλλουσιν: 'they also sent an embassy . . . northward from the city.'

The other envoys who had been sent to Athens met 5 with no success. When they returned, *The envoys return* the Mytilenaeans and the rest of Lesbos, *from Athens without* with the exception of Methymna, com- *success. A battle en-* menced hostilities; the Methymnaeans, *sues, in which the* with the Imbrians, Lemnians, and a few *Mytilenaeans have the* of the allies, had come to the support *advantage; but they re-* of the Athenians. The Mytilenaeans *main inactive, awaiting* with their whole force sallied out against the Athenian *aid from Peloponnesus.* camp, and a battle took place, in which they got the better; but they had no confidence in themselves, and, instead of encamping on the field, retired. They then remained quiet, being unwilling to risk an engagement without the additional help which they were expecting from Peloponnesus and elsewhere. For Meleas a Lacedaemonian, and Hermaeondas a Theban, had now arrived at Mytilenè; they had been sent before the revolt, but the Athenian fleet anticipated them, and they sailed in by stealth after the battle in a single trireme. The envoys recommended the Mytilenaeans to send an embassy of their own in another trireme to accompany them on their return to Sparta; which they accordingly did.

The Athenians, greatly encouraged by the inactivity of 6 their adversaries, summoned their *The Athenians block-* allies, who came all the more readily *ade Mytilenè by sea.* because they saw that the Lesbians displayed no energy. They then anchored the fleet round the south of the city, and having fortified two camps, one on either side of it, they established a blockade of both the harbours. Thus they excluded the Mytilenaeans from the sea. They like-wise held the country in the immediate neighbourhood of their two camps; but the Mytilenaeans and the other Lesbians, who had now taken up arms, were masters of the rest of the island. At Malea the Athenians had, not a camp, but a station for their ships and for their market.

Such was the course of the war in Lesbos. In the same 7 summer, and about the same time, the Athenians sent

thirty ships to Peloponnesus; they were placed under
Asopius with thirty Athenian ships ravages the Laconian coast, and, dismissing eighteen, sails to Oeniadae, which he is unable to capture. the command of Asopius, the son of Phormio; for the Acarnanians had desired them to send out a son or relation of Phormio to be their leader. The ships in passing ravaged the coast of Laconia, and then Asopius sent most of them home, but kept twelve, with which he sailed to Naupactus. Next he made a general levy of the Acarnanians and led his forces against Oeniadae, his ships sailing up the river Achelous, while his army ravaged the country by land. As the inhabitants refused to yield, he disbanded his land-forces, but himself sailed to Leucas and made a descent upon *He is killed in a descent upon Leucas.* Nericus, where he and part of his army in returning to their ships were slain by the inhabitants, assisted by a few Peloponnesian guards. The Athenians then put to sea, and received their dead from the Leucadians under a flag of truce.

8   The envoys whom the Mytilenaeans had sent out in *The Mytilenaean envoys meet the allies in council at Olympia. Their speech.* their first vessel were told by the Lacedaemonians to come to the Olympic festival, in order that the allies, as well as themselves, might hear them and determine what should be done. So they went to Olympia, The Olympiad was that in which the Rhodian Dorieus won his second victory. When the festival was over, the allies met in council, and the ambassadors spoke as follows:—

9   'We know, Lacedaemonians and allies, that all Hel-*There is a natural feeling against those who desert their friends, but the friendship must be real and equal.* lenes entertain a fixed sentiment against those who in time of war revolt and desert an old alliance. Their new allies are delighted with them in as far as they profit by their aid; but they do not respect them, for they deem them traitors to their former friends. And this opinion is reasonable enough; but only when the rebels, and those from whom they sever

themselves, are naturally united by the same interests and feelings and equally matched in power and resources, and when there is no reasonable excuse for a revolt.   But our relation to the Athenians was of another sort, and no one should be severe upon us for deserting them in the hour of danger although we were honoured by them in time of peace.

' Since an alliance is our object, we will first address 10 ourselves to the question of justice and honour.   We know that no friendship between man and man, no league between city and city, can ever be per- manent unless the friends or allies have a good opinion of each other's honesty, and are similar in general character. For the diversity in men's minds makes the difference in their actions.

Before asking for your alliance, we must show that we deserve your respect.

' Now our alliance with the Athenians first began when you ceased to take part in the Persian War, and they remained to complete the work.   But we were never the allies of the Athenians in their design of subjugating Hellas; we were really the allies of the Hellenes, whom we sought to liberate from the Persians. And while in the exercise of their com- mand they claimed no supremacy, we were very ready to follow them.   But our fears began to be aroused when we saw them relaxing their efforts against the Persians and imposing the yoke of their dominion upon the allies, who could not unite and defend themselves, for their interests were too various.   And so they were all enslaved, except ourselves and the Chians.   We forsooth were independent allies, free men—that was the word— who fought at their side.   But, judging from previous ex- amples, how could we any longer have confidence in our leaders?   For they had subjugated others to whom, equally with ourselves, their faith was pledged; and how

We became allies of the Athenians because we wanted to complete the deliverance of Hellas from the Persians. But when we saw the allies, excepting the Chians and ourselves, succes- sively enslaved by them, what wonder that we lost confidence in them!

could we who survived expect to be spared if ever they had the power to destroy us?

11   'Had all the allies retained their independence,we should

We were an offence to them, but they left us free because (1) our voluntary adherence was a testimony to their character, (2) they wanted to use the strong against the weak, and so isolate us, (3) they feared our navy, (4) we paid court to their demagogues.

have had better assurance that they would leave us as we were; but when the majority had been subjugated by them, they might naturally be expected to take offence at our footing of equality; they would contrast us who alone main-tained this equality with the majority who had submitted to them; they would also observe that in proportion as their strength was increasing, our isolation was increasing too. Mutual fear is the only solid basis of alliance; for he who would break faith is deterred from aggression by the consciousness of inferiority. And why were we left independent? Only because they thought that to gain an empire they must use fair words and win their way by policy and not by violence. On the one hand, our position was a witness to their character. For, having an equal vote with them, we could not be supposed to have fought in their wars against our will, but those whom they attacked must have been in the wrong. On the other hand, they were thus enabled to use the powerful against the weak; they thought that they would leave us to the last; when the lesser states were removed, the stronger would fall an easier prey. But if they had begun with us while the power of the allies was still intact, and we might have afforded a rallying-point, they would not so easily have mastered them. Besides, our navy caused them some apprehension; they were afraid that we might join you, or some other great power, and that the union would be dangerous to them. For a time, too, we saved ourselves by paying court to the people and to the popular leaders of the day. But we were not likely to have survived long, judging by the conduct of the Athe-nians towards others, if this war had not arisen.

'What trust then could we repose in such a friendship 12 or such a freedom as this? The civility which we showed to one another was at variance with our real feelings. They courted us in time of war because they were afraid of us, and we in time of peace paid a like attention to them. And the faith which is generally assured by mutual good-will had with us no other bond but mutual fear; from fear, and not from love, we were constrained to maintain the alliance, and which ever of us first thought that he could safely venture would assuredly have been the first to break it. And therefore if any one imagines that we do wrong in striking first, because they delay the blow which we dread, and thinks that we should wait and make quite sure of their intentions, he is mistaken. If we were really on an equality with them and in a position to counteract their designs and imitate their threatening attitude, how was it consistent with this equality that we had still to be at their mercy? The power of attack is always in their hands, and the power of anticipating attack should always be in ours.

It was not mutual love but mutual fear which united us. We struck first because we were not on an equality with them; we were always liable to be attacked, and were therefore at their mercy.

'These were the reasons, Lacedaemonians and allies, 13 and the grievances which led us to revolt. They were clear enough to prove to all hearers the justice of our cause, and strong enough to alarm us and drive us to seek some deliverance. We have acted from no sudden impulse; long ago, before the war began, we sent envoys to you, and proposed to revolt. But we could not, because you refused our request. Now, however, when the Boeotians have invited us, we have at once obeyed the call. We were intending to make a double severance of ourselves, from the

Our revolt, though premature, was not rash; it had a double motive: we feared the Athenians and sympathised with Hellas. But we look to you for help. Now is your opportunity for attacking Athens by sea. The battle must be fought in the countries on which Athens depends.

Hellenes and from the Athenians; from the guilt, that is, of oppressing the Hellenes, in concert with the Athenians, instead of aiding in their liberation, and from the ruin which the Athenians were sooner or later sure to bring upon us, unless we anticipated them. But the step has been taken hastily and without due preparation; hence you are the more bound to receive us into alliance and to send us speedy help, thereby showing that you are ready to protect those who have claims upon you and to strike a blow at your enemies. Never was there such an opportunity before. The Athenians are exhausted by pestilence and by a costly war; some of their ships are cruising about your shores; the remainder are threatening us; so that they are not likely to have many to spare if you, in the course of this summer, make a second attack upon them by land and by sea. They will not be able to meet you at sea; or, if they do, they will have to withdraw their forces both from Lesbos and from Peloponnesus. And let no one say to himself that he is going to incur a danger which will be his own on behalf of a country which is not his own. He may think that Lesbos is a long way off; but he will find that the help which we bring will be very near him. For the war will not be fought in Attica, as might be imagined; but in those countries by which Attica is supported. The revenues of the Athenians are derived from their allies, and, if they subdue us, will be greater than ever; no one will revolt again, and our resources will be added to theirs; and we shall suffer worse things than those who have been enslaved already. But, if you assist us heartily, you will gain the alliance of a great naval power, and a navy is your chief want; you will draw away the allies of the Athenians, who will fearlessly come over to you; thus you will more easily overthrow the power of Athens. And you will no longer incur, as in times past, the reproach of deserting those who revolt [a].

---

[a] Cp. i. 40 fin.; i. 69.

If you come forward as their liberators your final triumph
will be assured.

'Do not then for very shame frustrate the hopes which **14**
the Hellenes rest on you, or dishonour   *Do not then betray*
the name of Olympian Zeus in whose   *us, for our cause is the*
temple we are in a manner suppliants,   *cause of Hellas.*
but be our allies and helpers.   Do not betray us ; we, the
people of Mytilenè, risk our lives alone in the common
cause of Hellas : universal will be the benefit which we
confer if we succeed, and still more universal the ruin if
you are inflexible and we fall.   Wherefore prove yourselves worthy of your reputation in Hellas, and be such as
we in our fear would have you.'

These were the words of the Mytilenaeans.

The Lacedaemonians and the allies immediately ac- **15**
cepted their proposals and took the   *The Mytilenaeans are*
Lesbians into alliance.   The con-   *taken into alliance, and*
federates, who were present at Olym-   *the confederates are*
pia, were told to make ready quickly   *directed to meet at the*
for another expedition into Attica, and   *isthmus, but come in*
    slowly.
to assemble at the isthmus, bringing the usual contingent
of two-thirds.   The Lacedaemonians arrived first, and at
once set to work making machines for hauling ships over
the isthmus, from Corinth to the Saronic Gulf.   For they
intended to attack the Athenians both by sea and land.
But although they were energetic themselves, the other
allies assembled slowly ; they were gathering in their fruits
and in no mood for war.

The Athenians, perceiving that the activity of the Lace- **16**
daemonians was due to a conviction of   *The Lacedaemonians*
their weakness, determined to show   *for the first time prepare*
them their mistake, and to prove that,   *to attack Attica by sea,*
without moving the fleet from Lesbos,   *but the Athenians man*
they were fully able to repel this new   *a hundred ships, and*
    the attempt is given up.
force which threatened them.   They manned a hundred
ships, in which they embarked, both metics and citizens [a],

---

[a] Cp. i. 143 init.

all but the highest class and the Knights; they then set
sail, and, after displaying their strength along the shores
of the isthmus, made descents upon the Peloponnesian
coast wherever they pleased. The Lacedaemonians were
astounded, and thought that the Lesbians had told them
what was not true. Their allies too had not yet arrived,
and they heard that the Athenians in the thirty ships[a]
which had been sent to cruise around Peloponnesus were
wasting their country districts; and so, not knowing what
else to do, they returned home. However, they afterwards prepared a fleet to go to Lesbos, and ordered the
allies to equip forty ships: these they placed under the
command of Alcidas, who was to take them out. When
the Athenians saw that the Peloponnesians had gone
home, they and their fleet of a hundred ships did the
same.

17   At the time when the fleet was at sea, the Athenians had
Perfection of the the largest number of ships which they
Athenian navy at this ever had all together, effective and in
time. Great expendi- good trim, although the mere number
ture on the navy and was as large or even larger at the com-
the siege of Potidaea in mencement of the war. For then there
the first year of the war. were a hundred which guarded Attica, Euboea, and Salamis, and another hundred which were cruising off Pelo-
ponnesus[b], not including the ships employed in blockading
Potidaea and at other places; so that in one and the same
summer their fleet in all numbered two hundred and fifty.
This and the money spent in the war against Potidaea
was the chief call upon their treasury. Every one of the
hoplites engaged in the siege received two drachmae[c]
a-day, one for himself, and one for his servant; the
original force amounted to three thousand[d], and this number was maintained as long as the siege lasted. Sixteen
hundred more came with Phormio, but went away before

---

[a] Cp. iii. 7 init.   [b] Cp. ii. 17 fin.   [c] About 1s. 4d.
[d] Cp. i. 57 fin.; 61 init.

the end [a]. The sailors in the fleet all received the same pay as the soldiers. So great was the drain on the resources of the Athenians in the early part of the war, and such was the largest number of ships which they ever manned.

While the Lacedaemonians were at the isthmus, the 18 Mytilenaeans and their auxiliaries marched against Methymna, which they expected to be betrayed to them, but, making an assault, and finding that they were mistaken, they went off to Antissa, Pyrrha, and Eresus; and, having strengthened the walls of these places and established their interest in them, they hastily returned. As soon

The Mytilenaeans make an unsuccessful attempt upon Methymna. The Methymnaeans attack Antissa, but are defeated. Reinforcements from Athens arrive under Paches, who blockades Mytilenè by land.

as they had retired, the Methymnaeans retaliated by making an expedition against Antissa; but the people of Antissa and their auxiliaries sallied out and defeated them with heavy loss; the survivors made a hasty retreat. The Athenians heard that the Mytilenaeans were masters of the country, and that their own troops in Lesbos were not sufficient to confine them within the walls. So about the beginning of autumn they sent to Mytilenè, under the command of Paches the son of Epicurus, a thousand Athenian hoplites who handled the oars themselves. On arriving, they surrounded the town with a single line of wall; and in some strong places forts were erected which formed part of the wall. Thus Mytilenè was effectually blockaded both by sea and by land. The winter now began to set in.

The Athenians, being in want of money to carry on the 19 siege, raised among themselves for the first time a property-tax of two hundred talents [b], and sent out twelve ships to collect tribute among the allies, under the command of Lysicles and four others. He sailed to various places and exacted

The Athenians raise a property-tax; and Lysicles is sent to collect tribute; he is killed in Caria.

---

[a] Cp. i. 64 med.; ii. 58 med.   [b] £40,000.

tribute; but as he was going up from Myus in Caria, through the plain of the Maeander, he was attacked at the hill of Sandius by the Carians and the Samians of Anaea [a], and, with a great part of his army, perished.

During the same winter the Plataeans, who were still
20   *The Plataeans resolve* besieged by the Peloponnesians and
to break out of Plataea, Boeotians, began to suffer from the
but only two hundred failure of provisions. They had no
and twenty persevere. hope of assistance from Athens and no
They estimate the height other chance of deliverance. So they
of the enemy's wall by and the Athenians who were shut up
the layers of bricks. with them contrived a plan of forcing their way over the enemy's walls. The idea was suggested by Theaenetus the son of Tolmides, a diviner, and Eupompidas, the son of Daïmachus, one of their generals. At first they were all desirous of joining, but afterwards half of them somehow lost heart, thinking the danger too great, and only two hundred and twenty agreed to persevere. They first made ladders equal in length to the height of the enemy's wall, which they calculated by the help of the layers of bricks on the side facing the town, at a place where the wall had accidentally not been plastered. A great many counted at once, and, although some might make mistakes, the calculation would be oftener right than wrong; for they repeated the process again and again, and, the distance not being great, they could see the wall distinctly enough for their purpose. In this manner they ascertained the proper length of the ladders, taking as a measure the thickness of the bricks.

21   The Peloponnesian wall was double, and consisted of
Plan of the Pelopon- an inner circle looking towards Plataea,
nesian wall. and an outer intended to guard against
an attack from Athens; they were at a distance of about sixteen feet from one another. This interval of sixteen feet was partitioned off into lodgings for the soldiers, by which the two walls were joined together, so that they appeared

---

[a] Cp. iii. 32 init.; iv. 75 med.

to form one thick wall with battlements on both sides. At every tenth battlement there were large towers, filling up the space between the walls, and extending both to the inner and outer face ; there was no way at the side of the towers, but only through the middle of them. During the night, whenever there was storm and rain, the soldiers left the battlements and kept guard from the towers, which were not far from each other and were covered overhead. Such was the plan of the wall with which Plataea was invested.

When the Plataeans had completed their preparations **22** they took advantage of a night on *The Plataeans sally* which there was a storm of wind and *forth.   They are dis-* rain and no moon, and sallied forth. *covered by an accident.* *Their friends in the city* They were led by the authors of the *make an attack from* attempt.   First of all they crossed *the opposite side.* the ditch which surrounded the town ; then they came right up to the wall of the enemy. The guard did not discover them, for the night was so dark that they could not be seen, while the clatter of the storm drowned the noise of their approach. They marched a good way apart from each other, that the clashing of their arms might not betray them ; and they were lightly equipped, having the right foot bare that they might be less liable to slip in the mud. They now set about scaling the battle-ments, which they knew to be deserted, choosing a space between two of the towers. Those who carried the ladders went first and placed them against the wall ; they were followed by twelve others, armed only with sword and breastplate, under the command of Ammeas the son of Coroebus : he was the first to mount ; after him came the twelve, ascending the wall and proceeding to the towers on the right and left, six to each[a]. To these succeeded more men lightly armed with short spears, others following who bore their shields, that they might have less difficulty in mounting the wall ; the shields were

---

[a] See note on the passage.

to be handed to them as soon as they were near the
enemy. A considerable number had ascended, when they
were discovered by the guards in the towers. One of the
Plataeans, taking hold of the battlements, threw down
a tile which made a noise in falling: immediately a shout
was raised and the army rushed out upon the wall; for
in the dark and stormy night they did not know what the
alarm meant. At the same time, in order to distract their
attention, the Plataeans who were left in the city made
a sally against the Peloponnesian wall on the side opposite
to the place at which their friends were getting over.
The besiegers were in great excitement, but every one
remained at his own post, and dared not stir to give
assistance, being at a loss to imagine what was happening.
The three hundred who were appointed to act in any
sudden emergency marched along outside the walls
towards the spot from which the cry proceeded; and
fire-signals indicating danger were raised towards Thebes.
But the Plataeans in the city had numerous counter
signals ready on the wall, which they now lighted and
held up, thereby hoping to render the signals of the
enemy unintelligible, that so the Thebans, misunderstanding the true state of affairs, might not arrive until
the men had escaped and were in safety.

23   Meanwhile the Plataeans were scaling the walls. The
first party had mounted, and, killing
The Plataeans, pro- the sentinels, had gained possession
tected by parties of men of the towers on either side. Their
who hold the towers, followers now began to occupy the
first get over the wall; passages, lest the enemy should come
they then cross the ditch.
through and fall upon them. Some of them placed ladders
upon the wall against the towers, and got up more men.
A shower of missiles proceeding both from the upper and
lower parts of the towers kept off all assailants. Meanwhile the main body of the Plataeans, who were still
below, applied to the wall many ladders at once, and,
pushing down the battlements, made their way over

through the space between the towers. As each man got
to the other side he halted upon the edge of the ditch,
whence they shot darts and arrows at any one who came
along under the wall and attempted to impede their
passage. When they had all passed over, those who had
occupied the towers came down, the last of them not
without great difficulty, and proceeded towards the ditch.
By this time the three hundred were upon them; they
had lights, and the Plataeans, standing on the edge of
the ditch, saw them all the better out of the darkness, and
shot arrows and threw darts at them where their bodies
were exposed; they themselves were concealed by the
darkness, while the enemy were dazed by their own
lights. And so the Plataeans, down to the last man of
them all, got safely over the ditch, though with great
exertion and only after a hard struggle; for the ice in it
was not frozen hard enough to bear, but was half water,
as is commonly the case when the wind is from the east
and not from the north. And the snow which the east
wind brought in the night had greatly swollen the water,
so that they [a] could scarcely accomplish the passage [a]. It
was the violence of the storm, however, which enabled
them to escape at all.

From the ditch the Plataeans, leaving on the right hand 24
the shrine of Androcrates, ran all *They first go towards*
together along the road to Thebes. *Thebes, and then strike*
They made sure that no one would *over the mountains to*
ever suspect them of having fled in *Athens.*
the direction of their enemies. On their way they saw the
Peloponnesians pursuing them with torches on the road
which leads to Athens by Cithaeron and Dryoscephalae.
For nearly a mile the Plataeans continued on the Theban
road; they then turned off and went by the way up the
mountain leading to Erythrae and Hysiae, and so, getting
to the hills, they escaped to Athens. Their number was

---

[a] Taking ὑπερέχειν in the sense of 'superare': or, 'could hardly keep
above the surface in crossing.'

two hundred and twelve [a], though they had been originally more, for some of them went back to the city and never got over the wall ; one who was an archer was taken at the outer ditch.   The Peloponnesians at length gave up the pursuit and returned to their lines.   But the Plataeans in the city, knowing nothing of what had happened, for those who had turned back had informed them that not one was left alive, sent out a herald at daybreak, wanting to make a truce for the burial of the dead ; they then discovered the truth and returned.   Thus the Plataeans scaled the wall and escaped.

25   At the end of the same winter Salaethus the Lacedaemonian was despatched in a trireme from Lacedaemon to Mytilenè.   He sailed to Pyrrha, and thence, proceeding on foot, made his way, by the channel of a torrent at a place where the line of the Athenian wall could be crossed, undiscovered into Mytilenè.   He told the government that there was to be an invasion of Attica, and that simultaneously the forty ships which were coming to their assistance would arrive at Lesbos ; he himself had been sent in advance to bring the news and take charge of affairs.   Whereupon the Mytilenaeans recovered their spirits, and were less disposed to make terms with the Athenians.   So the winter ended, and with it the fourth year in the Peloponnesian War of which Thucydides wrote the history.

Salaethus is sent from Lacedaemon to Mytilenè, with the news that help is on the way.

26   With the return of summer the Peloponnesians despatched the two and forty ships which they intended for Mytilenè in charge of Alcidas, the Lacedaemonian admiral. They and their allies then invaded Attica, in order that the Athenians, embarrassed both by sea and land, might have their attention distracted from the ships sailing to Mytilenè. Cleomenes led the invasion.   He was acting in the place

B.C. 427.
Ol. 88, 2.

After despatching a fleet under Alcidas to Lesbos, the Peloponnesians invade Attica, causing great distress.

---

[a] Cp. iii. 20 med.

of his nephew, the king Pausanias, son of Pleistoanax, who was still a minor. All the country which they had previously overrun, wherever anything had grown up again, they ravaged afresh, and devastated even those districts which they had hitherto spared. This invasion caused greater distress to the Athenians than any, except the second. For the Peloponnesians, who were daily expecting to hear from Lesbos of some action on the part of the fleet, which they supposed by this time to have crossed the sea, pursued their ravages far and wide. But when none of their expectations were realised, and their food was exhausted, they retired and dispersed to their several cities.

Meanwhile the Mytilenaeans, finding as time went on 27 that the ships from Peloponnesus never came, and that their provisions had run short, were obliged to make terms with the Athenians. The immediate *Salaethus, despairing of help, arms the people, who turn upon the nobles.* cause was as follows :—Salaethus himself began to despair of the arrival of the ships, and therefore he put into the hands of the common people (who had hitherto been light-armed) shields and spears, intending to lead them out against the Athenians. But, having once received arms, they would no longer obey their leaders ; they gathered into knots and insisted that the nobles should bring out the corn and let all share alike ; if not, they would themselves negotiate with the Athenians and surrender the city.

The magistrates, knowing that they were helpless, and 28 that they would be in peril of their lives if they were left out of the convention, concluded a general agreement with Paches and his army, stipulating that the fate of the Mytilenaeans should be left in the hands of the Athenians at home. They were to receive him *The government, feeling their helplessness, surrender the city to Paches, on condition that the Athenians at home should decide on the fate of the inhabitants.* and his forces into the city ; but might send an embassy to Athens on their own behalf. Until the envoys returned, Paches was not to bind, enslave, or put to death any Mytilenaean. These were the terms of the capitulation. Nevertheless, when the army entered, those Mytilenaeans who had been principally concerned with the Lacedaemonians were in an agony of fear, and could not be satisfied until they had taken refuge at the altars. Paches raised them up, and promising not to hurt them, deposited them at Tenedos until the Athenians should come to a decision. He also sent triremes to Antissa, of which·he gained possession, and took such other military measures as he deemed best.

29   The forty ships of the Peloponnesians, which should
The Peloponnesian fleet intended for Mytilenè wastes time. Alcidas, hearing of its fall, sails to Embatum, and holds a council. Speech of Teutiaplus.   have gone at once to Mytilenè, lost time about the Peloponnese, and proceeded very leisurely on their voyage. They arrived safely at Delos, before they were heard of at Athens ; but on touching at Icarus and Myconus they found, too late, that Mytilenè was taken. Wanting to obtain certain information, they sailed to Embatum near Erythrae, which they reached, but not until seven days after the fall of Mytilenè. Having now made sure of the fact, they consulted as to what measures should next be taken, and Teutiaplus, an Elean, addressed them as follows :—

30   ' My opinion, Alcidas, and you, my fellow-commanders
Let us hurry on to Mytilenè. We shall find the Athenians off their guard. The art of the general is to surprise others, never to be surprised.   of the Peloponnesian forces, is that we should attack Mytilenè at once, just as we are, before our arrival is known. In all probability we shall find that men who have recently gained possession of a city will be much off their guard, and entirely so at sea, on which element they do not fear the attack of an enemy, and where at this moment we can strike with effect. Probably too their land forces, in the carelessness of victory, will be scattered up and

down among the houses of the city. If we were to fall
upon them suddenly by night, with the help of our friends
inside, should there be any left, I have no doubt that
Mytilenè would be ours. The danger should not deter
us ; for we should consider that the execution of a military
surprise is always dangerous, and that the general who is
never taken off his guard himself, and never loses an
opportunity of striking at an unguarded foe, will be most
likely to succeed in war.'

His words failed to convince Alcidas ; whereupon some **31**
Ionian exiles and the Lesbians who *It is also proposed to*
were on board the fleet [a] recommended *occupy some town, and*
that, if this enterprise appeared too *raise a revolt in Ionia.*
But Alcidas rejects both
hazardous, he should occupy one of *propositions. He hur-*
the Ionian towns or the Aeolian Cymè : *ries home.*
having thus established their head-quarters in a city, the
Peloponnesians might raise the standard of revolt in
Ionia. There was a good chance of success, for every
one was glad of his arrival ; they might cut off a main
source of Athenian revenue ; and although they themselves
would incur expense, for the Athenians would blockade
them [b], the attempt was worth making. Pissuthnes might
very likely be persuaded to co-operate. But Alcidas
objected to this proposal equally with the last ; his only
idea was, now that he had failed in saving Mytilenè, to
get back as fast as he could to Peloponnesus.

Accordingly he sailed from Embatum along the coast, **32**
touching at Myonnesus in the terri- *The Samian exiles*
tory of Teos ; he there slew most of *remonstrate with him*
the captives whom he had taken on his *for his impolicy in slay-*
voyage. He then put into harbour at *ing the captives whom*
he had taken.
Ephesus, where a deputation from the
Samians of Anaea [c] came to him. They told him that it
was an ill manner of liberating Hellas, to have put to death

---

[a] i.e. the envoys who had been sent to Sparta. Cp. iii. 4 fin., 5 fin.
[b] Adopting with Bekker the conjecture ἐφορμοῦσιν.   [c] Cp. iii. 19 fin.;
iv. 75 med.

men who were not his enemies and were not lifting a hand
against him, but were allies of Athens from necessity: if
he went on in this way he would convert few of his enemies
into friends, and many of his friends into enemies. He
was convinced by them, and allowed such of the Chian
prisoners as he had not yet put to death and some others
to go free. They had been easily taken, because, when
people saw the ships, instead of flying, they came close up
to them under the idea that they were Athenian; the
thought never entered into their minds that while the
Athenians were masters of the sea, Peloponnesian ships
would find their way across the Aegean to the coast of
Ionia.

33   From Ephesus Alcidas sailed away in haste, or rather

He sails from Ephe- fled; for while he was at anchor near
sus direct for Pelo- Clarus he had been sighted by the
ponnesus, having been Athenian sacred vessels, Paralus and
sighted by the Paralus
and Salaminia, and is Salaminia, which happened to be on
pursued as far as Pat- a voyage from Athens. In fear of
mos by Paches. pursuit he hurried through the open
sea, determined to stop nowhere, if he could help it, until
he reached Peloponnesus. News of him and his fleet was
brought to Paches from the country of Erythrae, and
indeed kept coming in from all sides. For Ionia not being
fortified, there was great apprehension lest the Peloponnesians, as they sailed along the coast, might fall upon the
cities and plunder them, even though they had no intention
of remaining. And the Paralus and Salaminia reported
that they had themselves seen him at Clarus. Paches
eagerly gave chase and pursued him as far as the island of
Patmos, but, seeing that he was no longer within reach, he
returned. Not having come up with the fleet of the
Peloponnesians upon the open sea, he congratulated himself that they had not been overtaken somewhere near
land, where they would have been forced to put in and
fortify themselves on shore, and the Athenians would have
had the trouble of watching and blockading them.

As he was sailing along the coast on his return he **34**
touched at Notium, the port of Colo-
phon.   Here some inhabitants of the   *Paches on his return*
upper town had taken up their abode ;   *puts in at Notium, the*
for it had been captured by Itamenes   *port of Colophon, on the*
and the Barbarians, who had been   *invitation of an anti-*
Persian faction which
invited into the city by a certain local   *had been driven out.*
faction.   The capture took place about   *He takes the citadel, and*
the time of the second invasion of   *treacherously kills the*
commander Hippias.
Attica.   The refugees who settled in   *The Athenians re-estab-*
Notium again quarrelled among them-   *lish the Colophonians*
in Notium.
selves.   The one party, having introduced Arcadian and
Barbarian auxiliaries whom they had obtained from
Pissuthnes, stationed them in a fortified quarter of the
town ; the Persian faction from the upper city of Colophon
joined them and were living with them.   The other party
had retired from the city, and being now in exile, called in
Paches.   He proposed to Hippias, the commander of the
Arcadians in the fortress, that they should hold a conference, undertaking, if they could not agree, to put him
back in the fort, safe and sound.   So he came out, and
Paches kept him in custody without fetters.   In the meantime he made an attack upon the unsuspecting garrison,
took the fortress, and slaughtered all the Arcadians and
Barbarians whom he found within.   He then conducted
Hippias into the fort, according to the agreement, and
when he was inside seized him and shot him to death
with arrows.   He next handed over Notium to the Colophonians, excluding the Persian party.   The Athenians
afterwards gathered together all the Colophonians who
could be found in the neighbouring cities and colonised
the place, to which they gave laws like their own, under
new founders whom they sent out from Athens.

On returning to Lesbos, Paches reduced Pyrrha and **35**
Eresus, and finding Salaethus, the   *Salaethus is captured*
Lacedaemonian governor, concealed in   *and sent to Athens with*
Mytilenè, sent him to Athens.   He   *the Mytilenaean rebels.*

also sent thither the Mytilenaeans whom he had deposited in Tenedos, and any others who seemed to have been implicated in the revolt. He then dismissed the greater part of his army, and, by the aid of the remainder, settled as seemed best to him the affairs of Mytilenè and Lesbos.

36   When the captives arrived at Athens the Athenians

The Athenians put Salaethus to death, and order the slaughter of all the grown-up citizens of Mytilenè. On the next day they begin to repent, and the Mytilenaean envoys persuade the magistrates to call another assembly.

instantly put Salaethus to death, although he made various offers, and among other things promised to procure the withdrawal of the Peloponnesians from Plataea, which was still blockaded. Concerning the other captives a discussion was held, and in their indignation the Athenians determined to put to death not only the men then at Athens, but all the grown-up citizens of Mytilenè, and to enslave the women and children; the act of the Mytilenaeans appeared inexcusable, because they were not subjects like the other states which had revolted, but free. That Peloponnesian ships should have had the audacity to find their way to Ionia and assist the rebels contributed to increase their fury; and the action showed that the revolt [a] was a long premeditated affair [a]. So they sent a trireme to Paches announcing their determination, and bidding him put the Mytilenaeans to death at once. But on the following day a kind of remorse seized them; they began to reflect that a decree which doomed to destruction not only the guilty, but a whole city, was cruel and monstrous. The Mytilenaean envoys who were at Athens [b] perceived the change of feeling, and they and the Athenians who were in their interest prevailed on the magistrates to bring the question again before the people; this they were the more willing to do, because they saw themselves that the majority of the citizens were anxious to have an opportunity given them of reconsidering

---

[a] Or, 'was part of an extensive scheme.'   [b] Cp. iii. 28 med.

their decision. An assembly was again summoned, and different opinions were expressed by different speakers. In the former assembly, Cleon the son of Cleaenetus had carried the decree condemning the Mytilenaeans to death. He was the most violent of the citizens, and at that time exercised by far the greatest influence over the people [a]. And now he came forward a second time and spoke as follows :—

Speech of Cleon.

'I have remarked again and again that a democracy 37 cannot manage an empire, but never more than now, when I see you regretting your condemnation of the Mytilenaeans. Having no fear or suspicion of one another in daily life [b], you deal with your allies upon the same principle, and you do not consider that whenever you yield to them out of pity or are misled by their specious tales, you are guilty of a weakness dangerous to yourselves, and receive no thanks from them. You should remember that your empire is a despotism [c] exercised over unwilling subjects, who are always conspiring against you; they do not obey in return for any kindness which you do them to your own injury, but in so far as you are their masters; they have no love of you, but they are held down by force. Besides, what can be more detestable than to be perpetually changing our minds? We forget that a state in which the laws, though imperfect, are inviolable, is better off than one in which the laws are good but ineffective [d]. Dullness and modesty are a more useful combination than cleverness and licence; and the more simple sort generally make better citizens than the more astute. For the latter desire to be thought wiser than the laws [e]; they want to be always getting their own way in public discussions; they think that they can

You do not know how to manage an empire; you are foolishly kind to your allies, who do not love you; and with your quick wits are always changing your minds.

---

[a] Cp. iv. 21 med.   [b] Cp. i. 68 init.   [c] Cp. ii. 63 med.
          [d] Cp. vi. 18 fin.   [e] Cp. i. 84 med.

nowhere have a finer opportunity of displaying their intelligence [a], and their folly generally ends in the ruin of their country; whereas the others, mistrusting their own capacity, admit that the laws are wiser than themselves: they do not pretend to criticise the arguments of a great speaker; and being impartial judges, not ambitious rivals, they hit the mark. That is the spirit in which we should act; not suffering ourselves to be so excited by our own cleverness in a war of wits as to advise the Athenian people contrary to our own better judgment.

38   'I myself think as I did before, and I wonder at those who have brought forward the case of the Mytilenaeans again, thus inter-posing a delay which is in the interest of the evil-doer. For after a time the anger of the sufferer waxes dull, and he pursues the offender with less keen-ness; but the vengeance which follows closest upon the wrong is most ade-quate to it and exacts the fullest retri-bution. And again I wonder who will answer me, and whether he will attempt to show that the crimes of the Mytilenaeans are a benefit to us, or that when we suffer, our allies suffer with us. Clearly he must be some one who has such confidence in his powers of speech as to con-tend [b] that you never adopted what was most certainly your resolution [b]; or else he must be some one who, under the inspiration of a bribe, elaborates a sophistical speech in the hope of diverting you from the point. In such rhetorical contests the city gives away the prizes to others, while she takes the risk upon herself. And you are to blame, for you order these contests amiss. When speeches are to be heard, you are too fond of using your eyes, but, where actions are concerned, you trust your ears; you estimate

Why is their punish-ment delayed? Will any one pretend that their crimes do us good? or would any one speak on their behalf if he was not well paid, and you were not blind to facts and at the mercy of every clever talker?

---

[a] Cp. iii. 40 init.

[b] Or, 'that what all men believe to be true is absolutely false.'

the possibility of future enterprises from the eloquence of an orator, but as to accomplished facts, instead of accepting ocular demonstration, you believe only what ingenious critics tell you[a]. No men are better dupes, sooner deceived by novel notions, or slower to follow approved advice. You despise what is familiar, while you are worshippers of every new extravagance. Not a man of you but would be an orator if he could ; when he cannot, he will not yield the palm to a more successful rival : he would fain show that he does not let his wits come limping after, but that he can praise a sharp remark before it is well out of another's mouth ; he would like to be as quick in anticipating what is said, as he is slow in foreseeing its consequences. You are always hankering after an ideal state, but you do not give your minds even to what is straight before you. In a word, you are at the mercy of your own ears, and sit like spectators attending a performance of sophists, but very unlike counsellors of a state.

'I want you to put aside this trifling, and therefore I say **39** to you that no single city has ever injured us so deeply as Mytilenè. I can excuse those who find our rule too heavy to bear, or who have revolted because the enemy has compelled them. But islanders who had walls, and were unassailable by our enemies, except at sea, and on that element were sufficiently protected by a fleet of their own, who were independent and treated by us with the highest regard, when they act thus, they have not revolted (that word would imply that they were oppressed), but they have rebelled, and entering the ranks of our bitterest enemies have conspired with them to seek our ruin. And

No city has done us so much harm as Mytilenè; none ever had so little reason. Our indulgence has made them insolent. Nobles and people should be punished alike, for they are equally guilty. If you pardon them your other subjects will be encouraged to revolt; and we must neglect our enemies to fight our own allies.

---

[a] Cp. vii. 48 med.

surely this is far more atrocious than if they had been led by motives of ambition to take up arms against us on their own account.   They learned nothing from the misfortunes of their neighbours who had already revolted and been subdued by us, nor did the happiness of which they were in the enjoyment make them hesitate to court destruction. They trusted recklessly to the future, and cherishing hopes which, if less than their wishes, were greater than their powers, they went to war, preferring might to right.   No sooner did they seem likely to win than they set upon us, although we were doing them no wrong.   Too swift and sudden a rise is apt to make cities insolent and, in general, ordinary good-fortune is safer than extraordinary.   Mankind apparently find it easier to drive away adversity than to retain prosperity.   We should from the first have made no difference between the Mytilenaeans and the rest of our allies, and then their insolence would never have risen to such a height; for men naturally despise those who court them, but respect those who do not give way to them.   Yet it is not too late to punish them as their crimes deserve. And do not absolve the people while you throw the blame upon the nobles.   For they were all of one mind when we were to be attacked.   Had the people deserted the nobles and come over to us, they might at this moment have been reinstated in their city; but they considered that their safety lay in sharing the dangers of the oligarchy, and therefore they joined in the revolt.   Reflect: if you impose the same penalty upon those of your allies who wilfully rebel and upon those who are constrained by the enemy, which of them will not revolt upon any pretext however trivial, seeing that, if he succeed, he will be free, and, if he fail, no irreparable evil will follow?   We in the meantime shall have to risk our lives and our fortunes against every one in turn.   When conquerors we shall recover only a ruined city, and, for the future, the revenues which are our strength will be lost to us[a].   But if we fail, the

----

[a] Cp. iii. 46 med.

number of our adversaries will be increased. And when
we ought to be employed in repelling the enemies with
whom we have to do, we shall be wasting time in fighting
against our own allies.

'Do not then hold out a hope, which eloquence can 40
secure or money buy, that they are to
be excused and that their error is to   *Do not be misled by*
be deemed human and venial. Their   *pity, fine words, or a*
                                          forgiving temper. If
attack was not unpremeditated; that   *you have no right to*
might have been an excuse for them;   *chastise rebels, you have*
but they knew what they were doing.   *no right to rule. Treat*
                                          them as they, fearing
This was my original contention, and   *your vengeance, would*
I still maintain that you should abide   *have treated you. You*
by your former decision, and not be   *will have no trouble*
                                          with your allies when
misled either by pity, or by the charm   *they know that rebellion*
of words, or by a too forgiving temper.   *will be punished by*
                                          death.
There are no three things more pre-
judicial to your power. Mercy should be reserved for the
merciful, and not thrown away upon those who will have
no compassion on us, and who must by the force of
circumstances always be our enemies. And our charming
orators will still have an arena[a], but one in which the
questions at stake will not be so grave, and the city will
not pay so dearly for her brief pleasure in listening to
them, while they for a good speech get a good fee. Lastly,
forgiveness is naturally shown to those who, being reconciled, will continue friends, and not to those who will
always remain what they were, and will abate nothing of
their enmity. In one word, if you do as I say, you will
do what is just to the Mytilenaeans, and also what is
expedient for yourselves; but, if you take the opposite
course, they will not be grateful to you, and you will be
self-condemned. For, if they were right in revolting, you
must be wrong in maintaining your empire. But if, right
or wrong, you are resolved to rule, then rightly or wrongly
they must be chastised for your good. Otherwise you must

------

[a] Cp. iii. 37 fin.

give up your empire, and, when virtue is no longer dangerous, you may be as virtuous as you please. Punish them as they would have punished you; let not those who have escaped appear to have less feeling than those who conspired against them. Consider: what might not they have been expected to do if they had conquered?—especially since they were the aggressors. For those who wantonly attack others always rush into extremes, and sometimes, like these Mytilenaeans, to their own destruction. They know the fate which is reserved for them by an enemy who is spared: [a] when a man is injured wantonly he is more dangerous if he escape than the enemy who has only suffered what he has inflicted [a]. Be true then to yourselves, and recall as vividly as you can what you felt at the time; think how you would have given the world to crush your enemies, and now take your revenge. Do not be soft-hearted at the sight of their distress, but remember the danger which was once hanging over your heads. Chastise them as they deserve, and prove by an example to your other allies that rebellion will be punished with death. If this is made quite clear to them, your attention will no longer be diverted from your enemies by wars against your own allies.'

41 Such were the words of Cleon; and after him Diodotus the son of Eucrates, who in the previous assembly had been the chief opponent of the decree which condemned the Mytilenaeans, came forward again and spoke as follows:—

Speech of Diodotus.

42 'I am far from blaming those who invite us to reconsider our sentence upon the Mytilenaeans, nor do I approve of the censure which has been cast on the practice of deliberating more than once about matters so critical. In my opinion the two things most adverse to good counsel are haste and passion; the former is generally a mark

---

[a] Or, referring the words to the Mytilenaeans: 'He who has gone out of his way to bring a calamity upon himself is more dangerous if he be allowed to escape than the enemy who only retaliates.'

of folly, the latter of vulgarity and narrowness of mind.
When a man insists that words ought
not to be our guides in action[a], he is *We are right in re-*
either wanting in sense or wanting in *considering the case of*
honesty: he is wanting in sense if he *the Mytilenaeans. He*
does not see that there is no other way *is foolish, even if he be*
honest, who would have
in which we can throw light on the *no deliberation: still*
unknown future; and he is not honest *worse is he who insinu-*
if, seeking to carry a discreditable *ates that his opponent*
is corrupt, instead of
measure, and knowing that he cannot *meeting him by fair*
speak well in a bad cause, he reflects *arguments. The wise*
that he can slander well and terrify *city makes room for all,*
and shows favour to
his opponents and his audience by *none.*
the audacity of his calumnies. Worst of all are those
who, besides other topics of abuse, declare that their
opponent is hired to make an eloquent speech. If they
accused him of stupidity only, when he failed in producing
an impression he might go his way having lost his reputation for sense but not for honesty; whereas he who is
accused of dishonesty, even if he succeed, is viewed with
suspicion, and, if he fail, is thought to be both fool and
rogue. And so the city suffers; for she is robbed of her
counsellors by fear. Happy would she be if such citizens
could not speak at all, for then the people would not be
misled. The good citizen should prove his superiority as
a speaker, not by trying to intimidate those who are to follow
him in debate, but by fair argument; and the wise city
ought not to give increased honour to her best counsellor,
any more than she will deprive him of that which he has;
while he whose proposal is rejected not only ought to
receive no punishment, but should be free from all
reproach. Then he who succeeds will not say pleasant
things contrary to his better judgment in order to gain
a still higher place in popular favour, and he who fails
will not be striving to attract the multitude to himself by
like compliances.

---

[a] Cp. ii. 40 med.

43   'But we take an opposite course; and still worse. Even

*But you are too clever:
you are always suspect-
ing that a speaker has
some interested motive.
You punish the giver
of bad advice, and not
yourselves for following
him.*

when we know a man to be giving the
wisest counsel, a suspicion of corruption
is set on foot; and from a jealousy
which is perhaps groundless we allow
the state to lose an undeniable advantage. It has come to this, that the
best advice when offered in plain terms

is as much distrusted as the worst; and not only he who
wishes to lead the multitude into the most dangerous
courses must deceive them, but he who speaks in the
cause of right must make himself believed by lying. In
this city, and in this city only, to do good openly and
without deception is impossible, because you are too
clever; and, when a man confers an unmistakeable benefit
on you, he is rewarded by a suspicion that, in some underhand manner, he gets more than he gives. But, whatever
you may suspect [a], when great interests are at stake, we
who advise ought to look further and weigh our words
more carefully than you whose vision is limited. And you
should remember that we are accountable for our advice
to you, but you who listen are accountable to nobody.
If he who gave and he who followed evil counsel suffered
equally, you would be more reasonable in your ideas; but
now, whenever you meet with a reverse, led away by the
passion of the moment you punish the individual who is
your adviser for his error of judgment, and your own
error you condone, if the judgments of many concurred
in it.

44   'I do not come forward either as an advocate of the

*The question is one
of policy, not of law.
Your anger ought not
to make you prefer jus-
tice to expediency.*

Mytilenaeans or as their accuser; the
question for us rightly considered is
not, what are their crimes? but, what
is for our interest? If I prove them
ever so guilty, I will not on that account

bid you put them to death, unless it is expedient. Neither,

---

[a] Reading ἀξιοῦντι.

if perchance there be some degree of excuse for them,
would I have you spare them, unless it be clearly for the
good of the state.   For I conceive that we are now concerned, not with the present, but with the future.   When
Cleon insists that the infliction of death will be expedient
and will secure you against revolt in time to come, I, like
him taking the ground of future expediency, stoutly maintain the contrary position ; and I would not have you be
misled by the apparent fairness of his proposal, and reject
the solid advantages of mine.   You are angry with the
Mytilenaeans, and the superior justice of his argument may
for the moment attract you ; but we are not at law with
them, and do not want to be told what is just ; we are
considering a question of policy, and desire to know how we
can turn them to account.

‘ To many offences less than theirs states have affixed 45
the punishment of death ; nevertheless, *Experience abun-*
excited by hope, men still risk their *dantly proves that the*
lives.   No one when venturing on a *penalty of death is no*
perilous enterprise ever yet passed *deterrent. Men, and*
still more states, are
a sentence of failure on himself.   And *carried away by their*
what city when entering on a revolt *passions and by trust*
ever imagined that the power which *in fortune.*
she had, whether her own or obtained from her allies, did
not justify the attempt ?   All are by nature prone to err
both in public and in private life, and no law will prevent
them.   Men have gone through the whole catalogue of
penalties in the hope that, by increasing their severity,
they may suffer less at the hands of evil-doers.   In early
ages the punishments, even of the worst offences, would
naturally be milder ; but as time went on and mankind
continued to transgress, they seldom stopped short of
death.   And still there are transgressors.   Some greater
terror then has yet to be discovered ; certainly death is no
deterrent.   For poverty inspires necessity with daring ;
and wealth engenders avarice in pride and insolence ; and
the various conditions of human life, as they severally fall

under the sway of some mighty and fatal power, lure men through their passions to destruction. Desire and hope are never wanting, the one leading, the other following the one devising the enterprise, the other suggesting that fortune will be kind; and they are the most ruinous, for, being unseen, they far outweigh the dangers which are seen. Fortune too assists the illusion, for she often presents herself unexpectedly, and induces states as well as individuals to run into peril, however inadequate their means; and states even more than individuals, because they are throwing for a higher stake, freedom or empire, and because when a man has a whole people acting with him, ᵃ he magnifies himselfᵃ out of all reason. In a word then, it is impossible and simply absurd to suppose that human nature when bent upon some favourite project can be restrained either by the strength of law or by any other terror.

46 'We ought not therefore to act hastily out of a mistaken

The threat of severe punishment will make rebels fight to the last, and, if we succeed, we shall only gain a ruined city. Our true policy is prevention, not punishment.

reliance on the security which the penalty of death affords. Nor should we drive our rebellious subjects to despair; they must not think that there is no place for repentance, or that they may not at any moment give up their mistaken policy. Consider: at present, although a city may actually have revolted, when she becomes conscious of her weakness she will capitulate while still able to defray the cost of the war and to pay tribute for the future; but if we are too severe, will not the citizens make better preparations, and, when besieged, resist to the last, knowing that it is all the same whether they come to terms early or late? Shall not we ourselves suffer? For we shall waste our money by sitting down before a city which refuses to surrender; when the place is taken it will be a mere wreck, and we shall in

---

ᵃ Or, reading αὐτῶν, ' he exaggerates the importance of his aims.'

future lose the revenues derived from it[a]; and in these revenues lies our military strength. Do not then weigh offences with the severity of a judge, when you will only be injuring yourselves, but have an eye to the future; let the penalties which you impose on rebellious cities be moderate, and then their wealth will be undiminished and at your service. Do not hope to find a safeguard in the severity of your laws, but only in the vigilance of your administration. At present we do just the opposite; a free people under a strong government will always revolt in the hope of independence; and when we have put them down we think that they cannot be punished too severely. But instead of inflicting extreme penalties on free men who revolt, we should practise extreme vigilance before they revolt, and never allow such a thought to enter their minds. When however they have been once put down we ought to extenuate their crimes as much as possible.

'Think of another great error into which you would fall 47 if you listened to Cleon. At present the popular party are everywhere our friends; either they do not join with the oligarchs, or, if compelled to do so, they are always ready to turn against the authors of the revolt; and so in going to war with a rebellious state you have the multitude on your side. But, if you destroy the people of Mytilenè who took no part in the revolt, and who voluntarily surrendered the city as soon as they got arms into their hands; in the first place they were your benefactors, and to slay them would be a crime; in the second place you will play into the hands of the oligarchic parties, who henceforward, in fomenting a revolt, will at once have the people on their side; for you will have proclaimed to

If you destroy the Mytilenaeans who put their city into your hands, you will show ingratitude and alienate the popular party everywhere. Even if they were guilty, it would be more expedient to pardon them.

---

[a] Cp. iii. 39 fin.

all that the innocent and the guilty will share the same fate. Even if they were guilty you should wink at their conduct, and not allow the only friends whom you have left to be converted into enemies. Far more conducive to the maintenance of our empire would it be to suffer wrong willingly, than for the sake of justice to put to death those whom we had better spare. Cleon may speak of a punishment which is just and also expedient, but you will find that, in any proposal like his, the two cannot be combined.

48 'Assured then that what I advise is for the best, and *Pass sentence at leisure on the prisoners sent hither by Paches, and spare the rest.* yielding neither to pity nor to lenity, for I am as unwilling as Cleon can be that you should be influenced by any such motives, but simply weighing the arguments which I have urged, accede to my proposal: Pass sentence at your leisure on the Mytilenaeans whom Paches, deeming them guilty, has sent hither ; but leave the rest of the inhabitants where they are. This will be good policy for the future, and will strike present terror into your enemies. For wise counsel is really more formidable to an enemy than the severity of unreasoning violence.'

49 Thus spoke Diodotus, and such were the proposals on *The motion of Diodotus is just carried. A trireme is despatched, which by great exertions arrives in time to save Mytilenè.* either side which most nearly represented the opposing parties. In spite of the reaction, there was a struggle between the two opinions; the show of hands was very near, but the motion of Diodotus prevailed. The Athenians instantly despatched another trireme, hoping that, if the second could overtake the first[a], which had a start of about twenty-four hours, it might be in time to save the city. The Mytilenaean envoys provided wine and barley for the crew, and promised them great rewards if they arrived first. And such was their energy that they continued rowing

---

[a] Reading δευτέρας.

whilst they ate their barley, kneaded with wine and oil, and slept and rowed by turns. Fortunately no adverse wind sprang up, and, the first of the two ships sailing in no great hurry on her untoward errand, and the second hastening as I have described, the one did indeed arrive sooner than the other, but not much sooner. Paches had read the decree and was about to put it into execution, when the second appeared and arrested the fate of the city.

So near was Mytilenè to destruction.

The captives whom Paches had sent to Athens as being 50 the most guilty numbered about a thousand, or rather more[a]; these the Athenians, upon the motion of Cleon, put to death. They razed the walls of the Mytilenaeans and took away their fleet. Then, instead of imposing tribute on them, they divided the whole island, exclusive of the territory of Methymna, into three thousand portions, of which they dedicated three hundred to the Gods ; the remainder they let out to cleruchi[b] taken from their own citizens, whom they chose by lot and sent to Lesbos. The Lesbians undertook to pay them a yearly rent of two minae[c] for each portion and cultivated the land themselves. The Athenians also took possession of the towns on the continent which the Mytilenaeans held[d], and these henceforward were subject to Athens.

The captives at Athens are put to death. The lands of Lesbos are divided among Athenian citizens.

Thus ended the revolt of Lesbos.

During the same summer, after the recovery of Lesbos, 51 the Athenians, under the command of Nicias the son of Niceratus, made an expedition against the island of Minoa, which lies in front of Megara ; the Megarians had built a fort there and used the island as a military station. But

The Athenians under Nicias capture and fortify the island of Minoa.

---

[a] See note. The number must be considered doubtful.   [b] Cleruchi, literally 'portioners,' Athenians who received land in a conquered country, but remained citizens.   [c] £6 13s. 4d.   [d] Cp. iv. 52 med.

Nicias wanted the Athenians to keep a watch over Megara, not as hitherto from Budorum in Salamis, but from this spot, which was nearer, the Peloponnesians would then be no longer able to send out triremes, as they had already done on one occasion [a], or privateers from the harbour unobserved, and nothing could be brought in by sea to Megara. First of all he took [b] two projecting towers on the side of the island towards Nisaea [b] by the help of engines from the sea, and, having thus freed a way into the channel dividing Minoa from the coast of Megara, he fortified the point nearest the mainland, where, by a bridge through a lagoon, aid could be brought by the enemy to the island, lying as it did at that point close to the shore. The work was completed in a few days. Nicias then proceeded to build a fort on the island, and, leaving a garrison, returned with the rest of his army.

52   In this summer and about the same time the Plataeans, who had exhausted their food and could no longer hold out, capitulated to the Peloponnesians. The enemy had assaulted their wall and they were unable to defend themselves. But the Lacedaemonian commander knew their weakness, and was desirous that the place should be surrendered and not stormed; he had instructions from home to this effect, the intention being that if some day a treaty of peace were concluded, and both parties agreed to give up all the places which they had taken by force of arms [c], Plataea might be excepted on the ground that the inhabitants had come to terms of their own accord. So he sent a herald to enquire whether they would surrender the place to the Lacedaemonians and submit to their decision; the guilty were to be punished, but no one without a just cause. The Plataeans,

The Plataeans surrender to the Lacedaemonians, and a commission of five is sent from Sparta to decide their fate. They obtain leave to speak in their own defence.

---

[a] Cp. ii. 93, 94.   [b] Or, 'two towers projecting from Nisaea.'
[c] Cp. v. 17 med.

now in the last stage of weakness, surrendered the city ;
and for a few days, until the five men who were appointed
judges came from Lacedaemon, the Peloponnesians
supplied them with food. On the arrival of the judges no
accusation was brought against them ; they were simply
asked one by one, Whether they had done any kind of
service to the Lacedaemonians or to their allies in the
present war. Before making their reply they requested
leave to speak at length, and appointed two of
their number, Astymachus the son of Asopolaus, and
Lacon the son of Aeimnestus, who was the Lacedaemonian proxenus, to be their advocates. They came
forward and spoke as follows :—

'Men of Lacedaemon, we surrendered our city because 53
we had confidence in you ; we were   *We hoped to have a*
under the impression that the trial to   *legal trial and to re-*
which we submitted would be legal,   *ceive justice at your*
and of a very different kind from this ; *hands, but we are dis-*
                                          appointed. We now fear
and when we accepted you and you   *that we are to be sacri-*
alone to be our judges, which indeed   *ficed to the Thebans.*
you are, we thought that at your hands we had the best
hope of obtaining justice. But we fear that we are doubly
mistaken, having too much reason to suspect that in this
trial our lives are at stake, and that you will turn out to be
partial judges. So we must infer, because no accusation
has been preferred against us calling for a defence, but
we speak at our own request ; and because your question
is a short one, to which the answer, if true, condemns us,
and, if false, is exposed at once. In the extremity of our
helplessness, our only and our safest course is to say
something, whatever may be our fate ; for men in our
condition are sure to reproach themselves with their
silence, and to fancy that the unuttered word, if spoken,
would have saved them.

'But by what arguments can we ever convince you ?
If we were unacquainted with one another we might with
advantage adduce in evidence matters of which you were

ignorant, but now you know all that we can say; and we are afraid, not that we are criminals in your eyes because you have decided that we fall short of your own standard of virtue [a], but that we are being sacrificed to please others, and that the cause which we plead is already prejudged.

54   'Still we may urge our claims of justice against our Theban enemies, and our claims of gratitude upon you and the other Hellenes; the recollection of our good deeds may perhaps move you. To your short question, "Whether in this war we have done any service to the Lacedaemonians and their allies," we reply that "if we are enemies you are not wronged, because you have received no good from us; and if you deem us friends, you who have made war upon us, and not we, are to blame." During the late peace and in the Persian War our conduct was irreproachable; we were not the first to violate the peace, and we were the only Boeotians who took part in repelling the Persian invader and in the liberation of Hellas. Although we are an inland city, we joined in the sea-fight off Artemisium; we were at your side when you fought in our land under Pausanias, and, whatever dangers the Hellenes underwent in those days, we took a share beyond our strength in all of them. And you, Lacedaemonians, more especially should remember how at the time when Sparta was panic-stricken by the rebellion of the Helots, who seized Ithomè after the earthquake [b], we sent a third part of our own citizens to your aid; these are things not to be forgotten.

Treat us either as friends or as open enemies. Remember our conduct (1) in the Persian War, (2) in the revolt of the Helots.

55   'Such was the spirit which animated us in the great days of old; not until later did we become your enemies, and that was originally your own fault. For when we sought your help against the violence of the Thebans, you had rejected us and had bade us turn to the Athenians, who were

---

[a] Cp. iii. 57 init.   [b] Cp. i. 101.

near, whereas you were at a distance.   Yet even in this
war you have neither suffered nor were ever likely to
suffer anything very atrocious at our *We only left you at*
hands.   If we refused to revolt from *the bidding of the Athe-*
the Athenians at your bidding, we *nians and you origin-*
were quite right; for they assisted us *ally forced us to be-*
come their allies. They
against the Thebans when you shrank *helped us then, and*
from the task; and after this it would *how could we abandon*
have been dishonourable to betray them. *them?*
They had been our benefactors; we had been at our
own request admitted to their alliance, and we shared the
rights of citizenship with them.   How could we refuse to
respond loyally to their call?   When you or they in the
exercise of your supremacy have acted, it may be, wrongly
and led your allies into evil courses, the leaders and not
the followers are to be blamed.

'The Thebans have inflicted many injuries upon us, 56
and their latest crime, as you are well *The Thebans attacked*
aware, is the cause of our present mis- *us in time of peace:*
fortunes.   They came, not only in time *were we wrong in re-*
sisting them? If we
of peace, but at a holy season, and *have erred at all, is not*
attempted to seize our city; we *the error outweighed by*
righteously and in accordance with *our former patriotism?*
univeral law defended ourselves and *Yet the same principle*
on which we acted then
punished the aggressor; and there is no *made us refuse to leave*
reason why we should now suffer for *the Athenians.*
their satisfaction.   If you take your own present advantage and their present hatred to be the measure of justice,
you will prove yourselves, not upright and impartial
judges, but the slaves of expediency.   The Thebans may
appear serviceable now, but of far greater service to you
were we and the other Hellenes when you were in far
greater danger.   For now you invade and menace others,
but in those days the Barbarian was threatening to enslave
us all, and they were on his side.   May we not fairly set
our former patriotism against our present offence, if indeed
we have offended?   You will find that the one more than

outweighs the other; for our service to you was performed at a time when very few Hellenes opposed their
courage to the power of Xerxes; they were then held in
honour, not [a] who, looking to their own advantage, made
terms with the invader [a] and were safe, but who, in the
face of danger, dared the better part.   Of that number
were we, and there was a time when we received the
highest honour at your hands, but now we fear that these
same principles, which have led us to prefer a just alliance
with the Athenians to an interested alliance with you,
will be our destruction.   Yet when men have been
consistent in their conduct, others should show themselves
consistent in their judgment of it [b].   For true expediency
is only this—to have an enduring sense of gratitude
towards good allies for their services, while we [c] do not
neglect our own immediate interest.

57   'Consider, before you act, that hitherto you have been

*Remember your own
reputation : do not out-
rage Hellenic sentiment
by allowing Plataea,
whose name your
fathers inscribed on the
Delphian tripod, to be
blotted out in order to
please the Thebans.*

generally esteemed among Hellenes to
be a pattern of nobility; if you decide
unjustly (and this judgment cannot be
hidden, for you, the judges, are famous,
and we, who are judged by you, are of
good repute), mankind will be indignant
at the strange and disgraceful sentence
which will have been passed against
good men by men still better [d].   They will not endure to see
spoils taken from us, the benefactors of Hellas, dedicated
by our enemies in the common temples.   Will it not be
deemed a monstrous thing that the Lacedaemonians should
desolate Plataea; that they, whose fathers inscribed the
name of the city on the tripod at Delphi in token of her
valour [e], should for the sake of the Thebans blot out the

---

[a] Or, reading αὐτοῖς, and referring the word to the Persians: 'who,
looking to advantage, forwarded the course of the invader.'   [b] This
may refer to the judgment of the Spartans on the Plataeans, or to the
adhesion of the Plataeans to the Athenians; see note.   [c] Reading
ἡμῖν.   [d] Cp. iii. 53 fin.   [e] Cp. i. 132 init.

whole people from the Hellenic world? For to this we have come at last. When the Persians conquered our land, we were all but ruined; and now, when we plead before you, who were once our dearest friends, the Thebans have prevailed against us. We have had to meet two terrible trials, the danger first of starvation, if we had not given up the city; and secondly, of condemnation to death. The Plataeans, who were zealous in the cause of Hellas even beyond their strength, are now friendless, spurned and rejected by all. None of our old allies will help us, and we fear that you, O Lacedaemonians, our only hope, are not to be depended upon.

'Yet once more for the sake of those Gods in whose 58 name we made a league of old, and for our services to the cause of Hellas, relent and change your minds, if the Thebans have at all influenced you: [a] in return for the wicked request which they make of you, ask of them the righteous boon that you should not slay us to your own dishonour [a]. Do not bring upon yourselves an evil name merely to gratify others. For, although you

Do not bring infamy upon yourselves by slaying suppliants. Your ancestors are buried in our land, and we have honoured them by yearly gifts. Will you give them up to their murderers and enslave the country in which the freedom of Hellas was won?

may quickly take our lives, you will not so easily obliterate the infamy of the deed. We are not enemies whom you might justly punish, but friends who were compelled to go to war with you; and therefore piety demands that you should spare our lives. Before you pass judgment, consider that we surrendered ourselves, and stretched out our hands to you; the custom of Hellas does not allow the suppliant to be put to death. Remember too that we have ever been your benefactors: Cast your eyes upon the sepulchres of your fathers slain by the Persians and buried in our land, whom we have honoured by a yearly public

---

[a] Or, 'ask of them the boon that you should not kill those whom you ought not, and receive an honest gratitude from us, instead of a disgraceful gratitude from them.'

offering of garments, and other customary gifts. We were their friends, and we gave them the firstfruits in their season of that friendly land in which they rest; we were their allies too, who in times past had fought at their side; and if you now pass an unjust sentence, will not your conduct strangely contrast with ours? Reflect: when Pausanias buried them here, he thought that he was laying them among friends and in friendly earth. But if you put us to death, and make Plataea one with Thebes, are you not robbing your fathers and kindred of the honour which they enjoy, and leaving them in a hostile land inhabited by their murderers? Nay more, you will enslave the land in which the Hellenes won their liberty; you bring desolation upon the temples in which they prayed when they conquered the Persians; and you will take away the sacrifices which our fathers instituted from the city which ordained and established them.

59 'These things, O Lacedaemonians, would not be for your honour. They would be an offence against the common feeling of Hellas and against your ancestors. You should be ashamed to put us to death, who are your benefactors and have never done you any wrong, in order that you may gratify the enmity of another. Spare us, and let your heart be softened towards us; be wise, and have mercy upon us, considering not only how terrible will be our fate, but who the sufferers are; think too of the uncertainty of fortune, which may strike any one however innocent. We implore you, as is becoming and natural in our hour of need, by the Gods whom the Hellenes worship at common altars, to listen to our prayers. We appeal to the oaths which your fathers swore, and entreat you not to forget them. We kneel at your fathers' tombs, and we call upon the dead not to let us be betrayed into the hands of the Thebans, their dearest

We entreat you by the common gods of Hellas, by your fathers' oaths, not to betray us. We did not surrender to the Thebans: we would rather have died of hunger: if you will not hear us, put us back in our city, and let us meet our fate.

friends to their bitterest enemies.   We remind you of the
day on which we shared in their glorious deeds—we who
on this day are in danger of meeting a fearful doom.   And
now we say no more ; to men in our case, though we must,
there is nothing harder than to make an end ; for with the
end comes the decisive hour.   Our last word is that we
did not surrender Plataea to the Thebans,—far rather
would we have perished from hunger, the most miserable
of deaths,—but to you, in whom we trusted, and, if you
will not listen to us, you ought at least to replace us in the
same position, and allow us to choose our destiny, whatever it may be.   We adjure you not to deliver us, the
Plataeans, who were so loyal to the cause of Hellas, and
who are now suppliants to you, O Lacedaemonians, out of
your own hands and your own good faith, into the hands
of the Thebans, our worst enemies.   Be our saviours.
You are liberating the other Hellenes; do not destroy us.'

Such were the words of the Plataeans ; whereupon the 60
Thebans, fearing that the Lacedae-   *The Thebans also*
monians might give way, came forward   *obtain leave to speak.*
and said that since, against their judgment, the Plataeans
had been allowed, instead of answering the question, to
make a long defence, they too wished to speak.   Permission was granted, and they spoke as follows :—

'We should never have asked to speak, if the Plataeans 61
had briefly answered the question which   *We should not have*
was put to them[a], and had not turned   *spoken if the Plataeans*
upon us and arraigned us while they   *had not. But you must*
made a long and irrelevant defence of   *hear our case as well as*
their own doings, excusing themselves   *theirs.   They separated*
from charges which nobody brought   *themselves from their*
against them, and praising what nobody   *own nation and went*
                                        over to the Athenians.
blamed.   We must answer their accusations of us, and
look a little closely into their glorification of themselves,

---

[a] Cp. i. 37 init. 73; vi. 82.

that neither our baseness nor their superior reputation may benefit them, and that, before you judge, you may hear the truth both about us and them. Our quarrel with them arose thus :—Some time after our first occupation of Boeotia[a] we settled Plataea and other places, out of which we drove a mixed multitude. But the Plataeans refused to acknowledge our leadership according to the original agreement, and, separating themselves from the other Boeotians, deserted the traditions of their ancestors. When force was applied to them they went over to the Athenians, and, assisted by them, did us a great deal of mischief; and we retaliated.

62　' They say that when the Barbarian invaded Hellas they were the only Boeotians who did not join the Persian; and this is their great glory, and our great reproach. But we say that if they did not side with the Persians, it was only because the Athenians did not; and on the same principle, they alone of all the Boeotians afterwards sided with the Athenians when the liberties of Hellas were attacked by them.

They say that we sided with the Persian in the war of liberation. To which we reply that we were not our own masters, and that afterwards we fought at Coronea for the liberation of Hellas from Athens, and are now fighting for it.

But, consider how different were the circumstances in which we and they acted. In those days our state was not governed by an oligarchy which granted equal justice to all, nor yet by a democracy; the power was in the hands of a small cabal, than which nothing is more opposed to law or to true political order, or more nearly resembles a tyranny. The rulers of the state, hoping to strengthen their private interest if the Persian won, kept the people down and brought him in. The city at large, when she acted thus, was not her own mistress; and she cannot be fairly blamed for an error which she committed when she had no constitution. After the Persian departed and she obtained a constitution, you may see how we fought against the Athenians when they became

[a] Cp. i. 12.

aggressive and endeavoured to subjugate us as well as the rest of Hellas. Owing to our divisions they actually conquered the greater part of the country; but we defeated them at Coronea, and liberated Boeotia[a]; and at this moment we are zealously co-operating in the liberation of Hellas, providing cavalry and munitions of war more largely than any of the allies. Thus much in answer to the charge respecting our Persian tendencies.

'And now we will proceed to show that you, and not we, have done the greater wrong to Hellas, and are deserving of every sort of punishment. You say that you became allies and citizens of Athens in order that you might be protected against us. If so, you ought to have *But they of their own free-will abetted the Athenians in their aggressions upon Hellas. They plead obligation, but no obligation can justify a crime.* invited their aid only against us, and not to have assisted them in their attacks upon others; such a course was certainly open to you: even if you had been in some degree constrained against your will by the Athenians, you had previously made the alliance with the Lacedaemonians against the Persians, to which you are so fond of appealing. That alliance would at any rate have restrained our hands, and above all would have secured to you freedom of deliberation. But you acted willingly, and were no longer under compulsion when you made common cause with the Athenians. Your allegation is that they were your benefactors and that you could not honourably betray them; but how far more dishonourable and wicked to betray all the Hellenes with whom you had sworn alliance, than the Athenians only, the one the liberators, the other the enslavers of Hellas! The return which you made to them is unequal, nay, infamous; you say that you invited them to assist you because you were wronged, and then you became their accomplices in wronging others. Surely ingratitude is shown in refusing to return an honourable kindness, when it can be done honourably, not in refusing to return

---

[a] Cp. iv. 92 fin.

a kindness which, however justly due, cannot be repaid without a crime.

64   'You have thus made it plain that, when you alone among

When they resisted the Persian it was only because the Athenians resisted him. They have now shown themselves in their true light, and have forfeited all their claims upon Hellas.

the Boeotians refused to join the Persian cause, this was not out of any love for Hellas[a], but because the Athenians did not[a]; and that you wanted to act with them and not with us; and now you claim the benefit of the virtue which others inspired in you. But this is not

reasonable; having once chosen the Athenians, fight on their side, and do not at the last moment be saying that the old alliance ought to save you. For you have abandoned it, and by the violation of it, instead of striving to

B.C. 456.
Ol. 81.

prevent, have aided in the enslavement of the Aeginetans and of other members of the alliance. And you were not, like us, under compulsion, but free, living under your ancient laws. Moreover, you persisted in refusing that last offer of peace and neutrality which we made to you before the siege began[b]. Who more thoroughly than you deserve the hatred of the Hellenes? than you who have only displayed your virtues to their injury? You have given proof that the merit which you claim for your former actions does not properly belong to you! Your true nature and constant desire are now revealed in the light of day; for you have followed the Athenians in the path of injustice. Thus much we have to say as to our involuntary dealings with the Persians, and your voluntary dealings with the Athenians.

65   'The last offence which you lay to our charge is that

They say that we broke into their city. True, because we were invited by the most influential and patriotic of their citizens.

we unlawfully assailed your city in time of peace, and at a holy season; even in that affair we do not think ourselves more in fault than you. We do not deny that we were wrong if of

---

[a] Or reading ὅτι οὐδ' 'Αθηναῖοι, ἡμεῖς δὲ, 'but because the Athenians did not and we did.'   [b] Cp. ii. 72, 73.

our own mere motion we went to your city, fought with
you, and ravaged your land. But when certain of the
noblest and richest of your citizens, who wished to
withdraw you from a foreign alliance and to bring you
back to the national institutions of Boeotia, came and
invited us, wherein are we to blame? As you say
yourselves, the leaders rather than the followers are
the transgressors[a]. But in our opinion, neither we nor
they were really guilty. Like yourselves they were citizens,
and they had a greater stake in the country than you
have; they opened their own gates and received us into
their native city, not as her enemies but as her friends.
They desired that the bad among you should not grow
worse, and that the good should have their reward. They
wanted to reform the principles of your citizens, and not
to banish their persons; they would have brought them
back into a natural union with their kindred, that Plataea
might be at peace with all and the enemy of none.

'And the proof that we acted in no hostile spirit is that 66
we did no harm to any one, but made *At first they were*
a proclamation that whoever wished *ready to join us, but*
to live under the national institutions *after a while they set*
upon us, and slew our
of Boeotia should join us. You came *citizens whom they had*
to us gladly, and, entering into an *sworn to spare.*
agreement, for a time offered no opposition; but afterwards, when you discovered that we were few, you turned
upon us. Even allowing that we did act somewhat incon-
siderately in entering your town without the consent of
your whole people, still how different was your conduct
and ours! For if you had followed our example you
would have used no violence, but thought only of getting
us out by persuasion, whereas you broke the agreement
and attacked us. Now we do not so much complain of
the fate of those whom you slew in battle—for they indeed
suffered by a kind of law — but there were others who

---

[a] Cp. iii. 55 fin.

stretched out their hands to you ; and although you gave
them quarter, and then promised to us that you would
spare them, in utter defiance of law you took their lives—
was not that a cruel act ? Here are three crimes which
you committed within a few hours ; the breach of the
agreement, the slaughter of the prisoners which followed,
and the lying promise which you made to us that you
would not slay them if we did no injury to your property
in the fields ; and yet you insist that we are the criminals,
and that you ought to be acquitted. Not so ; if the
Lacedaemonians give just judgment : but for all these
offences you shall suffer.

67   'We have entered into particulars, Lacedaemonians,

You should know the both for your sakes and for our own,
truth about the Plat- that you may know the sentence which
aeans. If they had you are going to pass on them to be
the virtues to which they
pretend, they deserve just, and still more righteous the ven-
a double punishment. geance which we have taken. Do not
Pity not them, but their let your hearts be softened by tales
victims. For their mis-
fortunes they may thank about their ancient virtues, if they ever
themselves.   Put the had any ; such virtues might plead for
question to them again. the injured, but should bring a double
penalty [a] on the authors of a base deed, because they are
false to their own character. Let them gain nothing by
their pitiful lamentations, or by appealing to your fathers'
tombs and their own desolate condition. We tell you that
a far sadder fate was inflicted by them on our murdered
youth, of whose fathers some fell at Coronea in the act
of bringing Boeotia to join you, while others are left in
their old age by their solitary hearths, and entreat you,
with far better reason, to punish the Plataeans. Men
who suffer an unworthy fate are indeed to be pitied, but
there should be joy over those who suffer justly, as these
do. For their present desolation they may thank themselves ; they might have chosen the worthier alliance, but

---

[a] Cp. i. 86 init.

they wilfully renounced it. They sinned against us though
we had never injured them ; the spirit of hatred and not
of justice possessed them, and even now they are not
punished half enough. For they are going to suffer by
a lawful sentence, not, as they pretend, stretching out their
suppliant hands on the field of battle, but delivering themselves up to justice under the terms of a capitulation.
Maintain then, Lacedaemonians, the common Hellenic
law which they have outraged, and give to us, who have
suffered contrary to law, the just recompense of our zeal
in your cause. Do not be moved by their words to spurn
and reject us [a], but show Hellas by example that, when
a cause is tried at your tribunal, deeds and not words will
prevail. If the deeds be good, a brief statement of them
is enough; if they be evil, speeches full of fine sentiments
do but veil them. If all persons in authority were like
you, and would sum up a case in a short question, and
pass sentence upon all the offenders at once, men would
be less tempted to seek out fair words in order to excuse
foul deeds.'

Thus spoke the Thebans. The Lacedaemonian judges 68
thought that no objection could be   *The Plataeans are*
made to their question, whether the   *put to death, and their*
Plataeans had done them any service   *city razed to the ground.*
in the war. [b] For they pretended to have expected
neutrality from them in the times before the war, on the
strength of the original treaty concluded with Pausanias
after the defeat of the Persians. And just before the
siege they had made to them a proposal [b] of neutrality
in accordance with the terms of the same treaty; but
the Plataeans had refused. Considering that they had
been wronged by them, after their own fair proposals

---

[a] Cp. iii. 57 fin.   [b] Or, taking ἠξίουν in a different sense, and repeating it before καὶ ὅτε ὕστερον : 'For they had been constantly requesting
them, as they said, to remain neutral in the times before the war, . . . and
they had repeated the request when just before the siege they had made
to them a proposal,' &c.

had released them from the obligations of the treaty, they again brought up the Plataeans one after another, and asked each of them separately, Whether he had done any service to the Lacedaemonians and their allies in the war? When he said No, they took him away and slew him; no one was spared. They put to death not less than two hundred Plataeans, as well as twenty-five Athenians who had shared with them in the siege; and made slaves of the women. For about a year the Thebans gave possession of the city to certain Megarians, who had been driven out by a revolution[a], and to any surviving Plataeans who were of their own party; but they afterwards razed the whole place to the very foundations, and built near the precinct of Herè an inn forming a square of two hundred feet; it had two stories, and chambers all round. They used the roofs and the doors of the Plataeans; and of the brass and iron articles of furniture found within the walls they made couches, which they dedicated to Herè; they also built in her honour a stone temple a hundred feet long. The Plataean territory they converted into public land, and let it out for terms of ten years; some of their own citizens occupied it. Throughout the whole affair the severity shown by the Lacedaemonians to the Plataeans was mainly promoted by a desire to gratify the Thebans, who seemed likely to be useful allies to them in the war then just beginning. Such was the fate of Plataea, which was overthrown in the ninety-third year after the Plataeans entered into alliance with Athens[b].

B.C. 519.
Ol. 65, 2.

69 The forty Peloponnesian ships which had been sent to the aid of Lesbos, as they fled

Return of Alcidas. He and Brasidas make ready an expedition to Corcyra.

through the open sea pursued by the Athenians[c], were caught in a storm near Crete, and, making their way in a straggling condition from Crete to the Peloponnesus, found at Cyllene thirteen Leucadian and Ambraciot

---

[a] Cp. iv. 66 init.   [b] Cp. Herod. vi. 108.   [c] Cp. iii. 33.

triremes, and Brasidas the son of Tellis, who had been
sent out as a commissioner to advise Alcidas. The Lacedaemonians at home, after the failure of their attempt on
Lesbos, had determined to increase their navy and sail
to Corcyra, which was in a state of revolution. The
Athenian squadron at Naupactus consisted of twelve
ships only, and the Lacedaemonians wanted to reach
the island before any more vessels could arrive from
Athens. Brasidas and Alcidas made their preparations
accordingly.

Now Corcyra had been in an unsettled state ever since 70
the return of the prisoners who were
taken at sea in the Epidamnian war [a],   *Unsettled state of
Corcyra, originating in
the intrigues of the
prisoners who had re-
turned from Corinth.*
and afterwards released by the Corinthians. They were nominally let out
on bail for a sum of eight hundred
talents [b] on the security of their proxeni, but in reality
they had been induced to try and gain over Corcyra to
the Corinthian interest. They went from one citizen
to another, and did their best with them to bring about
a revolt from Athens. On the arrival of an Athenian and
also of a Corinthian vessel conveying ambassadors, there
was a discussion in the assembly, and the Corcyraeans
voted that they would continue allies of Athens according
to their agreement [c], but would renew their former friendship with the Peloponnesians. A certain Peithias, who
voluntarily acted as the proxenus of   *Trial of Peithias, the
popular leader. His
acquittal. Trial of the
oligarchs, and murder
of Peithias and of sixty
others.*
the Athenians and was the popular
leader, was summoned by the partisans
of the Peloponnesians to take his trial,
they affirming that he wanted to bring
Corcyra under the yoke of Athens. He was acquitted,
and then he in turn summoned their five richest men,
declaring that they were in the habit of cutting poles for
vines in the sacred precinct of Zeus and Alcinous ; now

---

[a] Cp. i. 55 med.   [b] £160,000.   [c] Cp. i. 44.

for each pole the penalty was fixed at a stater [a].   They
were condemned; but the fine was so excessive that they
went and sat as suppliants in the temple of Zeus and
Alcinous, begging that they might pay the money by
instalments.   Peithias, who happened to be a member of
the senate as well as the popular leader, persuaded the
senators to put the law in execution.   The culprits,
knowing that the law was against them, and perceiving
that Peithias [b] as long as he remained in the senate would
try to induce the people [b] to make an alliance offensive
and defensive with Athens, conspired together, and, rushing into the council chamber with daggers in their hands,
slew him and others to the number of sixty, as well private
persons as senators.   A few who were of the same party
with him took refuge in the Athenian trireme, which had
not yet left.

71   The next step taken by the conspirators was to assemble
Temporary triumph   the people and tell them that they had
of the oligarchs.   acted for the best, and in order to
secure them against the tyranny of Athens.   For the future
they should receive neither Athenians nor Peloponnesians,
unless they came peaceably with one ship; to bring more
should be deemed the act of an enemy; and this proposal
they compelled the people to ratify.   They also sent
envoys to Athens, who were to put the most favourable
colour on the affair, and to dissuade the refugees who had
fled thither from taking any inconvenient step which might
lead to a counter-revolution.

72   When the envoys arrived, the Athenians arrested them
Envoys from Corcyra   as disturbers of the peace, and de-
are arrested at Athens.   posited them in Aegina, together with
Defeat of the popular   any of the refugees whom they had
party.   gained over.   In the meantime, the

---

[a] If the gold stater, about 16s.; if the silver Athenian stater, about
2s. 8d.; if the silver Corinthian stater (didrachmon) (tetradrachmon),
about 1s. 4d.

[b] Or, 'before he ceased to be a senator would persuade the people.'

Corcyraean oligarchs who were now in power, on the arrival of a Corinthian trireme and Lacedaemonian envoys, attacked and defeated the people, who at nightfall took refuge in the Acropolis and the higher parts of the city, and there concentrated their forces. They also held the Hyllaic harbour; the other party seized the Agora, where most of them lived, and the adjacent harbour which looked towards the continent.

On the following day they skirmished a little, and both 73 parties sent messengers round the country inviting the slaves to join *Reinforcements arrive.* them, and promising them liberty; the greater number came to the aid of the people, while the other faction was reinforced by eight hundred auxiliaries from the mainland.

After resting a day they fought again, and the people, 74 who had the advantage in numbers and in the strength of their positions, gained *In a second conflict the people are victorious.* the victory. Their women joined vigorously in the fray, hurling tiles from the housetops, and showing amid the uproar a fortitude beyond their sex. The conflict was decided towards evening; the oligarchy, fearing lest the people should take the arsenal with a sudden rush and so make an end of them, set fire to the private houses which surrounded the Agora, as well as to the larger blocks of buildings, sparing neither their own property nor that of any one else in their determination to stop them. Much merchandise was burnt, and the whole city would have been destroyed if the wind had carried the flame in that direction. Both parties now left off fighting, and kept watch in their own positions during the night. When the popular cause triumphed, the Corinthian vessel stole away and most of the auxiliaries crossed over unobserved to the continent.

On the following day, Nicostratus the son of Diitrephes, 75 an Athenian general, arrived from Naupactus with twelve ships and five hundred Messenian hoplites. He tried to

effect a reconciliation between the two parties, and on
his suggestion they agreed to bring to
*Arrival of twelve
Athenian ships under
Nicostratus, who vainly
tries to reconcile the
contending parties.*
trial ten of the most guilty persons, who
immediately fled.   The rest were to live
together, and to make peace with one
another, and with Athens an alliance
offensive and defensive.   Having accomplished his purpose he was about to sail away, when the leaders of the
people induced him to leave five of his own vessels, that
the enemy might be less inclined to stir, promising to man
five ships of their own and send them with him.   He
agreed, and they selected the crews of the ships out of the
opposite faction.   But the men were afraid of being sent
to Athens, and sat as suppliants in the temple of the
Dioscuri.   Nicostratus sought to raise them up and reassure them, but they would not trust him ; whereupon the
people armed themselves, arguing that their mistrust and
unwillingness to sail was a proof of their evil designs.   They
took their enemies' arms out of their houses, and some of
them whom they chanced to meet would have been slain if
Nicostratus had not interfered.   The rest, to the number of
about four hundred, when they saw what was going on,
took refuge afresh in the temple of Herè.   But the people,
fearing that they would resort to violence, persuaded them
to rise and conveyed them at once to the island that lies in
front of the temple of Herè, whither provisions were
regularly sent to them.

76   At this stage of the revolution, on the fourth or fifth
day after the suppliants had been con-
*Appearance of the
Peloponnesian fleet.*
veyed to the island, the Peloponnesian
ships from Cyllene, which since the expedition to Ionia
had been in harbour there [a], arrived on the scene, fifty-three
in number, still under the command of Alcidas.   Brasidas
his adviser was on board.   They anchored for the night at
Sybota, a harbour on the mainland, and when the morning
broke they sailed upon Corcyra.

----

[a] Cp. iv. 69.

The whole place was in an uproar; the people dreaded 77
their enemies within the city no less   *Confused battle of*
than the Peloponnesian fleet. They   *the Corcyraeans and*
hastened to equip sixty ships, and as   *Athenians against the*
fast as they were manned sent them out   *Peloponnesians.*
against the Peloponnesians, although the Athenians entreated to be allowed to sail out first, leaving them to follow
as soon as they had got their fleet together. But when in
this straggling fashion their ships approached the enemy,
two of them at once deserted ; in others the crews were
fighting with one another, and everything was in disorder.
The Peloponnesians, seeing the confusion, employed
twenty ships only against the Corcyraeans, and opposed
the remainder of their fleet to the twelve Athenian ships,
of which two were the Salaminia and Paralus.

The Corcyraeans, coming up few at a time and in this 78
disorderly fashion, had trouble enough   *Diversion effected by*
among themselves. The Athenians,   *the Athenians, who*
afraid of being surrounded by superior   *slowly retreat.*
numbers, did not attack the main body nor the centre of
those opposed to them, but fell upon the wings and sank
a single ship ; then, the enemy forming in a circle, they
sailed round them and endeavoured to throw them into
confusion. But those who were opposed to the Corcyraeans, seeing this movement and fearing a repetition
of what happened at Naupactus [a], came to the rescue,
and the united fleet charged the Athenians. Thereupon
they rowed astern, hoping that by retreating very
leisurely they might give the Corcyraeans time to escape,
especially as the attack of the enemy was now directed
against themselves. The naval engagement ended at
sunset.

The Corcyraeans, who were afraid that the victorious 79
enemy would sail to the city and have recourse to some
decisive measure, such as taking on board the prisoners

---

[a] Cp. ii. 84.

in the island, conveyed them back to the temple of Herè

The Peloponnesian and guarded the city. But the Pelo-
fleet, instead of attack- ponnesians, although they had won the
ing the city, retire; battle, did not venture to attack the city,
but returned to their station on the mainland with thirteen
Corcyraean ships which they had taken. On the next day
they still hesitated, although there was great panic and
confusion among the inhabitants. It is said that Brasidas
advised Alcidas to make the attempt, but he had not an
equal vote with him. So they only disembarked at the
promontory of Leucimnè and ravaged the country.

80   Meanwhile the people of Corcyra, dreading that the fleet

and soon afterwards, of the Peloponnesians would attack
hearing that sixty Athe- them, held a parley with the other
nian vessels are ap- faction, especially with the suppliants,
proaching, return home. in the hope of saving the city; they
even persuaded some of them to go on board the fleet; for
the Corcyraeans still contrived to man thirty ships. But
the Peloponnesians, after devastating the land till about
midday, retired. And at nightfall the approach of sixty
Athenian vessels was signalled to them from Leucas.
These had been sent by the Athenians under the command
of Eurymedon the son of Thucles, when they heard of the
revolution and of the intended expedition of Alcidas to
Corcyra.

81   The Peloponnesians set out that very night on their way

Massacre of the oli- home, keeping close to the land, and
garchs. transporting the ships over the Leucadian isthmus, that they might not be seen sailing round [a].
When the Corcyraeans perceived that the Athenian fleet
was appoaching, while that of the enemy had disappeared,
they took the Messenian troops, who had hitherto been
outside the walls, into the city, and ordered the ships
which they had manned to sail round into the Hyllaic
harbour. These proceeded on their way. Meanwhile

---

[a] Cp. iv. 8 init.

they killed any of their enemies whom they caught in the city. On the arrival of the ships they disembarked those whom they had induced to go on board, and despatched them [a]; they also went to the temple of Herè, and persuading about fifty of the suppliants to stand their trial condemned them all to death. The majority would not come out, and, when they saw what was going on, destroyed one another in the enclosure of the temple where they were, except a few who hung themselves on trees, or put an end to their own lives in any other way which they could. And, during the seven days which Eurymedon after his arrival remained with his sixty ships, the Corcyraeans continued slaughtering those of their fellow-citizens whom they deemed their enemies; they professed to punish them for their designs against the democracy, but in fact some were killed from motives of personal enmity, and some because money was owing to them, by the hands of their debtors. Every form of death was to be seen; and everything, and more than everything, that commonly happens in revolutions, happened then. The father slew the son, and the suppliants were torn from the temples and slain near them; some of them were even walled up in the temple of Dionysus, and there perished. To such extremes of cruelty did revolution go; and this seemed to be the worst of revolutions, because it was the first.

For not long afterwards nearly the whole Hellenic world **82** was in commotion; in every city the chiefs of the democracy and of the oligarchy were struggling, the one to bring in the Athenians, the other the Lacedaemonians. Now in time of peace, men would have had no excuse for introducing either, and no desire to do so; but, when they were

The conflict of democracy and oligarchy, encouraged as it is by the hope of Athenian or Lacedaemonian help, ruins states and disorganises society.

---

[a] Reading with a few MSS. ἀπεχρῶντο, (which is quoted from Thucydides by the Lexicographers,) instead of ἀνεχώρησαν, which gives no sense.

at war [a], the introduction of a foreign alliance on one side or the other to the hurt of their enemies and the advantage of themselves was easily effected by the dissatisfied party [a]. And revolution brought upon the cities of Hellas many terrible calamities, such as have been and always will be while human nature remains the same, but which are more or less aggravated and differ in character with every new combination of circumstances. In peace and prosperity both states and individuals are actuated by higher motives, because they do not fall under the dominion of imperious necessities; but war, which takes away the comfortable provision of daily life, is a hard master and tends to assimilate men's characters to their conditions.

Changes in men's moral principles and in their use of language. When troubles had once begun in the cities, those who followed carried the revolutionary spirit further and further, and determined to outdo the report of all who had preceded them by the ingenuity of their enterprises and the atrocity of their revenges. The meaning of words had no longer the same relation to things, but was changed by them as they thought proper. Reckless daring was held to be loyal courage ; prudent delay was the excuse of a coward ; moderation was the disguise of unmanly weakness; to know everything was to do nothing. Frantic energy was the true quality of a man. A conspirator who wanted to be safe was a recreant in disguise. The lover of violence was always trusted, and his opponent suspected. He who succeeded in a plot was deemed knowing, but a still greater master in craft was he who detected one. On the other hand, he who plotted from the first to have nothing to do with plots was a breaker up of parties and a poltroon who was afraid of the enemy. In a word, he who could outstrip another in a bad action was

---

[a] Omitting the comma inserted in Bekker's text after προσποιήσει, or retaining it 'and both sides could easily obtain allies to the hurt of their enemies and the advantage of themselves, the dissatisfied party were only too ready to invoke foreign aid' ; see note on the passage.

applauded, and so was he who encouraged to evil one who had no idea of it. The tie of party was stronger than the tie of blood, because a partisan was more ready to dare without asking why. (For party associations are not based upon any established law, nor do they seek the public good; they are formed in defiance of the laws and from self-interest.) The seal of good faith was not divine law, but fellowship in crime. If an enemy when he was in the ascendant offered fair words, the opposite party received them not in a generous spirit,[a] but by a jealous watchfulness of his actions[a]. Revenge was dearer than self-preservation. Any agreements sworn to by either party, when they could do nothing else, were binding as long as both were powerless. But he who on a favourable opportunity first took courage, and struck at his enemy when he saw him off his guard, had greater pleasure in a perfidious than he would have had in an open act of revenge; he congratulated himself that he had taken the safer course, and also that he had overreached his enemy and gained the prize of superior ability. In general the dishonest more easily gain credit for cleverness than the simple for goodness; men take a pride in the one, but are ashamed of the other.

The cause of all these evils was the love of power, originating in avarice and ambition, and the party-spirit which is engendered by them when men are fairly embarked in a contest. *Causes and effects of the revolutionary spirit. Disregard of all laws, human and divine.* For the leaders on either side used specious names, the one party professing to uphold the constitutional equality of the many, the other the wisdom of an aristocracy, while they made the public interests, to which in name they were devoted, in reality their prize. Striving in every way to overcome each other, they committed the most monstrous crimes; yet even these were surpassed by the magnitude of their revenges

---

[a] Or, 'but by active precautions.'

which they pursued to the very utmost [a], neither party
observing any definite limits either of justice or public
expediency, but both alike making the caprice of the
moment their law.   Either by the help of an unrighteous
sentence, or grasping power with the strong hand, they
were eager to satiate the impatience of party-spirit.
Neither faction cared for religion; but any fair pretence
which succeeded in effecting some odious purpose was
greatly lauded.   And the citizens who were of neither
party fell a prey to both; either they were disliked
because they held aloof, or men were jealous of their
surviving.

83   Thus revolution gave birth to every form of wickedness
Universal distrust. in Hellas.   The simplicity which is so
Force of character, not large an element in a noble nature was
intellect, prevailed. laughed to scorn and disappeared.   An
attitude of perfidious antagonism everywhere prevailed;
for there was no word binding enough, nor oath terrible
enough to reconcile enemies.   Each man was strong only
in the conviction that nothing was secure; he must look
to his own safety, and could not afford to trust others.
Inferior intellects generally succeeded best.   For, aware
of their own deficiencies, and fearing the capacity of their
opponents, for whom they were no match in powers of
speech, and whose subtle wits were likely to anticipate
them in contriving evil, they struck boldly and at once.
But the cleverer sort, presuming in their arrogance that
they would be aware in time, and disdaining to act when
they could think, were taken off their guard and easily
destroyed.

84   Now in Corcyra most of these deeds were perpetrated,
and for the first time.   There was every crime which men
could commit in revenge who had been governed not
wisely, but tyrannically, and now had the oppressor at
their mercy.   There were the dishonest designs of others

---

[a] Placing the comma after μείζους instead of after ἐπεξῇεσάν τε.

who were longing to be relieved from their habitual
poverty, and were naturally animated   (1) *Fury of the op-*
by a passionate desire for their neigh-   *pressed,* (2) *discontent*
bour's goods ; and there were crimes   *of the poor,* (3) *party*
of another class which men commit,   *hatred among equals,*
not from covetousness, but from the   *were the great incentives*
enmity which equals foster towards one   *to crime.   Human*
another until they are carried away by   *nature when inspired*
their blind rage into the extremes of   *by revenge is too much*
    for justice, conscience, or
    prudence.
pitiless cruelty.   At such a time the life of the city was all
in disorder, and human nature, which is always ready to
transgress the laws, having now trampled them under foot,
delighted to show that her passions were ungovernable,
that she was stronger than justice, and the enemy of
everything above her.   If malignity had not exercised
a fatal power, how could any one have preferred revenge
to piety, and gain to innocence?   But, when men are
retaliating upon others, they are reckless of the future, and
do not hesitate to annul those common laws of humanity
to which every individual trusts for his own hope of
deliverance should he ever be overtaken by calamity ; they
forget that in their own hour of need they will look for
them in vain.

Such were the passions which the citizens of Corcyra 85
first of all Hellenes displayed towards   *The surviving olig-*
one another.   After the departure of   *archs seize some forts*
Eurymedon and the Athenian fleet the   *on the opposite coast,*
surviving oligarchs, who to the number   *but soon return to the*
    island   and   occupy
of five hundred had escaped, seized   *Mount Istonè.*
certain forts on the mainland, and thus became masters of
the territory on the opposite coast which belonged to
Corcyra.   Thence issuing forth, they plundered the
Corcyraeans in the island, and did much harm, so that there
was a great famine in the city.   They also sent ambassadors
to Lacedaemon and Corinth, begging that they might
be restored, but, failing of their object, they procured
boats and auxiliaries, and passed over to Corcyra about six

hundred in all; then, burning their boats, that they might have no hope but in the conquest of the island, they went into Mount Istonè, and building a fort there, became masters of the country to the ruin of the inhabitants of the city.

86   At the end of the same summer the Athenians sent

War in Sicily between the Syracusans and Leontines; the latter obtain assistance from Athens.

twenty ships to Sicily under the command of Laches the son of Melanopus, and Charoeades the son of Euphiletus. Syracuse and Leontini were now at war with one another. All the Dorian cities, except Camarina, were in alliance with Syracuse; they were the same which at the beginning of the war were reckoned in the Lacedaemonian confederacy, but they had taken no active part[a]. The allies of the Leontines were the Chalcidian cities and Camarina. In Italy the Locrians sided with the Syracusans, and the Rhegians with the Leontines, who were their kinsmen[b]. The Leontines and their allies sent to Athens, and on the ground, partly of an old alliance, partly of their Ionian descent, begged the Athenians to send them ships, for they were driven off both sea and land by their Syracusan enemies. The Athenians sent the ships, professedly on the ground of relationship, but in reality because they did not wish the Peloponnesians to obtain corn from Sicily. Moreover they meant to try what prospect they had of getting the affairs of Sicily into their hands. So the commanders of the fleet came to Rhegium in Italy, where they established themselves, and carried on the war in concert with their allies. Thus the summer ended.

87   In the following winter the plague, which had never

Reappearance of the plague after it had abated. At the same time numerous earthquakes occur.

entirely disappeared, although abating for a time, again attacked the Athenians. It continued on this second occasion not less than a year, having previously lasted for two years. To the power of Athens certainly nothing was more ruinous; not less than

---

[a] Cp. ii. 7 med.   [b] Cp. vi. 44 fin.

four thousand four hundred Athenian hoplites who were
on the roll died, and also three hundred horsemen; how
many of the common people could never be ascertained.
This too was the time when the frequent earthquakes
occurred at Athens, in Euboea, and in Boeotia, especially
at Orchomenos [a].

During the same winter the Athenians in Sicily and the **88**
Rhegians made an expedition with   *Fruitless expedition*
thirty ships against the islands of   *against the Aeolian*
Aeolus, as they are called, which in *islands.*
summer time cannot be attacked owing to the want of
water.   These islands belong to the Liparaeans, who are
colonists of the Cnidians: they inhabit one of them, which
is not large, and is called Lipara; from this they go and
cultivate the rest, Didymè, Strongylè, and Hiera.   The
inhabitants believe that the forge of Hephaestus is in
Hiera, because the island sends up a blaze of fire in the
night-time and clouds of smoke by day.   The Aeolian
islands lie off the territory of the Sicels and Messenians;
they were in alliance with Syracuse.   The Athenians
wasted the country, but finding that the inhabitants would
not yield, sailed back to Rhegium.   And so ended the
winter, and with it the fifth year in the Peloponnesian
War of which Thucydides wrote the history.

In the ensuing summer the Peloponnesians and their **89**
allies, under the command of Agis the   *The earthquakes con-* B.C. 426.
son of Archidamus, the Lacedae-   *ceived by Thucydides to* Ol. 88, 3.
monian king, came as far as the   *have been the cause of*
isthmus.   They intended to invade   *the great ebb and flow*
Attica, but were deterred from proceed-   *of the sea at Orobiae in*
ing by numerous earthquakes [b], and   *Euboea, and at Ata-*
                                          lantè.
no invasion took place in this year.   About the time when
these earthquakes prevailed, the sea at Orobiae in Euboea,
retiring from what was then the line of coast and rising in
a great wave, overflowed a part of the city; and although

---

[a] Cp. ch. 89, and i. 23 med.   [b] Cp. ch. 87.

it subsided in some places, yet in others the inundation was permanent, and that which was formerly land is now sea. All the people who could not escape to the high ground perished. A similar inundation occurred in the neighbourhood of Atalantè, an island on the coast of the Opuntian Locri, which carried away a part of the Athenian fort [a], and dashed in pieces one of two ships which were drawn up on the beach. At Peparethus also the sea retired, but no inundation followed; an earthquake, however, overthrew a part of the wall, the Prytaneum, and a few houses. I conceive that, where the force of the earthquake was greatest, the sea was driven back, and the suddenness of the recoil made the inundation more violent; and I am of opinion that this was the cause of the phenomenon, which would never have taken place if there had been no earthquake.

90   During the same summer war was going on in various *Capture by Laches of* parts of Sicily, the Hellenes in Sicily *Mylae in Sicily, and* fighting against one another, the *submission of Messenè.* Athenians helping their own allies. I will mention the chief actions in which the Athenians took part, whether by the help of their allies attacking, or attacked by their enemies. Charoeades, the Athenian general, had been killed in battle by the Syracusans, and, Laches having taken the entire command of the fleet, he and the allies made an expedition against Mylae, a town belonging to Messenè. Two tribes of the Messenians were keeping guard there, and they had set an ambuscade for the force which they were expecting to land; but the Athenians and their allies put to flight with heavy loss the troops which came out of the ambush. Then, attacking the fortress, they compelled its defenders to come to terms, surrender the citadel, and march with them against Messenè. Finally, upon the approach of the Athenians and their allies, the Messenians themselves came to terms,

----

[a] Cp. ii. 32.

giving hostages and the other pledges which were required of them.

In the same summer the Athenians sent thirty ships *91* round the Peloponnese under the com- *Thirty Athenian ships* mand of Demosthenes the son of *under Demosthenes sail* Alcisthenes, and Procles the son of *round the Peloponnese.* Theodorus. They also sent sixty ships *Sixty more under Nicias* and two thousand hoplites to Melos, *ravaging the island* under the command of Nicias the son *sail to Oropus. At* of Niceratus, wishing to subdue the *Tanagra his troops, in* Melians, who, although they were *ian land-forces, defeat* islanders, resisted them and would not *the inhabitants.* join their alliance ª.   So they ravaged their country, but finding that the Melians would not yield, they sailed away to Oropus, opposite Euboea.   There they put in at nightfall, and the hoplites disembarking went at once by land to Tanagra in Boeotia.   Meanwhile the entire Athenian force, under the command of Hipponicus the son of Callias, and Eurymedon the son of Thucles, upon a signal given marched to meet them at the same spot.   There they encamped, and all together devastated the country, remaining at Tanagra during that day and the following night.   On the morrow they defeated the Tanagraeans who sallied out upon them, and also some Thebans who had come to their aid ; they then took up the arms of the slain, raised a trophy, and returned, the one part of the forces back again to the city, the other to their ships. Nicias with his sixty ships then sailed to the coast of Locris ; after ravaging the country he returned home.

About the same time the Lacedaemonians founded *92* Heraclea, their colony in Trachinia. *To help the Trachin-* The intention was as follows :—The *ians and their own* Trachinians are one of the three Melian *mother state Doris, the* tribes ; the other two being the Paral- *Lacedaemonians found* ians and the Hiereans. These Tra- *the colony of Heraclea.* chinians, having suffered greatly in war from their neigh-

---

ª Cp. v. 84.

bours the Oetaeans, at first thought of attaching themselves
to the Athenians, but, fearing that they could not trust
them [a], sent Tisamenus, whom they appointed their envoy,
to Lacedaemon.   The Dorians, who were the mother state
of Lacedaemon, joined in the embassy and also requested
help, for they too were suffering from the Oetaeans.   The
Lacedaemonians heard their appeal, and, being desirous
of assisting both the Trachinians and Dorians, made up
their minds to send out a colony.   They also thought
that the situation of the new city would be convenient for
carrying on the war against the Athenians.   There a navy
could be equipped if they wanted to attack Euboea, which
was quite near, and the station would be handy for the
conveyance of troops to Chalcidicè.   For every reason
they were eager to colonise the place.   First they enquired
of the God at Delphi; he bade them go, and they sent out
settlers taken from their own citizens and the Perioeci,
announcing that any Hellenes who desired, not being of
the Ionian, Achaean, or certain other races, might accompany them.   The leaders of the colony were three Lacedaemonians, Leon, Alcidas, and Damagon.   They set to
work and built afresh the walls of the city, which received
the name of Heraclea, and is situated about four miles and
a half from Thermopylae and a little more than two from
the sea.   They also constructed docks [b], beginning the
works near Thermopylae, at the pass, that the city might
be perfectly defended.

93   While the new colonists were collecting at Heraclea,

*The new colony is
gradually worn out by
the persistent opposition
of the Thessalians, and
by the brutality of the
Lacedaemonian govern-
ors.*

the Athenians grew alarmed; the
scheme appeared to be aimed at Euboea, for Cape Cenaeum on the opposite coast is within a short sail.   But
their fears were not realised; no harm
whatever ensued.   The reasons were
these :—In the first place the Thessalians are strong in

---

[a] Cp. iii. 113 fin.

[b] Or, reading εἶρξαν τὸ ——, 'and blockaded the defile at Thermopylae.'

that part of the country, and fearing that Heraclea, which
was built to control them, would be a powerful and
dangerous neighbour, they carried on uninterrupted war
against the young colony until they completely wore the
settlers out, although originally they had been very
numerous. For every one joined without hesitation,
encouraged by the promise of security which a Lacedaemonian colony seemed to offer. But another great cause
of the ruin and depopulation of the place was the conduct
of the governors sent out from Lacedaemon, who frightened
the people away by their severe and often unjust administration [a]. Thus the Heracleans fell an easy prey to their
neighbours.

During the same summer, and just about the same time 94
when the Athenians were engaged at *Attack upon Leucas.*
Melos, the troops which were cruising *Demosthenes, instead of*
in the thirty Athenian ships [b] about *completing the blockade,*
Peloponnesus set an ambuscade at *Messenians to invade*
Ellomenus in Leucadia and killed a *Aetolia.*
few of the guards of the country. They next attacked
Leucas itself with a larger armament, consisting of the
Acarnanians, who followed them with their whole forces,
all but the inhabitants of Oeniadae [c], and some Zacynthians
and Cephallenians, together with fifteen ships from Corcyra.
The Leucadians saw their territory both on the mainland
and within the isthmus, where the town of Leucas and the
temple of Apollo are situated, ravaged by the enemy; but
being powerless against a superior force, they remained
inactive. The Acarnanians begged Demosthenes, the
Athenian general, to cut Leucas off by a wall, thinking that
they could easily take the city and so rid themselves of an
old enemy. But just then he was persuaded by the Messenians that, having such an army in the field, it would be
a great thing to attack the Aetolians : they were the
enemies of Naupactus, and if he defeated them he would

----

[a] Cp. v. 52 init.   [b] Cp. iii. 91 init.   [c] Cp. ii. 102 init.

easily subjugate the adjoining part of the mainland to the Athenians. The Aetolians, they said, though a large and warlike people, dwelt in unwalled villages, which were widely scattered, and as they had only light-armed soldiers, they would be subdued without difficulty before they could combine. They told him that he should first attack the Apodotians, then the Ophioneans, and after them the Eurytanians. The last are the largest tribe of the Aetolians; they speak a dialect more unintelligible than any of their neighbours, and are believed to eat raw flesh. They said that, if he conquered these, the rest would readily come over to him.

95   He was influenced by his regard for the Messenians,

He determines to make his way through Aetolia and Phocis into Boeotia, which he hopes to attack with an allied force.

and still more by the consideration that without reinforcements from Athens, and with no other help than that of the allies on the mainland, to whom he hoped to add the Aetolians, he could make his way by land to attack Boeotia. He might proceed through the Ozolian Locri to the Dorian Cytinium, keeping Mount Parnassus on the right, until he came down upon the Phocians. They would probably be eager to join in the expedition because they had always been friendly to Athens, or, if unwilling, they might be coerced; and once in Phocis he would be on the borders of Boeotia. So he left Leucas with all his army, much against the will of the Acarnanians, and sailed to Sollium. He there communicated his design to them, but they would not accompany him because he had refused to blockade Leucas; so with the remainder of his army, which consisted of Cephallenians, Messenians, Zacynthians, and three hundred marines belonging to the Athenian fleet [a], the fifteen Corcyraean vessels having left, he marched against the Aetolians, starting from Oeneon in Locris. The Ozolian Locrians were allies of the Athenians, and

---

[a] Cp. ch. 94 init.

they were to meet him with their whole force in the interior of the country. They dwelt on the border of the
Aetolians, and as they were armed in a similar manner
and knew their country and ways of fighting, their help
in the expedition seemed likely to be very valuable.

He encamped the first night at the temple of Nemean 96
Zeus, where the poet Hesiod is said to   *The Aetolians collect*
have been killed by the inhabitants in   *their forces.*
fulfilment of an oracle which foretold that he should die
at Nemea. Early the next morning he proceeded on his
march into Aetolia. On the first day he took Potidania,
on the second Crocyleium, on the third Teichium. There
he stayed and sent back the spoils to Eupalium in Locris.
For he did not intend to attack the Ophioneans yet ; when
he had subjugated the rest of the country he would return
to Naupactus and make a second expedition against them
if they continued to resist. The Aetolians were aware of
his designs from the very first ; and no sooner did he enter
their territory than they all collected in great force ; even
the most distant of the Ophioneans, the Bomieans and
Callieans who reach down towards the Malian Gulf, came
to the aid of their countrymen.

The Messenians repeated the advice which they had 97
originally given to Demosthenes. They   *Demosthenes hurries*
assured him that there would be no   *on against the Aetolian*
difficulty in conquering the Aetolians,   *villages, but receives a*
and told him to march as quickly as he   *check at Aegitium.*
could against the villages. He should not wait until they
could combine and meet him with an army, but should
endeavour to take any place which was nearest. He,
trusting to their advice, and confident in his good fortune
since everything was going favourably, did not wait for the
Locrians, who should have supplied his deficiency in
javelin-men, but at once marched towards Aegitium, which
he attacked, and forced his way in. The inhabitants had
stolen away and taken up a position on the top of the
hills overhanging the town, which was itself built upon

heights at a distance of about nine miles from the sea.
The other Aetolians, who had by this time come to the
rescue of Aegitium, attacked the Athenians and their
allies.   Some ran down from one hill and some from
another and hurled darts at them; when the Athenian
army advanced they retired, and when the Athenians retreated they pressed upon them.   The battle, which lasted
long, was nothing but a series of pursuits and retreats, and
in both the Athenians were at a disadvantage.

98   While their archers had arrows and were able to use

The Aetolians press them, the Athenians maintained their
upon the Athenians, ground, for the Aetolians, being light-
who at length fly.   The armed, were driven back by the arrows.
survivors with difficulty But at length the captain of the archers
return to Naupactus, was slain, and the forces under his
and thence to Athens. command no longer kept together.
Demosthenes remains The Athenians themselves grew weary
behind.
of the long and tedious struggle.   The Aetolians came
closer and closer, and never ceased hurling darts at them.
At last they turned and fled, and falling into ravines,
out of which there was no way, or losing themselves in
a strange country, they perished.   Their guide, Chromon
the Messenian, had been killed.   The Aetolians, who were
light-armed and swift of foot, followed at their heels, hurling darts, and caught and slew many of them in the actual
rout.   The greater number missed their way and got into
the woods, out of which no path led; and their enemies
brought fire and burnt the wood about them.   So the
Athenian army tried every means of escape and perished
in all manner of ways.   The survivors with difficulty made
their way to the sea at Oeneon in Locris, whence they had
set out.   Many of the allies fell, and of the Athenian heavy-
armed about a hundred and twenty, all in the flower of
their youth; they were the very finest men whom the city
of Athens lost during the war.   Procles, one of the two
generals, was also killed.   When they had received the
bodies of their dead under a flag of truce from the Aetol-

ians, they retreated to Naupactus, and returned in their ships to Athens. Demosthenes remained behind in Naupactus and the neighbourhood; for, after what had happened, he feared the anger of the Athenians.

About the same time the Athenian forces engaged in 99 Sicily, sailing to the territory of Locri *The Italian Locrians* and there disembarking, defeated the *defeated.* Locrians who came out to meet them, and took a small garrison fort, which was situated upon the river Halex.

During the same summer the Aetolians, who had some 100 time before despatched Tolophus the *The Aetolians per-* Ophionean, Boriades the Eurytanian, *suade the Lacedae-* and Tisander the Apodotian on an *monians to send an* embassy to Corinth and Lacedaemon, *expedition against Nau-* induced the Lacedaemonians to aid *pactus.* them by sending an army against Naupactus, in order to punish the inhabitants for inviting the Athenian invasion [a]. So in the autumn they sent out three thousand hoplites of their allies, including five hundred from Heraclea, the newly-founded city in Trachis. Eurylochus, a Spartan, was general, and with him were associated in the command Macarius and Menedaeus, also Spartans.

When the army was collected at Delphi, Eurylochus 101 sent a herald to the Ozolian Locrians, *Eurylochus the Lace-* for he had to pass through their country *daemonian commander* on the way to Naupactus; and he also *starts from Delphi and* wished to detach them from the Athen- *marches through Locris.* ian alliance. Of the Locrians, the inhabitants of Amphissa were most willing to co-operate with him, being anxious for protection against their enemies the Phocians; they were the first who gave hostages, and by them the other Locrians, who were alarmed at the impending invasion, were persuaded to do the like:—first their neighbours the Myoneans, who commanded the most difficult pass into Locris; then the Ipneans, Messapians, Tritaeeans,

---

[a] Cp. iii. 94 med.

Chalaeans, Tolophonians, Hessians, and Oeantheans; all these tribes also joined the expedition. The Olpaeans gave hostages but did not join; the Hyaeans would not give hostages until the Lacedaemonians had taken one of their villages, called Polis.

102   When everything was ready, and Eurylochus had de-

Demosthenes with the help of the Acarnanians saves Naupactus. The Lacedaemonians retire, and in concert with the Ambraciots project an attack on the Amphilochian Argos.

posited the hostages at Cytinium of the Dorians, he marched with his army against Naupactus, through the territory of the Locrians. On his march he took Oeneon [a] and Eupalium [b], two Locrian towns which refused to come to terms. When they had arrived in the territory of Naupactus and the Aetolians had at length joined them, they devastated the country, and after taking the unwalled suburbs of the town marched against Molycrium, a colony of the Corinthians subject to Athens, which they captured. But Demosthenes the Athenian, who after his misfortune in Aetolia was still in the neighbourhood of Naupactus, having previous intelligence, and fearing for the town, went and persuaded the Acarnanians, much against their will—for they had not forgotten his withdrawal from Leucas—to assist Naupactus. So they sent with him on board the Athenian ships [c] a thousand hoplites; these got in and saved the place, which was in danger of having to capitulate, owing to the extent of the wall and the paucity of its defenders. Eurylochus and his soldiers, when they saw that the garrison had been reinforced, and that there was no possibility of taking the city by storm, instead of going back to Peloponnesus, retired into the country of Aeolis, which is now called by the names of the towns Calydon and Pleuron, and to other places in the neighbourhood; also to Proschium in Aetolia. For the Ambraciots sent and persuaded them to take part in an attack on the Amphilochian Argos and the rest of Amphi-

---

[a] Cp. iii. 95 fin.   [b] Cp. iii. 96 med.   [c] Cp. iii. 105 fin

lochia and Acarnania, declaring that, if they gained possession of these places, all the tribes of the mainland would
at once come over to the Lacedaemonians. Eurylochus
assented and, dismissing the Aetolians, waited with his
army in that region until the time for the Ambraciots to
make their expedition and for him to join them in the
neighbourhood of Argos. Thus the summer ended.

In the following winter the Athenians in Sicily and their 103
Hellenic allies made an attack upon *The Athenians are*
the Sicel fort of Inessa, a Sicel town *defeated at Inessa, but*
of which the citadel was held by the *are victorious in Locris.*
Syracusans. They were joined by many of the Sicels,
who had formerly been allies to the Syracusans, and,
having been held down by them, had now revolted to the
Athenians. The attempt failed, and they retreated. But
during their retreat the Syracusans sallied out and fell
upon the allies who were in the rear of the Athenians,
routed them, and put to flight a part of their forces with
great loss. Soon afterwards, Laches and the Athenians
in the fleet made several descents upon Locris. At the
river Caecinus they defeated about three hundred Locrians
who came out to meet them under Proxenus the son of
Capaton, took arms from the slain, and returned.

In the same winter the Athenians, by command of an 104
oracle, purified the island of Delos. *The Athenians renew*
Pisistratus the tyrant had already *the purification of Delos*
purified it, but imperfectly, for the *and restore the Delian*
purification only extended to that part *games.*
which was within sight of the temple. The whole island
was now purified in the following manner :—The Athenians
took away all the coffins of the dead which were in Delos[a],
and passed a decree that henceforward no one should die
or give birth to a child there, but that the inhabitants when
they were near the time of either should be carried across
to Rhenea. Now Rhenea is near to Delos, so near

---

[a] Cp. i. 8 init. ; v. 1.

indeed that Polycrates the tyrant of Samos, who for a time had a powerful navy, attached this island, which he conquered with the rest of the islands and dedicated to the Delian Apollo, by a chain to Delos. After the purification, the Athenians for the first time celebrated the Delian games, which were held every four years. There had been in ancient days a great gathering of the Ionians and the neighbouring islanders at Delos; whither they brought their wives and children to be present at the Delian games, as the Ionians now frequent the games at Ephesus. Musical and gymnastic contests were held there, and the *The old festival of Delos* cities celebrated choral dances. The *is celebrated by Homer.* character of the festival is attested by Homer in the following verses, which are taken from the hymn to Apollo :—

> 'At other times, Phoebus, Delos is dearest to thy heart,
> Where are gathered together the Ionians in flowing robes,
> With their wives and children in thy street :
> There do they delight thee with boxing and dancing and song,
> Making mention of thy name when they gather at the assembly.'

And that there were musical contests which attracted competitors is implied in the following words of the same hymn. After commemorating the Delian dance of women, Homer ends their praises with these lines, in which he alludes to himself :—

> 'And now may Apollo and Artemis be gracious,
> And to all of you, maidens, I say farewell.
> Yet remember me when I am gone ;
> And if some other toiling pilgrim among the sons of men
> Comes and asks : O maidens,
> Who is the sweetest minstrel of all who wander hither,
> And in whom do you delight most ?
> Make answer with one voice, in gentle words,
> The blind old man of Chios' rocky isle.'

Thus far Homer, who clearly indicates that even in days of old there was a great gathering and festival at Delos. In after ages the islanders and the Athenians led choruses in procession, and sacrificed. But the games and the greater part of the ceremonies naturally fell into disuse,

owing to the misfortunes of Ionia.   The Athenians now
restored the games and for the first time introduced
horse-races.

During the same winter the Ambraciots, in fulfilment 105
of the promise by which they had
induced Eurylochus and his army to
remain[a], made an expedition against
the Amphilochian Argos with three
thousand hoplites.   They invaded the
Argive territory and seized Olpae, a
strong fort on a hill by the sea-side,
which in former days the Acarnanians
had fortified and used as a common hall
*Eurylochus and the
Ambraciots combine
their forces against the
Amphilochian Argos,
which the Amphilo-
chians, Acarnanians,
and Athenians unite to
protect. TheAmbraciots
seize Olpae, and send
for reinforcements.*

of justice.   The place is about three miles from Argos, which
is also on the sea-shore.   One division of the Acarnanians
came to the aid of Argos, while another encamped at a spot
called the Wells, where they could lie in wait for Eurylochus and the Peloponnesians, and prevent them from
joining the Ambraciots unobserved.   They also despatched
a messenger to Demosthenes, who had led the Athenian
expedition into Aetolia, asking him to be their commander,
and sent for twenty Athenian ships which were just then
cruising about the Peloponnese under the command of
Aristoteles the son of Timocrates, and Hierophon the son
of Antimnestus.   The Ambraciots sent a messenger from
Olpae to their own citizens, bidding them come and help
them with their entire force; for they were afraid that
Eurylochus and his followers might not be able to make
their way through the Acarnanians, and then they would
have either to fight alone, or to attempt a hazardous
retreat.

Eurylochus and the Peloponnesians, when they heard 106
that the Ambraciots had arrived at
Olpae, left Proschium and went with
all speed to help them.   Passing over
the river Achelous they marched through
*March of the Pelo-
ponnesians, who effect
a junction with the Am-
braciots at Olpae.*

_____

[a] Cp. iii. 102 fin.

Acarnania, leaving the city and garrison of Stratus on the right hand, and the rest of Acarnania on their left. The land was deserted, for the inhabitants had gone to the assistance of Argos. Crossing the territory of Stratus they proceeded through Phytia and by the extreme border of Medeon, and so through Limnaea; at last they left Acarnania, and reached the friendly territory of the Agraeans. Then taking to Mount Thyamus, which is open country, they marched on and descended into the plain of Argos after dark. Making their way unobserved between the city of Argos and the Acarnanian force stationed at the Wells, they at length reached the Ambraciots at Olpae.

107 The two armies having effected this junction moved at

Athenian reinforcements arrive. Demosthenes takes the command. He encamps near Olpae, where preparing for action he places troops in an ambuscade.

break of day to a place called Metropolis, and there encamped. Soon afterwards the Argives received the expected reinforcement of twenty Athenian ships, which arrived in the Ambracian Gulf. With them came Demosthenes, who brought two hundred Messenian hoplites and sixty Athenian archers. The ships anchored about the hill of Olpae, while the Acarnanians and a few of the Amphilochians (the greater part of them were prevented from stirring by the Ambraciots [a]), having mustered at Argos, were now preparing to give battle. They associated Demosthenes with their own generals in the command of the allied forces. He led them to the neighbourhood of Olpae, and there encamped at a place where they were divided from the enemy by a great ravine. During five days they remained inactive; on the sixth day both armies drew up in battle array. Demosthenes, fearing that he would be surrounded by the Peloponnesians who were more numerous and extended beyond his own line, placed hoplites and light-armed troops,

----

[a] Cp. iii. 114 fin.

numbering altogether four hundred, in a deep lane over-
grown with brushwood, intending them to lie in wait until
the moment of conflict, when they were to rush out from
the rear on the line of the enemy where it overlapped.
The preparations of both armies were now complete and
they engaged. Demosthenes led his own right wing, on
which were the Messenians and a few Athenians, while
the other was held by the Acarnanians, who were disposed
according to their cities, and by the Amphilochian javelin-
men who were in the battle. The Peloponnesians and
Ambraciots were intermingled, with the exception of the
Mantineans, who were all collected on the left wing; but
the extremity of the wing was occupied by Eurylochus and
his division, who were opposed to the Messenians under
Demosthenes.

When the two armies were at close quarters, the left 108
wing of the Peloponnesians out-flanked
the right wing of their opponents and *The Peloponnesian*
threatened to surround them; where- *left wing is panic-*
upon the Acarnanians, coming upon *stricken by the troops*
coming out of the am-
them from behind out of the ambuscade, *bush, and flies. The*
charged and turned them. They fled *right wing is victorious*
without striking a blow, and their panic *at first, but finally*
driven back to Olpae.
caused the greater part of the army to run with them.
For, when they saw Eurylochus and their best troops
routed, they lost whatever courage they had. The Messenians, who were in this part of the field under the
command of Demosthenes, were foremost in the action.
The right wing of the enemy, however, and the Ambraciots,
who are the most warlike nation in those parts, vanquished
their opponents and drove them back to Argos. But,
returning, they saw the greater part of the army defeated,
and were hard pressed by the victorious division of the
Acarnanians, whereupon, escaping with difficulty, they
made their way to Olpae. Numbers of the defeated were
killed, for they dashed into the fort wildly and in confusion,
except the Mantineans, who kept together and retreated

in better order than any other part of the army. The battle, which had lasted until evening, now ended.

109   On the next day Menedaeus took the command, for

Difficulties of the Lacedaemonian commander, who negotiates with Demosthenes a secret treaty for the Peloponnesians only.

Eurylochus and Macarius, the two other generals, had been slain[a]. He knew not what to do after so serious a defeat. He could not hope, if he remained, to stand a siege, hemmed in as he was by land, and at sea blockaded by the Athenian ships; neither could he safely retire; so entering into a parley with Demosthenes and the Acarnanian generals about the burial of the dead, he tried to negotiate with them at the same time for a retreat. The Athenians gave back to the enemy their dead, erected a trophy, and took up their own dead, in number about three hundred. They would not openly agree to the proposal for a general retreat, but Demosthenes and his Acarnanian colleagues made a secret treaty with the Mantineans, and Menedaeus, and the other Peloponnesian generals and chief persons, allowing their army to depart. He wanted partly to isolate the Ambraciots and their foreign mercenary troops, but much more to take away the character of the Lacedaemonians and Peloponnesians among the Hellenes in those parts and convict them of selfishness and treachery. Accordingly the Peloponnesians took up their dead, and burying them quickly as well as they could, consulted secretly how those who had permission could best depart.

110   Meanwhile news was brought to Demosthenes and the

Approach of the main army of the Ambraciots. Demosthenes prepares to cut them off.

Acarnanians that the whole remaining force of the Ambraciots, who some time previously had been summoned from the city[b] to join the troops in Olpae, were now on their way through the territory of the Amphilochians and were in entire ignorance of what had occurred. Whereupon he at once sent forward a part of

---

[a] Cp. iv. 38 init.   [b] Cp. iii. 105 fin.

his army to lie in ambush in the roads and to occupy the strong places, himself at the same time preparing to support them with the rest of his forces.

In the meantime the Mantineans and the others who 111 were included in the truce went out on pretence of gathering herbs and sticks, and stole away one by one, picking up as they went along what they pretended to be looking for. But, as they got *The Peloponnesians steal away from Olpae, and escape to Agraea. The Ambraciots who try to follow them are slain.* farther away from Olpae, they quickened their steps, and then the Ambraciots and others who happened to collect on the instant, when they saw that they were leaving, ran after them at full speed, wanting to get up with them. The Acarnanians at first thought that none of those who were going away were protected by a truce, and pursued the Peloponnesians. Some of the generals tried to keep them back and explained how matters stood; whereupon a soldier, suspecting that there was treachery, hurled a javelin at them. At length the soldiers understood, and let the Mantineans and other Peloponnesians go, but began to kill the Ambraciots. There was great dispute and uncertainty as to who was an Ambraciot and who a Peloponnesian. Of the former they killed about two hundred; the Peloponnesians escaped into the neighbouring country of Agraea, and were received by king Salynthius who was their friend.

Meanwhile the reinforcement from the city of Ambracia 112 had reached Idomenè, which is the name of two lofty peaks. The higher of the two had been already occupied unobserved at nightfall by the troops which Demosthenes had sent forward; of the lower the Ambraciots first obtained possession and encamped there. *Demosthenes, having sent on forces which occupy the hill opposite to that whereon the Ambraciots are encamped at Idomenè, surprises and routs them.* As soon as it was dark, after supper, Demosthenes advanced with the rest of his army, himself leading half of them towards the pass between the mountains, while the rest made their way

through the Amphilochian hills. At the first dawn of day
he fell upon the Ambraciots, who were still half-asleep,
and so far from knowing anything of what had happened
that they imagined his troops to be their own comrades.
For Demosthenes had taken care to place the Messenians
in the first rank and desired them to speak to the enemy
in their own Doric dialect, thereby putting the sentinels
off their guard ; and as it was still dark, their appearance
could not be distinguished. So they fell upon the Ambraciots and routed them. Most of them were slain on
the spot ; the remainder fled over the mountains. But the
paths were beset; the Amphilochians were lightly-armed,
and in their own country which they knew, while their
enemies were heavy-armed and the country was strange to
them. And so, not knowing which way to turn, they fell
into ravines and into ambuscades which had been set for
them, and perished. Every means of escape was tried.
Some even fled to the sea which was not far distant, and
seeing the Athenian ships which were sailing by while the
action was taking place, swam out to them, thinking in the
terror of the moment that they had better be killed, if
die they must, by the Athenians in the ships than by
their barbarous and detested enemies the Amphilochians.
So the Ambraciots were cut to pieces, and but few out
of many returned home to their city. The Acarnanians,
having despoiled the dead and raised trophies, returned to
Argos.

113   On the following day there arrived a herald from the
Despair of the herald   Ambraciots who had escaped out of
who came from the fugi-   Olpae to the Agraeans. He came to
tive Ambraciots when   recover the bodies of the dead who had
he heard of the second   been slain subsequently to the first
and greater defeat.   engagement, when, unprotected by the
treaty, they tried to get out of Olpae in company with the
Mantineans and others protected by it. The herald saw
the arms of the Ambraciot troops from the city and
wondered at the number of them ; he knew nothing of the

later disaster, and he imagined that they belonged to his own division of the army.   Some one present thought that the herald had come from the army defeated at Idomenè, and asked why he looked so astonished, and how many of their men had fallen ; he replied, 'about two hundred [a] '; whereupon the other rejoined, 'These which you see are not the arms of two hundred men, but of more than a thousand.'   The herald replied, 'Then they cannot be the arms of our men.'   The other answered, 'They must be, if you were fighting yesterday at Idomenè.'   'But yesterday we did not fight at all ; it was the day before, in the retreat.'   'All I know is that we fought yesterday with these men, who were marching to your aid from Ambracia.' When the herald heard these words, and knew that the army coming from the city had perished, he uttered a cry of anguish, and, overwhelmed by the greatness of the blow, went away at once without doing his errand, no longer caring to demand the dead.   And indeed in the whole war no such calamity happened within so few days to any Hellenic state [b].   I have not ventured to set down the number of those who fell, for the loss would appear incredible when compared with the size of the city.   Of this I am certain, that if the Acarnanians had been willing to destroy Ambracia as Demosthenes and the Athenians desired, they might have taken it at the first onset.   But they were afraid that the Athenians, if they once got possession of the place, would be more troublesome neighbours than the Ambraciots [c].

After assigning a third part of the spoils to the Athen- 114 ians, the Acarnanians divided the remainder among their cities.   The *Division of the spoils.* spoils of the Athenians were captured on the voyage. But three hundred panoplies which were allotted to Demosthenes he brought home with him, and they are still preserved in the Athenian temples.   This good service

---

[a] Cp. iii. 111 fin.   [b] Cp. vii. 30 fin.   [c] Cp. iii. 92 init.

of his enabled him to return to Athens with less appre-

Return of Demo- hension after his misfortune in Aetolia.
sthenes and the Athen- The twenty Athenian ships sailed away
ian fleet. Treaty of the to Naupactus. The Acarnanians and
Acarnanians and Am- Amphilochians, after the Athenians and
philochians with the Amphilochians, after the Athenians and
Ambraciots. Demosthenes had left them, granted
a truce to the Ambraciots and Peloponnesians who had
fled to Salynthius and the Agraeans; they were thus
enabled to return home from Oeniadae, whither they had
removed from the country of Salynthius. The Acarnanians
and Amphilochians now made a treaty of alliance for one
hundred years with the Ambraciots, of which the terms
were as follows:—'The Ambraciots shall not be required
to join the Acarnanians in making war on the Peloponnesians, nor the Acarnanians to join the Ambraciots in
making war on the Athenians. But they shall aid in the
defence of one another's territory. The Ambraciots shall
give up such places or hostages of the Amphilochians as
they possess [a], and they shall not assist Anactorium'
(which was hostile to the Acarnanians) [b]. Upon these
terms they put an end to the war. Soon afterwards the
Corinthians sent a force of their own, consisting of three
hundred hoplites under the command of Xenocleidas the
son of Euthycles, to guard Ambracia, whither they made
their way with some difficulty by land. Such was the end
of the Ambracian war.

115   During the same winter the Athenian fleet in Sicily,

The Athenians re- sailing to Himera, made a descent
solve to take a more upon the country in concert with the
active part in the affairs Sicels, who had invaded the extreme
of Sicily. They send border of the Himeraeans from the in-
out Pythodorus. terior; they also attacked the Aeolian
Isles. Returning to Rhegium, they found that Pythodorus
son of Isolochus, one of the Athenian generals, had superseded Laches in the command of the fleet. The allies of

---

[a] Cp. iii. 107 init.   [b] Cp. i. 55 init.

the Athenians in Sicily had sailed to Athens, and persuaded the Athenians to send a larger fleet to their aid ;
for their territory was in the power of the Syracusans, and
they were kept off the sea by a few ships only; so they
were preparing to resist, and had begun to collect a navy.
The Athenians manned forty ships for their relief, partly
hoping to finish the war in Sicily the sooner, partly because
they wanted to exercise their fleet.   They despatched one
of the commanders, Pythodorus, with a few ships, intending to send Sophocles the son of Sostratides, and
Eurymedon the son of Thucles, with the larger division of
the fleet afterwards.   Pythodorus, having now succeeded
Laches in the command, sailed at the end of the winter
against the Locrian fort which Laches had previously
taken[a], but he was defeated by the Locrians and retired.

In the early spring the burning lava, not for the first time, 116
issued from Mount Aetna, which is the *Eruption of Aetna.*
highest mountain in Sicily, and devas-
tated a portion of the territory of the Catanaeans who
dwell on the skirts of Aetna.   The last eruption is said to
have taken place fifty years before ; and altogether three
eruptions are recorded since the Hellenes first settled in
Sicily.   Such were the events of the winter ; and so
ended the sixth year in the Peloponnesian War of which
Thucydides wrote the history.

---

[a] Cp. iii. **99.**

BOOKS IV–VIII

BOOK IV

1 In the following summer, about the time when the corn

B.C. 425.
Ol. 88, 4.

The Syracusans and Locrians induce Messenè to revolt from the Athenians. The Locrians at the same time invade the territory of Rhegium.

comes into ear, ten Syracusan and ten Locrian ships took possession of Messenè in Sicily, whither they had gone by the invitation of the inhabitants. And so Messenè revolted from the Athenians. The Syracusans took part in this affair chiefly because they saw that Messenè was the key to Sicily. They were afraid that the Athenians would one day establish themselves there and come and attack them with a larger force. The Locrians took part because the Rhegians were their enemies, and they wanted to crush them by sea as well as by land. They had already invaded the territory of Rhegium with their whole army, in order to hinder the Rhegians from assisting the Messenians; they were also partly instigated by certain Rhegian exiles who had taken refuge with them. For the Rhegians had been for a long time torn by revolution, and in their present condition could not resist the Locrians, who for this very reason were the more disposed to attack them. After wasting the country, the Locrians withdrew their land forces; but the ships remained to protect Messenè. Another fleet which the allies were manning was intended to lie in the harbour of Messenè, and to carry on the war from thence.

2 During the spring and about the same time, before the

Fifth invasion of Attica.

corn was in full ear, the Peloponnesians and their allies invaded Attica, under the command of Agis the son of Archidamus, the

Lacedaemonian king. They encamped and ravaged the country.

The Athenians sent to Sicily the forty ships [a], which were now ready, under the command of Eurymedon and Sophocles, the third general, Pythodorus, having gone thither beforehand. Orders were given to them, as they passed Corcyra, to

The Athenians send forty additional ships to Sicily. Demosthenes accompanies them on a special commission.

assist the Corcyraeans in the city, who were harassed by the exiles in the mountain [b]. The Peloponnesians had already sent sixty ships to the assistance of the exiles, expecting to make themselves masters of the situation with little difficulty; for there was a great famine in the city. Demosthenes, since his return from Acarnania, had been in no command, but now at his own request the Athenians allowed him to make use of the fleet about the Peloponnese according to his judgment.

When they arrived off the coast of Laconia and heard 3 that the Peloponnesian ships were already at Corcyra, Eurymedon and Sophocles wanted to hasten thither, but Demosthenes desired them first to

Demosthenes wants the generals to fortify Pylos. They ridicule his arguments.

put in at Pylos and not to proceed on their voyage until they had done what he wanted. They objected, but it so happened that a storm came on and drove them into Pylos. Instantly Demosthenes urged them to fortify the place; this being the project which he had in view when he accompanied the fleet [c]. He pointed out to them that there was abundance of timber and stone ready to their hand, and that the position was naturally strong, while both the place itself and the country for a long way round was uninhabited. Pylos is distant about forty-six miles from Sparta, and is situated in the territory which once belonged to the Messenians; by the Lacedaemonians it is

---

[a] Cp. iii. 115 med.   [b] Cp. iii. 85 fin.

[c] Reading with many good MSS. ξυνέπλευσε, and ἐπὶ τοῦτο.

called Coryphasium. The other generals argued that there were plenty of desolate promontories on the coast of Peloponnesus which he might occupy if he wanted to waste the public money. But Demosthenes thought that this particular spot had exceptional advantages. There was a harbour ready at hand; the Messenians, who were the ancient inhabitants of the country and spoke the same language with the Lacedaemonians, would make descents from the fort and do the greatest mischief; and they would be a trusty garrison.

4   As neither generals nor soldiers would listen to him, he *The Athenians are* at last communicated his idea to the *detained by stress of* officers of divisions; who would not *weather. At length the* listen to him either. The weather was *idea is taken up and* *carried out by the com-* still unfit for sailing; he was therefore *mon soldiers.* compelled to remain doing nothing; until at length the soldiers, who had nothing to do, were themselves seized with a desire to come round and fortify the place forthwith. So they put their hands to the work; and, being unprovided with iron tools, brought stones which they picked out and put them together as they happened to fit; if they required to use mortar, having no hods, they carried it on their backs, which they bent so as to form a resting-place for it, clasping their hands behind them that it might not fall off. By every means in their power they hurried on the weaker points, wanting to finish them before the Lacedaemonians arrived. The position was in most places so strongly fortified by nature as to have no need of a wall.

5   The Lacedaemonians, who were just then celebrating a festival[a], made light of the news, *The fort is completed* *in six days; five ships* being under the impression that they *are left with Demo-* could easily storm the fort whenever *sthenes, the rest go on to* they chose to attack it, even if the *Corcyra.* Athenians did not run away of themselves at their approach. They were also delayed by the

---

[a] Cp. v. 54; v. 82 init.

absence of their army in Attica. In six days the Athenians finished the wall on the land side, and in places towards the sea where it was most required; they then left Demosthenes with five ships to defend it, and with the rest hastened on their way to Corcyra and Sicily.

The Peloponnesian army in Attica, when they heard 6 that Pylos had been occupied, quickly *Recall of the Pelo-* returned home, Agis and the Lacedae- *ponnesians from Attica.* monians thinking that this matter touched them very nearly. The invasion had been made quite early in the year while the corn was yet green, and they were in want of food for their soldiers; moreover the wet and unseasonable weather had distressed them, so that on many grounds they were inclined to return sooner than they had intended. This was the shortest of all the Peloponnesian invasions; they only remained fifteen days in Attica.

About the same time Simonides, an Athenian general, 7 collecting a few troops from the Athen- *Temporary capture* ian garrisons, and a larger force from *and subsequent loss of* their allies in that neighbourhood, took *a place called Eion.* Eion in Chalcidicè, a colony of Mendè, which had been hostile to Athens; the place was betrayed to him. But the Chalcidians and Bottiaeans quickly came to the rescue and he was driven out with considerable loss.

On the return of the Peloponnesians from Attica, the 8 Spartans and the Perioeci[a] in the *The Spartans go to* neighbourhood of the city[a] went at *Pylos; they summon* once to attack Pylos, but the other *their allies and sixty* Lacedaemonians, having only just re- *ships which they had* turned from an expedition, were slower *sent to Corcyra.* in arriving. A message was sent round the Peloponnesus bidding the allies come without a moment's delay and meet at Pylos; another message summoned the sixty Peloponnesian ships from Corcyra. These were carried over the

---

' Or, 'in the neighbourhood of Pylos.'

Leucadian isthmus [a], and, undiscovered by the Athenian ships, which were by this time at Zacynthus, reached Pylos, where their land forces had already assembled. While the Peloponnesian fleet was still on its way, Demosthenes succeeded in despatching unobserved two vessels to let Eurymedon and the Athenian fleet know of his danger, and to bid them come at once.

While the Athenian ships were hastening to the assist-

The Lacedaemonians prepare to attack the fort. ance of Demosthenes in accordance with his request, the Lacedaemonians prepared to attack the fort both by sea and by land ; they thought that there would be little difficulty in taking a work hastily constructed and defended by a handful of men. But as they expected the speedy arrival of the Athenian fleet they meant to close the entrances to the harbour, and prevent the Athenians from anchoring there should they fail in taking the fort before their arrival.

The island which is called Sphacteria stretches along

The harbour of Pylos is formed by the island Sphacteria, which the Lacedaemonians occupy with four hundred and twenty men. the land and is quite close to it, making the harbour safe and the entrances narrow ; there is only a passage for two ships at the one end, which was opposite Pylos and the Athenian fort, while at the other the strait between the island and the mainland [b] is wide enough to admit eight or nine. The length of the island is about a mile and three-quarters ; it was wooded, and being uninhabited had no roads. The Lacedaemonians were intending to block up the mouths of the harbour by ships placed close together with their prows outwards ; meanwhile, fearing lest the Athenians should use the island for military operations, they conveyed thither some hoplites, and posted others along the shore of the mainland. Thus both the island and the mainland would be hostile to the Athenians ; and nowhere on the mainland would there

---

[a] Cp. iii. 81 init.   [b] It is really very much wider.

be a possibility of landing. For on the shore of Pylos itself, outside the entrance of the strait, and where the land faced the open sea, there were no harbours, and the Athenians would find no position from which they could assist their countrymen. Meanwhile the Lacedaemonians, avoiding the risk of an engagement at sea, might take the fort, which had been occupied in a hurry and was not provisioned. Acting on this impression they conveyed their hoplites over to the island, selecting them by lot out of each division of the army. One detachment relieved another; those who went over last and were taken in the island were four hundred and twenty men, besides the Helots who attended them; they were under the command of Epitadas the son of Molobrus.

Demosthenes, seeing that the Lacedaemonians were 9 about to attack him both by sea and by land, made his own preparations. He drew up on shore under the fort the three triremes remaining[a] to him out of the five which had not gone on to Corcyra, and protected them by a stockade; their crews he armed with shields, but of a poor sort, most of them made of wicker-work. In an uninhabited country there was no possibility of procuring arms, and these were only obtained from a thirty-oared privateer and a light boat belonging to some Messenians who had just arrived. Of these Messenians about forty were hoplites, whom Demosthenes used with the others. He placed the greater part of his forces, armed and unarmed, upon the side of the place which looks towards the mainland and was stronger and better fortified; these he ordered, if they should be attacked, to repel the land forces, while he himself selected out of the whole body of his troops sixty hoplites and a few archers, and marched out of the fort to the sea-shore at the point where the Lacedaemonians seemed most likely to attempt a landing. The spot which he chose lay towards the

Skilful use made by Demosthenes of the small means at his disposal.

---

[a] Reading αἱ περιῆσαν αὐτῷ.

open sea, and was rocky and dangerous; but he thought that the enemy would be attracted thither and would be sure to make a dash at that point because the fortifications were weaker. For the Athenians, not expecting to be defeated at sea, had left the wall just there less strong, while if the enemy could once force a landing, the place would easily be taken. Accordingly, marching down to the very edge of the sea, he there posted his hoplites; he was determined to keep the enemy off if he could, and in this spirit he addressed his men:—

10   'My companions in danger, let none of you now on the eve of battle desire to display his wits

Demosthenes advises his men not to think too much before they fight. The chances are in their favour. The place is inaccessible if they keep their ground, but if they retire, very accessible indeed. They are on land, the enemy on water. Let them stand firm, and keep him off the beach.

by reckoning up the sum of the perils which surround us; let him rather resolve to meet the enemy without much thought, but with a lively hope that he will survive them all. In cases like these, when there is no choice, reflection is useless, and the sooner danger comes the better. I am sure that our chances are more than equal if we will only stand firm, and, having so many advantages, do not take fright at the numbers of the enemy and throw them all away. The inaccessibility of the place is one of them; this, however, will only aid us if we maintain our position; when we have once retreated, the ground, though difficult in itself, will be easy enough to the enemy, for there will be no one to oppose him. And if we turn and press upon him he will be more obstinate than ever; for his retreat will be next to impossible. On ship-board the Peloponnesians are easily repelled, but once landed they are as good as we are. Of their numbers again we need not be so much afraid; for, numerous as they are, few only can fight at a time, owing to the difficulty of bringing their ships to shore. We are contending against an army superior indeed in numbers, but they are not our equals in other respects;

for they are not on land but on water, and ships require
many favourable accidents before they can act with advantage.   So that I consider their embarrassments to
counterbalance our want of numbers.   You are Athenians,
who know by experience the difficulty of disembarking in
the presence of an enemy, and that if a man is not
frightened out of his wits at the splashing of oars and
the threatening look of a ship bearing down upon him,
but is determined to hold his ground, no force can
move him.   It is now your turn to be attacked, and I
call on you to stand fast and not to let the enemy touch
the beach at all.   Thus you will save yourselves and
the place.'

The Athenians, inspirited by the words of Demosthenes, 11
went down to the shore and formed   *Difficulty of effecting*
a line along the water's edge.   The   *a landing.   Brasidas*
Lacedaemonians now began to move,   *greatly   distinguishes*
and assaulted the fort with their army   *himself.*
by land, and with their fleet, consisting of forty-three ships,
by sea.   The admiral in command was Thrasymelidas, son
of Cratesicles, a Spartan; he made his attack just where
Demosthenes expected.   The Athenians defended themselves both by sea and land.   The Peloponnesians had
divided their fleet into relays of a few ships—the space
would not allow of more—and so resting and fighting by
turns they made their attack with great spirit, loudly exhorting one another to force back the enemy and take the
fort.   Brasidas distinguished himself above all other men
in the engagement; he was captain of a ship, and seeing
his fellow-captains and the pilots, even if they could touch
anywhere, hesitating and afraid of running their ships on
the rocks, he called out to them: 'Not to be sparing of
timber when the enemy had built a fort in their country;
let them wreck their ships to force a landing': this he said
to his own countrymen, and to the allies that 'they should
not hesitate at such a moment to make a present of their
ships to the Lacedaemonians, who had done so much for

them ; they must run aground, and somehow or other get to land and take the fort and the men in it.'

12   While thus upbraiding the others he compelled his own

But he is wounded and loses his shield. Paradoxical character of the battle.

pilot to run his ship aground, and made for the gangway. But in attempting to disembark he was struck by the Athenians, and, after receiving many wounds, he swooned away and fell into the fore part of the ship ; his shield slipped off his arm into the sea, and, being washed ashore, was taken up by the Athenians and used for the trophy which they raised in commemoration of this attack. The Peloponnesians in the other ships made great efforts to disembark, but were unable on account of the roughness of the ground and the tenacity with which the Athenians held their position. It was a singular turn of fortune which drove the Athenians to repel the Lacedaemonians, who were attacking them by sea, from the Lacedaemonian coast, and the Lacedaemonians to fight for a landing on their own soil, now hostile to them, in the face of the Athenians. For in those days it was the great glory of the Lacedaemonians to be a land power distinguished for their military prowess, and of the Athenians to be a nation of sailors and the first sea power in Hellas.

13   The Peloponnesians, having continued their efforts

For two days the Peloponnesians continue their efforts. Fifty Athenian ships arrive and pass the night at Protè.

during this day and a part of the next, at length desisted ; on the third day they sent some of their ships to Asinè for timber with which to make engines, hoping by their help to take the part of the fort looking towards the harbour where the landing was easier, although it was built higher. Meanwhile the Athenian ships arrived from Zacynthus ; they had been increased in number to fifty by the arrival of some guard-ships from Naupactus and of four Chian vessels. Their commanders saw that both the mainland and the island were full of hoplites, and that the ships were in the harbour

and were not coming out : so, not knowing where to find
anchorage, they sailed away for the present to the island of
Protè, which is close at hand and uninhabited, and there
passed the night.   Next day, having made ready for action,
they put off to sea, intending, if, as they hoped, the
Peloponnesians were willing to come out against them, to
give battle in the open; if not, to sail into the harbour.
The Peloponnesians did not come out, and had somehow
neglected to close the mouths as they had intended.   They
showed no sign of moving, but were on shore, manning
their ships and preparing to fight, if any one entered the
harbour, which was of considerable size.

The Athenians, seeing how matters stood, rushed in **14**
upon them at both mouths of the har-
bour.   Most of the enemies' ships had
by this time got into deep water and
were facing them.   These they put to
flight and pursued them as well as they
could in such a narrow space, damaging
many and taking five, one of them with
the crew.   They charged the remaining

*The Athenians rush
in at both mouths of
the harbour, which the
enemy had neglected to
close.   The Lacedae-
monians are defeated
after a sharp conflict,
and the men stationed
in the island are cut off.*

vessels even after they had reached the land, and there
were some which they disabled while the crews were
getting into them and before they put out at all.   Others
they succeeded in tying to their own ships and began to
drag them away empty, the sailors having taken flight.
At this sight the Lacedaemonians were in an agony, for
their friends were being cut off in the island ; they hurried
to the rescue, and dashing armed as they were into the sea,
took hold of the ships and pulled them back ; [a] that was
a time when every one thought that the action was at
a stand where he himself was not engaged[a].   The confusion was tremendous ; the two combatants in this
battle for the ships interchanging their usual manner of

---

[a] Or, taking κεκωλῦσθαι with ἕκαστος : 'that was a time when every
one felt that he was under a restraint because he was unable to be everywhere and to do everything.'

fighting ; for the Lacedaemonians in their excitement and desperation did, as one may say, carry on a sea-fight from the land, and the Athenians, who were victorious and eager to push their good fortune to the utmost, waged a land-fight from their ships. At length, after giving each other much trouble and inflicting great damage, they parted. The Lacedaemonians saved their empty ships, with the exception of those which were first taken. Both sides retired to their encampments ; the Athenians then raised a trophy, gave up the dead, and took possession of the wrecks. They lost no time in sailing round the island and establishing a guard over the men who were cut off there. The Peloponnesians on the mainland, who had now been joined by all their contingents, remained in their position before Pylos.

15   At Sparta, when the news arrived, there was great consternation ; it was resolved that the magistrates should go down to the camp and see for themselves ; they could then take on the spot any measures which they thought necessary.

Consternation at Sparta. Finding that nothing can be done, the Spartans make a truce and send ambassadors to ask for peace.

Finding on their arrival that nothing could be done for their soldiers in the island, and not liking to run the risk of their being starved to death or overcome by force of numbers [a], they decided that with the consent of the Athenian generals they would suspend hostilities at Pylos, and sending ambassadors to ask for peace at Athens, would endeavour to recover their men as soon as possible.

16   The Athenian commanders accepted their proposals, and a truce was made on the following conditions :—

Terms of the truce. The Lacedaemonians agree to give up all their ships of war to the Athenians while the truce lasts.

'The Lacedaemonians shall deliver into the hands of the Athenians at Pylos the ships in which they fought, and shall also bring thither and deliver over any other ships of war which are in Laconia ; and they shall make no assault

---

[a] Omitting ἤ after βιασθέντας.

upon the fort either by sea or land. The Athenians shall permit the Lacedaemonians on the mainland to send to those on the island a fixed quantity of kneaded flour, viz. two Attic quarts [a] of barley-meal for each man, and a pint of wine, and also a piece of meat; for an attendant, half these quantities; they shall send them into the island under the inspection of the Athenians, and no vessel shall sail in by stealth. The Athenians shall guard the island as before, but not land, and shall not attack the Peloponnesian forces by land or by sea. If either party violate this agreement in any particular, however slight, the truce is to be at an end. The agreement is to last until the Lacedaemonian ambassadors return from Athens, and the Athenians are to convey them thither and bring them back in a trireme. When they return the truce is to be at an end, and the Athenians are to restore the ships in the same condition in which they received them.' Such were the terms of the truce. The ships, which were about sixty in number, were given up to the Athenians. The ambassadors went on their way, and arriving at Athens spoke as follows :—

'Men of Athens, the Lacedaemonians have sent us to 17 negotiate for the recovery of our countrymen in the island, in the hope that you may be induced to grant us terms such as will be at once advantageous to you and not inglorious to us in our present misfortune. If we speak *We use few or many words as the occasion requires. You have now a great opportunity of placing yourselves above the chances of fortune.* at length, this will be no departure from the custom of our country. On the contrary, it is our manner not to say much where few words will suffice, but to be more liberal of speech [b] when something important has to be said and words are the ministers of action [b]. Do not receive what

---

[a] The choenix was about two pints, dry measure; the cotylè about half a pint.

[b] Or, taking λόγοις with διδάσκοντας: 'when some weighty communication has to be made by words, if anything is to be really done.'

we say in a hostile spirit, or imagine that we deem you ignorant and are instructing you, but regard us simply as putting you in mind [a] of what you already know to be good policy. For you may turn your present advantage to excellent account, not only keeping what you have won, but gaining honour and glory as well. You will then escape the reverse which is apt to be experienced by men who attain any unusual good fortune; for, having already succeeded beyond all expectation, they see no reason why they should set any limit to their hopes and desires. Whereas they who have oftenest known the extremes of either kind of fortune ought to be most suspicious of prosperity; and this may naturally be expected to be the lesson which experience has taught both us and you.

18   'Look only at the calamity which has just overtaken us, who formerly enjoyed the greatest prestige of any Hellenic state, but are now come hither to ask of you the boon which at one time we should have thought ourselves better able to confer.

Take warning from our disaster. In your hour of prosperity show that you know when to stop.

You cannot attribute our mishap to any want of power; nor to the pride which an increase of power fosters. We were neither stronger nor weaker than before, but we erred in judgment, and to such errors all men are liable. Therefore you should not suppose that, because your city and your empire are powerful at this moment, you will always have fortune on your side. The wise ensure their own safety by not making too sure of their gains, and when disasters come they can meet them more intelligently; they know that war will go on its way whithersoever chance may lead, and will not restrict itself to the limits which he who begins to meddle with it would fain prescribe. They of all men will be least likely to meet with reverses, because they are not puffed up with military success, and they will be most inclined to end the struggle

---

[a] Cp. iv. 95 init.; iv. 126 init.; v. 60 fin.

in the hour of victory.   It will be for your honour,
Athenians, to act thus towards us.   And then the victories
which you have gained already cannot be attributed to
mere luck; as they certainly will be if, rejecting our
prayer, you should hereafter encounter disasters, a thing
which is not unlikely to happen.   Whereas you may if you
will leave to posterity a reputation for power and wisdom
which no danger can affect.

'The Lacedaemonians invite you to make terms with 19
them and to finish the war. They offer *We invite you to*
peace and alliance and a general *make peace. Great en-*
friendly and happy relation, and they *mities are best reconciled*
ask in return their countrymen who *rous and binds his*
when the victor is gene-
are cut off in the island.   They think *adversary to him by ties*
it better that neither city should run *of gratitude.*
any further risk, you of the escape of the besieged, who
may find some means of forcing their way out, we of their
being compelled to surrender and passing absolutely into
your hands.   We think that great enmities are most
effectually reconciled, not when one party seeks revenge
and, getting a decided superiority, binds his adversary by
enforced oaths and makes a treaty with him on unequal
terms, but when, having it in his power to do all this, he
from a generous and equitable feeling overcomes his
resentment, and by the moderation of his terms surprises
his adversary, who, having suffered no violence at his
hands, is bound to recompense his generosity not with
evil but with good, and who therefore, from a sense of
honour, is more likely to keep his word.   And mankind
are more ready to make such a concession to their greater
enemies than to those with whom they have only a slight
difference[a].   Again, they joyfully give way to those who
first give way themselves, although against overbearing
power they will risk a conflict even contrary to their own
better judgment.

---

[a] Cp. v. 91 init.

20   'Now, if ever, is the time of reconciliation for us both,

Reconciliation is still possible; for nothing irreparable has happened. Who began the war is a disputed point, but you will have the credit of ending it. Once united, we are the lords of Hellas.

before either has suffered any irremediable calamity, which must cause, besides the ordinary antagonism of contending states, a personal and inveterate hatred, and will deprive you of the advantages which we now offer. While the contest is still undecided, while you may acquire reputation and our friendship, and while our disaster can be repaired on tolerable terms, and disgrace averted, let us be reconciled, and choosing peace instead of war ourselves, let us give relief and rest to all the Hellenes. The chief credit of the peace will be yours. Whether we or you drove them into war is uncertain ; but to give them peace lies with you, and to you they will be grateful. If you decide for peace, you may assure to yourselves the lasting friendship of the Lacedaemonians freely offered by them, you on your part employing no force but kindness only. Consider the great advantages which such a friendship will yield. If you and we are at one, you may be certain that the rest of Hellas, which is less powerful than we, will pay to both of us the greatest deference.'

21   Thus spoke the Lacedaemonians, thinking that the

The Athenians at the instigation of Cleon insist on impossible terms.

Athenians, who had formerly been desirous of making terms with them, and had only been prevented by their refusal [a], would now, when peace was offered to them, joyfully agree and would restore their men. But the Athenians reflected that, since they had the Lacedaemonians shut up in the island, it was at any time in their power to make peace, and they wanted more. These feelings were chiefly encouraged by Cleon the son of Cleaenetus, a popular leader of the day who had the greatest influence over the multitude [b]. He persuaded

---

[a] Cp. ii. 59.   [b] Cp. iii. 36 fin.

them to reply that the men in the island must first of all give up themselves and their arms and be sent to Athens; the Lacedaemonians were then to restore Nisaea, Pegae, Troezen, and Achaia—places which had not been taken in war, but had been surrendered under a former treaty [a] in a time of reverse, when the Athenians [b] were more anxious to obtain peace than they now were [b]. On these conditions they might recover the men and make a treaty of such duration as both parties should approve.

To this reply the Lacedaemonians said nothing, but 22 only requested that the Athenians would appoint commissioners to discuss with them the details of the agreement and quietly arrive at an understanding about them if they could. This proposal was assailed by Cleon in unmeasured lan-

The proposal of the Lacedaemonians to discuss matters of detail in private is scornfully rejected. They are compelled to break off negotiations.

guage: he had always known, he said, that they meant no good, and now their designs were unveiled; for they were unwilling to speak a word before the people, but wanted to be closeted with a select few [c]; if they had any honesty in them, let them say what they wanted to the whole city. But the Lacedaemonians knew that, although they might be willing to make concessions under the pressure of their calamities, they could not speak openly before the assembly (for if they spoke and did not succeed, the terms which they offered might injure them in the opinion of their allies); they saw too that the Athenians would not grant what was asked of them on any tolerable conditions. So, after a fruitless negotiation, they returned home.

Upon their return the truce at Pylos instantly came to 23 an end, and the Lacedaemonians demanded back their

[a] Cp. i. 115 init.
[b] Or, 'were making and not receiving offers of peace.'
[c] Cp. v. 85.

ships according to the agreement.   But the Athenians accused them of making an assault upon the fort, and of some other petty infractions of the treaty which seemed

The Athenians refuse to restore the Peloponnesian fleet, insisting on some trivial infraction of the treaty.   They blockade Sphacteria.

hardly worth mentioning.   Accordingly they refused to restore them, insisting upon the clause which said that if 'in any particular, however slight,' the agreement were violated, the treaty was to be at an end.   The Lacedaemonians remonstrated, and went away protesting against the injustice of detaining their ships.   Both parties then renewed the war at Pylos with the utmost vigour.   The Athenians had two triremes sailing round Sphacteria in opposite directions throughout the day, and at night their whole fleet was moored about the island, except on the side towards the sea when the wind was high.   Twenty additional ships had come from Athens to assist in the blockade, so that the entire number was seventy.   The Peloponnesians lay encamped on the mainland and made assaults upon the fort, watching for any opportunity which might present itself of rescuing their men.

24   Meanwhile in Sicily the Syracusans and the allies brought up the fleet which they had

The Syracusans and Locrians renew the war against Rhegium from Messenè.   Hopes of the Syracusans.

been equipping[a] to Messenè, and joining the other fleet which was keeping guard there, carried on the war from thence.   They were instigated chiefly by the Locrians, who hated the Rhegians, and had already invaded their territory with their whole force.   They were eager to try their fortune in a naval engagement, for they saw that the Athenians had only a few ships actually on the spot, the larger portion of the fleet which had been despatched to Sicily being, as they heard, engaged in the siege of Sphacteria.   If they conquered at sea they hoped to blockade Rhegium both by sea and land; they would

---

[a] Cp. iv. 1 fin.

easily master the place, and their affairs would then be
really gaining strength. Rhegium, the extreme point of
Italy, and Messenè, of Sicily, are close to one another;
and if Rhegium were taken the Athenians would not be
able to lie there and command the strait. Now the strait
is that portion of sea between Rhegium and Messenè
where Sicily is nearest to the continent; it is the so-called
Charybdis by which Odysseus is said to have passed.
The channel was naturally considered dangerous; for
the strait is narrow, and the sea flowing into it from
two great oceans, the Tyrrhenian and Sicilian, is full of
currents.

In this strait the Syracusans and their allies, who had 25
somewhat more than thirty ships, were
compelled to fight late in the day for
a vessel which was sailing through.
They put out against sixteen Athenian
and eight Rhegian ships; but, being
*Partial defeat of the
Syracusan fleet by the
Athenians and Rheg-
ians in the straits of
Messenè.*
defeated by the Athenians, they made a hasty retreat, each
ship as it best could, to their stations at Messenè and near
Rhegium; one ship was lost. Night closed the engagement. After this the Locrians quitted the Rhegian
territory, and the Syracusans and their
confederates united their fleet and
anchored at the promontory of Pelorus
*Partial success of the
Syracusans, who take
two Athenian ships.*
near Messenè, where their land-forces were also stationed.
The Athenians and Rhegians, sailing up to them, and
seeing that the crews were not there, fell upon the empty
vessels, but an iron grapnel was thrown out at them, and
they in their turn lost a ship, from which the crew escaped
by swimming. Then the Syracusans embarked, and, as
they were being towed along the shore towards Messenè,
the Athenians again attacked them. Making a sudden
twist outwards they struck the first blow at the Athenians,
who lost another ship. Thus both in the movement along
the coast and in the naval engagement which ensued, the
Syracusans proved themselves quite a match for the

Athenians, and at length made their way into the harbour at Messenè.

The Athenians, hearing that Camarina was to be betrayed *Unsuccessful attempts of the Messenians upon Naxos, and of the Leontines and Athenians upon Messenè. The Athenians for a time withdraw from the contest.* to the Syracusans by a certain Archias and his confederates, sailed thither. Meanwhile the Messenians, with their whole power by land and with the allied fleet, made war upon Naxos, a Chalcidian city which was their neighbour. On the first day they forced the Naxians to retire within their walls and ravaged the country; on the morrow they sailed round to the mouth of the river Acesines, again ravaged the country, and with their land-forces made incursions right up to the city. But in the meantime a large body of Sicels came down over the heights to assist the Naxians against the Messenians. Perceiving this the besieged took heart, and shouting to one another that the Leontines and their other Hellenic allies were coming to succour them, they sallied out of the city, charged the Messenians, and put them to flight with a loss of more than a thousand men ; the rest with difficulty escaped, for the barbarians fell upon them in the roads and destroyed most of them. The allied fleet, putting into Messenè, broke up and returned home. Whereupon the Leontines and their allies, in concert with the Athenians, marched against the now enfeebled Messenè. The Athenian fleet attempted an assault of the harbour while the army attacked the city. But the Messenians and a Locrian garrison under Demoteles, which after their disaster at Naxos had been left to protect the place, suddenly falling upon them put to flight the main body of the Leontines with great loss ; whereupon the Athenians disembarked, came to their aid, and, falling on the Messenians while they were still in confusion, chased them back to the city. They then erected a trophy and retired to Rhegium. After this the Hellenes in Sicily went on fighting against one another by land ; but the Athenians took no part in their operations.

At Pylos meanwhile the Athenians continued to blockade **26**
the Lacedaemonians in the island, and
the Peloponnesian forces on the mainland remained in their old position.
The watch was harassing to the Athenians, for they were in want both of
food and water ; there was only one
small well, which was in the acropolis,
and the soldiers were commonly in the
habit of scraping away the shingle on

*The blockade of Pylos
was difficult, owing (1)
to want of food and
water; (2) to the con-
fined space; (3) to the
impossibility of anchor-
ing in shore; (4) to the
measures taken by the
Lacedaemonians for the
introduction of supplies.*

the sea-shore, and drinking such water as they could
get. The Athenian garrison was crowded into a narrow
space, and, their ships having no regular anchorage, the
crews took their meals on land by turns; one half of the
army eating while the other lay at anchor in the open sea.
The unexpected length of the siege was a great discouragement to them ; they had hoped to starve their enemies out
in a few days, for they were on a desert island, and had
only brackish water to drink. The secret of this protracted
resistance was a proclamation issued by the Lacedaemonians offering large fixed prices, and freedom if he were
a Helot, to any one who would convey into the island
meal, wine, cheese or any other provision suitable for
a besieged place. Many braved the danger, especially the
Helots; they started from all points of Peloponnesus, and
before daybreak bore down upon the shore of the island
looking towards the open sea. They took especial care to
have a strong wind in their favour, since they were less
likely to be discovered by the triremes when it blew hard
from the sea. The blockade was then impracticable, and
the crews of the boats were perfectly reckless in running
them aground; for a value had been set upon them, and
Lacedaemonian hoplites were waiting to receive them
about the landing-places of the island. All however who
ventured when the sea was calm were captured. Some too
dived and swam by way of the harbour, drawing after
them by a cord skins containing pounded linseed and

poppy-seeds mixed with honey. At first they were not found out, but afterwards watches were posted. The two parties had all sorts of devices, the one determined to send in food, the other to detect them.

27   When the Athenians heard that their own army was

The situation is reported to be critical. Cleon denies the reports. The Athenians want to send commissioners to Pylos. Cleon blames the generals, and proposes to send, not commissioners, but a fleet. He would soon take the men if he were general.

suffering and that supplies were introduced into the island, they began to be anxious and were apprehensive that the blockade might extend into the winter. They reflected that the conveyance of necessaries round the Peloponnese would then be impracticable. Their troops were in a desert place, to which, even in summer, they were not able to send a sufficient supply. The coast was without harbours; and therefore it would be impossible to maintain the blockade. Either the watch would be relaxed and the men would escape; or, taking advantage of a storm, they might sail away in the ships which brought them food. Above all they feared that the Lacedaemonians, who no longer made overtures to them, must now be reassured of the strength of their own position, and they regretted having rejected their advances. Cleon, knowing that he was an object of general mistrust because he had stood in the way of peace, challenged the reports of the messengers from Pylos; who rejoined that, if their words were not believed, the Athenians should send commissioners of their own. And so Theogenes and Cleon himself were chosen commissioners. As he knew that he could only confirm the report of the messengers whom he was calumniating, or would be convicted of falsehood if he contradicted them, observing too that the Athenians were now more disposed to take active measures, he advised them not to send commissioners, which would only be a loss of valuable time, but, if they were themselves satisfied with the report, to send a fleet against the island. Pointedly alluding to Nicias the son of Niceratus, who was one of the generals and an enemy of his, he declared sarcastically that, if the generals were men, they might easily sail with an expedition to the island and take the garrison, and that this was what he would certainly have done, had he been general.

Nicias perceived that the multitude were murmuring at Cleon, and asking 'why [a] he did not sail in any case—now was his time if he thought the capture of Sphacteria to be such an easy matter '; and hearing him find fault, he told him that, as far as they, the generals, were concerned, he might take any force which he required and try. Cleon at first imagined that the offer

The people murmur at him. Nicias resigns in his favour. He at first holds back, but is afterwards compelled to sail. He then declares that he will return victorious within twenty days. The Athenians laugh at him.

28

of Nicias was only a pretence, and was willing to go ; but finding that he was in earnest, he tried to back out, and said that not he but Nicias was general. He was now alarmed, for he never imagined that Nicias would go so far as to give up his place to him. Again Nicias bade him take the command of the expedition against Pylos, which he formally gave up to him in the presence of the assembly. And the more Cleon declined the proffered command and tried to retract what he had said, so much the more the multitude, as their manner is, urged Nicias to resign and shouted to Cleon that he should sail. At length, not knowing how to escape from his own words, he undertook the expedition, and, coming forward, said that he was not afraid of the Lacedaemonians, and that he would sail without taking a single man from the city if he were allowed to have the Lemnian and Imbrian forces now at Athens, the auxiliaries from Aenus, who were targeteers, and four hundred archers from other places. With these and with the troops already at Pylos he gave his word that within twenty days he would either bring the Lacedaemonians alive or kill them on the spot. His vain words moved the Athenians to laughter ; nevertheless the wiser

---

[a] Reading ὅ τι.

sort of men were pleased when they reflected that of two good things they could not fail to obtain one—either there would be no more trouble with Cleon, which they would have greatly preferred, or, if they were disappointed, he would put the Lacedaemonians into their hands.

29   When he had concluded the affair in the assembly, and the Athenians had passed the necessary vote for his expedition, he made choice of Demosthenes, one of the generals at Pylos, to be his colleague, and proceeded to sail with all speed. He selected Demosthenes because he heard that he was already intending to make an attack upon the island ; for the soldiers, who were suffering much from the discomfort of the place, in which they were rather besieged than besiegers [a], were eager to strike a decisive blow. He had been much encouraged by a fire which had taken place in the island. It had previously been nearly covered with wood and was pathless, having never been inhabited; and he had feared that the nature of the country would give the enemy an advantage. For, however large the force with which he landed, the Lacedaemonians might attack him from some place of ambush and do him much injury. Their mistakes and the character of their forces would be concealed by the wood ; whereas all the errors made by his own army would be palpable, and so the enemy, with whom the power of attack would rest, might come upon them suddenly wherever they liked. And if they were compelled to go into the wood and there engage, a smaller force which knew the ground would be more than a match for the larger number who were unacquainted with it. Their own army, however numerous, would be destroyed without knowing it, for they would not be able to see where they needed one another's assistance.

He selects Demosthenes to be his colleague, hearing that he is already meditating an attack upon the island. The design is encouraged by an accidental fire.

---

[a] Cp. vii. 11 fin.

Demosthenes was led to make these reflections from his 30 experience in Aetolia[a], where his de- *The burning of the* feat had been in a great measure owing *wood discovers the num-* to the forest. However, while the *ber and position of the* Athenian soldiers were taking their mid- *enemy.* day meal, with a guard posted in advance, at the extremity of the island, compelled as they were by want of room to land on the edge of the shore at meal-times, some one unintentionally set fire to a portion of the wood; a wind came on; and from this accident, before they knew what was happening, the greater part of it was burnt. Demosthenes, who had previously suspected that the Lacedaemonians when they sent in provisions to the besieged had exaggerated their number, saw that the men were more numerous than he had imagined. He saw too[b] the increased zeal of the Athenians, who were now convinced that the attempt was worth making; and the island seemed to him more accessible. So he prepared for the descent, despatching messengers to the allies in the neighbourhood for additional forces and putting all in readiness. Cleon sent and announced to Demosthenes his approach, and soon afterwards, bringing with him the army which he had requested, himself arrived at Pylos. On the meeting of the two generals they first of all sent a herald to the Lacedaemonian force on the mainland, proposing that they should avoid any further risk by ordering the men in the island to surrender with their arms; they were to be placed under surveillance but well treated until a general peace was concluded.

Finding that their proposal was rejected, the Athenians 31 waited for a day, and on the night of the day following put off, taking with *Disposition of the* them all their heavy-armed troops, *Lacedaemonian forces* whom they had embarked in a few *in three stations, the* ships. A little before dawn they *main body occupying* landed on both sides of the island, towards the sea and

---

[a] Cp. iii. 98.   [b] Reading τό τε.

towards the harbour, a force amounting in all to about
eight hundred men. They then ran as fast as they could
to the first station on the island. Now the disposition of
the enemy was as follows: This first station was garrisoned
by about thirty hoplites, while the main body under the
command of Epitadas was posted near the spring in the
centre of the island, where the ground was most level.
A small force guarded[a] the furthest extremity of the
island opposite Pylos, which was precipitous towards the
sea, and on the land side the strongest point of all, being
protected to some extent by an ancient wall made of rough
stones, which the Spartans thought would be of use to them
if they were overpowered and compelled to retreat. Such
was the disposition of the Lacedaemonian troops.

32   The Athenians rushed upon the first garrison and cut

*The Athenian hop-
lites land. The first of
the three garrisons is
cut down. The rest of
the Athenian forces
which land later are dis-
tributed in small parties
and occupy the higher
points of the island.*

them down, half asleep as they were
and just snatching up their arms.
Their landing had been unobserved,
the enemy supposing that the ships
were only gone to keep the customary
watch for the night. When the dawn
appeared, the rest of the army began
to disembark. They were the crews
of rather more than seventy ships, including all but the
lowest rank of rowers, variously equipped. There were
also archers to the number of eight hundred, and as many
targeteers, besides the Messenian auxiliaries and all who
were on duty about Pylos, except the guards who could
not be spared from the walls of the fortress. Demosthenes
divided them into parties of two hundred more or less,
who seized the highest points of the island in order that the
enemy, being completely surrounded and distracted by the
number of their opponents, might not know whom they
should face first, but might be exposed to missiles on every
side. For if they attacked those who were in front, they

---

[a] Reading αὐτὸ τὸ ἔσχατον, or, αὐτὸ τοὔσχατον.

would be assailed by those behind; and if those on one flank, by those posted on the other; and whichever way they moved, the light-armed troops of the enemy were sure to be in their rear. These were their most embarrassing opponents, because they were armed with bows and javelins and slings and stones, which could be used with effect at a distance. Even to approach them was impossible, for they conquered in their very flight, and when an enemy retreated, pressed close at his heels. Such was the plan of the descent which Demosthenes had in his mind, and which he now carried into execution.

The main body of the Lacedaemonians on the island 33 under Epitadas, when they saw the first garrison cut to pieces and an army approaching them, drew up in battle array. The Athenian hoplites were *The Lacedaemonian hoplites are unable to cope with the light-armed Athenian troops.* right in front, and the Lacedaemonians advanced against them, wanting to come to close quarters; but having light-armed adversaries both on their flank and rear, they could not get at them or profit by their own military skill, for they were impeded by a shower of missiles from both sides. Meanwhile the Athenians instead of going to meet them remained in position, while the light-armed again and again ran up and attacked the Lacedaemonians, who drove them back where they pressed closest. But though compelled to retreat they still continued fighting, being lightly equipped and easily getting the start of their enemies. The ground was difficult and rough, the island having been uninhabited; and the Lacedaemonians, who were incumbered by their arms, could not pursue them in such a place.

For some little time these skirmishes continued. But 34 soon the Lacedaemonians became too weary to rush out upon their assailants, *They are sorely distressed.* who began to be sensible that their resistance grew feebler. The sight of their own number, which was many times that of the enemy, encouraged them more than anything; they soon found that their losses were trifling compared with what they had expected; and familiarity made them think their opponents much less formidable than when they first landed cowed by the fear of facing Lacedaemonians. They now despised them and with a loud cry rushed upon them in a body, hurling at them stones, arrows, javelins, whichever came first to hand. The shout with which they accompanied the attack dismayed the Lacedaemonians, who were unaccustomed to this kind of warfare. Clouds of dust arose from the newly-burnt wood, and there was no possibility of a man's seeing what was before him, owing to the showers of arrows and stones hurled by their assailants which were flying amid the dust. And now the Lacedaemonians began to be sorely distressed, for their felt cuirasses did not protect them against the arrows, and the points of the javelins broke off where they struck them. They were at their wits' end, not being able to see out of their eyes or to hear the word of command, which was drowned by the cries of the enemy. Destruction was staring them in the face, and they had no means or hope of deliverance.

35 At length, finding that so long as they fought in the

They retreat to the fortification at the extremity of the island, and defend themselves with greater success because they are now less exposed.

same narrow spot more and more of their men were wounded, they closed their ranks and fell back on the last fortification of the island, which was not far off, and where their other garrison was stationed. Instantly the light-armed troops of the Athenians pressed upon them with fresh confidence, redoubling their cries. Those of the Lacedaemonians who were caught by them on the way were killed, but the greater number escaped to the fort and ranged themselves with the garrison, resolved to defend the heights wherever they were assailable. The Athenians followed, but the strength of the position made it impossible to surround and cut them off, and so they attacked them in face and tried to force them back. For a long time, and indeed during the greater part of the day, both armies, although suffering from the battle and thirst and the heat of the sun, held their own ; the one endeavouring to thrust their opponents from the high ground, the other determined not to give way.   But the Lacedaemonians now defended themselves with greater ease, because they were not liable to be taken in flank.

There was no sign of the end.   At length the general of 36 the Messenian contingent came to Cleon and Demosthenes and told them that the army was throwing away its pains, but if they would give him some archers and light-armed troops and let

The Messenian general finds a way round by the rocks and reappears suddenly in their rear.

him find a path by which he might get round in the rear of the Lacedaemonians, he thought that he could force the approach.   Having obtained his request he started from a point out of sight of the enemy, and making his way wherever the broken ground afforded a footing and where the cliff was so steep that no guards had been set, he and his men with great difficulty got round unseen and suddenly appeared on the summit in their rear, striking panic into the astonished enemy and redoubling the courage of his own friends who were watching for his reappearance. The Lacedaemonians were now assailed on both sides, and to compare a smaller thing to a greater, were in the same case with their own countrymen at Thermopylae.   For as they perished when the Persians found a way round by the path, so now the besieged garrison were attacked on both sides, and no longer resisted.   The disparity of numbers, and the failure of bodily strength arising from want of food, compelled them to fall back, and the Athenians were at length masters of the approaches.

Cleon and Demosthenes saw that if the Lacedaemonians 37 gave way one step more they would be destroyed by the Athenians ; so they stopped the engagement and held back their own army, for they wanted, if possible, to bring them alive to Athens.   They were in

Cleon and Demosthenes invite the Lacedaemonians to surrender.

hopes that when they heard the offer of terms their courage might be broken, and that they might be induced by their desperate situation to yield up their arms. Accordingly they proclaimed to them that they might, if they would, surrender at discretion to the Athenians themselves and their arms.

38   Upon hearing the proclamation most of them lowered their shields and waved their hands in

The Lacedaemonians on the mainland give their consent, and the offer is accepted. The prisoners brought to Athens number two hundred and ninety-two, of whom a hundred and twenty are Spartans.

token of their willingness to yield. A truce was made, and then Cleon and Demosthenes on the part of the Athenians, and Styphon the son of Pharax on the part of the Lacedaemonians, held a parley. Epitadas, who was the first in command, had been already slain; Hippagretas, who was next in succession, lay among the slain for dead; and Styphon had taken the place of the two others, having been appointed, as the law prescribed, in case anything should happen to them. He and his companions expressed their wish to communicate with the Lacedaemonians on the mainland as to the course which they should pursue. The Athenians allowed none of them to stir, but themselves invited heralds from the shore ; and after two or three communications, the herald who came over last from the body of the army brought back word, ' The Lacedaemonians bid you act as you think best, but you are not to dishonour yourselves.' Whereupon they consulted together, and then gave up themselves and their arms. During that day and the following night the Athenians kept guard over them ; on the next day they set up a trophy on the island and made preparations to sail, distributing the prisoners among the trierarchs. The Lacedaemonians sent a herald and conveyed away their own dead. The number of the dead and the prisoners was as follows :—Four hundred and twenty hoplites in all passed over into the island ; of these, two hundred and ninety-two were brought to Athens alive, the remainder had perished. Of the survivors the Spartans numbered about a hundred and twenty. But few Athenians fell, for there was no regular engagement.

Reckoned from the sea-fight to the final battle in the island, the time during which the blockade *Duration of the block-* lasted was ten weeks and two days. *ade. Supply of food.* For about three weeks the Lacedaemonians were supplied with food while the Spartan ambassadors were gone to solicit peace, but during the rest of this time they lived on what was brought in by stealth. A store of corn and other provisions was found in the island at the time of the capture ; for the commander Epitadas had not served out full rations. The Athenians and Peloponnesians now withdrew their armies from Pylos and returned home. And the mad promise of Cleon was fulfilled ; for he did bring back the prisoners within twenty days, as he had said.

Nothing which happened during the war caused greater amazement in Hellas ; for it was uni- *Astonishment of Hel-* versally imagined that the Lacedae- *las at the surrender of* monians would never give up their *the Lacedaemonians.* arms, either under the pressure of famine or in any other extremity, but would fight to the last and die sword in hand. No one would believe that those who surrendered were men of the same quality with those who perished. There is a story of a reply made by a captive taken in the island to one of the Athenian allies who had sneeringly asked ' Where were their brave men—all killed ? ' [a] He answered that ' The spindle ' (meaning the arrow) ' would be indeed a valuable weapon if it picked out the brave.' He meant to say that the destruction caused by the arrows and stones was indiscriminate.

On the arrival of the captives the Athenians resolved

---

[a] Literally, ' Were their dead brave ? ' implying that the living were not.

to put them in chains until peace was concluded, but if in the meantime the Lacedaemonians invaded Attica, to bring them out and put them to death. They placed a garrison in Pylos ; and the Messenians of Naupactus, regarding the place as their native land (for Pylos is situated in the territory which was once Messenia),

The prisoners are detained as securities for Attica. The Messenians of Naupactus garrison Pylos. The Lacedaemonians are distressed and sue for peace.

sent thither some of themselves, being such troops as were best suited for the service, who ravaged Laconia and did great harm, because they spoke the same language with the inhabitants. The Lacedaemonians had never before experienced this irregular and predatory warfare ; and finding the Helots desert, and dreading some serious domestic calamity, they were in great trouble. Although reluctant to expose their condition before the Athenians, they sent envoys to them and endeavoured to recover Pylos and the prisoners. But the Athenians only raised their terms, and at last, after they had made many fruitless journeys, dismissed them. Thus ended the affair of Pylos.

42   During the same summer and immediately afterwards the Athenians attacked the Corinthian territory with eighty ships, two thousand heavy-armed, and cavalry to the number of two hundred conveyed in horse transports. They were accompanied by allies from Miletus, Andros, and Carystus.

Athenian troops land near Solygea. The Corinthians, who are warned from Argos, come out to meet them.

Nicias the son of Niceratus, and two others, were in command. Very early in the morning they put in between the promontory Chersonesus and the stream Rhetus, to that part of the coast which is overhung by the Solygean ridge ; there in ancient times Dorian invaders had taken up their position and fought against their Aeolian enemies in Corinth, and to this day there is a village, called Solygea, on the hill which they occupied. From the beach where the crews landed this village is distant nearly a mile

and a-half, the city of Corinth about seven miles, and
the isthmus about two miles and a quarter. The Corinthians, having had early intimation from Argos of the
intended invasion, came in good time to the isthmus. The
whole population, with the exception of those who dwelt
to the north of the isthmus and five hundred troops
who were employed in protecting Ambracia and Leucadia [a], was on the watch to see where the Athenians
would land. But, having sailed in before daylight, they
were not discovered; the Corinthians however were
soon informed by signals of their landing; and so, leaving
half their troops at Cenchreae in case the Athenians
should attack Crommyon, they came to the rescue with
all speed.

Battus, one of the two generals who were present in the 43
engagement, taking a single division *Obstinate conflict on*
of the force, went to Solygea, intend- *the hill of Solygea. The*
ing to protect the village, which was *two armies drive one*
not fortified; Lycophron with the re- *another backwards and*
mainder of the army attacked the enemy. *forwards.*
The Corinthians first of all assailed the right wing of the
Athenians, which had only just landed in front of the
Chersonesus, and then engaged with the rest. The conflict was stubborn, and all hand to hand. The Athenians,
who were on the right wing, and the Carystians, who were
on the extreme right, received the Corinthians, and with
some difficulty drove them back. They retired behind
a loose stone wall, and the whole place being a steep
hill-side, threw the stones down from above; but soon
they raised the paean and again came on. Again the
Athenians received them, and another hand-to-hand fight
ensued, when a division of the Corinthians coming to the
aid of their left wing, forced back the right wing of the
Athenians and pursued them to the sea; but the Athenians
and Carystians in their turn again drove them back from

---

[a] Cp. iii. 114 fin.

the ships.   Meanwhile the rest of the two armies had been fighting steadily.   On the right wing of the Corinthians, where Lycophron was opposed to the Athenian left, the defence was most energetic ; for he and his troops were apprehensive that the Athenians would move on the village of Solygea.   For a long time neither would give way, but
44

The Athenians gain a partial victory, but, alarmed at the approach of a reinforcement, they retreat to their ships.

at length the Athenians, having an advantage in cavalry, with which the Corinthians were unprovided, drove them back, and they retired to the summit of the ridge ; where they grounded their arms and remained inactive, refusing to come down.   In this defeat of their right wing the Corinthians incurred the heaviest loss, and Lycophron their general was slain.   The whole army was now forced back upon the high ground, where they remained in position ; they were not pursued far, and made a leisurely retreat. The Athenians seeing that they did not return to the attack, at once erected a trophy and began to spoil the enemies' dead and take up their own.   The other half of the Corinthians who were keeping guard at Cenchreae, lest the Athenians should sail against Crommyon, had their view of the battle intercepted by Mount Oneum.   But when they saw the dust and knew what was going on, they instantly came to the rescue.   The elder men of Corinth hearing of the defeat likewise hastened to the spot.   The united army then advanced against the Athenians, who fancying that a reinforcement had come from the neighbouring states of Peloponnesus, quickly retreated to their ships, taking their spoils and their own dead, with the exception of two whom they could not find ; they then embarked and sailed to the neighbouring islands.   Thence they sent a herald asking for a truce, and recovered the two dead bodies which were missing.   The Corinthians lost two hundred and twelve men ; the Athenians hardly so many as fifty.

45   On the same day the Athenians sailed from the islands to

Crommyon, which is in the territory of Corinth, nearly
fourteen miles from the city, and, there
anchoring, they ravaged the country
and encamped for the night.   On the
following day they sailed along the
coast to Epidaurus, where they made
a descent, and then passed onward and
came to Methonè, which is situated
between Epidaurus and Troezen.   They built a wall
across the isthmus, and so cut off the peninsula on which
Methonè stands.   There they established a garrison, which
continued for some time to ravage the country of Troezen,
Halieis, and Epidaurus.   The fleet, when the fortification
was completed, returned home.

Second descent of the Athenians upon the territory of Corinth. After ravaging the neighbourhood of Crommyon and then of Epidaurus they cut off Methonè by a wall and leave a garrison.

Just about this time Eurymedon and Sophocles, who had 46
started from Pylos on their voyage to
Sicily with the Athenian fleet, arrived at Corcyra, and in concert with
the popular party attacked the Corcyraean oligarchs, who after the revolution
had crossed over into the island and
settled in Mount Istonè.   Here they
had become masters of the country again, and were doing
great mischief [a].   The Athenians assaulted and took their
fortress; the garrison, who had fled in a body to a peak
of the hill, came to terms, agreeing to give up their auxiliaries and surrender their arms, but stipulating that their
own fate should be decided by the Athenian people.   The
garrison themselves were conveyed by the generals to the
island of Ptychia and kept there under a promise of safety
until they could be sent to Athens ; on condition however
that if any of them were caught attempting to escape, they
should all lose the benefit of the agreement.   Now the
leaders of the Corcyraean democracy feared that when the
captives arrived at Athens they would not be put to death ;
so they devised the following trick :—They sent to the

The Athenians on their way to Sicily stop at Corcyra. The oligarchs in Mount Istone surrender on condition that their fate shall be left to the Athenian people.

---

[a] Cp. iii. 85.

island friends of the captives, whom with seeming good-will they instructed to tell them that they had better escape as fast as they could, for the fact was that the Athenian generals were about to hand them over to the Corcyraean democracy; they would themselves provide a vessel.

47   The friends of the captives persuaded a few of them,

The captive oligarchs are induced by a trick to break their parole and are delivered up to the vengeance of the Corcyraeans.

and the vessel was provided. The prisoners were taken sailing out; the truce was at an end, and they were all instantly delivered up to the Corcyraeans. The feeling which the Athenian generals displayed greatly contributed to the result; for, being compelled to proceed to Sicily themselves, they were well known to wish that no one else should gain the credit of bringing the prisoners to Athens; [a] and therefore the agreement was interpreted to the letter [a], and the contrivers of the trick thought that they could execute it with impunity. The Corcyraeans took the prisoners and shut them up in a large building; then, leading them out in bands of twenty at a time, they made them pass between two files of armed men; they were bound to one another and struck and pierced by the men on each side, whenever any one saw among them an enemy of his own; and there were men with whips, who accompanied them to the place of execution and quickened the steps of those who lingered.

48   In this manner they brought the prisoners out of the

They are cruelly massacred. The Athenian commanders, who did not want them to be carried by others to Athens, look on with indifference. They now pursue their voyage to Sicily.

building, and slew them to the number of sixty undiscovered by the rest, who thought that they were taking them away to some other place. But soon they found out what was happening, for some one told them, and then they called upon the Athenians, if they wanted them to die, to take their lives

---

[a] Or, 'and so the pretext turned out to be the exact truth;' or, 'and so the pretext seemed to correspond to the facts.'

themselves. Out of the building they refused to stir, and threatened that into it, if they could help, no one should enter. The Corcyraean populace had not the least intention of forcing a way in by the door, but they got upon the roof and, making an opening, threw tiles and shot arrows down from above. The prisoners sought to shelter themselves as they best could. Most of them at the same time put an end to their own lives ; some thrust into their throats arrows which were shot at them, others strangled themselves with cords taken from beds which they found in the place, or with strips which they tore from their own garments. This went on during the greater part of the night, which had closed upon their sufferings, until in one way or another, either by their own hand or by missiles hurled from above, they all perished. At daybreak the Corcyraeans flung the dead bodies cross-wise on waggons and carried them out of the city. The women who were taken in the fortress on Mount Istonè were reduced to slavery. Thus the Corcyraeans in the mountain were destroyed by the people, and, at least while the Peloponnesian war lasted, there was an end of the great sedition ; for there was nothing left of the other party worth mentioning. The Athenians then sailed for Sicily, their original destination[a], and there fought in concert with their allies.

At the end of the summer the Athenian forces in 49 Naupactus and some Acarnanians made an expedition against Anacto- *Anactorium is occupied by the Acarnanians.* rium, a Corinthian town at the mouth of the Ambracian Gulf, which was betrayed to them. The Acarnanians expelled the Corinthians, and sent a colony of their own, taken from the whole nation, to occupy the place. So the summer ended.

During the ensuing winter Aristides the son of Arch- 50 ippus, one of the commanders of the Athenian vessels which collected tribute from the allies, captured, at Eion upon the Strymon, Artaphernes a Persian, who was on

---

[a] Cp. iv. 4 fin. ; iv. 46 init.

his way from the King to Sparta. He was brought to

Seizure of a Persian envoy bearing despatches from the King, in which he complains of the Spartans. The Athenians send him back with an envoy of their own, but, arriving at the time of Artaxerxes' death, the embassy returns.

Athens, and the Athenians had the despatches which he was carrying and which were written in the Assyrian character translated, and read them; there were many matters contained in them, but the chief point was a remonstrance addressed to the Lacedaemonians by the King, who said that he could not understand what they wanted; for, although many envoys had come to him, no two of them agreed. If they meant to make themselves intelligible, he desired them to send to him another embassy with the Persian envoy. Shortly afterwards the Athenians sent Artaphernes in a trireme to Ephesus, and with him an embassy of their own, but they found that Artaxerxes the son of Xerxes had recently died; for the embassy arrived just at that time. Whereupon they returned home.

51　　During the same winter the Chians dismantled their new

The Chians, suspected of rebellion, are required to dismantle their walls.

walls by order of the Athenians, who suspected that they meant to rebel, not however without obtaining from the Athenians such pledges and assurances as they could, that no violent change should be made in their condition. So the winter came to an end; and with it the seventh year in the Peloponnesian War of which Thucydides wrote the history.

52　　Early in the ensuing summer there was a partial eclipse

B.C. 424.
Ol. 89.

An eclipse of the sun and an earthquake occur.

of the sun at the time of the new moon, and within the first ten days of the same month an earthquake.

The main body of the refugees who had escaped from

The Lesbian refugees, who had settled on the continent, take Rhoeteum and Antandrus.

Mitylenè and the rest of Lesbos had established themselves on the continent. They hired mercenaries from Peloponnesus or collected them on the spot, and took Rhoeteum, but on receiving a payment of

two thousand Phocaean staters [a], they restored the town
uninjured.   They then made an expedition against Antandrus and took the city, which was betrayed into their
hands.   They hoped to liberate the other so-called 'cities
of the coast,' which had been formerly in the possession of
the Mytilenaeans and were now held by the Athenians [b],
but their principal object was Antandrus itself, which they
intended to strengthen and make their head-quarters.
Mount Ida was near and would furnish timber for ship-
building, and by the help of a fleet and by other means
they could easily harass Lesbos which was close at hand,
and reduce the Aeolian towns on the continent.   Such
were their designs.

During the same summer the Athenians with sixty ships, 53
two thousand hoplites, and a few *The Athenians send*
cavalry, taking also certain Milesian *an expedition against*
and other allied forces, made an *Cythera. Importance of*
expedition against Cythera, under the *the island.*
command of Nicias the son of Niceratus, Nicostratus the
son of Diotrephes, and Autocles the son of Tolmaeus.
Cythera is an island which lies close to Laconia off Cape
Malea ; it is inhabited by Lacedaemonian Perioeci, and
a Spartan officer called the Judge of Cythera was sent
thither every year.   The Lacedaemonians kept there a
garrison of hoplites, which was continually relieved, and
took great care of the place.   There the merchant vessels
coming from Egypt and Libya commonly put in ; the
island was a great protection to the Lacedaemonians
against depredation by sea, on which element, though
secure by land, they were exposed to attack, for the
whole of Laconia runs out towards the Sicilian and Cretan
seas [c].

The Athenian fleet appeared off Cythera, and with a 54

---

[a] The value of the Phocaean stater is not precisely known : it was
somewhat less than that of the Attic stater (about 16*s*.).

[b] Cp. iii. 50 fin.   [c] Cp. Herod. vii. 235.

detachment of ten ships and two thousand Milesian hoplites

The Athenians cap-
ture Scandea. An
engagement takes place
in which the Cytherians
are defeated, and the
island capitulates. The
Athenians ravage the
coast of Laconia.

took Scandea, one of the cities on the sea-shore. The rest of their army disembarked on the side of the island looking towards Malea, and moved on to the lower city of the Cytherians, which is also on the sea-coast ; there they found all the inhabitants encamped in force.

A battle was fought in which the Cytherians held their ground for some little time, and then, betaking themselves to flight, retired to the upper city. They at length surrendered to Nicias and his colleagues, placing themselves at the disposal of the Athenians, but stipulating that their lives should be spared. Nicias had already contrived to enter into communication with some of them, and in consequence the negotiations were speedier, and lighter terms were imposed upon them both at the time and afterwards [a]. Else the Athenians would have expelled them, because they were Lacedaemonians and their island was close to Laconia. After the capitulation they took into their own hands Scandea, the city near the harbour, and secured the island by a garrison. They then sailed away, made descents upon Asinè, Helos, and most of the other maritime towns of Laconia, and, encamping wherever they found convenient, ravaged the country for about seven days.

55   The Lacedaemonians seeing that the Athenians had got

The Lacedaemonians
lose confidence in them-
selves. They act on the
defensive. Hesitation in
their counsels and panic
at their reverses.

possession of Cythera, and anticipating similar descents on their own shores, nowhere opposed them with their united forces, but distributed a body of hoplites in garrisons through the country where their presence seemed to be needed. They kept strict watch, fearing lest some domestic revolution should break out. Already a great and unexpected blow had fallen

---

[a] Cp. iv. 57 fin.

upon them at Sphacteria; Pylos and Cythera were in the hands of the Athenians, and they were beset on every side by an enemy against whose swift attacks precaution was vain. Contrary to their usual custom they raised a force of four hundred cavalry and archers. Never in their history had they shown so much hesitation in their military movements. They were involved in a war at sea, an element to which they were strange, against a power like the Athenians, in whose eyes to miss an opportunity was to lose a victory[a]. Fortune too was against them, and they were panic-stricken by the many startling reverses which had befallen them within so short a time. They feared lest some new calamity like that of the island might overtake them; and therefore they dared not venture on an engagement, but expected all their undertakings to fail; they had never hitherto known misfortune, and now they lost all confidence in their own powers.

While the Athenians were ravaging their coasts they hardly ever stirred; for each garrison at the places where they happened to land considered in their depressed state of mind that they were too few to act. *The small garrisons stationed in the country are afraid to move.* 56 One of them however, which was in the neighbourhood of Cotyrta and Aphrodisia, did offer some resistance, and by a sudden rush put to flight the multitude of light-armed troops who had been scattered, but, being encountered by the hoplites, they again retired with the loss of some few men and arms. The Athenians, raising a trophy, sailed back to Cythera. Thence they coasted round to Epidaurus Limera and, after devastating some part of its territory, to Thyrea, which is situated in the country called Cynuria, on the border of Argolis and Laconia. The Lacedaemonians, who at that time held the town, had settled there the Aeginetan exiles[b], whom they wished to requite for services rendered to them at the time of the earthquake and the Helot revolt, and

---

[a] Cp i. 70 med. [b] Cp. ii. 27.

also because they had always been partisans of theirs, although subjects of the Athenians.

57　　Before the Athenian ships had actually touched, the Aeginetans quitted a fort on the sea-shore which they were just building and retired to the upper city, where they lived, a distance of rather more than a mile. One of the country garrisons of the Lacedaemonians which was helping to build the fort was entreated by the Aeginetans to enter the walls, but refused, thinking that to be shut up inside them would be too dangerous. So they ascended to the high ground, and then, considering the enemy to be more than a match for them, would not come down. Meanwhile the Athenians landed, marched straight upon Thyrea with their whole army, and took it. They burnt and plundered the city, and carried away with them to Athens all the Aeginetans who had not fallen in the battle, and the Lacedaemonian governor of the place, Tantalus the son of Patrocles, who had been wounded and taken prisoner. They also had on board a few of the inhabitants of Cythera, whose removal seemed to be required as a measure of precaution. These the Athenians determined to deposit in some of the islands; at the same time they allowed the other Cytherians to live in their own country, paying a tribute of four talents[a]. They resolved to kill all the Aeginetans whom they had taken in satisfaction of their long-standing hatred, and to put Tantalus in chains along with the captives from Sphacteria.

Athenian attack upon Thyrea, where the Aeginetan exiles are settled. The Lacedaemonian garrisons refuse to enter the town, which is taken, and its inhabitants put to death by the Athenians.

58　　During the same summer the people of Camarina and Gela in Sicily made a truce, in the first instance with one another only. But after a while all the other Sicilian states sent envoys to Gela, where they held a conference in the hope of effecting a reconciliation.

A conference is held at Gela between the representatives of the Sicilian states.

-----

[a] £800.

Many opinions were expressed on both sides; and the representatives of the different cities wrangled and put in claims for the redress of their several grievances. At length Hermocrates the son of Hermon, a Syracusan, [a] whose words chiefly influenced their decision[a], addressed the conference in the following speech:—

'Sicilians, the city to which I belong is not the least in 59 Sicily, nor am I about to speak because Syracuse suffers more than other cities in the war, but because I want to lay before you the policy which seems to me best fitted to promote the common good of the whole country. You well know, and therefore I shall not rehearse to you at length, all the misery of war.

Speech of Hermo-crates. Why do men go to war? Because they expect to gain more than they will lose. But if they will lose more than they gain they had better make peace.

Nobody is driven into war by ignorance, and no one who thinks that he will gain anything from it is deterred by fear. The truth is that the aggressor deems the advantage to be greater than the suffering; and the side which is attacked would sooner run any risk than suffer the smallest immediate loss. But when such feelings on the part of either operate unseasonably, the time for offering counsels of peace has arrived, and such counsels, if we will only listen to them, will be at this moment invaluable to us. Why did we go to war? Simply from a consideration of our own individual interests, and with a view to our interests we are now trying by means of discussion to obtain peace; and if, after all, we do not before we separate succeed in getting our respective rights, we shall go to war again. But at the same 60 time we should have the sense to see that this conference is not solely concerned with our private interests, but with those of the whole country. Sicily is in my opinion at this moment imperilled by the designs of the Athenians, and we must try, if not too late, to save her.

The interests of the whole country and not of individual cities only are at stake. For the Athenians are upon us.

The Athenians are a much more

---

[a] Or, 'who had been the chief agent in bringing them together.'

convincing argument of peace than any words of mine can
be.   They are the greatest power in Hellas; they come
hither with a few ships to spy out our mistakes; though
we are their natural enemies, they assume the honourable
name of allies, and under this flimsy pretence turn our
enmity to good account.   For when we go to war and
invite their assistance (and they are fond of coming whether
they are invited or not) we are taxing ourselves for our
own destruction, and at the same time paving the way for
the advance of their empire.   And at some future day,
when they see that we are exhausted, they are sure to
come again with a larger armament, and attempt to bring
all Sicily under their yoke [a].

61   'And yet if we must call in allies and involve ourselves

We gain nothing by   in dangers, as men of sense, looking
war.   We only invite   to the interest of our several states, we
the common enemy.   should set before us the prospect of
The Athenians care   gaining an increase of dominion, not
nothing about Dorian
and Ionian: they want   of losing what we already have.   We
Sicily.   should consider that internal quarrels
more than anything else are the ruin of Sicily and her
cities; we Sicilians are fighting against one another at
the very time when we are threatened by a common enemy.
Knowing this, we should be reconciled man to man, city
to city, and make an united effort for the preservation of
all Sicily.   Let no one say to himself, "The Dorians
among us may be enemies to the Athenians, but the Chalcidians, being Ionians, are safe because they are their
kinsmen."   For the Athenians do not attack us because
we are divided into two races, of which one is their enemy
and the other their friend, but because they covet the good
things of Sicily which we all share alike [b].   Is not their
reception of the Chalcidian appeal a proof of this? [c]   They
have actually gone out of their way to grant the full

----

[a] Cp. iv. 1 med.   [b] Cp. vi. 77, 79.

[c] Cp. iii. 86.

privileges of their old treaty to those who up to this hour
have never aided them as required by the terms of that
treaty. The ambition and craft of the Athenians are
pardonable enough. I blame not those who wish to rule,
but those who are willing to serve. The same human
nature which is always ready to domineer over the subservient, bids us defend ourselves against the aggressor.
And if, knowing all these things, we continue to take no
thought for the future, and have not, every one of us, made
up our minds already that first and foremost we must all
deal wisely with the danger which threatens all, we are
grievously in error.

'Now a mutual reconciliation would be the speediest
way of deliverance from this danger; *Let us make peace*
for the Athenians do not come direct *and then they will have*
from their own country, but first plant *no footing in Sicily.*
themselves in that of the Sicilians who have invited them.
Instead of finishing one war only to begin another, we
should then quietly end our differences by peace. And
those who came at our call and had so good a reason for
doing wrong will have a still better reason for going away
and doing nothing.

'Such is the great advantage which we obtain by sound 62
policy as against the Athenians. And *Why should we not*
why, if peace is acknowledged by all *secure the blessings of*
to be the greatest of blessings, should *peace instead of relying*
we not make peace among ourselves? *on the chances of war?*
Whatever good or evil is the portion of any of us, is not
peace more likely than war to preserve the one and to
alleviate the other? And has not peace honours and
glories of her own unattended by the dangers of war?
(But it is unnecessary to dilate on the blessings of peace
any more than on the miseries of war.) Consider what
I am saying, and instead of despising my words, may
every man seek his own safety in them! And should
there be some one here present who was hoping to gain
a permanent advantage either by right or by force, let him

not take his disappointment to heart. For he knows that many a man before now who has sought a righteous revenge, far from obtaining it, has not even escaped himself; and many an one who in the consciousness of power has grasped at what was another's, has ended by losing what was his own. The revenge of a wrong is not always successful merely because it is just; nor is strength most assured of victory when it is most full of hope. The inscrutable future is the controller of events, and, being the most treacherous of all things, is also the most beneficent; for when there is mutual fear, men think twice before they make aggressions upon one another.

63   'And now, because we know not what this hidden future may bring forth, and because the Athenians, who are dangerous enemies, are already at our gates,—having these two valid reasons for alarm, let us acquiesce in our disappointment, deem-

Send away the Athenians: even if they punish your enemies, they will make you the enemies of your friends.

ing that the obstacles ᵃ to the fulfilment of our individual hopes ᵃ are really insuperable. Let us send out of the country the enemies who threaten us, and make peace among ourselves, if possible for ever; but if not, for as long as we can, and let our private enmities bide their time. If you take my advice, rest assured that you will maintain the freedom of your several cities; from which you will go forth your own masters, and recompense, like true men, the good or evil which is done to you. But if you will not believe me, and we are enslaved by others, the punishment of our enemies will be out of the question. Even supposing we succeed in obtaining vengeance to our hearts' content, we may perhaps become the friends of our greatest enemies, we certainly become the enemies of our real friends.

ᵃ Or, reading ἕκαστός τι : ' to the accomplishment of those things which each of us in whatever degree was hoping to effect.'

'As I said at first, I am the representative of a great **64**
city which is more likely to act on the   *Though I represent a*
aggressive than on the defensive ; and   *great city I am willing*
yet with the prospect of these dangers   *to make concessions,*
before me I am willing to come to   *and I ask others to do*
                                          the like. We are breth-
terms, and not to injure my enemies in   *ren.   Sicily for the*
such a way that I shall doubly injure   *Sicilians.*
myself.   Nor am I so obstinate and foolish as to imagine
that, because I am master of my own will, I can control
fortune, of whom I am not master ; but I am disposed to
make reasonable concessions.   And I would ask the other
Sicilians to do the same of their own accord, and not to
wait until the enemy compels them.   There is no disgrace
in kinsmen yielding to kinsmen, whether Dorians to
Dorians, or Chalcidians to the other Ionians.   Let us
remember too that we are all neighbours, inhabitants
of one island home, and called by the common name of
Sicilians.   When we see occasion we will fight among ourselves, and will negotiate and come to terms among
ourselves.   But we shall always, if we are wise, unite as
one man against the invader ; for when a single state
suffers, all are imperilled.   We will never again introduce
allies from abroad, no, nor pretended mediators.   This
policy will immediately secure to Sicily two great blessings ;
she will get rid of the Athenians, and of civil war.   And
for the future we shall keep the island free and our own,
and none will be tempted to attack us.'

Such were the words of Hermocrates.   The Sicilians **65**
took his advice and agreed among   *Terms of the treaty*
themselves to make peace, on the   *'uti possidetis.'   The*
understanding that they should all   *Athenians are dissatis-*
retain what they had ; only Morgantinè   *fied with their generals,*
                                          and believe that they
was handed over to the Camarinaeans,   *might have conquered*
who were to pay in return a fixed   *Sicily if they had not*
sum to the Syracusans.   The cities in   *been bribed.*
alliance with Athens sent for the Athenian generals and
told them that a treaty was about to be made in which they

might join if they pleased. They assented; the treaty was concluded; and so the Athenian ships sailed away from Sicily. When the generals returned the Athenians punished two of them, Pythodorus and Sophocles, with exile, and imposed a fine on the third, Eurymedon, believing that they might have conquered Sicily but had been bribed to go away. For in their present prosperity they were indignant at the idea of a reverse; they expected to accomplish everything, possible or impossible, with any force, great or small. The truth was that they were elated by the unexpected success of most of their enterprises, which inspired them with the liveliest hope.

66   During the same summer the citizens of Megara were hard pressed by the Athenians, who

The citizens of Megara, thinking it better to have one enemy than two, propose to restore the exiles. The popular leaders in alarm enter into negotiation with the Athenians.

twice every year invaded the country with their whole army [a], as well as by their own exiles in Pegae, who had been driven out by the people in a revolution [b], and were continually harassing and plundering them. So they conferred together upon the advisability of recalling the exiles, lest they should expose the city to destruction from the attacks of two enemies at once. The friends of the exiles became aware of the agitation and ventured to urge the measure more openly than hitherto. But the popular leaders, knowing that their partisans were in great extremity and could not be trusted to hold out in support of them much longer, took alarm and entered into negotiation with the Athenian generals, Hippocrates the son of Ariphron, and Demosthenes the son of Alcisthenes. They thought that they would incur less danger by surrendering the city to them than by the restoration of the exiles whom they had themselves expelled. So they agreed that the Athenians should in the first place seize their Long Walls [c], which were

---

[a] Cp. ii. 31.   [b] Cp. iii. 68 med.   [c] Cp. i. 103 fin.

a little less than a mile in length and extended from the
city to their harbour Nisaea. They wanted to prevent
the Peloponnesians interfering from Nisaea, of which they
formed the sole garrison, being stationed there to secure
Megara. The conspirators were then to try and place in
the hands of the Athenians the upper city, which would be
more ready to come over when they once had possession
of the Long Walls.

Both parties had now made all necessary preparations, 67
both in word and act. The Athenians *Disposition of the*
sailed at nightfall to Minoa, the island in *Athenian troops before*
front of Megara, with six hundred hop- *Megara. The gates are*
opened to them by their
lites under the command of Hippocrates. *Megarian confederates,*
They then took up their position not *and they mount the*
far from the Long Walls, in a pit out *Long Walls.*
of which the bricks for the walls had been dug.   A
second division of the Athenian army, consisting of light-
armed Plataeans and of a part of the force employed in
guarding the frontier, under the command of Demosthenes
the other general, lay in ambush at the temple of Ares,
which is nearer still.   During the night no one knew what
they were about, except the men who were immediately
concerned. Just before daybreak the conspirators executed their plan. They had long ago provided that the
gates should be open when required ; for by the permission of the commander, who supposed them to be
privateering, they had been in the habit of conveying
a sculling-boat out of the town by night. This they placed
upon a waggon, and carried it down to the sea through
the trench ; they then sailed out, and just before day broke
the boat was brought back by them on the waggon and
taken in at the gates ; their object being, as they pretended, to baffle the Athenian watch at Minoa, as no
vessel would be seen in the harbour at all. The waggon
had just arrived at the gates, which were opened for the
boat to enter, when the Athenians, with whom the whole
affair had been preconcerted, seeing this movement, rushed

out of the ambuscade, wanting to get in before the gates
were shut again and while the waggon was still in them,
and prevented them from being closed. At the same
instant their Megarian confederates cut down the guards
stationed at the gates. First of all the Plataeans and the
frontier guard under Demosthenes rushed in where the
trophy now stands. No sooner were they within the gates
than the Peloponnesians who were nearest and saw what
was going on hastened to the rescue; but they were overpowered by the Plataeans, who secured the gates for the
entrance of the Athenian hoplites as they came running up.

68   Then the Athenians entered, and one after another

The Peloponnesians, proceeded to mount the wall. A few
supposing the Megar- Peloponnesian guards at first resisted
ians to have gone over and some of them were killed; but the
to the enemy, fly to greater part took to flight; they were
Nisaea. The plot is de- terrified at the night attack of the
tected by the oligarchical enemy, and fancied, when they saw
party in time to save the Megarians who were in the con-
Megara itself.

spiracy fighting against them, that all the Megarians
had betrayed them. It had occurred at the same time
to the Athenian herald, without orders, to make proclamation that any Megarian who pleased might join the
ranks of the Athenians. When the Lacedaemonians heard
the proclamation none of them remained any longer, but
thinking that the Megarians were really fighting on the
Athenian side they fled into Nisaea.

When the morning dawned and the Long Walls were
already captured, Megara was in a tumult, and those who
had negotiated with the Athenians and a large number of
others who were in the plot insisted upon opening the
gates and going out to battle. Now they had agreed
that the Athenians should immediately rush in; and they
were themselves to be anointed with oil; this was the
mark by which they were to be distinguished, that they
might be spared in the attack. There was the less danger
in opening the gates, since there had now arrived four

thousand Athenian hoplites and six hundred horse, who by a previous arrangement had come from Eleusis during the night. When they were anointed and had collected about the gates some one in the secret acquainted the other party, who instantly came upon them in a compact body and declared that there should be no going out; even when they were stronger than at present they had not ventured to take the field; the danger to the city was too palpable; if any one opposed them the battle would have to be fought first within the walls. They did not betray their knowledge of the plot, but assumed the confident tone of men who were recommending the best course. At the same time they kept watch about the gates; and thus the conspiracy was foiled.

The Athenian generals became aware that some diffi- 69 culty had arisen, and that they could not carry the city by storm. So they immediately set about the circum- vallation of Nisaea, thinking that, if they could take it before any assist- ance arrived, Megara itself would be more likely to capitulate. Iron and other things needful, as well as masons, were quickly procured from Athens. Beginning from the wall which they already held they intercepted the approach from Megara by a cross wall, and from that drew another on either side of Nisaea down to the sea. The army divided among them the execution of the trench and walls, obtaining stones and bricks from the suburbs of the town. They also cut down timber and fruit-trees and made palisades where they were needed. The houses in the suburbs were of themselves a sufficient fortification, and only required battlements. All that day they continued working; on the following day, towards evening, the wall was nearly finished, and the terrified inhabitants of Nisaea having no food (for they depended for their daily supplies on the upper city), and imagining that Megara had gone over to the enemy, despairing too

The Athenians cut off Nisaea by a cross wall.

The town, which is in danger of starvation, capitulates.

of any aid soon arriving from Peloponnesus, capitulated to the Athenians. The conditions were as follows :— They were to go free, every man paying a fixed ransom and giving up his arms ; but the Athenians might deal as they pleased with the Lacedaemonian commander and any Lacedaemonian who was in the place. Upon these terms they came out, and the Athenians, having broken down the Long Walls between Megara and Nisaea, took possession of Nisaea and prepared for further action.

70 But it so happened that Brasidas, son of Tellis, the *Brasidas collects* Lacedaemonian, who was equipping an *troops and sends to the* expedition intended for Chalcidicè, was *Boeotians for an army.* in the neighbourhood of Sicyon and Corinth at the time. Hearing of the capture of the Long Walls, and fearing for the safety of the Peloponnesians in Nisaea, and of Megara itself, he sent to the Boeotians, desiring them to bring an army and meet him with all speed at Tripodiscus. The place so called is a village of Megara situated under Mount Geranea. Thither he also came himself, bringing two thousand seven hundred Corinthian, four hundred Phliasian, and six hundred Sicyonian hoplites, as well as the followers whom he had previously collected[a]. He had hoped to find Nisaea still untaken ; but the news of the capture reached him on his exit from the hills at Tripodiscus, where he did not arrive until night. He immediately took with him a body of three hundred chosen men, and before his arrival in the country was reported reached Megara, undiscovered by the Athenians, who were near the sea. He professed that he wanted, and he really meant if he could, to attempt the recovery of Nisaea ; but the great point was to get into Megara and make that safe. So he demanded admission, saying that he had hopes of regaining Nisaea.

[a] Cp. iv. 80 fin.

The two factions in Megara were both equally afraid to 71
receive him—the one lest he should
introduce the exiles and drive them   *He tries to enter Me-*
out, the other lest the people, fearing   *gara, but neither faction*
this very thing, should set upon them   *is as yet willing to re-*
                                         ceive him.
and ruin the city, which would then be distracted by civil
war and at the same time beset by the Athenians. And
so both parties determined to wait and see what would
happen. For they both expected a battle to ensue between the Athenians and the army which had come to
the relief of the city, and when the victory was won the
party whose friends had conquered could more safely
join them. Brasidås, thus failing in his purpose, returned
to the main body of his troops.

At dawn of day the Boeotians appeared. Even before 72
they were summoned by Brasidas they   *The Boeotians arrive.*
had intended to relieve Megara; for   *Indecisive action of*
the danger came home to them; and   *Boeotian and Athenian*
their whole force was already collected   *cavalry.*
at Plataea. When his messenger arrived they were more
resolved than ever, and sent forward two thousand two
hundred heavy-armed and six hundred horse, allowing the
greater number to return. The entire army of Brasidas
now amounted to six thousand hoplites. The Athenian
hoplites were drawn up near Nisaea and the sea, and their
light-armed troops were scattered over the plain, when
the Boeotian cavalry came riding up, fell upon the light-
armed, and drove them to the shore. The attack was
unexpected, for in no former invasion had aid come to
the Megarians from any quarter. The Athenian cavalry
now rode forward and there was a long engagement, in
which both parties claimed to have won a victory. The
Athenians drove the general of the Boeotian cavalry and
a few other horsemen up [a] to the walls of Nisaea, and

---

[a] Or, reading προσελάσαντας and omitting καὶ before ἀποκτείναντες,
'who had ridden up to the walls.'

there slew them and took their arms. As they retained possession of the dead bodies, and only restored them under a flag of truce, they raised a trophy. Still in respect of the whole engagement neither side when they parted had a decided advantage. The Boeotians retired to their main body, and the Athenians to Nisaea.

73   Brasidas and his army then moved nearer to the sea

The Peloponnesians, having shown that they are ready to engage, do not care to risk a battle. The Athenians are even more unwilling to fight than the Peloponnesians. The result is that Brasidas is admitted into Megara by the oligarchical party.

and to the town of Megara, and there, taking up a convenient position and marshalling their forces, they remained without moving. They were expecting the Athenians to attack them, and knew that the Megarians were waiting to see who would be the conquerors. They were very well satisfied, for two reasons. In the first place they were not the assailants, and had not gone out of their way to risk a battle, although they had clearly shown that they were ready to engage; and so they might fairly claim a victory without fighting. Again, the result in regard to Megara was good: for if they had not put in an appearance they would have had no chance at all, but would have been as good as beaten, and beyond a doubt would immediately have lost the city. Whereas now the Athenians themselves might be unwilling to fight; and, if so, they would gain their object without striking a blow. And this turned out to be the fact; for the Megarians did in the end receive Brasidas. At first the Athenians came out and drew up near the Long Walls, but not being attacked they likewise remained inactive. The generals on their side were restrained by similar reflections. They had gained the greater part of what they wanted; they would be offering battle against a superior force; and their own danger would be out of proportion to that of the enemy. They might be victorious and take Megara, but if they failed the loss would fall on the flower of their infantry. Whereas the Peloponnesians were naturally more willing to encounter a risk which would be divided among the several contingents making up the army now in the field; and each of these was but a part of their whole force, present and absent.   Both armies waited for a time, and, when neither saw the other moving, the Athenians first of the two retired into Nisaea and the Peloponnesians returned to their previous position.   Whereupon the party in Megara friendly to the exiles took courage, opened the gates, and received Brasidas and the generals of the other cities, considering that the Athenians had finally made up their minds not to fight, and that he was the conqueror.   They then entered into negotiations with him; for the other faction which had conspired with the Athenians was now paralysed.

After this the allies dispersed to their several cities and 74 Brasidas returned to Corinth, where he made preparations for his expedition into Chalcidicè, his original destination.   When the Athenians had also gone home, such of the Megarians *Megara now passes into the hands of the oligarchs, who cruelly and treacherously put to death their opponents.* as had been chiefly concerned with them, knowing that they were discovered, at once slipped away.   The rest of the citizens, after conferring with the friends of the exiles, recalled them from Pegae[a], first binding them by the most solemn oaths to consider the interests of the state and to forget old quarrels.   But no sooner had they come into office than, taking the opportunity of a review and drawing up the divisions apart from one another, they selected about a hundred of their enemies, and of those who seemed to have been most deeply implicated with the Athenians, and compelled the people to give sentence upon them by an open vote; having obtained their condemnation, they put them to death.   They then established in the city an extreme oligarchy.   And no government based on a counter revolution effected by so few ever lasted so long a time.

---

[a] Cp iv. 66 init.

75   During the same summer Demodocus and Aristides,

Antandrus, which had become the headquarters of the Lesbian exiles, is taken by the Athenians.

two commanders of the Athenian fleet which collected tribute from the allies, happened to be in the neighbourhood of the Hellespont; there were only two of them, the third, Lamachus, having sailed with ten ships into the Pontus. They saw that the Lesbian exiles were going to strengthen Antandrus as they had intended [a], and they feared that it would prove as troublesome an enemy to Lesbos as Anaea had been to Samos [b]; for the Samian refugees, who had settled there, aided the Peloponnesian navy by sending them pilots; they likewise took in fugitives from Samos and kept the island in a state of perpetual alarm. So the Athenian generals collected troops from their allies, sailed to Antandrus, and, defeating a force which came out against them, recovered the place. Not long afterwards Lamachus, who had sailed into the Pontus and had anchored in the territory of Heraclea at the mouth of the river Calex, lost his ships by a sudden flood which a fall of rain in the upper country had brought down. He and his army returned by land through the country of the Bithynian Thracians who dwell on the Asiatic coast across the water, and arrived at Chalcedon, the Megarian colony at the mouth of the Pontus.

76   In the same summer, and immediately after the with-

The Athenians enter into communication with the democratical party in Boeotia, who undertake to betray Siphae, while the Athenians seize Delium.

drawal of the Athenians from Megara, the Athenian general Demosthenes arrived at Naupactus with forty ships. A party in the cities of Boeotia, who wanted to overthrow their constitution and set up a democracy like that of Athens, had entered into communications with him and with Hippocrates, and a plan of operations had been concerted, chiefly under the direction of Ptoeodorus,

---

[a] Cp. iv. 52.   [b] Cp. iii. 19; iii. 32 init.

a Theban exile. Some of the democratical party undertook to betray Siphae, which is a seaport on the Crisaean
Gulf in the Thespian territory, and certain Orchomenians
were to deliver up to the Athenians Chaeronea, which is
a dependency of the Boeotian, or as it was formerly called
the Minyan, Orchomenus. A body of Orchomenian
exiles had a principal hand in this design and were
seeking to hire a Peloponnesian force. The town of
Chaeronea is at the extremity of Boeotia near the territory
of Phanoteus in Phocis, and some Phocians took part in
the plot. The Athenians meanwhile were to seize Delium,
a temple of Apollo which is in the district of Tanagra and
looks towards Euboea. In order to keep the Boeotians
occupied with disturbances at home, and prevent them
from marching in a body to Delium, the whole movement
was to be made on a single day, which was fixed beforehand. If the attempt succeeded and Delium was fortified,
even though no revolution should at once break out in the
states of Boeotia, they might hold the places which they
had taken and plunder the country. The partisans of
democracy in the several cities would have a refuge near
at hand to which in case of failure they might retreat.
Matters could not long remain as they were ; and in time,
the Athenians acting with the rebels, and the Boeotian
forces being divided, they would easily settle Boeotia in
their interest. Such was the nature of the proposed
attempt.

Hippocrates himself with a force from the city was 77
ready to march into Boeotia when the   *Demosthenes with a*
moment came. He had sent Demo-   *fleet from Naupactus*
sthenes beforehand with the forty ships   *and Hippocrates with*
to Naupactus, intending him to collect   *an army from Athens*
an army of Acarnanians and other   *agree to invade Boeotia*
on a fixed day.
allies of the Athenians in that region and sail against
Siphae, which was to be betrayed to them. These operations were to be carried out simultaneously on the day
appointed.

Demosthenes on his arrival found that the confederate
Oeniadae forced into Acarnanians had already compelled
the Athenian alliance. Oeniadae to enter the Athenian
alliance. He then himself raised all the forces of the
allies in those parts and proceeded first to make war upon
Salynthius and the Agraeans[a]. Having subdued them,
he took the necessary steps for keeping his appointment
at Siphae.

78   During this summer, and about the same time, Brasidas
Brasidas, escorted by set out on his way to Chalcidicè with
the leading men of the seventeen hundred hoplites. When
country, makes his way he arrived at Heraclea in Trachis he
through Thessaly. His
politic language. despatched a messenger to Pharsalus,
where he had friends, with a request that they would
conduct him and his army through the country. Accordingly there came to meet him at Melitia, in Achaea
Phthiotis, Panaerus, Dorus, Hippolochidas, Torylaus, and
Strophacus who was the proxenus of the Chalcidians.
Under their guidance he started. Other Thessalians
also conducted him; in particular, Niconidas a friend of
Perdiccas from Larissa. Under any circumstances it
would not have been easy to cross Thessaly without an
escort, and certainly for an armed force to go through
a neighbour's country without his consent was a proceeding
which excited jealousy among all Hellenes. Besides, the
common people of Thessaly were always well disposed
towards the Athenians. And if the traditions of the
country had not been in favour of a close oligarchy,
Brasidas could never have gone on; even as it was, some
of the opposite party met him on his march at the river
Enipeus and would have stopped him, saying that he had
no business to proceed without the consent of the whole
nation. His escort replied that they would not conduct him
if the others objected, but that he had suddenly presented
himself and they were doing the duty of hosts in accom-

---

[a] Cp. iii. 111 fin.

panying him. Brasidas himself added that he came as
a friend to the Thessalian land and people, and that he
was making war upon his enemies the Athenians, and not
upon them. He had never heard that there was any ill-
feeling between the Thessalians and Lacedaemonians
which prevented either of them from passing through the
territory of the other; however, if they refused their consent, he would not and indeed could not go on; but such
was not the treatment which he had a right to expect from
them. Upon this they departed, and he by the advice of
his escort, fearing that a large force might collect and stop
him, marched on at full speed and without a halt. On the
same day on which he started from Melitia he arrived at
Pharsalus, and encamped by the river Apidanus. Thence
he went on to Phacium, and thence to Perrhaebia. Here
his Thessalian escort returned; and the Perrhaebians,
who are subjects of the Thessalians, brought him safe to
Dium in the territory of Perdiccas, a city of Macedonia
which is situated under Mount Olympus on the Thessalian
side.

Thus Brasidas succeeded in running through Thessaly 79
before any measures were taken to *Brasidas reaches Per-*
stop him, and reached Perdiccas and *diccas.*
Chalcidicè. He and the revolted tributaries of the
Athenians, alarmed at their recent successes, had invited
the Peloponnesians. The Chalcidians were expecting that
the first efforts of the Athenians would be directed against
them : their cities in the neighbourhood also which had
not revolted secretly joined in the invitation. Perdiccas
was not a declared enemy of Athens, but was afraid that
the old differences between himself and the Athenians
might revive, and he was especially anxious to subdue
Arrhibaeus, king of the Lyncestians.

The Lacedaemonians were the more willing to let the 80
Chalcidians have an army from Peloponnesus owing to
the unfortunate state of their affairs. For now that the
Athenians were infesting Peloponnesus, and especially

Laconia, they thought that a diversion would be best
effected if they could retaliate on them by sending troops to help their dissatisfied allies, who moreover were offering to maintain them, and had asked for assistance from Sparta with the intention of revolting. They were also glad of a pretext for sending out of the way some of the Helots, fearing that they would take the opportunity of rising afforded by the occupation of Pylos. Most of the Lacedaemonian institutions were specially intended to secure them against this source of danger. Once, when they were afraid of the number and vigour [a] of the Helot youth, this was what they did :—They proclaimed that a selection would be made of those Helots who claimed to have rendered the best service to the Lacedaemonians in war, and promised them liberty. The announcement was intended to test them ; it was thought that those among them who were foremost in asserting their freedom would be most high-spirited, and most likely to rise against their masters. So they selected about two thousand, who were crowned with garlands and went in procession round the temples ; they were supposed to have received their liberty ; but not long afterwards the Spartans put them all out of the way, and no man knew how any one of them came by his end.—And so they were only too glad to send with Brasidas seven hundred Helots as hoplites. The rest of his army he hired from Peloponnesus [b]. He himself was even more willing to go

81 than they were to send him. The Chalcidians too desired to have him, for at Sparta he had always been considered a man of energy. And on this expedition he proved invaluable to the Lacedaemonians. At the time he gave an impression of justice

Side notes:

The Lacedaemonians encourage the expedition of Brasidas in the hope of making a diversion, and getting rid of the Helots. Their monstrous cruelty and treachery.

Justice and moderation of Brasidas remembered afterwards in Hellas.

---

[a] Or, reading σκαιότητα, ' obstinacy.'   [b] Cp. iv. 70 med.

and moderation in his behaviour to the cities, which induced most of them to revolt, while others were betrayed
into his hands. Thus the Lacedaemonians were able to
lighten the pressure of war upon Peloponnesus; and when
shortly afterwards they desired to negotiate, they had
places to give in return for what they sought to recover.
And at a later period of the war, after the Sicilian expedition, the honesty and ability of Brasidas which some
had experienced, and of which others had heard the fame,
mainly attracted the Athenian allies to the Lacedaemonians. [a] For he was the first Spartan who had gone out to
them, and he proved himself[a] to be in every way a good
man. Thus he left in their minds a firm conviction that
the others would be like him.

The Athenians, hearing of the arrival of Brasidas in 82
Chalcidicè, and believing that Perdiccas *The Athenians de-*
was the instigator of the expedition, *clare Perdiccas an*
declared war against the latter and *enemy.*
kept a closer watch over their allies in that region.

Perdiccas, at once uniting the soldiers of Brasidas with 83
his own forces, made war upon Arrhi- *The alliance between*
baeus the son of Bromerus, king of the *Perdiccas and Brasidas*
Lyncestians, a neighbouring people of *soon begins to cool.*
Macedonia; for he had a quarrel with *baeus.*
him and wanted to subdue him. But when he and Brasidas
and the army arrived at the pass leading into Lyncus,
Brasidas said that before appealing to arms he should like
to try in person the effect of negotiations, and see if he
could not make Arrhibaeus an ally of the Lacedaemonians.
He was partly influenced by messages which came from
Arrhibaeus expressing his willingness to submit any
matter in dispute to the arbitration of Brasidas: and the
Chalcidian ambassadors who accompanied the expedition
recommended him not to remove from Perdiccas' path all

---

[a] Or, taking πρῶτος closely with δόξας : ' For of all the Spartans who
had been sent out, he was the first who proved himself,' &c.

his difficulties, lest, when they were wanting him for their own affairs, his ardour should cool. Besides, the envoys of Perdiccas when at Sparta had said something to the Lacedaemonians about his making many of the neighbouring tribes their allies, and on this ground Brasidas claimed to act jointly with Perdiccas in the matter of Arrhibaeus. But Perdiccas answered that he had not brought Brasidas there to arbitrate in the quarrels of Macedonia; he had meant him to destroy his enemies when he pointed them out. While he, Perdiccas, was maintaining half the Lacedaemonian army, Brasidas had no business to be holding parley with Arrhibaeus. But in spite of the opposition and resentment of Perdiccas, Brasidas communicated with Arrhibaeus, and was induced by his words to withdraw his army without invading the country. From that time Perdiccas thought himself ill-used, and paid only a third instead of half the expenses of the army.

84   During the same summer, immediately on his return

Brasidas is admitted into Acanthus and addresses the citizens. from Lyncus, and a little before the vintage, Brasidas, reinforced by Chalcidian troops, marched against Acanthus, a colony of Andros. The inhabitants of the city were not agreed about admitting him; those who in concert with the Chalcidians had invited him being opposed to the mass of the people. So he asked them to receive him alone, and hear what he had to say before they decided; and to this request the multitude, partly out of fear for their still ungathered vintage, were induced to consent. Whereupon, coming forward to the people (and for a Lacedaemonian he was not a bad speaker), he addressed them as follows:—

85   'Men of Acanthus, the Lacedaemonians have sent me out at the head of this army to justify the declaration which we made at the beginning of the war—that we were going to fight against the Athenians for the liberties of Hellas. If we have been long in coming, the reason is that we were disappointed in the result of the war nearer

home ; for we had hoped that, without involving you in danger, we might ourselves have made a speedy end of the Athenians. And therefore let no one blame us ; we have come as soon as we could, and with your help will do our best to overthrow them. But how is it that you close your gates against me, and do not greet my arrival ? We Lacedaemonians thought that we were coming to those

We come to you as the liberators of Hellas: why do you close your gates against us ? Your refusal to admit us will have a bad effect on other cities. We are able and willing to help you. We were too strong for the Athenians at Nisaea.

who even before we came in act were our allies in spirit, and would joyfully receive us; having this hope we have braved the greatest dangers, marching for many days through a foreign country, and have shown the utmost zeal in your cause. And now, for you to be of another mind and to set yourselves against the liberties of your own city and of all Hellas would be monstrous ! The evil is not only that you resist me yourselves, but wherever I go people will be less likely to join me ; they will take it amiss when they hear that you to whom I first came, representing a powerful city and reputed to be men of sense, did not receive me, and I shall not be able to give a satisfactory explanation, [a] but shall have to confess either that I offer a spurious liberty, or that I am weak [a] and incapable of protecting you against the threatened attack of the Athenians. And yet when I brought assistance to Nisaea in command of the army which I have led hither, the Athenians, though more numerous, refused to engage with me ; and they are not likely now, when their forces must be conveyed by sea, to send an army against you equal to that which they had at Nisaea [b]. And I myself, 86 why am I here ? I come, not to injure, but to emancipate the Hellenes. And I have bound the government of Lacedaemon by the most solemn oaths to respect the inde-

---

[a] Or, taking ἐπιφέρειν after αἰτίαν ἕξω : 'but shall be deemed either to offer a spurious liberty, or to be weak.'   [b] Cp. iv. 108 fin.

pendence of any states which I may bring over to their side.

I am not the repre-sentative of a faction; and shall not enslave either the few or the many. The Lacedae-monians, unlike the Athenians, have a char-acter to lose.
I do not want to gain your alliance by force or fraud, but to give you ours, that we may free you from the Athenian yoke. I think that you ought not to doubt my word when I offer you the most solemn pledges, nor should I be regarded as an inefficient champion; but you should confidently join me.

'If any one among you hangs back because he has a personal fear of anybody else, and is under the impression that I shall hand over the city to a party, him above all I would reassure. For I am not come hither to be the tool of a faction; nor do I conceive that the liberty which I bring you is of an ambiguous character; I should forget the spirit of my country were I to enslave the many to the few, or the minority to the whole people. Such a tyranny would be worse than the dominion of the foreigner, and we Lacedaemonians should receive no thanks in return for our trouble, but, instead of honour and reputation, only reproach. We should lay ourselves open to the charges which are our best weapons against the Athenians, and in a far more detestable form, for they have never been great examples of virtue. For to men of character there is more disgrace in seeking aggrandisement by specious deceit than by open violence[a]; the violent have the justification of strength which fortune gives them, but a policy of intrigue is insidious and wicked.

'So careful are we where our highest interests are at

87　*If you will not be our friends, we must be your enemies. Having a duty to perform, we cannot tolerate your opposition.*
stake. And not to speak of our oaths, you cannot have better assurance than they give whose actions, when compared with their professions, afford a convincing proof that it is their interest to keep their word.

---

[a] Cp. i. 77 med.

'But if you plead that you cannot accept the proposals which I offer, and insist that you ought not to suffer for the rejection of them because you are our friends; if you are of opinion that liberty is perilous and should not in justice be forced upon any one, but gently brought to those who are able to receive it,—I shall first call the Gods and heroes of the country to witness that I have come hither for your good, and that you would not be persuaded by me: I shall then use force and ravage your country without any more scruple. I shall deem myself justified by two overpowering arguments. In the first place, I must not permit the Lacedaemonians to suffer by your friendship, and suffer they will through the revenues which the Athenians will continue to derive from you if you do not join me; and in the second place, the Hellenes must not lose their hope of liberation by your fault. On any other ground we should certainly be wrong in taking such a step; it is only for the sake of the general weal that we Lacedaemonians have any right to be forcing liberty upon those who would rather not have it. For ourselves, we are far from desiring empire, but we want to overthrow the empire of others. And having this end in view, we should do injustice to the majority if, while bringing independence to all, we tolerated opposition in you. Wherefore be well advised. Strive to take the lead in liberating Hellas, and lay up a treasure of undying fame. You will save your own property, and you will crown your city with glory.'

Thus spoke Brasidas. The Acanthians, after much had **88** been said on both sides, partly under the attraction of his words, and partly because they were afraid of losing their vintage, determined by a majority, voting *The Acanthians, who are afraid of losing their vintage, determine to revolt from Athens.* secretly, to revolt from Athens. They pledged Brasidas to stand by the engagement to which the government of Sparta had sworn before they sent him out, to respect the independence of all whom he brought over to the Lacedaemonian alliance. They then admitted his army;

and shortly afterwards Stagirus, a colony of the Andrians, revolted also. Such were the events of the summer.

89　　Meanwhile the betrayal of Boeotia into the hands of Hippocrates and Demosthenes, the Athenian generals, was on the eve of accomplishment. At the beginning of the ensuing winter Demosthenes and his fleet were to appear at Siphae, and Hippocrates simultaneously to march upon Delium. But there was a mistake about the day, and Demosthenes, with his Acarnanian and numerous other allies drawn from that neighbourhood, sailed to Siphae too soon. His attempt failed; for the plot was betrayed by Nicomachus a Phocian, of the town of Phanoteus, who told the Lacedaemonians, and they the Boeotians. Whereupon there was a general levy of the Boeotians, for Hippocrates, who was to have been in the country and to have distracted their attention, had not yet arrived; and so they forestalled the Athenians by the occupation of Siphae and Chaeronea. When the conspirators in the Boeotian cities saw that there had been a mistake they made no movement from within.

The plot for the betrayal of Boeotia is discovered.

90　　Hippocrates had called out the whole force of Athens, metics as well as citizens, and all the strangers who were then in the city. But he did not arrive at Delium until after the Boeotians had quitted Siphae. He encamped and fortified Delium, which is a temple of Apollo. His army dug a trench around the temple and the sacred precinct, the earth which they threw up out of the trench forming a rampart; along this rampart they drove in a double palisade, and cutting down the vines in the neighbourhood of the temple threw them in between. They made a like use of the stones and bricks of the houses near, which they pulled down, and by every means in their power strove to increase the height of the rampart. Where the temple buildings did not extend they erected wooden towers at convenient places; the cloister which

The Athenians under Hippocrates fortify Delium. The main body of the army then leaves the Boeotian territory.

had once existed had fallen down. They began their work on the third day after their departure from Athens, and continued all this day and the next and the following day until the midday meal. When it was nearly finished the army retired from Delium to a distance of a little more than a mile, intending to go home. The greater part of the light-armed troops proceeded on their march, but the hoplites piled their arms and rested. Hippocrates, who had remained behind, was occupied in placing the guards at their posts, and in superintending the completion of that part of the outworks which was still unfinished.

Meanwhile the Boeotians were gathering at Tanagra. 91 All the forces from the different cities had now arrived. They saw that the Athenians were already marching homewards, and most of the Boeotarchs (who are in number eleven) disapproved *The Boeotians at the instigation of Pagondas determine to pursue the Athenians across the border.* of giving battle, because the enemy had left the Boeotian territory. For when the Athenians rested in their march they were just on the borders of Oropia. But Pagondas the son of Aeoladas, one of the two Boeotarchs from Thebes, who was in command at the time (the other being Arianthidas the son of Lysimachidas), [a] wanted to fight [a], believing that the risk was worth encountering. So calling the soldiers to him in successive divisions, that they might not all leave their arms at once, he exhorted the Boeotians to march against the Athenians and to hazard battle, in the following words :—

'Men of Boeotia, no one among us generals should ever 92 have allowed the thought to enter his mind that we ought not to fight with the Athenians, even although we may not overtake them on Boeotian soil. They have crossed our frontier ; it is Boeotia in which they have built a fort, and Boeotia which they intend to lay waste. Our enemies

---

[a] Or, omitting the words 'who was in command at the time': 'wanted to fight while he held the command.'

they clearly are wherever we find them, and therefore
in that country out of which they came

*The Athenians are
our inveterate enemies,
wherever we find them.
They are the aggressors,
and we must defend
ourselves against them
without stopping to
think. Neighbours are
always dangerous, and
they are the most dan-
gerous of all. Once we
were at their mercy;
but we recovered our
liberty at Coronea, and
must again show them
that we cannot be at-
tacked with impunity.*

and did us mischief. But perhaps not
to fight may appear to some one to be
the safer course. Well then, let him
who thinks so think again. When
a man being in full possession of his
own goes out of his way to attack others
because he covets more, he cannot
reflect too much; but when a man is
attacked by another and has to fight for
his own, prudence does not allow of
reflection. In you the temper has been
hereditary which would repel the foreign
invader, whether he be in another's
country or in your own; the Athenian invader above all
others should be thus repelled, because he is your next
neighbour. For among neighbours antagonism is ever
a condition of independence, and against men like these,
who are seeking to enslave not only near but distant
countries, shall we not fight to the last? Look at their
treatment of Euboea just over the strait, and of the greater
part of Hellas. I would have you know, that whereas
other men fight with their neighbours about the lines of
a frontier, for us, if we are conquered, there will be no
more disputing about frontiers, but one fixed boundary,
including our whole country, for the Athenians will come
in and take by force all that we have. So much more
dangerous are they than ordinary neighbours. And men
who, like them, wantonly assail others, will not hesitate to
attack him who remains quietly at home and only defends
himself; but they are not so ready to overbear the
adversary who goes out of his own country to meet them,
and when there is an opportunity strikes first. We have
proved this in our own dealings with the Athenians.
Once, owing to our internal dissensions, they took
possession of our land, but we overcame them at Coronea,

and gave Boeotia that complete security which has lasted to this day[a].   Remember the past: let the elder men among us emulate their own earlier deeds, and the younger who are the sons of those valiant fathers do their best not to tarnish the virtues of their race.   Confident that the God whose temple they have impiously fortified and now occupy will be our champion, and relying on the sacrifices, which are favourable to us, let us advance to meet them. They may satisfy their greed by attacking those who do not defend themselves; but we will show them that from men whose generous spirit ever impels them to fight for the liberties of their country, and who will not see that of others unjustly enslaved,—from such men they will not part without a battle.'

With this exhortation Pagondas persuaded the Boeotians to march against the Athenians, and quickly moved his army forward (for the day was far advanced).   As soon as he approached the enemy he took up a position where a hill intercepted the view, and there drew up his army and prepared for action.

The Boeotian army, numbering not less than eighteen thousand five hundred in all, the Theban division arranged twenty-five deep, appears over the crest of a hill.

Hippocrates, who was still at Delium, heard that the Boeotians were advancing, and sent a message to the army bidding them get into position.   He himself came up shortly afterwards, having left three hundred cavalry at Delium, in order that they might protect the place if assailed, and also might watch their opportunity and attack the Boeotians while the battle was going on.   To these the Boeotians opposed a separate force.   When everything was ready they appeared over the crest of the hill, and halted in the order which they proposed to maintain in the engagement; they numbered about seven thousand hoplites, more than ten thousand light-armed troops, a thousand cavalry, and five hundred targeteers.

---

[a] Cp. iii. 62 fin.

The Thebans and the Boeotians who served in their ranks occupied the right wing. In the centre were the men of Haliartus, Coronea, and Copae, and the other dwellers about the Lake Copais. On the left wing were the Thespians, Tanagraeans, and Orchomenians; the cavalry and light-armed troops were placed on both wings. The Thebans were formed in ranks of five and twenty deep; the formation of the others varied. Such was the character and array of the Boeotian forces.

94   All the hoplites of the Athenian army were arranged in

Numbers of the Athenian hoplites about the same as of the Boeotian: they are drawn up eight deep.

ranks eight deep; in numbers they equalled the hoplites of the enemy; the cavalry were stationed on either wing. No regular light-armed troops accompanied them, for Athens had no organised force of this kind. Those who originally joined the expedition were many times over the number of their opponents; but they were to a great extent without proper arms, for the whole force, strangers as well as citizens, had been called out. Having once started homewards, there were but few of them forthcoming in the engagement. When the Athenians were ranged in order of battle and on the point of advancing, Hippocrates the general, proceeding along the lines, exhorted them as follows:—

95   ' Men of Athens, there is not much time for exhortation,

We are fighting not only to gain Boeotia, but for the safety and liberties of Athens. We ought to have a spirit worthy of her, worthy of the victors at Oeno- phyta.

but to the brave a few words are as good as many; I am only going to remind, not to admonish you[a]. Let no man think that because we are on foreign soil we are running into great danger without cause. Although in Boeotian territory we shall be fighting for our own. If we are victors, the Peloponnesians, deprived of the Boeotian cavalry, will never invade our

---

[a] Cp. iv. 17 med.; iv. 126 init.; v. 69 fin.

land again, so that in one battle you win Boeotia and win
at the same time for Attica a more complete freedom.
Meet them in a spirit worthy of the first city in Hellas—of
that Athens which we are all proud to call our country;
in a spirit too worthy of our fathers, who in times past
under Myronides at Oenophyta overcame these very
Boeotians and conquered their land.'

Thus spoke Hippocrates, and had gone over half the 96
army, not having had time for more,   *The right wing of*
when the Boeotians (to whom Pagondas   *the Athenians over-*
just before engaging had been making   *comes the Boeotians, and*
a second short exhortation) raised the   *the right wing of the*
Boeotians   overcomes
paean, and came down upon them   *the Athenians. On the*
from the hill. The Athenians hastened   *sudden appearance of*
some Boeotian cavalry
forward, and the two armies met at   *the Athenians are finally*
a run. The extreme right and left of   *defeated.*
either army never engaged, for the same reason ; they were
both prevented by water-courses. But the rest closed, and
there was a fierce struggle and pushing of shield against
shield. The left wing of the Boeotians as far as their
centre was worsted by the Athenians, who pressed hard
upon this part of the army, especially upon the Thespians.
For the troops ranged at their side having given way they
were surrounded and hemmed in; and so the Thespians
who perished were cut down fighting hand to hand. Some
of the Athenians themselves in surrounding the enemy
were thrown into confusion and unwittingly slew one
another. On this side then the Boeotians were overcome,
and fled to that part of the army which was still fighting;
but the right wing, where the Thebans were stationed,
overcame the Athenians, and forcing them back, at first
step by step, were following hard upon them, when
Pagondas, seeing that his left wing was in distress, sent
two squadrons of horse unperceived round the hill. They
suddenly appeared over the ridge; the victorious wing of
the Athenians, fancying that another army was attacking
them, was struck with panic; and so at both points, partly

owing to this diversion, and partly to the pressure of the advancing Thebans who broke their line, the rout of the Athenian army became general. Some fled to the sea at Delium, others towards Oropus, others to Mount Parnes, or in any direction which gave hope of safety. The Boeotians, especially their cavalry and that of the Locrians which arrived when the rout had begun, pursued and slaughtered them. Night closed upon the pursuit, and aided the mass of the fugitives in their escape. On the next day those of them who had reached Oropus and Delium, which, though defeated, they still held, were conveyed home by sea. A garrison was left in the place.

97   The Boeotians, after raising a trophy, took up their own dead, and despoiled those of the enemy. They then left them under the care of a guard, and retiring to Tanagra concerted an attack upon Delium. The herald of the Athenians,

The Athenians are refused permission to bury their dead, on the ground that they have been guilty of sacrilege.

as he was on his way to ask for their dead, met a Boeotian herald, who turned him back, declaring that he would get no answer until he had returned himself. He then came before the Athenians and delivered to them the message of the Boeotians, by whom they were accused of transgressing the universally recognised customs of Hellas. Those who invaded the territory of others ever abstained from touching the temples, whereas the Athenians had fortified Delium and were now dwelling there, and doing all that men usually do in an unconsecrated place. They were even drawing, for common use, the water which the Boeotians themselves were forbidden to use except as holy water for the sacrifices. They therefore on behalf both of the God and of themselves, invoking Apollo and all the divinities who had a share in the temple, bade the Athenians depart and carry off what belonged to them.

98   Upon the delivery of this message the Athenians sent to the Boeotians a herald of their own, who on their behalf

declared 'that they had done no wilful injury to the
temple, and would not damage it if they could help it;
they had not originally entered it with any injurious
intent, but in order that from it they
might defend themselves against those *The Athenians de-*
who were really injuring them. Ac- *fend themselves against*
cording to Hellenic practice, they who *the charge of sacrilege,*
were masters of the land, whether *which they retort upon*
their opponents.
much or little, invariably had possession of the temples, to
which they were bound to [a] show the customary reverence,
but in such ways only as were possible [a].   There was
a time when the Boeotians themselves and most other
nations, including all who had driven out the earlier
inhabitants of the land which they now occupied, attacked
the temples of others, and these had in time become their
own.   So the Boeotian temples would have become theirs
if they had succeeded in conquering more of Boeotia.   So
much of the country as they did occupy was their own, and
they did not mean to leave it until compelled. As to
meddling with the water, they could not help themselves;
the use of it was a necessity which they had not incurred
wantonly; they were resisting the Boeotians who had
begun by attacking their territory.   When men were constrained by war, or by some other great calamity, there
was every reason to think that their offence was forgiven
by the God himself.   He who has committed an involuntary misdeed finds a refuge at the altar, and men are said
to transgress, not when they presume a little in their
distress, but when they do evil of their own free will.
The Boeotians, who demanded a sacred place as a ransom
for the bodies of the dead, were guilty of a far greater
impiety than the Athenians who refused to make such an
unseemly exchange.   They desired the Boeotians to let
them take away their dead, not adding the condition " if
they would quit Boeotia," for in fact they were in a spot

---

[a] Or, ' were bound to show reverence in such ways as they could in
addition to the customary observances.'

which they had fairly won by arms and not in Boeotia, but simply saying, "if they would make a truce according to ancestral custom." '

99   The Boeotians replied that if they were in Boeotia they

The Boeotians quibble about the spot in which the dead bodies lie.

might take what belonged to them, but must depart out of it; if they were in their own land they could do as they pleased. They knew that the territory of Oropus, in which the dead lay (for the battle took place on the border), was actually in the possession of Athens, but that the Athenians could not take them away without their leave, ª and they were unwilling as they pretended to make a truce respecting a piece of ground which did not belong to them ª. And to say in their reply 'that if they would quit Boeotian ground they might take what they asked for,' sounded plausible. Thereupon the Athenian herald departed, leaving his purpose unaccomplished.

100   The Boeotians immediately sent for javelin-men and

They attack, and, by the help of an ingenious machine, take Delium seventeen days after the battle.

slingers from the Malian Gulf. They had been joined after the battle by the Corinthians with two thousand hoplites, and by the Peloponnesian garrison which had evacuated Nisaea ᵇ, as well as by some Megarians. They now marched against Delium and attacked the rampart, employing among other military devices an engine, with which they succeeded in taking the place; it was of the following description. They sawed in two and hollowed out a great beam, which they joined together again very exactly, like a flute, and suspended a vessel by chains at the end of the beam; the iron mouth of a bellows directed downwards into the vessel was attached to the beam, of which a great part was itself overlaid with iron. This machine they brought

---

ª Or, taking δῆθεν with ὑπὲρ τῆς ἐκείνων: 'and they were unwilling to make a truce respecting a piece of ground which was claimed by the Athenians.'   ᵇ Cp. iv. 69 fin.

up from a distance on carts to various points of the rampart where vine stems and wood had been most extensively used, and when it was quite near the wall they applied a large bellows to their own end of the beam, and blew through it. The blast, prevented from escaping, passed into the vessel which contained burning coals and sulphur and pitch; these made a huge flame, and set fire to the rampart, so that no one could remain upon it. The garrison took flight, and the fort was taken. Some were slain; two hundred were captured; but the greater number got on board their ships and so reached home.

Delium was captured seventeen days after the battle. 101 The Athenian herald came shortly afterwards in ignorance of its fate to ask again for the dead, and now the Boeotians, instead of repeating their former answer, gave them up. In the battle the Boeotians lost somewhat less than five hundred; the Athenians not quite a thousand, and Hippocrates their general; also a great number of light-armed troops and baggage-bearers.

They now give up the dead, numbering about a thousand; among them is Hippocrates the general.

Shortly after the battle of Delium, Demosthenes, on the failure of the attempt to betray Siphae, against which he had sailed with forty ships[a], employed the Agraean and Acarnanian troops together with four hundred Athenian hoplites whom he had on board in a descent on the Sicyonian coast. Before all the fleet had reached the shore the Sicyonians came out against the invaders, put to flight those who had landed, and pursued them to their ships, killing some, and making prisoners of others. They then erected a trophy, and gave back the dead under a flag of truce.

Failure of a descent made by Demosthenes on Sicyonia.

While the affair of Delium was going on, Sitalces the Odrysian king died; he had been engaged in an ex-

---

[a] Cp. iv. 77 init., 89.

pedition against the Triballi, by whom he was defeated in

Death of Sitalces, who is succeeded by his nephew Seuthes.

battle. Seuthes the son of Spara-docus[a], his nephew, succeeded him in the kingdom of the Odrysians and the rest of his Thracian dominions.

102   During the same winter, Brasidas and his Chalcidian

The first, second, and third foundation of Amphipolis.

allies made an expedition against Amphipolis upon the river Strymon, the Athenian colony. The place where the city now stands is the same which Aristagoras of

B.C. 497.
Ol. 70, 4.

Miletus in days of old, when he was fleeing from King Darius, attempted to colonise; he was driven out by

B.C. 465.
Ol. 78, 4.

the Edonians[b]. Two and thirty years afterwards the Athenians made another attempt; they sent a colony of ten thousand, made up partly of their own citizens, partly of any others who liked to join; but these also were attacked by the Thracians at Drabescus, and perished[c]. Twenty-nine years later the Athenians came again, under the leadership of Hagnon the son of Nicias,

B.C. 437.
Ol. 85, 4.

drove out the Edonians, and built a town on the same spot, which was formerly called 'The Nine Ways.' Their base of operations was Eion, a market and seaport which they already possessed, at the mouth of the river, about three miles from the site of the present town. Wanting to enclose the newly-founded city, which on two sides is surrounded by the river Strymon, Hagnon cut it off by a long wall reaching from the upper part of the river to the lower, and called the place Amphipolis, because it strikes the eye both by sea and land.

103   Against Amphipolis Brasidas now led his army. Starting

Brasidas is received by the inhabitants of Argilus, who conduct his army to the bridge near Amphipolis.

from Arnae in Chalcidicè, towards evening he reached Aulon and Bro-miscus at the point where the lake Bolbè flows into the sea; having there supped, he marched on during the

---

[a] Cp. ii. 101 fin.   [b] Cp. Herod. v. 124.   [c] Cp. i. 100 fin.

night.   The weather was wintry and somewhat snowy;
and so he pushed on all the quicker; he was hoping that
his approach might be known at Amphipolis only to those
who were in the secret.   There dwelt in the place settlers
from Argilus, a town which was originally colonised from
Andros; these and others aided in the attempt, instigated
some by Perdiccas, others by the Chalcidians.   The town
of Argilus is not far off, and the inhabitants were always
suspected by the Athenians, and were always conspiring
against Amphipolis.   For some time past, ever since the
arrival of Brasidas had given them an opportunity, they
had been concerting measures with their countrymen inside
the walls for the surrender of the city.   They now revolted
from the Athenians on that very night, and received him
into their town, and before dawn [a] they conducted the army
to the bridge over the river, which is at some distance
from the town.   At that time no walls had been built down
to the river, as they have since been; a small guard was
posted there.   Brasidas easily overcame the guard, owing
partly to the plot within the walls, partly to the severity
of the weather and the suddenness of his attack; he then
crossed the bridge, and at once was master of all the
possessions of the Amphipolitans outside the walls.   For
they lived scattered about in the country.

The passage of the river was a complete surprise to the 104
citizens within the walls.   Many who
happened to be outside were taken. *The country outside
the walls is now at his*
Others fled into the town.   The Am- *mercy.   He is anxious*
phipolitans were in great consternation, *to take the place before*
for they suspected one another.   [b] It *Thucydides arrives,*
is even said that Brasidas, if, instead of allowing his army
to plunder, he had marched direct to the place, would
probably [b] have captured it.   But he merely occupied
a position, and overran the country outside the walls;

---

[a] Reading πρὸ ἔω.   [b] Or, 'It is said to have been the impression
that Brasidas' &c., omitting 'probably.'

and then, finding that his confederates within failed in accomplishing their part, he took no further step. Meanwhile the opponents of the conspirators, being superior in number, prevented the immediate opening of the gates, and acting with Eucles, the general to whose care the place had been committed by the Athenians, sent for help to the other general in Chalcidicè, Thucydides the son of Olorus, who wrote this history; he was then at Thasos, an island colonised from Paros, and distant from Amphipolis about half a day's sail. As soon as he heard the tidings he sailed quickly to Amphipolis with seven ships which happened to be on the spot; he wanted to get into Amphipolis if possible before it could capitulate, or at any rate to occupy Eion.

105   Meanwhile Brasidas, fearing the arrival of the ships from Thasos, and hearing that Thucydides had the right of working gold mines in the neighbouring district of Thrace, and was consequently one of the leading men of the country, did his utmost to get possession of the city before his arrival. He was afraid that, if Thucydides once came, the people of Amphipolis would no longer be disposed to surrender. For their hope would be that he would bring in allies from the islands or maritime towns or from the interior of Thrace, and relieve them. He therefore offered moderate terms, proclaiming that any Amphipolitan or Athenian might either remain in the city and have the enjoyment of his property on terms of equality; or, if he preferred, might depart, taking his goods with him, within five days.

and therefore offers moderate terms,

106   When the people heard the proclamation they began to waver; for very few of the citizens were Athenians, the greater number being a mixed multitude. Many within the walls were relatives of those who had been captured outside. In their alarm they thought the terms reasonable; the Athenian

which are accepted by the inhabitants. Thucydides saves Eion, but is too late to save Amphipolis.

population because they were too glad to withdraw, reflecting how much greater their share of the danger was, and not expecting speedy relief; the rest of the people because they retained all their existing rights, and were delivered from a fate which seemed inevitable. The partisans of Brasidas now proceeded to justify his proposals without disguise, for they saw that the mind of the whole people had changed, and that they no longer paid any regard to the Athenian general who was on the spot. So his terms were accepted, and the city was surrendered and delivered up to him. On the evening of the same day Thucydides and his ships sailed into Eion, but not until Brasidas had taken possession of Amphipolis, missing Eion only by a night. For if the ships had not come to the rescue with all speed, the place would have been in his hands on the next morning.

Thucydides now put Eion in a state of defence, desiring 107 to provide not only against any im- *Brasidas sails down* mediate attempt of Brasidas, but also *the river to Eion, but* against future danger. He received *fails in taking the place.* the fugitives who had chosen to quit Amphipolis according to the agreement and wished to come into Eion. Brasidas suddenly sailed with a number of small craft down the river to Eion, hoping that he might take the point which runs out from the wall, and thereby command the entrance to the harbour; at the same time he made an attack by land. But in both these attempts he was foiled. Whereupon he returned, and took measures for the settlement of Amphipolis. Myrcinus a city in the Edonian country joined him, Pittacus the king of the Edonians having been assassinated by the children of Goaxis and Brauro his wife. Soon afterwards Galepsus and Oesymè (both colonies from Thasos) came over to him. Perdiccas likewise arrived shortly after the taking of Amphipolis, and assisted him in settling the newly-acquired towns.

The Athenians were seriously alarmed at the loss of 108

Amphipolis; the place was very useful to them, and supplied them with a revenue, and with
timber which they imported for ship-
building.   As far as the Strymon the
Lacedaemonians could always have
found a way to the allies of Athens, if
the Thessalians allowed them to pass;
but until they gained possession of the
bridge they could proceed no further,
because, for a long way above, the
river forms a large lake, and below,
towards Eion, there were triremes on guard.   All difficulty
seemed now to be removed, and the Athenians feared that
more of their allies would revolt.   For Brasidas in all his
actions showed himself reasonable, and whenever he made
a speech lost no opportunity of declaring that he was sent
to emancipate Hellas.   The cities which were subject to
Athens, when they heard of the taking of Amphipolis and
of his promises and of his gentleness, were more impatient
than ever to rise, and privately sent embassies to him,
asking him to come and help them, every one of them
wanting to be first.   They thought that there was no
danger, for they had under-estimated the Athenian power,
which afterwards proved its greatness and the magnitude
of their mistake; they judged rather by their own illusive
wishes than by the safe rule of prudence.   For such
is the manner of men; what they like is always seen by
them in the light of unreflecting hope, what they dislike
they peremptorily set aside by an arbitrary conclusion.
Moreover, the Athenians had lately received a blow in
Boeotia, and Brasidas told the allies what was likely to
attract them, but untrue, that at Nisaea the Athenians had
refused to fight with his unassisted forces[a].   And so they
grew bold, and were quite confident that no army would
ever reach them.   Above all, they were influenced by the

The Athenians are alarmed at the revolt of Amphipolis because it opens the way to their other allies in Thrace. The revolting cities miscalculated, but it was natural that they should be influenced by the character of Brasidas. Jealousy of his enterprises at Sparta.

---

[a] Cp. iv. 73, 85 fin.

pleasurable excitement of the moment; they were now for the first time going to find out of what the Lacedaemonians were capable when in real earnest, and therefore they were willing to risk anything. The Athenians were aware of their disaffection, and as far as they could, at short notice and in winter time, sent garrisons to the different cities. Brasidas also despatched a message to the Lacedaemonians requesting them to let him have additional forces, and he himself began to build triremes on the Strymon. But they would not second his efforts because their leading men were jealous of him, and also because they preferred to recover the prisoners taken in the island and bring the war to an end.

In the same winter the Megarians recovered their Long 109 Walls which had been in the hands of the Athenians [a], and razed them to the ground.

Recovery of their Long Walls by the Megarians.

After the taking of Amphipolis, Brasidas and his allies marched to the so-called Actè, or coast-land, which runs out from the canal made by the Persian King and extends into the peninsula; it ends in Athos, a high mountain projecting into the Aegean sea [b]. There are cities in the peninsula, of which one is Sanè, an Andrian colony on the edge of the canal looking towards the sea in the direction of Euboea; the others are Thyssus, Cleonae, Acrothoi, Olophyxus, and Dium; their inhabitants are a mixed multitude of barbarians, speaking Greek as well as their native tongue. A few indeed are Chalcidian; but the greater part are Pelasgians (sprung from the Tyrrhenians who once inhabited Lemnos and Athens), or Bisaltians, Crestonians, Edonians. They all dwell in small cities. Most of them joined Brasidas, but Sanè and Dium held out; whereupon he remained there for a time and wasted their territory.

Description of Actè and its cities. Brasidas marches thither, and is joined by most of them.

---

[a] Cp. iv. 68, 69.   [b] Cp. Herod. vii. 22.

110   Finding that they would not yield, he promptly made
Brasidas makes an an expedition against Toronè in Chalcid-
expedition against To- icè, which was held by the Athenians.
ronè. He halts outside He was invited by a few of the in-
the town, and contrives
to introduce a few of his habitants, who were ready to deliver
soldiers.   the city into his hands.   Arriving at
night, or about daybreak, he took up a position at the
temple of the Dioscuri, which is distant about three
furlongs from the city.   The great body of the inhabitants
and the Athenian garrison never discovered him; but
those Toronaeans who were in his interest, and knew
that he was coming, were awaiting his approach; some
few of them had privately gone to meet him.   When his
confederates found that he had arrived, they introduced
into the city, under the command of Lysistratus an
Olynthian, seven light-armed soldiers carrying daggers
(for of twenty who had been originally appointed to that
service, only seven had the courage to enter).   These
men slipped in undiscovered by way of the wall where
it looks towards the sea.   They ascended the side of the
hill on the slope of which the city is built, and slew
the sentinels posted on the summit; they then began to
break down the postern-gate towards the promontory of
Canastraeum.

111   Meanwhile Brasidas advanced a little with the rest of
They and his par- his army, and then halting, sent forward
tisans in Toronè break a hundred targeteers, that as soon as
open a postern-gate. any of the gates were opened, and the
signal agreed upon displayed, they might rush in first.
There was a delay, and they, wondering what had happened,
drew by degrees nearer and nearer to the city.   Their
partisans in Toronè, acting with the soldiers who had
already got inside, had now broken through the postern-
gate, and proceeded to cut the bar which fastened the
gates near the market-place.   They then brought round
some of the targeteers by way of the postern-gate, and
introduced them into the city, hoping to strike panic into

the unconscious citizens by the sudden appearance of an armed force in their rear and on both sides of them at once. Their next step was to raise the fire-signal according to agreement; they then received the rest of the targeteers through the gates by the market-place.

Brasidas, when he saw the signal, gave his army the 112 word to advance, and ran forward. *The army of Brasi-* Raising with one voice a shout which *das, on a signal given* struck great terror into the inhabitants, *from the town, rush in.* they followed him. Some of them dashed in by the gates; others found a way in at a place where the wall had fallen down and was being repaired, getting up by some planks which were placed against it, intended for drawing up stones. He himself with the main body of his army ascended to the upper part of the city, wanting to make the capture thorough and secure; the rest of his soldiers overran the town.

While the capture was proceeding the Toronaeans 113 generally, who knew nothing about the *The Athenian gar-* plot, were in confusion. The con- *rison take refuge in* spirators and their party at once joined *Lecythus.* the assailants. Of the Athenian hoplites, who to the number of fifty chanced to be sleeping in the Agora, a few were cut down at once, but the greater number, when they saw what had happened, fled, some by land, others to the Athenian guard-ships, of which two were on the spot, and reached safely the fort of Lecythus, a high point of the city which the Athenians had occupied and retained in their own hands; it runs out into the sea, and is only joined to the mainland by a narrow isthmus; thither fled also such Toronaeans as were friendly to the Athenians.

It was now daylight, and the city being completely in 114 his power, Brasidas made proclamation to the Toronaeans who had taken refuge with the Athenians, that if they liked they might come out and return to their homes; they would suffer no harm in the city. He also sent a herald to the Athenians, bidding them take what was their own and depart under a flag of truce out of Lecythus. The place,

Brasidas summons the Athenians to sur-render. At their request he grants them a short truce. He addresses pacific words to the people of Toronè. he said, belonged to the Chalcidians, and not to them. They refused to go, but asked him to make a truce with them for a day, that they might take up their dead, and he granted them two days. During these two days he fortified the buildings which were near Lecythus, and the Athenians strengthened the fort itself. He then called a meeting of the Toronaeans, and addressed them much in the same terms which he had used at Acanthus[a]. He told them that they ought not to think badly of those citizens who had aided him, much less to deem them traitors; for they were not bribed and had not acted with any view of enslaving the city, but in the interest of her freedom and welfare. Those of the inhabitants who had not joined in the plot were not to suppose that they would fare worse than the rest; for he had not come thither to destroy either the city or any of her citizens. In this spirit he had made the proclamation to those who had taken refuge with the Athenians, and he thought none the worse of them for being their friends; when they had a similar experience of the Lacedaemonians their attach-ment to them would be still greater, for they would recognise their superior honesty; they were only afraid of them now because they did not know them. They must all make up their minds to be faithful allies, and expect henceforward to be held responsible if they offended; but in the past the Lacedaemonians had not been wronged by them; on the contrary, it was they who had been wronged by a power too great for them, and were to be excused if they had opposed him.

115   With these words he encouraged the citizens. On the expiration of the truce he made his intended attack upon Lecythus. The Athenians defended themselves

---

[a] Cp. iv. 85–87.

from the fortress, which was weak, and from some houses
which had battlements. For a whole
day they repulsed the assault; but
on the morrow an engine was brought
against them, from which the Lacedaemonians proposed to throw fire upon the wooden
breastwork. Just as the army was drawing near the wall,
the Athenians raised a wooden tower upon the top of
a building at a point where the approach was easiest and
where they thought that the enemy would be most likely
to apply the engine. To this tower they carried up
numerous jars and casks of water and great stones; and
many men mounted upon it. Suddenly the building, being
too heavily weighted, fell in with a loud crash. This
only annoyed and did not much alarm the Athenians who
were near and saw what had happened, but the rest were
terrified, and their fright was the greater in proportion as
they were further off. They thought that the place had
been taken at that spot, and fled as fast as they could to
the sea where their ships lay.

The fall of a wooden tower frightens the Athenians, who fly to their ships.

　　Brasidas witnessed the accident and observed that they
were abandoning the battlements. He
at once rushed forward with his army,
captured the fort, and put to death all
whom he found in it. Thus the
Athenians were driven out; and in their ships of war and
other vessels crossed over to Pallenè. There happened
to be in Lecythus a temple of Athenè; and when Brasidas
was about to storm the place he had made a proclamation
that he who first mounted the wall should receive thirty
minae[a]; but now, believing that the capture had been
effected by some more than human power, he gave the
thirty minae to the Goddess for the service of the temple,
and then pulling down Lecythus and clearing the ground,
he consecrated the whole place. The rest of this winter he

Brasidas takes the fort of Lecythus and puts to death those who are found in it.

116

------

[a] About £100.

spent in settling the administration of the towns which he already held, and in concerting measures against the rest.   At the end of the winter ended the eighth year of the war.

117   Early in the following spring the Lacedaemonians and

*The Athenians be-
cause they are appre-
hensive of the growing
success of Brasidas, the
Lacedaemonians   be-
cause they want to re-
cover the captives, make
peace for a year.*

Athenians made a truce for a year. The Athenians hoped to prevent Brasidas from gaining over any more of their allies for the present; the interval would give them leisure for preparation; and hereafter, if it was for their interest, they might come to a general understanding.   The Lacedaemonians had truly divined the fears of the Athenians, and thought that, having enjoyed an intermission of trouble and hardship, they would be more anxious to make terms, restore the captives taken in the island, and conclude a durable peace.   Their main object was to recover their men while the good fortune of Brasidas lasted; when, owing to his successful career and the balance which he had established between the contending powers, they did not feel the loss of them, and yet by retaliating on equal terms with the remainder of their forces might have a fair prospect of victory[n].   So they made a truce for themselves and their allies in the following terms:—

118   'I. Concerning the temple and oracle of the Pythian

Terms of peace.

Apollo, it seems good to us that any one who will shall ask counsel thereat without fraud and without fear, according to his ancestral customs.   To this we, the Lacedaemonians and their allies here present, agree, and we will send heralds to the Boeotians and Phocians, and do our best to gain their assent likewise.

'II. Concerning the treasures of the God, we will take

---

[n] See the note on this passage in Barton and Chavasse's edition of Thucydides, Book IV.

measures for the detection of evil-doers, both you and we, according to our ancestral customs, and any one else who will, according to his ancestral customs, proceeding always with right and equity. Thus it seems good to the Lacedaemonians and their allies in respect of these matters.

'III. It further seems good to the Lacedaemonians and their allies that, if the Athenians consent to a truce, either party shall remain within his own territory, retaining what he has. The Athenians at Coryphasium shall keep between Buphras and Tomeus. They shall remain at Cythera[a], but shall not communicate with the Lacedaemonian confederacy, neither we with them nor they with us. The Athenians who are in Nisaea[b] and Minoa[c] shall not cross the road which leads from the gates of the shrine of Nisus to the temple of Poseidon, and from the temple of Poseidon goes direct to the bridge leading to Minoa; neither shall the Megarians and their allies cross this road; the Athenians shall hold the island which they have taken, neither party communicating with the other. They shall also hold what they now hold near Troezen[d], according to the agreement concluded between the Athenians and Troezenians.

'IV. At sea the Lacedaemonians and their allies may sail along their own coasts and the coasts of the confederacy, not in ships of war, but in any other rowing vessel whose burden does not exceed five hundred talents[e].

'V. There shall be a safe-conduct both by sea and land for a herald, with envoys and any number of attendants which may be agreed upon, passing to and fro between Peloponnesus and Athens, to make arrangements about the termination of the war and about the arbitration of disputed points.

'VI. While the truce lasts, neither party, neither we nor you, shall receive deserters, either bond or free.

---

[a] Cp. iv. 53, 54. [b] Cp. iv. 69. [c] Cp. iii. 51. [d] Cp. iv. 45.
[e] About 12 tons.

'VII. And we will give satisfaction to you and you shall give satisfaction to us according to our ancestral customs, and determine disputed points by arbitration and not by arms.

'These things seem good to us, the Lacedaemonians, and to our allies. But if you deem any other condition more just or honourable, go to Lacedaemon and explain your views; neither the Lacedaemonians nor their allies will reject any just claim which you may prefer.

'And we desire you, as you desire us, to send envoys invested with full powers.

'This truce shall be for a year.'

'The Athenian people passed the following decree. The
During the armistice prytanes were of the tribe Acamantis,
heralds and envoys are Phaenippus was the registrar, Niciades
to pass to and fro and was the president. Laches moved that
discuss the terms of a a truce be concluded on the terms to
permanent peace. which the Lacedaemonians and their
allies had consented; and might it be for the best interests of the Athenian people! Accordingly the assembly agreed that the truce shall last for a year, beginning from this day, being the fourteenth day of the month Elaphebolion[a]. During the year of truce ambassadors and heralds are to go from one state to another and discuss proposals for the termination of the war. The generals and prytanes shall proceed to hold another assembly, at which the people shall discuss, first of all, the question of peace, whatever proposal the Lacedaemonian embassy may offer about the termination of the war. The embassies now present shall bind themselves on the spot, in the presence of the assembly, to abide for a year by the truce just made.'

119   To these terms the Lacedaemonians assented, and they
Formal ratification of and their allies took oath to the Athen-
the truce. ians and their allies on the twelfth day
of the Spartan month Gerastius. Those who formally

a March—April.

ratified the truce were, on behalf of Lacedaemon, Taurus the son of Echetimidas, Athenaeus the son of Periclidas, Philocharidas the son of Eryxidaidas; of Corinth, Aeneas the son of Ocytus, Euphamidas the son of Aristonymus; of Sicyon, Damotimus the son of Naucrates, Onasimus the son of Megacles; of Megara, Nicasus the son of Cecalus, Menecrates the son of Amphidorus; of Epidaurus, Amphias the son of Eupaïdas; and on behalf of Athens, Nicostratus the son of Diitrephes, Nicias the son of Niceratus, Autocles the son of Tolmaeus. Such were the terms of the armistice; during its continuance fresh negotiations for a final peace were constantly carried on.

About the time when the envoys engaged in the negotia- 120 tions were passing to and fro, Scionè, *Meanwhile Scionè* a town of Pallenè, revolted from the *revolts. Brasidas sails* Athenians and joined Brasidas. The *thither by night in a* Scionaeans, according to their own *small boat, and having summoned the citizens,* account, sprang originally from Pellenè *warmly praises their* in Peloponnesus, but their ancestors *conduct.* returning from Troy were carried by the storm which the Achaean fleet encountered to Scionè, where they took up their abode. Brasidas, when he heard of the revolt, sailed thither by night, sending before him a friendly trireme, while he himself followed at some distance in a small boat, thinking that if he met any vessel, not a trireme, larger than the boat, the trireme would protect him [a], while if another trireme of equal strength came up, it would fall, not upon the boat, but upon the larger vessel, and in the meantime he would be able to save himself. He succeeded in crossing, and having summoned a meeting of the Scionaeans, he repeated what he had said at Acanthus and Toronè, adding that their conduct was deserving of the highest praise; for at a time when the Athenians were holding Potidaea and the isthmus of Pallenè, and they, being cut off from the mainland, were

---

[a] Reading αὐτῷ; or, reading αὐτή, ‘the mere presence of the trireme would protect him.’

as defenceless as if they had been islanders, they had taken the side of liberty unbidden. They were not such cowards as to wait until they were compelled to do what was obviously for their own interest; and this was a sufficient proof that they would endure like men any hardships, however great, if only their aspirations could be realised. He should reckon them the truest and most loyal friends of the Lacedaemonians, and pay them the highest honour.

121   The Scionaeans were inspirited by his words; and one

Honours showered on Brasidas. He enters into communication with Mendè and Potidaea.

and all, even those who had previously been against the movement, took courage and determined to bear cheerfully the burdens of the war. They received Brasidas with honour, and in the name of the city crowned him with a golden crown as the liberator of Hellas; many too, in token of their personal admiration, placed garlands on his head, and congratulated him, as if he had been a victor in the games. For the present he left a small garrison with them and returned, but soon afterwards again crossed the sea with a larger army, being desirous, now that he had the help of the Scionaeans, to attempt Mendè and Potidaea; he made sure that the Athenians would follow him with their ships to Pallenè, which they would consider an island; and he wished to anticipate them. Moreover he had entered into negotiations with these cities, and had some hope of their being betrayed to him.

122   But before he had executed his intentions, a trireme

Meanwhile he is stopped in his career by the announcement of the truce, which had really been made before the revolt of Scionè. Brasidas refuses to give the place up. Fury of the Athenians.

arrived conveying the ambassadors who went round to proclaim the truce, Aristonymus from Athens, and Athenaeus from Lacedaemon. His army then returned to Toronè, and the truce was formally announced to him. All the allies of the Lacedaemonians in Chalcidicè agreed to the terms. Aristonymus the Athenian assented generally, but finding on a calculation of the days that the Scionaeans had revolted after the conclusion of the truce, refused to admit them. Brasidas insisted that they were in time, and would not surrender the city. Whereupon Aristonymus despatched a message to Athens. The Athenians were ready at once to make an expedition against Scionè. The Lacedaemonians, however, sent an embassy to them and protested that such a step would be a breach of the truce. They laid claim to the place, relying on the testimony of Brasidas, and proposed to have the matter decided by arbitration. But the Athenians, instead of risking an arbitration, wanted to send an expedition instantly ; for they were exasperated at discovering that even the islanders were now daring to revolt from them, in a futile reliance on the Lacedaemonian power by land. The greater right was on their side ; for the truth was that the Scionaeans had revolted two days after the truce was made. They instantly carried a resolution, moved by Cleon, to destroy Scionè and put the citizens to the sword ; and, while abstaining from hostilities elsewhere, they prepared to carry out their intentions.

In the meantime Mendè, a city of Pallenè and an 123 Eretrian colony, revolted from them. *Brasidas receives the* Brasidas felt justified in receiving the *Mendaeans after the* Mendaeans, although, when they came *declaration of the truce.* to him, the peace had unmistakably been declared, because there were certain points in which he too charged the Athenians with violating the treaty. His attitude encouraged them to take this bold step ; they saw his zeal in the cause, which they likewise inferred from his unwillingness to hand over Scionè to the Athenians. Moreover the persons who negotiated with him were few in number, and having once begun, would not give up their purpose. For they feared the consequences of detection, and therefore compelled the multitude to act contrary to their own wishes. When the Athenians heard of the revolt they were more angry than ever, and made preparations against both cities. Brasidas, in expectation of their attack, conveyed away the wives and children of the Scionaeans [a] and Mendaeans to Olynthus in Chalcidicè, and sent over five hundred Peloponnesian hoplites and three hundred Chalcidian targeteers, under the sole command of Polydamidas, to their aid. The two cities concerted measures for their defence against the Athenians, who were expected shortly to arrive.

124   Brasidas and Perdiccas now joined their forces, and

Brasidas and Per- made a second expedition to Lyncus
diccas again invade the against Arrhibaeus. Perdiccas led his
country of Arrhibaeus own Macedonian army and a force of
and defeat his army. hoplites supplied by the Hellenic inhabitants of the country. Brasidas, beside the Peloponnesians who remained with him, had under his command a body of Chalcidians from Acanthus and other cities which supplied as many troops as they severally could. The entire heavy-armed Hellenic forces numbered about three thousand; the Chalcidian and Macedonian cavalry nearly a thousand, and there was also a great multitude of barbarians. They entered the territory of Arrhibaeus, and there finding the Lyncestians ready for battle, they took up a position in face of them. The infantry of the two armies was stationed upon two opposite hills, and between them was a plain, into which the cavalry of both first descended and fought. Then the Lyncestian heavy-armed troops began to advance from the hill, and forming a junction with their cavalry, offered battle. Brasidas and Perdiccas now drew out their army and charged; the Lyncestians were put to flight and many slain; the rest escaped to the high ground, and there remained inactive. The conquerors raised a trophy, and waited for two or three days expecting the arrival of some Illyrians whom Perdiccas had hired. Then Perdiccas wanted, instead of sitting idle, to push on against the villages of Arrhibaeus, but Brasidas was anxious about Mendè, and apprehensive that the

---

[a] But cp. v. 32 init.

Athenians might sail thither and do some mischief before he returned. The Illyrians had not appeared ; and for both reasons he was more disposed to retreat than to advance.

But while they were disputing, the news arrived that the 125 Illyrians had just betrayed Perdiccas and joined Arrhibaeus, whereupon they both resolved to retreat ; for they were afraid of the Illyrians, who are a nation of warriors. Owing to the dispute nothing had been determined respecting the time of their departure.

Meanwhile some Illyrians who had been hired by Perdiccas, join Arrhibaeus. This treachery causes panic and flight in the army of Perdiccas. The Illyrians pursue.

Night came on, and the Macedonians and the mass of the barbarians were instantly seized with one of those unaccountable panics to which great armies are liable[a]. They fancied that the Illyrians were many times their real number, and that they were close at their heels ; so, suddenly betaking themselves to flight, they hastened homewards. And they compelled Perdiccas, when he understood the state of affairs, which at first he did not, to go away without seeing Brasidas, for the two armies were encamped at a considerable distance from one another. At dawn Brasidas, finding that Arrhibaeus and the Illyrians were coming on and that the Macedonians had already decamped, resolved to follow them. So he formed his hoplites into a compact square, and placed his light-armed troops in the centre. He selected the youngest of his soldiers to run out upon the enemy at whatever point the attack might be made. He himself proposed during the retreat to take his post in the rear with three hundred chosen men, meaning to stop the foremost of his assailants and beat them off. Before the Illyrians came up he exhorted his soldiers, as far as the shortness of the time permitted, in the following words :—

'Did I not suspect, men of Peloponnesus, that you may 126 be terrified because you have been deserted by your

---

[a] Cp. vii. 80 med.

companions and are assailed by a host of barbarians, I
should think only of encouraging and
not of instructing you [a]．But now that
we are left alone in the face of numerous enemies, I shall endeavour in
a few words to impress upon you the
main points which it concerns you to
be informed of and to remember．For
you ought to fight like men not merely
when you happen to have allies present,
but because courage is native to you;
nor should you fear any number of
foreign troops．Remember that in the cities from which
you come, not the many govern the few, but the few
govern the many, and have acquired their supremacy
simply by successful fighting．Your enemies are barbarians, and you in your inexperience fear them．But
you ought to know, from your late conflicts with the
Macedonian portion of them [b]—and any estimate which
I can form, or account of them which I receive from others,
would lead me to infer—that they will not prove so very
formidable．An enemy often has weak points which wear
the appearance of strength ; and these, when their nature
is explained, encourage rather than frighten their oppo-
nents．As, on the other hand, where an army has a real
advantage, the adversary who is the most ignorant is also
the most foolhardy．The Illyrians, to those who have no
experience of them, do indeed at first sight present a
threatening aspect．The spectacle of their numbers is
terrible, their cries are intolerable, and the brandishing of
their spears in the air has a menacing effect．But in action
they are not the men they look, if their opponents will
only stand their ground ; for they have no regular order,
and therefore are not ashamed of leaving any post in which
they are hard pressed ; to fly and to advance being alike

Brasidas encourages his troops : You are few against many, but so you are at home ; and you are fighting against barbarians．Do not be frightened by their outlandish cries and gestures．They make a vain flourish but have no discipline, and, if withstood quietly, retreat.

---

[a] Cp iv. 17 med. ; iv. 95 init. ; v. 69 fin.　　[b] Cp. iv. 124 med.

honourable, no imputation can be thrown on their courage. When every man is his own master in battle he will readily find a decent excuse for saving himself. They clearly think that to frighten us at a safe distance is a better plan than to meet us hand to hand; else why do they shout instead of fighting? You may easily see that all the terrors with which you have invested them are in reality nothing; they do but startle the sense of sight and hearing. If you repel their tumultuous onset, and, when opportunity offers, withdraw again in good order, keeping your ranks, you will sooner arrive at a place of safety, and will also learn the lesson that mobs like these, if an adversary withstand their first attack, do but threaten at a distance and make a flourish of valour, although if he yields to them they are quick enough to show their courage in following at his heels when there is no danger.'

Brasidas, having addressed his army, began to retreat. 127 Whereupon the barbarians with loud noise and in great disorder pressed hard upon him, supposing that he was flying, and that they could overtake *The Illyrians, finding that they make no impression, seize a pass on the border.* and destroy his troops. But, wherever they attacked, the soldiers appointed for the purpose ran out and met them, and Brasidas himself with his chosen men received their charge. Thus the first onset of the barbarians met with a resistance which surprised them, and whenever they renewed the attack the Lacedaemonians received and repelled them again, and when they ceased, proceeded with their march. Thereupon the greater part of the barbarians abstained from attacking Brasidas and his Hellenes in the open country; but leaving a certain number to follow and harass them, they ran on after the fugitive Macedonians and killed any with whom they fell in. They then secured beforehand the narrow pass between two hills which led into the country of Arrhibaeus, knowing that this was the only path by which Brasidas could retreat. And as he was approaching the most dangerous point of the defile they began to surround him in the hope of cutting him off.

128   Perceiving their intention, he told his three hundred to

Brasidas dislodges them, and they follow no further. Ill-feeling increases between Brasidas and Perdiccas.

leave their ranks and run every man as fast as he could to the top of one of the hills, being the one which he thought the barbarians would be most likely to occupy ; and before a larger number of them could come up and surround them, to dislodge those who were already there [a]. They accordingly attacked and defeated them ; and so the main body of his army more easily reached the summit ; for the barbarians, seeing their comrades defeated and driven from the high ground, took alarm ; they considered too that the enemy were already on the borders of the country, and had got away from them, and therefore followed no further. Brasidas had now gainèd the high ground and could march unmolested ; on the same day he arrived at Arnissa, which is in the dominion of Perdiccas. The soldiers were enraged at the hasty retreat of the Macedonians, and when they came upon carts of theirs drawn by oxen, or any baggage which had been dropped in the flight, as was natural in a retreat made in a panic and by night, they of themselves loosed the oxen and slaughtered them, and appropriated the baggage. From that time forward Perdiccas regarded Brasidas in the light of a foe, and conceived a new hatred of the Peloponnesians, which was not a natural feeling in an enemy of the Athenians. Nevertheless, disregarding his own nearest interests, he took steps to make terms with the one and get rid of the other.

129   Brasidas returned from Macedonia to Toronè, and when

Nicias attempts to take Mendè, but fails.

he arrived there found the Athenians already in possession of Mendè. Thinking it now too late to cross over to Pallenè and assist Mendè and Scionè, he remained quiet and guarded

---

[a] Adopting with Poppo the correction ἐπόντας.

Toronè. While he was engaged with the Lyncestians, the Athenians, having completed their preparations, had sailed against Mendè and Scionè with fifty ships, of which ten were Chian, conveying a thousand hoplites of their own, six hundred archers, a thousand Thracian mercenaries, and targeteers furnished by their allies in the neighbourhood. They were under the command of Nicias the son of Niceratus, and Nicostratus the son of Diitrephes. Sailing from Potidaea and putting in near the temple of Poseidon they marched against the Mendaeans. Now they and three hundred Scionaeans who had come to their aid, and their Peloponnesian auxiliaries, seven hundred hoplites in all, with Polydamidas their commander, had just encamped outside the city on a steep hill. Nicias, taking with him for the assault a hundred and twenty Methonaean light-armed troops, sixty select Athenian hoplites and all the archers, made an attempt to ascend the hill by a certain pathway, but he was wounded and failed to carry the position. Nicostratus with the remainder of his troops approaching the hill, which was hard of access, by another and more circuitous route was thrown into utter confusion, and the whole army of the Athenians were nearly defeated. So on this day the Athenians, finding that the Mendaeans and their allies refused to give way, retreated and encamped ; and when night came on, the Mendaeans likewise returned to the city.

On the following day the Athenians sailed round to the 130 side of Mendè looking towards Scionè ; they took the suburb, and during the whole of that day devastated the country. No one came out to meet them ; for a division had arisen in the *Soon, in consequence of internal divisions, the place falls into the hands of the Athenians. The Peloponnesians are shut up in the citadel.* city, and on the following night the three hundred Scionaeans returned home. On the next day Nicias with half his army went as far as the Scionaean frontier and devastated the country on his march, while Nicostratus with the other half sat down before the upper gates of

Mendè, out of which the road leads to Potidaea. In this
part of the city within the walls the Mendaeans and their
allies chanced to have their arms deposited, and Polydamidas, arraying his forces in order of battle, was just
exhorting the Mendaeans to go forth. Some one of the
popular faction answered in the heat of party that he would
not go out, and that he did not care to fight, but no sooner
had he uttered the words than he was seized by the
Peloponnesian commander and roughly handled. Whereupon the people lost patience, caught up their arms, and
made a furious rush upon the Peloponnesians and the
opposite party who were in league with them. They soon
put them to flight, partly because the onslaught was sudden,
and also because the gates were thrown open to the
Athenians, which greatly terrified them. For they thought
that the attack upon them was premeditated. All the
Peloponnesians who were not killed on the spot fled to
the citadel, which they had previously kept in their own
hands. Nicias had now returned and was close to the
city, and the Athenians rushed into Mendè with their
whole force. As the gates had been opened without any
previous capitulation they plundered the town as if it had
been stormed ; and even the lives of the citizens were with
difficulty saved by the efforts of the generals. The Mendaeans were then told that they were to retain their former
constitution, and bring to trial among themselves any whom
they thought guilty of the revolt. At the same time the
Athenians blockaded the garrison in the Acropolis by a
wall extending to the sea on either side and established
a guard. Having thus secured Mendè, they proceeded
against Scionè.

131   The inhabitants of Scionè and the Peloponnesian garri-
The Athenians block- son had come out to meet them and
ade Scionè. The gar- occupied a steep hill in front of the
rison of Mendè force city. The hill had to be taken by the
their way into the place. Athenians before they could effect the
circumvallation of the place. So they made a furious

attack and dislodged those who were stationed there[a];
they then encamped, and after raising a trophy, prepared
to invest the city. Soon afterwards, while they were
engaged in the work, the Peloponnesian auxiliaries who
were besieged in the Acropolis of Mendè, forcing their
way out by the sea-shore, broke through the watch and
came to Scionè by night. Most of them eluded the
Athenians who were encamped outside, and got into the
town.

While the circumvallation of Scionè was proceeding, 132
Perdiccas, who, after what had oc-
curred in the retreat from Lyncus,
hated Brasidas, sent heralds to the
Athenian generals, and came to an
understanding with them, [b] which without loss of time he took measures to
carry out[b]. It so happened that Ischagoras the Lacedaemonian was then on the eve of marching
with an army to reinforce Brasidas. Perdiccas was told
by Nicias that, having now made friends with the Athenians, he should give them some evidence of his sincerity.
He himself too no longer wished the Peloponnesians to
find their way into his country. And so by his influence
over the Thessalian chiefs, with whom he was always on
good terms, he put a stop to the whole expedition ; indeed,
the Lacedaemonians did not even attempt to obtain the
consent of the Thessalians. Nevertheless, Ischagoras,
Ameinias, and Aristeus, who had been sent by the Lacedaemonian government to report on the state of affairs,
found their way to Brasidas. They brought with them,
though contrary to law, certain young Spartans, intending
to make them governors of the cities, instead of leaving
the care of them to chance persons. Accordingly Brasidas

Perdiccas makes an alliance with the Athenians. To prove his sincerity he puts a stop to the passage of Peloponnesian reinforcements through Thessaly.

---

[a] Reading ἐπόντας.   [b] Or, ‘ having commenced negotiations
immediately after the retreat’ (cp. iv. 128 fin.) ; in which case, however,
εὐθὺς τότε ἀρξάμενος and ἐτύγχανε τότε must refer to different times.

appointed Clearidas the son of Cleonymus governor of
Amphipolis, and Pasitelidas[a] the son of Hegesander
governor of Toronè.

133   During the same summer the Thebans dismantled the
wall of the Thespians, charging them
Harshness and in- with Athenian tendencies. This was
gratitude of the Thebans an object which they always had in
towards the Thespians. view, and now they had their oppor-
Burning of the temple
of Herè near Argos. tunity, because the flower of the Thespian army had fallen in the battle of Delium[b]. During the
same summer the temple of Herè near Argos was burnt
down; Chrysis the priestess had put a light too near the
sacred garlands, and had then gone to sleep, so that the
whole place took fire and was consumed. In her fear of
the people she fled that very night to Phlius; and the
Argives, as the law provided, appointed another priestess
named Phaeinis. Chrysis had been priestess during eight
years of the war and half of the ninth when she became
an exile. Towards the close of the summer Scionè was
completely invested, and the Athenians, leaving a guard,
retired with the rest of their army.

134   In the following winter the Athenians and Lacedaemonians remained inactive, in con-
Indecisive action be- sequence of the armistice; but the
tween the Tegeans and Mantineans and the Tegeans with their
Mantineans.
respective allies fought a battle at Laodicium in the territory of Orestheum; the victory was disputed. For the
troops of both cities defeated the allies on the wing
opposed to them, and both erected trophies, and sent
spoils to Delphi. The truth is that, although there was
considerable slaughter on both sides, and the issue was
still undecided when night put an end to the conflict, the
Tegeans encamped on the field and at once erected

---

[a] Reading, according to Dobree's conjecture, Πασιτελίδαν, not Ἐπιτε-
λίδαν. Pasitelidas is mentioned, v. 3, as governor of Toronè

[b] Cp. iv. 96 med.

a trophy, while the Mantineans retreated to Bucolion and raised a rival trophy, but afterwards.

At the close of the same winter, towards the beginning 135 of spring, Brasidas made an attempt on Potidaea. He approached the place by night and planted a ladder against the walls.   *Unsuccessful attempt made by Brasidas on Potidaea.*   Thus far he proceeded undiscovered; for the ladder was fixed at a point which the sentinel who was passing on the bell had just quitted, and before he had returned to his post.   But Brasidas had not yet mounted the ladder when he was detected by the garrison: whereupon he withdrew his army in haste without waiting for the dawn.   So the winter ended, and with it the ninth year in the Peloponnesian War of which Thucydides wrote the history.

BOOK V

WITH the return of summer the year of the truce expired, but hostilities were not resumed *Expiration of the truce and subsequent resumption of hostilities. Second purification of Delos.* until after the Pythian games. During the armistice the Athenians removed the Delians from Delos ; they considered them impure and unworthy of their sacred character by reason of a certain ancient offence. The island had been purified before, when they took up the coffins of the dead as I have already narrated [a] ; but this purification, which seemed sufficient at the time, was now thought unsatisfactory because the inhabitants had been suffered to remain. Pharnaces gave to the Delians an asylum at Adramyttium in Asia, and whoever chose went and settled there.

2   When the armistice was over, Cleon, having obtained the consent of the people, sailed on an *Cleon sails to Chalcidicè, and after touching at Scionè goes on to Toronè.* expedition to the Chalcidian cities with thirty ships conveying twelve hundred Athenian hoplites, three hundred Athenian horsemen, and numerous allies. Touching first at Scionè (which was still blockaded), and taking from thence some hoplites of the besieging force, he sailed into the so-called Colophonian port, which was near the city of Toronè ; there learning from deserters that Brasidas was not in Toronè, and that the garrison was too weak to

---

[a] Cp. i. 8 init.; iii. 104 init.; v. 32 init.; viii. 108 med.

resist, he marched with his army against the town, and sent ten ships to sail round into the harbour. First he came to the new line of wall which Brasidas had raised when, wanting to take in the suburbs, he broke down a part of the old wall and made the whole city one.

But Pasitelidas, the Lacedaemonian governor, and the 3 garrison under his command came to *While Pasitelidas is* the defence of this quarter of the town, *defending a suburb the* and fought against their assailants, who *Athenian fleet sails into* pressed them hard. Meanwhile the *town is taken. Betrayal* Athenian fleet was sailing round into *of Panactum.* the harbour, and Pasitelidas feared that the ships would take the city before he could return and defend it, and that the new fortifications would be captured and himself in them. So he left the suburb and ran back into the city. But the enemy were too quick; the Athenians from the ships having taken Toronè before he arrived; while their infantry followed close upon him, and in a moment dashed in along with him at the breach in the old wall. Some of the Peloponnesians and Toronaeans were slain upon the spot, others were captured, and among them Pasitelidas the governor. Brasidas was on his way to the relief of Toronè at the time, but, hearing that the place was taken, he stopped and returned; he was within four miles and a half at the time of the capture. Cleon and the Athenians erected two trophies, one at the harbour and the other near the new wall. The women and children were made slaves; the men of Toronè and any other Chalcidians, together with the Peloponnesians, numbering in all seven hundred, were sent to Athens. The Peloponnesian captives were liberated at the peace which was concluded shortly afterwards; the rest were recovered by the Olynthians in exchange for a like number of the captives held by them. About the same time Panactum, a fortress on the Athenian frontier, was betrayed to the Boeotians. Cleon, putting a garrison into Toronè, sailed round Mount Athos, intending to attack Amphipolis.

4   About the same time three envoys, of whom one was

Revolution in Leon-tini. The oligarchy by the help of the Syracus-ans drive out the people. They then settle in Syracuse, but some of them soon grow dis-contented and return home, when they are joined by the people. They fight against Syracuse. The Athen-ians try to combine Sicily against Syra-cuse.

Phaeax the son of Erasistratus, were sent by the Athenians with two ships to Italy and Sicily. After the general peace and the withdrawal of the Athenians from Sicily [a], the Leontines had enrolled many new citizens, and the people contemplated a redistribution of the land. The oligarchy, perceiving their intention, called in the Syracus-ans and drove out the people, who separated and wandered up and down the island. The oligarchy then made an agreement with the Syracusans ; and, leaving their own city deserted, settled in Syracuse, and received the privileges of citizenship. Not long afterwards some of them grew discontented, and, quitting Syracuse, seized a place called Phocaeae, which was a part of the town of Leontini, and Bricinniae, a fortress in the Leontine territory. Here they were joined by most of the common people who had been previously driven out, and from their strongholds they carried on a continual warfare against Syracuse. It was the report of these events which induced the Athenians to send Phaeax to Sicily. He was to warn the Sicilians that the Syracusans were aiming at supremacy, and to unite the allies of Athens, and if possible the other cities, in a war against Syracuse. The Athenians hoped that they might thus save the Leontine people. Phaeax suc-ceeded in his mission to the Camarinaeans and Agri-gentines, but in Gela he failed, and, convinced that he could not persuade the other states, went no further. Returning by land through the country of the Sicels, and by the way going to Bricinniae and encouraging the exiles, he arrived at Catana, where he embarked for Athens.

---

[a] Cp. iv. 65 init.

On his voyage, both to and from Sicily, he made pro- 5 posals of friendship to several of the   *The Italian Locrians* Italian cities. He also fell in with   *make a treaty with* some Locrian settlers who had been   *Athens.* driven out of Messenè. After the agreement between the Sicilian towns, a feud had broken out at Messenè, and one of the two parties called in the Locrians, who sent some of their citizens to settle there ; thus Messenè was held for a time by the Locrians. They were returning home after their expulsion when Phaeax fell in with them, but he did them no harm ; for the Locrians had already agreed with him to enter into a treaty with the Athenians. At the general reconciliation of the Sicilians, they alone of the allies had not made peace with Athens. And they would have continued to hold out had they not been constrained by a war with the Itoneans and Melaeans, who were their neighbours and colonists from their city. Phaeax then returned to Athens.

Cleon had now sailed round from Toronè against Am- 6 phipolis, and making Eion his head-
quarters, attacked Stagirus[a], a colony   *Cleon remains at* of the Andrians, which he failed to   *Eion waiting for rein-* take. He succeeded, however, in   *forcements; Brasidas* storming Galepsus[b], a Thasian colony.   *ascends the hill of Cer-*
    dylium to reconnoitre.
He sent an embassy to Perdiccas, desiring him to come with an army, according to the terms of the alliance[c], and another to Polles, the king of the Odomantian Thracians, who was to bring as many Thracian mercenaries as he could ; he then remained quietly at Eion waiting for these reinforcements. Brasidas, hearing of his movements, took up a counter-position on Cerdylium. This is a high ground on the right bank of the river, not far from Amphipolis, belonging to the Argilians. From this spot he commanded a view of the country round, so that Cleon was sure to be seen by him if,—as Brasidas fully expected,—despising the

---

^a Cp. iv. 88 fin.   ^b Cp. iv. 107 fin.   ^c Cp. iv. 132 init.

numbers of his opponents, he should go up against Amphipolis without waiting for his reinforcements. At the same time he prepared for a battle, summoning to his side fifteen hundred Thracian mercenaries and the entire forces of the Edonians, who were targeteers and horsemen ; he had already one thousand Myrcinian and Chalcidian targeteers, in addition to the troops in Amphipolis. His heavy-armed, when all mustered, amounted to nearly two thousand, and he had three hundred Hellenic cavalry. Of these forces about fifteen hundred were stationed with Brasidas on Cerdylium, and the remainder were drawn up in order of battle under Clearidas in Amphipolis.

7   Cleon did nothing for a time, but he was soon compelled to make the movement which Brasidas. expected. For the soldiers were disgusted at their inaction, and drew comparisons between the generals ; what skill and enterprise might be expected on the one side, and what ignorance and cowardice on the other. And they remembered how unwilling they had been to follow Cleon when they left Athens. He, observing their murmurs, and not wanting them to be depressed by too long a stay in one place, led his army forward. He went to work in the same confident spirit which had already been successful at Pylos, and of which the success had given him a high opinion of his own wisdom. That any one would come out to fight with him he never even imagined; he said that he was only going to look at the place. If he waited for a larger force, this was not because he thought that there was any risk of his being defeated should he be compelled to fight, but that he might completely surround and storm the city. So he stationed his army upon a steep hill above Amphipolis, whence he surveyed with his own eyes the lake formed by the river Strymon, and the lie of the country on the side towards

Feelings of the soldiers towards Cleon contrast greatly with his own confidence in himself. At length he is compelled by their murmurs to move forward; he ascends a hill commanding a view of the country.

Thrace. He thought that he could go away without fighting whenever he pleased. For indeed there was no one to be seen on the walls, nor passing through the gates, which were all closed. He even imagined that he had made a mistake in coming up against the city without siege-engines; had he brought them he would have taken Amphipolis, for there was no one to prevent him.

No sooner did Brasidas see the Athenians in motion, than he himself descended from Cerdylium, and went into Amphipolis. He did not go out and draw up his forces in order of battle; he feared too much the inferiority of his own troops, not in their numbers (which were about equal to those of the enemy) but in quality; for the Athenian forces were the flower of their army, and they were supported by the best of the Lemnians and Imbrians. So he determined to employ a manœuvre, thinking that, if he showed them the real number and meagre equipment of his soldiers, he would be less likely to succeed than if he came upon them before there had been time to observe him, and when as yet they had no real grounds for their contempt of him. Selecting a hundred and fifty hoplites, and handing over the rest to Clearidas, he resolved to make a sudden attack before the Athenians retired, considering that, if their reinforcements should arrive, he might never again have an opportunity of fighting them by themselves. So he called together all his troops, and wishing to encourage them, and explain his plan, spoke as follows:—

Brasidas descends from Cerdylium. Fearing the inferiority of his own troops he determines to fall upon the Athenians in two separate detachments.

'Men of Peloponnesus, I need not waste words in telling you that we come from a land which has always been brave, and therefore free [a], and that you are Dorians [b], and are about to fight with Ionians whom you have beaten again and again. But I must explain to you my plan of

---

[a] Cp. iv. 28 med.

[b] Cp. i. 124 init.; vi. 77 med.; vii. 5 fin.: viii. 25 med. and fin.

attack, lest you should be disheartened at the seeming
disproportion of numbers, because we
We are Dorians and go into battle not with our whole force
may be expected to beat but with a handful of men. Our enemies,
Ionians. But you must if I am not mistaken, despise us; they
understand my plan.
The enemy are off their believe that no one will come out against
guard and ready to them, and so they have ascended the
retreat. First, I will hill, where they are busy looking about
sally forth out of one
gate and surprise them, them in disorder, and making but
then Clearidas from small account of us. Now, he is the
another, to complete most successful general[a] who discerns
their discomfiture.
most clearly such mistakes when made by his enemies,
and adapts his attack to the character of his own
forces, not always assailing them openly and in regular
array, but acting according to the circumstances of the
case. And the greatest reputation is gained by those
stratagems in which a man deceives his enemies most completely, and does his friends most service. Therefore
while they are still confident and unprepared, and, if
I read their intentions aright, are thinking of withdrawing
rather than of maintaining their ground, while they are off
their guard and before they have recovered their presence
of mind, I and my men will do our best to anticipate their
retreat, and will make a rush at the centre of the army.
Then, Clearidas, when you see me engaged, and I hope
striking panic into them, bring up your troops, the
Amphipolitans and the other allies, open the gates
suddenly, run out, and lose no time in closing with them.
This is the way to terrify them; for reinforcements are
always more formidable to an enemy than the troops
with which he is already engaged. Show yourself a brave
man and a true Spartan, and do you, allies, follow man-
fully, remembering that readiness, obedience, and a sense
of honour are the virtues of a soldier. To-day you have
to choose between freedom and slavery; between the

---

[a] Cp. iii. 29 fin.

name of Lacedaemonian allies, which you will deserve if you are brave, and of servants of Athens. For even if you should be so fortunate as to escape bonds or death, servitude will be your lot, a servitude more cruel than hitherto; and what is more, you will be an impediment to the liberation of the other Hellenes. Do not lose heart; think of all that is at stake; and I will show you that I can not only advise others, but fight myself.'

When Brasidas had ·thus spoken, he prepared to sally 10 forth with his own division, and stationed the rest of his army with Clearidas at the so-called Thracian gate, that they might come out and support him, in accordance with his instructions. He had been seen descending from Cerdylium into Amphipolis, [a] and then offering up sacrifice at the temple of Athenè within the walls; for the interior of the city was visible from the surrounding country. While he was thus employed, a report was brought to Cleon, who [a] had just gone forward to reconnoitre, that the whole army of the enemy could plainly be seen collected inside the town, and that the feet of numerous men and horses ready to come forth were visible under the gate. He went to the spot and saw for himself; but, not wishing to hazard a regular engagement until his allies arrived, and thinking he could get away soon enough, he gave a general signal for retreat, at the same time ordering his forces to retire slowly on the left wing, which was the only direction possible, towards Eion.   They appeared to linger; whereupon he caused his own right wing to face round, and so with his unshielded side exposed to the enemy began to lead off his army. Meanwhile Brasidas,

Cleon orders his army to retreat, but he is suddenly attacked by Brasidas, who is seconded by Clearidas. The Athenians are routed. Brasidas is wounded mortally and Cleon slain. Brasidas hears of the victory and dies.

---

[a] Or, taking the words καὶ ταῦτα πράσσοντος as subordinate to φανεροῦ γενομένου : 'and then offering up sacrifice at the temple of Athenè within the walls, for the interior of the city, &c., . . . and making preparations. A report was brought to Cleon, who,' &c.

seeing that the Athenians were on the move and that his
opportunity was come, said to his companions and to the
troops: 'These men do not mean to face us; see how
their spears and their heads are shaking; such behaviour
always shows that an army is going to run away. Open
me the gates there as I ordered, and let us boldly attack
them at once.' Thereupon he went out himself by the
gate leading to the palisade and by the first gate of the
long wall which was then standing, and ran at full speed
straight up the road, where, on the steepest part of the
hill, a trophy now stands: he then attacked the centre of
the Athenians, who were terrified at his audacity and
their own disorder, and put them to flight. Then
Clearidas, as he was bidden, sallied forth by the Thracian gate with his division, and charged the Athenians.
The sudden attack at both points created a panic among
them. Their left wing, which had proceeded some little
way along the road towards Eion, broke off and instantly
fled. They were already in full retreat, and Brasidas was
going on to the right wing when he was wounded; the
Athenians did not observe his fall, and those about him
carried him off the field. The right wing of the Athenians
was more disposed to stand. Cleon indeed, who had
never intended to remain, fled at once, and was overtaken
and slain by a Myrcinian targeteer. But his soldiers
rallied where they were on the top of the hill, and repulsed
Clearidas two or three times. They did not yield until
the Chalcidian and Myrcinian cavalry and the targeteers
hemmed them in and put them to flight with a shower of
darts. And so the rout became general, and those of the
Athenians who were not slain at once in close combat
or destroyed by the Chalcidian horse and the targeteers,
hard-pressed and wandering by many paths over the hills,
made their way back to Eion. Brasidas was carried
safely by his followers out of the battle into the city. He
was still alive, and knew that his army had conquered, but
soon afterwards he died. The rest of the army returning

with Clearidas from the pursuit, spoiled the dead, and
erected a trophy.

Brasidas was buried in the city with public honours in 11
front of what is now the Agora. The   *Funeral of Brasidas.*
whole body of the allies in military   *The Amphipolitans give*
array followed him to the grave. The   *him the honours of a*
                                          hero and founder, super-
Amphipolitans enclosed his sepulchre,   *seding Hagnon who*
and to this day they sacrifice to him   *was their real founder.*
as to a hero, and have also instituted games and yearly
offerings in his honour. They likewise made him their
founder, and dedicated their colony to him, pulling down
ᶜthe buildings which Hagnon had erected ᵃ, and obliterating
any memorials which might have remained to future time
of his foundation ᵇ. For they considered Brasidas to have
been their deliverer, and under the present circumstances
the fear of Athens induced them to pay court to their
Lacedaemonian allies. That Hagnon should retain the
honours of a founder, now that they were enemies of the
Athenians, seemed to them no longer in accordance with
their interests, and likely to be displeasing to him.

They gave back to the Athenians their dead, who numbered about six hundred, while only seven were slain on
the other side. For there was no regular engagement,
but an unforeseen circumstance led to the battle ; and the
Athenians were panic-stricken before it had well begun.
After the recovery of the dead the Athenians went home
by sea. Clearidas and his companions remained and
administered the affairs of Amphipolis.

At the end of the summer, a little before this time, a 12
reinforcement of nine hundred heavy-   *A reinforcement sent*
armed, under the command of the   *by the Lacedaemonians*
Lacedaemonian generals Rhamphias,   *to Amphipolis arrives*
                                           at Heraclea,
Autocharidas, and Epicydidas, set out
for Chalcidicè. Coming first to Heraclea in Trachis ᶜ, they
regulated whatever appeared to them to be amiss. They

ᵃ Or, 'the shrine of Hagnon.'   ᵇ Cp. iv. 102 fin.   ᶜ Cp. iii. 92, 93.

were staying there when the battle of Amphipolis occurred. And so the summer came to an end.

13   The following winter Rhamphias and his army went as *but is not allowed to* far as Pierium in Thessaly, but as the *pass through Thessaly.* Thessalians would not let them proceed [a], and Brasidas, for whom these reinforcements were intended, was dead, they returned home, thinking that the time for action had gone by. They felt that they were not competent to carry out the great designs of Brasidas, and the Athenians had now left the country defeated. But their chief reason for not proceeding was that the Lacedaemonians, at the time when they left Sparta, were inclined towards peace.

14   After the battle of Amphipolis and the return of Rham-
Both the Athenians phias from Thessaly, neither side
and Lacedaemonians, undertook any military operations.
being alike disappointed Both alike were inclined to peace. The
in their hopes, now Athenians had been beaten at Delium,
desire peace. and shortly afterwards at Amphipolis;
and so they had lost that confidence in their own strength which had indisposed them to treat at a time when temporary success seemed to make their final triumph certain. They were afraid too that their allies would be elated at their disasters, and that more of them would revolt; they repented that after the affair at Pylos, when they might honourably have done so, they had not come to terms. The Lacedaemonians on the other hand inclined to peace because the course of the war had disappointed their expectations. There was a time when they fancied that, if they only devastated Attica, they would crush the power of Athens within a few years [b]; and yet they had received a blow at Sphacteria such as Sparta had never experienced until then; their country was continually ravaged from Pylos and Cythera; the Helots were deserting, and they were always fearing lest those who had not deserted,

---

[a] Cp. iv. 132 med.   [b] Cp. i. 81 fin.

relying on the help of those who had, should seize their opportunity and revolt, as they had done once before. Moreover, the truce for thirty years which they had made with Argos was on the point of expiring; the Argives were unwilling to renew it unless Cynuria were restored to them, and the Lacedaemonians deemed it impossible to fight against the Argives and Athenians combined. They suspected also that some of the Peloponnesian cities would secede and join the Argives, which proved to be the case.

Upon these grounds both governments thought it de- 15 sirable to make peace. The Lacedae-monians were the more eager of the two, because they wanted to recover the prisoners taken at Sphacteria; for the Spartans among them were of high rank, and all alike related to themselves. They had negotiated for their recovery immediately after they were taken, but the Athenians, in the hour of their prosperity, would not as yet agree to fair terms[a]. After their defeat at Delium, the Lacedaemonians were well aware that they would now be more compliant, and therefore they had at once made a truce for a year, during which the envoys of the two states were to meet and advise about a lasting peace. When Athens had received a second blow at 16 Amphipolis, and Brasidas and Cleon, who had been the two greatest enemies of peace,—the one because the war brought him success and reputation, and the other because he fancied that in quiet times his rogueries would be more transparent and his slanders less credible,—had fallen in the battle, [b] the two chief aspirants for political power at Athens and Sparta, Pleistoanax [b] the son of Pausanias,

The desire of the Lacedaemonians is the stronger because they want to recover the prisoners.

Brasidas and Cleon for very different reasons had been both enemies to peace. But now they are dead, and Nicias and Pleistoanax, the two leading men of their respective states, have each a strong motive for putting an end to the war.

---

[a] Cp. iv. 41 fin.   [b] Reading οἱ ἐν before ἑκατέρᾳ. Or, omitting οἱ ἐν and inserting a comma after ἡγεμονίαν : 'these (i. e. Cleon and

king of the Lacedaemonians, and Nicias the son of
Niceratus the Athenian, who had been the most fortunate
general of his day, became more eager than ever to make
an end of the war.   Nicias desired, whilst he was still
successful and held in repute, to preserve his good fortune;
he would have liked to rest from toil, and to give the
people rest; and he hoped to leave behind him to other
ages the name of a man who in all his life had never
brought disaster on the city.   He thought that the way to
gain his wish was to trust as little as possible to fortune,
and to keep out of danger; and that danger would be best
avoided by peace.   Pleistoanax wanted peace, because his
enemies were always stirring up the scruples of the Lacedaemonians against him, and insisting whenever misfortunes
came that they were to be attributed to his illegal return
from exile.   For they accused him and Aristocles his
brother of having induced the priestess at Delphi, whenever Lacedaemonian envoys came to enquire of the oracle,
constantly to repeat the same answer: ' Bring back the
seed of the hero son of Zeus from a strange country to
your own; else you will plough with a silver ploughshare':
until, after a banishment of nineteen years, he persuaded
the Lacedaemonians to bring him home again with dances
and sacrifices and such ceremonies as they observed when
they first enthroned their kings at the foundation of Lacedaemon.   He had been banished on account of his retreat
from Attica, when he was supposed to have been bribed [a].
While in exile at Mount Lycaeum he had occupied a
house half within the sacred precinct of Zeus, through fear
of the Lacedaemonians.

17   He was vexed by these accusations, and thinking that
in peace, when there would be no mishaps, and when
the Lacedaemonians would have recovered the captives,

Brasidas) being at the time the two great champions of the supremacy
of their respective states; Pleistoanax ' &c.

   [a] Cp. i. 114; ii. 21 init.

he would himself be less open to attack, whereas in war leading men must always have the misfortunes of the state laid at their door, he was very anxious to come to terms. Negotiations were commenced during the winter. Towards spring the Lacedaemonians sounded a note of preparation by announcing to the allies *The negotiations proceed. Both parties agree to give up what they had gained by arms. Only the Thebans retain Plataea and the Athenians Nisaea, which had been surrendered.* that their services would be required in the erection of a fort; they thought that the Athenians would thereby be induced to listen to them. At the same time, after many conferences and many demands urged on both sides, an understanding was at last arrived at that both parties should give up what they had gained by arms. The Athenians, however, were to retain Nisaea, for when they demanded the restoration of Plataea the Thebans protested that they had obtained possession of the place not by force or treachery, but by agreement [a]; to which the Athenians rejoined that they had obtained Nisaea in the same manner[b]. The Lacedaemonians then summoned their allies; and although the Boeotians, Corinthians, Eleans, and Megarians were dissatisfied, the majority voted for peace. And so the peace was finally concluded and ratified by oaths and libations, the Lacedaemonians binding themselves to the Athenians and the Athenians to the Lacedaemonians in the following terms :—

'The Athenians and Lacedaemonians and their respective 18 allies make peace upon the following terms, to which they swear, each city separately :— *Terms of the treaty.*

' I. Touching the common temples, any one who pleases may go and sacrifice in them and enquire at them, on behalf either of himself or of the state, according to the custom of his country, both by land and sea, without fear.

' II. The precinct and the temple of Apollo at Delphi and

---

[a] Cp. iii. 52 init.   [b] Cp. iv. 69 fin.

the Delphian people shall be independent, and shall retain their own revenues and their own courts of justice, both for themselves and for their territory, according to their ancestral customs.

'III. The peace between the Athenians and their confederates and the Lacedaemonians and their confederates shall endure fifty years, both by sea and land, without fraud or hurt.

'IV. They shall not be allowed to bear arms to the hurt of one another in any way or manner; neither the Lacedaemonians and their allies against the Athenians and their allies, nor the Athenians and their allies against the Lacedaemonians and their allies; and they shall determine any controversy which may arise between them by oaths and other legal means in such sort as they shall agree.

'V. The Lacedaemonians and their allies shall restore Amphipolis to the Athenians.

'VI. The inhabitants of any cities which the Lacedaemonians deliver over to the Athenians may depart whithersoever they please, and take their property with them. The said cities shall be independent, but shall pay the tribute which was fixed in the time of Aristides. After the conclusion of the treaty the Athenians and their allies shall not be allowed to make war upon them to their hurt, so long as they pay the tribute. The cities are these— Argilus [a], Stagirus [b], Acanthus [c], Scolus, Olynthus [d], Spartolus [e]: these shall be allies neither of the Lacedaemonians nor of the Athenians, but if the Athenians succeed in persuading them, having their consent, they may make them allies.

'VII. The Mecybernaeans, Sanaeans [f], and Singaeans shall dwell in their own cities on the same terms as the Olynthians and Acanthians.

---

[a] Cp. iv. 103 med.   [b] Cp. iv. 88 fin.   [c] Cp. iv. 88.
[d] Cp. i. 58 med.   [e] Cp. ii. 79 init.   [f] Cp. iv. 109 fin.

'VIII. The Lacedaemonians and the allies shall restore Panactum [a] to the Athenians. The Athenians shall restore to the Lacedaemonians Coryphasium [b], Cythera [c], Methonè [d], Pteleum, and Atalantè [e].

'IX. The Athenians shall surrender the Lacedaemonian captives whom they have in their public prison, or who are in the public prison of any place within the Athenian dominions, and they shall let go the Peloponnesians who are besieged in Scionè, and any other allies of the Lacedaemonians who are in Scionè, and all whom Brasidas introduced into the place [f], and any of the allies of the Lacedaemonians who are in the public prison at Athens, or in the public prison of any place within the Athenian dominions. The Lacedaemonians and their allies in like manner shall restore those of the Athenians and their allies who are their prisoners.

'X. Respecting Scionè [g], Toronè [h], and Sermylè, or any cities which are held by the Athenians, the Athenians shall do with the inhabitants of the said cities, or of any cities which are held by them, as they think fit.

'XI. The Athenians shall bind themselves by oath to the Lacedaemonians and their allies, city by city, and the oath shall be that which in the several cities of the two contracting parties is deemed the most binding. The oath shall be in the following form :—'I will abide by this treaty and by this peace truly and sincerely.' The Lacedaemonians and their allies shall bind themselves by a similar oath to the Athenians. This oath shall be renewed by both parties every year ; and they shall erect pillars at Olympia, Delphi, and the Isthmus, at Athens in the Acropolis, at Lacedaemon in the temple of Apollo at Amyclae.

'XII. If anything whatsoever be forgotten on one side or the other, either party may, without violation of their

---

[a] Cp. v. 3 fin.   [b] Cp. iv. 3 med.   [c] Cp. iv. 54.   [d] Cp. iv. 45.
[e] Cp. ii. 32.   [f] Cp. iv. 123 fin.   [g] Cp. v. 32 init.   [h] Cp. v. 3.

oaths, take honest counsel and alter the treaty in such manner as shall seem good to the two parties, the Athenians and Lacedaemonians.'

19   The treaty begins, at Lacedaemon in the Ephorate of

Ratification.

Pleistolas, and on the twenty-seventh day of the month Artemisium, and at Athens in the Archonship of Alcaeus, on the twenty-fifth day of the month Elaphebolion [a]. The following persons took the oaths and ratified the treaty:—On behalf of the Lacedaemonians, Pleistolas, Damagetus, Chionis, Metagenes, Acanthus, Daïthus, Ischagoras, Philocharidas, Zeuxidas, Antippus, Tellis, Alcinidas, Empedias, Menas, Laphilus; on behalf of the Athenians, Lampon, Isthmionicus, Nicias, Laches, Euthydemus, Procles, Pythodorus, Hagnon, Myrtilus, Thrasycles, Theagenes, Aristocrates, Iolcius, Timocrates, Leon, Lamachus, Demosthenes.

20   This treaty was concluded at the end of winter, just at

The war had lasted almost exactly ten years.

the beginning of spring, immediately after the city Dionysia. Ten years, with a difference of a few days, had passed since the invasion of Attica and the commencement of the war. I would have a person reckon the actual periods of time, and not rely upon catalogues of the archons or other official personages whose names may be used in different cities to mark the dates of past events. For whether an event occurred in the beginning, or in the middle, or whatever might be the exact point, of a magistrate's term of office is left uncertain by such a mode of reckoning. But if he measure by summers and winters as they are here set down, and count each summer and winter as a half year, he will find that ten summers and ten winters passed in the first part of the war.

21   The Lacedaemonians—for the lot having fallen upon them they had to make restitution first—immediately released their prisoners, and sending three envoys, Ischa-

---

[a] March—April.

goras, Menas, and Philocharidas, to Chalcidicè, commanded
Clearidas to deliver up Amphipolis to *The Lacedaemonians*
the Athenians, and the other cities to *restore their prisoners,*
accept the articles of the treaty which *but Clearidas refuses to*
severally concerned them. But they *deliver up Amphipolis,*
and the Chalcidian
did not approve of the terms, and *cities will not accept the*
refused. Clearidas, who acted in the *treaty.*
interest of the Chalcidians, would not give up the place,
and said that it was not in his power to do so against their
will. Accompanied by envoys from the Chalcidian cities, he
himself went direct to Lacedaemon, intending to defend
himself in case Ischagoras and his colleagues should
accuse him of insubordination; he also wanted to know
whether the treaty could still be reconsidered. On his
arrival he found that it was positively concluded, and he
himself was sent back to Thrace by the Lacedaemonians,
who commanded him to give up Amphipolis, or, if he could
not, at any rate to withdraw all the Peloponnesian forces
from the place. So he returned in haste.

The representatives of the other allies were present at **22**
Lacedaemon, and the Lacedaemonians *The allies are dis-*
urged the reluctant states to accept the *satisfied; but the Lace-*
treaty. But they refused for the same *daemonians, fearing a*
renewal of hostilities
reasons as before[a], and insisted that *from Argos, dismiss*
they must have more equitable condi- *them and form an*
tions. Finding that they would not *alliance with Athens.*
come in, the Lacedaemonians dismissed them, and proceeded on their own account to make an alliance with the
Athenians. They thought that the Argives, whose hostile
intentions had been manifested by their refusal to renew
the peace at the request of Ampelidas and Lichas, the
Lacedaemonian envoys who had gone thither, being now
unsupported by the Athenians, would thus be least
dangerous and that the rest of Peloponnesus would be least
likely to stir. For the Athenian alliance, to which they
would otherwise have had recourse, would now be closed

---

[a] Cp. v. 17 fin.

to them.   There were present at the time Athenian envoys,
and after a negotiation the two parties took oaths, and
made an alliance, of which the terms were as follows :—

23   'The Lacedaemonians shall be allies of the Athenians
Terms of the alliance.   for fifty years, on the following conditions :—

'I. If any enemy invade the Lacedaemonian territory and
harm the Lacedaemonians, the Athenians shall assist the
Lacedaemonians in any way which they can, and to the
utmost of their power ; and if the enemy ravage their
territory and depart, the offending city shall be the enemy
of the Lacedaemonians and Athenians, and shall suffer at
the hands of both of them, and neither city shall cease from
war before the other.   These things shall be performed
honestly, and zealously, and sincerely.

'II. If any enemy invade the Athenian territory and
harm the Athenians, the Lacedaemonians shall assist them
in any way which they can, and to the utmost of their
power ; and if the enemy ravage their territory and depart,
the offending city shall be the enemy of the Athenians and
Lacedaemonians, and shall suffer at the hands of both of
them, and neither city shall cease from war before the
other.   These things shall be performed honestly, and
zealously, and sincerely.

'III. If the slaves rebel, the Athenians shall aid the
Lacedaemonians with all their might and to the utmost of
their power.

'IV. These provisions shall be sworn to on both sides by
the same persons who swore to the former treaty.   Every
year the Lacedaemonians shall go to Athens at the
Dionysia and renew the oath, and the Athenians shall go
to Lacedaemon at the Hyacinthia and renew the oath.
Both parties shall erect pillars, one in Lacedaemon at the
temple of Apollo in Amyclae, another at Athens in the
Acropolis at the temple of Athenè.

'V. If the Lacedaemonians and Athenians agree that anything shall be added to or taken away from the treaty of

alliance, whatever it be, this may be done without violation of their oaths.'

On behalf of the Lacedaemonians there took the oaths, 24 Pleistoanax, Agis, Pleistolas, Damag- *Ratification.* etus, Chionis, Metagenes, Acanthus, Daïthus, Ischagoras, Philocharidas, Zeuxidas, Antippus, Alcinadas, Tellis, Empedias, Menas, Laphilus. On behalf of the Athenians there took the oaths, Lampon, Isthmionicus, Laches, Nicias, Euthydemus, Procles, Pythodorus, Hagnon, Myrtilus, Thrasycles, Theagenes, Aristocrates, Iolcius, Timocrates, Leon, Lamachus, Demosthenes.

This alliance was made shortly after the treaty; at the same time the Athenians restored to *Restoration of the* the Lacedaemonians the prisoners *prisoners taken at* taken at Sphacteria. The summer of *Sphacteria.* the eleventh year then began. During the previous ten years the first war, of which the history has now been written, went on without intermission.

The treaty and the alliance which terminated the ten 25 years' war were made in the Ephorate of Pleistolas at Lacedaemon, and the *First Corinth and* Archonship of Alcaeus at Athens. *other Peloponnesian* Those who accepted the treaty were *cities, and afterwards* now at peace ; but the Corinthians and *the Athenians them-* several of the Peloponnesian cities did *selves, show signs of discontent.* what they could to disturb the arrangement. And so before long a new cause of quarrel set the allies against the Lacedaemonians ; who also, as time went on, incurred the suspicion of the Athenians, because in certain particulars they would not *The war renewed.* execute the provisions of the treaty. For six years and ten months the two powers abstained from invading each other's territories, but abroad the cessation of arms was intermittent, and they did each other all the harm which they could. At last they were absolutely compelled to break the treaty made at the end of the first ten years, and engaged once more in open war.

26   The same Thucydides of Athens continued the history,

The peace was merely nominal, and may fairly be reckoned in the twenty-seven years' war. The prediction of 'thrice nine years' was the only oracle which was verified by the event. I myself lived through the whole war, and being for twenty years in banishment had the opportunity of knowing both sides.

following the order of events, which he reckoned by summers and winters, up to the destruction of the Athenian empire and the taking of Piraeus and the Long Walls by the Lacedaemonians and their allies.   Altogether the war lasted twenty-seven years, for if any one argue that the interval during which the truce continued should be excluded, he is mistaken.   If he have regard to the facts of the case, he will see that the term 'peace' can hardly be applied to a state of things in which neither party gave back or received all the places stipulated; moreover in the Mantinean and Epidaurian wars and in other matters there were violations of the treaty on both sides; the Chalcidian allies maintained their attitude of hostility towards Athens, and the Boeotians merely observed an armistice terminable at ten days' notice.   So that, including the first ten years' war, the doubtful truce which followed, and the war which followed that, he who reckons up the actual periods of time will find that I have rightly given the exact number of years with the difference only of a few days. He will also find that this was the solitary instance in which those who put their faith in oracles were justified by the event.   For I well remember how, from the beginning to the end of the war, there was a common and often-repeated saying that it was to last thrice nine years.   I lived through the whole of it, being of mature years and judgment, and I took great pains to make out the exact truth. For twenty years I was banished from my country after I held the command at Amphipolis, and associating with both sides, with the Peloponnesians quite as much as with the Athenians, because of my exile, I was thus enabled to watch quietly the course of events.   I will now proceed to narrate the quarrels which after the first ten years broke up the treaty, and the events of the war which followed.

After the conclusion of the fifty years' peace and of the 27 subsequent alliance, the ambassadors who had been invited to the conference from the other states of Peloponnesus left Lacedaemon. They all went home except the Corinthians, who turned aside to Argos and opened communications with certain of the Argive magistrates, saying that the Lacedaemonians had made peace and alliance with the Athenians, hitherto their mortal enemies, to no good end, but for the enslavement of Peloponnesus, and that the Argives were bound to take measures for its deliverance. They ought to pass a vote that any independent Hellenic city which would allow a settlement of disputes on equal terms might enter into a defensive alliance with them. The negotiation should not be carried on with the assembly, but the Argives should appoint a few commissioners having full powers, lest, if any states appealed to the people and were rejected, their failure should become public. They added that hatred of the Lacedaemonians would induce many to join them. Having offered this recommendation, the Corinthians returned home.

The Corinthians go to Argos and flatter the Argives with the notion that they must become the centre of a great anti-Laconian confederacy.

The Argive magistrates, after hearing these proposals, 28 referred them to their colleagues and the people. The Argives passed a vote accordingly, and elected twelve commissioners; through these any of the Hellenes who pleased might make an alliance with them, except the Athenians and Lacedaemonians, who could only be admitted to the league with the sanction of the Argive people. The Argives were the more inclined to take this course because, their truce with the Lacedaemonians being about to expire, they saw that war was imminent. Moreover they were en-

The Argives, seeing that war with Lacedaemon was imminent and hoping to lead Peloponnesus, enter warmly into the idea.

couraged by the hope of becoming the leaders of Peloponnesus. For at this time the reputation of Lacedaemon had fallen very low; her misfortunes had brought her into contempt, while the resources of Argos were unimpaired. For the Argives had not taken part in the war with Athens, and, being at peace with both parties, had reaped a harvest from them.

29   The first to enter the alliance offered by the Argives

The Mantineans join the Argives. Great uneasiness is caused by the powers which the treaty gave to the Athenians and Lacedaemonians. to any Hellenes who were willing to accept it were the Mantineans and their allies, who joined through fear of the Lacedaemonians. For, during the war with Athens, they had subjected a part of Arcadia, which they thought that the Lacedaemonians, now that their hands were free, would no longer allow them to retain. So they gladly joined Argos, reflecting that it was a great city, the constant enemy of Sparta, and, like their own, governed by a democracy. When Mantinea seceded, a murmur ran through the other states of Peloponnesus that they must secede too ; they imagined that the Mantineans had gone over to the Argives because they had better information than themselves, and also they were angry with the Lacedaemonians, chiefly on account of that clause in the treaty with Athens which provided that the Lacedaemonians and Athenians, if agreed, might add to or take away from it whatever they pleased[a]. This clause aroused great uneasiness among the Peloponnesians, and made them suspect that the Lacedaemonians meant to unite with the Athenians in order to enslave them[b]; they argued that the power of altering the treaty ought to have been given only to the whole confederacy. Entertaining these fears they generally inclined towards Argos, and every state was eager to follow the example of Mantinea and form an alliance with her.

---

[a] Cp. v. 18. § 12.   [b] Cp. iv. 20 fin,

The Lacedaemonians perceived that great excitement 30 prevailed in Peloponnesus, and that the Corinthians had inspired it and were themselves on the point of making a treaty with Argos. So they sent envoys to Corinth, desiring to antici- pate what might happen. They laid *The Lacedaemonians accuse the Corinthians of deserting their alli- ance; to which the Corinthians reply that they cannot betray the Chalcidian cities.* the blame of having instigated the whole movement on the Corinthians, and protested that, if they deserted them and joined the Argives, they would be forsworn ; indeed they were already much to blame for not accepting the peace made with Athens, although there was an article in their league which said that what the majority of the allies voted should be binding unless there was some impediment on the part of Gods or heroes. Now the Corinthians had previously summoned those of the allies who, like them- selves, had rejected the treaty : and, replying in their presence, they were unwilling to speak out and state their grievances, of which the chief was that the Lacedaemonians had not recovered for them Sollium[a] or Anactorium[b]. But they pretended that they could not betray their allies in Thrace, to whom, when they originally joined in the revolt of Potidaea, they had sworn a separate oath[c], and had afterwards renewed it. They denied therefore that they were violating the terms of the league by refusing to join in the peace with the Athenians ; for, having sworn in the name of the Gods to their allies, they would be violating their oaths if they betrayed them : the treaty said ‘unless there was some impediment on the part of Gods or heroes,’ and this did appear to them to be an impedi- ment of that nature. Thus far they pleaded their former oaths ; as to the Argive alliance they would take counsel with their friends, and do whatever was right. So the Lacedaemonians returned home. Now there happened to be at that time Argive envoys present at Corinth who urged

---

[a] Cp. ii. 30 init.　　　　[b] Cp. iv. 49.　　　　[c] Cp. i. 58.

the Corinthians to join the alliance without more delay, and
the Corinthians told them to come to their next assembly.

31   Soon afterwards envoys from Elis likewise arrived at
Corinth, who, first of all making an
The Lepreans, having alliance with the Corinthians, went on
agreed to pay a rent to Argos, and became allies of the
to the Eleans, break Argives in the manner prescribed.
this agreement. They Now the Eleans had a quarrel with
are supported by the the Lacedaemonians about the town of
Lacedaemonians. The the Lacedaemonians about the town of
Eleans in a rage join Lepreum.   A war had arisen between
the Argive league. The the Lepreans and certain Arcadian
Corinthians and Chal- tribes, and the Eleans having been
cidians join likewise; tribes, and the Eleans having been
not so the Boeotians called in by the Lepreans came to
and Megarians.
assist them, on condition of receiving half their territory.
When they had brought the war to a successful end the
Eleans allowed the inhabitants of Lepreum to cultivate
the land themselves, paying a rent of a talent to Olympian
Zeus.   Until the Peloponnesian war they had paid the
talent, but taking advantage of the war they ceased to pay,
and the Eleans tried to compel them.   The Lepreans then
had recourse to the Lacedaemonians, who undertook to
arbitrate.   The Eleans suspected that they would not
have fair play at their hands; they therefore disregarded
the arbitration and ravaged the Leprean territory.   Nevertheless the Lacedaemonians went on with the case and
decided that Lepreum was an independent state, and that
the Eleans were in the wrong.   As their award was rejected by the Eleans, they sent a garrison of hoplites to
Lepreum.   The Eleans, considering that the Lacedaemonians had taken into alliance a city which had seceded
from them, appealed to the clause of the agreement which
provided that whatever places any of the confederates had
held previous to the war with Athens should be retained
by them at its conclusion, and acting under a sense of
injustice they now seceded to the Argives and, like the
rest, entered into the alliance with them in the manner
prescribed.   Immediately afterwards the Corinthians and

the Chalcidians of Thrace joined; but the Boeotians and
the Megarians agreed to refuse [a], and, jealously watched
by the Lacedaemonians, stood aloof; for they were well
aware that the Lacedaemonian constitution was far more
congenial to their own oligarchical form of government
than the Argive democracy.

During the same summer, and about this time, the 32
Athenians took Scionè which they
were blockading [b], put to death all the
grown-up men, and enslaved the
women and children; they then gave
possession of the land to the Plataeans.
They also replaced the Delians in
Delos [c], moved partly by the defeats
*Capture of Scionè.
Restoration of the Del-
ians. The Tegeans
refuse to join the new
alliance. The Corin-
thians get frightened
and have recourse to
the Boeotians.*
which they had sustained, partly by an oracle of the
Delphic God. About this time too the Phocians and
Locrians went to war. The Corinthians and Argives (who
were now allies) came to Tegea, which they hoped to withdraw from the Lacedaemonian alliance, thinking that if
they could secure so important a part of Peloponnesus they
would soon have the whole of it. The Tegeans however
said that they could have no quarrel with the Lacedaemonians; and the Corinthians, who had hitherto been
zealous in the cause, now began to cool, and were seriously
afraid that no other Peloponnesian state would join them.
Nevertheless they applied to the Boeotians and begged
them to become allies of themselves and of the Argives,
and generally to act with them; they further requested
that they would accompany them to Athens and procure
an armistice terminable at ten days' notice, similar to that
which the Athenians and Boeotians had made with one
another shortly after the conclusion of the fifty years'
peace. If the Athenians did not agree, then the Corinthians demanded of the Boeotians that they should
renounce the armistice and for the future make no truce

---

[a] Cp. v. 38 init.   [b] Cp. iv. 130.   [c] Cp. v. 1.

without them.   The Boeotians on receiving this request desired the Corinthians to say no more about alliance with the Argives.   But they went together to Athens, where the Boeotians failed to obtain the armistice for the Corinthians, the Athenians replying that the original truce[a] extended to them, if they were allies of the Lacedaemonians.   The Boeotians however did not renounce their own armistice, although the Corinthians expostulated, and argued that such had been the agreement.   Thus the Corinthians had only a suspension of hostilities with Athens, but no regular truce.

33   During the same summer the Lacedaemonians with

The Lacedaemonians free the Parrhasians from the Mantineans.

their whole force, commanded by their king Pleistoanax the son of Pausanias, made war upon the Parrhasians of Arcadia, who were subjects of the Mantineans[b].   They had been invited by a faction among the Parrhasians ; and moreover they wanted to demolish a fortress in the Parrhasian town of Cypsela, threatening the Laconian district of Sciritis, which the Mantineans had built and garrisoned.   The Lacedaemonians devastated the country of the Parrhasians ; and the Mantineans, leaving the custody of their own city to a force of Argives, themselves garrisoned the territory of their allies.   But being unable to save either the fort of Cypsela or the cities of Parrhasia, they went home again ; whereupon the Lacedaemonians, having demolished the fort and restored the independence of the Parrhasians, returned home likewise.

34   In the course of the same summer the troops serving in

The Helots who served with Brasidas are emancipated and settled at Lepreum.   The captives from the island are for a time deprived of citizenship.

Thrace, which had gone out under Brasidas and were brought home by Clearidas after the conclusion of peace, arrived at Lacedaemon.   The Lacedaemonians passed a vote that the Helots who had fought under Brasidas should be free and might dwell wherever they pleased.

---

[a] Cp. v. 18.   [b] Cp. v. 29 init.

Not long afterwards, they settled them, together with the Neodamodes, at Lepreum, which is on the borders of Laconia and Elis, being now enemies of the Eleans. Fearing lest their own citizens who had been taken in the island and had delivered up their arms might expect to be slighted in consequence of their misfortune, and, if they retained the privileges of citizens, would attempt revolution, they took away the right of citizenship from them, although some of them were holding office at the time. By this disqualification they were deprived of their eligibility to offices, and of the legal right to buy and sell. In time, however, their privileges were restored to them.

During this summer the Dictidians took Thyssus, a town 35 of Mount Athos, which was in alliance with the Athenians. During the whole summer intercourse continued between the Athenians and Peloponnesians. But almost as soon as the peace was concluded both Athenians and Lace- *The Lacedaemonians do not give up Amphipolis. The Athenians retain Pylos. They agree however to withdraw the Messenians and Helots.* daemonians began to mistrust one another, because the places mentioned in the treaty were not given up. For the Lacedaemonians, who were to make restitution first, according to the lot, had not surrendered Amphipolis and the other less important places which they held, and had not made their allies in Chalcidicè, nor the Boeotians, nor the Corinthians accept the treaty, but only kept declaring that they would join the Athenians in coercing them if they continued to refuse. They even fixed a time, though they did not commit themselves in writing, within which those who would not come into the treaty were to be declared the enemies of both parties. The Athenians, seeing that nothing was being really done, suspected the Lacedaemonians of dishonesty, and therefore they would not give up Pylos when the Lacedaemonians required it; they even repented that they had restored the prisoners taken at Sphacteria, and resolved to keep the other places until the Lacedaemonians had fulfilled their part of the contract. The Lacedaemonians replied that they had done what they could. They had delivered up the Athenian prisoners who were in their hands, and had withdrawn their soldiers from Chalcidicè; they had neglected nothing which lay within their power. But they could not give up Amphipolis, of which they were not entirely masters; they would however try to bring the Boeotians and Corinthians into the treaty, to get back Panactum, and recover all the Athenian captives who were in the hands of the Boeotians. They still continued to insist on the restoration of Pylos, or at any rate on the withdrawal of the Messenians and Helots, now that the Lacedaemonians had withdrawn their troops from Chalcidicè; the Athenians might, if they liked, garrison the place themselves. After many long conferences held during the summer, they persuaded the Athenians to withdraw the Messenians, Helots, and Lacedaemonian deserters: these the Athenians settled at Cranii in Cephallenia. So during this summer there was peace and intercourse between Athens and Sparta.

36   Before the following winter the Ephors under whom the *New Ephors come into office, who are in the interest of the war party. They suggest that the Boeotians shall first join the Argive and Corinthian alliance and then reconcile the Argives with the Lacedaemonians.* peace was concluded were succeeded by others, of whom some were actually opposed to it. During the winter, embassies from the allied states arrived at Sparta, including representatives of Athens, Boeotia, and Corinth. Much was said with no result. As the ambassadors were departing, Cleobulus and Xenares, the Ephors who were most desirous of renewing the war, entered into a private negotiation with the Boeotians and Corinthians, recommending them to unite as closely as possible, and suggesting that the Boeotians should first enter the Argive alliance and then try and make the Argives, as well as themselves, allies of the Lacedaemonians. The

Boeotians would thus escape the necessity of accepting the peace with Athens; for the Lacedaemonians would prefer the friendship and alliance of Argos to anything which they might lose by the enmity of Athens and the dissolution of the treaty. The two Ephors knew that a satisfactory alliance with Argos was an object which the Lacedaemonians always had at heart, perceiving as they did that it would enable them to carry on the war beyond the Peloponnesus with greater freedom. At the same time they entreated the Boeotians to give up Panactum to the Lacedaemonians, in order that they might exchange it for Pylos, and so be in a better position for renewing the war with Athens.

The Boeotians and Corinthians, having received from Xenares and Cleobulus and their other Lacedaemonian friends the instructions which they were to convey to their own governments, returned to their respective cities. On their way home two Argives high in office, who had been waiting for them on the road, entered into communications with them, in the hope that the Boeotians, like the Corinthians, Eleans, and Mantineans, might join their alliance; if this could only be accomplished, and they could act together, they might easily, they said, go to war or make peace, either with Lacedaemon or with any other power. The Boeotian envoys were pleased at the proposal, for it so happened that the request of the Argives coincided with the instructions of their Lacedaemonian friends. Whereupon the Argives, finding that their proposals were acceptable to the Boeotians, promised to send an embassy to them, and so departed. When the Boeotians returned home they told the Boeotarchs what they had heard, both at Lacedaemon and from the Argives who had met them on their way. The Boeotarchs were glad, and their zeal was quickened when they discovered that the request made to them by their friends in Lacedaemon fell in with the

37

The Boeotians agree. Two Argives make a similar proposal to them.

projects of the Argives. Soon afterwards the envoys from Argos appeared, inviting the Boeotians to fulfil their engagement. The Boeotarchs encouraged their proposals, and dismissed them; promising that they would send envoys of their own to negotiate the intended alliance.

38   In the meantime the Boeotarchs and the envoys from *But the negotiation* Corinth, Megara, and Chalcidicè deter-*afterwards fails through* mined that they would take an oath to *mismanagement.* one another, pledging themselves to assist whichever of them was at any time in need, and not go to war or make peace without the consent of all. When they had got thus far, the Megarians and Boeotians, who acted together in the matter[a], were to enter into an agreement with the Argives. But before the oath was sworn, the Boeotarchs communicated their intentions to the Four Councils of the Boeotians, whose sanction is always necessary, and urged that oaths of alliance should be offered to any cities which were willing to join with them for mutual protection. But the Boeotian Councils, fearing that they might offend the Lacedaemonians if they swore alliance to the Corinthians who had seceded from them, rejected their proposals. For the Boeotarchs did not tell them what had passed at Lacedaemon, and how two of the Ephors, Cleobulus and Xenares, and their friends had advised them first to become allies of Argos and Corinth, and then to make a further alliance with the Lacedaemonians. They thought that the Councils, whether informed of this or not, would be sure to ratify their foregone decision when it was communicated to them. So the plan broke down, and the Corinthian and the Chalcidian envoys went away without effecting their purpose. The Boeotarchs, who had originally intended, if they succeeded, to do their best to effect an alliance with the Argives, gave up the idea of bringing this latter measure before the Councils, and did not fulfil their

---

[a] Cp. v. 31 fin.

promise of sending envoys to Argos; but the whole business was neglected and deferred.

During the same winter the Olynthians made a sudden attack upon Mecyberna[a], which was held by an Athenian garrison, and took it. The Athenians and Lacedaemonians still continued to negotiate about the places which had not been restored, the Lacedaemonians hoping *39*

The Lacedaemonians, wanting to recover Pylos, persuade the Boeotians, with whom they make a separate alliance, to give up Panactum.

that, if the Athenians got back Panactum from the Boeotians, they might themselves recover Pylos. So they sent an embassy to the Boeotians, and begged of them to give up Panactum and the Athenian prisoners to themselves, that they might obtain Pylos in return for them. But the Boeotians refused to give them up unless the Lacedaemonians made a separate alliance with them as they had done with the Athenians. Now the Lacedaemonians knew that, if they acceded to this request, they would be dealing unfairly with Athens, because there was a stipulation which forbade either state to make war or peace without the consent of the other; but they were eager to obtain Panactum and thereby, as they hoped, recover Pylos. At the same time the party who wished to break the peace with Athens were zealous on behalf of the Boeotians. So they made the alliance about the end of winter and the beginning of spring. The Boeotians at once commenced the demolition of Panactum; and the eleventh year of the war ended. *B. C. 420. Ol. 90.*

Immediately on the commencement of spring, the Argives, observing that the envoys whom the Boeotians promised to send had not arrived, that Panactum was being demolished, and that a private alliance had been made between the Lacedaemonians and the Boeotians, began to fear that they would be isolated, and that the *40*

The Argives are alarmed at the seeming agreement of the Boeotians and Lacedaemonians, in which they suppose the Athenians to be included.

---

a Cp. v. 18. § 7.

whole confederacy would go over to the Lacedaemonians.
For they thought that the Boeotians were demolishing
Panactum by the desire of the Lacedaemonians, and had
likewise been induced by them to come into the Athenian
treaty; and that the Athenians were cognisant of the
whole affair. But, if so, they could no longer form an
alliance even with Athens, although they had hitherto
imagined that the enmity of the two powers would secure
them an alliance with one or the other, and that if they
lost the peace with Lacedaemon, they might at any rate
become allies of the Athenians. So in their perplexity,
fearing that they might have to fight Lacedaemon, Tegea,
Boeotia, and Athens, all at once, the Argives, who at the
time when they were proudly hoping to be the leaders of
Peloponnesus had refused to make a treaty with Lacedaemon, now sent thither two envoys, Eustrophus and
Aeson, who were likely to be well regarded by the Spartans.
For under present circumstances it seemed to them that
nothing better could be done than to make a treaty with
the Lacedaemonians on any terms whatever, and keep out
of war.

41   The envoys arrived, and began to confer with the Lace-

They send envoys to daemonians respecting the conditions
Lacedaemon, who, after on which the peace should be made.
making a foolish stipu- The Argives at first demanded that the
lation about Cynuria, old quarrel about the border-land of
prepare to conclude a Cynuria, a district which contains the
peace with the Lacedae- cities of Thyrea and Anthenè and is
monians for fifty years.

occupied by the Lacedaemonians, should be referred to the
arbitration of some state or person. Of this the Lacedaemonians would not allow a word to be said, but they
professed their readiness to renew the treaty on the old
terms. The Argives at length induced them to make
a fifty years' peace, on the understanding however that
either Lacedaemon or Argos, provided that neither
city were suffering at the time from war or plague, might
challenge the other to fight for the disputed territory, as

they had done once before when both sides claimed the
victory; but the conquered party was not to be pursued
over their own border. The Lacedaemonians at first
thought that this proposal was nonsense; however, as they
were desirous of having the friendship of Argos on any
terms, they assented, and drew up a written treaty. But
they desired the envoys, before any of the provisions took
effect, to return and lay the matter before the people of
Argos; if they agreed, they were to come again at the
Hyacinthia and take the oaths. So they departed.

While the Argives were thus engaged, the envoys of the 42
Lacedaemonians—Andromedes, Phae-
dimus, and Antimenidas—who were *Indignation of the*
Athenians at the separ-
appointed to receive Panactum and the *ate alliance and at the*
demolition of Panac-
prisoners from the Boeotians, and give *tum, which should have*
them up to the Athenians, found *been restored intact.*
Panactum already demolished by the Boeotians. They
alleged that the Athenians and Boeotians in days of old
had quarrelled about the place, and had sworn that neither
of them should inhabit it, but both enjoy the use of it.
However, Andromedes and his colleagues conveyed the
Athenian prisoners who were in the hands of the Boeotians
to Athens, and restored them; they further announced the
destruction of Panactum, ᵃ maintaining that they were
restoring that too ᵃ, inasmuch as no enemy of the Athenians
could any longer dwell there. Their words raised a violent
outcry among the Athenians; they felt that the Lacedaemonians were dealing unfairly with them in two respects:
first, there was the demolition of Panactum, which should
have been delivered standing; secondly, they were
informed of the separate alliance which the Lacedaemonians
had made with the Boeotians, notwithstanding their promise that they would join in coercing those who did not
accept the peace. They called to mind all their other

ᵃ Or, 'maintaining that this,' i. e. its destruction, 'was equivalent to
its restoration' (καὶ τοῦτο, τὴν καθαίρεσιν, ἀπόδοσιν εἶναι).

shortcomings in the fulfilment of the treaty, and conscious that they had been deceived, they answered the envoys roughly, and sent them away.

43 When the difference between the Lacedaemonians and

Alcibiades, the youthful Athenian leader, irritated at the want of confidence shown in him by the Lacedaemonians, opposes them at Athens.

Athenians had gone thus far, the war party at Athens in their turn lost no time in pressing their views. Foremost among them was Alcibiades the son of Cleinias, a man who would have been thought young in any other city, but was influential by reason of his high descent: he sincerely preferred the Argive alliance, but at the same time he took part against the Lacedaemonians from temper, and because his pride was touched. For they had not consulted him, but had negotiated the peace through Nicias and Laches, despising his youth, and disregarding an ancient connexion with his family, who had been their proxeni; a connexion which his grandfather had renounced, and he, by the attention which he had paid to the captives from Sphacteria, had hoped to have renewed. Piqued at the small respect which was shown to all his claims, he had originally opposed the negotiations; declaring that the Lacedaemonians were not to be trusted, and that their only object in making terms was that they might by Athenian help crush the Argives, and afterwards attack the Athenians themselves when they had no friends. As soon as the rupture occurred he promptly despatched a private message to the Argives, bidding them send an embassy as quickly as they could, together with representatives of Mantinea and Elis, and invite the Athenians to enter the alliance; now was the time, and he would do his utmost to assist them.

44 The Argives received his message, and thus became aware that the alliance with the Boeotians had been made without the consent of the Athenians, and that a violent quarrel had broken out between Athens and Lacedaemon. So they thought no more about their

ambassadors who were at that very moment negotiating the peace with Lacedaemon, but turned their thoughts towards Athens. They reflected that Athens was a city which had been their friend of old[a]; like their own it was governed by a democracy, and would be a powerful ally to them at sea, if they were involved in war. They at once sent envoys *At his suggestion the Argives, who are partly influenced by the memory of an ancient connexion, partly by democratic sympathy, and also by the hope of a naval alliance, join the Athenians.* to negotiate an alliance with the Athenians; the Eleans and Mantineans joined in the embassy. Thither also came in haste three envoys from Lacedaemon, who were thought likely to be acceptable at Athens—Philocharidas, Leon, and Endius[b]. They were sent because the Lacedaemonians were afraid that the Athenians in their anger would join the Argive alliance. The envoys while they demanded the restoration of Pylos in return for Panactum, were to apologise for the alliance with the Boeotians, and to explain that it was not made with any view to the injury of Athens.

They delivered their message to the council, adding that they came with full power to ‘treat about all differences. Alcibiades took alarm; he feared that if the envoys made a similar statement to the people they would win them over to their side, and that the Argive alliance would be rejected. Whereupon he devised the 45 *Alcibiades by a trick deceives the Lacedaemonian envoys. They are persuaded to deny in the assembly the powers which they have acknowledged in the council.* following trick : he solemnly assured the Lacedaemonians that if they would not communicate to the people the extent of their powers, he would restore Pylos to them, for he would use his influence in their favour instead of against them, and would arrange their other differences. But his real aim all the time was to alienate them from Nicias, and to bring about an alliance with Argos, Elis,

---

[a] Cp. i. 102 fin.   [b] Cp. viii. 6 med.

and Mantinea, which he hoped to effect, if he could only
discredit them in the assembly, and create the impression
that their intentions were not honest, and that they never
told the same tale twice.   And he succeeded; for when
the envoys appeared before the assembly, and in answer
to the question whether they had full powers replied ' No,'
in direct contradiction to what they had said in the council,
the patience of the Athenians was exhausted, and Alcibiades declaimed against the Lacedaemonians more violently
than ever.   The people were carried away and were ready
to have in the Argives, and make an alliance with them
and their confederates on the spot.   But an earthquake
occurred before the final vote was taken, and the assembly
was adjourned.

46   The trick which had deceived the Lacedaemonians

The trick deceives Nicias, who nevertheless continues to support the Lacedaemonians; he is himself sent to demand satisfaction at Sparta.   The ' nego- tiation fails.

themselves completely deceived Nicias,
who could not understand the dis-
avowal of their powers.   Nevertheless
in the assembly which met on the following day he still continued to maintain that the Athenians ought to prefer
the friendship of Sparta, and not to
conclude the Argive alliance until they had sent to the
Lacedaemonians and ascertained their intentions.   He
urged them not to renew the war now, when it could be
put off with honour to themselves and discredit to the
Lacedaemonians; they were successful and should seek
to preserve their good fortune as long as they could, but
the Lacedaemonians were in a bad way, and would be
only too glad to fight as soon as possible at all hazards.
And he prevailed on them to send envoys, of whom he
was himself one, requiring the Lacedaemonians, if they
were sincere in their intentions, to rebuild and restore
Panactum, to restore Amphipolis, and to renounce their
alliance with the Boeotians unless they came into the
treaty, according to the stipulation which forbade the
contracting parties to make a new alliance except by

mutual consent. If we, they added, had wanted to deal
unfairly, we should already have accepted an alliance with
the Argives, whose ambassadors have come hither to offer
it. They entrusted the representation of these and their
other grievances to Nicias and his colleagues, and sent
them away to Sparta. These, on their arrival, delivered
their message, which they concluded by declaring that,
unless the Lacedaemonians renounced their alliance with
the Boeotians in case the latter still refused to accept the
peace, the Athenians on their part would enter into an
alliance with the Argives and their confederates. The
Lacedaemonians refused to give up their Boeotian alliance,
Xenares the Ephor, with his friends and partisans, carrying
this point. However they consented to ratify their former
oaths at the request of Nicias, who was afraid that he
would return without having settled anything, and would
incur the blame of failure, as indeed he did, because he
was held to be responsible for the original treaty with the
Lacedaemonians. When the Athenians learned on his
return that the negotiations with Sparta had miscarried,
they were furious ; and acting under a sense of injustice,
entered into an alliance with the Argives and their allies,
whose ambassadors were present at the time, for Alcibiades had introduced them on purpose. The terms were
as follows :—

'I. The Athenians and the Argives, Mantineans, and 47
Eleans, on their own behalf and that of *Terms of an alliance*
the allies over whom they severally *between the Athenians*
rule, make a peace to continue for a *and the Argive con-*
hundred years both by sea and land, *federacy.*
without fraud or hurt. The Argives, Eleans, Mantineans,
and their allies shall not make war against the Athenians
and the allies over whom they rule, and the Athenians and
their allies shall not make war against the Argives, Eleans,
Mantineans, and their allies, in any sort or manner.

'II. Athens, Argos, Elis, and Mantinea shall be allied
for a hundred years on the following conditions :—If

enemies invade the territory of the Athenians, the Argives, Eleans, and Mantineans shall go to Athens and render the Athenians any assistance which they may demand of them, in the most effectual manner, and to the utmost of their power. And if the enemy spoil their territory and depart, the offending city shall be an enemy to Argos, Mantinea, Elis, and Athens, and suffer at the hands of all these cities; and it shall not be lawful for any of them to make peace with the offending city, unless they have the consent of all the rest. And if enemies shall invade the territory of the Eleans or Argives or Mantineans, the Athenians shall go to Argos, Mantinea, or Elis, and render these cities any assistance which they may demand of them, in the most effectual manner, and to the utmost of their power. If an enemy spoil their territory and depart, the offending city shall be an enemy to Athens, Argos, Mantinea, and Elis, and shall suffer at the hands of all these cities; and it shall not be lawful for any of them to make peace with the offending city, unless they have the consent of all the rest.

'III. The confederates shall not allow armed men to pass through their own territory, or that of the allies over whom they severally rule or may rule, or to pass by sea, with hostile intent, unless all the cities have formally consented to their passage—that is to say, Athens, Argos, Mantinea, and Elis.

'IV. The city which sends troops to help another shall supply them with provisions for thirty days, counting from the time of their arrival at the city which summons them; it shall also provide for them at their departure. But if the city which summons the troops wishes to employ them for a longer time, it shall give them provisions at the rate of three Aeginetan obols[a] a day for heavy-armed and light-armed troops and for archers, and an Aeginetan drachma[b] for cavalry.

---

[a] About **6d.**   [b] About *1s.*

'V. The city which sent for the troops shall have the command when the war is carried on in her territory. Or, if the allied cities agree to send out a joint expedition, then the command shall be equally shared among all the cities.

'VI. The Athenians shall swear to the peace on their own behalf and on that of their allies ; the Argives, Mantineans, and Eleans, and their allies shall swear city by city. The oath shall be taken over full-grown victims, and shall be that oath which in the countries of the several contracting parties is deemed the most binding. The form of oath shall be as follows :—

"I will be true to the alliance, and will observe the agreement in all honesty and without fraud or hurt ; I will not transgress it in any way or manner." '

At Athens the senate and the home magistrates shall swear, and the prytanes shall administer the oath ; at Argos the senate and the council of eighty and the artynae *Provisions for the ratification of the treaty and for changes.* shall swear, and the eighty shall administer the oath ; at Mantinea the demiurgi and the senate and the other magistrates shall swear, and the theori and the polemarchs shall administer the oath. At Elis the demiurgi and the supreme magistrates and the six hundred shall swear, and the demiurgi and the guardians of the law shall administer the oath. Thirty days before the Olympian games the Athenians shall go to Elis, to Mantinea, and to Argos, and renew the oath. Ten days before the Great Panathenaea the Argives, Eleans, and Mantineans shall go to Athens and renew the oath. The agreement concerning the treaty and the oaths and the alliance shall be inscribed on a stone column in the Acropolis by the Athenians, by the Argives on a similar column in the temple of Apollo in the Agora, and by the Mantineans in the temple of Zeus in the Agora. They shall together erect at Olympia a brazen column at the coming Olympic games. And if these cities think it desirable to make any improvement in the treaty, they shall add it to the provisions of it. Whatever the cities agree upon in common shall hold good.

48   Thus the peace and the alliance were concluded.

The Corinthians re- Nevertheless the previous treaty be-
fuse to join the Argives tween the Lacedaemonians and the
in the Athenian alliance. Athenians was not on that account
renounced by either party. The Corinthians, although allies of the Argives, took no part in the new alliance; they had already refused to swear to an offensive and defensive alliance which the Eleans, Argives, and Mantineans had previously made with one another. They said that they were satisfied with the original defensive alliance which bound them only to assist one another when attacked, but not to join in offensive movements. Thus the Corinthians severed themselves from the allies, and were again beginning to turn their thoughts to the Lacedaemonians.

49   During the summer the Olympic games were celebrated,

The Lacedaemonians the Olympiad being that in which An-
are excluded from the drosthenes, an Arcadian, won his first
Olympic games on the victory in the pancratium. The Lace-
ground that they had daemonians were excluded from the
attacked Phyrcus and temple by the Eleans, and so could
entered Lepreum during neither sacrifice nor contend in the
the Olympic truce, and games. For they had refused to pay
had refused to pay the the fine which, according to Olympic
fine imposed upon them.
law, the Eleans had imposed upon them, alleging that they had brought an armed force against the fortress of Phyrcus, and had introduced some hoplites of their own into Lepreum during the Olympic truce. The fine amounted to two thousand minae [a], being two minae [b] for each hoplite, which is the penalty imposed by the law. The Lacedaemonians sent envoys who argued that the sentence was unjust, for at the time when their troops entered Lepreum the truce had not been announced at Lacedaemon. The

---

[a] About £6,660.   [b] About £6 12s.

Eleans replied that the truce (which they always proclaim first to themselves) had already begun with them, and that while they were quietly observing the truce, and expecting nothing less, the Lacedaemonians had treacherously attacked them. The Lacedaemonians rejoined by asking why the Eleans proclaimed the truce at all at Lacedaemon if they considered them to have broken it already—they could not really have thought so when they made the proclamation ; and from the moment when the announcement reached Lacedaemon all hostilities had ceased. The Eleans were still positive that the Lacedaemonians were in the wrong, and said that they would never be persuaded of the contrary. But if the Lacedaemonians were willing to restore Lepreum to them, they offered to remit their own share of the penalty, and pay on their behalf that part which was due to the God.

As this proposal was rejected, the Eleans made another : 50 the Lacedaemonians need not give up Lepreum if they did not like, but since they wanted to have access to the temple of Olympian Zeus, they might go up to *Fear of a disturbance at the games, which turns out to be unfounded.* his altar and swear before all the Hellenes that they would hereafter pay the fine. But neither to this offer would the Lacedaemonians agree ; they were therefore excluded from the temple and from the sacrifices and games, and sacrificed at home. The other Hellenes, with the exception of the people of Lepreum, sent representatives to Olympia. The Eleans however, fearing that the Lacedaemonians would force their way into the temple and offer sacrifice, had a guard of young men under arms ; there came to their aid likewise a thousand Argives, and a thousand Mantineans, and certain Athenian horsemen, who had been awaiting the celebration of the festival at Argos. The whole assembly were in terror lest the Lacedaemonians should come upon them in arms, and their fears were redoubled when Lichas, the son of Arcesilaus, was struck by the officers. As a Lacedaemonian he had been excluded from the lists, but his chariot had been entered in the name of the Boeotian state, and was declared victorious. He had then come forward into the arena and placed a garland on the head of his charioteer, wishing to show that the chariot was his own. When the blows were given the anxiety became intense, and every one thought that something serious would happen. But the Lacedaemonians did not stir, and the festival passed off quietly.

The Olympic games being over, the Argives and their allies went to Corinth, and requested the Corinthians to join them. An embassy from Lacedaemon was also present. After much discussion nothing was concluded, for an earthquake broke up the assembly, and the envoys from the several states returned home. So the summer ended.

51   In the following winter there was a battle between the Heracleans of Trachis and the Oeni-anians, Dolopes, Malians, and certain Thessalians. These were neighbouring tribes hostile to the place, for it was in order to control them that it was originally fortified ; they had been enemies to it from the first, and had done it all the damage in their power. In this battle they gained a victory over the Heracleans. Xenares, son of Cnidis, the Lacedaemonian governor, and many of the Heracleans were killed. Thus ended the winter, and with it the twelfth year of the war.

The Heracleans defeated by the neighbouring tribes.

52   At the beginning of the following summer the Boeotians took possession of Heraclea, which after the battle was in a miserable plight. They dismissed Hegesippidas, the Lacedaemonian governor, for his misconduct [a], and occupied the place themselves. They were afraid that now, when the Lacedaemonians were embroiled in Peloponnesus, the Athenians

B.C. 419.
Ol. 90, 2.

The Boeotians take possession of Heraclea.

_____

[a] Cp. iii. 93 fin.

would take it if they did not.   But, for all that, the Lacedaemonians were offended.

During the same summer, Alcibiades, the son of Cleinias, now one of the Athenian generals, *Activity of Alcibiades* acting in concert with the Argives and *in Achaia and other* their allies, led into Peloponnesus *parts of Peloponnesus.* a small Athenian force of hoplites and archers.   He collected other troops from the Athenian allies in the Peloponnese, and, marching with his army through the country, organised the affairs of the confederacy.   Coming to Patrae, he persuaded the citizens to build walls reaching down to the sea.   He was intending also to erect a fort himself on the promontory of Rhium in Achaia.   But the Corinthians, Sicyonians, and others to whose interests the fort would have been injurious, came and prevented him.

In the same summer there broke out a war between the 53 Epidaurians   and   the   Argives.   The   *The Argives on a* occasion of the war was as follows :— *flimsy pretext make* The Epidaurians were bound to send *war against the Epi-* a victim as a tribute for ^a the meadows ^a *daurians.* to the temple of Apollo Pythaeus over which the Argives had chief authority, and they had not done so.   But this charge was a mere pretext; for in any case Alcibiades and the Argives had determined, if possible, to attach Epidaurus to their league, that they might keep the Corinthians quiet, and enable the Athenians to bring forces to Argos direct from Aegina instead of sailing round the promontory of Scyllaeum.   So the Argives prepared to invade Epidauria, as if they wished on their own account to exact payment of the sacrifice.

About the same time the Lacedaemonians with their 54 whole force, under the command of king Agis the son of Archidamus, likewise made an expedition.   They marched as far as Leuctra, a place on their own frontier in the direction of Mount Lycaeum.   No one, not even the cities

---

^a Or, reading παραποταμίων, 'the water meadows.'

whence the troops came, knew whither the expedition was

The Lacedaemonians intending to make war upon Argos are deterred by the sacrifices and the sacred month. The latter obligation is evaded by the Argives, who go on with the expedition against Epidaurus.

going. But at the frontier the sacrifices proved unfavourable; so they returned, and sent word to their allies that, when the coming month was over, which was Carneus, a month held sacred by the Dorians, they should prepare for an expedition. When they had retreated, the Argives, setting out on the twenty-seventh day of the month before Carneus, and continuing the observance of this day during the whole time of the expedition, invaded and devastated the territory of Epidaurus. The Epidaurians summoned their allies, but some of them refused to come, pleading the sanctity of the month; others came as far as the frontier of Epidauria and there stopped.

55   While the Argives were in Epidauria, envoys from the

Conference held at Mantinea. War between Epidaurus and Argos intermitted and then renewed.

different cities met at Mantinea, on the invitation of the Athenians. A conference was held, at which Euphamidas the Corinthian remarked that their words and their actions were at variance;

for they were conferring about peace while the Argives and the Epidaurians with their allies were in the field against each other; first let envoys from both parties go and induce the armies to disband, and then they might come back and discuss the peace. His advice was approved; so they went straight to the Argives and compelled them to withdraw from Epidauria. But, when they re-assembled, they were still unable to agree, and the Argives again invaded and began to ravage the Epidaurian territory. Whereupon the Lacedaemonians likewise made an expedition as far as Caryae; but again the sacrifices at the frontier proved unfavourable, and they returned home. The Argives, after devastating about one-third of Epidauria, also returned home. One thousand Athenian hoplites, under the command of Alcibiades, had come to their aid. But hearing that the Lacedaemonian expedition was over, and seeing that there was no longer any need of them, they departed. And so passed the summer.

In the following winter the Lacedaemonians, unknown 56 to the Athenians, sent by sea to Epidaurus a garrison of three hundred under the command of Agesippidas. The Argives came to the Athenians and complained that, notwithstanding the clause in the treaty which forbade the passage of enemies through the territory of any of the contracting

The Lacedaemonians send a garrison by sea to Epidaurus. The Argives remonstrate with the Athenians for allowing the Lacedaemonians to pass. The Athenians declare the treaty broken.

parties[a], they had allowed the Lacedaemonians to pass by sea along the Argive coast. If they did not retaliate by replacing the Messenians and Helots in Pylos, and letting them ravage Laconia, they, the Argives, would consider themselves wronged. The Athenians, by the advice of Alcibiades, inscribed at the foot of the column on which the treaty was recorded [b] words to the effect that the Lacedaemonians had not abided by their oaths, and thereupon conveyed the Helots recently settled at Cranii [c] to Pylos that they might plunder the country, but they took no further steps. During the winter the war between the Argives and Epidaurians continued; there was no regular engagement, but there were ambuscades and incursions in which losses were inflicted, now on one side, now on the other. At the end of winter, when the spring was approaching, the Argives came with scaling-ladders against Epidaurus, expecting to find that the place was stripped of its defenders by the war, and could be taken by storm. But the attempt failed, and they returned. So the winter came to an end, and with it the thirteenth year of the war.

In· the middle of the following summer, the Lacedae- 57 monians, seeing that their Epidaurian allies were in great B. C. 418. distress, and that several cities of Peloponnesus had Ol. 90, 3.

[a] Cp. v. 47. § 3.   [b] Cp. v. 18. § 4; 23. § 5.   [c] Cp. v. 35 fin.

seceded from them, while others were disaffected, and knowing that if they did not quickly take measures of precaution the evil would spread, made war on Argos with their whole forces, including the Helots, under the command of Agis the son of Archidamus, the Lacedaemonian king. The Tegeans and the other Arcadian allies of the Lacedaemonians took part in the expedition. The rest of their allies, both from within and without the Peloponnesus, mustered at Phlius. Among the other contingents there came from Boeotia five thousand heavy-armed, and as many light-armed, five hundred cavalry, and attached to each horseman a foot-soldier; and from Corinth two thousand heavy-armed, while the Phliasians joined with their whole force, because the army was to assemble in their country.

The Lacedaemonians at length take the field in earnest. Their allies muster at Phlius.

58   The Argives, having had previous notice of the Lacedaemonian preparations, and seeing that they were actually on their march to join the rest of the army at Phlius, now took the field themselves. The Mantineans and their allies and three thousand Elean hoplites came to their aid. They advanced to the territory of Methydrium in Arcadia, where they fell in with the Lacedaemonians. The two armies each occupied a hill, and the Argives, thinking that they now had the Lacedaemonians alone, prepared for action. But in the night Agis removed his forces unknown to them and went to join the allies at Phlius. At dawn the Argives became aware of his departure, and moved first towards Argos, then to the Nemean road, by which they expected the Lacedaemonians and their allies to descend into the plain. But Agis, instead of taking the road by which he was expected, led the Lacedaemonians, Arcadians, and Epidaurians by a more difficult path, and so made his way down; the Corinthians, Pellenians, and Phliasians went by another

The Argives and their allies march into Arcadia; there they find the Lacedaemonians isolated. But Agis evades them and joins the rest of the army at Phlius.

steep pass; the Boeotians, Megarians, and Sicyonians he commanded to descend by the Nemean road, where the Argives had taken up their position, in order that, if the Argives should return and attack his own division of the army in the plain, they might be pursued and harassed by their cavalry. Having made these dispositions, and having come down into the plain, he began to devastate Saminthus and the neighbourhood.

It was now daylight, and the Argives, who had become 59 aware of his movements, quitted Nemea *The Argives are sur-* and went in search of the enemy. *rounded by the enemy,* Encountering the Phliasian and Cor- *who enter the Argive* inthian forces, they killed a few of the *territory in three di-* Phliasians, and had rather more of their *visions; they are in* own troops killed by the Corinthians. *the utmost danger, of* The Boeotians, Megarians, and Sicyon- *which they are wholly* *unconscious, when two* ians marched as they were ordered *of their leading men* towards Nemea, but found the Argives no longer there, *propose a truce.* for by this time they had descended from the high ground, and seeing their lands ravaged were drawing up their troops in order of battle. The Lacedaemonians prepared to meet them. The Argives were now surrounded by their enemies; for on the side of the plain the Lacedaemonians and their division of the army cut them off from the city; from the hills above they were hemmed in by the Corinthians, Phliasians and Pellenians, towards Nemea by the Boeotians, Sicyonians, and Megarians, and in the absence of the Athenians, who alone of their allies had not arrived, they had no cavalry. The main body of the Argives and their allies had no conception of their danger. They thought that their position was a favourable one, and that they had cut off the Lacedaemonians in their own country and close to the city of Argos. But two of the Argives, Thrasyllus one of the five generals, and Alciphron the proxenus of the Lacedaemonians, came to Agis when the armies were on the point of engaging, and urged him privately not to fight; the Argives were ready to offer and accept a fair arbitration, if the Lacedaemonians had any complaint to make of them ; they would gladly conclude a treaty, and be at peace for the future.

60   These Argives spoke of their own motion ; they had no *The truce is accepted* authority from the people ; and Agis, *by Agis. The magnifi-* likewise on his own authority, accepted *cent army of the Pelo-* their proposals, not conferring with his *ponnesians now returns* *home. They find great* countrymen at large, but only with one *fault with their com-* of the Lacedaemonian magistrates who *manders,* accompanied the expedition. He made a treaty with the Argives for four months, within which they were to execute their agreement, and then, without saying a word to any of the allies, he at once withdrew his army.   The Lacedaemonians and their allies followed Agis out of respect for the law, but they blamed him severely among themselves.   For they believed that they had lost a glorious opportunity ; their enemies had been surrounded on every side both by horse and foot ; and yet they were returning home having done nothing worthy of their great effort.—No finer Hellenic army had ever up to that day been collected ; its appearance was most striking at Nemea while the host was still one ; the Lacedaemonians were there in their full strength ; arrayed by their side were Arcadians, Boeotians, Corinthians, Sicyonians, Pellenians, Phliasians, and Megarians, from each state chosen men—they might have been thought a match not only for the Argive confederacy, but for another as large.—So the army returned and dispersed to their homes, much out of humour with Agis.

The Argives on their part found still greater fault with *and the Argives still* those who had made the peace, *greater.* unauthorised by the people ; they too thought that such an opportunity would never recur, and that it was the Lacedaemonians who had escaped, for the combat would have taken place close to their own city, and they had numerous and brave allies.   And so, as they were retreating and had reached the bed of the Charadrus, where they hold military trials before they enter the city, they began to stone Thrasyllus. He saved his life by flying to the altar, but they confiscated his property.

Soon afterwards there arrived an Athenian reinforce- 61 ment of a thousand hoplites and three hundred horse, under the command of Laches and Nicostratus. The Argives, although dissatisfied with the truce, were reluctant to break it, so they bade them depart; and, when they desired to treat, they would not present them to the assembly until they were compelled by the importunity of their Mantinean and Elean allies, who had not yet left Argos. The Athenians then, speaking by the mouth of their ambassador Alcibiades, told the Argives in the presence of the rest that they had no right to make the truce at all independently of their allies, and that, the Athenians having arrived at the opportune moment, they should fight at once. The allies were convinced, and they all, with the exception of the Argives, immediately marched against Orchomenus in Arcadia; the Argives, though consenting, did not join them at first, but they came afterwards. The united forces then sat down before Orchomenus, which they assailed repeatedly; they were especially anxious to get the place into their hands, because certain Arcadian hostages had been deposited there by the Lacedaemonians. The Orchomenians, considering the weakness of their fortifications and the numbers of the enemy, and beginning to fear that they might perish before any one came to their assistance, agreed to join the alliance: they were to give hostages of their own to the Mantineans, and to deliver up those whom the Lacedaemonians had deposited with them.

Alcibiades and the allies refuse to acknowledge the truce. The Argives reluctantly consent to its violation. The united forces besiege Orchomenus, which surrenders to them.

The allied force, now in possession of Orchomenus, 62 considered against what town they should next proceed; the Eleans wanted them to attack Lepreum, the Mantineans Tegea. The Argives and Athenians sided with the Mantineans; whereupon the Eleans, indignant that

The Argives and their allies now quarrel among themselves. The Eleans return home; the rest of the allies prepare to attack Tegea.

they had not voted for the expedition against Lepreum, returned home, but the remainder of the allies made preparations at Mantinea to attack Tegea. They were assisted by a party within the walls who were ready to betray the place to them.

63   The Lacedaemonians, when after making the four

The Lacedaemonians are furious with Agis. He pacifies them. Nevertheless they appoint ten Spartans to be his advisers.

months' truce they had returned home, severely blamed Agis because he had not conquered Argos, and had lost an opportunity of which, in their own judgment, they had never before had

the like. For it was no easy matter to bring together a body of allies so numerous and brave. But when the news came that Orchomenus had fallen they were furious, and in a fit of passion, which was unlike their usual character, they had almost made up their minds to raze his house and fine him in the sum of a hundred thousand drachmae [a]. But he besought them not to punish him, promising that he would atone for his error by some brave action in the field; if he did not keep his word they might do as they pleased with him. So they did not inflict the fine or demolish his house, but on this occasion they passed a law which had no precedent in their history, providing that ten Spartans should be appointed his counsellors [b], who were to give their consent before he could lead the army out of the city.

64   Meanwhile word was brought from their friends in Tegea that they must come at once, since Tegea was about to secede and had almost seceded already to the Argives and their allies. Whereupon the Lacedaemonians

---

[a] About £4,600, supposing the sum to be given in Aeginetan drachmae.   [b] Cp. the cases of Cnemus, ii. 85 init.; Alcidas, iii. 69 med.; Astyochus, viii. 39 med., for a somewhat similar proceeding.

led out their whole force, including the Helots, with an alacrity which they had never before displayed, and marched to Orestheum in Maenalia. They told their Arcadian allies to assemble and follow them at once to Tegea. *The Lacedaemonians again lead forth their whole force to the support of Tegea.* When the army had proceeded as far as Orestheum they dismissed the sixth part, including the elder and the younger men, who were to keep guard at home, and arrived at Tegea with the rest of their troops. Not long afterwards the Arcadian allies appeared. They had also sent to the Corinthians, and to the Boeotians, Phocians, and Locrians, whom they summoned to meet them with all speed at Mantinea. But the notice given to the allies was short, and their passage was barred by the enemies' country, which they could not easily traverse unless they waited for one another and came all together. However, they did their best. The Lacedaemonians, accompanied by their Arcadian allies, invaded the territory of Mantinea, and pitching their camp near the temple of Heracles, wasted the country.

When the Argives and their allies saw the enemy they took up a steep and hardly assailable position, and arranged themselves in order of battle. The Lacedaemonians instantly charged them, and had proceeded within a javelin or stone's throw when one of the elder Spartans, seeing the strength of the ground which they were attacking, called out to Agis that he was trying to mend one error by another; *The Argives occupy a hill. The Lacedaemonians charge them. Agis nearly commits a second fatal error, but is induced to withdraw his troops. After a while the Argives, who are again dissatisfied with their generals, follow him.* he meant to say that his present mistaken forwardness was intended to repair the discredit of his former retreat. And, either in consequence of this exclamation or because ᵃ some new thought suddenly struck him ᵃ, he

---

ᵃ Or, 'some new thought, or the same thought (which had occurred to the Spartan elder), suddenly struck him.'

withdrew his army in haste without actually engaging. He marched back into the district of Tegea, and proceeded to turn the water into the Mantinean territory. This water is a constant source of war between the Mantineans and Tegeans, on account of ᵃ the great harm which is done[a] to one or other of them according to the direction which the stream takes. Agis hoped that the Argives and their allies when they heard of this movement would come down from the hill and try to prevent it; he could then fight them on level ground. Accordingly he stayed about the water during the whole day, diverting the stream. Now the Argives and their confederates were at first amazed at the sudden retreat of their enemies when they were so near, and did not know what to think. But when the Lacedaemonians had retired and disappeared from view, and they found themselves standing still and not pursuing, they once more began to blame their own generals. Their cry was that they had already let the Lacedaemonians slip when they had them at a disadvantage close to Argos; and now they were running away and no one pursued them; the enemy were just allowed to escape, while their own army was quietly betrayed. The commanders were at first bewildered by the outcry; but soon they quitted the hill, and advancing into the plain took up a position with the intention of attacking.

66   On the following day the Argives and their allies drew *The Lacedaemonians* themselves up in the order in which they *are surprised. Organi-* intended to fight should they meet with *sation of their army.* the enemy. Meanwhile the Lacedaemonians returned from the water to their old encampment near the temple of Heracles. There they saw quite close to them the Argive army, which had moved on from the hill, and was already in order of battle. Never within their recorded history were the Lacedaemonians more dismayed than at that instant; not a moment was to be

---

ᵃ Or, 'the harm which is commonly done.'

this great war has been undertaken and all these preparations made. It would be best for you to join with us,
and observe the oaths yourselves which you would have
us observe. But if you prefer to be neutral, a course
which we have already once proposed to you, retain
possession of your lands, and receive both sides in
peace, but neither for the purposes of war ; and we shall
be satisfied.'

The Plataean ambassadors then returned to the city and
reported these words of Archidamus to
the people, who made answer that they
could not do what they were asked
without the sanction of the Athenians,
in whose power they had left their
*The Plataeans reply
that they cannot act
without the Athenians,
and also that they dis-
trust the Thebans.*
wives and children, and that they also feared for the very
existence of their state. When the Lacedaemonians were
gone the Athenians might come and not allow them to
carry out the treaty ; or the Thebans, who would be
included in the clause requiring them 'to receive both
sides,' might again attempt to seize their town. To this
Archidamus, wanting to reassure them, made the following
answer :—

' Then deliver over your city and houses to the Lacedaemonians ; mark the boundaries of
your land, and number your fruit-trees
and anything else which can be counted.
Go yourselves whithersoever you
*Archidamus then asks
them to surrender the
city till the end of the
war.*
please, while the war lasts, and on the return of peace we
will give back to you all that we have received. Until then
we will hold your property in trust, and will cultivate
your ground, paying you such a rent as will content you.'

Upon hearing these words the envoys again returned into the city,
and, after holding a consultation with
the people, told Archidamus that
they wished first to communicate his
*The Plataeans, ob-
taining permission to
consult the Athenians,
are encouraged by them
to resist.*
73
proposals to the Athenians, and if they could get their

say, for the secrecy of the government did not allow the
Numbers of neither army could be accurately ascertained. strength of the Lacedaemonian army to be known, and the numbers on the other side were thought to be exaggerated by the vanity natural to men when speaking of their own forces. However, the following calculation may give some idea of the Lacedaemonian numbers. There were seven divisions in the field, besides the Sciritae who numbered six hundred; in each division there were four pentecosties, in every pentecosty four enomoties, and of each enomoty there fought in the front rank four. The depth of the line was not everywhere equal, but was left to the discretion of the generals commanding divisions; on an average it was eight deep. The front line consisted of four hundred and forty-eight men, exclusive of the Sciritae [a].

69   The two armies were now on the point of engaging, but
The Mantineans, Argives, and Athenians received eloquent exhortations from their leaders. But the Lacedaemonians had no need of them. first the several commanders addressed exhortations to their own contingents. The Mantineans were told that they were not only about to fight for their country, but would have to choose between dominion [b] or slavery; having tried both, did they want to be deprived of the one, or to have any more acquaintance with the other? The Argives were reminded that in old times they had been sovereign, and more recently the equals of Sparta, in Peloponnesus; would they acquiesce for ever in the loss of their supremacy, and lose at the same time the chance of revenging themselves upon their hateful neighbours, who had wronged them again and again? The Athenians were told that it was glorious to be fighting side by side with a host of brave allies and to be found equal to the bravest. If they could conquer a Lacedaemonian army in

---

[a] The whole number of the Lacedaemonians is 3584 without the Sciritae, or with them 4184.   [b] Cp. v. 29 init.

Peloponnesus, they would both extend and secure their
dominion, and need never fear an invader again.   Such
were the exhortations addressed to the Argives and to
their allies.   But the Lacedaemonians, both in their war-
songs and in the words which a man spoke to his comrade,
did but remind one another of what their brave spirits
knew already[a].   For they had learned that true safety
was to be found in long previous training, and not in
eloquent exhortations uttered when they were going into
action.

At length the two armies went forward.   The Argives 70
and their allies advanced to the charge
with great fury and determination. *The Argives march
into battle with great*
The Lacedaemonians moved slowly *fury; the Lacedae-*
and to the music of many flute-players, *monians quietly to the*
who were stationed in their ranks, and *sound of music.*
played, not as an act of religion, but in order that the
army might march evenly and in true measure, and that
the line might not break, as often happens in great armies
when they go into battle.

Before they had actually closed a thought occurred to 71
Agis.   All armies, when engaging, are *Agis tries to extend
his left wing by moving*
apt to thrust outwards their right wing; *the Sciritae further off,*
and either of the opposing forces tends *thus leaving a gap*
to outflank his enemy's left with his *which he endeavours to*
own right, because every soldier in- *fill by a detachment*
dividually fears for his exposed side, *from his right.*
which he tries to cover with the shield of his comrade on
the right, conceiving that the closer he draws in the better
he will be protected.   The first man in the front rank of
the right wing is originally responsible for the deflection,
for he always wants to withdraw from the enemy his own
exposed side, and the rest of the army, from a like fear,
follow his example.   In this battle the line of the Mantineans, who were on the Argive right wing, extended far

---

[a] Cp. iv. 17 med , 95 init., 126 init.

beyond the Sciritae : and still further, in proportion as the army to which they belonged was the larger, did the Lacedaemonians and Tegeans on the Lacedaemonian right wing extend beyond the Athenian left. Agis was afraid that the Lacedaemonian left wing would be surrounded, and, thinking that the Mantineans outflanked them too far, he signalled to the Sciritae and the old soldiers of Brasidas to make a lateral movement away from his own division of the army, and so cover the line of the Mantineans : to fill up the space thus left vacant he ordered Hipponoidas and Aristocles, two of the polemarchs, to bring up their two divisions from the right wing, thinking that he would still have more troops than he wanted there, and that he would thus strengthen that part of his line which was opposed to the Mantineans.

72   He had given the order at the last moment, when the charge had already begun, and Aristocles and Hipponoidas refused to make the movement. (For the cowardice which they were supposed to have shown on this occasion they were afterwards banished from Sparta.) The enemy were upon him before he was ready, and as the two divisions would not advance into the place left by the Sciritae, Agis ordered the Sciritae themselves to close up, but he found that it was too late, and that they also were now unable to fill the vacant space. Then the Lacedaemonians showed in a remarkable manner that, although utterly failing in their tactics, they could win by their courage alone. When they were at close quarters with the enemy, the Mantinean right put to flight the Sciritae and the soldiers of Brasidas. The Mantineans and their allies and the thousand chosen Argives dashed in through the gap in the Lacedaemonian ranks and completed their defeat ; they surrounded and routed them, and so drove them to their waggons, where they killed some of the elder men who were appointed to guard them. In this part of

But the detachment refusing to stir, the Mantineans and Argives rush through the gap and defeat the left wing of the Lacedaemonians.

the field the Lacedaemonians were beaten, but elsewhere, and especially in the centre of the army, where the king Agis and the three hundred Knights, as they are called, who attend him, were posted, they charged the elder Argives, the Five Divisions as they are termed, the Cleonaeans, Orneatae, and those of the Athenians who were ranged with them, and put them to flight. Most of them never even struck a blow, but gave way at once on the approach of the Lacedaemonians ; some were actually trodden under foot, being overtaken by the advancing host.

When the allies and the Argives had yielded in this 73 quarter, they became severed from their comrades to the left as well as to the right of the line ; meanwhile the extended right wing of the Lacedaemonians and the Tegeans threatened to surround the Athenians. They were in great danger ; their men were being hemmed in at one point and were already defeated at another ; and but *Danger of the Athenians, which is only averted by the retirement of the Lacedaemonians on the right wing, who go to the assistance of their own defeated troops on the left. The Lacedaemonians win the battle, but do not pursue far.* for their cavalry, which did them good service, they would have suffered more than any other part of the army. Just then Agis, observing the distress of the Lacedaemonian left wing, which was opposed to the Mantineans and the thousand select Argives, commanded his whole forces to go and assist their own defeated troops. Whereupon the Athenians, when their opponents turned aside and began to move away from them, quietly made their escape, and along with them the defeated Argives. The Mantineans and their allies and the chosen force of Argives, seeing their army conquered and the Lacedaemonians bearing down upon them, gave up all thoughts of following up their advantage and fled. The loss incurred by the chosen Argives was small, that of the Mantineans more serious. The pursuit was not fierce nor the flight protracted, for the Lacedaemonians fight long and refuse to move until they have put an enemy to flight, but, having once defeated him, they do not follow him far or long.

74 Thus, or nearly thus, went the battle, by far the greatest

Numbers of the slain.

of Hellenic battles which had taken place for a long time, and fought by the most famous cities. The Lacedaemonians exposed the arms of the enemies' dead, and made a trophy of them ; they then plundered the bodies, and taking up their own dead carried them away to Tegea, where they were buried ; the enemies' dead they gave back under a flag of truce. Of the Argives, Orneatae, and Cleonaeans there fell seven hundred, of the Mantineans two hundred, and of the Athenians, including their settlers in Aegina [a], two hundred, and both their generals. As to the Lacedaemonians, their allies were not hard pressed and did not incur any considerable loss ; how many of themselves fell it was hard to ascertain precisely, but their dead are reported to have numbered about three hundred.

75 Just before the battle, Pleistoanax, the other king, led

The Lacedaemonians go home and celebrate the Carnea. Great moral effect of the battle.

out of Sparta a reinforcement composed of the elder and younger citizens [b] ; he had proceeded as far as Tegea when he heard of the victory, and returned. The Lacedaemonians sent and countermanded the reinforcements from Corinth and beyond the Isthmus ; they then went home themselves and, dismissing the allies, celebrated the festival of the Carnea, for which this happened to be the season. Thus, by a single action, they wiped out the charge of cowardice, which was due to their misfortune at Sphacteria, and of general stupidity and sluggishness, then current against them in Hellas. They were now thought [c] to have been hardly used by fortune [c], but in character to be the same as ever.

The very day before the battle, the Epidaurians with

---

[a] Cp. ii. 27 med. [b] Cp. v. 64 med. [c] Or, 'to have incurred disgrace through a mishap.'

their whole force invaded the territory of Argos, expecting
to find it deserted; they killed many of the men who
had been left to protect the country when the main army
took the field a. After the battle three thousand Elean
hoplites came to the aid of the Mantineans, and a second
detachment of a thousand from Athens. While the Lacedaemonians were still celebrating the Carnea they marched
all together against Epidaurus, and began to surround the
city with a wall, dividing the task among them. The other
allies did not persevere, but the Athenians soon completed
their own portion, the fortification of the promontory on
which the temple of Herè stood. In this part of the works
a garrison was left, to which all furnished a contingent;
they then returned to their several cities. So the summer
ended.

At the very beginning of the following winter, after the 76
celebration of the Carnea, the Lacedae-
monians led out an army as far as
Tegea, whence they sent proposals of
peace to the Argives. There had
*The Lacedaemonian
party at Argos, intend-
ing to put down the
democracy, make peace.*
always been some partisans of Lacedaemon in the city, who
had wanted to put down the democracy. After the battle
it was far easier for this party to draw the people into an
alliance with Sparta. Their intention was to make first of
all a peace, and then an alliance, with the Lacedaemonians,
and, having done so, to set upon the people. And now
there arrived in Argos, Lichas the son of Arcesilaus, the
proxenus of the Argives, offering them one of two alternatives : There were terms of peace, but they might also
have war if they pleased. A warm discussion ensued, for
Alcibiades happened to be in the place. The party which
had been intriguing for the Lacedaemonians, and had at
last ventured to come forward openly, persuaded the
Argives to accept the terms of peace, which were as
follows :—

---

a Reading ἐξελθόντων αὐτῶν.

77   'It seems good to the Lacedaemonian assembly to make
The terms of the first   an agreement with the Argives on the
treaty.   following terms:—

'I. The Argives shall restore to the Orchomenians [a] the
youths, and to the Maenalians the men whom they hold as
hostages, and to the Lacedaemonians [a] the men who were
deposited in Mantinea.

'II. They shall also evacuate Epidauria, and demolish
the fortifications which they have erected there. If the
Athenians refuse to evacuate Epidauria, they shall be
enemies to the Argives and Lacedaemonians, and to the
allies of the Lacedaemonians, and to the allies of the
Argives.

'III. If the Lacedaemonians have any youths belonging
to any of the allies in their country, they shall restore
them to their several cities.

'IV. Concerning the sacrifice to the God, the Epidaurians
shall be permitted to take an oath which the Argives shall
formally tender to them.

'V. The cities in Peloponnesus, both small and great,
shall be all independent, according to their ancestral
laws.

'VI. If any one from without Peloponnesus comes against
Peloponnesus with evil intent, the Peloponnesians shall
take council together and shall repel the enemy; and the
several states shall bear such a share in the war as may
seem equitable to the Peloponnesians.

'VII. The allies of the Lacedaemonians without Peloponnesus shall be in the same position as the other allies
of the Lacedaemonians and the allies of the Argives, and
they shall retain their present territory.

'VIII. The Argives [b] may if they think fit show this

---

[a] Cp. v. 61 fin.   [b] Or, taking αὐτοῖς of the allies : 'may show
this agreement to their allies and make terms with them if the allies
think fit ;' or, referring ξυμβαλέσθαι to the original agreement and giving
a different sense to the words αἵ κα αὐτοῖς δοκῇ : ' may show the agree-

agreement to their allies and make terms with them [b], but if the allies raise any objection, they shall dismiss them to their homes.'

When the Argives had accepted these propositions in 78 the first instance, the Lacedaemonian army returned home from Tegea. The two states now began to hold intercourse with one another, and not long *The alliance of Argos with Mantinea, Athens, and Elis is dissolved.* afterwards the same party which had negotiated the treaty contrived that the Argives should renounce their alliance with Mantinea, Athens, and Elis, and make a new treaty of alliance with Lacedaemon on the following terms :—

'It seems good to the Lacedaemonians and to the 79 Argives to make peace and alliance for fifty years on the following conditions :— *The terms of the second treaty include an alliance which extends to all the Peloponnesian cities, with fuller provisions for their independence and, in case of dispute, for arbitration.*

'I. They shall submit to arbitration on fair and equal terms, according to their ancestral customs.

'II. The other cities of Peloponnesus shall participate in the peace and alliance, and shall be independent and their own masters, retaining their own territory and submitting to arbitration on fair and equal terms, according to their ancestral customs.

'III. All the allies of the Lacedaemonians outside Peloponnesus shall share in the same terms as the Lacedaemonians, and the allies of the Argives shall be in the same position as the Argives, and shall retain their present territory.

'IV. If it shall be necessary to make an expedition in common against any place, the Lacedaemonians and the Argives shall consult together and fix the share in the war which may be equitably borne by the allies.

―――――――――――

ment to their allies before they conclude it, in case they are willing to come into it.'

B.C. 418.
Ol. 90, 3.

'V. If any of the states, either within or without Peloponnesus, have a dispute about a frontier, or any other
matter, the difference shall be duly settled. But should
a quarrel break out between two of the allied cities, they
shall appeal to some state which both the cities deem to
be impartial.

'VI. Justice shall be administered to the individual
citizens of each state according to their ancestral customs.'

80   Thus the peace and the alliance were concluded, and

*The Lacedaemonians
and Argives now act
together against the
Athenians. They in-
duce the Chalcidian cities
and Perdiccas to join
them. Evacuation of
Epidaurus.*

the Lacedaemonians and Argives
settled with each other any difference
which they had about captures made in
the war, or about any other matter.
They now acted together, and passed
a vote that no herald or embassy
should be received from the Athenians,

unless they evacuated the fortifications which they held in
Peloponnesus and left the country; they agreed also
that they would not enter into alliance or make war
except in concert. They were very energetic in all their
doings, and jointly sent ambassadors to the Chalcidian
cities in Thrace, and to Perdiccas whom they persuaded
to join their confederacy. He did not, however, immediately desert the Athenians, but he was thinking of
deserting, being influenced by the example of the Argives;
for he was himself of Argive descent[a]. The Argives and
Lacedaemonians renewed the oaths formerly taken by the
Lacedaemonians to the Chalcidians and swore new ones[b].
The Argives also sent envoys to the Athenians bidding
them evacuate the fortifications which they had raised at
Epidaurus. They, seeing that their troops formed but
a small part of the garrison, sent Demosthenes to bring
them away with him. When he came he proposed to hold
a gymnastic contest outside the fort; upon this pretext he
induced the rest of the garrison to go out, and then shut

---

[a] See note.   [b] Cp. i. 58 med.; v. 31 fin.

the gates upon them. Soon afterwards the Athenians renewed their treaty with the Epidaurians, and themselves restored the fort to them.

When the Argives deserted the alliance the Mantin- 81 eans held out for a time, but without *The   Mantineans* the Argives they were helpless, and so *make terms with the* they too came to terms with the Lace- *Lacedaemonians. The* daemonians, and gave up their claim *Argive democracy put* *down by force.* to supremacy over the cities in Arcadia which had been subject to them[a]. Next the Lacedaemonians and the Argives, each providing a thousand men, made a joint expedition: first the Lacedaemonians went alone and set up a more oligarchical government at Sicyon; then they and the Argives uniting their forces put down the democracy at Argos, and established an oligarchy which was in the interest of the Lacedaemonians. These changes were effected at the close of winter towards the approach of spring, and so ended the fourteenth year of the war.

In the ensuing summer the Dictidians in Mount Athos 82 revolted from the Athenians to the   B.C. 417. Chalcidians; and the Lacedaemonians *The popular party at* Ol. 90, 4. resettled the affairs of Achaia upon *Argos, availing them-* a footing more favourable to their *selves of a Lacedae-* interests than hitherto. The popular *monian festival, attack* *and defeat the oligarchy.* party at Argos, reconstituting them- *They renew the Athen-* selves by degrees, plucked up courage, *ian alliance and begin* and, taking advantage of the festival *to build Long Walls to* *the sea.* of the Gymnopaediae at Lacedaemon, attacked the olig- archy. A battle took place in the city: the popular party won, and either killed or expelled their enemies. The oligarchy had sought help from their friends the Lace- daemonians, but they did not come for some time; at last they put off the festival and went to their aid. When they arrived at Tegea they heard that the oligarchs had been

---

[a] Cp. v. 29 init.

defeated.   They would proceed no further, but in spite of the entreaties of the fugitives returned home and resumed the celebration of the festival. Not long afterwards envoys came to them both from the party now established in Argos and from those who had been driven out, and in the presence of their allies, after hearing many pleas from both sides, they passed a vote condemning the victorious faction; they then resolved to send an expedition to Argos, but delays occurred and time was lost.   Meanwhile the democracy at Argos, fearing the Lacedaemonians, and again courting the Athenian alliance in which their hopes were centred, began building Long Walls to the sea, in order that if they were blockaded by land they might have the advantage, with Athenian help, of introducing provisions by water.   Certain other states in Peloponnesus were privy to this project.   The whole Argive people, the citizens themselves, their wives, and their slaves, set to work upon the wall, and the Athenians sent them carpenters and masons from Athens.   So the summer ended.

83   In the ensuing winter the Lacedaemonians, hearing of the progress of the work, made an *The unfinished walls are captured and destroyed by the Lacedaemonians.* expedition to Argos with their allies, all but the Corinthians; there was also a party at Argos itself acting in their interest.   Agis the son of Archidamus, king of the Lacedaemonians, led the army.   The support which they expected to find at Argos was not forthcoming; the walls however, which were not yet finished, were captured by them and razed to the ground; they also seized Hysiae, a place in the Argive territory, and put to death all the free men whom they caught; they then withdrew, and returned to their several cities.   Next the Argives in their turn made an expedition into the territory of Phlius, which they ravaged because the Phliasians had received the Argive refugees, most of whom had settled there; they then returned home.

During the same winter the Athenians blockaded Perdiccas in Macedonia, complaining *The Athenians block-* of the league which he had made with *ade Perdiccas.* the Argives and Lacedaemonians; and also that he had been false to their alliance when they had prepared to send an army against the Chalcidians and against Amphipolis under the command of Nicias the son of Niceratus. The army was in fact disbanded chiefly owing to his withdrawal. So he became their enemy. Thus the winter ended, and with it the fifteenth year of the war.

In the ensuing summer, Alcibiades sailed to Argos 84 with twenty ships, and seized any of *Alcibiades seizes the* B.C. 416. the Argives who were still suspected *suspected Argives. The* Ol. 91. to be of the Lacedaemonian faction, *Athenians, enraged at* to the number of three hundred; and *the independence of the* the Athenians deposited them in the *island of Melos, send* subject islands near at hand. The *thither an expedition.* Athenians next made an expedition *But first they try ne-* *gotiation.* against the island of Melos with thirty ships of their own, six Chian, and two Lesbian, twelve hundred hoplites and three hundred archers besides twenty mounted archers of their own, and about fifteen hundred hoplites furnished by their allies in the islands. The Melians are colonists of the Lacedaemonians who would not submit to Athens like the other islanders. At first they were neutral and took no part. But when the Athenians tried to coerce them by ravaging their lands, they were driven into open hostilities[a]. The generals, Cleomedes the son of Lycomedes and Tisias the son of Tisimachus, encamped with the Athenian forces on the island. But before they did the country any harm they sent envoys to negotiate with the Melians. Instead of bringing these envoys before the people, the Melians desired them to explain their errand to the magistrates and to the dominant class. They spoke as follows:—

---

[a] Cp. iii. 91 init.

85 'Since we are not allowed to speak to the people, lest,
Since we are to be forsooth, a multitude should be deceived
closeted with you, let us by seductive and unanswerable [a] argu-
converse and not make ments which they would hear set forth
speeches. in a single uninterrupted oration (for
we are perfectly aware that this is what you mean in bringing us before a select few), you who are sitting here may
as well make assurance yet surer. Let us have no set
speeches at all, but do you reply to each several statement
of which you disapprove, and criticise it at once.   Say
first of all how you like this mode of proceeding.'

86   The Melian representatives answered:—'The quiet
We do not object. But interchange of explanations is a reason-
discussion between you able thing, and we do not object to that.
and us is a mockery, But your warlike movements, which
and can only end in are present not only to our fears but
our ruin. to our eyes, seem to belie your words.
We see that, although you may reason with us, you mean
to be our judges ; and that at the end of the discussion, if
the justice of our cause prevail and we therefore refuse to
yield, we may expect war ; if we are convinced by you,
slavery.'

87   *Ath.* 'Nay, but if you are only going to argue from
In any case you must fancies about the future, or if you meet
face the facts. us with any other purpose than that of
looking your circumstances in the face and saving your
city, we have done ; but if this is your intention we will
proceed.'

88   *Mel.* 'It is an excusable and natural thing that men in
It must be as you, our position should neglect no argu-
and not as we, please. ment and no view which may avail.
But we admit that this conference has met to consider the
question of our preservation ; and therefore let the argument proceed in the manner which you propose.'

89   *Ath.* 'Well, then, we Athenians will use no fine

---

[a] Or, 'unexamined.'

words ; we will not go out of our way to prove at length that we have a right to rule, because we overthrew the Persians[a] ; or that we attack you now because we are suffering any injury at your hands.   We should not convince you if we did ; nor must you expect to convince us by arguing that, although a colony of the Lacedaemonians, you have taken no part in their expeditions, or that you have never done us any wrong. But you and we should say what we really think, and aim only at what is possible, for we both alike know that into the discussion of human affairs the question of justice only enters where there is equal power to enforce it, and that the powerful exact what they can, and the weak grant what they must.'

No use in talking about right; expediency is the word.

Mel. 'Well, then, since you set aside justice and invite us to speak of expediency, in our judgment it is certainly expedient that you should respect a principle which is for the common good ; that to every man when in peril a reasonable claim should be accounted a claim of right, and that any plea which he is disposed to urge, even if failing of the point a little, should help his cause.   Your interest in this principle is quite as great as ours, [b] inasmuch as you, if you fall, will incur the heaviest vengeance, and will be the most terrible example to mankind [b].'

For your own sakes, then, it is expedient that you should not be too strict.

Ath. 'The fall of our empire, if it should fall, is not an event to which we look forward with dismay ; for ruling states such as Lacedaemon are not cruel to their vanquished enemies.   [c] With the Lacedaemonians, however, we are not

For ourselves we have no fears. It is you who have to learn the lesson of what is expedient both for us and you.

90

91

---

[a] Cp. vi. 83 init.   [b] Or, ' inasmuch as you, if you disregard it, will by your example justify others in inflicting the heaviest vengeance on you should you fall.'

[c] Taking ἔστι δὲ . . . ὁ ἀγών as a parenthesis and giving a different

now contending ; the real danger is from our many subject states, who may of their own motion rise up and overcome their masters ᶜ. But this is a danger which you may leave to us.   And we will now endeavour to show that we have come in the interests of our empire, and that in what we are about to say we are only seeking the preservation of your city. For we want to make you ours with the least trouble to ourselves, and it is for the interests of us both that you should not be destroyed.'

92   *Mel.* 'It may be your interest to be our masters,

For you, yes. But how for us? but how can it be ours to be your slaves ? '

93   *Ath.* 'To you the gain will be that by submission you

You will suffer less and we shall gain more. will avert the worst; and we shall be all the richer for your preservation.'

94   *Mel.* 'But must we be your enemies? Will you not

May we not be neutral ? receive us as friends if we are neutral and remain at peace with you ? '

95   *Ath.* 'No, your enmity is not half so mischievous to

Our subjects would not understand that. us as your friendship ; for the one is in the eyes of our subjects an argument of our power, the other of our weakness.'

96   *Mel.* 'But are your subjects really unable to distin-

But we are not a colony of yours. guish between states in which you have no concern, and those which are chiefly your own colonies, and in some cases have revolted and been subdued by you ? '

97   *Ath.* 'Why, they do not doubt that both of them have

You are talking about justice again.   We say that we cannot allow freedom to insignificant islanders. a good deal to say for themselves on the score of justice, but they think that states like yours are left free because they are able to defend themselves, and that we do not attack them because we

---

sense to πoυ and αὐτoί. Or, 'And we are fighting not so much against the Lacedaemonians, as against our own subjects who may some day rise up and overcome their former masters.'

dare not. So that your subjection will give us an increase of security, as well as an extension of empire. For we are masters of the sea, and you who are islanders, and insignificant islanders too, must not be allowed to escape us.'

Mel. 'But do you not recognise another danger? For, **98** once more, since you drive us from the plea of justice [a] and press upon us your doctrine of expediency [a], we must show you what is for our interest, and, if it be for yours also, may hope to convince you:—Will you not be making enemies of all who are now neutrals? When they see how you are treating us they will expect you some day to turn against them; and if so, are you not strengthening the enemies whom you already have, and bringing upon you others who, if they could help, would never dream of being your enemies at all?' *Note*

But will not your policy convert all neutrals into enemies?

Ath. 'We do not consider our really dangerous ene- **99** mies to be any of the peoples inhabiting the mainland who, secure in their freedom, may defer indefinitely any measures of precaution which they take against us, but islanders who, like you, happen to be under no control, and all who may be already irritated by the necessity of submission to our empire—these are our real enemies, for they are the most reckless and most likely to bring themselves as well as us into a danger which they cannot but foresee.'

The neutral peoples of the mainland have nothing to fear from us, and therefore we have nothing to fear from them. Our subjects and the free islanders are our danger.

Mel. 'Surely then, if you and your subjects will brave **100** all this risk, you to preserve your empire and they to be quit of it, how base and cowardly would it be in us, who retain our freedom, not to do and suffer anything rather than be your slaves.'

If you fight for empire and your subjects for freedom, shall we be slaves?

---

[a] Or, ' and insist upon our compliance with your interests.

101   *Ath.* 'Not so, if you calmly reflect: for you are not

There is no coward- fighting against equals to whom you
ice in yielding to cannot yield without disgrace, but you
superior force. are taking counsel whether or no you
shall resist an overwhelming force. The question is not
one of honour but of prudence.'

102   *Mel.* 'But we know that the fortune of war is sometimes

But we hope that impartial, and not always on the side
fortune may befriend of numbers. If we yield now, all is
us. over; but if we fight, there is yet a
hope that we may stand upright.'

103   *Ath.* 'Hope is a good comforter in the hour of danger,

Hope is a great de- and when men have something else to
ceiver; and is only de- depend upon, although hurtful, she is
tected when men are not ruinous. But when her spend-
already ruined. thrift nature has induced them to stake
their all, ᵃ they see her as she is in the moment of their
fall, and not till then. While the knowledge of her might
enable them to be ware of her, she never fails ᵃ. You are
weak and a single turn of the scale might be your ruin.
Do not you be thus deluded; avoid the error of which so
many are guilty, who, although they might still be saved
if they would take the natural means, when visible grounds
of confidence forsake them, have recourse to the invisible,
to prophecies and oracles and the like, which ruin men by
the hopes which they inspire in them.'

104   *Mel.* 'We know only too well how hard the struggle

Heaven will protect must be against your power, and against
the right and the Lace- fortune, if she does not mean to be
daemonians will suc- impartial. Nevertheless we do not
cour us. despair of fortune; for we hope to
stand as high as you in the favour of heaven, because we
are righteous and you against whom we contend are un-

ᵃ Or, 'they see her as she is in the moment of their fall; and afterwards, when she is known and they might be ware of her, she leaves
them nothing worth saving.'

righteous; and we are satisfied that our deficiency in power will be compensated by the aid of our allies the Lacedaemonians; they cannot refuse to help us, if only because we are their kinsmen, and for the sake of their own honour. And therefore our confidence is not so utterly blind as you suppose.'

Ath. 'As for the Gods, we expect to have quite as much of their favour as you: for we are not doing or claiming anything which goes beyond common opinion about divine or men's desires about human things. For of the Gods we believe, and of men we know, that by a law of their nature wherever they can rule they will. This law was not made by us, and we are not the first who have acted upon it; we did but inherit it, and shall bequeath it to all time, and we know that you and all mankind, if you were as strong as we are, would do as we do. So much for the Gods; we have told you why we expect to stand as high in their good opinion as you. And then as to the Lacedaemonians—when you imagine that out of very shame they will assist you, we admire the innocence of your idea, but we do not envy you the folly of it. The Lacedaemonians are exceedingly virtuous among themselves, and according to their national standard of morality ᵃ. But, in respect of their dealings with others, although many things might be said, they can be described in few words—of all men whom we know they are the most notorious for identifying what is pleasant with what is honourable, and what is expedient with what is just. But how inconsistent is such a character with your present blind hope of deliverance!'

105 *That the stronger should rule over the weaker is a principle common to Gods and men. Therefore the Gods are as likely to favour us as you. And the Lacedaemonians look only to their interest.*

Mel. 'That is the very reason why we trust them; they will look to their interest, and therefore will not 106

ᵃ Cp. i. 68 init.

be willing to betray the Melians, who are their own

But their interest will colonists, lest they should be distrusted
induce them to assist us. by their friends in Hellas and play
into the hands of their enemies.'

107 *Ath.* 'But do you not see that the path of expediency

Not when there is any is safe, whereas justice and honour in-
danger. volve danger in practice, and such
dangers the Lacedaemonians seldom care to face?'

108 *Mel.* 'On the other hand, we think that whatever perils

But they may need there may be, they will be ready to
our aid, and they are face them for our sakes, and will con-
our kinsmen. sider danger less dangerous where we
are concerned. For a if they need our aid a we are close
at hand, and they can better trust our loyal feeling because
we are their kinsmen.'

109 *Ath.* 'Yes, but what encourages men who are invited

The aid which you to join in a conflict is clearly not the
can give is not sufficient good-will of those who summon them
to make them run into to their side, but a decided superiority
danger for your sakes. in real power. To this no men look
They will not come more keenly than the Lacedaemonians;
alone to an island.
so little confidence have they in their own resources, that
they only attack their neighbours when they have numerous
allies, and therefore they are not likely to find their way
by themselves to an island, when we are masters of the
sea.'

110 *Mel.* 'But they may send their allies: the Cretan sea is

Their ships may find a large place; and the masters of the
their way to us; and sea will have more difficulty in over-
they may themselves in- taking vessels which want to escape
vade Attica and draw than the pursued in escaping. If the
away your allies. attempt should fail they may invade
Attica itself, and find their way to allies of yours whom
Brasidas did not reach: and then you will have to fight,
not for the conquest of a land in which you have no

---

a Or, ' when we need their aid.'

concern, but nearer home, for the preservation of your confederacy and of your own territory.'

Ath. 'Help may come from Lacedaemon to you as it 111 has come to others, and should you *Wait and you will* ever have actual experience of it, then *see. Nothing which you* you will know that never once have *say is to the point. You* the Athenians retired from a siege *sense of honour. Think* through fear of a foe elsewhere. You *again.* told us that the safety of your city would be your first care, but we remark that, in this long discussion, not a word has been uttered by you which would give a reasonable man expectation of deliverance. Your strongest grounds are hopes deferred, and what power you have is not to be compared with that which is already arrayed against you. Unless after we have withdrawn you mean to come, as even now you may, to a wiser conclusion, you are showing a great want of sense. For surely you cannot dream of flying to that false sense of honour which has been the ruin of so many when danger and dishonour were staring them in the face. Many men with their eyes still open to the consequences have found the word "honour" too much for them, and have suffered a mere name to lure them on, until it has drawn down upon them real and irretrievable calamities; through their own folly they have incurred a worse dishonour than fortune would have inflicted upon them. If you are wise you will not run this risk; you ought to see that there can be no disgrace in yielding to a great city which invites you to become her ally on reasonable terms, keeping your own land, and merely paying tribute; and that you will certainly gain no honour if, having to choose between two alternatives, safety and war, you obstinately prefer the worse. To maintain our rights against equals, to be politic with superiors, and to be moderate towards inferiors is the path of safety. Reflect once more when we have withdrawn, and say to yourselves over and over again that you are deliberating about your one and only country, which may be saved or may be destroyed by a single decision.'

112   The Athenians left the conference: the Melians, after
The Melians refuse consulting among themselves, resolved
to yield. to persevere in their refusal, and made
answer as follows :—' Men of Athens, our resolution is unchanged; and we will not in a moment surrender that liberty which our city, founded seven hundred years ago, still enjoys; we will trust to the good fortune which, by the favour of the Gods, has hitherto preserved us, and for human help to the Lacedaemonians, and endeavour to save ourselves. We are ready however to be your friends, and the enemies neither of you nor of the Lacedaemonians, and we ask you to leave our country when you have made such a peace as may appear to be in the interest of both parties.'

113   Such was the answer of the Melians; the Athenians, as
Last words of the they quitted the conference, spoke as
Athenians. follows :—' Well, we must say, judging
from the decision at which you have arrived, that you are the only men who deem the future to be more certain than the present, and regard things unseen as already realised in your fond anticipation, and that the more you cast yourselves upon the Lacedaemonians and fortune and hope, and trust them, the more complete will be your ruin.'

114   The Athenian envoys returned to the army; and the
The Athenians block- generals, when they found that the
ade Melos. Melians would not yield, immediately
commenced hostilities. They surrounded the town of Melos with a wall, dividing the work among the several contingents. They then left troops of their own and of their allies to keep guard both by land and by sea, and retired with the greater part of their army; the remainder carried on the blockade.

115   About the same time the Argives made an inroad into Phliasia, and lost nearly eighty men, who were caught in an ambuscade by the Phliasians and the Argive exiles.

The Athenian garrison in Pylos took much spoil from the Lacedaemonians; nevertheless the latter did not renounce the peace and go to war, but only notified by a proclamation that if any one of their own people had a mind to make reprisals on the Athenians he might. The Corinthians next declared war upon the Athenians on some private grounds, but the rest of the Peloponnesians did not join them. The Melians took that part of the Athenian wall which looked towards the agora by a night assault, killed a few men, and brought in as much corn and other necessaries as they could; they then retreated and remained inactive. After this the Athenians set a better watch. So the summer ended.

Inroad of Argives into Phliasia. Athenians at Pylos. Quarrel between Athens and Corinth. Check of Athenians before Melos.

In the following winter the Lacedaemonians had intended 116 to make an expedition into the Argive territory, but finding that the sacrifices which they offered at the frontier were unfavourable [a] they returned home. The Argives, suspecting that the threatened invasion was instigated by citizens of their own, apprehended some of them; others however escaped.

The Lacedaemonians intending to invade Argolis are again deterred by the sacrifices.

About the same time the Melians took another part of the Athenian wall; for the fortifications were insufficiently guarded. Whereupon the Athenians sent fresh troops, under the command of Philocrates the son of Demeas. The place was now closely invested, and there was treachery among the citizens themselves. So the Melians were induced to surrender at discretion. The Athenians thereupon put to death all who were of military age, and made slaves of the women and children. They then colonised the island, sending thither five hundred settlers of their own.

Melos taken and the male inhabitants put to death.

---

[a] Cp. v. 54, 55.

BOOK VI

1 DURING the same winter the Athenians conceived a

The Athenians, ig-
norant of the size and
resources of the island,
determine to send a
great expedition to
Sicily.

desire of sending another expedition to Sicily, larger than those commanded by Laches and Eurymedon [a]. They hoped to conquer the island. Of its great size and numerous population, barbarian as well as Hellenic, most of them knew nothing, and they never reflected that they were entering on a struggle almost as arduous as the Peloponnesian War. The voyage in a merchant-vessel round Sicily takes up nearly eight days, and this great island is all but a part of the mainland, being divided from it by a sea not much more than two miles in width.

2 I will now describe the original settlement of Sicily,

Thucydides describes
the races by which the
island was inhabited.
1. The mythical Cyclop-
es and Laestrygones.
2. The Sicanians from
Spain said to be auto-
chthons. 3. Some Tro-
jans, and 4. some
Phocians, who came to
Sicily after the fall of
Troy. 5. The Sicels
from Italy. 6. The
Phoenicians.

and enumerate the nations which it contained. Oldest of all were (1) the Cyclopes and Laestrygones, who are said to have dwelt in a district of the island; but who they were, whence they came, or whither they went, I cannot tell. We must be content with the legends of the poets, and every one must be left to form his own opinion. (2) The Sicanians appear to have succeeded these early races, although according to their own account they were still older; for they profess to have been children of the soil.

---

[a] Cp. iii. 86, 115.

But the fact proves to be that they were Iberians, and were driven from the river Sicanus in Iberia by the Ligurians. Sicily, which was originally called Trinacria, received from them the name Sicania. To this day the Sicanians inhabit the western parts of the island. (3) After the capture of Troy, some Trojans who had escaped from the Achaeans came in ships to Sicily; they settled near the Sicanians, and took the common name of Elymi but had two separate cities, Eryx and Egesta. (4) These were joined by certain Phocians, who had also fought at Troy, and were driven by a storm first to Libya and thence to Sicily. (5) The Sicels were originally inhabitants of Italy, whence they were driven by the Opici, and passed over into Sicily;—according to a probable tradition they crossed upon rafts, taking advantage of the wind blowing from the land, but they may have found other ways of effecting a passage; there are Sicels still in Italy, and the country itself was so called from Italus a Sicel king. They entered Sicily with a large army, and defeating the Sicanians in battle, drove them back to the southern and western parts of the country; from them the island, formerly Sicania, took the name of Sicily. For nearly three hundred years after their arrival until the time when the Hellenes came to Sicily they occupied the most fertile districts, and they still inhabit the central and northern regions. (6) The Phoenicians at one time had settlements all round the island. They fortified headlands on the sea-coast, and settled in the small islands adjacent, for the sake of trading with the Sicels; but when the Hellenes began to find their way by sea to Sicily in greater numbers they withdrew from the larger part of the island, and forming a union established themselves in Motyè, Soloeis, and Panormus, in the neighbourhood of the Elymi, partly trusting to their alliance with them, and partly because this is the point at which the passage from Carthage to Sicily is shortest. Such were the Barbarian nations who inhabited Sicily, and these were their settlements.

3   (7) The first Hellenic colonists sailed from Chalcis in

Euboea under the leadership of Thucles,

7. The Hellenic colonies:—(1) Naxos, from Chalcis, founded about 735 B.C. (2) Syracuse, from Corinth, about 734 B.C. (3) Leontini, 730 B.C., and (4) Catana, from Naxos.

and founded Naxos; there they erected an altar in honour of Apollo the Founder, [a] which is still standing without the city [a], and on this altar religious embassies sacrifice before they sail from Sicily.   (8) In the following year Archias, one of the Heraclidae, came from Corinth and founded Syracuse, first driving the Sicels out of the island of Ortygia; in which, though it is no longer surrounded by the sea, the inner city now stands; in process of time the outer city was included within the walls and became populous.   (9) In the fifth year after the foundation of Syracuse Thucles and the Chalcidians went forth from Naxos, and driving out the Sicels by force of arms, founded first Leontini, then Catana.   The Catanaeans however chose a founder of their own, named Evarchus.

4   (10) About the same time Lamis came from Megara

bringing a colony to Sicily, where he

(5) Trotilus, (6) Thapsus, and (7) the Hyblaean Megara, from Megara, about 728 B.C. (8) Selinus, from the Hyblaean Megara, 628 B.C. (9) Gela, from Rhodes and Crete, 690 B.C. (10) Agrigentum, from Gela, 582 B.C. (11) Zanclè or Messenè from Cymè.

occupied a place called Trotilus, upon the river Pantacyas; but he soon afterwards joined the settlement of the Chalcidians at Leontini; with them he dwelt a short time, until he was driven out; he then founded Thapsus, where he died.   His followers quitted Thapsus and founded the city which is called the Hyblaean Megara; Hyblon, a Sicel king, had betrayed the place to them and guided them thither.   There they remained two hundred and forty-five years, and were then driven out of their town and land by Gelo the tyrant of Syracuse; but before they were driven out, and a hundred years after

---

[a] Or, 'which is now outside the city.'

their own foundation, they sent out Pamillus and founded
Selinus; he had come from Megara, their own mother
state, to take part in the new colony. (11) In the forty-fifth
year after the foundation of Syracuse, Antiphemus of
Rhodes and Entimus of Crete came with their followers
and together built Gela. The city was named from the
river Gela, but the spot which is now the Acropolis and
was first fortified is called Lindii. The institutions of the
new settlement were Dorian. Exactly a hundred and
eight years after their own foundation the inhabitants of
Gela founded Agrigentum (Acragas), which they named
from the river Acragas; they appointed Aristonous and
Pystilus founders of the place, and gave to it their own
institutions. (12) Zanclè was originally colonised by
pirates who came from Cymè, the Chalcidian city in
Opicia; these were followed by a large body of colonists
from Chalcis and the rest of Euboea, who shared in the
allotment of the soil. The first settlement was led by
Perieres of Cymè, the second by Crataemenes of Chalcis.
Zanclè was the original name of the place, a name given
by the Sicels because the site was in shape like a sickle,
for which the Sicel word is *zanclon*. These earlier
settlers were afterwards driven out by the Samians and
other Ionians, who when they fled from the Persians B.C. 494.
found their way to Sicily [a]. Not long afterwards Anaxilas, Ol. 71, 3.
the tyrant of Rhegium, drove out these Samians. He
then repeopled their city with a mixed multitude, and
called the place Messenè after his native country.

Himera was colonised from Zanclè by Euclides, Simus, 5
and Sacon. Most of the settlers were   (12) *Himera, from* B.C. 648?
Chalcidian, but the so-called Myletidae, *Zanclè.* (13) *Acrae,* Ol. 33?
Syracusan exiles who had been defeated   664 B.C., *and* (14)
in a civil war, took part in the colony. *Casmenae,* 644 B.C.,
Their language was a mixture of the   *from Syracuse.* (15)
Chalcidian and Doric dialects, but their *Camarina, from Syra-*
institutions were mainly Chalcidian. (13) Acrae and Cas- *cuse,* 599 B.C.

---

[a] Cp. Herod. vi. 22, 23.

menae were founded by the Syracusans, Acrae seventy years after Syracuse, and Casmenae nearly twenty years after Acrae. Camarina was originally founded by the Syracusans exactly a hundred and thirty-five years after the foundation of Syracuse; the founders were Dascon and Menecolus. But the Camarinaeans revolted, and as a punishment for their revolt were violently expelled by

B.C. 498-491. Ol. 70, 3-72, 2.

the Syracusans. After a time Hippocrates the tyrant of Gela, receiving the territory of Camarina [a] as the ransom of certain Syracusan prisoners, became the second founder

B.C. 491-478. Ol. 72, 2-75, 3.

of the place, which he colonised anew. The inhabitants were once more driven out by Gelo, [b] who himself colonised the city for the third time [b].

6

B.C. 416. Ol. 91.

Ambition was the real motive of the Sicilian expedition, for which the Athenians found an occasion in the war between Egesta and Selinus. The Egestaean envoys.

These were the nations, Hellenic or Barbarian, who inhabited Sicily, and such was the great island on which the Athenians were determined to make war. They virtuously professed that they were going to assist their own kinsmen and their newly-acquired allies [c], but the simple truth was that they aspired to the empire of Sicily. They were principally instigated by an embassy which had come from Egesta and was urgent in requesting aid. The Egestaeans had gone to war with the neighbouring city of Selinus about certain questions of marriage and about a disputed piece of land. The Selinuntians summoned the Syracusans to their assistance, and their united forces reduced the Egestaeans to great straits both by sea and land. The Egestaean envoys reminded the Athenians of the alliance which they had made [d] with the Leontines under Laches in the former war [d],

---

[a] Cp. Herod vii. 154.   [b] Or, adopting the conjecture Γελώων : 'and the city was colonised for the third time by the inhabitants of Gela.' This accords with the statement of Diodorus, xi. 76.   [c] The Camarinaeans and Agrigentines, v. 4 fin., and some of the Sicels, iii. 103 init., 115 init.   [d] Or 'with Egesta under Laches in the former war on behalf of the Leontines.' See note. Cp. for either rendering iii. 86.

and begged them to send ships to their relief. Their chief argument was that, if the Syracusans were not punished for the expulsion of the Leontines, but were allowed to destroy the remaining allies of the Athenians, and to get the whole of Sicily into their own hands, they would one day come with a great army, Dorians assisting Dorians, who were their kinsmen, and colonists assisting their Peloponnesian founders, and would unite in over-throwing Athens herself. Such being the danger, the Athenians would be wise in combining with the allies who were still left to them in Sicily against the Syracusans, especially since the Egestaeans would themselves provide money sufficient for the war. These arguments were constantly repeated in the ears of the Athenian assembly by the Egestaeans and their partisans; at length the people passed a vote that they would at all events send envoys to ascertain on the spot whether the Egestaeans really had the money which they professed to have in their treasury and in their temples, and to report on the state of the war with Selinus. So the Athenian envoys were despatched to Sicily.

During the same winter the Lacedaemonians and their **7** allies, all but the Corinthians, made an expedition into the Argive territory, of which they devastated a small part, and, having brought with them waggons, carried away a few loads of corn. They settled the Argive exiles at Orneae, where they left a small garrison, and *The Lacedaemonians invade Argolis; they settle at Orneae the Argive exiles, who are treacherously attacked by the Argive people, assisted by the Athenians, but escape.* having made an agreement that the inhabitants of Orneae and the Argives should not injure one another's land for a given time, returned home with the rest of their army. Soon afterwards the Athenians arrived with thirty ships and six hundred hoplites. They and the people of Argos with their whole power went out and blockaded Orneae for a day, but at night the Argive exiles within the walls got away unobserved by the besiegers, who were encamped at some distance. On the following day the Argives, perceiving what had happened, razed Orneae to the ground and returned. Soon afterwards the Athenian fleet returned likewise.

The Athenians also conveyed by sea cavalry of their *The Athenians ravage* own, and some Macedonian exiles who *Macedonia.* had taken refuge with them, to Methonè on the borders of Macedonia, and ravaged the territory of Perdiccas. Whereupon the Lacedaemonians sent to the Thracian Chalcidians, who were maintaining an armistice terminable at ten days' notice with the Athenians, and commanded them to assist Perdiccas, but they refused. So the winter ended, and with it the sixteenth year in the Peloponnesian War of which Thucydides wrote the history.

8   Early in the next spring the Athenian envoys returned

B. C. 415.
Ol. 91, 2.
The Athenians after the return of their envoys convoke an assembly, which decides in favour of war. At a second assembly, called for the purpose of voting supplies, Nicias still endeavours to deter them from going to war at all.

from Sicily. They were accompanied by Egestaeans who brought sixty talents [a] of uncoined silver, being a month's pay for sixty vessels which they hoped to obtain from Athens. The Athenians called an assembly, and when they heard both from their own and from the Egestaean envoys, amongst other inviting but untrue statements, that there was abundance of money lying ready in the temples and in the treasury of Egesta [b], they passed a vote that sixty ships should be sent to Sicily; Alcibiades the son of Cleinias, Nicias the son of Niceratus, and Lamachus the son of Xenophanes were appointed commanders with full powers. They were to assist Egesta against Selinus; if this did not demand all their military strength they were empowered to restore the Leontines, and generally to further in such manner as they deemed best the Athenian interests in Sicily. Five days afterwards

---

[a] £12,000.　　　　　[b] Cp. vi. 46.

another assembly was called to consider what steps should
be taken for the immediate equipment of the expedition,
and to vote any additional supplies which the generals
might require.   Nicias, who had been appointed general
against his will, thought that the people had come to a
wrong conclusion, and that upon slight if specious grounds
they were aspiring to the conquest of Sicily, which was no
easy task.   So, being desirous of diverting the Athenians
from their purpose, he came forward and admonished them
in the following terms :—

'I know that we are assembled here to discuss the 9
preparations which are required for
our expedition to Sicily, but in my   *I must say what I*
believe to be the truth.
judgment it is still a question whether   *This war is impolitic*
we ought to go thither at all; we   *and ill-timed.*
should not be hasty in determining a matter of so much
importance, or allow ourselves to enter into an impolitic
war at the instigation of foreigners.   Yet to me personally
war brings honour; and I am as careless as any man
about my own life : not that I think the worse of a citizen
who takes a little thought about his life or his property,
for I believe that the sense of a man's own interest will
quicken his interest in the prosperity of the state.   But
I have never in my life been induced by the love of reputation to say a single word contrary to what I thought ;
neither will I now : I will say simply what I believe to be
best.   If I told you to take care of what you have and not
to throw away present advantages in order to gain an
uncertain and distant good, my words would be powerless
against a temper like yours.   I would rather argue that
this is not the time for vigorous action, and that your great
aims will not be easily realised.

'I tell you that in going to Sicily you are leaving many 10
enemies behind you, and seem to be bent on bringing new
ones hither.   You are perhaps relying upon the treaty
recently made, which if you remain quiet may retain the
name of a treaty; for to a mere name the intrigues of

certain persons both here and at Lacedaemon have nearly

The state of our affairs in Hellas is uncertain, and while we are dreaming of conquests abroad we shall be attracting enemies at home. The Chalcidians are still in rebellion.

succeeded in reducing it. But if you meet with any serious reverse, your enemies will be upon you in a moment, for the agreement was originally extracted from them by the pressure of misfortune, and the discredit of it was on their side not on ours [a]. In the treaty itself there are many disputed points; and, unsatisfactory as it is, to this hour several cities, and very powerful cities too, persist in rejecting it. Some of these are at open war with us already [b]; others may declare war at ten days' notice [c]; and they only remain at peace because the Lacedaemonians are indisposed to move. And in all probability, if they find our power divided (and such a division is precisely what we are striving to create), they will eagerly join the Sicilians, whose alliance in the war they would long ago have given anything to obtain. These considerations should weigh with us. The state is far from the desired haven, and we should not run into danger and seek to gain a new empire before we have fully secured the old. The Chalcidians in Thrace have been rebels all these years and remain unsubdued, and there are other subjects of ours in various parts of the mainland who are uncertain in their allegiance. And we forsooth cannot lose a moment in avenging the wrongs of our allies the Egestaeans, while we still defer the punishment of our revolted subjects, whose offences are of long standing.

11　'And yet if we subdue the Chalcidian rebels we may

Sicily, even if conquered, cannot be retained.

retain our hold on them; but Sicily is a populous and distant country, over which, even if we are victorious, we shall hardly be able to maintain our dominion. And how foolish it is to select for attack a land which no conquest can secure, while he who fails to conquer will not be where he was before!

---

[a] Cp. v. 46 init.　　　[b] Cp. v. 115 med.　　　[c] Cp. v. 26 med., vi. 7 fin.

' I should say that the Sicilian cities are not dangerous
to you,—certainly not in their present *The Sicilians, if they*
condition, and they would be even less *were united, would not*
so if they were to fall under the sway *help Sparta to make*
of the Syracusans (and this is the pro- *they would fear that a*
spect with which the Egestaeans would *united Hellas might*
fain scare you). At present individuals *make war upon them.*
might cross the sea out of friendship *known, the more he is*
for the Lacedaemonians; but if the *feared. Familiarity*
states of Sicily were all united in one *makes you despise*
empire they would not be likely to *but they are biding their*
make war upon another empire. For *time.*
whatever chance they may have of overthrowing us if they
unite with the Peloponnesians, there will be the same
chance of their being overthrown themselves if the Peloponnesians and Athenians are ever united against them [a].
The Hellenes in Sicily will dread us most if we never
come; in a less degree if we display our strength and
speedily depart; but if any disaster occur, they will despise
us and be ready enough to join the enemies who are
attacking us here. We all know that men have the
greatest respect for that which is farthest off, and for that
of which the reputation has been least tested; and this,
Athenians, you may verify by your own experience.
There was a time when you feared the Lacedaemonians
and their allies, but now you have got the better of them,
and because your first fears have not been realised you
despise them, and even hope to conquer Sicily. But you
ought not to be elated at the chance mishaps of your
enemies; before you can be confident you should have
gained the mastery over their minds [b]. Remember that
the Lacedaemonians are sensitive to their disgrace, and
that their sole thought is how they may even yet find
a way of inflicting a blow upon us which will retrieve their
own character; the rather because they have laboured so

---

[a] Cp. viii. 46.   [b] Cp. ii. 87 init.; vi. 72 init.

earnestly and so long to win a name for valour. If we
are wise we shall not trouble ourselves about the barbarous
Egestaeans in Sicily; the real question is how we can
make ourselves secure against the designs of an insidious
oligarchy.

12   'We must remember also that we have only just re-

We have plenty of
work at home, and had
better leave these ad-
venturers to themselves.

covered in some measure from a great
plague and a great war, and are beginning to make up our losses in men
and money. It is our duty to expend
our new resources upon ourselves at home, and not upon
begging exiles who have an interest in successful lies;
who find it expedient only to contribute words, and let
others fight their battles; and who, if saved, prove ungrateful; if they fail, as they very likely may, only involve
their friends in a common ruin.

'I dare say there may be some young man here who is

Alcibiades is too
young to command
such an expedition, and
he only wants to indulge
his taste for horses at
the public expense.

delighted at holding a command, and
the more so because he is too young for
his post [a]; and he, regarding only his
own interest, may recommend you to
sail; he may be one who is much
admired for his stud of horses, and wants to make something out of his command which will maintain him in his
extravagance. But do not you give him the opportunity
of indulging his own magnificent tastes at the expense of
the state. Remember that men of this stamp impoverish
themselves and defraud the public. An expedition to
Sicily is a serious business, and not one which a mere
13 youth can plan and carry into execution off-hand. The
youth of whom I am speaking has summoned to his side
young men like himself, whom, not without alarm, I see
sitting by him in this assembly, and I appeal against
them to you elder citizens. If any of you should be placed
next one of his supporters, I would not have him

---

[a] Omitting the comma after ἐκπλεῖν.

ashamed, or afraid, of being thought a coward if he does
not vote for war. Do not, like them,

He has his youthful supporters, who rather alarm me. They will charge you with cowardice, but never mind that. Do not interfere in Sicily; let the Egestaeans fight their own battles.

entertain a desperate craving for things
out of your reach ; you know that by
prevision many successes are gained,
but few or none by mere greed. On
behalf of our country, now on the brink
of the greatest danger which she has
ever known, I entreat you to hold
up your hands against them. Do not interfere with the
boundaries which divide us from Sicily; I mean the Ionian
gulf which parts us if we sail along the coast, the Sicilian
sea if we sail through the open water ; these are quite
satisfactory. The Sicilians have their own country ; let
them manage their own concerns. And let the Egestaeans
in particular be informed that, having originally gone to
war with the Selinuntians on their own account, they must
make peace on their own account. Let us have no more
allies such as ours have too often been, whom we are
expected to assist when they are in misfortune, but to
whom we ourselves when in need may look in vain.

'And you, Prytanis, as you wish to be a good citizen, 14
and believe that the welfare of the state

The Prytanis need not fear to bring before you once more the question of the expedition itself.

is entrusted to you, put my proposal to
the vote, and lay the question once
more before the Athenians. If you
hesitate, remember that in the presence
of so many witnesses there can be no question of breaking
the law, and that you will be the physician of the state at
the critical moment. The first duty of the good magistrate
is to do the very best which he can for his country, or, at
least, to do her no harm which he can avoid.'

Such were the words of Nicias. Most of the Athenians 15
who came forward to speak were in favour of war, and
reluctant to rescind the vote which had been already passed,
although a few took the other side. The most enthusiastic supporter of the expedition was Alcibiades the son of

Cleinias; he was determined to oppose Nicias, who was

*The Athenians re-
fuse to rescind the
former vote. The war
is strongly advocated
by Alcibiades, who wants
to gain an empire and
to pay his own debts.
Thucydides thinks that
his wild courses went
far to ruin the state.
For notwithstanding his
extraordinary talents he
was not trusted, and
the conduct of the war
was committed to in-
ferior men.*

always his political enemy and had just now spoken of him in disparaging terms; but the desire to command was even a stronger motive with him. He was hoping that he might be the conqueror of Sicily and Carthage; and that success would repair his private fortunes, and gain him money as well as glory. He had a great position among the citizens and was devoted to horse-racing and other pleasures which outran his means. And in the end his wild courses went far to ruin the Athenian state. For the people feared the extremes to which he carried the lawlessness of his personal habits, and the far-reaching purposes which invariably animated him in all his actions. They thought that he was aiming at a tyranny and set themselves against him. And therefore, although his talents as a military commander were unrivalled, they entrusted the administration of the war to others, because they personally objected to his private habits; and so they speedily shipwrecked the state. He now came forward and spoke as follows:—

16   'I have a better right to command, men of Athens, than

*My private extravag-
ance is a public benefit.
And why should men
complain of being looked
down upon by the for-
tunate? For they look
down upon the un-
fortunate themselves.
Great men have great
ambitions, but their
merits are not acknow-
ledged during their life-
time. This foolish youth
gained for you the
Argive alliance.*

another; for as Nicias has attacked me, I must begin by praising myself; and I consider that I am worthy. Those doings of mine for which I am so much cried out against are an honour to myself and to my ancestors, and a solid advantage to my country. In consequence of the distinguished manner in which I represented the state at Olympia, the other Hellenes formed an idea of our power which even exceeded the reality, although

they had previously imagined that we were exhausted by
war.   I sent into the lists seven chariots,—no other private
man ever did the like; I was victor, and also won the
second and fourth prize; and I ordered everything in
a style worthy of my victory.   Apart from the conventional
honour paid to such successes, the energy which is shown
by them creates an impression of power.   At home, again,
whenever I gain distinction by providing choruses or by
the performance of some other public duty, although the
citizens are naturally jealous of me, to strangers these
acts of munificence are a new argument of our strength.
There is some use in the folly of a man who at his own
cost benefits not only himself, but the state.   And where
is the injustice, if I or any one who feels his own
superiority to another refuses to be on a level with him?
The unfortunate keep their misfortunes to themselves.
We do not expect to be recognised by our acquaintance
when we are down in the world; and on the same principle why should any one complain when treated with
disdain by the more fortunate?   He who would have
proper respect shown to him should himself show it
towards others.   I know that men of this lofty spirit, and
all who have been in any way illustrious, are hated while
they are alive, by their equals especially, and in a lesser
degree by others who have to do with them; but that they
leave behind them to after-ages a reputation which leads
even those who are not of their family to claim kindred
with them, and that they are the glory of their country,
which regards them, not as aliens or as evil-doers, but as
her own children, of whose character she is proud.   These
are my own aspirations, and this is the reason why my
private life is assailed; but let me ask you, whether in the
management of public affairs any man surpasses me.   Did
I not, without involving you in any great danger or
expense, combine the most powerful states of Peloponnesus against the Lacedaemonians, whom I compelled to
stake at Mantinea all that they had upon the fortune of

one day? And even to this hour, although they were victorious in the battle, they have hardly recovered courage.

17   ' These were the achievements of my youth, and of what

*And now abide by
your intention. There
is nothing to fear in
Sicily. The Sicilians
are a mixed multitude,
ill provided with in-
fantry; and many of
the barbarians will
assist us. At home we
are more than a match
for the Peloponnesians.*

is supposed to be my monstrous folly;
thus did I by winning words conciliate
the Peloponnesian powers, and my
heartiness made them believe in me
and follow me. And now do not be
afraid ᵃ of me because I am young, but
while I am in the flower of my days
and Nicias enjoys the reputation of
success, use the services of us both.

Having determined to sail, do not change your minds
under the impression that Sicily is a great power. For
although the Sicilian cities are populous, their inhabitants
are a mixed multitude, and they readily give up old forms
of government and receive new ones from without. No
one really feels that he has a city of his own; and so the
individual is ill provided with arms, and the country has
no regular means of defence. A man looks only to what
he can win from the common stock by arts of speech or by
party violence; hoping, if he is overthrown, at any rate to
carry off his prize and enjoy it elsewhere. They are
a motley crew, who are never of one mind in counsel, and
are incapable of any concert in action. Every man is for
himself, and will readily come over to anyone who makes
an attractive offer; the more readily if, as report says, they
are in a state of internal discord. They boast of their
hoplites, but, as has proved to be the case in all Hellenic
states, the number of them is grossly exaggerated. Hellas
has been singularly mistaken about her heavy infantry;
and even in this war it was as much as she could do to
collect enough of them. The obstacles then which will
meet us in Sicily, judging of them from the information
which I have received, are not great; indeed, I have over-

ᵃ Adopting the conjecture πεφόβησθε, and placing a full stop after ἔπεισε.

rated them, for there will be many barbarians who, through fear of the Syracusans, will join us in attacking them [a]. And at home there is nothing which, viewed rightly, need interfere with the expedition.   Our forefathers had the same enemies whom we are now told that we are leaving behind us, and the Persian besides; but their strength lay in the greatness of their navy, and by that and that alone they gained their empire.   Never were the Peloponnesians more hopeless of success than at the present moment; and let them be ever so confident, they will only invade us by land, which they can equally do whether we go to Sicily or not.   But on the sea they cannot hurt us, for we shall leave behind us a navy equal to theirs.

'What reason can we give to ourselves for hesitation ? what excuse can we make to our allies for denying them aid ? We have sworn to them, and have no right to argue that they never assisted us [b]. In seeking their alliance we did not intend that they should come and help us here, but that they should harass our enemies in Sicily, and prevent them from coming hither.   Like all other imperial powers, 18

Why then hesitate? For an imperial power the true policy of defence is to attack. We cannot lose, and we shall probably become masters of Hellas. Let young and old act together and not allow the state to rust from want of energy.

we have acquired our dominion by our readiness to assist any one, whether Barbarian or Hellene, who may have invoked our aid.   If we are all to sit and do nothing, or to draw distinctions of race when our help is requested, we shall add little to our empire, and run a great risk of losing it altogether.   For mankind do not await the attack of a superior power, they anticipate it.   We cannot cut down an empire as we might a household; but having once gained our present position, we must, while keeping a firm hold upon some, contrive occasion against others; for if we are not rulers we shall be subjects.   You cannot afford to regard inaction in the same light as others might, unless

---

[a] Cp. vi. 88 init., 98 init., 103 med.   [b] Cp. iv. 61 med.

you impose a corresponding restriction on your practice. Convinced then that we shall be most likely to increase our power here if we attack our enemies there, let us sail. We shall humble the pride of the Peloponnesians when they see that, scorning the delights of repose, we have attacked Sicily. By the help of our acquisitions there, we shall probably become masters of all Hellas; at any rate we shall injure the Syracusans, and at the same time benefit ourselves and our allies. Whether we succeed and remain, or depart, in either case our navy will ensure our safety; for at sea we shall be more than a match for all Sicily. Nicias must not divert you from your purpose by preaching indolence, and by trying to set the young against the old; rather in your accustomed order, old and young taking counsel together, after the manner of your fathers who raised Athens to this height of greatness, strive to rise yet higher. Consider that youth and age have no power unless united; but that the shallower and the more exact and the middle sort of judgment, when duly attempered, are likely to be most efficient. The state, if at rest, like everything else will wear herself out by internal friction. Every pursuit which requires skill will tend to decay, whereas by conflict the city will always be gaining fresh experience and learning to defend herself, not in theory, but in practice. My opinion in short is, that a state used to activity will quickly be ruined by the change to inaction; and that they of all men enjoy the greatest security who are truest to themselves and their institutions even when they are not the best.'

19   Such were the words of Alcibiades. After hearing him

The people are bent on war: Nicias now dwells on the magnitude of the forces required.

and the Egestaeans and certain Leontine exiles who came forward and earnestly entreated assistance, reminding the Athenians of the oaths which they had sworn [a], the people were more than ever resolved

---

[a] Cp. iii. 86.

upon war. Nicias, seeing that his old argument would no longer deter them, but that he might possibly change their minds if he insisted on the magnitude of the force which would be required, came forward again and spoke as follows :—

'Men of Athens, as I see that you are thoroughly deter- 20 mined to go to war, I accept the decision, and will advise you accordingly, trusting that the event will be such as we all wish. The cities which we are about to attack are, I am informed, powerful, and independent of one another; they are not inhabited by slaves, who would gladly pass out of a harder into an easier condition of life; and they are very unlikely to accept our rule in exchange for their present liberty[a]. As regards numbers, although Sicily is but one island, it contains a great many Hellenic states. Not including Naxos and Catana (of which the inhabitants, as I hope, will be our allies because they are the kinsmen of the Leontines), there are seven other cities fully provided with means of warfare similar to our own, above all Selinus and Syracuse, the cities against which our expedition is particularly directed. For they have numerous hoplites, archers, and javelin-men, and they have many triremes which their large population will enable them to man; besides their private wealth, they have the treasures of the Selinuntian temples; and the Syracusans receive a tribute which has been paid them from time immemorial by certain barbarian tribes. Moreover, they have a numerous cavalry, and grow their own corn instead of importing it : in the two last respects they have a great advantage over us.

The Hellenic cities in Sicily are free and powerful; they have numerous hoplites and cavalry.

'Against such a power more is needed than an insignifi- 21 cant force of marines; if we mean to do justice to our design, and not to be kept within our lines by the numbers

---

[a] Cp. vii. 55 fin.

of their cavalry, we must embark a multitude of infantry.

And we must take with us a corresponding force of hoplites and, if not of cavalry, of javelin-men and archers, for we shall be in a distant country.
For what if the Sicilians in terror combine against us, and we make no friends except the Egestaeans who can furnish us with horsemen capable of opposing theirs? To be driven from the island or to send for reinforcements, because we were wanting in forethought at first, would be disgraceful. We must take a powerful armament with us from home, in the full knowledge that we are going to a distant land, and that the expedition will be [a] of a kind very different from any which you have hitherto made among your subjects against some enemy in this part of the world, yourselves the allies of others. Here a friendly country is always near, and you can easily obtain supplies. There [b] you will be dependent on a country [b] which is entirely strange to you, and whence during the four winter months hardly even a message can be sent hither.

22   'I say, therefore, that we must take with us a large
Food must be brought from home, and we must have the command of the sea that we may be able to procure supplies from elsewhere.
heavy-armed force both of Athenians and of allies, whether our own subjects or any Peloponnesians whom we can persuade [c] or attract by pay [d] to our service; also plenty of archers and javelin-men to act against the enemy's cavalry. Our naval superiority must be overwhelming, that we may not only be able to fight, but may have no difficulty in bringing in supplies. And there is the food carried from home, such as wheat and parched barley, which will have to be conveyed in merchant-vessels; we must also have bakers, drafted in a certain proportion from each mill, who will receive pay, but will be forced to serve, in order that, if

---

[a] Reading στρατευσόμενοι and ἀπαρτήσοντες.   [b] Or, 'you will be removed to a country'; or, reading with Bekker ἀπαρτήσαντες, 'you will find yourselves dependent on,' or 'will have been removed to a country.' [c] Cp. vi. 29 med.   [d] Cp. vi. 43 med.; vii. 57 fin.

we should be detained by a calm, the army may not want food; for it is not every city that will be able to receive so large a force as ours. We must make our preparations as complete as possible, and not be at the mercy of others; above all, we must take out with us as much money as we can; for as to the supplies of the Egestaeans which are said to be awaiting us, we had better assume that they are imaginary.

'Even supposing we leave Athens with a force of our own, not merely equal to that of the enemy, but in every way superior, except indeed as regards the number of hoplites which they can put into the field, for in that respect equality is impossible, still it will be no easy task to conquer Sicily, or indeed to preserve ourselves. You ought to consider that we are like men going to found a city in a land of strangers and enemies, who on the very day of their disembarkation must have command of the country; for if they meet with a disaster they will have no friends. And this is what I fear. We shall have much need of prudence; still more of good fortune (and who can guarantee this to mortals?). Wherefore I would trust myself and the expedition as little as possible to accident, and would not sail until I had taken such precautions as will be likely to ensure our safety. This I conceive to be the course which is the most prudent for the whole state, and, for us who are sent upon the expedition, a condition of safety. If any one thinks otherwise, to him I resign the command.'

We must leave nothing to chance. 23

These were the words of Nicias. He meant either to deter the Athenians by bringing home to them the vastness of the undertaking, or to provide as far as he could for the security of the expedition if he were compelled to proceed. The result disappointed him. Far from losing their enthusiasm at the disagreeable prospect, they were more deter-

The Athenians are not deterred by the vast force required; the greater the preparation the more they are assured of safety. 24

mined than ever; they approved of his advice, and were
confident that every chance of danger was now removed.
All alike were seized with a passionate desire to sail, the
elder among them convinced that they would achieve the
conquest of Sicily,—at any rate such an armament could
suffer no disaster; the youth were longing to see with
their own eyes the marvels of a distant land, and were
confident of a safe return; the main body of the troops
expected to receive present pay, and to conquer a country
which would be an inexhaustible mine of pay for the
future. The enthusiasm of the majority was so overwhelming that, although some disapproved, they were
afraid of being thought unpatriotic if they voted on the
other side, and therefore held their peace.

25   At last an Athenian came forward and, calling upon

Nicias gives a provi- Nicias, said that they would have no
sional estimate of the more excuses and delays; he must
forces required. speak out and say what forces the
people were to vote him. He replied, with some unwillingness, that he would prefer to consider the matter
at leisure with his colleagues, but that, as far as he could
see at present, they ought to have at least a hundred
triremes of their own; of these a certain number might
be used as transports ᵃ, and they must order more triremes
from their allies. Of heavy-armed troops they would
require in all, including Athenians and allies, not less
than five thousand, and more if they could possibly have
them; the rest of the armament must be in proportion,
and should comprise archers to be procured both at home
and from Crete, and slingers. These forces, and whatever else seemed to be required, the generals would make
ready before they started.

26   Upon this the Athenians at once decreed that the

Preparations for war. generals should be empowered to act
as they thought best in the interest of
the state respecting the numbers of the army and the

ᵃ Cp. ch. 31 init., 43 init.

whole management of the expedition. Then the preparations began. Lists for service were made up at home and orders given to the allies. The city had newly recovered from the plague and from the constant pressure of war; a new population had grown up; there had been time for the accumulation of money during the peace; so that there was abundance of everything at command.

While they were in the midst of their preparations, the **27** Hermae or square stone figures carved *Meanwhile occurs the* after the ancient Athenian fashion, and *outrage on the Hermae:* standing everywhere at the doorways *the unknown authors* both of temples and private houses, *of it are suspected of* in one night had nearly all of them *designs against the* throughout the city their faces mutilated. The offenders *democracy.* were not known, but great rewards were publicly offered for their detection, and a decree was passed that any one, whether citizen, stranger, or slave, might without fear of punishment disclose this or any other profanation of which he was cognisant. The Athenians took the matter greatly to heart—it seemed to them ominous of the fate of the expedition; and they ascribed it to conspirators who wanted to effect a revolution and to overthrow the democracy.

Certain metics and servants gave information, not **28** indeed about the Hermae, but about *Information is given* the mutilation of other statues which *about some other pro-* had shortly before been perpetrated by *fane acts. Alcibiades* some young men in a drunken frolic : *and others are accused* they also said that the mysteries were *of celebrating the myste-* repeatedly profaned by the celebration *ries in private houses.* of them in private houses, and of this impiety they accused, among others, Alcibiades. A party who were jealous of his influence over the people, which interfered with the permanent establishment of their own, thinking that if they could get rid of him they would be supreme[a], took up and exaggerated

---

[a] Cp. ii. 65 fin.

the charges against him, clamorously insisting that both
the mutilation of the Hermae and the profanation of the
mysteries were part of a conspiracy against the democracy,
and that he was at the bottom of the whole affair. In
proof they alleged the excesses of his ordinary life, which
were unbecoming in the citizen of a free state.

29   He strove then and there to clear himself of the
He begs to be tried charges, and also offered to be tried
before he sails; but his before he sailed (for all was now ready),
enemies think that they in order that, if he were guilty, he
will have more chance might be punished, and if acquitted,
of obtaining a con- might retain his command. He ad-
demnation if the trial
is deferred. jured his countrymen to listen to no
calumnies which might be propagated against him in his
absence; and he protested that they would be wiser in
not sending a man who had so serious an imputation
hanging over him on a command so important. But his
enemies feared that if the trial took place at once he
would have the support of the army; and that the people
would be lenient, [a] and would not forget that [a] he had
induced the Argives and some Mantineans to join in the
expedition. They therefore exerted themselves to post-
pone the trial. To this end they suborned fresh speakers,
who proposed that he should sail now and not delay the
expedition, but should return and stand his trial within
a certain number of days. Their intention was that he
should be recalled and tried when they had stirred up
a stronger feeling against him, which they could better
do in his absence. So it was decided that Alcibiades
should sail.

30   About the middle of summer the expedition started
Conflict of emotions for Sicily. Orders had been previously
among the Athenians given to most of the allies, to the corn-
at the moment of part- ships, the smaller craft, and generally
ing. to the vessels in attendance on the

---

[a] Or supplying αὐτόν with θεραπεύων : 'being well disposed to him
because' etc.

armament, that they should muster at Corcyra, whence the whole fleet was to strike across the Ionian gulf to the promontory of Iapygia. Early in the morning of the day appointed for their departure, the Athenian forces and such of their allies as had already joined them went down to the Piraeus and began to man the ships. Almost the entire population of Athens accompanied them, citizens and strangers alike. The citizens came to take farewell, one of an acquaintance, another of a kinsman, another of a son, and as they passed along were full of hope and full of tears; hope of conquering Sicily, tears because they doubted whether they would ever see their friends again, when they thought of the long voyage on which they were going away. At the last moment of parting the danger was nearer; and terrors which had never occurred to them when they were voting the expedition now entered into their souls. Nevertheless their spirits revived at the sight of the armament in all its strength and of the abundant provision which they had made. The strangers and the rest of the multitude came out of curiosity, desiring to witness an enterprise of which the greatness exceeded belief.

No armament so magnificent or costly had ever been 31 sent out by any single Hellenic power, though in mere number of ships and hoplites that which sailed to Epidaurus under Pericles and afterwards under Hagnon to Potidaea[a] was not inferior. For that expedition consisted of a hundred Athenian and fifty Chian and Lesbian triremes, conveying four thousand hoplites all Athenian citizens, three hundred cavalry, and a multitude of allied troops. Still the voyage was short and the equipments were poor, whereas this expedition was intended to be long absent, and was thoroughly provided both for sea and land service, wherever its presence might

Beauty and precision of the armament. Vast expenses connected with it.

---

[a] Cp. ii. 56, 58.

be required.   On the fleet the greatest pains and
expense had been lavished by the trierarchs and the
state.   The public treasury gave a drachma[a] a day to
each sailor, and furnished empty hulls for sixty swift-
sailing vessels, and for forty transports carrying hoplites.
All these were manned with the best crews which could
be obtained.   The trierarchs, besides the pay given by
the state, added somewhat more out of their own means
to the wages of the upper ranks of rowers and of[b] the
petty officers[b].   The figure-heads and other fittings
provided by them were of the most costly description.
Every one strove to the utmost that his own ship
might excel both in beauty and swiftness.   The infantry
had been well selected and the lists carefully made
up.   There was the keenest rivalry among the soldiers
in the matter of arms and personal equipment.   And
while at home the Athenians were thus competing with
one another in the performance of their several duties,
to the rest of Hellas the expedition seemed to be a grand
display of their power and greatness, rather than a preparation for war.   If any one had reckoned up the whole
expenditure, both of the state and of individual soldiers
and others, including in the first not only what the city
had already laid out, but what was entrusted to the
generals, and in the second what either at the time or
afterwards private persons spent upon their outfit, or the
trierarchs upon their ships, the provision for the long
voyage which every one may be supposed to have carried
with him over and above his public pay, and what soldiers
or traders may have taken for purposes of exchange, he
would have found that altogether an immense sum
amounting to many talents was withdrawn from the city.
Men were quite amazed at the boldness of the scheme
and the magnificence of the spectacle, which were every-

---

[a] 8d.   [b] Others translate ' the crews generally,' or ' the soldiers'
servants.'

where spoken of, no less than at the great disproportion of the force when compared with that of the enemy against whom it was intended.   Never had a greater expedition been sent to a foreign land ; never was there an enterprise in which the hope of future success seemed to be better justified by actual power.

When the ships were manned and everything required 32 for the voyage had been placed on board, silence was proclaimed by the sound of the trumpet, and all with one voice before setting sail offered up the customary prayers ; these were recited, not in each ship separately, but by a single herald, the whole fleet accompanying him. On every deck both the officers and the marines, mingling wine in bowls, made libations from vessels of gold and silver.   The multitude of citizens and other well-wishers who were looking on from the land joined in the prayer. The crews raised the paean and, when the libations were completed, put to sea.   After sailing out for some distance in single file, the ships raced with one another as far as Aegina ; thence they hastened onwards to Corcyra, where the allies who formed the rest of the army were assembling.

Prayers offered by the whole fleet and by the spectators.   The sailors make libations and raise the paean. The ships race as far as Aegina.

Meanwhile reports of the expedition were coming in to Syracuse from many quarters, but for a long time nobody gave credit to them.   At length an assembly was held.   Even then different opinions were expressed, some affirming and others denying that the expedition was coming.   At last Hermocrates the son of Hermon, believing that he had certain information, came forward, and warned the Syracusans in the following words :—

Rumours of the expedition reach Syracuse.

'I dare say that, like others, I shall not be believed 33 when I tell you that the expedition is really coming ; and I am well aware that those who are either the authors or reporters of tidings which seem incredible not only fail to convince others, but are thought fools for their pains. Yet, when the city is in danger, fear shall not stop

Speech of Hermo-crates. They are com-ing and you must pre-pare for them. If you are prepared there is nothing to fear; Sicily will unite against them; and great expeditions never come to good.
my mouth; for I am convinced in my own mind that I have better informa-tion than anybody.   The Athenians, wonder as you may, are coming against us with a great fleet and army; they profess to be assisting their Egestaean allies and to be restoring the Leont-ines.   But the truth is that they covet Sicily, and especially our city.   They think that, if they can conquer us, they will easily conquer the rest.   They will soon be here, and you must consider how with your present resources you can make the most successful defence.   You should not let them take you by surprise because you despise them, or neglect the whole matter because you will not believe that they are coming at all. But to him who is not of this unbelieving temper I say:— And do not you be dismayed at their audacity and power. They cannot do more harm to us than we can do to them; the very greatness of their armament may be an advantage to us; it will have a good effect on the other Sicilian cities, who will be alarmed, and in their terror will be the more ready to assist us.   Then, again, if in the end we over-power them, or at any rate drive them away baffled, for I have not the slightest fear of their accomplishing their purpose, we shall have achieved a noble triumph.   And of this I have a good hope.   Rarely have great expeditions, whether Hellenic or Barbarian, when sent far from home, met with success.   They are not more numerous than the inhabitants and their neighbours, who all combine through fear; and if owing to scarcity of supplies in a foreign land they miscarry, although their ruin may be chiefly due to themselves, they confer glory on those whom they meant to overthrow.   The greatness of these very Athenians was based on the utter and unexpected ruin of the Persians [a], who were always supposed to have directed

---

[a] Cp. i. 69 fin.

their expedition against Athens. And I think that such
a destiny may very likely be reserved for us.

'Let us take courage then, and put ourselves into a 34
state of defence ; let us also send en-   *Let us summon our*
voys to the Sicels, and, while we make   *old Sicel allies and make*
sure of our old allies, endeavour to   *new ones. Let us ob-*
gain new ones. We will despatch en-   *tain help from the rest*
voys to the rest of Sicily, and point out   *of Sicily, Italy, Car-*
                                             thage, Lacedaemon, and
that the danger is common to all ; we   *Corinth. If you would*
                                             take my advice you
will also send to the Italian cities in   *would go and meet the*
the hope that they may either join us,   *Athenians half way.*
or at any rate refuse to receive the   *We should very likely*
                                             defeat them, and even
Athenians. And I think that we should   *if we did not fight*
send to the Carthaginians ; the idea of   *should still embarrass*
an Athenian attack is no novelty to   *them. They might be*
                                             so dismayed by our
them ; they are always living in appre-   *boldness as to give up*
hension of it. They will probably feel   *the expedition.*
that if they leave us to our fate, the trouble may reach
themselves, and therefore they may be inclined in some
way or other, secretly, if not openly, to assist us. If
willing to help, of all existing states they are the best able ;
for they have abundance of gold and silver, and these
make war, like other things, go smoothly. Let us also
send to the Lacedaemonians and Corinthians and entreat
them to come to our aid speedily, and at the same time to
revive the war in Hellas. I have a plan which in my
judgment is the best suited to the present emergency,
although it is the last which you in your habitual indolence
will readily embrace [a]. Let me tell you what it is. If all
the Sicilian Greeks, or at least if we and as many as will
join us, taking two months' provisions, would put out to
sea with all our available ships and prepare to meet the
Athenians at Tarentum and the promontory of Iapygia,
thereby proving to them that before they fight for Sicily
they must fight for the passage of the Ionian Sea, we

---

[a] Cp. i. 143 fin.

should strike a panic into them. They would then reflect that at Tarentum (which receives us), we, the advanced guard of Sicily, are among friends, and go forth from a friendly country, and that the sea is a large place not easy to traverse with so great an armament as theirs. They would know that after a long voyage their ships will be unable to keep in line, and coming up slowly and few at a time will be at our mercy. On the other hand, if they lighten their vessels and meet us in a compact body with the swifter part of their fleet, they may have to use oars, and then we shall attack them when they are exhausted. Or if we prefer not to fight, we can retire again to Tarentum. Having come over with slender supplies and prepared for a naval engagement, they will not know what to do on these desolate coasts. If they remain they will find themselves blockaded ; if they attempt to sail onwards they will cut themselves off from the rest of their armament, and will be discouraged ; for they will be far from certain whether the cities of Italy and Sicily will receive them. In my opinion the anticipation of these difficulties will hamper them to such a degree, that they will never leave Corcyra. While they are holding consultations, and sending out spies to discover our number and exact position, they will find themselves driven into winter ; or in dismay at the unexpected opposition, they may very likely break up the expedition ; especially if, as I am informed, the most experienced of their generals has taken the command against his will, and would gladly make any considerable demonstration on our part an excuse for retreating. I am quite sure that rumour will exaggerate our strength. The minds of men are apt to be swayed by what they hear ; and they are most afraid of those who commence an attack, or who at any rate show to the aggressor betimes that he will meet with resistance ; for then they reflect that the risk is equally divided. And so it will be with the Athenians. They are now attacking us because they do not believe that we shall defend our-

selves, and in this opinion they are justified by our neglect
to join with the Lacedaemonians in putting them down.
But, if they see that they were mistaken, and that we
boldly venture [a], they will be more dismayed at our unexpected resistance than at our real power. Take my
advice ; if possible, resolve on this bold step, but if not,
adopt other measures of defence as quickly as possible.
Remember each and all of you that the true contempt of
an invader is shown by deeds of valour in the field,
and that meanwhile the greatest service which you can
render to the state is to act as if you were in the
presence of danger, considering that safety depends on
anxious preparation [b]. The Athenians are coming ; I am
certain that they are already on the sea and will soon
be here.'

Thus spoke Hermocrates. Great was the contention 35
which his words aroused among the
Syracusan people, some asserting that *People said, They
the Athenians would never come, and will never come; and,
What harm will they
that he was not speaking truth, others do? A few saw the
asking, 'And if they should come, what danger.*
harm could they do to us nearly so great as we could do
to them ? ' while others were quite contemptuous, and
made a jest of the whole matter. A few only believed
Hermocrates and realised the danger. At last Athenagoras, the popular leader, who had at that time the
greatest influence with the multitude, came forward and
spoke as follows : —

'He is either a coward or a traitor who would not 36
rejoice to hear that the Athenians are so mad as to come
hither and deliver themselves into our hands. The audacity of the people who are spreading these alarms does
not surprise me, but I do wonder at their folly if they
cannot see that their motives are transparent. Having

---

[a] Cp. ii. 89 med.   [b] Cp. ii. 11 med.

private reasons for being afraid, they want to strike terror

Speech of Athen-
agoras. These alarms
are spread by traitors,
who want to divert
public attention from
their own designs. The
whole story is exceed-
ingly improbable.
into the whole city [a] that they may hide themselves [a] under the shadow of the common fear. And now, what is the meaning of these rumours? They do not grow of themselves; they have been got up by persons who are the troublers of our state. And you, if you are wise, will not measure probabilities by their reports, but by what we may assume to be the intentions of shrewd and experienced men such as I conceive the Athenians to be. They are not likely to leave behind them a power such as Peloponnesus. The war which they have already on their hands is far from settled, and will they go out of their way to bring upon themselves another as great? In my opinion they are only too glad that we are not attacking them, considering the number and power of our states.

37   'Even if the rumour of their coming should turn out to

Sicily is more than
a match for the Athen-
ians; and another
Syracuse, if they had
possession of it, could
not conquer Syracuse.
be true, I am sure that Sicily is more fit than Peloponnesus to maintain a great war. The whole island is better supplied in every way, and our own city is herself far more than a match for the army which is said to be threatening us; aye, and for another as great. I know that they will not bring cavalry with them, and will find none here, except the few horsemen which they may procure from Egesta. They cannot provide a force of hoplites equal to ours [b], for they have to cross the sea; and to come all this distance, if only with ships and with no troops or lading, would be work enough [c]. I know too that an armament which is directed against so great a city as ours will require

---

[a] Or, 'that they may hide their own consciousness of guilt.'   [b] Cp. vi. 23 init.   [c] Placing a colon after ἐλθόντας and taking μέγα γάρ . . . κομισθῆναι as a parenthesis.

immense supplies[a].   Nay, I venture to assert that if they
came hither, having at their command another city close
upon our border as large as Syracuse, and could there
settle and carry on war against us from thence, they would
still be destroyed to a man; how much more when the
whole country will be their enemy (for Sicily will unite),
and when they must pitch their camp the moment they
are out of their ships, and will have nothing but their
wretched huts and meagre supplies, being prevented by
our cavalry from advancing far beyond their lines?
Indeed I hardly think that they will effect a landing at all.
So far superior, in my judgment, are our forces to theirs.

'The Athenians, I repeat, know all that I am telling 38
you, and do not mean to throw away   *The Athenians are*
what they have got: I am pretty sure   *a shrewd people and*
of that.   But some of our people are   *not likely to ruin them-*
fabricating reports which neither are, *selves.   These reports*
nor are ever likely to be, true. I know, *are fabricated by olig-*
and have always known, that by words   *archical conspirators,*
like these, and yet more mischievous,   *who want to get the*
if not by acts, they want to intimidate *government into their*
                                        hands. I shall resist
                                        them to the last.
you, the Syracusan people and make themselves chiefs of
the state.   And I am afraid that if they persevere they will
succeed at last, and that we shall be delivered into their
hands before we have had the sense to take precautions
or to detect and punish them.   This is the reason why
our city is always in a state of unrest and disorganisation,
fighting against herself quite as much as against foreign
enemies, and from time to time subjected to tyrants and to
narrow and wicked oligarchies.   If the people will only
support me I shall endeavour to prevent any such misfortunes happening in our day.   With you I shall use
persuasion, but to these conspirators I shall apply force;
and I shall not wait until they are detected in the act (for
who can catch them?), but I shall punish their intentions

----

[a] Cp. vi. 21 med.

and the mischief which they would do if they could.   For
the thoughts of our enemies must be punished before they
have ripened into deeds.   If a man does not strike first, he
Tirade against the will be the first struck.   As to the rest
young oligarchs.   of the oligarchical party, I must expose
them and have an eye on their designs; I must also
instruct them; that, I think, will be the way by which
I can best deter them from their evil courses.   Come now,
young men, and answer me a question which I have often
asked myself.   "What can you want?"   To hold office
already?   But the law forbids.   And the law was not
intended to slight you had you been capable; it was
passed because you were incapable.   And so you would
rather not be on an equality with the many?   But when
there is no real difference between men, why should there
be a privileged class?

39   'I shall be told that democracy is neither a wise nor
The true state is a just thing, and that those who have
composed of various the money are most likely to govern
elements; while an well.   To which I answer, first of all,
oligarchy takes all the that the people is the name of the
good and gives the
people their full share whole, the oligarchy of a part; secondly,
of the evil.   that the rich are the best guardians of
the public purse, the wise the best counsellors, and the
many, when they have heard a matter discussed, the best
judges [a]; and that each and all of these classes have in
a democracy equal privileges.   Whereas an oligarchy,
while giving the people the full share of danger, not
merely takes too much of the good things, but absolutely
monopolises them.   And this is what the powerful among
you and the young would like to have, and what in a great
city they will never obtain.

40   'O most senseless of men, for such you are indeed if
you do not see the mischief of your own schemes; never
in all my experience have I known such blindness among

---

[a] Cp. ii. 40 med.

Hellenes, or such wickedness if you have your eyes open
to what you are doing. Yet even now *Blind fools, if you*
learn if you are stupid, repent if you *are not knaves, the city*
are guilty; and let your aim be the *will never be imposed*
welfare of the whole country. Re- *upon by you.*
member that the good among you will have an equal or
larger share in the government of it than the people [a];
while if you want more you will most likely lose all.
Away with 'these reports; we know all about them, and
are determined to suppress them. Let the Athenians
come, and Syracuse will repel her enemies in a manner
worthy of herself; we have generals who will look to the
matter. But if, as I believe, none of your tales are true,
the state is not going to be deceived, and will not in
a moment of panic admit you to power, or impose upon
her own neck the yoke of slavery. She will take the
matter into her own hands, and when she gives judgment
will reckon words to be equally criminal with actions.
She will not be talked out of her liberty by you, but will
do her utmost to preserve it; she will be on her guard,
and will put you down with a strong hand.'

Thus spoke Athenagoras. Whereupon one of the 41
generals rose, and suffering no one *One of the generals*
else to come forward, closed the *deprecates the use of*
discussion himself in the following *bad language: he thinks*
the report of the danger
words :— *a good opportunity for*
'There is little wisdom in exchanging *increasing the army.*
abuse or in sitting by and listening to it; let us rather, in
view of the reported danger, see how the whole city and
every man in it may take measures for resisting the
invaders worthily. Why should not the city be richly
furnished with arms, horses, and all the pride and pomp
of war; where is the harm even if they should not be
wanted? We, who are generals, will take in hand all
these matters and examine into them ourselves; and we

---

[a] Cp. ii. 37 init.

will send messengers to the neighbouring cities in order to obtain information, and for any other purpose which may be necessary.   Some precautions we have taken already, and whatever comes to our notice we will communicate to you.'   When the general had thus spoken, the assembly dispersed.

42   The Athenians and their allies were by this time gathered

The Athenians at Corcyra make a final review of their armament, which is formed into three divisions.

at Corcyra.   There the generals began by holding a final review of the ships, and disposed them in the order in which they were to anchor at their stations.   The fleet was divided into three squadrons, and one of them assigned by lot to each of the three generals, in order to avoid any difficulties which might occur, if they sailed together, in finding water, anchorage, and provisions where they touched ; they also thought that the presence of a general with each division would promote good order and discipline throughout the fleet. They then sent before them to Italy and Sicily three ships, which had orders to find out what cities in those regions would receive them, and to meet them again on their way, that they might know before they put in.

43   At length the great armament proceeded to cross from

At length they cross the sea in a hundred and thirty-four triremes and two penteconters, conveying five thousand one hundred hoplites, four hundred and eighty archers, seven hundred slingers, a hundred and twenty Megarian light-armed, and thirty horsemen.

Corcyra to Sicily.   It consisted of a hundred and thirty-four triremes in all, besides two Rhodian vessels of fifty oars.   Of these a hundred were Athenian ; sixty being swift vessels, and the remaining forty transports : the rest of the fleet was furnished by the Chians and other allies.   The hoplites numbered in all five thousand one hundred, of whom fifteen hundred were Athenians taken from the roll, and seven hundred who served as marines were of the fourth and lowest class of Athenian citizens.   The remainder of the hoplites were furnished by the allies, mostly by the subject states ;

but five hundred came from Argos, besides two hundred and fifty Mantinean and other mercenaries. The archers were in all four hundred and eighty, of whom eighty were Cretans. There were seven hundred Rhodian slingers, a hundred and twenty light-armed Megarians who were exiles[a]; and one horse transport which conveyed thirty horsemen and horses.

Such were the forces with which the first expedition 44 crossed the sea. For the transport of provisions thirty merchant-ships, which also conveyed bakers, masons, carpenters, and tools such as are required in sieges, were included in the armament. It was likewise attended by a hundred small vessels; these, as well as the merchant-vessels, were pressed into the service. Other merchant-vessels and lesser craft in great numbers followed of their own accord for purposes of trade. The whole fleet now struck across the Ionian sea from Corcyra. They arrived at the promontory of Iapygia and at Tarentum, each ship taking its own course, and passed along the coast of Italy. The Italian cities did not admit them within their walls, or open a market to them, but allowed them water and anchorage; Tarentum and Locri refused even these. At length they reached Rhegium, the extreme point of Italy, where the fleet reunited. As they were not received within the walls they encamped outside the city at the temple of Artemis; there they were provided by the inhabitants with a market, and drawing up their ships on shore they took a rest. They held a conference with the Rhegians, and pressed them, being Chalcidians themselves, to aid their Chalcidian kinsmen the Leontines. But the Rhegians replied that they would be neutral, and would only act in accordance with the decision of all

The fleet included thirty merchant-ships and a hundred small vessels. Arriving at Rhegium they are refused admittance into the city, but are supplied with provisions and allowed to anchor.

---

[a] Cp. iv. 74.

the Italian Greeks. The Athenian commanders now began to consider how they could best commence operations in Sicily. Meanwhile they were expecting the ships which had gone on and were to meet them from Egesta ; for they wanted to know whether the Egestaeans really had the money of which the messengers had brought information to Athens.

45   From many quarters the news began to reach the

The Syracusans re-
solve to defend them-
selves in earnest.

Syracusans that the Athenian fleet was at Rhegium, and the report was confirmed by their spies. They now no longer doubted, but fell to work heart and soul. To some of the Sicel towns they sent troops, to others envoys ; they also garrisoned the forts in the territory of Syracuse, and within the city itself inspected the horses and arms, and saw that they were in good condition. In short, they made every preparation, as for a war which was rapidly approaching, and almost at their gates.

46   The three ships which had gone forward to Egesta now

Trick practised by the
Egestaeans, who had
borrowed the plate
which the Athenian
envoys saw at Egesta.

returned to the Athenians at Rhegium ; they reported that of the money which had been promised thirty talents [a] only were forthcoming and no more. The spirits of the generals fell at once on receiving this their first discouragement. They were also disappointed at the unfavourable answer of the Rhegians, whom they had asked first, and who might naturally have been expected to join them because they were kinsmen of the Leontines, and had always hitherto been in the Athenian interest. Nicias had expected that the Egestaeans would fail them [b] ; to the two others their behaviour appeared even more incomprehensible than the defection of the Rhegians. The fact was that when the original envoys came from Athens to inspect the treasure, the Egestaeans had practised a trick upon them. They

---

[a] £6,000.   [b] Cp. vi. 22 fin.

brought them to the temple of Aphrodìtè at Eryx, and showed them the offerings deposited there, consisting of bowls, flagons, censers, and a good deal of other plate. Most of the vessels were only of silver, and therefore they made a show quite out of proportion to their value. They also gave private entertainments to the crews of the triremes : on each of these occasions they produced, as their own, drinking-vessels of gold and silver not only collected in Egesta itself, but borrowed from the neighbouring towns, Phoenician as well as Hellenic. All of them exhibiting much the same vessels and making everywhere a great display, the sailors were amazed, and on their arrival at Athens told every one what heaps of wealth they had seen. When the news spread that the Egestaeans had not got the money, great was the unpopularity incurred throughout the army by these men, who having been first imposed upon themselves had been instrumental in imposing upon others.

The generals now held a council of war. Nicias was 47 of opinion that they should sail with the whole fleet against Selinus, which was their main errand : if the Egestaeans provided pay for all their forces, they would shape their course accordingly ; if not, they would demand maintenance for sixty ships, the number

Opinions of the three generals. Nicias would sail against Selinus, making the Egestaeans pay. Then, after displaying the power of Athens, he would return home.

which the Egestaeans had requested [a], and remain on the spot until they had brought the Selinuntians to terms either by force or by negotiation. They would then pass along the coast before the eyes of the other cities and display the visible power of Athens, while they proved at the same time her zeal in the cause of her friends and allies ; after this they would return home, unless a speedy way of relieving the Leontines or obtaining support from some of the other cities should unexpectedly present

---

[a] Cp. vi. 8 init.

itself. But they should not throw away their own resources and imperil the safety of Athens.

48   Alcibiades urged that it would be a disgrace to have

Alcibiades would do more; he would attack both Selinus and Syracuse, first gaining over the other Sicilian states.
gone forth with so great an armament
and to return without achieving any·
thing. They should send envoys to
every city of Sicily, with the exception
of Selinus and Syracuse; they should
also negotiate with the Sicels, making friends of the
independent tribes, and persuading the rest to revolt from
the Syracusans. They would thus obtain supplies and
reinforcements. They should first appeal to the Messenians, whose city being on the highway of traffic was the
key of Sicily, and possessed a harbour from which the
Athenian forces could most conveniently watch the enemy.
Finally, when they had brought the cities over to them and
knew who would be on their side in the war, they should
attack Selinus and Syracuse, unless the Selinuntians would
come to terms with the Egestaeans, and the Syracusans
would permit the restoration of the Leontines.

49   Lamachus was of opinion that they ought to sail direct

Lamachus thinks that the Athenians should sail to Syracuse and fight at once. They should establish their fleet at Megara.
to Syracuse, and fight as soon as pos-
sible under the walls of the city, while
the inhabitants were unprepared and
the consternation was at its height.
He argued that all armies are most
terrible at first; if the appearance of them is long delayed the spirits of men revive, and, when they actually
come, the sight of them only awakens contempt[a]. If the
Athenians could strike suddenly, while their opponents
were still in fear and suspense, that would be the best
chance of victory. Not only the sight of the armament
which would never seem so numerous again, but the near
approach of suffering, and above all the immediate peril
of battle, would create a panic among the enemy. Many

---

[a] Cp. vii. 42 med.

of the Syracusans would probably be cut off in the country, not believing in the approach of an invader; and while the villagers were trying to convey their property into the city, their own army, which would be encamped close under the walls, would be masters of the field and could have no lack of provisions. In the end, the other Sicilian Greeks, instead of joining the Syracusan alliance, would come over to them, and would no longer hesitate and look about them to see which side would conquer. He was also of opinion that they should make Megara their naval station, ᵃ the fleet returning thither from Syracuse and anchoring in the harbour ᵃ. The place was deserted, and was not far distant from Syracuse either by land or by sea.

Lamachus having thus spoken nevertheless gave his own voice for the proposal of Alci-50
biades. Whereupon Alcibiades sailed *The plan of Alci-*
across in his admiral's ship to Messenè *biades is pursued, and*
and proposed an alliance to the inhab- *he himself goes as envoy*
itants. He failed to convince them, *to Messenè, but is not*
for they refused to receive the Athen- *admitted. An Athen-*
ians into the city, although they *ian force is received at*
Naxos, but excluded at
Catana. They go on
to Syracuse.
offered to open a market for them out-
side the walls. So he sailed back to Rhegium. The generals at once manned sixty ships, selecting the crews indifferently out of the entire fleet, and taking the necessary provisions coasted along to Naxos; they left the rest of the armament and one of themselves at Rhegium. The Naxians received them into their city, and they sailed on to Catana; but the Catanaeans, having a Syracusan party within their walls, denied admission to them; so they moved to the river Terias and there encamped. On the following day they went on to Syracuse in long file with all their ships, except ten, which they had sent forward to sail into the Great Harbour and

---

ᵃ Reading ἐφορμισθέντας, a conjecture of Schaefer's adopted by Poppo; or, following the MSS. and reading ἐφορμηθέντας: 'there taking up a secure position and thence attacking Syracuse.'

see whether there was any fleet launched.   On their
approaching the city a herald was to proclaim from the
decks that the Athenians had come to restore their allies
and kinsmen the Leontines to their homes, and that
therefore any Leontines who were in Syracuse should
regard the Athenians as their friends and benefactors,
and join them without fear.   When the proclamation had
been made, and the fleet had taken a survey of the city,
and harbours, and of the ground which was to be the
scene of operations, they sailed back to Catana.

51   The Catanaeans now held an assembly and, although
They   return   to   they still refused to receive the army,
Catana,   where   the   they told the generals to come in and
soldiers find a way in   say what they had to say.   While Alci-
while   Alcibiades   is
speaking.   The whole   biades was speaking and the people of
fleet   removes   thither   the city had their attention occupied
from Rhegium.   with the assembly, the soldiers broke
down unobserved a postern gate which had been badly
walled up, and finding their way into the town began to
walk about in the market-place.   Those of the Catanaeans who were in the Syracusan interest, when they
saw that the enemy had entered, took alarm and stole
away.   They were not numerous, and the other Catanaeans voted the alliance with the Athenians, and told
them to bring up the rest of their armament from Rhegium.
The Athenians then sailed back to Rhegium, and with
their entire force moved to Catana, where on their
arrival they began to establish their camp.

52   But meanwhile news came from Camarina that if they
The Athenians sail   would go thither the Camarinaeans
first to Syracuse, which   would join them.   They also heard
has as yet no fleet ;   that the Syracusans were manning a
then to Camarina, but
they are not received   navy.   So they sailed with their whole
there.   force first to Syracuse, but they found
that there was no fleet in preparation ; they then passed
on to Camarina, and putting in to the open beach they
sent a herald to the city.   The citizens would not receive

them, declaring that their oath[a] bound them not to receive the Athenians if they came with more than one ship, unless they themselves sent for a greater number. So they sailed away without effecting their purpose. They then disembarked on a part of the Syracusan territory, which they ravaged. But a few Syracusan horse coming up killed some of their light-armed troops who were straggling. They then returned to Catana.

There they found that the vessel Salaminia had come 53 from Athens to fetch Alcibiades, who had been put upon his trial by the state and was ordered home to defend himself. With him were summoned certain of the soldiers, who were accused at the same time, some of profaning the mysteries, others of mutilation of the Hermae. For after the departure of the expedition the Athenians prosecuted both enquiries as keenly as ever. They did not investigate the character of the informers, but in their suspicious mood listened to all manner of statements, and seized and imprisoned some of the most respectable citizens on the evidence of wretches; they thought it better to sift the matter and discover the truth; and they would not allow even a man of good character, against whom an accusation was brought, to escape without a thorough investigation, merely because the informer was a rogue. For the people, who had heard by tradition that the tyranny of Pisistratus and his sons ended in great oppression, and knew moreover that their power was overthrown, not by Harmodius or any efforts of their own, but by the Lacedaemonians[b], were in a state of incessant fear and suspicion.

The Salaminia comes to fetch Alcibiades. Excitement of the Athenians, who connect the mutilation of the Hermae with the tradition of the Pisistratidae.

Now the attempt of Aristogiton and Harmodius arose 54 out of a love affair, which I will narrate at length; and the narrative will show that the Athenians themselves give quite an inaccurate account of their own tyrants, and

---

[a] Cp. iv. 65 init.   [b] Cp. Herod. v. 65.

of the incident in question, and know no more than other

B.C. 527.
Ol. 63, 2.

Not Hippias the reigning tyrant, but Hipparchus his brother, was slain by Harmodius and Aristogiton. The attempt

B.C. 514.
Ol. 66, 3.

arose out of a love affair. The Pisistratidae, though tyrants, were not without virtues or wanting in moderation: they retained the ancient laws, but kept their hold over the offices.

Hellenes [a]. Pisistratus died at an advanced age in possession of the tyranny, and then, not, as is the common opinion, Hipparchus, but Hippias (who was the eldest of his sons) succeeded to his power.—Harmodius was in the flower of youth, and Aristogiton, a citizen of the middle class, became his lover. Hipparchus made an attempt to gain the affections of Harmodius, but he would not listen to him, and told Aristogiton. The latter was naturally tormented at the idea, and fearing that Hipparchus who was powerful would resort to violence, at once formed such a plot as a man in his station might for the overthrow of the tyranny. Meanwhile Hipparchus made another attempt; he had no better success, and thereupon he determined, not indeed to take any violent step, but to insult Harmodius [b] in some secret place [b], so that his motive could not be suspected. To use violence would have been at variance with the general character of his rule, which was not unpopular or oppressive to the many; in fact no tyrants ever displayed greater merit or capacity than these. Although the tax on the produce of the soil which they exacted amounted only to five per cent., they improved and adorned the city, and carried on successful wars; they were also in the habit of sacrificing in the temples. The city meanwhile was permitted to retain her ancient laws; but the family of Pisistratus took care that one of their own number should always be in office. Among others who thus held the annual archonship at Athens was Pisistratus, a son of the tyrant Hippias. He was named after his grandfather Pisistratus, and

---

[a] Cp. i. 20.   [b] Reading τύπῳ with all the MSS.; or, reading τρόπῳ: 'in some underhand manner.'

during his term of office he dedicated the altar of the Twelve Gods in the Agora, and another altar in the temple of the Pythian Apollo. The Athenian people afterwards added to one side of the altar in the Agora and so concealed the inscription upon it; but the other inscription on the altar of the Pythian Apollo may still be seen, although the letters are nearly effaced. It runs as follows :—

'Pisistratus the son of Hippias dedicated this memorial of his archonship in the sacred precinct of the Pythian Apollo.'

That Hippias was the eldest son of Pisistratus and 55 succeeded to his power I can positively affirm from special information which has been transmitted to me. But there is other evidence. Of the legitimate sons of Pisistratus he alone had children; this is indicated by the altar just mentioned, and by the column which the Athenians set up in the Acropolis to commemorate the oppression of the tyrants. For on that column no son of Thessalus or of Hipparchus is named, but five of Hippias who were born to him of Myrrhinè the daughter of Callias the son of Hyperechides; now there is a presumption that the son who married first would be the eldest. Moreover, his name is inscribed ᵃ on the same column ᵃ immediately after his father's; this again is a presumption that he was his eldest son and succeeded him. I think too that Hippias would have found a difficulty in seizing the tyranny if Hipparchus had been tyrant at the time of his death and he had tried to step into his place. As it was, owing to the habitual dread which he had inspired in the citizens, and the strict discipline which he maintained among his body-guard, he held the government with the

Various proofs of the fact that Hippias was the elder son.

ᵃ Reading ἐν τῇ αὐτῇ στήλῃ. Or, reading with the MSS. ἐν τῇ πρώτῃ στήλῃ : 'on the front part of the column.' But the words can hardly bear this meaning. The word πρώτῃ is probably derived from πρῶτος which follows.

most perfect security and without the least difficulty. Nor did he behave at all like a younger brother, who would not have known what to do ᵃ because he had not been regularly used to command ᵃ. Yet Hipparchus by reason of his violent end became famous, and obtained in after ages the reputation of having been the tyrant.

56   When Hipparchus found his advances repelled by Har-

The rest of the story. The revenge of Harmodius and Aristogiton.

modius he carried out his intention of insulting him. There was a young sister of his whom Hipparchus and his friends first invited to come and carry a sacred basket in a procession, and then rejected her, declaring that she had never been invited by them at all because she was unworthy. At this Harmodius was very angry, and Aristogiton, for his sake, more angry still. They and the other conspirators had already laid their preparations, but were waiting for the festival of the great Panathenaea, when the citizens who took part in the procession assembled in arms ; for to do so on any other day would have aroused suspicion. Harmodius and Aristogiton were to begin the attack, and the rest were immediately to join in, and engage with the guards. The plot had been communicated to a few only, the better to avoid detection ; but they hoped that, however few struck the blow, the crowd who would be armed, although not in the secret, would at once rise and assist in the recovery of their own liberties.

57   The day of the festival arrived, and Hippias went out

Harmodius and Aristogiton, suspecting that they have been betrayed, leave Hippias and fall upon Hipparchus. The manner of his and their deaths.

of the city to the place called the Ceramicus, where he was occupied with his guards in marshalling the procession. Harmodius and Aristogiton, who were ready with their daggers, stepped forward to do the deed. But seeing one of the conspirators in familiar conversation

---

ᵃ Or, giving a more precise sense to ξυνεχῶς: 'because he had succeeded to the command and not been used to it.'

with Hippias, who was readily accessible to all, they took alarm, and imagined that they had been betrayed and were on the point of being seized. Whereupon they determined to take their revenge first on the man who had outraged them and was the cause of their desperate attempt. So they rushed, just as they were, within the gates. They found Hipparchus near the Leocorium, as it was called, and then and there falling upon him with all the blind fury, one of an injured lover, the other of a man smarting under an insult, they smote and slew him. The crowd ran together, and so Aristogiton for the present escaped the guards; but he was afterwards taken and not very gently handled. Harmodius perished on the spot.

The news was carried to Hippias at the Ceramicus; he **58** went at once, not to the place, but to *Hippias, dissembling* the armed men who were to march in *his feelings, contrives* the procession and, being at a distance, *to disarm the citizens* were as yet ignorant of what had hap- *and arrest the sus-* pened. Betraying nothing in his looks of the calamity *pected.* which had befallen him, he bade them leave their arms and go to a certain spot which he pointed out. They, supposing that he had something to say to them, obeyed, and then bidding his guards seize the arms, he at once selected those whom he thought guilty, and all who were found carrying daggers; for the custom was to march in the procession with spear and shield only.

Such was the conspiracy of Harmodius and Aristogiton, **59** which began in the resentment of a *The rule of Hippias* lover; the reckless attempt which fol- *grows oppressive. He* lowed arose out of a sudden fright. *is deposed by the Lace-* To the people at large the tyranny *daemonians, and goes* simply became more oppressive, and *to the court of Persia.* Hippias, after his brother's death living *Epitaph of his daughter* *Archedicè.* in great fear, slew many of the citizens; he also began to look abroad in hope of securing an asylum should a revolution occur. Himself an Athenian, he married his daughter Archedicè to a Lampsacene, Aeantides, son of Hippoclus the tyrant of Lampsacus; for he observed that the family of Hippoclus had great influence with King Darius.   Her tomb is at Lampsacus, and bears this inscription :—

> 'This earth covers Archedicè the daughter of Hippias,
> A man who was great among the Hellenes of his day.
> Her father, her husband, her brothers, and her sons were tyrants,
> Yet was not her mind lifted up to vanity.'

Hippias ruled three years longer over the Athenians. In the fourth year he was deposed by the Lacedaemonians and the exiled Alcmaeonidae.   He retired under an agreement, first to Sigeum, and then to Aeantides at Lampsacus.   From him he went to the court of Darius, whence returning twenty years later with the Persian army he took part in the expedition to Marathon, being then an old man.

B.C. 510.
Ol. 67, 3.

60   The Athenian people, recalling these and other traditions of the tyrants which had sunk deep into their minds, were suspicious and savage against the supposed profaners of the mysteries; the whole affair seemed to them to indicate some conspiracy aiming at oligarchy or tyranny. Inflamed by these suspicions they had already imprisoned many men of high character.   There was no sign of returning quiet, but day by day the movement became more furious and the number of arrests increased.   At last one of the prisoners, who was believed to be deeply implicated, was induced by a fellow-prisoner to make a confession—whether true or false I cannot say; opinions are divided, and no one knew at the time, or to this day knows, who the offenders were.   His companion argued that even if he were not guilty he ought to confess and claim a pardon[a]; he would thus save his own life, and at the same time deliver Athens from the prevailing state

B.C. 415.
Ol. 91, 2.

The Athenians become more and more excited about the acts of irreligion, which they believe to indicate some design against the democracy.   Confession of one of the prisoners.

---

[a] Cp. vi. 27.

of suspicion.   His chance of escaping would be better if
he confessed his guilt in the hope of a pardon, than if he
denied it and stood his trial.   So he gave evidence both
against himself and others in the matter of the Hermae.
The Athenians were delighted at finding out what they
supposed to be the truth ; they had been in despair at the
thought that the conspirators against the democracy would
never be known, and they immediately liberated the
informer and all whom he had not denounced.   The
accused they brought to trial, and executed such of them
as could be found.   Those who had fled they condemned
to death, and promised a reward to any one who would
kill them.   No one could say whether the sufferers were
justly punished ; but the beneficial effect on the city at the
time was undeniable.

The enemies of Alcibiades, who had attacked him before 61
he sailed, continued their machinations,
and popular feeling was deeply stirred   *Suspicion of Alcibia-*
against him.   The Athenians now   *des increased by the ap-*
thought that they knew the truth about   *pearance of a Lacedae-*
                                          monian force at the
the Hermae, and they were more than   *Isthmus.   The people*
ever convinced that the violation of the   *are beside themselves.*
mysteries which had been laid to his   *The suspicion extends*
charge was done by him with the same   *to Argos.   The Sala-*
                                          minia is sent to arrest
purpose, and was a part of the con-   *him, but he escapes at*
spiracy.   It so happened that while   *Thurii and crosses to*
                                          Peloponnesus.
the city was in this state of excitement a small Lacedaemonian force proceeded as far as the Isthmus, having
something to do in Boeotia.   They were supposed to have
come, not in the interest of the Boeotians, but by a secret
understanding with Alcibiades ; and the Athenians really
believed that but for their own alacrity in arresting the
accused persons the city would have been betrayed.   For
one whole night the people lay in arms in the temple of
Theseus which is within the walls.   About this time too
the friends of Alcibiades at Argos were suspected of conspiring against the Argive democracy, and accordingly the

Argive hostages who had been deposited in the islands[a] were at once given up by the Athenians to the vengeance of the Argive people. From every quarter suspicion had gathered around Alcibiades, and the Athenian people were determined to have him tried and executed ; so they sent the ship Salaminia to Sicily bearing a summons to him and to others against whom information had been given. He was ordered to follow the officers home and defend himself, but they were told not to arrest him ; the Athenians, having regard to their interests in Sicily, were anxious not to cause excitement in their own camp or to attract the attention of the enemy, and above all not to lose the Mantineans and Argives, whom they knew to have been induced by his influence to join in the expedition[b]. He in his own ship, and those who were accused with him, left Sicily in company with the Salaminia, and sailed for Athens. When they arrived at Thurii they followed no further, but left the ship and disappeared, fearing to return and stand their trial when the prejudice against them was so violent. The crew of the Salaminia searched for them, but after a time, being unable to find them, gave up the search and went home. Alcibiades, now an exile, crossed not long afterwards in a small vessel from Thurii to Peloponnesus, and the Athenians on his non-appearance sentenced him and his companions to death.

62   The two Athenian generals who remained in Sicily now

Expedition to Egesta. divided the fleet between them by lot,
Capture of Hyccara. and sailed towards Selinus and Egesta ;
The Athenian army they wanted to know whether the
returns by land to Ca- Egestaeans would give them the pro-
tana. Failure to take mised money, and also to ascertain the
Hybla. condition of the Selinuntians and the nature of their quarrel with the Egestaeans. Sailing along the north coast of Sicily, which looks towards the Tyrrhenian Gulf, they touched at Himera, the only Hellenic city in this part of

---

the island. But they were not received, and passed on.
On their voyage they took Hyccara, a city on the sea-shore
which, although of Sicanian origin, was hostile to the
Egestaeans [a]. They reduced the inhabitants to slavery,
and handed the place over to the Egestaeans, whose
cavalry had now joined them.   The Athenian troops then
marched back through the country of the Sicels until they
arrived at Catana ; the ships which conveyed the prisoners
going round the coast to meet them.   Nicias had sailed
straight from Hyccara to Egesta, where he did his business,
and having obtained thirty talents [b] of silver, rejoined the
army at Catana.   The Athenians on their return disposed
of their slaves [c]; the sum realised by the sale was about
a hundred and twenty talents [d].   They next sailed round
to their Sicel allies and bade them send reinforcements.
Then with half of their army they marched against Hybla
Geleatis, a hostile town, which they failed to take.   And
so ended the summer.

Early in the ensuing winter the Athenians made pre- 63
parations for an attack upon Syracuse ;   *The Syracusans begin*
the Syracusans likewise prepared to *to despise the Athen-*
take the offensive. For when they found *ians.*
that their enemies did not assail them at once, as in their
first panic they had expected, day by day their spirits rose.
And now the Athenians, after cruising about at the other
end of Sicily, where they seemed to be a long way off, had
gone to Hybla, and their attack upon it had failed.   So
the Syracusans despised them more than ever.   After the
manner of the populace when elated, they insisted that
since the Athenians would not come to them, their generals
should lead them against Catana.   Syracusan horsemen,
who were always riding up to the Athenian army and
watching their movements, would ask insultingly whether,
instead of resettling the Leontines in their old home, they

---

[a] Cp. vi. 2 med.   [b] Cp. vi. 46 init.   [c] Cp. vii. 13 fin.
                         [d] £24,000.

were not themselves going to settle down with their good friends the Syracusans in a new one.

64   The generals were aware of the state of affairs. They *The Athenians de-* determined to draw the whole Syra-*ceive the Syracusans by* cusan army as far as possible out of *a fictitious message and* the city, and then in their absence sail *draw them off to Ca-* thither by night and take up a con-*tana,* venient position unmolested. They knew that they would fail of their purpose [a] if they tried to disembark their men in the face of an enemy who was prepared to meet them, or if they marched openly by land and were discovered, for they had no cavalry of their own, and the Syracusan horse which were numerous would do great harm to their light-armed troops and the mass of attendants. Whereas if they sailed thither by night they would be enabled to take up a position in which the cavalry could do them no serious mischief.—The exact spot near the temple of Olympian Zeus which they afterwards occupied was indicated by Syracusan exiles who accompanied them.— Accordingly the generals devised the following plan ; they sent to Syracuse a man of whose fidelity they were assured, but whom the Syracusan leaders believed to be a friend of theirs. He was a Catanaean, and professed to come from adherents of their party whose names were familiar to them, and whom they knew to be still remaining in Catana[b]. He told them that the Athenians lay within the city every night away from the camp in which their arms were deposited, and if at dawn on a set day the Syracusans with their whole force would come and attack the troops left in the camp, their partisans in Catana would themselves [c] shut the Athenians up in the town [c] and fire their ships ; meanwhile the Syracusans might assault the palisade, and easily take the camp—preparations had been made [d], and

---

[a] Omitting καὶ before εἰ ἐκ τῶν νεῶν.   [b] Cp. vi. 51.   [c] Reading αὐτοὺς after ἀποκλῄσειν : or, reading τοὺς instead of αὐτοὺς : ' shut up those of the Athenians who were in the town.'   [d] Placing a comma after ἤδη.

many of the Catanaeans were in the plot; from them he came.

The Syracusan generals were already in high spirits, and 65 before this proposal reached them had made up their minds to have all things in readiness for a march to Catana. So they trusted the man the more recklessly, and at once fixed the day on which they would arrive. They then sent him back, and issued orders for an expedition to their whole army, including the Selinuntians and the rest of the allies, who had now joined them. When they were ready and the appointed day drew near they marched towards Catana, and encamped by the river Symaethus in the Leontine territory. The Athenians, aware of the approach of the Syracusans, took all their own army and Sicel or other allies on board their ships and smaller craft, and sailed away at nightfall to Syracuse. At dawn they disembarked opposite the temple of Olympian Zeus, intending to seize a place for their camp; almost at the same moment the Syracusan horse who had advanced before the rest to Catana discovered that the whole Athenian army had put out to sea, whereupon they returned and told the infantry: and then all together hurried back to protect the city.

while they quietly sail away by night and disembark at Syracuse.

The march from Catana to Syracuse was long, and 66 in the meantime the Athenians had quietly established themselves in an advantageous position, where they could give battle whenever they pleased, and the Syracusan horse were least likely to harass them either before or during the engagement. On one side they were protected by walls, and houses, and trees, and a marsh; on another by a line of cliffs. They felled the trees near, and bringing them down to the sea made a palisade to protect their ships; on the shore of Dascon too they hurriedly raised a fortification of rough stones and logs at a point where the ground was most accessible to

They occupy a strong position. The Syracusans return from Catana.

the enemy, and broke down the bridge over the river Anapus. No one came out from the walls to hinder them in their work. The first to appear at all were the returning cavalry; after a while the whole body of infantry came up and re-formed. They at once marched right up to the Athenian position, but the Athenians did not come out to meet them; so they retired and encamped on the other side of the Helorine road.

67   On the next day the Athenians and their allies prepared

The Athenians pre- to give battle. Their order was as
pare for battle; they are follows:—The Argives and Mantineans
drawn up eight deep
and the Syracusans six- formed the right wing, the Athenians
teen deep. held the centre; on the left wing were
the remaining allies. Half of their army which formed the van was ranged eight deep. The other half was drawn up likewise eight deep close to their sleeping-places, in a hollow oblong. The latter were told to watch the engagement, and to move up to the support of any part of the line which might be distressed. In the midst of the reserve thus disposed were placed the baggage-bearers. The Syracusans drew up their heavy-armed sixteen deep; the army consisted of the whole Syracusan people and their allies, chiefly the Selinuntians, who were in the city; they had also two hundred horsemen from Gela, and twenty, with about fifty archers, from Camarina. The cavalry, numbering in all twelve hundred, were placed upon the right wing, and beside them the javelin-men. The Athenians determined to begin the attack. Just before the battle Nicias went up and down, and addressed the following words to all and each of the various peoples who composed the army:—

68   'What need, soldiers, is there of a long exhortation when we are all here united in the same cause [a]? The mere sight of this great army is more likely to put courage into you than an eloquent speech and an inferior force [b].

---

[a] Cp. vii. 61 init.   [b] Cp. v. 69 fin.; vii. 61 fin., 77 med.

We are Argives and Mantineans, and Athenians and
the chief of the islanders; and must   *We are picked men,*
not the presence of so many brave   *and they are the popu-*
allies inspire every one of us with a   *lace of a city. They*
good hope of victory, especially when   *despise us, but will not*
we reflect that our opponents are   *from home and retreat*
not like ourselves picked soldiers, but a   *is impossible.*
whole city which has turned out to meet us? They are
Sicilians too, who, although they may despise us, will not
stand their ground against us; for their skill is not equal
to their courage. Consider again that we are far from
home, and that there is no friendly land near but what
you can win with your swords[a]. The generals of the
enemy, as I know well, are appealing to very different
motives. They say to them, "you are fighting for your
own country," but I say to you that you are fighting in
a country which is not your own, and from which, if you
do not conquer, retreat will be impossible, for swarms of
cavalry will follow at your heels. Remember your own
reputation, and charge valiantly, deeming the difficulties
and necessities of your position to be more formidable
than the enemy.'

Nicias having thus exhorted his men led them at once 69
to the charge. The Syracusans did   *The Syracusans are*
not expect that they would have to   *unprepared for the at-*
fight just at that moment, and some of   *tack; they have plenty*
them had even gone away into the   *ficient in skill. Motives*
city, which was close at hand; others   *of the two armies.*
came running up as fast as they could, and, although late,
joined the main body one by one at the nearest point.
For they showed no want of spirit or daring in this or any
other engagement; in courage they were not a whit inferior
to their enemies, had their skill only been adequate, but
when it failed, they could no longer do justice to their
good intentions. On this occasion they were compelled

---

[a] Cp. vii. 77 fin.

to make a hasty defence, for they felt sure that the Athenians would not begin the attack. Nevertheless they took up their arms and immediately went forward to meet them. For a while the throwers of stones, and slingers, and archers skirmished in front of the two armies, driving one another before them after the manner of light-armed troops. Then the soothsayers brought out the customary victims, and the trumpets sounded and called the infantry to the charge. The two armies advanced; the Syracusans to fight for their country, and every man for life now, and liberty hereafter; on the opposite side the Athenians to gain a new country, and to save the old from the disaster of defeat; the Argives and the independent allies eager to share the good things of Sicily, and, if they returned victorious, to see their own homes once more. The courage of the subject allies was chiefly inspired by a lively consciousness that their only chance of life was in victory; they had also a distant hope that, if they assisted the Athenians in overthrowing others, their own yoke might be lightened.

70   The armies met, and for a long time the issue was

The Syracusans are doubtful. During the battle there came
defeated, but they are on thunder and lightning, and a deluge
saved in their retreat by of rain; these added to the terror of
their cavalry.
the inexperienced who were fighting
for the first time, but experienced soldiers ascribed the storm to the time of year, and were much more alarmed
ᵃ at the stubborn resistance of the enemy ᵃ. First the Argives drove back the left wing of the Syracusans; next the Athenians the right wing which was opposed to them. Whereupon the rest of the army began to give way and were soon put to flight. Their opponents did not pursue them far, for the Syracusan horsemen, who were numerous and had not shared in the defeat, interposed, and wherever

---

ᵃ Or, giving a slightly different meaning to the present: 'at the prospect of the enemy's success.'

they saw hoplites advancing from the ranks attacked and drove them back.   The Athenians pursued in a body as far as they safely could, and then returned and raised a trophy.   The Syracusans rallied on the Helorine road, and did their best to reform after their defeat.   They did not neglect to send some of their forces as a guard to the Olympieum, fearing lest the Athenians should plunder the treasures of the temple.   The rest of the army returned to the city.

The Athenians, however, did not go to the temple at all, but collecting their dead, and laying them on a pyre, they passed the night where they were.   On the following day they gave back the Syracusan dead under a flag of truce, and gathered from the pyre the bones of their own dead.   There had fallen of the Syra-

The Athenians, sensible of their deficiency in cavalry, return to Catana and Naxos, where they intend to winter while they obtain reinforcements from Athens and Sicily.

cusans and of their allies about two hundred and sixty; of the Athenians and their allies not more than fifty.   The Athenians then taking with them the spoils of their enemies, sailed back to Catana.   Winter had now set in, and they thought that before they could do anything more at Syracuse they must send for horsemen from Athens, and collect others from their Sicilian allies ; without them they would be at the mercy of the Syracusan cavalry. They also wanted to obtain both in Sicily and from Athens a supply of money, and to gain over some of the Sicilian cities.   These would be more willing to listen to them after their victory.   They had likewise to provide supplies, and to make the other requisite preparations for attacking Syracuse in the spring.   Accordingly they sailed away to Naxos and Catana, intending to winter.

The Syracusans, after burying their dead, called an assembly.   Hermocrates the son of Hermon, a man of first-rate ability, of distinguished bravery, and also of great military experience, came forward and encouraged them. He told them not to be disheartened at the result of the battle; for their resolution had not been defeated [a]; but

Hermocrates points out to the Syracusans the causes of their defeat. They should have fewer generals with more power, better discipline, and greater secrecy. they had suffered from want of discipline. Yet they had proved less unequal than might have been expected; and they should remember that they had been contending against the most experienced soldiers of Hellas; [b] they were unskilled workmen, and the Athenians masters in their craft [b]. Another great source of weakness had been the number of generals (there were fifteen of them); the division of authority had produced disorganisation and disorder among the troops. If they had a few experienced generals, and during the winter got their hoplites into order, providing arms for those who had none, and so raising the number of their forces to the utmost, while at the same time they insisted on strict drill and discipline, they would have a good chance of victory; for they had courage already, and only wanted steadiness in action. Both qualities would improve together; they would learn steadiness in the school of danger, and their natural courage would be reinforced by the confidence which skill inspires. The generals whom they elected should be few in number and should be entrusted with full power, the people taking a solemn oath to them that they would be allowed to command according to their own judgment. The secrets of the army would then be better kept, and everything would be done in a more orderly and straightforward manner.

73   The Syracusans listened to him, and voted all that he

The Syracusans follow his advice, and send envoys to Corinth and Lacedaemon. desired. They chose three generals and no more; Hermocrates himself, Heraclides the son of Lysimachus, and Sicanus the son of Execestus. They also sent ambassadors to Corinth and to Lacedaemon

---

[a] Cp. ii. 87 init.; vi. 11 fin.   [b] Reading χειροτέχναις.   Or reading χειροτέχνας with Bekker and the MSS.; 'themselves were untrained handicraftsmen.

requesting aid as allies, and urged the Lacedaemonians to make war openly and decidedly against the Athenians on their behalf; thus they would either draw them off from Sicily, or at any rate prevent them from sending reinforcements to the army which was there already.

No sooner had the Athenians returned in the fleet to 74 Catana than they sailed to Messenè, expecting that the city would be betrayed to them. But they were disappointed. For Alcibiades, when he was recalled and gave up his command, foreseeing that he would be an exile, communicated to the Syracusan party at Messenè the plot of which he was cognisant [a]. They at once put to death the persons whom he indicated; and on the appearance of the Athenians the same party, rising and arming, prevented their admission. The Athenians remained there about thirteen days, but the weather was bad, their provisions failed, and they had no success. So they went to Naxos, and having surrounded their camp with a palisade, proposed to pass the winter there. They also despatched a trireme to Athens for money and cavalry, which were to arrive at the beginning of spring.

Alcibiades having contrived that Messenè should be betrayed, now betrays the betrayers. The Athenians take up their winter quarters at Naxos.

The Syracusans employed the winter in various defensive 75 works. Close to the city they built a wall, which took in the shrine of Apollo Temenites and extended all along that side of Syracuse which looks towards Epipolae; they thus enlarged the area of the city, and increased the difficulty of investing it in case of defeat. They fortified and garrisoned Megara, and also raised a fort at the Olympieum [b], besides fixing stockades at all the landing-places along the shore. They knew that the Athenians were wintering at Naxos, and so, marching out with their whole army to Catana, they

The Syracusans extend the line of their walls, burn the Athenian camp at Catana, and send an embassy to Camarina.

---

[a] Cp. vi. 50 init.   [b] Cp. vii. 4 fin.

ravaged the country and burnt the huts and the camp of
the Athenians; they then returned home. They heard
that the Athenians were sending an embassy to gain over
the Camarinaeans on the strength of their former alliance,
which had been made under Laches[a], and they despatched
a counter embassy of their own. They suspected that the
Camarinaeans had not been over-zealous in sending their
contingent to the first battle, and would not be willing to
assist them any longer now that the Athenians had gained
a victory; old feelings of friendship would revive, and they
would be induced to join them. Accordingly Hermocrates
came with an embassy to Camarina, and Euphemus with
another embassy from the Athenians. An assembly of
the Camarinaeans was held, at which Hermocrates, hoping
to raise a prejudice against the Athenians, spoke as
follows :—

76   'We are not here, Camarinaeans, because we suppose

We fear not the that the presence of the Athenian army
swords but the words will dismay you; we are more afraid
of the Athenians. They of their as yet unuttered words, to
pretend to be liberators, which you may too readily lend an ear
but they are really en- if you hear them without first hearing
slavers of Hellas, abroad us. You know the pretext on which
as well as at home, the they have come to Sicily, but we can
new masters whom all guess their real intentions. If I am
Hellas has taken in ex-
change for the Persians.

not mistaken they want, not to restore the Leontines to
their city, but to drive us out of ours. Who can believe
that they who desolate the cities of Hellas mean to restore
those of Sicily, or that the enslavers and oppressors of
the Chalcidians in Euboea have any feeling of kindred
towards the colonists of these Chalcidians in Leontini?
In their conquests at home, and in their attempt to
conquer Sicily, is not the principle upon which they act
one and the same? The Ionians and other colonists of
theirs who were their allies, wanting to be revenged on

---

[a] Cp. iii. 86.

the Persian, freely invited them to be their leaders; and
they accepted the invitation. But soon they charged them,
some with desertion, and some with making war upon
each other[a]; any plausible accusation which they could
bring against any of them became an excuse for their overthrow. It was not for the liberties of Hellas that Athens,
or for her own liberty that Hellas, fought against the
Persian; they fought, the Athenians that they might
enslave Hellas to themselves instead of him, the rest of
the Hellenes that they might get a new master, who may
be cleverer, but certainly makes a more dishonest use of
his wits.

'However, the character of the Athenians is known to 77
you already, and we do not come here
to set forth their enormities, which *The old tales and the old tricks are being repeated here. Shall we allow ourselves to be taken in by them and to succumb one by one?*
would be an easy task, but rather to
accuse ourselves. We have had a
warning in the fate of the Hellenes
elsewhere; we know that they were reduced to slavery
because they would not stand by one another, And when
the same tricks are practised upon us[b], and we hear the
old tale once more about the restoration of "our kinsmen
the Leontines," and the succour of "our allies the Egestaeans," why do we not all rise as one man and show
them that here they will find, not Ionians, nor yet Helles-
pontians, nor islanders, who must always be the slaves, if
not of the Persian, of some other master; but Dorians[c]
and free inhabitants of Sicily, sprung from the independent soil of Peloponnesus? Are we waiting till our
cities are taken one by one, when we know that this is the
only way in which we can be conquered? We see what
their policy is: how in some cases their cunning words
sow ill-feeling; in others they stir up war by the offer of
alliance; or again, by some well-invented phrase specially

---

[a] Cp. i. 99.   [b] Cp. iv. 61 med.   [c] Cp. i. 124 init.; v. 9 init.;
vii. 5 fin.; viii. 25 med.

agreeable to an individual state they do it all the mischief which they can. And does any one suppose that, if his countryman at a distance perishes, the danger will not reach him, or that he who suffers first will have no companions in ruin?

78   'If any one fancies that not he, but the Syracusan, is

In fighting for us you are fighting for yourselves. You might like us to be humbled, but you cannot secure the right amount of humiliation; and when we are fallen you will want to have us back. You should have offered help, and not have waited to be asked.

the enemy of the Athenian, and asks indignantly " Why should I risk myself for you?" let him consider that in fighting for my country he will be at the same time fighting in mine for his own [a]. And he will fight with less danger, because I shall still be in existence; he will not carry on the struggle alone, for he will have me for an ally [b]. Let him consider that the Athenian is not really seeking to chastise the enmity of the Syracusan, but under pretence of attacking me may be quite as desirous of drawing hard and fast the bonds of friendship with him. And if any one from envy, or possibly from fear (for greatness is exposed to both), would have Syracuse suffer that we may receive a lesson, but survive for his own security, he is asking to have a thing which human power cannot compass. For a man may regulate his own desires, but he is not the dispenser of fortune [c]; the time may come when he will find himself mistaken, and while mourning over his own ruin he may possibly wish that he could still have my prosperity to envy. But he cannot bring me back again when he has once abandoned me and has refused to take his share in the common danger, which, far from being imaginary, is only too real. For though in name you may be saving me, in reality you will be saving yourselves. And you especially, Camarinaeans, who are our next neighbours, and on whom the danger will fall next, should have

---

[a] Cp. iii. 13 med.   [b] Reading ἔρημος.   [c] Cp. iv. 64 init.

anticipated all this, and not be so slack in your alliance. Instead of our coming to you, you should have come to us. Suppose the Athenians had gone to Camarina first, would you not at this moment be begging and praying for assistance? Then why did not you present yourselves at Syracuse, and say to us in our time of danger, "Never yield to the enemy"? But, hitherto, neither you nor any of the Sicilians have shown a spirit like this.

'You may perhaps disguise your cowardice under the 79 pretence of impartiality; you may balance between us and the invaders, and plead that you have an alliance with the Athenians. But that alliance was made on the supposition that you *You may pretend impartiality, but you will really be conspiring with your enemies against your friends.* were invaded by an enemy, not against a friend; and you promised to assist the Athenians if they were wronged by others, not when, as now, they are doing wrong themselves. Are the Rhegians who are Chalcidians so very anxious to join in the restoration of their Leontine kinsmen[a]? And yet how monstrous that they, suspecting the real meaning of this plausible claim, should display a prudence for which they can give no reason; and that you, who have every reason for a like prudence, should be eager to assist your natural enemies, and to conspire with them for the destruction of those who by a higher law are your still more natural kinsmen. This should not be. You must make a stand against them. And do not be afraid of their armament. There is no danger if we hold together; the danger is in disunion, and they want to disunite us. Even when they engaged with our unaided forces[b], and defeated us in battle, they failed in their main purpose, and quickly retired.

'If then we can once unite, there is no reason for dis- 80 couragement. But there is every reason why you, who are our allies, should meet us more cordially. We may

----

[a] Cp. vi. 44 fin., 46 init.   [b] But cp. vi. 65 init., 67 med.

be sure that help will come to us from Peloponnesus, and

Union will be strength. the Peloponnesians are far better soldiers
If you join neither side, than the Athenians.   Let no one think
you will really be un- that the caution which professes to be
true to both. in league with both, and therefore
gives aid to neither, is just to us or safe for you.
Such a policy, though it may pretend to impartiality, is
really unjust.   For if through your absence the victor
overcomes and the vanquished falls, have you not abandoned the one to his fate, and allowed the other to commit
a crime?   How much nobler would it be to join your
injured kinsmen, and thereby maintain the common
interest of Sicily and save the Athenians, whom you call
your friends, from doing wrong!

'To sum up:—We Syracusans are quite aware that

You who are Dori- there is no use in our dilating to you
ans should not betray or to any one else on matters which
your kinsmen to Ioni- you know as well as ourselves.   But
ans. If they conquer, we prefer a prayer to you; and
you will be absorbed by solemnly adjure you to consider, that,
them; if we conquer,
we shall punish you. if you reject us, we, who are Dorians
like yourselves, are betrayed by you to Ionians, our inveterate enemies, who are seeking our ruin.   If the
Athenians subdue us, your decision will have gained them
the day; but the honour will be all their own, and the
authors of their victory will be the prize of their victory.
If on the other hand we conquer, you who have brought
the peril upon us will have to suffer the penalty.   Reflect
then, and take your choice: will you have present safety
and slavery, or the hope of delivering yourselves and us,
and thereby escaping the dishonour of submitting to the
Athenian yoke, and the danger of our enmity, which will
not be short-lived?'

81   Thus spoke Hermocrates. Euphemus, the Athenian
envoy, replied as follows:—

82   'We had come to renew our former alliance, but the
attack made upon us by the Syracusan envoy renders it

necessary for us to vindicate our title to empire[a]. He
himself bore the strongest witness in   *True, we are Ionians,*
our favour when he said that Dorians   *and the enmity of Dor-*
and Ionians are inveterate enemies.   *ian and Ionian is the*
                                           justification of our em-
And so they are. We Ionians dwelling   *pire. We had to de-*
in the neighbourhood of the Pelopon-   *fend ourselves, and if*
nesians (who are Dorians and more   *we enslaved our kins-*
                                           men, they were slaves
numerous than ourselves) have had to   *already, and would*
consider the best way of securing our·   *have made slaves of us.*
independence. After the Persian War we were delivered
by the help of our newly-acquired navy from the rule and
supremacy of Lacedaemon ; they had no more right to
domineer over us than we over them, except the right of
the stronger, which at the time they possessed. We then
assumed the leadership of the King's former subjects,
which we still retain ; if we were not to be the slaves
of the Peloponnesians we thought that we must have the
means of self-defence. And what if we did subjugate
those kinsmen of ours whom the Syracusans say that we
have enslaved, the Ionians and the islanders ? On the
strictest principles, where was the injustice ? For we
were their mother-city, and they joined in the Persian
invasion. They had not the courage to revolt from him
and to destroy their homes, as we did when we left our
city. But they chose slavery for their own portion, and
would have imposed it upon us.

'We rule then, in the first place, because we deserve to 83
rule ; for we provided the largest navy   *We come hither for*
and showed the most patriotic alacrity   *our own sake as well*
in the cause of Hellas[a] ; while those   *as for yours; and for*
who became our subjects were willing   *yours as well as for our*
                                             own.
slaves to the Persian, and were doing
us mischief.   And secondly, we were anxious to gain
additional strength against the Peloponnesians. We use
no fine words : we do not tell you that we have a right to

---

[a] Cp. i. 37 init. ; i. 73 init.   [a] Cp. i. 74 init.

rule on the ground that we alone overthrew the Barbarians[a], nor do we pretend that we fought for the liberty
of our allies, and not equally for the general liberty and
for our own[b]. Can any man be blamed because he makes
the natural provision for his own safety[c]? The same
care of our safety has brought us hither, and we can see
that our presence here is for your benefit as well as for
ours. This we will prove to you ; and our proofs shall be
drawn from the calumnies of our enemies, and from the
suspicions and fears which most sway your minds. For we
know that those who are timorous and mistrustful may be
won for the moment by alluring words, but that when the
time of action comes they follow their own interests.

'We have told you already that fear makes us main-

It is for our interest that you should be independent. We are quite consistent in restoring the Chalcidians in Sicily and in subjecting the Chalcidians in Euboea.

84

tain our empire at home ; and that a
like fear brings us to your shores. For
we desire by the help of our friends to
secure our position in Sicily. And we
have not come to enslave you, but to
save you from being enslaved. Let no
one imagine that your welfare is no business of ours, for
if you are preserved, and are strong enough to hold out
against the Syracusans, they will be less likely to aid the
Peloponnesians, and so to injure us. Thus you become
at once our first concern. And we are quite consistent
in restoring the Leontines, not to be subjects, like their
kinsmen in Euboea, but to be as strong as ever we can
make them, that from their position on the border they
may harass the Syracusans and do our work. In Hellas
we are a match for our enemies single-handed ; and as to
our subjection of the Chalcidians at home, which Hermocrates finds so inconsistent with our emancipation of the
Chalcidians here, it is for our advantage, on the one hand,
that the cities of Euboea should have no armed force and
contribute money only, and, on the other hand, that the

---

[a] Cp. v. 89 init.   [b] Cp. vi. 76 fin.   [c] Cp. i. 75 fin.

Leontines and our friends in Sicily should be as independent as possible.

'Now to a tyrant or to an imperial city [a] nothing is 85 inconsistent which is expedient, and no man is a kinsman who cannot be trusted. In each case we must make friends or enemies according to circumstances, and here our interest requires, not that we should weaken our friends, but that our friends should be too strong for our enemies. Do not mistrust us. In Hellas we act upon the same principle, managing our allies as our interest requires in their several cases. The Chians and Methymnaeans furnish us with ships, and are their own masters; the majority are less independent, and pay a tribute; others, although they are islanders and might be easily conquered, enjoy complete freedom, because they are situated conveniently for operations about Peloponnesus [b]. So that in Sicily too our policy is likely to be determined by our interest, and, as I was saying, by our fear of the Syracusans. For they desire to be your masters, but first they must unite you in a common suspicion of us, and then either by force, or through your isolation, when we have failed and retired, they will dominate Sicily. This is inevitable if you now join them. Your united power will be more than we can manage, and the Syracusans, when we are gone, will be too much for you. He who thinks otherwise is convicted out of his own mouth. For when you originally invited us, the danger which we should incur if we allowed you to fall into the hands of the Syracusans was precisely what you held before our eyes, and now you ought not to distrust the argu-

We act upon principle, and that principle requires a different policy in different cases.

You told us that Syracuse would rule Sicily, and we give you back your words. You have nothing to fear from us, who are at a distance, but much to fear from the Syracusans, who are your neighbours and can always get at you. You will be sorry some day that you have lost us. 86

---

[a] Cp. ii. 63; iii. 37 init.　　　　[b] Cp. ii. 7 fin.; vii. 57 med.

ment which you thought good enough for us. Nor should
you suspect us because we bring hither a force larger
than before; for we have to contend against the power
of Syracuse. Much more to be mistrusted are they.
Without your aid we cannot even remain where we are,
and if we were so dishonourable as to make conquests
we should be unable to retain them[a], for the voyage is
long, and it would be a hopeless task to garrison great
cities which, though situated on an island, have the
resources of a continent. Whereas these men are your
nearest neighbours. And they dwell, not in a camp, but
in a city far more powerful than the forces which we have
brought to Sicily; they are always scheming against you,
and never miss a chance, as they have often shown,
especially in their conduct towards the Leontines. And
now they have the impudence to stir you up against those
who resist them, and have thus far saved Sicily from
passing under their yoke. As if you had no eyes! Far
more real than the security offered by them is that to
which we invite you, a security which we and you gain from
one another, and we beseech you not to throw it away.
Reflect: the Syracusans are so numerous that with or
without allies they can always find their way to you, but
you will not often have the chance of defending yourself
with the aid of an army like ours. And if from any
suspicion you allow us to depart unsuccessful, or perhaps
defeated, the time may come when you will desire to see
but a fraction of that army, although, if it came, it would
be too late to save you.

87   'But we would not have either you, Camarinaeans, or
others moved by their calumnies. We have told you the
whole truth about the suspicions which are entertained
of us; we will now sum up our arguments, and we
think that they ought to convince you. We rule over
the cities of Hellas in order to maintain our independence,
and we emancipate the cities of Sicily that they may not

---

[a] Cp. vi. 11 init.

be used against us. And we are compelled to adopt a
policy of interference because we have many interests to
guard. Lastly, we come now, as we *Enough of these sus-*
came before, not uninvited, but upon *picions. We come at*
your own invitation to assist those of *your own invitation;*
you who are suffering wrong. Do not *and you had better use*
us if we can be of use
sit in judgment upon our actions, or *to you. Do not judge*
seek to school us into moderation and *or advise us but avail*
so divert us from our purpose (the time *yourselves of our power,*
which is everywhere the
for good advice has gone by), but in as *terror of the oppressor*
far as our busy, meddlesome spirit can *and the friend of the*
be of service to you as well as to our- *oppressed, in your in-*
evitable contest with the
selves, take and use us, remembering *Syracusans.*
that these qualities, so far from being injurious to all
alike, actually benefit great numbers of the Hellenes. For
in all places—however remote from our sphere—both he
who fears and he who intends injustice, the one because
he has a lively hope that from us he will obtain redress,
and the other because he may well be alarmed for the
consequences if we answer to the call, must both alike
submit, the one to learn moderation against his will, the
other to receive at our hands a deliverance which costs
him nothing. Do not reject the common salvation which
is offered to you at this moment, as well as to all who
seek it, but following the example of your countrymen
join with us and, instead of having always to watch the
Syracusans, assert your equality and threaten them as
they have long been threatening you.'

Thus spoke Euphemus. Now the Camarinaeans were 88
swayed by opposite feelings; they had
a good will to the Athenians, tempered *The Camarinaeans*
suspect the designs of
by a suspicion that they might be in- *the Athenians and are*
tending to enslave Sicily, whereas the *afraid of their Syra-*
Syracusans, from their proximity, were *cusan neighbours. They*
resolve to assist, if
always at feud with them. But they *either, the Syracusans,*
were not so much afraid of the *but to profess neutral-*
Athenians as of their Syracusan neigh- *ity.*

bours, who, as they thought, might win without their assistance. This was the reason why they sent them the small body of horse which took part in the first battle; and in a like spirit they now determined that for the future they would give real assistance only to the Syracusans, but to a very moderate extent. For the present however, that they might seem to deal equal justice to the Athenians, especially after their recent victory, they resolved to return the same answer to both. Such were the considerations which led them to reply that, as two of their allies were at war with one another, they thought that under the circumstances the best way of observing their oaths would be to assist neither. So the two embassies departed.

The Athenians in the Sicel country. They remove from Naxos to Catana, send envoys to Carthage and Tyrrhenia, and prepare for the siege of Syracuse.

The Syracusans proceeded with their own preparations for the war, and the Athenians who were encamped at Naxos tried by negotiation to gain over as many of the Sicels as they could. The dwellers in the plain who were subjects of the Syracusans mostly stood aloof, but the Sicel settlements in the interior (which had always been independent) at once, with a few exceptions, joined the Athenians, and brought down food to the army; in some cases money also. Against those who were recalcitrant troops were despatched by the Athenians; and some of them were forced into submission, but others were protected by the garrisons which the Syracusans sent to their aid. They then transferred their station from Naxos to Catana and, reconstructing the camp which had been burnt by the Syracusans [a], passed the winter there. In the hope of obtaining assistance they sent a trireme to Carthage with a proposal of friendship; likewise to Tyrrhenia, since some of the cities there were offering of themselves to join them in the war: to the various Sicel tribes [b] and to the Egestaeans they issued orders that they were to send

---

    [a] Cp. vi. 75 med.   [b] Cp. vi. 98 init.

as many horse as possible. They further prepared bricks, tools, and whatever else was requisite for siege operations, intending, when the spring arrived, to prosecute the war with vigour.

The envoys whom the Syracusans had sent to Corinth and Lacedaemon [a] endeavoured on the voyage to persuade the Italian Greeks that they were equally threatened by the Athenian designs, and should take an interest in the war. When they arrived at Corinth they appealed to the Corinthians for aid on the ground of relationship. The Corinthians, taking the lead of all the Hellenic states, voted that they would assist Syracuse with all possible energy. They sent with the Syracusan envoys ambassadors of their own to the Lacedaemonians, bearing a joint request that they would resume open hostilities at home, and unite with them in sending help to Sicily. At Lacedaemon the Corinthian ambassadors met Alcibiades and his fellow exiles. He had sailed at once from Thurii in a trading vessel to Cyllenè in Elis, and thence proceeded to Lacedaemon on the invitation of the Lacedaemonians themselves, first obtaining a safe-conduct; for he was afraid of them after his proceedings in the matter of the Mantinean league [b]. And so it came to pass that the Corinthians, the Syracusans, and Alcibiades appeared simultaneously in the Lacedaemonian assembly, and concurred in urging the same request. The ephors and the magistrates were already intending to send envoys to the Syracusans bidding them make no terms with the Athenians, although they were not disposed to assist them actively. But now Alcibiades came forward and stimulated the energies of the Lacedaemonians in the following words:—

The Corinthians are the first who promise aid to the Syracusan envoys. They go with them to Sparta, where they meet Alcibiades, who had come thither under a safe conduct.

'I must endeavour first of all to remove a prejudice 89

---

[a] Cp. vi. 73.   [b] Cp. v. 43 ff., 61 ff.

against myself, lest through suspicion of me you should

I must offer explana-
tions. I wanted to
serve you, but you were
ungrateful, and I re-
taliated. I was not a de-
magogue but an heredi-
tary leader of the state
as a whole. Democracy,
however liable to abuse,
was our natural form
of government, and we
could not change it.

turn a deaf ear to considerations of public interest. My ancestors in consequence of some misunderstanding renounced the office of Lacedaemonian proxenus; I myself resumed it, and did you many good offices, especially after your misfortune at Pylos. My anxiety to serve you never ceased, but when you were making peace with Athens you negotiated through my enemies, thereby conferring power on them, and bringing dishonour upon me [a]. And if I then turned to the Mantineans and Argives and opposed you in that or in any other way, you were rightly served, and any one who while the wound was recent may have been unduly exasperated against me should now take another and a truer view. Or, again, if any one thought the worse of me because I was inclined to the people, let him acknowledge that here too there is no real ground of offence. Any power adverse to despotism is called democracy, and my family have always retained the leadership of the people in their hands because we have been the persistent enemies of tyrants. Living too under a popular government, how could we avoid in a great degree conforming to circumstances? However, we did our best to observe political moderation amid the prevailing licence. But there were demagogues, as there always have been, who led the people into evil ways, and it was they who drove me out [b]. Whereas we were the leaders of the state as a whole [c], and not of a part only; it was our view that all ought to combine in maintaining that form of government which had been inherited by us, and under which the city enjoyed the greatest freedom and glory. Of course, like all sensible men, we knew only too well what democracy

---

[a] Cp. v. 43.   [b] Cp. viii. 65 med.   [c] Cp. vi. 39 init.

is, and I better than any one, who have so good a reason for abusing it. The follies of democracy are universally admitted, and there is nothing new to be said about them. But we could not venture to change our form of government when an enemy like yourselves was so near to us.

'Such is the truth about the calumnies under which 90 I labour. And now I will speak to you of the matter which you have in hand, and about which I, in so far as I have better information, am bound to instruct you. We sailed to Sicily hoping in the first place to conquer the Sicilian cities; then to proceed against the Hellenes of Italy; and lastly, to make an attempt on the Carthaginian dominions, and on Carthage itself. If all or most of these enterprises succeeded, we meant finally to attack Peloponnesus, bringing with us the whole Hellenic power which we had gained abroad, besides many barbarians whom we intended to hire—Iberians and the neighbouring tribes, esteemed to be the most warlike barbarians that now are[a]. Of the timber which Italy supplies in such abundance we meant to build numerous additional triremes, and with them to blockade Peloponnesus. At the same time making inroads by land with our infantry, we should have stormed some of your cities and invested others. Thus we hoped to crush you easily, and to rule over the Hellenic world. For the better accomplishment of our various aims our newly-acquired territory would supply money and provisions enough, apart from the revenue which we receive in Hellas.

The Athenian designs embraced Sicily, Italy, Carthage; if we succeeded we were going to invest Peloponnesus; the empire of Hellas would then have been ours.

'You have heard the objects of our expedition from 91 him who knows them best; the generals who remain will persevere and carry them out if they can. And now let me

---

[a] Reading μαχιμωτάτους and placing a comma after ἐκεῖ.

prove to you that if you do not come to the rescue Sicily will
be lost.   If the Greeks would all unite
they might even now, notwithstanding
their want of military skill, resist
with success ; but the Syracusans alone,
whose whole forces have been already
defeated, and who cannot move freely
at sea, will be unable to withstand the
power which the Athenians already
have on the spot.   And Syracuse once
taken, the whole of Sicily is in their

*Sicily is lost unless
you come to the rescue.
The Sicilians will not
unite, and Syracuse
alone is no match for
the Athenians.   Send
hoplites and a Spartan
commander at once, and
fortify Decelea.   I know
best what the Athenians
most dread.   You must
be up and doing.*

hands ; the subjugation of Italy will follow ; and the
danger which, as I was saying, threatens you from that
quarter, will speedily overwhelm you.   And therefore
remember every one of you that the safety, not of Sicily
alone, but of Peloponnesus, is at stake.   No time should
be lost.   You must send to Sicily a force of hoplites who will
themselves handle the oars and will take the field immediately on landing.   A Spartan commander I conceive to
be even more indispensable than an army ; his duty will
be to organise the troops which are already enlisted, and
to press the unwilling into the service.   Thus you will
inspire confidence in your friends and overcome the fears
of the wavering.   Here too in Hellas you should make
open war.   The Syracusans, seeing that you have not
forgotten them, will then persevere in their resistance,
while the Athenians will have greater difficulty in rein-
forcing their army.   You ought also to fortify Decelea in
Attica ; the Athenians are always in particular dread of
this ; to them it seems to be the only peril of which they
have not faced the worst in the course of the war.   And
the way to hurt an enemy most surely is to inform yourself
exactly about the weak points of which you see that he
is conscious, and strike at them.   For every man is likely
to know best himself the dangers which he has most to
fear.   I will sum up briefly the chief though by no means
all the advantages which you will gain, and the disad-

vantages which you will inflict, by the fortification of Decelea. The whole stock of the country will fall into your hands. The slaves will come over to you of their own accord; what there is besides will be seized by you. The Athenians will at once be deprived of the revenues which they obtain from the silver mines of Laurium, and of all the profits which they make by the land or by the law courts: above all, the customary tribute will cease to flow in; for their allies, when they see that you are now carrying on the war in earnest, will not mind them. How far these plans are executed, and with how much speed and energy, Lacedaemonians, depends on you; for I am confident that they are practicable, and I am not likely to be mistaken.

'You ought not in fairness to think the worse of me because, having been once distinguished as a lover of my country, I now cast in my lot with her worst foes and attack her with all my might; or suspect that I speak only with the eagerness of an exile.

Athens has compelled me to be her enemy. She is no longer my country. Yet I do her evil only that I may regain her.

An exile I am indeed; I have lost an ungrateful country, but I have not lost the power of doing you service, if you will listen to me. The true enemies of my country are not those who, like you, have injured her in open war, but those who have compelled her friends to become her enemies. I love Athens, not in so far as I am wronged by her, but in so far as I once enjoyed the privileges of a citizen. The country which I am attacking is no longer mine, but a lost country which I am seeking to regain. He is the true patriot, not who, when unjustly exiled, abstains from attacking his country, but who in the warmth of his affection seeks to recover her without regard to the means. I desire therefore that you, Lacedaemonians, will use me without scruple in any service however difficult or dangerous, remembering that, according to the familiar saying, "the more harm I did you as an enemy, the more good can I do you as a friend." For

I know the secrets of the Athenians, while I could only guess at yours. Remember the immense importance of your present decision, and do not hesitate to send an expedition to Sicily and Attica. By despatching a fraction of your forces to co-operate in Sicily you may save great interests, and may overthrow the Athenian power once and for ever. And so henceforward you may dwell safely yourselves and be leaders of all Hellas, which will follow you, not upon compulsion, but from affection.'

93   Thus spoke Alcibiades: the Lacedaemonians, who had

The Lacedaemonians determine to fortify Decelea and to send Gylippus to Syracuse.

been intending to send an army against Athens, but were still hesitating and looking about them, were greatly strengthened in their resolution when they heard all these points urged by him who, as they thought, knew best. Accordingly they now turned their thoughts to the fortification of Decelea, and determined to send immediate assistance to the Syracusans. They appointed Gylippus the son of Cleandridas commander of the Syracusan forces, and desired him to co-operate with the Syracusan and Corinthian representatives, and send aid to Sicily in the speediest and most effective manner which the circumstances admitted. Whereupon he told the Corinthians to despatch immediately two ships to him at Asinè, and to fit out as many more as they meant to send ; the latter were to be ready for sea when the season arrived. Coming to this understanding the envoys departed from Lacedaemon.

About this time the trireme which the Athenian generals had despatched from Sicily for money and cavalry [a] arrived at Athens. The Athenians, hearing their request, voted money and a force of cavalry for the army. So the winter ended, and with it the seventeenth year in the Peloponnesian War of which Thucydides wrote the history.

------

[a] Cp. vi. 74 fin.

At the very beginning of the following spring the *Athenians quitted Catana, and sailed along the coast towards the Sicilian Megara; this place, as I have already mentioned[a], in the days of Gelo the tyrant was depopulated by the Syra-* cusans, who still retain possession of the country. They disembarked, and after ravaging the fields proceeded to attack a small Syracusan fortress[b], but without success; they then moved on some by land and some by sea to the river Terias, and going up the country wasted the plain and burned the corn. They encountered a few Syra- cusans, some of whom they killed, and setting up a trophy returned to their ships. They then sailed back to Catana, and having taken in provisions marched with their whole force against Centoripa, a Sicel town, which capitulated. Thence they returned, and on their way burned the corn of the Inessians and the Hyblaeans. Arriving at Catana they found that the horsemen, for whom they had sent, to the number of two hundred and fifty had come from Athens, with their equipments, but without horses, which they were expected to procure on the spot. Thirty mounted archers and three hundred talents of silver[c] had arrived also.

94

B.C. 414.
Operations of Athen- Ol. 91, 3.
ians in the eastern district of Sicily. Arrival of horsemen and money from Athens.

During the same spring the Lacedaemonians led an army against Argos, and advanced as far as Cleonae, but retired in conse- quence of an earthquake. The Argives in their turn invaded the neighbouring district of Thyrea, and took a great deal of spoil from the Lacedaemonians, which was sold for no less than twenty-five talents[d]. Somewhat later the populace of Thespiae[e] made an attack upon the govern- ment, but the attempt did not succeed; for the Thebans

95

A Lacedaemonian invasion of Argolis stopped by an earth- quake. Argives invade Thyrea. Rising at Thespiae.

---

[a] Cp. vi. 4 init.   [b] Cp. vi. 75 init.   £60 000
[d] £5,000.   [e] Cp. iv. 133 init.

came to the rescue. Some of the insurgents were apprehended, others fled to Athens.

96 The Syracusans heard that the Athenians had received their cavalry, and that they

The Syracusans determine to guard Epipolae, but are anticipated, while holding a review, by the Athenians; would soon be upon them. They considered that, unless the Athenians gained possession of Epipolae (which was a steep place looking down upon

Syracuse), the city could not easily be invested, even if they were defeated in battle; they therefore determined to guard the paths leading to the summit that the enemy might not get up by stealth. At all other points the place was secure, as it lies high and slopes right down to the city, from the interior of which it can all be seen; the Syracusans call it Epipolae (or the plateau), because it is above the level of the adjacent country. Hermocrates and his colleagues had now entered upon their command. The whole people went out at break of day to the meadow skirting the river Anapus, and proceeded to hold a review of their forces. A selection was at once made of six hundred hoplites, who were appointed to guard Epipolae, and to run in a body to any point at which they were needed. They were commanded by Diomilus, an Andrian exile.

97 On the very same morning the Athenians were likewise holding a muster of their army. They

who land, unobserved, north of the city. They gain the summit of Epipolae and put to flight the Syracusan hoplites. had come from Catana with their whole force, and had put in unobserved near a place called Leon, which is distant from Epipolae not quite a mile;

there they disembarked their troops. Their ships cast anchor at Thapsus, which is a peninsula with a narrow isthmus, running out into the sea, and not far from Syracuse either by land or water. The Athenian sailors made a stockade across the isthmus and remained at Thapsus, while the troops ran to Epipolae, and gained the summit by the way of the Euryelus before the Syracusans saw

them or could come up to them from the meadow where
the review was going on.   Nevertheless Diomilus with
his six hundred hurried to the spot, accompanied by the
rest of the army, each man running as fast he could ; but
the distance from the meadow which they had to traverse
before they could engage was not less than three miles ;
consequently they were in disorder when they closed with
the Athenians.   They were defeated in the engagement
which ensued on Epipolae, and retired into the city.
Diomilus and about three hundred others were slain.
The Athenians erected a trophy, and gave up to the
Syracusans the bodies of the dead under a flag of truce.
On the following day they went down to the city itself,
but as the Syracusans did not come out against them,
they retired and built a fort upon Labdalum, at the edge
of the cliffs of Epipolae looking towards Megara, in order
that when they advanced either to fight or to construct
lines, the place might serve as a depository for their
baggage and their property.

Not long afterwards the Athenians were joined by three 98
hundred Egestaean horsemen, and
about a hundred more furnished by the
Sicels, Naxians, and others.   They
had two hundred and fifty of their own,
for some of whom they received horses
from the Egestaeans and Catanaeans ;
other horses they bought.   The whole
number of their cavalry was now raised

*The Athenians now
muster six hundred and
fifty horse. They begin
to construct a wall round
Syracuse.   The Syra-
cusans go out to meet
them, but retire, and
some of their cavalry
are defeated.*

to six hundred and fifty.   They placed a garrison in
Labdalum and went down to Sycè, where they took up
a position and immediately commenced building ᵃ a wall
round the city ⁿ.   The Syracusans were amazed at the
celerity of the work.   They saw that they must interfere,
and made up their minds to go out and fight.   The two
armies were already preparing to engage when the Syra-

ᵃ Or 'a circular fort.'   See note.

Chalaeans, Tolophonians, Hessians, and Oeantheans; all these tribes also joined the expedition. The Olpaeans gave hostages but did not join; the Hyaeans would not give hostages until the Lacedaemonians had taken one of their villages, called Polis.

102   When everything was ready, and Eurylochus had de-

Demosthenes with the help of the Acarnanians saves Naupactus. The Lacedaemonians retire, and in concert with the Ambraciots project an attack on the Amphilochian Argos.

posited the hostages at Cytinium of the Dorians, he marched with his army against Naupactus, through the territory of the Locrians. On his march he took Oeneon [a] and Eupalium [b], two Locrian towns which refused to come to terms. When they had arrived in the territory of Naupactus and the Aetolians had at length joined them, they devastated the country, and after taking the unwalled suburbs of the town marched against Molycrium, a colony of the Corinthians subject to Athens, which they captured. But Demosthenes the Athenian, who after his misfortune in Aetolia was still in the neighbourhood of Naupactus, having previous intelligence, and fearing for the town, went and persuaded the Acarnanians, much against their will—for they had not forgotten his withdrawal from Leucas—to assist Naupactus. So they sent with him on board the Athenian ships [c] a thousand hoplites; these got in and saved the place, which was in danger of having to capitulate, owing to the extent of the wall and the paucity of its defenders. Eurylochus and his soldiers, when they saw that the garrison had been reinforced, and that there was no possibility of taking the city by storm, instead of going back to Peloponnesus, retired into the country of Aeolis, which is now called by the names of the towns Calydon and Pleuron, and to other places in the neighbourhood; also to Proschium in Aetolia. For the Ambraciots sent and persuaded them to take part in an attack on the Amphilochian Argos and the rest of Amphi-

---

[a] Cp. iii. 95 fin.   [b] Cp. iii. 96 med.   [c] Cp. iii. 105 fin

The Athenians did not interfere with their work, for 100
they were afraid of dividing and *These, when partly*
weakening their forces; and they were *finished, are taken by a*
pressing forward that part of the line *sudden attack of the*
on which they were employed. So the *Athenians.*
Syracusans when they had sufficiently completed a part
of their stockade and cross-wall, leaving one division to
guard the work, retreated into the city with the rest of
their army. The Athenians now destroyed their conduits,
which were laid underground to bring drinking-water into
the city. Then, choosing their time at noon when the
Syracusan guard remained within their tents (some of
them had even retired into the city) and when the vigilance of their sentinels at the stockade was relaxed, they
took a body of three hundred chosen hoplites of their own
and some light-armed troops, picked soldiers, to whom they
had given heavy arms, and bade them run quickly to the
cross-wall. The rest of the army proceeded in two divisions
under the two generals, one towards the city in case the
enemy should come to save the wall, the other to that part
of the stockade which adjoined the postern-gate of the city.
The three hundred attacked and captured the further end
of the stockade, from which the guards retired and fled
inside the new outer wall which enclosed the shrine of
Apollo Temenites[a]. The pursuers pressed forward and
made their way in after them; but they were forced out
again by the Syracusans; and some Argives and a few
of the Athenians fell there. Then the whole army, turning
back, destroyed the cross-wall, tore up the stockades,
carried the stakes to their camp, and raised a trophy.

On the following day the Athenians, beginning at one 101
end of the unfinished circle, began to bring the wall [b] down
over[b] the cliff which on this side of Epipolae looks across
the marsh towards the Great Harbour, intending to carry
on the line by the shortest way to the harbour right

---

[a] Cp. vi. 75 init.   [b] Or, 'along.'

through the level of the marsh. Meanwhile the Syra-

*The Athenians pro-
ceed to carry their wall
southwards towards the
Great Harbour. They
take the stockade which
is intended to intercept
them. After defeating
the Syracusans they fall
into partial confusion
themselves. Lamachus
is slain.*
cusans also came out, and beginning
from the city, proceeded to carry
another stockade through the middle of
the marsh, with a ditch at the side, in
order to prevent the Athenians from
completing their line to the sea. The
latter, having finished their work as
far as the cliff, attacked the new
Syracusan stockade and ditch. They
ordered the ships to sail round from Thapsus into the
Great Harbour of the Syracusans; with the first break
of day they descended themselves from Epipolae to the
level ground; and passing through the marsh where the
soil was clay and firmer than the rest, over planks and
gates which they laid down, they succeeded at sunrise in
taking nearly the whole of the stockade and the ditch, and
the remainder not long afterwards. A battle took place in
which the Athenians were victorious, and the Syracusans
on the right wing fled to the city, those on the left along
the river. The three hundred chosen Athenian troops
pressed on at full speed towards the bridge, intending to
stop their passage, but the Syracusans, fearing that they
would be cut off, and having most of their horsemen on
the spot, turned upon the three hundred, and putting them
to flight, charged the right wing of the Athenians. The
panic now extended to the whole division[a] at the extremity
of the wing. Lamachus saw what had happened, and
hastened to the rescue from his own place on the left
wing, taking with him a few archers and the Argive
troops; but pressing forward across a certain ditch he and
a few who had followed him were cut off from the rest, and
he fell with five or six others. The Syracusans hastily
snatched up their bodies, and carried them across the
river out of the reach of the enemy. But when they saw

[a] Reading φυλή.

the rest of the Athenian army advancing towards them they retreated.

Meanwhile the Syracusans who fled first into the city, 102 observing the resistance made by the left wing, took courage, and coming out drew up against that part of the Athenian line which was opposed to them. They also sent a detachment against the wall of circumvallation a on Epipolae, supposing that it was undefended, and might be taken. They did indeed take and demolish the outwork, which was about a thousand feet in length ; but Nicias, who happened to have been left there because he was ill, saved the lines a themselves. He commanded the attendants of the camp to set fire to the engines and to the timber which had been left lying in front of the wall, for being without troops he knew that there was no other way of escape. The expedient succeeded ; and in consequence of the fire the Syracusans gave up the attack. The Athenian army too was now hastening from the plain to the surrounding wall a, with the intention of beating off the enemy ; while the ships, as they had been ordered, were sailing from Thapsus into the Great Harbour. The Syracusans on the heights, seeing this combined movement, quickly retreated, together with the rest of the army, into the city, thinking that with their present force they were no longer able to prevent the completion of the line of wall towards the sea.

Meanwhile the Syracusans attack the deserted walls on Epipolae, which are only saved by Nicias setting fire to some timber and engines.

The Athenians then erected a trophy and restored the 103 Syracusan dead under a flag of truce. The Syracusans delivered to them the bodies of Lamachus and his companions. The whole Athenian forces, both naval and military, were now on the spot, and they proceeded to cut off the Syracusans

Despair of the Syracusans at the progress of the wall. They parley with Nicias, and are suspicious of their generals whom they depose.

---

a Or ' the circle.'

by a double wall, beginning at the southern cliff of Epipolae and extending to the sea. Provisions came to their army in abundance from various parts of Italy. Many of the Sicel tribes who had hitherto been hesitating now joined the Athenians, and three penteconters came from the Tyrrhenians. Everything began to answer to their hopes. The Syracusans despaired of saving the city by arms, for no help reached them even from Peloponnesus. Within the walls they were talking of peace, and they began to enter into communications with Nicias, who, now that Lamachus was dead, had the sole command. But no definite result was attained; although, as might be expected when men began to feel the pressure of the siege and their own helplessness, many proposals were made to him, and many more were discussed in the city. Their calamities even made them suspicious of one another; accordingly they deposed their generals, attributing the misfortunes which had befallen the city since they were appointed either to their ill-luck or to their treachery. In their room they chose Heraclides, Eucles, and Tellias.

104   Meanwhile Gylippus the Lacedaemonian and the ships

Gylippus arrives at Tarentum. Nicias despises the smallness of his force.

from Corinth [a] were already at Leucas hastening to their relief. They were alarmed at the reports which were continually pouring in, all false, but all agreeing that the Athenian lines round Syracuse were now complete. Gylippus had no longer any hope of Sicily, but thought that he might save Italy; so he and Pythen the Corinthian sailed across the Ionian Gulf to Tarentum as fast as they could, taking two Laconian and two Corinthian ships. The Corinthians were to man ten ships of their own, two Leucadian, and three Ambracian, and to follow. Gylippus on his arrival at Tarentum went on a mission to Thurii, of which his father had formerly been a citizen; he had hoped to gain over the Thurians, but failed; he

---

[a] Cp. vi. 93 med.

then continued his voyage from Tarentum along the coast
of Italy. He was caught in the Terinaean gulf[a] by a wind
which in this region blows violently and steadily from the
north, and was carried into the open sea. After ex-
periencing a most violent storm he returned to Tarentum,
where he drew up those of his ships which had suffered
in the gale and refitted them. Nicias heard of his approach, but despised the small number of his ships; in
this respect he was like the Thurians. He thought that
he had come on a mere privateering expedition, and for
some time set no watch[b].

During the same summer, about the same time, the 105
Lacedaemonians and their allies in-
vaded Argolis and wasted most of the   *Athenians violate the
Argive territory. The Athenians as-   peace with the Lacedae-
sisted the Argives with thirty ships.   monians by devastating
The use which they made of them was a   the Laconian coast.*
glaring violation
of the treaty with the Lacedaemonians. Hitherto they
had only gone out on marauding expeditions from Pylos;
when they landed, it was not upon the shores of Laconia,
but upon other parts of the Peloponnese; and they had
merely fought as the allies of the Argives and Mantineans.
The Argives had often urged them just to land soldiers
on Lacedaemonian ground, and to waste some part of
Laconia, however small, without remaining, and they had
refused. But now, under the command of Pythodorus,
Laespodias, and Demaratus, they landed at Epidaurus
Limera, Prasiae, and other places, and wasted the country.
Thereby the Athenians at last gave the Lacedaemonians
a right to complain of them and completely justified
measures of retaliation. After the Athenian fleet had
departed from Argos, and the Lacedaemonians had likewise retired, the Argives invaded Phliasia, and having
ravaged the country and killed a few of the Phliasians,
returned home.

---

[a] See note.   [b] Cp. vii. 1 med.

BOOK VII

1 GYLIPPUS and Pythen, after refitting their ships at

Gylippus arrives at Himera and, with an army numbering about three thousand in all, marches towards Syracuse.

Tarentum, coasted along to the Epizephyrian Locri. They now learned the truth, that Syracuse was not as yet completely invested, but that an army might still enter by way of Epipolae.

So they considered whether they should steer their course to the left or to the right of Sicily. They might attempt to throw themselves into Syracuse by sea, but the risk would be great; or they might go first to Himera, and gathering a force of the Himeraeans, and of any others whom they could induce to join them, make their way by land. They determined to sail to Himera, especially as the straits were unguarded. Nicias, when he heard that they were at Locri, although he had despised them at first, now sent out four Athenian ships to intercept them; but these had not as yet arrived at Rhegium, and came too late. So they sailed through the strait and, touching by the way at Rhegium and Messenè, reached Himera. They persuaded the Himeraeans to make common cause with them, and not only to join in the expedition themselves, but to supply arms to all their unarmed sailors, for they had beached their ships at Himera. They then sent to the Selinuntians and told them to come and meet them with their whole army at an appointed place. The Geloans and certain of the Sicels also promised to send them a small force; the latter with the more alacrity because Archonides, a Sicel king in these parts who was a powerful man and

friendly to the Athenians, had recently died, and because
Gylippus seemed to have come from Lacedaemon with
hearty good-will. And so, taking with him about seven
hundred of his own sailors and marines for whom he had
obtained arms, about a thousand Himeraean infantry,
heavy and light-armed included, and a hundred Himeraean
horsemen, some light-armed troops and cavalry from
Selinus, a few more from Gela, and of the Sicels about
a thousand in all, Gylippus marched towards Syracuse.

In the meantime the Corinthian ships[a] had put to sea 2
from Leucas and were coming with all
speed to the relief of the besieged.
Gongylus, one of the Corinthian commanders, who started last in a single
ship, arrived at Syracuse before the
rest of the fleet, and a little before
Gylippus. He found the citizens on
the point of holding an assembly at which the question of
peace was to be discussed; from this intention he dis-
suaded them by the encouraging announcement that more
ships, and Gylippus the son of Cleandridas, whom the
Lacedaemonians had sent to take the command, were on
their way. Whereupon the Syracusans were reassured,
and at once went forth with their whole army to meet
Gylippus, who, as they were informed, was now close at
hand. He had shortly before captured the Sicel fort Geta
on his march, and drawing up his men in readiness to fight,
came to Epipolae, which he ascended by the Euryelus;
where the Athenians had found a way before him [b]. Having
formed a junction with the Syracusans, he marched against
the Athenian lines. He arrived just at the time when the
Athenians had all but finished their double wall [c], nearly
a mile long, reaching to the Great Harbour; there remained only a small portion toward the sea, upon which
they were still at work. Along the remainder of the line

The Syracusans are a'out to make terms when Gongylus sails in and encourages them with the news that Gylippus is at hand. They go out to meet him.

---

[a] Cp. vi. 93 med., 104 med.   [b] Cp. vi. 97 med.   [c] Cp. vi. 103 init.

of wall, which extended towards Trogilus and the northern sea, the stones were mostly lying ready; a part was half-finished, a part had been completed and left.   So near was Syracuse to destruction.

3   The Athenians, though at first disconcerted by the

Gylippus and the Syracusans offer battle to Nicias on Epipolae, but as Nicias remains by the Athenian lines they soon withdraw. Labdalum taken by the Syracusans.

sudden advance of Gylippus and the Syracusans, drew up their forces in order of battle.   He halted as he approached, and sent a herald to them offering a truce if they were willing to quit Sicily within five days taking what belonged to them.   But they despised his offer, and sent away the herald without an answer. Whereupon both armies set themselves in order of battle. Gylippus, seeing that the Syracusans were in confusion, and could with difficulty form, led back his troops to the more open ground.   Nicias did not follow, but lay still, close to his own wall.   When Gylippus observed that the Athenians remained where they were, he led away his army to the height called Temenites; there they passed the night.   On the following day he stationed the greater part of his troops in front of the Athenian wall that the enemy might not despatch a force to any other point, and then sent a detachment against the fort of Labdalum, which was out of sight of the Athenian lines.   He took the place, and killed every one whom he found in it.   On the same day an Athenian trireme which was keeping watch over the mouth of the harbour was taken by the Syracusans.

4   The Syracusans and their allies now [a] began to build [a]

The third counter-work. Failure of an attack on the Athenian lines.

a single line of wall starting from the city and running upwards across Epipolae at an angle with the Athenian wall; this was a work which, unless it could be stopped by the Athenians, would make the investment of the city impossible.   Towards the sea the Athenian

---

[a] Or, omitting 'upwards': 'began to build on the high ground.'

wall was now completed, and their forces had come up to
the high ground. Gylippus, knowing that a part of the
wall was weak, instantly went by night with his army to
attack it. But the Athenians, who happened to be passing
the night outside the walls, perceived this movement and
marched to oppose him; whereupon he at once withdrew.
They then raised the weak portion of their wall higher;
and guarded it themselves, while they posted the allies on
the other parts of the fortification in the places severally
assigned to them.

Nicias now determined to fortify Plemmyrium, a promontory which runs out opposite the *The Athenians by*
city and narrows the entrance to the *the fortification of*
Great Harbour. He thought that this *Plemmyrium obtain*
measure would facilitate the introduc- *greater command of*
tion of supplies [a]. His forces would *the harbour; but the*
removal of the army
then be able to watch the harbour of *exposes their foragers to*
the Syracusans from a nearer point, *the Syracusan cavalry.*
whereas they had hitherto been obliged to put out from the
further corner of the Great Harbour whenever a Syracusan
ship threatened to move. He was inclined to pay more
attention than hitherto to naval operations; for since the
arrival of Gylippus the Athenian prospects by land were
not so encouraging. Having therefore transferred his
ships and a portion of his army to Plemmyrium, he built
three forts in which the greater part of the Athenian stores
were deposited; and the large boats as well as the ships
of war were now anchored at this spot. The removal was
a first and main cause of the deterioration of the crews.
For when the sailors went out to procure forage and water,
of which there was little, and that only to be obtained from
a distance, they were constantly cut off by the Syracusan
cavalry, who were masters of the country, a third part of
their force having been posted in a village at the Olympieum [b] expressly in order to prevent the enemy at Plem-

---

[a] Cp. vii. 13 init., 24 fin.   [b] Cp. vi. 75 init.

myrium from coming out and doing mischief. About this
time Nicias was informed that the rest of the Corinthian
fleet [a] was on the point of arriving, and he sent twenty
ships, which were ordered to lie in wait for them about
Locri and Rhegium and the approach to Sicily.

5   While Gylippus was building the wall across Epipolae,

*Gylippus, engaging
the Athenians in a con-
fined space between· the
walls, is defeated.*
employing the stones which the Athenians had previously laid there for
their own use, he at the same time
constantly led out and drew up in front
of the wall the Syracusans and their allies, and the Athenians on their part drew up in face of them. When he
thought that the moment had arrived he offered battle;
the two armies met and fought hand to hand between the
walls. But there the Syracusan cavalry was useless ; the
Syracusans and their allies were defeated, and received
their dead under a flag of truce, while the Athenians
raised a trophy. Gylippus then assembled his army and
confessed that the fault was his own and not theirs ; for by
confining their ranks too much between the walls he had
rendered useless both their cavalry and their javelin-
men. So he would lead them out again. And he
reminded them that in material force they were equal to
their enemies, while as for resolution they ought to be
far superior. That they, who were Peloponnesians and
Dorians [b], should allow a mixed rabble of Ionians and
islanders to remain in the country and not determine to
master them and drive them out, was a thing not to be
thought of.

6   On the first opportunity he led them out again. Nicias
and the Athenians had determined that, whether the
Syracusans would offer battle or not, they must not allow
them to carry on their counter-work. For already it had
almost passed the end of the Athenian wall, and if the

---

[a] Cp. vii 2 init.
25 med.

[b] Cp. i. 124 init. ; v. 9 init.; vi. 77 med. ; viii.

work advanced any further it would make no difference to the Athenians whether they fought and conquered in every battle, or never fought at all. So they went out to meet the Syracusans. Gylippus before engaging led his heavy-armed further outside the walls than on the former *But renewing the conflict on more open ground, where his cavalry can act, he is victorious. The cross-wall is now carried past the Athenian wall.* occasion; his cavalry and javelin-men he placed on the flanks of the Athenians in the open space between the points at which their respective lines of walls stopped. In the course of the battle the cavalry attacked the left wing of the Athenians which was opposed to them, and put them to flight; the defeat became general, and the whole Athenian army was driven back by main force within their lines. On the following night the Syracusans succeeded in carrying their wall past the works of the enemy. Their operations were now no longer molested by them, and the Athenians, whatever success they might gain in the field, were utterly deprived of all hope of investing the city.

Not long afterwards the remaining Corinthian with the 7 Ambraciot and Leucadian ships [a] sailed in, under the command of Erasinides the Corinthian, having eluded the Athenian guardships. They assisted the Syracusans in completing what remained of the Syracusan wall up to *Arrival of fresh reinforcements. Gylippus collects allies in Sicily. Second embassy to Corinth and Lacedaemon. Syracusans man a fleet.* the Athenian wall which it crossed. Gylippus meanwhile had gone off into Sicily to collect both naval and land forces, and also to bring over any cities which either were slack in the Syracusan cause or had stood aloof from the war. More ambassadors, Syracusan and Corinthian, were despatched to Lacedaemon and Corinth, requesting that reinforcements might be sent across the sea in merchant-ships or small craft, or by any other available means, since

---

[a] Cp. vii. 4 fin.

the Athenians were sending for assistance. The Syracusans, who were in high spirits, also manned a fleet, and began to practise, intending to try their hand at this new sort of warfare.

8   Nicias observing how they were employed, and seeing that the strength of the enemy and the helplessness of the Athenians was daily increasing, sent to Athens a full report of his circumstances, as he had often done before, but never in such detail.

Day by day the Syracusans are gaining and the Athenians losing strength. Nicias writes to Athens.

He now thought the situation so critical that, if the Athenians did not at once recall them or send another considerable army to their help, the expedition was lost. Fearing lest his messengers, either from inability to speak or ª from want of intelligence ª, or because they desired to please the people, might not tell the whole truth, he wrote a letter, that the Athenians might receive his own opinion of their affairs unimpaired in the transmission, and so be better able to judge of the real facts of the case. The messengers departed carrying his letter and taking verbal instructions. He was now careful to keep his army on the defensive, and to run no risks which he could avoid.

9   At the end of the same summer, Euetion an Athenian general, in concert with Perdiccas and assisted by a large force of Thracians, made an attack upon Amphipolis, which he failed to take. He then brought round triremes into the Strymon and besieged the place from the river, making Himeraeum his head-quarters. So the summer ended.

Failure of an attack upon Amphipolis.

10   In the following winter the messengers from Nicias arrived at Athens. They delivered their verbal instructions, and answered any questions which were put to them. They also pre-

The messengers of Nicias arrive at Athens.

ª Or, reading μνήμης instead of γνώμης : ' from defect of memory.'

sented his letter, which the registrar of the city, coming forward, read to the Athenian people. It ran as follows :—

'Athenians, in many previous despatches I have re- 11 ported to you the course of events up to this time, but now there is greater *The arrival of Gy-* need than ever that you should inform *lippus has entirely al-* yourselves of our situation, and come *besiegers are now be-* to some decision. After we had en- *sieged.* gaged the Syracusans, against whom you sent us, in several battles, and conquered in most of them, and had raised the lines within which we are now stationed, Gylippus a Lacedaemonian arrived, bringing an army from Peloponnesus and from certain of the cities of Sicily. In the first engagement he was defeated by us, but on the following day we were overcome by numerous horsemen and javelin-men, and retired within our lines. We have therefore desisted from our siege-works and remain idle, since we are overpowered by the superior numbers of the enemy, and indeed cannot bring our whole army into the field, for the defence of our wall absorbs a large part of our heavy-armed. The enemy meanwhile have built a single wall which crosses ours, and we cannot now invest them, unless a large army comes up and takes this cross-wall. So that we, who are supposed to be the besiegers, are really the besieged [a], at least by land ; and the more so because we cannot go far even into the country, for we are prevented by their horsemen.

'Moreover they have sent ambassadors to Peloponnesus 12 asking for reinforcements, and Gylippus *The Syracusans are* has gone to the cities in Sicily intending *seeking reinforcements* to solicit those who are at present *in Peloponnesus and* neutral to join him, and to obtain from *Sicily, and mean to* his allies fresh naval and land forces. *ships and crews are in* For they purpose, as I hear, to attack *good order; whereas* our walls by land, and at the same time *our ships are decaying.*

---

[a] Cp. iv. 29 init.

to make an effort at sea.   And let no one be startled when
I say "at sea."   Our fleet was originally in first-rate
condition : the ships were sound and the crews were in
good order, but now, as the enemy are well aware, the
timbers of the ships, having been so long exposed to the
sea, are soaked, and the efficiency of the crews is destroyed.
We have no means of drawing up our vessels and airing
them, because the enemy's fleet is equal or even superior
in numbers to our own, and we are always expecting an
attack from them.   They are clearly trying their strength ;
they can attack us when they please, and they have far
greater facilities for drying their ships, since they are not,
like us, engaged in a blockade.

13   'Even if we had a great superiority in the number of our
ships, and were not compelled as we
Our supplies are with   are to employ them all in keeping
difficulty conveyed to us;
our crews are demoral-   guard, we could hardly have the like
ised and our sailors   advantage.   For our supplies have to
desert.
pass so near the enemy's city that they
are with difficulty conveyed to us now, and if we relax our
vigilance ever so little we shall lose them altogether.

'It has been, and continues to be the ruin of our crews,
that the sailors, having to forage and fetch water and wood
from a distance, are cut off by the Syracusan horse[a], while
our servants, since we have been reduced to an equality
with the enemy, desert us.   Of the foreign sailors, some
who were pressed into the service run off at once to the
Sicilian cities ; others, having been originally attracted by
high pay, and fancying that they were going to trade and
not to fight, astonished at the resistance which they encounter, and especially at the naval strength of the enemy,
either find an excuse for deserting to the Syracusans, or
they effect their escape into the country ; and Sicily is
a large place.   Others, again, have persuaded the trierarchs
to take Hyccarian slaves in their room while they them-

---

[a] Cp. vii. 4 fin.

selves are busy trading; and thus the precision of the
service is lost.

'You to whom I am writing know that the crew of a 14
vessel does not long remain at its
prime, ᵃ and that the sailors who really   *I cannot prevent these*
start the ship and keep the rowing to-   *abuses; for your Athen-*
gether are but a fraction of the whole   *ian tempers will not*
number ᵃ.   The most hopeless thing of   *submit to discipline.*
all is that, although I am general, I am   *We are in danger of*
not able to put a stop to these disorders,   *being starved out. It*
for tempers like yours are not easily   *is better that you should*
                                           know the truth, how-
                                           ever painful.
controlled, and that we cannot even fill up the crews,
whereas the enemy can obtain recruits from many sources.
Our daily waste in men and stores can only be replaced
out of the supplies which we brought with us; and these
we have no means of increasing, for the cities which are
now our confederates, Naxos and Catana, are unable to
maintain us.   There is only one advantage more which
the Syracusans can gain over us: if the towns of Italy
from which our provisions are derived, seeing in what
a plight we are and that you do not come to our help, go
over to the enemy, we shall be starved out, and they will
have made an end of the war without striking a blow.
I could have written you tidings more cheering than these,
but none more profitable; for you should be well-informed
of our circumstances if you are to take the right steps.
Moreover I know your dispositions; you like to hear
pleasant things, but afterwards lay the fault on those who
tell you them if they are falsified by the event; therefore
I think it safer to speak the truth.

'And now, do not imagine that your soldiers and their 15
generals have failed in the fulfilment of the duty which
you originally imposed upon them.   But when all Sicily
is uniting against us, and the Syracusans are expecting

ᵃ Or, 'and that there are few sailors who can start a ship and keep
the rowing together.'

another army from Peloponnesus, it is time that you

We have done our duty, but the enemy and their allies are too much for us; I am sick and want to resign. Whatever you do, do quickly. should make up your minds. For the troops which we have here certainly cannot hold out even against our present enemies, and therefore you ought either to recall us or to send another army and fleet as large as this, and plenty of money. You should also send a general to succeed me, for I have a disease in the kidneys and cannot remain here. I claim your indulgence; while I retained my health I often did you good service when in command. But do whatever you mean to do at the very beginning of spring, and let there be no delay. The enemy will obtain reinforcements in Sicily without going far, and although the troops from Peloponnesus will not arrive so soon, yet if you do not take care they will elude you; their movements will either be too secret for you, as they were before[a], or too quick.'

16   Such was the condition of affairs described in the letter

The Athenians resolve to send a second expedition, of which Demosthenes and Eurymedon are appointed commanders. of Nicias. The Athenians, after hearing it read, did not release Nicias from his command, but they joined with him two officers who were already in Sicily, Menander and Euthydemus, until regular colleagues could be elected and sent out, for they did not wish him to bear the burden in his sickness alone. They also resolved to send a second fleet and an army of Athenians taken from the muster-roll and of allies. As colleagues to Nicias they elected Demosthenes the son of Alcisthenes, and Eurymedon the son of Thucles. Eurymedon was despatched immediately to Sicily about the winter solstice; he took with him ten ships conveying a hundred and twenty[b] talents of silver, and was to tell the army in Sicily that they should receive assistance and

17 should not be neglected. Demosthenes remained behind,

---

[a] Cp. vii. 2 init.   [b] £24,000.

and busied himself in getting ready the expedition which he was to bring out in the spring. He *The Athenians and* announced to the allies that troops *Peloponnesians get* would be required, collected money, *ready their forces.* and mustered ships, and hoplites at Athens. The Athenians also sent twenty ships to cruise off the Peloponnesian coast and intercept any vessels trying to pass to Sicily from the Peloponnesus or Corinth. The Sicilian envoys [a] had now arrived at Corinth, and the Corinthians had heard from them that affairs were looking better in Sicily. Seeing how opportune had been the arrival of the ships which they had already despatched they were more zealous than ever. They prepared to convey hoplites to Sicily in merchant-vessels; the Lacedaemonians were to do the like from Peloponnesus. The Corinthians also proceeded to man twenty-five ships of war, intending to hazard a naval engagement against the Athenian squadron stationed at Naupactus. They hoped that, if the attention of the Athenians was diverted by an opposing force, they would be unable to prevent their merchant-vessels from sailing.

The Lacedaemonians also prepared for their already 18 projected invasion of Attica [b]. They *The Lacedaemonians,* were kept to their purpose by the Syra- *at the instigation of* cusans and Corinthians, who, having *Alcibiades, prepare to* heard of the reinforcements which the *fortify Decelea. In the* Athenians were sending to Sicily, hoped *former war the Lace-* they might be stopped by the invasion. *daemonians were guilty* Alcibiades was always at hand insisting *of violating the treaty;* *in this, the Athenians.* upon the importance of fortifying Decelea and of carrying on the war with vigour. Above all, the Lacedaemonians were inspirited by the thought that the Athenians would be more easily overthrown now that they had two wars on hand, one against themselves, and another against the Sicilians. They considered also that this time they had been the first offenders against the treaty, whereas in the

---

[a] Cp. vii. 7.   [b] Cp. vi. 93 init.

former war the transgression had rather been on their own side. For the Thebans had entered Plataea in time of peace [a], and they themselves had refused arbitration when offered by the Athenians, although the former treaty forbade war in case an adversary was willing to submit to arbitration [b]. They felt that their ill success was deserved, and they took seriously to heart the disasters which had befallen them at Pylos and elsewhere. But now the Athenians with a fleet of thirty ships had gone forth from Argive territory and ravaged part of the lands of Epidaurus and Prasiae, besides other places [c]; marauding expeditions from Pylos were always going on; and whenever quarrels arose about disputed points in the treaty and the Lacedaemonians proposed arbitration, the Athenians refused it. Reflecting upon all this, the Lacedaemonians concluded that the guilt of their former transgression was now shifted to the Athenians, and they were full of warlike zeal. During the winter they bade their allies provide iron, and themselves got tools in readiness for the fortification of Decelea. They also prepared, and continually urged the other Peloponnesians to prepare, the succours which they intended to send in merchant-vessels to the Syracusans. And so the winter ended, and with it the eighteenth year in the Peloponnesian War of which Thucydides wrote the history.

19   At the very beginning of the next spring, and earlier

The Lacedaemonians enter Attica and fortify Decelea. than ever before, the Lacedaemonians and their allies entered Attica under the command of Agis the son of Archidamus the Lacedaemonian king. They first devastated the plain and its neighbourhood. They then began to fortify Decelea, dividing the work among the cities of the confederacy. Decelea is distant about fourteen miles from Athens, and not much further from Boeotia. The fort was

---

[a] Cp. ii. 2 foll.; iii. 56 init.   [b] Cp. i. 78 fin , 85, 140 med.

[c] Cp. vi. 105.

designed for the devastation of the plain and the richest parts of the country, and was erected on a spot within sight of Athens.

While the Peloponnesians and their allies in Attica were thus engaged, the Peloponnesians at home were despatching the hoplites in the merchant-vessels to Sicily. The Lacedaemonians selected the best of the Helots and Neodamodes, numbering *Reinforcements leave for Sicily, from which the attention of the Athenians is diverted by the Corinthians at Naupactus.* in all six hundred, and placed them under the command of Eccritus, a Spartan. The Boeotians furnished three hundred hoplites, who were commanded by two Thebans, Xenon and Nicon, and by Hegesander, a Thespian. These started first and put out into the open sea from Taenarus in Laconia. Not long afterwards the Corinthians sent five hundred heavy-armed, some of them from Corinth itself, others who were Arcadian mercenaries; they were all placed under the command of Alexarchus, a Corinthian. The Sicyonians also sent with the Corinthians two hundred hoplites under the command of Sargeus, a Sicyonian. Meanwhile the twenty five ships which the Corinthians had manned in the winter lay opposite to the twenty Athenian ships at Naupactus until the merchant-vessels conveying the heavy-armed troops had got safely off. So the design succeeded, and the attention of the Athenians was diverted from the merchant-ships to the triremes.

At the beginning of spring, whilst the Lacedaemonians 20 were fortifying Decelea, the Athenians sent thirty ships under the command of Charicles the son of Apollodorus to cruise about Peloponnesus. He was told to touch at Argos, and there to *Charicles with thirty ships sent to Laconia. The second armament under Demosthenes musters at Aegina.* summon and take on board a force of heavy-armed which the Argives, being allies of the Athenians, were bound to furnish. Meanwhile they despatched under Demosthenes their intended expedition to Sicily: it consisted of sixty

Athenian ships and five Chian, twelve hundred heavy-
armed Athenians taken from the roll, and as many others
as could possibly be obtained from the different islanders;
they had also collected from their subject-allies supplies of
all sorts for the war.   Demosthenes was told first of all to
co-operate with Charicles on the coast of Laconia.   So he
sailed to Aegina, and there waited until the whole of his
armament was assembled and until Charicles had taken on
board the Argives.

21   In the same spring and about the same time Gylippus
Gylippus and Her- returned to Syracuse, bringing from
mocrates incite the each of the cities which he had per-
Syracusans to try the suaded to join him as many troops as
sea; they should imitate
the daring spirit of their he could obtain.   He assembled the
foes. Syracusans and told them that they
should man as large a fleet as possible and try their fortune
at sea; he hoped to obtain a decisive result which would
justify the risk.   Hermocrates took the same view, and
urged them strongly not to be faint-hearted at the prospect
of attacking with their ships.   He said that the Athenians
had not inherited their maritime skill, [a] and would not
retain it for ever[a]; there was a time when they were less
of a naval people than the Syracusans themselves[b], but
they had been made sailors from necessity by the Persian
invasion.   To daring men like the Athenians those who
emulated their daring were the most formidable foes.   The
same reckless courage which had often enabled the
Athenians, although inferior in power, to strike terror into
their adversaries might now be turned against them by
the Syracusans.   He was quite sure that if they faced the
Athenian navy suddenly and unexpectedly, they would gain
more than they would lose; the consternation which they
would inspire would more than counterbalance their own
inexperience and the superior skill of the Athenians.   He
told them therefore to try what they could do at sea, and

---

[a] Or, ' or been sailors from all time.'   [b] Cp. i. 14.

not to be timid.   Thus under the influence of Gylippus,
Hermocrates, and others, the Syracusans, now eager for
the conflict, began to man their ships.

When the fleet was ready, Gylippus, under cover of 22
night, led forth the whole land-army,   *At dawn Gylippus*
intending to attack in person the forts   *attacks the forts on*
on Plemmyrium.   Meanwhile the tri-   *Plemmyrium,   while*
remes of the Syracusans, at a concerted   *their fleet encounters the*
signal, sailed forth, thirty-five from the   *Athenians in the har-*
bour.
greater harbour and forty-five from the lesser, where they
had their arsenal.   These latter sailed round into the
Great Harbour, intending to form a junction with the other
ships inside and make a combined attack on Plemmyrium,
that the Athenians, assailed both by sea and land, might be
disconcerted.   The Athenians however quickly manned
sixty ships; and with twenty-five of them engaged the
thirty-five of the Syracusans which were in the Great
Harbour: with the remainder they encountered those
which were sailing round from the arsenal.   These two
squadrons met at once before the mouth of the Great
Harbour: the struggle was long and obstinate, the
Syracusans striving to force an entrance, the Athenians
to prevent them.

Meanwhile Gylippus, quite early in the morning, while 23
the Athenians in Plemmyrium who had   *In the sea-fight the*
gone down to the water-side had their   *Syracusans   are de-*
minds occupied by the sea-fight, made   *feated, but the forts are*
a sudden attack upon their forts.   He   *taken.*
captured the largest of them first, then the two lesser, their
garrisons forsaking them when they saw the largest so
easily taken.   Those who escaped from the fortress first
captured, getting into a merchant-vessel and some boats
which were moored at Plemmyrium, found their way to
the main station of the Athenians, but with difficulty; for
they were chased by a swift trireme, the Syracusans at that
time having the advantage in the Great Harbour.   But
when the two lesser fortresses were taken, the Syracusans

were already losing the day, and the fugitives got past
them with greater ease. For the Syracusan ships which
were fighting before the mouth of the harbour, having
forced their way through the enemy, entered in disorder,
and falling foul of one another gave away the victory to
the Athenians, who routed not only these, but also the
others by whom they were at first worsted inside the
harbour. Eleven Syracusan ships were disabled; the
crews in most of them were slain, in three, made prisoners.
The Athenians themselves lost three ships. They now
drew to land the wrecks of the Syracusan ships, and
erecting a trophy on the little island in front of Plemmyrium
returned to their own station.

24   But although the Syracusans were unsuccessful in the
The loss of Plem- sea-fight, still they had taken the fort-
myrium disastrous to resses of Plemmyrium. They erected
the Athenians. three trophies, one for each fort. Two
out of the three forts they repaired and garrisoned, but
one of the two which were captured last they demolished.
Many perished and many prisoners were made at the
capture of the forts, and abundant spoil of different kinds
was taken, for the Athenians had used them as a store,
and much corn and goods of traders were deposited in
them; also much property belonging to the trierarchs,
including the sails and other fittings of forty triremes
which fell into the enemy's hands, and three triremes
which had been drawn up on the beach. The loss of
Plemmyrium was one of the greatest and severest blows
which befell the Athenians. For now they could no longer
even introduce provisions with safety, but the Syracusan
ships lay watching to prevent them, and they had to fight
for the passage [a]. General discouragement and dismay
prevailed throughout the army.

25   The Syracusans next sent out twelve ships under the
command of Agatharchus, a Syracusan. One of these

---

[a] Cp. vii. 4 med., 13 init.

hastened to Peloponnesus conveying envoys who were to
report their improved prospects, and   *The Syracusans send*
to urge more strongly than ever the   *a third embassy to Pelo-*
prosecution of the war in Hellas. The   *ponnesus, and despatch*
remaining eleven sailed to Italy, hear-   *a squadron which inter-*
ing that ships laden with supplies were   *cepts some Athenian*
on their way to the Athenians. They fell in with and
destroyed most of these ships, and burnt a quantity of
ship-timber which was lying ready for the Athenians in
the territory of Caulonia. Then they came to Locri,
and while they were at anchor there, one of the merchant-
vessels from Peloponnesus sailed in, bringing some
Thespian hoplites[a]. These the Syracusans took on
board, and sailed homewards. The Athenians watched
for them near Megara with twenty ships and took one
ship with the crew, but the rest made their escape to
Syracuse.

There was some skirmishing in the harbour about the
palisades which the Syracusans had
fixed in the sea in front of their old   *The Athenians pull*
dock-houses, that their ships might ride   *up the palisade which*
at anchor in the enclosed space, where   *the Syracusans had*
they could not be struck by the enemy,   *driven in to protect their*
                                            ships.
and would be out of harm's way. The Athenians brought
up a ship of ten thousand talents[b] burden, which had
wooden towers and bulwarks ; and from their boats they
tied cords to the stakes and [c]wrenched and tore them
up[c] ; or dived and sawed them through underneath the
water. Meanwhile the Syracusans kept up a shower of
missiles from the dock-houses, which the men in the ship
returned. At length the Athenians succeeded in pulling
up most of the palisade. The stakes which were out of
sight were the most dangerous of all, there being some
which were so fixed that they did not appear above the

---

[a] Cp. vii. 19 med.   [b] About 250 tons.   [c] Or, 'wrenched
them up and broke them off.'

water; and no vessel could safely come near. They were like a sunken reef, and a pilot, not seeing them, might easily catch his ship upon them. Even these were sawn off by men who dived for hire; but the Syracusans drove them in again. Many were the contrivances employed on both sides, as was very natural, when two armies confronted each other at so short a distance. There were continual skirmishes, and they practised all kinds of stratagems.

The Syracusans also sent to the Siciliot cities Corin-

A second embassy, asking for help, is sent from Syracuse to the cities of Sicily. thian, Ambraciot, and Lacedaemonian ambassadors announcing the taking of Plemmyrium, and explaining that in the sea-fight they had been defeated

not so much by the superior strength of the enemy as through their own disorder. They were also to report their great hopes of success, and to ask for assistance both by land and sea. They were to add that the Athenians were expecting reinforcements; if they could succeed in destroying the army then in Sicily before these arrived, there would be an end of the war. Such was the course of events in Sicily.

26   Demosthenes, when the reinforcements which he was

Devastation of Laconia and erection of a second Pylos opposite Cythera. Demosthenes, having assisted in these operations, sails forward to Corcyra. to take to Sicily had all been collected, sailed from Aegina to Peloponnesus and joined Charicles and his thirty ships [a]. He embarked the Argive hoplites, and, proceeding to Laconia, first devastated some part of the lands

of Epidaurus Limera. Next the Athenians landed in the district of Laconia opposite Cythera, where there is a temple of Apollo. They ravaged various parts of the country, and fortified a sort of isthmus in the neighbourhood, that the Helots of the Lacedaemonians might desert and find a refuge there, and that privateers might make

---

[a] Cp. vii. 20 init.

the place, as they did Pylos, their head-quarters for
marauding expeditions. Demosthenes assisted in the
occupation, and then sailed for Corcyra, intending to collect
additional forces from the allies in that region, and to
make his way with all speed to Sicily. Charicles waited
until he had completed the fort, and then leaving a garrison
he sailed home with his thirty ships, accompanied by the
Argives.

During the same summer there arrived at Athens 27
thirteen hundred Thracian targeteers *The Dian Thracians*
of the Dian race, who carried dirks; *arrive too late to join*
they were to have sailed with Demo- *the expedition.*
sthenes to Sicily, but came too late, and the Athenians
determined to send them back to their native country.
Each soldier was receiving a drachma[a] per day; and
to use them against Decelea would have been too
expensive.

For during this summer Decelea had been fortified by
the whole Peloponnesian army, and *Thucydides digresses*
was henceforward regularly occupied *to speak of the great*
for the annoyance of the country by *sufferings caused by the*
a succession of garrisons sent from the *fortification of Decelea,*
allied cities, whose incursions did *which permanently com-*
immense harm to the Athenians : the *manded the whole coun-*
destruction of property and life which *try. Desertion of twenty*
ensued did as much as anything to ruin *thousand slaves ; great*
the city. Hitherto the invasions had been brief and did not *destruction of cattle and*
injury to cavalry.
prevent them from getting something from the soil in the
interval ; but now the Peloponnesians were continually on
the spot ; and sometimes they were reinforced by additional
troops, but always the regular garrison, who were compelled to find their own supplies, overran and despoiled
the country. The Lacedaemonian king, Agis, was present in person, and devoted his whole energies to the
war. The sufferings of the Athenians were terrible. For

---

[a] 8*d.*

they were dispossessed of their entire territory; more than twenty thousand slaves had deserted [a], most of them workmen; all their sheep and cattle had perished, and now that the cavalry had to go out every day and make descents upon Decelea or keep guard all over the country, their horses were either wounded by the enemy, or lamed by the roughness of the ground and the incessant fatigue.

28   Provisions, which had been formerly conveyed by the *Provisions brought a long way round. Citizens on guard by turns in the day, and the whole population by night, summer and winter. Two wars instead of one; the besiegers besieged. The great paradox.* shorter route from Euboea to Oropus and thence overland through Decelea, were now carried by sea round the promontory of Sunium at great cost. Athens was obliged to import everything from abroad, and resembled a fort rather than a city. In the daytime the citizens guarded the battlements by relays; during the night every man was on service except the cavalry; some at their places of arms, others on the wall [b], summer and winter alike, until they were quite worn out. But worse than all was the cruel necessity of maintaining two wars at once; and they carried on both with a determination which no one would have believed unless he had actually seen it. That, blockaded as they were by the Peloponnesians, who had raised a fort in their country, they should refuse to let go Sicily, and, themselves besieged, persevere in the siege of Syracuse, which as a mere city might rank with Athens, and— whereas the Hellenes generally were expecting at the beginning of the war, some that they would survive a year, others two or perhaps three years, certainly not more, if the Peloponnesians invaded Attica—that in the seventeenth year from the first invasion, after so exhausting a struggle, the Athenians should have been strong enough and bold enough to go to Sicily at all, and to plunge into a fresh

---

[a] Cp. viii. 40 med.   [b] Cp. ii. 13 fin. ; viii. 69 init.

war as great as that in which they were already engaged—
how contrary was all this to the expectation of mankind!
Through the vast expense thus incurred, above all through
the mischief done by Decelea, they were now greatly
impoverished. It was at this time that they imposed upon
their allies, instead of the tribute, a   *New financial mea-*
duty of five per cent. on all things   *sure.*
imported and exported by sea, thinking that this would be
more productive. For their expenses became heavier and 29
heavier as the war grew in extent, and at the same time
their sources of revenue were drying up.

And so, being in extreme want of money, and desirous
to economise, they at once sent away   *The Thracians are*
the Thracians who came too late for   *sent home by the Athen-*
Demosthenes, ordering Diitrephes to   *ians,   who   cannot*
convey them home, but, as they must   *afford to keep them.*
                                        Being desired to do what
needs sail through the Euripus, to   *mischief they can by the*
employ them in any way which he   *way, they sack Myca-*
could against the enemy. He landed   *lessus.   The   pathetic*
                                        tale   of   its   sufferings
them at Tanagra and there made a   *moves   Thucydides   to*
hasty raid; in the evening he sailed   *pity.*
from Chalcis in Euboea across the Euripus, and disembarking his troops in Boeotia led them against the town of
Mycalessus. He passed the night unperceived at the
temple of Hermes, which is distant from Mycalessus about
two miles, and at the dawn of day he assaulted and captured
the city, which is not large. The inhabitants were taken
off their guard; for they never imagined that an enemy
would come and attack them at so great a distance from
the sea. The walls were weak, and in some places had
fallen down; in others they were built low; while the
citizens, in their sense of security, had left their gates
open. The Thracians dashed into the town, sacked the
houses and temples, and slaughtered the inhabitants.
They spared neither old nor young, but cut down, one
after another, all whom they met, the women and children,
the very beasts of burden, and every living thing which they

saw. ªFor the Thracians, when they dare, can be as bloody as the worst barbarians ª. There in Mycalessus the wildest panic ensued, and destruction in every form was rife. They even fell upon a boys' school, the largest in the place, which the children had just entered, and massacred them every one. No calamity could be worse than this, touching as it did the whole city, none was ever so sudden or so terrible.

30   When the news reached the Thebans they hastened to the rescue. Coming upon the Thracians

The Thebans soon come upon them and they are driven back with loss to their ships.

before they had gone far, they took away the spoil and, putting them to flight, pursued them to the Euripus, where the ships which had brought them were moored. Of those who fell, the greater number were slain in the attempt to embark ; for they did not know how to swim, and the men on board, seeing what was happening, had anchored their vessels out of bow-shot ᵇ. In the retreat itself the Thracians made a very fair defence against the Theban cavalry which first attacked them, running out and closing in again, after the manner of their country ; and their loss was trifling. But a good many who remained for the sake of plunder were cut off within the city and slain. The whole number who fell was two hundred and fifty, out of thirteen hundred. They killed, however, some of the Thebans and others who came to the rescue, in all about twenty, both horsemen and hoplites. Scirphondas, one of the Theban Boeotarchs, was slain. A large proportion of the Mycalessians perished. Such was the fate of Mycalessus ; considering the size of the city, no calamity more deplorable occurred during the war ᶜ.

31   Demosthenes, who after helping to build the fort on the

ª Or, 'For the Thracians, like all very barbarous tribes, are most bloody when they are least afraid.'   ᵇ Reading τοξεύματος with Valla's translation.   ᶜ Cp. iii. 113 fin.

Laconian coast, had sailed away to Corcyra [a], on his way thither destroyed a merchant-vessel anchored at Phea in Elis, which was intended to convey some of the Corinthian hoplites to Sicily. But the crew escaped, and sailed in another vessel. He went on to Zacynthus and Cephallenia, where he took on board some hoplites, and sent to the Messen-

Demosthenes sailing up the west coast meets Eurymedon, who brings news from Sicily. They collect troops for Sicily and send reinforcements to Naupactus.

ians of Naupactus for others; he then passed over to the mainland of Acarnania, and touched at Alyzia and Anactorium [b], which were at that time occupied by the Athenians. While he was in those regions he met Eurymedon returning from Sicily, whither he had been sent during the winter in charge of the money which had been voted to the army [c]; he reported, among other things, the capture of Plemmyrium by the Syracusans, of which he had heard on his voyage home. Conon too, the governor of Naupactus, brought word that the twenty-five Corinthian ships [d] which were stationed on the opposite coast were still showing a hostile front, and clearly meant to fight. He requested the generals to send him reinforcements, since his own ships—eighteen in number—were not able to give battle against the twenty-five of the enemy. Demosthenes and Eurymedon sent ten ships, the swiftest which they had, to the fleet at Naupactus, while they themselves completed the muster of the expedition. Eurymedon, sailing to Corcyra, ordered the Corcyraeans to man fifteen ships, and himself levied a number of hoplites. He had turned back from his homeward voyage, and was now holding the command, to which, in conjunction with Demosthenes, he had been appointed. Demosthenes meanwhile had been collecting slingers and javelin-men in the neighbourhood of Acarnania.

The ambassadors from Syracuse who had gone to the 32

---

[a] Cp. vii. 26.   [b] Cp. iv. 49; v. 30 med.   [c] Cp. vii. 16 fin.
[d] Cp. vii. 17 fin., 19 fin.

cities of Sicily after the taking of Plemmyrium, and had
Part of the reinforce- persuaded them to join in the war,
ments sent by the cities were now about to bring back the
of Sicily to Syracuse are army which they had collected. Nic-
destroyed in an ambus-
cade by the Sicel allies ias, having previous information, sent
of the Athenians. word to the Sicel allies of Athens who
commanded the road, such as the Centoripes and Alicyaei,
and told them not to let the forces of the enemy pass, but
to unite and stop them; there was no likelihood, he said,
that they would even think of taking another road, since
they were not allowed to go through the country of the
Agrigentines. So when the forces of the Sicilian towns
were on their way, the Sicels, complying with the request
of the Athenians, set an ambush in three divisions, and
falling upon them suddenly when they were off their guard,
destroyed about eight hundred of them, and all the envoys
except the Corinthian; he brought the survivors, numbering
fifteen hundred, to Syracuse.

33 About the same time arrived a reinforcement from
Camarina[a] of five hundred hoplites,
Reinforcements from three hundred javelin-men, and three
Camarina and Gela.
Nearly the whole of hundred archers. The Geloans also
Sicily unites against sent five ships with four hundred
the Athenians. javelin-men and two hundred horsemen.
Hitherto the Sicilian cities had only watched the course
of events, but now the whole island, with the exception of
Agrigentum, which was neutral, united with the Syracusans
against the Athenians.

After their misfortune in the Sicel country, the Syra-
The Athenian fleet cusans deferred their intended attack
crosses to Iapygia. They for a time. The forces which Demo-
are received at Thurii, sthenes and Eurymedon had collected
where they hold a review. from Corcyra and the mainland were
now ready, and they passed over the Ionian Sea to the
promontory of Iapygia. Proceeding onwards, they touched

---

[a] Cp vi. 88 init.

at the Iapygian islands called Choerades, and took on
board a hundred and fifty Iapygian javelin-men of the
Messapian tribe. After renewing an ancient friendship
with Artas, a native prince who had furnished the javelin-
men, they went on to Metapontium in Italy. They
persuaded the Metapontians, who were their allies, to let
them have two triremes and three hundred javelin-men ;
these they took with them and sailed to Thurii. At
Thurii they found that the party opposed to the Athenians
had just been driven out by a revolution. Wishing
to hold another muster and inspection of their whole
army, and to be sure that no one was missing, they
remained there for some time. They also did their best
to gain the hearty co-operation of the Thurians, and to
effect an offensive and defensive alliance with them, now
that they had succeeded in expelling the anti-Athenian
party.

About the same time the Peloponnesians in their fleet of 34
twenty-five ships, which was stationed
opposite the Athenian fleet at Naupactus to protect the passage of the
merchant-vessels going to Sicily, made
ready for action. They manned some
additional ships, which raised their
number nearly to that of the Athenians,

*Indecisive naval ac-
tion in the Corinthian
gulf between the Corin-
thians and the Athen-
ians. The former
greatly assisted by an
improvement in the
structure of their ships.*

and anchored at Erineus off Achaia, which is in the
territory of Rhypae. The bay, off the shore of which they
were stationed, has the form of a crescent, and the infantry
of the Corinthians and of the allies, which had come from
the country on both sides to co-operate with the fleet, was
disposed on the projecting promontories. The ships,
which were under the command of Polyanthes the Corinthian, formed a close line between the two points. The
Athenians sailed out against them from Naupactus with
thirty-three ships, under the command of Diphilus. For
a while the Corinthians remained motionless ; in due time
the signal was raised and they rushed upon the Athenians

and engaged with them. The battle was long and obstinate. Three Corinthian ships were destroyed. The Athenians had no ships absolutely sunk, but about seven of them were rendered useless ; for they were struck full in front by the beaks of the Corinthian vessels, which had the projecting beams of their prows designedly built thicker, and their bows were stoven in. The engagement was undecided and both sides claimed the victory ; but the Athenians gained possession of the wrecks because the wind blew them towards the open sea and the Corinthians did not put out again. So the two fleets parted. There was no pursuit, nor were any prisoners taken on either side. For the Corinthians and Peloponnesians were fighting close to the land and thus their crews escaped, while on the Athenian side no ship was sunk. As soon as the Athenians had returned to Naupactus the Corinthians set up a trophy, insisting that they were the victors, because they had disabled more of the enemy's ships than the enemy of theirs. They refused to acknowledge defeat on the same ground which made the Athenians unwilling to claim the victory. For the Corinthians considered themselves conquerors, if they were not severely defeated ; but the Athenians thought that they were defeated because they had not gained a signal victory. When however the Peloponnesians had sailed away and the land-army was dispersed, the Athenians raised another trophy in Achaia, at a distance of about two miles and a quarter from the Corinthian station at Erineus. Such was the result of the engagement.

35   Demosthenes and Eurymedon, when the Thurians had

The Thurians join the Athenians. The Athenian fleet and army pass along the Italian coasts to Rhegium.

been prevailed upon to help them, and had furnished seven hundred hoplites and three hundred javelin-men, commanded the ships to sail towards the territory of Crotona, and themselves, after holding a review of all their infantry at the river Sybaris, led them through the territory of Thurii. On their arrival at the river Hylias the people of Crotona sent to them, and said that they could not allow the army to march through their country. So they directed their march down to the sea and passed the night at the mouth of the river, where they were met by their ships. On the following day they re-embarked the army and coasted along, touching at the cities which they passed, with the exception of Locri [a], until they came to the promontory of Petra near Rhegium.

The Syracusans, hearing of their approach, desired to have another trial of the fleet, and to use the army which they had collected with the express purpose of bringing on an engagement before Demosthenes and Eurymedon arrived in Sicily. Profiting by the experience which they had acquired in the last sea-fight, they devised several improvements in the construction of their vessels. They cut down and strengthened the prows, and also made the beams which pro-

The Syracusans make preparations for another sea-fight. They adopt the Corinthian invention of flattening the prows of their ships and strengthening the projecting beams, a device well suited to the narrow space, in which the Athenians had no room to manœuvre, and to the inferior skill of their own pilots.

jected from them thicker; these latter they supported underneath with stays of timber extending from the beams to and through the sides of the ship a length of nine feet within and nine without, after the fashion in which the Corinthians had refitted their prows before they fought with the squadron from Naupactus. For the Syracusans hoped thus to gain an advantage over the Athenian ships, which were not constructed to resist such improvements, but had their prows slender, because they were in the habit of rowing round an enemy and striking the side of his vessel instead of meeting him prow to prow. The plan would be the more effectual, because they were going to fight in the Great Harbour, where many ships would be crowded in a narrow space. They would charge full in

36

---

[a] Cp. vi. 44 med.

face, and presenting their own massive and solid beaks would stave in the hollow and weak forepart of their enemies' ships[a]; while the Athenians, confined as they were, would not be able to wheel round them or break their line before striking, to which manœuvres they mainly trusted—the want of room would make the one impossible, and the Syracusans themselves would do their best to prevent the other. What had hitherto been considered a defect of skill on the part of their pilots, the practice of striking beak to beak, would now be a great advantage, to which they would have constant recourse; for the Athenians, when forced to back water, could only retire towards the land, which was too near, and of which but a small part, that is to say, their own encampment, was open to them. The Syracusans would be masters of the rest of the harbour, and, if the Athenians were hard pressed at any point, they would all be driven together into one small spot, where they would run foul of one another and fall into confusion. (Which proved to be the case; for nothing was more disastrous to the Athenians in all these sea-fights than the impossibility of retreating, as the Syracusans could, to any part of the harbour.) Again, while they themselves had command of the outer sea and could charge from it and back water into it whenever they pleased, the Athenians would be unable to sail into the open and turn before striking[b]; besides, Plemmyrium was hostile to them, and the mouth of the harbour was narrow.

37   Having thus adapted their plans to the degree of naval

Gylippus and the land-forces attack the Athenian lines, and at the same time eighty Syracusan ships sail out suddenly; they are met by seventy-five Athenian ships.

skill and strength which they possessed, the Syracusans, greatly encouraged by the result of the previous engagement, attacked the Athenians both by sea and land. A little before the fleet sailed forth, Gylippus led the land-forces out of the city against that part of the

---

[a] Omitting the comma at αὐτοῖς.   [b] Cp. ii. 91 med.

Athenian wall which faced Syracuse, while some of the
heavy-armed troops, which together with the cavalry and
light infantry were stationed at the Olympieum, approached
the lines of the enemy from the opposite side.   Nearly at
the same instant the ships of the Syracusans and their
allies sailed out.   The Athenians at first thought that they
were going to make an attempt by land only, but when
they saw the ships suddenly bearing down upon them they
were disconcerted.   Some mounted the walls or prepared
to meet their assailants in front of them ; others went out
against the numerous cavalry and javelin-men, who were
hastening from the Olympieum and the outer side of the
wall ; others manned the ships or prepared to fight on
the beach.   When the crews had got on board they sailed
out with seventy-five ships ; the number of Syracusan ships
being about eighty.

During a great part of the day the two fleets continued 38
advancing and retreating and skirmish-   *Slight result of the*
ing with one another.   Neither was   *first day's fighting.*
able to gain any considerable advan-   *Nicias repairs his ships*
tage, only the Syracusans sank one or   *and places merchant-*
vessels so as to protect
two ships of the Athenians; so they   *them if defeated.*
parted, and at the same time the infantry retired from
the walls.   On the following day the Syracusans remained
quiet and gave no sign of what they meant to do next.
Seeing how close the conflict had been, Nicias expected
another attack ; he therefore compelled the trierarchs to
repair their ships wherever they were injured, and anchored merchant-vessels in front of the palisades which
the Athenians had driven into the sea so as to form
a kind of dock for the protection of their own ships ;
these he placed at a distance of about two hundred
feet from one another, in order that any ship which was
hard pressed might have a safe retreat and an opportunity of going out again at leisure.   These preparations
occupied the Athenians for a whole day from morning
to night.

39   On the next day, in the same manner as before but

The second day is wearing away without a serious engagement, when the Syracusans retire and take their midday meal on the beach. at an earlier hour, the Syracusans attacked the Athenians both by sea and land. Again the ships faced one another, and again a great part of the day was passed in skirmishing. At length Ariston the son of Pyrrhichus, a Corinthian, who was the ablest pilot in the Syracusan fleet, persuaded the commanders to send a message to the proper authorities in the city desiring them to have the market transferred as quickly as possible to the shore, and to compel any one who had food for sale to bring his whole stock thither. The sailors would thus be enabled to disembark and take their midday meal close to the ships ; and so after a short interval they might, without waiting until the next day, renew the attack upon the Athenians when least expected.

40   The generals, agreeing to the proposal, sent the message,

They soon return, to the great surprise of the Athenians, who are now compelled to charge and fight. and the market was brought down to the shore. Suddenly the Syracusans backed water and rowed towards the city ; then disembarking they at once took their meal on the spot. The Athenians, regarding their retreat as a confession of defeat, disembarked at leisure, and among other matters set about preparing their own meal, taking for granted that there would be no more fighting that day. Suddenly the Syracusans manned their ships and again bore down upon them ; the Athenians, in great disorder and most of them fasting, hurried on board, and with considerable difficulty got under weigh. For some time the two fleets looked at one another, and did not engage ; after a while the Athenians thought they had better not delay until they had fairly tired themselves out, but attack at once. So, cheering on one another, they charged and fought. The Syracusans remained firm, and meeting the enemy prow to prow, as they had resolved, stove in by the strength of their beaks a great part of the bows of the Athenian ships. Their javelin-men on the decks greatly injured the enemy. Still more mischief was done by Syracusans who rowed about in light boats and dashed in upon the blades of the enemy's oars, or ran up alongside and threw darts at the sailors.

By such expedients as these the Syracusans, who made 41 a great effort, gained the victory; and the Athenians, retreating between the merchant-vessels, took refuge at their own moorings. The ships of the enemy pursued them as far as the entrance, but they were prevented from following further by leaden dolphins, which were suspended aloft from beams placed in the merchant-vessels. Two Syracusan ships, in the exultation of victory, approached too near and were disabled; one of them was taken with its whole crew. The Syracusans damaged many of the Athenian ships and sank seven; the crews were either killed or taken prisoners. They then retired and raised trophies of the two sea-fights. They were now quite confident that they were not only equal but far superior to the Athenians at sea, and they hoped to gain the victory on land as well. So they prepared to renew the attack on both elements.

The Athenians are defeated and return to their moorings with a loss of seven ships. Two Syracusan vessels following too closely are caught in the entrance to the dock.

But in the midst of their preparations Demosthenes and 42 Eurymedon arrived with the Athenian reinforcements. They brought a fleet, including foreign ships, of about seventy-three sail, carrying five thousand heavy infantry of their own and of their allies, numerous javelin-men, slingers, and archers, both Hellenic and Barbarian, and abundant supplies of every kind. The Syracusans and their allies were in consternation. It seemed to them as if their perils would never have an end when they saw, notwithstanding the

While the Syracusans are making preparations for a fresh attack, Demosthenes arrives. Being determined to strike hard and at once, he plans an attack upon the Syracusan cross-wall by way of the Euryelus.

fortification of Decelea, another army arriving nearly equal to the former, and Athens displaying such varied and exuberant strength ; while the first Athenian army regained a certain degree of confidence after their disasters. Demosthenes at once saw how matters stood ; he knew that there was no time to be lost, and resolved that it should not be with him as it had been with Nicias. For Nicias was dreaded at his first arrival, but when, instead of at once laying siege to Syracuse, he passed the winter at Catana, he fell into contempt, and his delay gave Gylippus time to come with an army from Peloponnesus. Whereas if he had struck hard at first, the Syracusans would never even have thought of getting fresh troops ; strong in their own self-sufficiency, they would have discovered their inferiority only when the city had been actually invested, and then, if they had been sent for reinforcements, they would have found them useless. Demosthenes, reflecting on all this, and aware that he too would never again be in a position to inspire such terror as on the day of his arrival, desired to take the speediest advantage of the panic caused by the appearance of his army. Accordingly, seeing that the cross-wall of the Syracusans which had prevented the Athenians from investing them was but a single line, and that if he could gain the command of the way up to Epipolae and take the camp which was on the high ground the wall would be easily captured, for no one would so much as stand his ground against them, he resolved to make the attempt at once. This would be the shortest way of putting an end to the war. If he succeeded, Syracuse would fall into his hands ; if he failed, he meant to bring away the expedition ; he would no longer wear out the Athenian army, and weaken the state to no purpose.

The Athenians began by ravaging the fields of the Syracusans about the Anapus, and regained their former superiority both by sea and land. At sea the Syracusans no longer opposed them ; and on land they merely sent out parties of cavalry and javelin-men from the Olympieum.

Before he attacked Epipolae, Demosthenes wished to 43
try what could be done with engines
against the counter-wall. But the
engines which he brought up were
burnt by the enemy, who fought from
the wall, and, after making assaults at
several points, the Athenian forces
were repulsed. He now determined to
delay no longer, and persuaded Nicias
and his colleagues to carry out the
plan of attacking Epipolae. To approach
during the daytime and ascend the
heights undetected appeared to be impossible ; so he resolved to attack by
night. He ordered provisions for five

*Failure of an attempt
to take the wall in front.
Leaving Nicias in the
camp, Demosthenes with
his army proceeds before
midnight by way of
the Euryelus to ascend
Epipolae ; he takes the
first fort and drives
back Gylippus and his
troops, who are amazed
at the sudden onset.
The Athenians are
hurrying forward when
they are met by the
Boeotians and put to
flight.*

days, and took with him all the masons and carpenters in
the army ; also a supply of arrows and of the various
implements which would be required for siege-works if he
were victorious. About the first watch he, Eurymedon,
and Menander led out the whole army and marched
towards Epipolae. Nicias was left in the Athenian fortifications. Reaching Epipolae at the Euryelus, where
their first army had originally ascended [a], and advancing
undiscovered by the garrison to the fort which the
Syracusans had there erected, they took it and killed
some of the guards. But the greater number made good
their escape and carried the news to the three fortified
camps, one of the Syracusans, one of the other Sicilian
Greeks, and one of the allies, which had been formed on
Epipolae ; they also gave the alarm to the six hundred
who were an advanced guard stationed on this part of
Epipolae [b]. They hastened to meet the enemy, but Demosthenes and the Athenians came upon them and, in spite of

---

[a] Cp. vi. 97 med.   [b] Cp. vi. 96 fin.

a vigorous resistance, drove them back. The Athenians immediately pressed forward; they were determined not to lose a moment or to slacken their onset until they had accomplished their purpose. Others captured the first part of the Syracusan counter-wall and, the guards taking to flight, began to drag off the battlements. Meanwhile the Syracusans, the allies, and Gylippus with his own troops, were hurrying from the outworks. The boldness of this night attack quite amazed them. They had not recovered from their terror when they met the Athenians, who were at first too strong for them and drove them back. But now the conquerors, in the confidence of victory, began to fall into disorder as they advanced; they wanted to force their way as quickly as they could through all that part of the enemy which had not yet fought, and they were afraid that if they relaxed their efforts the Syracusans might rally. The Boeotians were the first to make a stand: they attacked the Athenians, turned, and put them to flight.

44   The whole army was soon in utter confusion, and the

All now becomes confusion. Those behind press on those before, who are already turning back. The moonlight, the dense masses, the narrow space, the watchword, the Paean, contribute to the rout. Friends attack friends. Many throw themselves from the cliffs, leaving their arms behind; others miss their way in the dark and are cut off.

perplexity was so great that from neither side could the particulars of the conflict be exactly ascertained. In the daytime the combatants see more clearly; though even then only what is going on immediately around them, and that imperfectly—nothing of the battle as a whole. But in a night engagement, like this in which two great armies fought—the only one of the kind which occurred during the war—who could be certain of anything? The moon was bright, and they saw before them, as men naturally would in the moonlight, the figures of one another, but were unable to distinguish with certainty who was friend or foe. Large bodies of heavy-armed troops, both Athenian and Syracusan, were moving about in a narrow space; of the

Athenians some were already worsted, while others, still
unconquered, were carrying on the original movement.
A great part of their army had not yet engaged, but either
had just mounted the heights, or were making the ascent;
and no one knew which way to go. For in front they
were defeated already; there was nothing but confusion,
and all distinction between the two armies was lost by
reason of the noise. The victorious Syracusans and their
allies, who had no other means of communication in the
darkness, cheered on their comrades with loud cries as
they received the onset of their assailants. The Athenians
were looking about for each other; and every one who
met them, though he might be a friend who had turned
and fled, they imagined to be an enemy. They kept
constantly asking the watchword (for there was no other
mode of knowing one another), and thus they not only
caused great confusion among themselves by all asking
at once, but revealed the word to the enemy. The watchword of the Syracusans was not so liable to be discovered,
because being victorious they kept together and were more
easily recognised. So that when they were encountered
by a superior number of the enemy they, knowing the
Athenian watchword, escaped; but the Athenians in a like
case, failing to answer the challenge, were killed. Most
disastrous of all were the mistakes caused by the sound
of the Paean, which, the same being heard in both armies,
was a great source of perplexity. For there were in the
battle Argives, Corcyraeans, and other Dorian allies of
the Athenians, and when they raised the Paean they
inspired as much alarm as the enemy themselves; so that
in many parts of the army, when the confusion had once
begun, not only did friends terrify friends and citizens
their fellow-citizens whom they had encountered, but they
attacked one another, and were with difficulty disentangled.
The greater number of those who were pursued and killed
perished by throwing themselves from the cliffs; for the
descent from Epipolae is by a narrow path. The fugitives

who reached the level ground, especially those who had served in the former army and knew the neighbourhood, mostly escaped to the camp. But of the newly-arrived many missed their way, and, wandering about until daybreak, were then cut off by the Syracusan cavalry who were scouring the country.

45   On the following day the Syracusans erected two *Syracusans erect two* trophies, one on Epipolae at the *trophies. More arms* summit of the ascent, the other at the *than dead taken.* spot where the Boeotians made the first stand. The Athenians received their dead under a flag of truce. A considerable number of them and of their allies had fallen; there were however more arms taken than there were bodies of the slain; for those who were compelled to leap from the heights, whether they perished or not, had thrown away their shields.

46   The confidence of the Syracusans was restored by their *Encouraged by their* unexpected success, and they sent *success the Syracusans* Sicanus with fifteen ships to Agrigen- *seek for the third time* tum, then in a state of revolution, that *aid in Sicily. They make* he might win over the place if he *an attempt on Agri-* could. Gylippus had gone off again *gentum.* by land to collect a new army in the other parts of Sicily, hoping after the victory of Epipolae to carry the Athenian fortifications by storm.

47   Meanwhile the Athenian generals, troubled by their *Athenian council of* recent defeat and the utter discourage- *war. There is sickness* ment which prevailed in the army, held *in the camp and the* a council of war. They saw that their *soldiers are dispirited.* attempts all failed, and that the soldiers *Demosthenes votes for* were weary of remaining. For they *immediate departure.* were distressed by sickness, proceeding from two causes: the season of the year was that in which men are most liable to disease; and the place in which they were encamped was damp and unhealthy. And they felt that the situation was in every way hopeless. Demosthenes gave his voice against remaining; he said that the decisive

attack upon Epipolae had failed, and, in accordance with
his original intention, he should vote for immediate departure while the voyage was possible, and while, with the
help of the ships which had recently joined them, they had
the upper hand at any rate by sea.   It was more expedient
for the city that they should make war upon the Peloponnesians, who were raising a fort in Attica, than against the
Syracusans, whom they could now scarcely hope to conquer; and there was no sense in carrying on the siege at
a vast expense and with no result.   This was the opinion
of Demosthenes.

Nicias in his own mind took the same gloomy view of 48
their affairs; but he did not wish openly
to confess their weakness, or by a
public vote given in a numerous
assembly to let their intention reach
the enemy's ears, and so lose the
advantage of departing secretly whenever they might choose to go.   He had
moreover still some reason to suppose
that the Syracusans, of whose condition
he was better informed than the other
generals, were likely to be worse off
than themselves if they would only
persevere in the siege; they would be
worn out by the exhaustion of their resources; and now
the Athenians with their additional ships had much greater
command of the sea.—There was a party in Syracuse
itself which wanted to surrender the city to the Athenians,
and they kept sending messages to Nicias and advising
him not to depart.   Having this information he was still
wavering and considering, and had not made up his mind.
But in addressing the council he positively refused to
withdraw the army; he knew, he said, that the Athenian
people would not forgive their departure if they left without
an order from home.   The men upon whose votes their
fate would depend would not, like themselves, have seen

Nicias, who is partly swayed by information from Syracuse, is in his own mind undecided. But in public he refuses to go. They will be censured at home, and even accused of treason by their own soldiers. Better to die at the hands of enemies than of friends. And the Syracusans, in debt and dependent on mercenaries, are worse off than themselves.

with their own eyes the state of affairs; they would only have heard the criticisms of others, and would be convinced by any accusations which a clever speaker might bring forward [a]. Indeed many or most of the very soldiers who were now crying out that their case was desperate would raise the opposite cry when they reached home, and would say that the generals were traitors, and had been bribed to depart; and therefore he, knowing the tempers of the Athenians, [b] would for his own part rather take his chance and fall, if he must, alone by the hands of the enemy, than die [b] unjustly on a dishonourable charge at the hands of the Athenians. And, after all, the Syracusans were in a condition worse than their own; for they had to maintain mercenary troops; they were spending money on garrisons, and had now kept up a large navy for a whole year; already in great difficulties, they would soon be in greater; they had expended two thousand talents [c], and were heavily in arrear; and if by a failure in the pay they suffer any diminution of their present forces their affairs would be ruined. For they depended on mercenaries, who, unlike the Athenian allies, were under no compulsion to serve. Therefore, he said, they ought to persevere in the siege, and not go away [d] disheartened by the greatness of the expense, for they were far richer than the enemy [d].

49   Nicias spoke thus decidedly because he knew exactly how matters stood in Syracuse; he was aware of their want of money, and of the secret existence of that party within the walls which wished well to the Athenians, and was continually sending word to him not to depart; and the confidence in his navy, if not in his army, which now possessed him

Demosthenes and Eurymedon at first insist that the expedition shall leave Syracuse and encamp elsewhere, but they afterwards hesitate, believing that Nicias has some secret reason for remaining.

---

[a] Cp. iii. 38 med.   [b] Or, 'would for his own part rather take his chance, and fall, if he must, by the hands of the enemy, like any private soldier, than die.'   [c] £40,000.   [d] Or, 'disheartened at the idea of the enemy's riches; for they were far richer themselves.'

was greater than ever.   But Demosthenes would not hear
for an instant of persisting in the siege ; if, he said, the
army must remain and ought not to be removed without
a vote of the assembly, then they should retire to Thapsus
or Catana, whence they might overrun the whole country
with their land-forces, maintaining themselves at the
expense of the enemy and doing him great damage.   They
would thus fight their battles, not cooped up in the harbour,
which gave an advantage to the enemy, but in the open
sea, where their skill would be available and their charges
and retreats would not be circumscribed by the narrow
space which now hampered their movements whenever
they had to put in or out.   In a word, he wholly disapproved of the Athenians continuing in their present
position ; they should with all speed break up the siege
and be gone.   Eurymedon took the same side.   Still
Nicias resisted ; there was delay and hesitation, and
a suspicion that he might have some ground which they
did not know for his unwillingness to yield.   And so the
Athenians stayed on where they were.

Meanwhile Gylippus and Sicanus returned to Syracuse. 50
Sicanus had not succeeded in his
design upon Agrigentum ; for while he *Gylippus returns with*
was at Gela on his way the party in- *reinforcements. Failure*
clined to friendship with the Syracusans *of Syracusan design on*
had been driven out.   But Gylippus *Agrigentum. Adven-*
brought back a large army, together *tures of Peloponnesian*
with the hoplites who had been sent in *ships on their way to*
merchant-vessels from Peloponnesus *Sicily. The Syracusans*
in the spring[a], and had come by way *prepare a new attack.*
of Libya to Selinus.   They had been *The Athenian generals*
driven to Libya by stress of weather, *now agree to depart,*
and the Cyrenaeans had given them two triremes and *when the moon is eclipsed. The soldiers and Nicias refuse to stir.*
pilots.   On their voyage they had made common cause
with the Evesperitae, who were besieged by the Libyans.

----

[b] Cp. vii. 19.

After defeating the Libyans they sailed on to Neapolis, a Carthaginian factory which is the nearest point to Sicily, the passage taking two days and a night only; thence they crossed and came to Selinus. On their arrival, the Syracusans immediately prepared to renew their attack upon the Athenians, both by land and sea. And the Athenian generals, seeing that their enemy had been reinforced by a new army, and that their own affairs, instead of improving, were daily growing worse in every respect, and being especially troubled by the sickness of their troops, repented that they had not gone before. Even Nicias now no longer objected, but only made the condition that there should be no open voting. So, maintaining such secrecy as they could, they gave orders for the departure of the expedition; the men were to prepare themselves against a given signal. The preparations were made and they were on the point of sailing, when the moon, being just then at the full, was eclipsed. The mass of the army was greatly moved, and called upon the generals to remain. Nicias himself, who was too much under the influence of divination and such like, refused even to discuss the question of their removal until they had remained thrice nine days, as the soothsayers prescribed. This was the reason why the departure of the Athenians was finally delayed.

51   And now the Syracusans, having heard what had
The Syracusans de- happened, were more eager than ever
termine not to let their to prosecute the war to the end; they
enemies go. They again saw in the intention of the Athenians
attack the Athenians to depart a confession that they were
and drive a small party no longer superior to themselves, either
of them within their
lines. by sea or land; and they did not want
them to settle down in some other part of Sicily where they would be more difficult to manage, but sought to compel them forthwith to fight at sea under the disadvantages of their present position. So they manned their ships and exercised for as many days as they thought

sufficient. When the time came they began by attacking
the Athenian lines. A small number both of the hoplites
and of the cavalry came out of some of the gates to meet
them ; they cut off however a portion of the hoplites, and,
putting the main body to flight, drove them within their
walls. The entrance was narrow, and the Athenians lost
seventy horses and a few infantry.

The Syracusan army then retired. On the morrow their 52
ships, in number seventy-six, sailed
forth, and at the same time their land- *Third sea-fight in*
forces marched against the walls. The *the harbour. Euryme-*
Athenians on their side put out with *don is cut off and the*
Athenians are defeated.
eighty-six ships ; and the two fleets met and fought.
Eurymedon, who commanded the right wing of the
Athenians, hoping to surround the enemy, extended his
line too far towards the land, and was defeated by the
Syracusans, who, after overcoming the Athenian centre,
cooped him up in the inner bay of the harbour. There he
was slain, and the vessels which were under his command
and had followed him were destroyed. The Syracusans
now pursued and began to drive ashore the rest of the
Athenian fleet.

Gylippus, observing the discomfiture of the enemy, who 53
were being defeated and driven to land
beyond their own palisade and the *The defeat is partially*
lines of their camp, hastened with a *compensated by an ad-*
part of his army to the causeway which *vantage which the Tyr-*
rhenians and Athen-
ran along the harbour, intending to *ians gain over Gylip-*
kill all who landed, and to assist the *pus near the marsh.*
Syracusans in capturing the ships, *A Syracusan fireship*
fails.
which could be more easily towed away if the shore was
in the hands of their friends. The Tyrrhenians, who
guarded this part of the Athenian lines, seeing Gylippus
and his forces advance in disorder, rushed out, and
attacking the foremost put them to flight, and drove them
into the marsh called Lysimelea. But soon the Syracusans and their allies came up in greater numbers. The

Athenians in fear for their ships advanced to the support of the Tyrrhenians, and joined in the engagement; the Syracusans were overcome and pursued, and a few of their heavy-armed slain.   Most of the Athenian ships were saved and brought back to the Athenian station.   Still the Syracusans and their allies took eighteen, and killed the whole of their crews.   Then, hoping to burn the remainder of the fleet, they procured an old merchant-vessel, which they filled with faggots and brands; these they lighted, and as the wind blew right upon the enemy they let the ship go. The Athenians, alarmed for the safety of their fleet, contrived means by which they extinguished their flames, and succeeded in keeping the fireship at a distance.   Thus the danger was averted.

54   The Syracusans now raised a trophy of their naval victory, and another marking their interception of the hoplites on the higher ground close to the wall at the place where they took the horses.

The Syracusans raise two trophies; the Athenians also raise a trophy.

The Athenians raised a trophy of the victory over the land-forces whom the Tyrrhenians drove into the marsh, and another of that which they had themselves gained with the rest of the army.

55   The Syracusans, who up to this time had been afraid of the reinforcements of Demosthenes, had now gained a brilliant success by sea as well as by land; the Athenians were in utter despair.   Great was their surprise at the result, and still greater

The Athenians in despair; they had never before contended with a democratic and populous city like their own.

their regret that they had ever come.   The Sicilian were the only cities which they had ever encountered similar in character to their own [a], having the same democratic institutions and strong in ships, cavalry, and population, They were not able by holding out the prospect of a change of government to introduce an element of discord

---

[a] Cp. viii. 96 fin

among them which might have gained them over [a], nor could they master them [b] by a [b] decided superiority of force. They had failed at almost every point, and were already in great straits, when the defeat at sea, which they could not have thought possible, reduced their fortunes to a still lower ebb.

The Syracusans at once sailed round the shore of the 56 harbour without fear, and determined to close the mouth, that the Athenians might not be able, even if they wanted, to sail out by stealth. For they were now striving, no longer to achieve their

The Syracusans prepare to close the mouth of the harbour. They aspire to take the lead in the liberation of Hellas.

own deliverance, but to cut off the escape of the Athenians; they considered their position already far superior, as indeed it was, and they hoped that if they could conquer the Athenians and their allies by sea and land, their success would be glorious in the eyes of all the Hellenes, who would at once be set free, some from slavery, others from fear. For the Athenians, having lost so much of their power, would never be able to face the enemies who would rise up against them. And the glory of the deliverance would be ascribed to the Syracusans, who would be honoured by all living men and all future ages. [c] The conflict was still further ennobled by the thought that they were now conquering [c], not only the Athenians, but a host of their allies. And they themselves were not alone, but many had come to their support; they were taking the command in a war by the side of Corinth and Lacedaemon; they had offered their own city to bear the brunt of the encounter, and they had made an immense advance in naval power. More nations met at Syracuse than ever gathered around any single city, although not so many as

---

[a] Cp. vi. 20 init.   [b] Or, 'by their.'   [c] Or, taking the words as a reflection, not of the Syracusans, but of Thucydides himself: ' And indeed there was everything to ennoble the conflict; for they were now conquering ' etc.

the whole number of nations enrolled in this war under the Athenians and Lacedaemonians.

57   I will now enumerate the various peoples who came to

Athenian allies. Sicily as friends or enemies, to share either in the conquest or in the defence of the country, and who fought before Syracuse [a], choosing their side, not so much from a sense of right, or from obligations of kinship, as from the accident of compulsion or of their own interest.

The Athenians themselves, who were Ionians, went of

(A) In Hellas proper. their own free will against the Syracusans, who were Dorians ; they were followed by the Lemnians and Imbrians [b] and the then

(i) Their own settlers. inhabitants of Aegina [c], and by the Hestiaeans dwelling at Hestiaea in Euboea [d] : all these were their own colonists, speaking the same language with them, and retaining the same institutions.

Of the rest who joined in the expedition, some were

(ii) Subjects, mostly subjects, others independent allies,
tributaries, who were some again mercenaries. Of the sub-
(1) Ionians. jects and tributaries, the Eretrians, Chalcidians, Styreans, and Carystians came from Euboea; the Ceans, Andrians, and Tenians from the islands ; the Milesians, Samians, and Chians from Ionia. Of these however the Chians [e] were independent, and instead of paying tribute, provided ships. All or nearly all were Ionians and descendants of the Athenians, with the exception of the Carystians, who are Dryopes. They were subjects and constrained to follow, but still they were Ionians fighting against Dorians. There were also

(2) Aeolians partly Aeolians, namely, the Methymnaeans [f],
subjects. who furnished ships but were not tributaries, and the Tenedians and Aenians, who paid

---

[a] Adopting the conjecture Συρακούσαις.   [b] Cp. iv. 28, n.
[c] Cp. ii. 27 med.   [d] Cp. i. 115 fin.   [e] Cp. vi. 85 med.   [f] Cp. iii. 50 med. ; vi. 85 med.

tribute. These Aeolians were compelled to fight against their Aeolian founders, the Boeotians, who formed part of the Syracusan army. The Plataeans were the only Boeotians opposed to Boeotians, a natural result of mutual hatred. The Rhodians and Cytherians were both Dorians; the Cytherians, although   *(3) Dorians, kindred* Lacedaemonian colonists, bore arms in   *against kindred.* the Athenian cause against the Lacedaemonians who came with Gylippus; and the Rhodians, though by descent Argive, were compelled to fight against the Syracusans, who were Dorians, and against the Geloans, who were actually their own colony[a], and were taking part with Syracuse. Of the islanders around Peloponnesus, the   *(iii) Allies called in-* Cephallenians and Zacynthians were   *dependent, who were* independent[b]; still, being islanders,   *really compelled: either* they followed under a certain degree   *(1) islanders, or (2)* of constraint; for the Athenians were   *cities having special* masters of the sea. The Corcyraeans, who were not only Dorians but actually Corinthians, were serving against Corinthians and Syracusans, although they were the colonists of the one and the kinsmen of the other; they followed under a decent appearance of compulsion, but quite readily, because they hated the Corinthians[c]. The Messenians too, as the inhabitants of Naupactus were now called, including the garrison of Pylos, which was at that time held by the Athenians, were taken by them to the war. A few Megarians[d], having the misfortune to be exiles, were thus induced to fight against the Selinuntians, who were Megarians like themselves[e].

The service of the remaining allies was voluntary. The Argives[f], not so much because they   *(iv) Voluntary allies.* were allies of Athens, as owing to their hatred of the Lacedaemonians, and the desire of each man

---

[a] Cp. vi. 4 med.   [b] Cp. ii. 7 fin.; vi. 85 med.   [c] Cp. i. 25 med.   [d] Cp. iv. 74; vi. 43 fin.   [e] Cp. vi. 4 init.
[f] Cp. vi. 43.

among them to better himself at the time, followed the
Athenians, who were Ionians, being themselves Dorians,
to fight against Dorians. The Mantineans and other
Arcadians were mercenaries accustomed to attack any
enemy who from time to time might be pointed out to
them, and were now ready, if they were paid, to regard the
Arcadians, who were in the service of the Corinthians [a],
as their enemies. The Cretans and Aetolians also served
for hire; the Cretans, who had once joined with the
Rhodians in the foundation of Gela [b], came with reluctance; nevertheless for pay they consented to fight against
their own colonists. Some of the Acarnanians came to
aid their Athenian allies, partly from motives of gain, but
much more out of regard for Demosthenes [c] and good-will
to Athens. All these dwelt on the eastern side of the
Ionian Gulf.

Of the Hellenes in Italy, the Thurians and Metapontians,

(B) Allies in Italy and Sicily, including barbarians. constrained by the necessities of a revolutionary period, joined in the enterprise; of the Hellenes in Sicily,
the Naxians and Catanaeans. Of Barbarians, there were
the Egestaeans, who invited the expedition, and the greater
part of the Sicels, and, besides native Sicilians, certain
Tyrrhenians [d] who had a quarrel with the Syracusans;
also Iapygians [e], who served for hire. These were the
nations who followed the Athenians.

58   The Syracusans, on the other hand, were assisted by

Syracusan allies (i) Inhabitants of Sicily, (1) from the southern, (2) from the northern district. the Camarinaeans, who were their nearest neighbours, and by the Geloans, who dwelt next beyond them; and then (for the Agrigentines, who came next, were neutral) by the still more distant
Selinuntians. All these inhabited the region of Sicily
which lies towards Libya. On the side looking towards

---

[a] Cp. vii. 19 fin.   [b] Cp. vi. 4 med.   [c] Cp. iii. 105 foll. ; vii. 31 fin.
[d] Cp. vi. 103 med.   [e] Cp. vii. 33 med.

the Tyrrhenian Gulf the Himeraeans, the only Hellenic
people in those parts, were also their only allies. These
were the Hellenic peoples in Sicily who fought on the side
of the Syracusans ; they were Dorians and independent.
As for Barbarians, they had only such of the Sicels as had
not gone over to the Athenians.

Of Hellenes who were not inhabitants of Sicily, the
Lacedaemonians provided a Spartan *(ii) Inhabitants of*
general ; the Lacedaemonian forces *Hellas Proper.*
were all Neodamodes and Helots. (The meaning of the
word Neodamode is freedman.) The Corinthians were
the only power which furnished both sea and land forces.
Their Leucadian and Ambraciot kinsmen accompanied
them ; from Arcadia came mercenaries sent by Corinth ;
there were also Sicyonians who served under compulsion [a] ;
and of the peoples beyond the Peloponnese, some Boeotians.—This external aid however was small compared
with the numerous troops of all kinds which the Sicilian
Greeks themselves supplied ; for they dwelt in great cities,
and had mustered many ships and horses and hoplites,
besides a vast multitude of other troops. And again, the
proportion furnished by the Syracusans themselves was
greater than that of all the rest put together ; their city
was the largest, and they were in the greatest danger.

Such were the allies who were assembled on both sides. 59
At that time they were all on the spot,
and nothing whatever came afterwards *These were all.*
to either army.

The Syracusans and the allies naturally thought that
the struggle would be brought to a *The Syracusans begin*
glorious end if, after having defeated *to close the harbour.*
the Athenian fleet, they took captive the whole of their
great armament, and did not allow them to escape either
by sea or land. So they at once began to close the mouth
of the Great Harbour, which was about a mile wide, by

[c] Cp. v. 81 med. ; vi. 19 fin.

means of triremes, merchant-vessels, and small boats, placed broadside, which they moored there. They also made every preparation for a naval engagement, should the Athenians be willing to hazard another; and all their thoughts were on a grand scale.

60   The Athenians, seeing the closing of the harbour and *The Athenians pre-* inferring the intentions of the enemy, *pare for a last struggle.* proceeded to hold a council. The *They withdraw from* generals and officers met and con- *the higher ground, and* sidered the difficulties of their position. *determine to fight their* *way out by sea, or if* The most pressing of all was the want *defeated, by land.* of food. For they had already sent to Catana, when they intended to depart, and stopped the supplies for the present; and they could get no more in the future unless they recovered the command of the sea. They resolved therefore to quit their lines on the higher ground and to cut off by a cross-wall a space close to their ships, no greater than was absolutely required for their baggage and for their sick; after leaving a guard there they meant to put on board every other man, and to launch all their ships, whether fit for service or not; they would then fight a decisive battle, and, if they conquered, go to Catana; but if not, they would burn their ships, and retreat by land in good order, taking the nearest way to some friendly country, Barbarian or Hellenic. This design they proceeded to execute, and withdrawing quietly from the upper walls manned their whole fleet, compelling every man of any age at all suitable for service to embark. The entire number of the ships which they manned was about a hundred and ten. They put on board numerous archers and javelin-men, Acarnanians, and other foreigners, and made such preparations for action as their difficult *Nicias, seeing the de-* situation and the nature of their plan *jection of his soldiers,* allowed. When all was nearly ready, *strives to encourage* Nicias, perceiving that his men were *them.* depressed by their severe defeat at sea, which was so new an experience to them, while at the

same time the want of provisions made them impatient
to risk a battle with the least possible delay, called the
whole army together, and before they engaged exhorted
them as follows :—

'Soldiers of Athens and of our allies, we have all the 61
same interest in the coming struggle [a] ;

If we win we may see our homes once more. We are not mere tyros, and ought not to be cast down by reverses.

every one of us as well as of our
enemies will now have to fight for his
life and for his country, and if only we
can win in the impending sea-fight,
every one may see his native city and his own home once
more. But we must not be faint-hearted, nor behave as if we
were mere novices in the art of war, who when defeated in
their first battle are full of cowardly apprehensions and
continually retain the impress of their disaster. You,
Athenians, have had great military experience ; and you,
allies, are always fighting at our side. Remember the
sudden turns of war ; let your hope be that fortune herself
may yet come over to us ; and prepare to retrieve your
defeat in a manner worthy of the greatness of your own
army which you see before you [b].

'We have consulted the pilots about any improvements 62
which seemed likely to avail against

We are going to fight a land-battle at sea ; and have new devices suggested by our recent experience.

the crowding of ships in the narrow
harbour, as well as against the force
on the enemy's decks, which in previous engagements did us so much
harm, and we have adopted them as far as we had the
means. Many archers and javelin-men will embark, and
a great number of other troops, whom if we were going
to fight in the open sea we should not employ because
they increase the weight of the ships, and therefore impede
our skill ; but here, where we are obliged to fight a land-
battle on ship-board [c], they will be useful. We have

---

[a] Cp. vi. 68 init.   [b] Cp. vi. 68 init. ; vii. 77 med.

[c] Cp. i. 49 init.

thought of all the changes which are necessary in the construction of our ships, and in order to counteract the thickness of the beams on the enemy's prows, for this did us more mischief than anything else, we have provided iron grapnels, which will prevent any ship striking us from getting off if the marines are quick and do their duty. For, as I tell you, we are positively driven to fight a land-battle on ship-board, and our best plan is neither to back water ourselves nor to allow the enemy to back water after we have once closed with him. Recollect that the shore, except so far as our land-forces extend, is in their hands.

63   'Knowing all this, you must fight to the last with all

To the soldiers I say: When once engaged you must not separate until you have swept the enemy's decks. To the sailors: You have more and better ships. To the allies: Remember the glory and the advantages of your connexion with Athens. Show that your weakness is more than another's strength.

your strength, and not be driven ashore. When ship strikes ship, refuse to separate until you have swept the enemy's heavy-armed from their decks. I am speaking to the hoplites rather than to the sailors; for this is the special duty of the men on deck. We may still reckon on the superiority of our infantry. The sailors I would exhort, nay I would implore them, not to be paralysed by their disasters; for they will find the arrangements on deck improved, and the numbers of the fleet increased. Some among you have long been deemed Athenians, though they are not; and to them I say, Consider how precious is that privilege, and how worthy to be defended. You were admired in Hellas because you spoke our language and adopted our manners, and you shared equally with ourselves in the substantial advantages of our empire, while you gained even more than we by the dread which you inspired in subject-states and in your security against wrong. You alone have been free partners in that empire; you ought not to betray it now. And so, despising the Corinthians whom you have beaten again and again, and the Sicilians who never dared to withstand us when our fleet was in its prime, repel your enemies, and show that your skill even amid weakness and disaster is superior to the strength of another in the hour of his success.

'Let me appeal once more to you who are Athenians, 64 and remind you that there are no more ships like these in the dockyards of the Piraeus, and that you have no more young men fit for service. In any event but victory your enemies here will instantly sail against Athens, *And you, Athenians, must not forget that the safety of your friends at home is at stake; and that the greatness and glory of Athens is all in your hands.* while our countrymen at home, who are but a remnant, will be unable to defend themselves against the attacks of their former foes reinforced by the new invaders. You who are in Sicily will instantly fall into the hands of the Syracusans (and you know how you meant to deal with them), and your friends at Athens into the hands of the Lacedaemonians. In this one struggle you have to fight for yourselves and them. Stand firm therefore now, if ever, and remember one and all of you who are embarking that you are both the fleet and army of your country, and that on you hangs the whole state and the great name of Athens: for her sake if any man exceed another in skill or courage let him display them now; he will never have a better opportunity of doing good to himself and saving his country.'

Nicias, as soon as he had done speaking, gave orders 65 to man the ships. Gylippus and the Syracusans could see clearly enough from the preparations which the Athenians were making that they were going to fight. But they had also *The Syracusans meet the Athenian improvements with counter-improvements. Gylippus exhorts them.* previous notice, and had been told of the iron grapnels; and they took precautions against this as against all the other devices of the Athenians. They covered the prows of their vessels with hides, extending a good way along the upper part of their sides, so that the grapnels might

slip and find no hold.   When all was ready, Gylippus and
the other generals exhorted their men in the following
words :—

66   ' That our actions so far have been glorious, and that

*Our past victories are
a pledge of our future
success, as the defeats of
the enemy in former
engagements are omin-
ous of a defeat in this.
They came hither to
enslave us with their
navy, but now the power
of the sea has departed
from them to us.*

in the coming conflict we shall be
fighting for a glorious prize, most of
you, Syracusans and allies, seem to be
aware : what else would have inspired
you with so much energy ?   But if any
one has failed to understand our position, we will enlighten him.   The
Athenians came hither intending to
enslave first of all Sicily, and then, if
they succeeded, Peloponnesus and the rest of Hellas, they
having already the largest dominion of any Hellenic power,
past or present.   But you set mankind the example of
withstanding that invincible navy ; which you have now
defeated in several engagements at sea, and which you
will probably defeat in this.   For when men are crippled
in what they assume to be their strength, any vestige of
self-respect is more completely lost than if they had never
believed in themselves at all.   When once their pride has
had a fall they throw away the power of resistance which
they might still exert.   And this we may assume to be the
condition of the Athenians.

67   ' Far otherwise is it with us.   The natural courage, which

*Success infuses cour-
age.   Their new inven-
tions are bad imitations
of ours, which they can-
not use.   Their ships
are weighed down with
fighting-men.   They are
simply desperate.*

even in the days of our inexperience
dared to risk all, is now better assured,
and when we have the further conviction
that he is the strongest who has overcome the strongest, the hopes of every
one are redoubled.   And in all enterprises the highest hopes infuse the
greatest courage.   Their imitation of our modes of fighting
will be useless to them.   To us they come naturally, and
we shall readily adapt ourselves to any arrangements of
ours which they have borrowed.   But to them the em-

ployment of troops on deck is a novelty; they will be
encumbered with crowds of hoplites and crowds of javelin-
men, Acarnanians and others, who are mere awkward
landsmen put into a ship, and will not even know how to
discharge their darts when they are required to keep their
places. Will they not make the ships unsteady? And
their own movements will be so unnatural to them that
they will all fall into utter confusion. The greater number
of the enemy's ships will be the reverse of an advantage to
him, should any of you fear your inequality in that respect;
for a large fleet confined in a small space will be hampered
in action and far more likely to suffer from our devices.
And I would have you know what I believe on the best
authority to be the simple truth. .Their misfortunes paralyse
them, and they are driven to despair at finding themselves helpless. They have grown reckless, and have
no confidence in their own plans. They will take
their chance as best they can, and either force a way
out to sea, or in the last resort retreat by land; for
they know that they cannot in any case be worse off
than they are.

'Against such disorder, and against hateful enemies 68
whose good fortune has run away from *Now is the time for*
them to us, let us advance with fury. *revenge, which is the*
We should remember in the first place *sweetest of all things.*
Safety we have already.
that men are doing a most lawful act *Let us do to them as*
when they take vengeance upon an *they would have done*
to us. We may gain
enemy and an aggressor, and that they *everything, and cannot*
have a right to satiate their heart's *lose much.*
animosity; secondly, that this vengeance, which is proverbially the sweetest of all things, will soon be within
our grasp. I need not tell you that they are our enemies,
and our worst enemies. They came against our land that
they might enslave us, and if they had succeeded they
would have inflicted the greatest sufferings on our men,
and the worst indignities upon our wives and children,
and would have stamped a name of dishonour upon our

whole city. Wherefore let no one's heart be softened towards them. Do not congratulate yourselves at the mere prospect of getting safely rid of them. Even if they conquer they can only depart. But supposing that we obtain, as we most likely shall, the fulness of our desires, in the punishment of the Athenians and in the confirmation to Sicily of the liberties which she now enjoys, how glorious will be our prize! Seldom are men exposed to hazards in which they lose little if they fail, and win all if they succeed.'

69   When Gylippus and the other Syracusan generals had,

The peril comes nearer and nearer, and Nicias once more repeats to the trierarchs the old tale of freedom and country, wives and children, and their fathers' Gods. They then go on board.

like Nicias, encouraged their troops, perceiving the Athenians to be manning their ships, they presently did the same. Nicias, overwhelmed by the situation, and seeing how great and how near the peril was (for the ships were on the very point of rowing out), feeling too, as men do on the eve of a great struggle, that all which he had done was nothing, and that he had not said half enough, again addressed the trierarchs, and calling each of them by his father's name, and his own name, and the name of his tribe, he entreated those who had made any reputation for themselves not to be false to it, and those whose ancestors were eminent not to tarnish their hereditary fame. He reminded them that they were the inhabitants of the freest country in the world, and how in Athens there was no interference with the daily life of any man[a]. He spoke to them of their wives and children and their fathers' Gods, as men will at such a time; for then they do not care whether their common-place phrases seem to be out of date or not, but loudly reiterate the old appeals, believing that they may be of some service at the awful moment. When he thought that he had exhorted them, not enough, but as much as the scanty time allowed, he retired, and led

---

[a] Cp. ii. 37.

the land-forces to the shore, extending the line as far as he could, so that they might be of the greatest use in encouraging the combatants on board ship. Demosthenes, Menander, and Euthydemus, who had gone on board the Athenian fleet to take the command, now quitted their own station, and proceeded straight to the closed mouth of the harbour, intending to force their way to the open sea where a passage was still left.

The Syracusans and their allies had already put out 70 with nearly the same number of ships as before. A detachment of them guarded the entrance of the harbour; the remainder were disposed all round it in such a manner that they might fall on the Athenians from every side at once, and that their land-forces might at the same time be able to co-operate wherever the ships retreated to the shore. Sicanus and Agatharchus commanded the Syracusan fleet, each of them a wing; Pythen and the Corinthians occupied the centre. When the Athenians approached the closed mouth

Disposition of the Syracusan fleet. The Athenians rush to the mouth of the harbour. The Syracusans bear down upon them. Fury and disorder of the conflict. Manœuvres of pilots, courage of the marines, crash of vessels, shouts of boatswains, the Athenians fighting for life, the Syracusans for glory. Will they find a home among their foes? Will they fly from the fliers?

of the harbour the violence of their onset overpowered the ships which were stationed there; they then attempted to loosen the fastenings. Whereupon from all sides the Syracusans and their allies came bearing down upon them, and the conflict was no longer confined to the entrance, but extended throughout the harbour. No previous engagement had been so fierce and obstinate. Great was the eagerness with which the rowers on both sides rushed upon their enemies whenever the word of command was given; and keen was the contest between the pilots as they manœuvred one against another. The marines too were full of anxiety that, when ship struck ship, the service on deck should not fall short of the rest; every one in the place assigned to him was eager to be

foremost among his fellows.   Many vessels meeting—and
never did so many fight in so small a space, for the two
fleets together amounted to nearly two hundred—they
were seldom able to strike in the regular manner, because
they had no opportunity of first retiring or breaking the
line ; they generally fouled one another as ship dashed
against ship in the hurry of flight or pursuit.   All the
time that another vessel was bearing down, the men on
deck poured showers of javelins and arrows and stones
upon the enemy ; and when the two closed, the marines
fought hand to hand, and endeavoured to board.   In many
places, owing to the want of room, they who had struck
another found that they were struck themselves ; often
two or even more vessels were unavoidably entangled
about one, and the pilots had to make plans of attack and
defence, not against one adversary only, but against several
coming from different sides.   The crash of so many ships
dashing against one another took away the wits of the
crews, and made it impossible to hear the boatswains,
whose voices in both fleets rose high, as they gave directions to the rowers, or cheered them on in the excitement
of the struggle.   On the Athenian side they were shouting
to their men that they must force a passage and seize the
opportunity now or never of returning in safety to their
native land.   To the Syracusans and their allies was
represented the glory of preventing the escape of their
enemies, and of a victory by which every man would exalt
the honour of his own city.   The commanders too, when
they saw any ship backing without necessity, would call
the captain by his name, and ask, of the Athenians,
whether they were retreating because they expected to
be more at home upon the land of their bitterest foes
than upon that sea [a] which had been their own so long [a] ;
on the Syracusan side, whether, when they knew per-

---

[a] Or, reading πόνου after ὀλίγου : 'which by the labour of years they
had made their own.'

fectly well that the Athenians were only eager to find
some means of flight, they would themselves fly from the
fugitives.

While the naval engagement hung in the balance the 71
two armies on shore had great trial and
conflict of soul. The Sicilian soldier
was animated by the hope of increasing
the glory which he had already won,
while the invader was tormented by
the fear that his fortunes might sink
lower still. The last chance of the
Athenians lay in their ships, and their
anxiety was dreadful. The fortune of
the battle varied; and it was not possible that the spectators on the shore

*Fearful anxiety of the
men drawn up on shore,
especially when the
battle wavers. They
accompany the conflict
with cries and move-
ments of the body. At
length the Athenians
are driven ashore. The
army seeing the ships
lost know themselves to
be lost, like the Lace-
daemonians at Pylos.*

should all receive the same impression of it. Being quite
close and having different points of view, they would some
of them see their own ships victorious; their courage
would then revive, and they would earnestly call upon the
Gods not to take from them their hope of deliverance.
But others, who saw their ships worsted, cried and shrieked
aloud, and were by the sight alone more utterly unnerved
than the defeated combatants themselves. Others again,
who had fixed their gaze on some part of the struggle
which was undecided, were in a state of excitement still
more terrible; they kept swaying their bodies to and fro in
an agony of hope and fear as the stubborn conflict went on
and on; for at every instant they were all but saved or all
but lost. And while the strife hung in the balance you
might hear in the Athenian army at once lamentation,
shouting, cries of victory or defeat, and all the various
sounds which are wrung from a great host in extremity of
danger. Not less agonising were the feelings of those on
board. At length the Syracusans and their allies, after
a protracted struggle, put the Athenians to flight, and
triumphantly bearing down upon them, and encouraging
one another with loud cries and exhortations, drove them

to land.   Then that part of the navy which had not been taken in the deep water fell back in confusion to the shore, and the crews rushed out of the ships into the camp [a]. And the land-forces, no longer now divided in feeling, but uttering one universal groan of intolerable anguish, ran, some of them to save the ships, others to defend what remained of the wall; but the greater number began to look to themselves and to their own safety.   Never had there been a greater panic in an Athenian army than at that moment.   They now suffered what they had done to others at Pylos.   For at Pylos the Lacedaemonians, when they saw their ships destroyed, knew that their friends who had crossed over into the island of Sphacteria were lost with them [b].   And so now the Athenians, after the rout of their fleet, knew that they had no hope of saving themselves by land unless events took some extraordinary turn.

72   Thus, after a fierce battle and a great destruction of ships and men on both sides, the Syra-

Demosthenes desires to renew the conflict. But the sailors are paralysed and refuse to embark. So it is decided to depart by land.

cusans and their allies gained the victory.   They gathered up the wrecks and bodies of the dead, and sailing back to the city, erected a trophy. The Athenians, overwhelmed by their misery, never so much as thought of recovering their wrecks or of asking leave to collect their dead.   Their intention was to retreat that very night.   Demosthenes came to Nicias and proposed that they should once more man their remaining vessels and endeavour to force the passage at daybreak, saying that they had more ships fit for service than the enemy.   For the Athenian fleet still numbered sixty, but the enemy had less than fifty.   Nicias approved of his proposal, and they would have manned the ships, but the sailors refused to embark; for they were paralysed by their defeat, and had no longer any hope of

---

[a] Cp. vii. 41 init., 74 fin.   [b] Cp. iv. 14 init.

succeeding.   So the Athenians all made up their minds to escape by land.

Hermocrates the Syracusan suspected their intention, 73 and dreading what might happen if their vast army, retreating by land and settling somewhere in Sicily, should choose to renew the war, he went to the authorities, and represented to them that they ought not to allow the Athenians to withdraw by night (mentioning his own suspicion of their intentions), but that all the Syracusans and their *Hermocrates, antici-* *pating their design,* *wants the Syracusans,* *who were keeping holi-* *day, to intercept them,* *but, the magistrates* *declaring the thing im-* *possible, he persuades* *the Athenians them-* *selves to delay their* *march;* allies should go out in advance, wall up the roads, and occupy the passes with a guard.   They thought very much as he did, and wanted to carry out his plan, but doubted whether their men, who were too glad to repose after a great battle, and in time of festival—for there happened on that very day to be a sacrifice to Heracles—could be induced to obey.   Most of them, in the exultation of victory, were drinking and keeping holiday, and at such a time how could they ever be expected to take up arms and go forth at the order of the generals ?   On these grounds the authorities decided that the thing was impossible.   Whereupon Hermocrates himself, fearing lest the Athenians should gain a start and quietly pass the most difficult places in the night, contrived the following plan : when it was growing dark he sent certain of his own acquaintance, accompanied by a few horsemen, to the Athenian camp. They rode up within earshot, and pretending to be friends (there were known to be men in the city who gave information to Nicias of what went on)[a] called to some of the soldiers, and bade them tell him not to withdraw his army during the night, for the Syracusans were guarding the roads ; he should make preparation at leisure and retire by day.   Having delivered their message they departed,

---

[a] Cp. vii. 48 med.

and those who had heard them informed the Athenian generals.

74   On receiving this message, which they supposed to be genuine, they remained during the night. And having once given up the intention of starting immediately, they decided to remain during the next day, that the soldiers might, as well as they could, put together their baggage in the most convenient form, and depart, taking with them the bare necessaries of life, but nothing else.

Meanwhile the Syracusans and Gylippus, going forth *and so gives the Syra-* before them with their land-forces, *cusans time to block the* blocked the roads in the country by *roads.* which the Athenians were likely to pass, guarded the fords of the rivers and streams, and posted themselves at the best points for receiving and stopping them. Their sailors rowed up to the beach and dragged away the Athenian ships. The Athenians themselves had burnt a few of them, as they had intended [a], but the rest the Syracusans towed away, unmolested and at their leisure, from the places where they had severally run aground, and conveyed them to the city.

75   On the third day after the sea-fight, when Nicias and *Misery of the depar-* Demosthenes thought that their pre- *ture. There are sights* parations were complete, the army *of death everywhere;* began to move. They were in a *the sick and wounded* dreadful condition; not only was there *are left behind, cursing* the great fact that they had lost their *their comrades; the* whole fleet, and instead of their ex- *vast army is in tears;* pected triumph had brought the utmost *the sense of disgrace,* peril upon Athens as well as upon *the want of food, and* themselves, but also the sights which *the contrast between* presented themselves as they quitted *their arrival and their* the camp were painful to every eye and *departure, quite over-* mind. The dead were unburied, and *power them. Yet more* *overwhelming is the* *thought of the future.* when any one saw the body of a friend lying on the ground

---

[a] Inserting a comma after διενοήθησαν.

he was smitten with sorrow and dread, while the sick or
wounded who still survived but had to be left were even
a greater trial to the living, and more to be pitied than
those who were gone.   Their prayers and lamentations
drove their companions to distraction ; they would beg
that they might be taken with them, and call by name any
friend or relation whom they saw passing ; they would
hang upon their departing comrades and follow as far as
they could, and, when their limbs and strength failed them,
and they dropped behind, many were the imprecations and
cries which they uttered.   So that the whole army was in
tears, and such was their despair that they could hardly
make up their minds to stir, although they were leaving
an enemy's country, having suffered calamities too great
for tears already, and dreading miseries yet greater in the
unknown future.   There was also a general feeling of
shame and self-reproach,—indeed they seemed, not like
an army, but like the fugitive population of a city captured
after a siege ; and of a great city too.   For the whole
multitude who were marching together numbered not less
than forty thousand.   Each of them took with him anything he could carry which was likely to be of use.   Even
the heavy-armed and cavalry, contrary to their practice
when under arms, conveyed about their persons their own
food, some because they had no attendants, others because
they could not trust them ; for they had long been deserting, and most of them had gone off all at once.   Nor was
the food which they carried sufficient ; for the supplies of
the camp had failed.   Their disgrace and the universality
of the misery, although there might be some consolation
in the very community of suffering, were nevertheless at that
moment hard to bear, especially when they remembered
from what pride and splendour they had fallen into their
present low estate.   Never had an Hellenic army [a] experienced such a reverse.   They had come intending to

------

[a] Omitting τῷ.

enslave others, and they were going away in fear that they would be themselves enslaved. Instead of the prayers and hymns with which they had put to sea, they were now departing amid appeals to heaven of another sort. They were no longer sailors but landsmen, depending, not upon their fleet, but upon their infantry. Yet in face of the great danger which still threatened them all these things appeared endurable.

76   Nicias, seeing the army disheartened at their terrible fall, went along the ranks and encouraged and consoled them as well

Address of Nicias.

as he could. In his fervour he raised his voice as he passed from one to another and spoke louder and louder, desiring that the benefit of his words might reach as far as possible.

77   ' Even now, Athenians and allies, we must hope : men have been delivered out of worse straits

We have suffered more than we deserve ; and I as much as any one ; though my life has been blameless. But we may hope that the Gods will now take pity upon us. Look at your own numbers, and remember that there is nowhere a refuge for the coward, but everywhere for the brave. We must get to the Sicels at once, for we have no more food. While Athenians live, Athens lives.

than these, and I would not have you judge yourselves too severely on account either of the reverses which you have sustained or of your present undeserved miseries. I too am as weak as any of you ; for I am quite prostrated by my disease, as you see. And although there was a time when I might have been thought equal to the best of you in the happiness of my private and public life, I am now in as great danger, and as much at the mercy of fortune, as the meanest. Yet my days have been passed in the performance of many a religious duty, and of many a just and blameless action. Therefore my hope of the future is still courageous, [a] and our calamities do not appal me as they might [a]. Who knows

---

[a] Or, taking κατ' ἀξίαν closely with φοβοῦσι : ' and our calamities do not appal me, as if they were deserved ;' or, ' although our calamities, undeserved as they are, do certainly appal me.'

that they may not be lightened? For our enemies have
had their full share of success, and if we were under the
jealousy of any God when our fleet started [a], by this time
we have been punished enough. Others ere now have
attacked their neighbours; they have done as men will do,
and suffered what men can bear. We may therefore begin
to hope that the Gods will be more merciful to us; for we
now invite their pity rather than their jealousy. And look
at your own well-armed ranks; see how many brave soldiers you are, marching in solid array [b], and do not be
dismayed; bear in mind that wherever you plant yourselves you are a city already, and that no city in Sicily will
find it easy to resist your attack, or can dislodge you if you
choose to settle. Provide for the safety and good order of
your own march, and remember every one of you that on
whatever spot a man is compelled to fight, there if he conquer he may find a native land and a fortress. We must
press forward day and night, for our supplies are but
scanty. The Sicels through fear of the Syracusans still
adhere to us, and if we can only reach any part of their
territory we shall be among friends, and you may consider
yourselves secure. We have sent to them, and they have
been told to meet us and bring food. In a word, soldiers,
let me tell you that you must be brave; there is no place
near to which a coward can fly [c]. And if you now escape
your enemies, those of you who are not Athenians will see
once more the home for which they long, while you Athenians will again rear aloft the fallen greatness of Athens.
For men, and not walls or ships in which are no men,
constitute a state.'

Thus exhorting his troops Nicias passed through the 78
army, and wherever he saw gaps in the ranks or the men
dropping out of line, he brought them back to their proper
place. Demosthenes did the same for the troops under

---

[a] Cp. vii. 50 fin.   [b] Cp. vi. 68 init.; vii. 61 fin.
          [c] Cp. vi. 68 med. and fin.

his command, and gave them similar exhortations. The army marched disposed in a hollow oblong: the division of Nicias leading, and that of Demosthenes following; the hoplites enclosed within their ranks the baggage-bearers and the rest of the host. When they arrived at the ford of the river Anapus they found a force of the Syracusans and of their allies drawn up to meet them; these they put to flight, and getting command of the ford, proceeded on their march. The Syracusans continually harassed them, the cavalry riding alongside, and the light-armed troops hurling darts at them. On this day the Athenians proceeded about four and a half miles and encamped at a hill. On the next day they started early, and, having advanced more than two miles, descended into a level plain, and encamped. The country was inhabited, and they were desirous of obtaining food from the houses, and also water which they might carry with them, as there was little to be had for many miles in the country which lay before them. Meanwhile the Syracusans had gone forward, and at a point where the road ascends a steep hill called the Acraean height, and there is a precipitous ravine on either side, were blocking up the pass by a wall. On the next day the Athenians advanced, although again impeded by the numbers of the enemy's cavalry who rode alongside, and of their javelin-men who threw darts at them. For a long time the Athenians maintained the struggle, but at last retired to their own encampment. Their supplies were now cut off, because the horsemen circumscribed their movements.

The Athenians move on in two divisions, one under Nicias, and the other under Demosthenes. They succeed in passing the river Anapus, and proceed a few miles southward. The Syracusans overtake them and occupy a steep pass on their route.

79   In the morning they started early and resumed their march. They pressed onwards to the hill where the way was barred, and found in front of them the Syracusan infantry drawn up to defend the wall, in deep array, for

The Athenians make no impression on the Syracusan position.

the pass was narrow.   Whereupon the Athenians advanced and assaulted the barrier, but the enemy, who were numerous and had the advantage of position, threw missiles upon them from the hill, which was steep, and so, not being able to force their way, they again retired and rested. During the conflict, as is often the case in the fall of the year, there came on a storm of rain and thunder, whereby the Athenians were yet more disheartened, for they thought that everything was conspiring to their destruction [a].   While they were resting, Gylippus and the Syracusans despatched a division of their army to raise a wall behind them across the road by which they had come ; but the Athenians sent some of their own troops and frustrated their intention. They then retired with their whole army in the direction of the plain and passed the night.   On the following day they again advanced.   The Syracusans now surrounded and attacked them on every side, and wounded many of them.   If the Athenians advanced they retreated, but charged them when they retired, falling especially upon the hindermost of them, in the hope that, if they could put to flight a few at a time, they might strike a panic into the whole army.   In this fashion the Athenians struggled on for a long time, and having advanced about three-quarters of a mile rested in the plain. The Syracusans then left them and returned to their own encampment.

The army was now in a miserable plight, being in want *80* of every necessary ; and by the continual assaults of the enemy great numbers of the soldiers had been wounded. Nicias and Demosthenes, perceiving their condition, resolved during the night to light as many watch-fires as possible and to lead off their forces.

The condition of the Athenians grows worse and worse. At night they change their route and go towards the sea. A panic occurs. Nicias crosses the Cacyparis.

They intended to take another route and march towards

---

[a] Cp. vi. 70 init.

the sea in the direction opposite to that from which the Syracusans were watching them. Now their whole line of march lay, not towards Catana, but towards the other side of Sicily, in the direction of Camarina and Gela, and the cities, Hellenic or Barbarian, of that region. So they lighted numerous fires and departed in the night. And then, as constantly happens in armies [a], especially in very great ones, and as might be expected when they were marching by night in an enemy's country, and with the enemy from whom they were flying not far off, there arose a panic among them, and they fell into confusion. The army of Nicias, which was leading the way, kept together, and got on considerably in advance, but that of Demosthenes, which was the larger half, was severed from the other division, and marched in worse order. At daybreak, however, they succeeded in reaching the sea, and striking into the Helorine road marched along it, intending as soon as they arrived at the Cacyparis to follow up the course of the river through the interior of the island. They were expecting that the Sicels for whom they had sent would meet them on this road. When they had reached the river they found there also a guard of the Syracusans cutting off the passage by a wall and palisade. They forced their way through and, crossing the river, passed on towards another river which is called the Erineus, this being the direction in which their guides led them.

81   When daylight broke and the Syracusans and their allies

The Syracusans soon overtake the division of Demosthenes, which is surrounded by them. saw that the Athenians had departed, most of them thought that Gylippus had let them go on purpose, and were very angry with him. They easily found the line of their retreat, and quickly following, came up with them about the time of the midday meal. The troops of Demosthenes were last; they were marching

---

[a] Cp. iv. 125 init.

slowly and in disorder, not having recovered from the panic of the previous night, when they were overtaken by the Syracusans,who immediately fell upon them and fought. Separated as they were from the others, they were easily hemmed in by the Syracusan cavalry and driven into a narrow space. The division of Nicias was now as much as six miles in advance, for he marched faster, thinking that their safety depended at such a time, not in remaining and fighting, if they could avoid it, but in retreating as quickly as they could, and resisting only when they were positively compelled. Demosthenes, on the other hand, who had been more incessantly harassed throughout the retreat, because marching last he was first attacked by the enemy, now, when he saw the Syracusans pursuing him, instead of pressing onward, ranged his army in order of battle. Thus lingering he was surrounded, and he and the Athenians under his command were in the greatest confusion. For they were crushed into a walled en-closure, having a road on both sides and planted thickly with olive-trees, and missiles were hurled at them from all points. The Syracusans naturally preferred this mode of attack to a regular engagement. For to risk themselves against desperate men would have been only playing into the hands of the Athenians. Moreover, every one was sparing of his life ; their good fortune was already assured, and they did not want to fall in the hour of victory. Even by this irregular mode of fighting they thought that they could overpower and capture the Athenians.

And so when they had gone on all day assailing them 82 with missiles from every quarter, and saw that they were quite worn out with their wounds and all their other suffer-ings, Gylippus and the Syracusans made a proclamation, first of all to the islanders, that any of them who pleased might come over to them and have their freedom. But

The troops are worn out ; offers of freedom to the islanders gener-ally refused. But at last the whole force is driven to capitulate.

only a few cities accepted the offer. At length an agreement was made for the entire force under Demosthenes. Their arms were to be surrendered, but no one was to suffer death, either from violence or from imprisonment, or from want of the bare means of life. So they all surrendered, being in number six thousand, and gave up what money they had. This they threw into the hollows of shields and filled four. The captives were at once taken to the city. On the same day Nicias and his division reached the river Erineus, which he crossed, and halted his army on a rising ground.

83   On the following day he was overtaken by the Syracus-

Nicias being informed of the surrender of Demosthenes tries in vain to negotiate with Gylippus. He attempts to steal away by night, but fails. Three hundred escape in the darkness.

ans, who told him that Demosthenes had surrendered, and bade him do the same. He, not believing them, procured a truce while he sent a horseman to go and see. Upon the return of the horseman bringing assurance of the fact, he sent a herald to Gylippus and the Syracusans, saying that he would agree, on behalf of the Athenian state, to pay the expenses which the Syracusans had incurred in the war, on condition that they should let his army go; until the money was paid he would give Athenian citizens as hostages, a man for a talent. Gylippus and the Syracusans would not accept these proposals, but attacked and surrounded this division of the army as they had the other, and hurled missiles at them from every side until the evening. They too were grievously in want of food and necessaries. Nevertheless they meant to wait for the dead of the night and then to proceed. They were just resuming their arms, when the Syracusans discovered them and raised the Paean. The Athenians, perceiving that they were detected, laid down their arms again, with the exception of about three hundred men who broke through the enemy's guard, and made their escape in the darkness as best they could.

When the day dawned Nicias led forward his army, and **84**
the Syracusans and the allies again
assailed them on every side, hurling   *The troops of Nicias*
javelins and other missiles at them.   *hurry on to the river*
                                           Assinarus; they rush
The Athenians hurried on to the   *in pell-mell; they are*
river Assinarus.   They hoped to   *attacked by the enemy,*
                                           the water runs blood,
gain a little relief if they forded the   *and the living and dead*
river, for the mass of horsemen and   *are huddled together in*
other troops overwhelmed and crushed   *the stream.*
them; and they were worn out by fatigue and thirst.
But no sooner did they reach the water than they lost
all order and rushed in; every man was trying to cross
first, and, the enemy pressing upon them at the same
time, the passage of the river became hopeless.   Being
compelled to keep close together they fell one upon
another, and trampled each other under foot: some at
once perished, pierced by their own spears; others got
entangled in the baggage and were carried down the stream.
The Syracusans stood upon the further bank of the river,
which was steep, and hurled missiles from above on the
Athenians, who were huddled together in the deep bed of
the stream and for the most part were drinking greedily.
The Peloponnesians came down the bank and slaughtered
them, falling chiefly upon those who were in the river.
Whereupon the water at once became foul, but was drunk
all the same, although muddy and dyed with blood, and
the crowd fought for it.

At last, when the dead bodies were lying in heaps upon **85**
one another in the water and the army   *Nicias at last sur-*
was utterly undone, some perishing in   *renders to Gylippus.*
the river, and any who escaped being   *The three hundred are*
cut off by the cavalry, Nicias surren-   *brought in. Greatness*
                                             of the slaughter. Many
dered to Gylippus, in whom he had more   *prisoners become the*
confidence than in the Syracusans. He   *property of the soldiers,*
entreated him and the Lacedaemonians   *and many escape.*
to do what they pleased with himself, but not to go on killing the men.   So Gylippus gave the word to make

prisoners. Thereupon the survivors, not including however a large number whom the soldiers concealed, were
brought in alive. As for the three hundred who had
broken through the guard in the night, the Syracusans
sent in pursuit and seized them. The total of the public
prisoners when collected was not great; for many were
appropriated by the soldiers, and the whole of Sicily was
full of them, they not having capitulated like the troops
under Demosthenes. A large number also perished; the
slaughter at the river being very great, quite as great as
any which took place in the Sicilian war; and not a few
had fallen in the frequent attacks which were made upon
the Athenians during their march. Still many escaped,
some at the time, others ran away after an interval of
slavery, and all these found refuge at Catana.

86   The Syracusans and their allies collected their forces
and returned with the spoil, and as
many prisoners as they could take
with them, into the city. The captive
Athenians and allies they deposited in
the quarries, which they thought would
be the safest place of confinement. Nicias and Demosthenes they put to the sword, although against the will of
Gylippus. For Gylippus thought that to carry home with
him to Lacedaemon the generals of the enemy, over and
above all his other successes, would be a brilliant triumph.
One of them, Demosthenes, happened to be the greatest foe,
and the other the greatest friend of the Lacedaemonians,
both in the same matter of Pylos and Sphacteria. For
Nicias had taken up their cause [a], and had persuaded the
Athenians to make the peace which set at liberty the
prisoners taken in the island. The Lacedaemonians were
grateful to him for the service, and this was the main
reason why he trusted Gylippus and surrendered himself
to him. But certain Syracusans, who had been in communication with him, were afraid (such was the report) that

*The public prisoners
are confined in the
quarries; Nicias and
Demosthenes are put to
death.*

---

[a] Cp. v. 16 med.

on some suspicion of their guilt he might be put to the torture and bring trouble on them in the hour of their prosperity. Others, and especially the Corinthians, feared that, being rich, he might by bribery escape and do them further mischief. So the Syracusans gained the consent of the allies and had him executed. For these or the like reasons he suffered death. No one of the Hellenes in my time was less deserving of so miserable an end; for he lived in the practice of every virtue.

Those who were imprisoned in the quarries were at the beginning of their captivity harshly treated by the Syracusans. There were great numbers of them, and they were crowded in a deep and narrow place. At first the sun by day was still scorching and suffocating, for they *Sufferings of the prisoners from cold, heat, noisome smells, scanty allowance of food and water. The whole number of them about seven thousand.* had no roof over their heads, while the autumn nights were cold, and the extremes of temperature engendered violent disorders. Being cramped for room they had to do everything on the same spot. The corpses of those who died from their wounds, exposure to heat and cold, and the like, lay heaped one upon another. The smells were intolerable; and they were at the same time afflicted by hunger and thirst. During eight months they were allowed only about half a pint of water and a pint of food a day. Every kind of misery which could befall man in such a place befell them. This was the condition of all the captives for about ten weeks. At length the Syracusans sold them, with the exception of the Athenians and of any Sicilian or Italian Greeks who had sided with them in the war. The whole number of the public prisoners is not accurately known, but they were not less than seven thousand.

Of all the Hellenic actions which took place in this war, or indeed, as I think, of all Hellenic actions which are on record, this was the greatest—the most glorious to the *Thus ended the greatest of all Hellenic actions.*

victors, the most ruinous to the vanquished ; for they were utterly and at all points defeated, and their sufferings were prodigious.   Fleet and army perished from the face of the earth ; nothing was saved, and of the many who went forth few returned home.

Thus ended the Sicilian expedition.

BOOK VIII

THE news was brought to Athens, but the Athenians could not believe that the armament had been so completely annihilated, although they had the positive assurances of [a] the very soldiers who [a] had escaped from the scene of action. At last they knew the truth ; and then they were furious with the orators who had joined in promoting the expedition —as if they had not voted it themselves [b]—and with the soothsayers, and prophets, and all who by the influence of religion had at the time inspired them with the belief that they would conquer Sicily. Whichever way they looked there was trouble ; they were overwhelmed by their calamity, and were in fear and consternation unutterable. The citizens and the city were alike distressed ; they had lost a host of cavalry and hoplites and the flower of their youth, and there were none to replace them [c]. And when they saw an insufficient number of ships in their docks, and no crews to man them, nor money in the treasury, they despaired of deliverance. They had no doubt that their enemies in Sicily, after the great victory which they had already gained, would at once sail against the Piraeus. Their enemies in Hellas, whose resources were now doubled, would likewise set upon them with all their might both by sea and land, and would be assisted by their own revolted allies. Still they determined, so far as their situation allowed, not to give

1

At first the Athenians will not believe the truth, and are furious when they know it. Their prospects are hopeless. However, they determine not to yield. They appoint a council of elders, and are disposed to economise and to behave well.

---

[a] Or, taking πάνυ with στρατιωτῶν : 'trustworthy soldiers who.'
[b] Cp. ii. 60 med., 61 med.   [c] Cp. vii. 64.

way. They would procure timber and money by whatever means they might, and build a navy. They would make sure of their allies, and above all of Euboea. Expenses in the city were to be economised, and they were to choose a council of the elder men, who should advise together, and lay before the people the measures which from time to time might be required. After the manner of a democracy, they were very amenable to discipline while their fright lasted. They proceeded to carry out these resolutions. And so the summer ended.

2   During the following winter all Hellas was stirred by

The neutral states, the Lacedaemonian and Athenian allies, are all alike eager to have a share in a war which appears to be nearly at an end and to involve no danger. Hopes of the Lacedaemonians.

the great overthrow of the Athenians in Sicily. The states which had been neutral determined that the time had come when, invited or not, they could no longer stand aloof from the war; they must of their own accord attack the Athenians. They considered, one and all, that if the Sicilian expedition had succeeded, they would sooner or later have been attacked by them. The war would not last long, and they might as well share in the glory of it. The Lacedaemonian allies, animated by a common feeling, were more eager than ever to make a speedy end of their great hardships. But none showed greater alacrity than the subjects of the Athenians, who were everywhere willing even beyond their power to revolt; for they judged by their excited feelings[a], and would not admit a possibility that the Athenians could survive another summer. To the Lacedaemonians themselves all this was most encouraging; and they had in addition the prospect that their allies from Sicily would join them at the beginning of spring with a large force of ships as well as men; necessity having at last compelled them to become a naval power. Everything looked hopeful, and they determined to strike promptly and vigorously. They considered that by the

---

[a] Cp. iv. 108 med.

successful termination of the war they would be finally delivered from dangers such as would have surrounded them if the Athenians had become masters of Sicily [a]. Athens once overthrown, they might assure to themselves the undisputed leadership of all Hellas.

At the beginning therefore of this winter, Agis the 3 Lacedaemonian king led out a body of troops from Decelea, and collected from the allies contributions towards the expenses of a navy. Then passing to the Malian Gulf, he carried off from the Oetaeans, who were old enemies [b], *Agis carries away the cattle of the Oetaeans, and exacts money from the Achaeans of Phthia. The Lacedaemonians and allies are to build a hundred ships.* the greater part of their cattle, and exacted money of them; from the Achaeans of Phthia, and from the other tribes in that region, without the leave and in spite of the remonstrance of the Thessalians, to whom they were subject, he likewise extorted money and took some hostages, whom he deposited at Corinth, and tried to force upon them the Lacedaemonian alliance. The whole number of ships which the allies were to build was fixed by the Lacedaemonians at a hundred: twenty-five were to be built by themselves and twenty-five by the Boeotians, fifteen by the Phocians and Locrians, fifteen by the Corinthians, ten by the Arcadians, Pellenians, and Sicyonians, ten by the Megarians, Troezenians, Epidaurians, and Hermionians. Every sort of preparation was made, for the Lacedaemonians were determined to prosecute the war at the first appearance of spring.

The Athenians also carried out their intended prepara- 4 tions during this winter. They collected timber and built ships; they fortified Sunium for the protection of their corn-ships on the voyage round to Athens; also they abandoned the *The Athenians build a fleet and fortify Sunium. They cut down expense and keep an eye upon their allies.* fort in Laconia which they had erected while sailing to Sicily [c], and cut down any expenses which seemed un-

---

[a] Cp. vi. 90.   [b] Cp. iii. 92 foll.   [c] Cp. vii. 26 med.

necessary. Above all, they kept strict watch over their allies, apprehending revolt.

5   During the same winter, while both parties were as

(1) The Euboeans; then (2) the Lesbians, who are supported by their Boeotian kinsmen, negotiate with Agis, who has more power than the home government.

intent upon their preparations as if the war were only just beginning, first among the Athenian subjects the Euboeans sent envoys to negotiate with Agis. Agis accepted their proposals, and summoned from Lacedaemon Alcamenes the son of Sthenelaidas,

and Melanthus, that they might take the command in Euboea. They came, accompanied by three hundred of the Neodamodes. But while he was making ready to convey them across the strait, there arrived envoys from Lesbos, which was likewise anxious to revolt; and as the Boeotians [a] were in their interest, Agis was persuaded to defer the expedition to Euboea while he prepared to assist the Lesbians. He appointed Alcamenes, who had been designed for Euboea, their governor; and he further promised them ten ships, the Boeotians promising ten more. All this was done without the authority of the Lacedaemonian government; for Agis, while he was with his army at Decelea, had the right to send troops whithersoever he pleased, to raise levies, and to exact money. And at that particular time he might be said to have far more influence over the allies than the Lacedaemonians at home, for he had an army at his disposal, and might appear in formidable strength anywhere at any time.

While he was supporting the Lesbians, certain Chians

(3) The Chians and Erythraeans assisted by Tissaphernes ask aid from Sparta. The King's tribute in question.

and Erythraeans (who were also ready to revolt) had recourse, not to Agis, but to Lacedaemon; they were accompanied by an envoy from Tissaphernes, whom King Darius the son of Artaxerxes had appointed to be military

---

[a] Cp. iii. 2 fin., 5 med., 13 init.; viii. 100 med.

governor of the provinces on the coast of Asia. Tissaphernes too was inviting the assistance of the Lacedaemonians, and promised to maintain their troops; for the King had quite lately been demanding of him the revenues due from the Hellenic cities in his province, which he had been prevented by the Athenians from collecting, and therefore still owed. He thought that if he could weaken the Athenians he would be more likely to get his tribute; he hoped also to make the Lacedaemonians allies of the King, and by their help either to slay or take alive, in accordance with the King's orders, Amorges the natural son of Pissuthnes, who had revolted in Caria.

While the Chians and Tissaphernes were pursuing their common object, Calligitus the son of Laophon, a Megarian, and Timagoras the son of Athenagoras, a Cyzicene, both exiles from their own country, who were residing at the court of Pharnabazus the son of Pharnaces, came to Lacedaemon. They had been commissioned by Pharnabazus to bring up a fleet to the Hellespont; like Tissaphernes he was anxious, if possible, to induce the cities in his province to revolt from the Athenians, that he might obtain the tribute from them; and he wanted the alliance between the Lacedaemonians and the King to come from himself. The two parties—that is to say, the envoys of Pharnabazus and those of Tissaphernes—were acting independently; and a vehement contest arose at Lacedaemon, the one party urging the Lacedaemonians to send a fleet and army to Ionia and Chios, the other to begin with the Hellespont. They were themselves far more favourable to the proposals of the Chians and Tissaphernes; for Alcibiades was in their interest, and he was a great hereditary friend of Endius, one of the Ephors of that year.—Through this friendship the Lacedaemonian name of Alcibiades had come into his family; for Alcibiades was the name of

(4) Pharnabazus, through two Greek exiles, invites the Lacedaemonian fleet to the Hellespont. The Chians having the support of Alcibiades are first received into alliance; they are promised the assistance of a Peloponnesian fleet.

Endius' father [a].—Nevertheless the Lacedaemonians, before giving an answer, sent a commissioner, Phrynis, one of their Perioeci, to see whether the Chians had as many ships as they said, and whether the power of the city was equal to her reputation. He reported that what they had heard was true. Whereupon they at once made alliance with the Chians and Erythraeans and voted them forty ships—there being at Chios already, as the Chians informed them, no less than sixty. Of the forty ships they at first intended to send out ten themselves under the command of Melancridas their admiral; but an earthquake occurred; so instead of Melancridas they appointed Chalcideus, and instead of the ten ships they prepared to send five only, which they equipped in Laconia. So the winter ended, and with it the nineteenth year in the Peloponnesian War of which Thucydides wrote the history.

7   At the beginning of the next summer the Chians were

The ships are to be dragged over the Isthmus. eager to get the fleet sent off at once. For their proposals, like those of the other allies, had been made secretly, and they were afraid that the Athenians would detect them. Thereupon the Lacedaemonians sent to Corinth three Spartans, who were to give orders that the ships then lying at the Isthmus should be as quickly as possible dragged over from the Corinthian gulf to the coast on the other side. They were all to be despatched to Chios, including the ships which Agis had been equipping for Lesbos. The allied fleet then at the Isthmus numbered in all thirty-nine.

8   Calligitus and Timagoras, who represented Pharnabazus,

Agis, who had originally favoured Lesbos, acquiesces in the expedition to Chios. took no part in the expedition to Chios, nor did they offer to contribute towards the expenses of it the money which they had brought with them,

---

[a] Literally, 'for Endius was called Endius the son of Alcibiades;' implying that in the family of Endius the names Endius and Alcibiades alternated.

amounting to twenty-five talents [a]; they thought of sailing later with another expedition.   Agis, when he saw that the Lacedaemonians were bent on going to Chios first, offered no opposition; so the allies held a conference at Corinth, and after some deliberation determined to sail, first of all to Chios, under the command of Chalcideus, who was equipping the five ships in Laconia, then to proceed to Lesbos, under the command of Alcamenes, whom Agis had previously designed to appoint to that island, and finally to the Hellespont; for this last command they had selected Clearchus the son of Rhamphias.   They resolved to carry over the Isthmus half the ships first; these were to sail at once, that the attention of the Athenians might be distracted between those which were starting and those which were to follow.   They meant to sail quite openly, taking it for granted that the Athenians were powerless, since no navy of theirs worth speaking of had as yet appeared.   In pursuance of their plans they conveyed twenty-one ships over the Isthmus.

They were in a hurry to be off, but the Corinthians were unwilling to join them until the conclusion of the Isthmian games, which were then going on.   Agis was prepared to respect their scruples and to take the responsibility of the expedition on himself.   But the Corinthians would not agree to this proposal, and there was delay.   In the meantime the Athenians began to discover the proceedings of the Chians, and despatched one of their generals, Aristocrates, to accuse them of treason.   They denied the charge; whereupon he desired them to send back with him a few ships as a pledge of their fidelity to the alliance; and they sent seven.   They could not refuse his request, for the Chian people were ignorant of the whole matter, while the oligarchs, who were in the plot, did not want to break with the multitude until they had secured their

9

The Corinthians are delayed by their Isthmian games.   Meanwhile the Athenians detect the treason of the Chians and exact pledges of them.

---

[a] £5,000.

ground.   And the Peloponnesian ships had delayed so
long that they had ceased to expect them.

10   Meanwhile the Isthmian games were celebrated.   The

The first Pelopon-
nesian   squadron   is
driven by the Athenians
into Piraeum and the
commander,   Alcame-
nes, slain.

Athenians, to whom they had been
formally notified, sent representatives
to them ; and now their eyes began to
be opened to the designs of the Chians.
On their return home they took imme-
diate measures to prevent the enemy's ships getting away
from Cenchreae unperceived.   When the games were over,
the Peloponnesians, under the command of Alcamenes,
with their twenty-one ships set sail for Chios ; the Athenians, with an equal number, first sailed up to them and
tried to draw them into the open sea.   The Peloponnesians did not follow them far, but soon turned back to
Cenchreae ; the Athenians likewise retired, because they
could not depend on the fidelity of the seven Chian ships
which formed a part of their fleet.   So they manned some
more ships, making the whole number thirty-seven, and
when the Peloponnesians resumed their voyage along the
coast they pursued them into Piraeum, a lonely harbour,
the last in the Corinthian territory before you reach Epidauria.   One ship was lost by the Peloponnesians at sea,
but they got the rest together and came to anchor in the
harbour.   Again the Athenians attacked them, not only on
the water, but also after they had landed ;   there was a
fierce struggle, but no regular engagement ;   most of the
enemy's ships were damaged by the Athenians on the
beach, and their commander, Alcamenes, was slain.   Some
Athenians also fell.

11   When the conflict was over, the conquerors left a suffi-

The ships are block-
aded by the Athenians.
Discouragement of the
Lacedaemonians, who
seem doomed to failure.

cient number of ships to watch the
enemy, and with the remainder they
lay to under a little island not far off,
where they encamped, and sent to
Athens,   requesting   reinforcements.
For on the day after the battle the Corinthians had come

to assist the Peloponnesian ships, and the other inhabitants of the country quickly followed them. Foreseeing how great would be the labour of keeping guard on so desolate a spot, the Peloponnesians knew not what to do ; they even entertained the idea of burning their ships, but on second thoughts they determined to draw them high up on shore, and to keep guard over them with their land-forces stationed near, until some good opportunity of escape should occur. Agis was informed of their condition, and sent Thermon, a Spartan, to them. The first tidings which had reached Sparta were to the effect that the ships had left the Isthmus (the Ephors having told Alcamenes to send a horseman announcing the fact), and immediately they determined to send out the five ships of their own which they had ready, under the command of Chalcideus, who was to be accompanied by Alcibiades. But when they were on the point of departure, a second messenger reported that the other squadron had been chased into Piraeum ; and then, disheartened by finding that they had begun the Ionian war with a failure, they determined to give up sending the ships from Laconia, and even to recall some others which had already sailed.

Alcibiades, seeing the state of affairs, advised Endius **12** and the Ephors to persevere in the expedition. They would arrive, he said, before the Chians had heard of the misadventure of the ships. He would himself, as soon as he reached *They are going to do nothing; but Alcibiades insists that the Lacedae-monian contingent shall at once put to sea.* Ionia, represent to the cities the weakness of the Athenians and the alacrity of the Lacedaemonians, and they would revolt at once ; for they would believe him sooner than any one. To Endius he argued in private 'ᵃ that he would win honour if he were the instrument of effecting a revolt in Ionia, and of gaining the alliance of the Kingᵃ; he

---

ᵃ Or, ' that he would win honour by effecting through his (Alcibiades') agency a revolt in Ionia and gaining the alliance of the King.'

should not allow such a prize to fall into the hands of Agis';—now Agis was a personal enemy of Alcibiades. His opinion prevailed with Endius and the other Ephors. So he put to sea with the .five ships, accompanied by Chalcideus the Lacedaemonian, and hastened on his way.

13 About this time sixteen Peloponnesian ships which had

Return of some ships remained with Gylippus to the end of
from Sicily. the Sicilian war were returning home.
They were caught in the neighbourhood of Leucadia and roughly handled by twenty-seven Athenian vessels, under the command of Hippocles the son of Menippus, which were on the watch for ships coming from Sicily; but all except one of them escaped the Athenians and sailed into Corinth.

14 Chalcideus and Alcibiades on their voyage seized every

(1) Chios, then (2) one whom they met in order that their
Erythrae, (3) Clazo- coming might not be reported. They
menae, are induced to touched first at the promontory of
revolt by Chalcideus and Corycus on the mainland, and there
Alcibiades.
releasing their prisoners they held a preliminary conference with certain of the Chians, who were in the plot, and who advised them to give no notice of their intention, but to sail at once to the city. So they appeared suddenly at Chios, to the great wonder and alarm of the people. The oligarchs had contrived that the council should be sitting at the time. Chalcideus and Alcibiades made speeches and announced that many more ships were on their way, but said nothing about the blockade of Piraeum. So Chios first, and afterwards Erythrae, revolted from Athens. They then sailed with three vessels to Clazomenae, which they induced to revolt. The Clazomenians at once crossed over to the mainland and fortified Polichnè, intending in case of need to retreat thither from the little island on which Clazomenae stands. All the revolted cities were occupied in raising fortifications and preparing for war.

The news of the revolt of Chios soon reached Athens; 15
and the Athenians realised at once the   *The Athenians, alive*
magnitude of the danger which now   *to their situation, pass*
surrounded them. The greatest city   *a decree allowing the*
of all had gone over to the enemy, and   *reserve of money and*
ships to be freely used.
the rest of their allies were certain to   *They resolve to send a*
rise. In the extremity of their alarm   *large fleet to Asia.*
they abrogated the penalties denounced against any one
who should propose or put to the vote the employment of
the thousand talents which throughout the war they had
hitherto jealously reserved[a]. They now passed a decree
permitting their use, and resolved to man a large number
of ships; also to send at once to Chios eight ships which
had been keeping guard at Piraeum, and had gone away
under the command of Strombichides the son of Diotimus
in pursuit of Chalcideus, but not overtaking him had
returned. Twelve other ships, under the command of Thrasycles, were to follow immediately; these too were to be
taken from the blockading force. They also withdrew the
seven Chian ships which were assisting them in the
blockade of Piraeum; and setting free the slaves in them,
put the freemen in chains. Other ships were then quickly
manned by them and sent to take the place of all those
which had been subtracted from the blockading squadron,
and they proposed to equip thirty more. They were full
of energy, and spared no effort for the recovery of Chios.

Meanwhile Strombichides with his eight ships arrived at 16
Samos, and thence, taking with him
an additional Samian vessel, sailed to   *Strombichides at Teos.*
He narrowly escapes
Teos and warned the inhabitants against   *Chalcideus and Alcib-*
revolt. But Chalcideus with twenty-   *iades, by whom he is*
three ships was on his way from Chios   *chased into Samos.* (4)
Teos revolts.
to Teos, intending to attack it; he was
assisted by the land-forces of Clazomenae and Erythrae,
which followed his movements on the shore. Strombichides saw him in time, and put out to sea before he arrived.

---

[a] Cp. ii 24.

When fairly away from land he observed the superior numbers of the fleet coming from Chios, and fled towards Samos, pursued by the enemy. The land-forces were not at first received by the Teians, but after the flight of the Athenians they admitted them. The troops waited a little for the return of Chalcideus from the pursuit, but as he did not come they proceeded without him to demolish the fort which the Athenians had built for the protection of Teos on the land side. A few barbarians under the command of Stages, a lieutenant of Tissaphernes, came and joined in the work of demolition.

17   Chalcideus and Alcibiades, when they had chased Strombichides to Samos, gave heavy arms to the crews of the ships which they had brought from Peloponnesus, and left them in Chios. Then, having manned their own vessels and twenty others with Chians, they sailed to Miletus, intending to raise a revolt.—For Alcibiades, who was on friendly terms with the principal Milesians, wanted to gain over the place before any more ships from Peloponnesus arrived, and, using the Chian troops and those of Chalcideus only, to spread revolt far and wide among the cities of Ionia. Thus he would gain the chief glory of the war for the Chians, for himself, for Chalcideus ; and, in fulfilment of his promise [a], for Endius, who had sent him out.—They were not observed during the greater part of their voyage, and, although narrowly escaping from Strombichides, and from Thrasycles who had just arrived with twelve ships from Athens and had joined Strombichides in the pursuit, they succeeded in raising a revolt in Miletus. The Athenians followed close behind them with nineteen ships, but the Milesians would not receive them, and they came to anchor at Ladè, the island opposite the town. Immediately after the revolt of Miletus the Lacedaemonians made their first alliance with the King of Persia,

Chalcideus and Alcibiades raise a revolt in (5) Miletus, in their turn narrowly escaping Strombichides and Thrasycles, who anchor at Ladè.

---

[a] Cp. viii. 12.

which was negotiated by Tissaphernes and Chalcideus.   It
ran as follows :—

'The Lacedaemonians and their allies make an alliance 18
with the King and Tissaphernes on the following terms :—

'I. All the territory and all the cities which are in
possession of the King, or were in
possession of his forefathers, shall be *Treaty of alliance:*
the King's [a], and whatever revenue or *all that ever was sub-*
other advantages the Athenians derived *ject to the Kings of*
from these cities, the King. and the *Persia shall be theirs*
still.
Lacedaemonians and their allies, shall combine to prevent
them from receiving such revenue or advantage.

'II. The King, and the Lacedaemonians and their allies,
shall carry on the war against the Athenians in common,
and they shall not make peace with the Athenians unless
both parties—the King on the one hand and the Lacedaemonians and their allies on the other—agree.

'III. Whosoever revolts from the King shall be the
enemy of the Lacedaemonians and their allies, and whosoever revolts from the Lacedaemonians and their allies
shall be the enemy of the King in like manner.'

Such were the terms of the alliance.

Shortly afterwards the Chians manned ten more ships 19
and sailed to Anaea, wanting to hear
whether the attempt on Miletus had *Zeal of the Chians.*
The Athenians take four
succeeded, and to draw fresh cities *of their ships.   Revolts*
into the revolt.   A message however *of (6) Lebedus and (7)*
was brought from Chalcideus, bidding *Erae.*
them return, and warning them that Amorges was coming
thither by land at the head of an army.   So they sailed to
the Temple of Zeus [b], where they caught sight of sixteen
Athenian ships which Diomedon, following Thrasycles, was
bringing from Athens.   They instantly fled ; one ship to
Ephesus, the remainder towards Teos.   Four of them the
Athenians took empty, the crews having got safe to land ;

---

[a] Cp. viii. 43 med.   [b] A place so called between Lebedus
and Colophon.

the rest escaped to Teos. The Athenians then sailed away to Samos. The Chians with their remaining ships put to sea again, and, assisted by the land-forces of their allies[a], caused first Lebedus, and afterwards Erae, to revolt. Both the army and the fleet then returned home.

20   About the same time the twenty Peloponnesian ships which had been chased into Piraeum,

Escape of the ships blockaded at Piraeum. They prepare to start for Chios.

and were now blockaded by a like number of Athenian ships, made a sally, defeated the Athenians, and took four ships; they then got away to Cenchreae, and once more prepared to sail to Chios and Ionia. At Cenchreae they were met by Astyochus, the admiral from Lacedaemon, to whom the whole of the Peloponnesian navy was about to be entrusted.

By this time the land-forces of Clazomenae and Erythrae[b]

Teos consents to neutrality.

had retired from Teos, and Tissaphernes, who had led a second army thither in person and overthrown what was left of the Athenian fort, had retired also. Not long after his departure, Diomedon arrived with ten ships, and made an agreement with the Teians, who promised to receive the Athenians as well as the Peloponnesians. He then sailed to Erae, which he attacked without success, and departed.

21   About the same time a great revolution occurred in Samos. The people, aided by the

The people of Samos rise against the nobles and set up a democracy. The Athenians grant them independence.

crews of three Athenian vessels which happened to be on the spot, rose against the nobles, slew in all about two hundred of them, and banished four hundred more; they then distributed their land and houses among themselves. The Athenian people, now assured of their fidelity, granted them independence; and henceforward the city was in the hands of the democracy. They denied to the former landed proprietors all the privi-

---

[a] Cp. viii. 16 init.   [b] Cp. viii. 16 init. ; 19 fin.

leges of citizenship, not even allowing them to contract marriage with any family belonging to the people, nor any of the people with them.

The zeal of the Chians did not abate.   They had already 22 begun to go out with armies and raise revolts independently of the Pelopon- *The Chians send a* nesians [a], and they wished to draw as *fleet to Lesbos. A land* many cities as they could into their *army co-operates with* own danger.   During the same summer *Mytilenè and (9) Meth-* they sent out a Chian fleet numbering *ymna to revolt.* thirteen ships.   The expedition was directed first against Lesbos, the Lacedaemonians having originally instructed their officers to proceed from Chios to Lesbos, and thence to the Hellespont [b].   It was placed under the command of Deiniadas, one of the Perioeci.   Meanwhile the infantry of the Peloponnesians and of the neighbouring allies, under Evalas, a Spartan, moved along the shore towards Clazo-menae and Cymè.   The fleet sailed to Lesbos, and first induced Methymna to rebel; there leaving four of their ships, with the remainder they raised a revolt in Mytilenè.

Meanwhile Astyochus the Lacedaemonian admiral, with 23 four ships, set forth, as he intended, *The Athenians first,* from Cenchreae, and arrived at Chios. *and afterwards Asty-* On the third day after his arrival a *ochus, who has newly* division of the Athenian fleet, number- *arrived from Cenchreae,* ing twenty-five ships, sailed to Lesbos *sail to Lesbos. Mytilenè* under the command of Leon and Dio- *is retaken by the Athen-* medon; Leon had arrived from Athens *ians, and the Chian* later than Diomedon with a reinforce- *ships captured. Attempt* ment of ten ships.   On the same day, *to support Methymna,* towards evening, Astyochus put to sea, *which fails, like all the* and taking with him one Chian ship, *plans of Astyochus in* sailed to Lesbos, that he might render *Lesbos. The Athenians* any assistance which he could to the *recover the whole of* *Lesbos, and afterwards* *Clazomenae.* Chian fleet.   He came to Pyrrha, and on the following day to Eresus, where

---

[a] Cp. viii. 19   [b] Cp. viii. 8 med.

he heard that Mytilenè had been taken by the Athenians
at the first blow.   The Athenian ships had sailed right into
the harbour when they were least expected, and captured
the Chian vessels ; the men on board had then landed, and
defeating in a battle a Mytilenean force which came out to
meet them, had taken possession of the city.   Astyochus
heard the news from the Eresians, and from the Chian
ships which had been left with Eubulus at Methymna.
They had fled when Mytilenè was taken, and had now
fallen in with him ; but only three out of the four, for one
of them had been captured by the Athenians.   Upon this,
instead of going on to Mytilenè, he raised a revolt in
Eresus, and armed the inhabitants : he then disembarked
the heavy-armed from his ships and sent them by land to
Antissa and Methymna under the command of Eteonicus ;
and with his own and the three Chian ships coasted thither
himself, hoping that the Methymnaeans would take courage
at the sight of them and persevere in their revolt.   But
everything went against him in Lesbos ; so he re-embarked
his troops and sailed back to Chios.   The land-forces from
the ships which were intended to go to the Hellespont [a]
also returned to their several homes.   Not long afterwards
six ships came to Chios from the allied forces of the Peloponnesians now collected at Cenchreae.   The Athenians,
when they had re-established their influence in Lesbos,
sailed away, and having taken Polichnè on the mainland,
which the Clazomenians were fortifying [b], brought them
all back to their city on the island, except the authors of
the revolt, who had escaped to Daphnus.   So Clazomenae
returned to the Athenian alliance.

24   During the same summer the Athenians, who were
The Athenians at stationed with twenty of their ships at
Ladè make a descent the island of Ladè [c] and were watching
the enemy in Miletus, made a descent upon Panormus in

---

the Milesian territory. Chalcideus the Lacedaemonian
general with a few followers came out
to meet them, but was killed. Three
days later they again sailed across and
set up a trophy, which the Milesians
pulled down, because the Athenians
were not really masters of the ground
at the time when they erected it. Leon
and Diomedon, who were at Lesbos
with the rest of the Athenian fleet, stationed their ships at the islands called
Oenussae which lie in front of Chios,
at Sidussa and Pteleum, which were
forts held by them in the Erythraean

*upon Miletus. Chal-
cideus is slain. The
Athenians at Lesbos
carry on the war against
the Chians, who are
defeated in three battles
and undergo great
sufferings.—Yet they
had been very rich, and
their government was
wise and moderate.
Nor was there any im-
prudence in their revolt.
Owing to their losses a reaction now sets in, which
has to be suppressed.*

territory, and at Lesbos itself, and carried on the war by
sea against the Chians. The marines whom they had on
board were hoplites taken from the roll and compelled to
serve. They made descents upon Cardamylè and Bolissus,
and having defeated with heavy loss the Chians who came
out to meet them, they devastated all that region. In
another battle at Phanae they defeated them again, and in
a third at Leuconium. Henceforward the Chians remained within their walls. The Athenians ravaged their
country, which was well stocked, and from the Persian
War until that time had never been touched by an
invader. No people as far as I know, except the Chians
and Lacedaemonians (but the Chians not equally with
the Lacedaemonians), have preserved moderation in
prosperity, and in proportion as their city has gained in
power have gained also in the stability of their administration. In this revolt they may seem to have shown
a want of prudence, yet they did not venture upon it until
many brave allies were ready to share the peril with them,
and until the Athenians themselves seemed to confess that
after their calamity in Sicily the state of their affairs was
hopelessly bad. And, if they were deceived through the
uncertainty of human things, this error of judgment was

common to many who, like them, believed that the Athenian power would speedily be overthrown. But now that they were driven off the sea and saw their lands ravaged, some of their citizens undertook to bring back the city to the Athenians. The magistrates perceived their design, but instead of acting themselves, they sent to Erythrae for Astyochus the admiral. He came with four ships which he had on the spot, and they considered together by what means the conspiracy might be suppressed with the least violence, whether by taking hostages or in some other way.

25   The Lacedaemonians were thus engaged in Chios when

Athenian reinforcements arrive. A battle takes place before the walls of Miletus, in which the Athenians defeat the Peloponnesians and the Argives are defeated by the Milesians. Alcibiades is fighting in the Milesian army. Attempt to invest Miletus.

towards the end of the summer there came from Athens a thousand Athenian hoplites and fifteen hundred Argives, of whom five hundred were originally light-armed, but the Athenians gave them heavy arms; also a thousand of the allies. They were conveyed in forty-eight ships, of which some were transports, under the command of Phrynichus, Onomacles, and Scironides. Sailing first to Samos they crossed over to Miletus, and there took up a position. The Milesians with a force of eight hundred heavy-armed of their own, the Peloponnesians who came with Chalcideus, and certain foreign mercenaries of Tissaphernes, who was there in person with his cavalry, went out and engaged the Athenians and their allies. The Argives on their own wing dashed forward, and made a disorderly attack upon the troops opposed to them, whom they despised; they thought that, being Ionians, they would be sure to run away[a]. But they were defeated by the Milesians, and nearly three hundred of them perished. The Athenians first overcame the Peloponnesians, and then forced back the barbarians and the inferior troops. But they never engaged the

---

[a] Cp. i. 124 init.; v. 9 init.; vi. 77 med.; vii. 5 fin.

Milesians, who, after routing the Argives, when they saw their other wing defeated, returned to the city. The Athenians, having won the day, took up a position close under the walls of Miletus. In this engagement the Ionians on both sides had the advantage of the Dorians ; for the Athenians vanquished the Peloponnesians who were opposed to them, and the Milesians vanquished the Argives [a]. The Athenians now raised a trophy, and prepared to build a wall across the isthmus which separates the city from the mainland, thinking that, if they could reduce Miletus, the other cities would quickly return to their allegiance.

But meanwhile, late in the afternoon, news was brought 26 to them that a fleet of fifty-five ships from Peloponnesus and Sicily was close at hand. Hermocrates the Syracusan had urged the Sicilians to assist in completing the overthrow of Athens. Twenty ships came from Syracuse, two from Selinus, and with them the Peloponnesian ships which had been in preparation [b]. The two squadrons were entrusted to Theramenes, who was to conduct them to Astyochus the admiral. They sailed first to Leros [c], an island lying off Miletus. Thence, finding that the Athenians were at Miletus, they sailed away to the Iasian Gulf, wanting to ascertain the fate of the town. Alcibiades came on horseback to Teichiussa in the Milesian territory, the point of the gulf at which the fleet had passed the night, and from him they received news of the battle. For he had been present, and had fought on the side of the Milesians and Tissaphernes. And he recommended them, if they did not mean to ruin their cause in Ionia and everywhere else, to assist Miletus at once, and break up the blockade.

Approach of thirty-three Peloponnesian and twenty - two Sicilian vessels under Hermocrates. Alcibiades advises them to go instantly to the relief of Miletus.

---

[a] Cp. iv. 12 fin.   [b] Cp. viii. 6 fin.   [c] According to the reading of the Vatican MS. adopted by Bekker : cp. infra, 27 init. Other MSS. 'Ελεον, a name otherwise unknown.

27   They determined to go at daybreak and relieve the

They agree; and the place.   But Phrynichus the Athenian
Athenians hearing of general had certain information from
their approach on the Leros of their approach, and, although
evening of their own his colleagues wanted to remain and
victory, by the advice of risk a battle, he refused and declared
Phrynichus, who over- that he would neither himself fight, nor
rules his colleagues, allow them or any one else to fight if he
withdraw to Samos.

could help it.   For when they might discover the exact
number of the enemy's ships and the proportion which
their own bore to them, and, before engaging, make ade-
quate preparations at their leisure, he would not be so
foolish as to risk all through fear of disgrace.   There was
no dishonour in Athenians retreating before an enemy's
fleet when circumstances required.   But there would be
the deepest dishonour under any circumstances in a defeat;
and the city would then not only incur disgrace, but would
be in the utmost danger.   Even if their preparations were
complete and satisfactory, Athens after her recent disasters
ought not to take the offensive, or in any case not without
absolute necessity; and now when they were not compelled,
why should they go out of their way to court danger?   He
urged them to put on board their wounded, and their
infantry, and all the stores which they had brought with
them, but to leave behind the plunder obtained from the
enemy's country, that their ships might be lighter; they
should sail back to Samos, and there uniting all their forces,
they might go on making attacks upon Miletus when oppor-

Character of Phry- tunity offered.   His advice was fol-
nichus.   lowed.   [a] And not on this occasion
only, but quite as much afterwards, whenever Phrynichus had to act, he showed himself to be a man of great
sagacity [b].—So the Athenians departed that very evening
from Miletus without completing their victory, and the

---

[a] Or 'And not on this occasion only, but whenever Phrynichus had
to act, he was acknowledged, afterwards if not at the time, to be' &c.

[b] Cp viii. 68 med.

Argives, hurrying away from Samos in a rage after their disaster, went home.

At dawn the Peloponnesians sailed from Teichiussa, and 28 on their arrival at Miletus found that the Athenians had left: after remaining one day, on the morrow they took the Chian ships which under the command of Chalcideus had previously been chased into Miletus[n], and resolved to go back to Teichiussa and fetch that

The Peloponnesians at the suggestion of Tissaphernes attack and take Iasus. Amorges is made prisoner. Pedaritus sets out for Chios, of which he had been appointed governor.

part of the tackle of which they had lightened the ships. There they found Tissaphernes, who had come with his infantry; he persuaded them to sail against Iasus, in which his enemy Amorges lay. So they attacked Iasus, which they took by a sudden assault; for it never occurred to the inhabitants that their ships were not Athenian. The Syracusans distinguished themselves greatly in the action. The Peloponnesians took captive Amorges the natural son of Pissuthnes, who had rebelled, and gave him to Tissaphernes, that, if he liked, he might convey him to the King in obedience to the royal command[b]. They then plundered Iasus, and the army obtained a great deal of treasure; for the city had been rich from early times. They did no harm to the mercenaries of Amorges, but received them into their own ranks; for most of them came from Peloponnesus. The town, and all their prisoners, whether bond or free, were delivered by them into the hands of Tissaphernes, who engaged to give them a Daric stater[c] for each man; they then returned to Miletus. Thence they despatched by land as far as Erythrae Pedaritus the son of Leon, whom the Lacedaemonians had sent out to be governor of Chios; he was escorted by the mercenaries who had been in the service of Amorges. To remain on the spot, and take charge of Miletus, they appointed Philip. So the summer ended.

---

[a] Cp. viii. 17 fin.   [b] Cp. viii. 5 fin.   [c] Twenty Attic drachmae, about 13s. 4d.

29   During the following winter, Tissaphernes, after he had

Reduction of pay. provided for the security of Iasus, came
Tissaphernes agrees to to Miletus.   There he distributed one
give three talents to month's pay among all the ships, at
every five ships, or the rate of an Attic drachma [a] a day
rather more than three per man, as his envoy had promised at
obols a day to each
sailor. Lacedaemon ; in future he proposed to
give half a drachma only until he had asked the King's
leave, promising that if he obtained it he would pay the
entire drachma.   On the remonstrance, however, of Hermocrates the Syracusan general (Theramenes, not being
himself admiral, but only taking charge of the ships which
he was to hand over to Astyochus, took no interest in the
matter of the pay), he promised to each man a payment of
somewhat more than three obols, reckoning the total sum
paid to every five ships.   For he offered to every five
ships, up to the number of fifty-five [b], three talents a month,
and to any ships in excess of this number he agreed to
give at a like rate.

30   During the same winter there arrived at Samos from

Arrival of reinforce- Athens thirty-five ships, under the com-
ments.   Muster at mand of Charminus, Strombichides,
Samos, and redistribu- and   Euctemon.   Whereupon   the
tion of the Athenian
fleet. Thirty-three ships generals assembled their whole fleet,
sent to Chios ; seventy- including the ships engaged at Chios [c],
four remain at Samos. their purpose being to make a distribution of their forces by lot.   The principal division was to
continue watching Miletus, while a second force of ships
and soldiers was to be sent to Chios.   Accordingly Strombichides, Onomacles, and Euctemon, with thirty ships,
besides transports in which they conveyed a portion of the
thousand heavy-armed who had joined the army at Miletus [d],
sailed away to Chios, the duty which the lot assigned to
them.   The other generals remaining at Samos with

---

[a] *8d.*   [b] Retaining, with the MSS., καὶ πεντήκοντα after ναῦς;
see note.   [c] Cp. viii. 24 init.   [d] Cp. viii. 25 init.

seventy-four ships, and having the mastery of the sea, prepared to make a descent upon Miletus.

Astyochus was at Chios selecting hostages as a pre- 31 caution against the betrayal of the island to Athens [a], but when he heard of the reinforcements which Theramenes had brought, and of the improved prospects of the allies, he desisted, and

Astyochus fails in an attack on Pteleum and Clazomenae. The weather is much against him.

taking with him his own Peloponnesian ships, ten in number [b], and ten Chian, he put to sea. Failing in an attack upon Pteleum he sailed on to Clazomenae, and demanded that the Athenian party should settle at Daphnus [c] on the mainland, and come over to the Peloponnesians: Tamos, one of the Persian lieutenants of Ionia, joined in the demand. But the Clazomenians would not listen to him; whereupon he assaulted the city (which was unwalled), but being unable to take it, sailed away with a strong wind. He was himself carried to Phocaea and Cymè, and the remainder of the fleet put into the islands, Marathussa, Pelè, and Drymussa, which lie off Clazomenae. There, being detained eight days by the weather, they spoiled and destroyed part of the property of the Clazomenians which had been deposited in the islands, and, taking part on board, they sailed away to Phocaea and Cymè, where they rejoined Astyochus.

While Astyochus was there, envoys came to him from 32 Lesbos; the Lesbians were once more eager to revolt, and he was willing to assist them; but the Corinthians and the other allies were disheartened by the previous failure. So he put to sea and sailed back to Chios. His ships were scattered by a storm, and reached

The Lesbians are again desirous to revolt. Astyochus is willing to assist, but Pedaritus, the new governor of Chios, and the Chians, refuse to join.

Chios from various places. Soon afterwards Pedaritus and his army [d] having come by land from Miletus to

---

[a] Cp. viii. 24 fin.   [b] Cp. viii. 23 init. and fin.   [c] Cp. viii. 23 fin.
[d] Cp. viii. 28 fin.

Erythrae, where he crossed the channel, arrived in Chios.
On his arrival he found at his disposal the sailors whom
Chalcideus had taken from his five ships [a] and left in
Chios fully armed, to the number of five hundred. Some
of the Lesbians renewing their proposal to revolt, Asty·
ochus suggested to Pedaritus and the Chians that they
should go with the fleet to Lesbos and raise the country;
they would thus increase the number of their allies, and,
even if the attempt did not wholly succeed, they would
injure the Athenians. But they would not listen, and
Pedaritus refused to let him have the Chian ships.

33   So Astyochus took five Corinthian ships [b] and a sixth

*Astyochus sets sail
for Miletus to assume
the command of the
fleet. He narrowly
escapes the Athenian
squadron sailing to
Chios. Trick of the
Erythraean prisoners.*

from Megara, one from Hermionè, and
the Lacedaemonian ships which he had
brought with him [c], and set sail for
Miletus in order to assume his command. He threatened the Chians,
again and again, that he would certainly
not help them when their time of need
came. Touching at Corycus in Erythraea he passed the
night there. The Athenian ships from Samos were now
on their way to Chios; they had put in at a place where
they were only divided from the Peloponnesians by a hill,
and neither fleet knew that the other was so near. But
that night there came a despatch from Pedaritus informing
Astyochus that certain Erythraean prisoners had been
released by the Athenians from Samos on condition of
betraying Erythrae, and had gone thither with that intention. Whereupon Astyochus sailed back to Erythrae. So
narrowly did he escape falling into the hands of the
Athenians. Pedaritus sailed over to meet him. They
then enquired about the supposed traitors, and found
that the whole matter was a trick which the men had
devised in order to get away from Samos; so they acquitted
them of the charge, and Pedaritus returned to Chios, while
Astyochus resumed his voyage to Miletus.

---

[a] Cp. viii. 17 init.   [b] Cp. viii. 23 fin.   [c] Cp. viii. 23 init.

In the meantime the Athenian fleet, sailing round the 34
promontory of Corycus towards Ar-
ginus, lighted upon three Chian ships
of war, to which they gave chase.   A
great storm came on, and the Chian

*Three Athenian ships
in pursuit of three
Chian are wrecked in a
storm.*

ships with difficulty escaped into their harbour, but of the
Athenian ships the three which were most zealous in the
pursuit were disabled and driven ashore near the city of
Chios ; the crews were either lost or taken captive.   The
remainder of the fleet found shelter in the harbour called
Phoenicus, lying under Mount Mimas, whence again setting
sail they put in at Lesbos, and made preparations for
building the fort which they meant to establish in
Chios.

During the same winter, Hippocrates the Lacedaemonian 35
sailed from the Peloponnese with one
Laconian, one Syracusan, and ten
Thurian ships ; of these last Dorieus
the son of Diagoras and two others
were the commanders.   They put in at
Cnidus, which under the influence of
Tissaphernes [a] had already revolted
from Athens.   The Peloponnesian

*(10) Cnidus, which
has revolted from
Athens, is attacked by
the Athenians. They
take six newly-arrived
ships of the allies, and
are nearly but not quite
successful in taking the
town.*

authorities at Miletus, when they heard of their arrival,
ordered one half of these ships to protect Cnidus,
and the other half to cruise off Triopium and seize the
merchant-vessels which put in there from Egypt.   This
Triopium is a promontory in the district of Cnidus on
which there is a temple of Apollo.   The Athenians, hearing of their intentions, sailed from Samos and captured the
six ships which were keeping guard at Triopium ; the
crews escaped.   They then sailed to Cnidus, and attacking
the town, which was unwalled, all but took it.   On the
following day they made a second attack, but during the

---

[a] Accepting Palmer's conjecture, ὑπό for ἀπό. But see note, and cp.
viii. 109 init.

night the inhabitants had improved their hasty defences, and some of the men who had escaped from the ships captured at Triopium had come into the city. So the Athenian assault was less destructive than on the first day ; and after retiring from the city and devastating the country belonging to it they sailed back to Samos.

36 About the same time Astyochus arrived at Miletus and

The Milesians are in earnest. The spoils of Iasus maintain the army. The Peloponnesians repent of their first treaty with Persia, and make another.

took the command of the fleet. He found the Peloponnesians still abundantly provided with all requisites. They had sufficient pay; the great spoils taken at Iasus were in the hands of the army, and the Milesians carried

on the war with a will. The Peloponnesians however considered the former treaty made between Tissaphernes and Chalcideus defective and disadvantageous to them ; so before the departure of Theramenes they made new terms of alliance, which were as follows :—

37 ' The Lacedaemonians and their allies make agreement

In this treaty the rights of the King are less directly stated than in the former.

with King Darius and the sons of the King, and with Tissaphernes, that there shall be alliance and friendship between them on the following

conditions : —

"I. Whatever territory and cities belong to King Darius, or formerly belonged to his father, or to his ancestors, against these neither the Lacedaemonians nor their allies shall make war, or do them any hurt, nor shall the Lacedaemonians or their allies exact tribute of them. Neither Darius the King nor the subjects of the King shall make war upon the Lacedaemonians or their allies, or do them any hurt.

"II. If the Lacedaemonians or their allies have need of anything from the King, or the King have need of anything from the Lacedaemonians and their allies, whatever they do by mutual agreement shall hold good.

"III. They shall carry on the war against the Athenians

and their allies in common, and if they make peace, shall make peace in common.

"IV. The King shall defray the expense of any number of troops for which the King has sent, so long as they remain in the King's country.

"V. If any of the cities who are parties to this treaty go against the King's country, the rest shall interfere and aid the King to the utmost of their power. And if any of the inhabitants of the King's country or any country under the dominion of the King shall go against the country of the Lacedaemonians or their allies, the King shall interfere and aid them to the utmost of his power".'

After the conclusion of the treaty, Theramenes, having delivered over the fleet to Astyochus, sailed away in a small boat and was no more heard of. The Athenians, who had now crossed over with their troops from Lesbos to Chios, and had the upper hand both by land and sea, began to fortify Delphinium, a place not far distant from the town of Chios, which had the double advantage of being strong by land and of possessing harbours. The Chians meanwhile remained inactive; they had been already badly beaten in several battles, and their internal condition was far from satisfactory; for Tydeus the son of Ion and his accomplices had been executed by Pedaritus on a charge of complicity with Athens, and the city was reduced by the strong hand to a mere oligarchy. Hence they were in a state of mutual distrust, and could not be persuaded that either they or the mercenaries [a] brought by Pedaritus were a match for the enemy. They sent however to Miletus and requested the aid of Astyochus, but he refused. Whereupon Pedaritus sent a despatch to Lacedaemon, complaining of his misconduct. So favourable to the Athenians was the

The Chians are reduced to inaction. The conspirators are executed, and the government becomes a close oligarchy. Pedaritus complains to Sparta of Astyochus.

38

---

[a] Cp. viii. 28 fin.

course of affairs in Chios. The main fleet, which they had left at Samos, from time to time made threatening movements against the enemy at Miletus, but as they would never come out, the Athenians at length retired to Samos and there remained.

39   During the same winter, about the solstice, twenty-seven

The Lacedaemonians resolve to assist Pharnabazus at the Hellespont. They send eleven assessors to control Astyochus.

ships which Calligitus of Megara and Timagoras of Cyzicus, the agents of Pharnabazus, had persuaded the Lacedaemonians to fit out in his interest [a], sailed for Ionia: they were placed under the command of Antisthenes, a Spartan. The Lacedaemonians sent at the same time eleven Spartans to act as advisers [b] to Astyochus, one of whom was Lichas the son of Arcesilaus [c]. Besides receiving a general commission to assist in the direction of affairs to the best of their judgment, they were empowered on their arrival at Miletus to send on, if they saw fit, these ships, or a larger or smaller number, to Pharnabazus at the Hellespont under the command of Clearchus [d] the son of Rhamphias, who sailed with them. The eleven might also, if they thought good, deprive Astyochus of his command and appoint Antisthenes in his place, for the despatch of Pedaritus had excited suspicion against him. So the ships sailed from Malea over the open sea until they came to Melos. There they lighted on ten Athenian ships; of these they took three without their crews and burned them. But then, fearing that the remainder which had escaped would, as in fact they did, give information of their approach to the fleet at Samos, they took the precaution of going by a longer route. And sailing round by Crete they put in at Caunus in Asia. They thought that they were now safe, and sent a messenger to the fleet at Miletus requesting a convoy.

----

[a] Cp. viii. 6 init.   [b] Cp. ii. 85 init.; iii. 69 med.; v. 63 fin.
[c] Cp. v. 50 med.   [d] Cp viii. 8 med.

Meanwhile the Chians and Pedaritus continued to send 40
messengers to Astyochus, who con-
tinued to delay. They implored him   *The Chians are block-*
to come to their help with his whole   *aded.   Their slaves*
fleet, saying that they were blockaded,   *desert. Astyochus is at*
and that he should not allow the chief   *last induced to go to*
their aid.
ally of Sparta in Ionia to be cut off from the sea and overrun and devastated by land. Now the Chians had more
domestic slaves than any other state with the exception of
Lacedaemon, and their offences were always more severely
punished because of their number; so that, when the
Athenian army appeared to be firmly settled in their
fortifications, most of them at once deserted to the enemy[a].
And they did the greatest damage, because they knew the
country. The Chians pressed upon the Lacedaemonians
the necessity of coming to their assistance while there was
still hope of interfering to some purpose; the fortification
of Delphinium, though not yet completed, was in progress,
and the Athenians were beginning to extend the lines of
defence which protected their army and ships. Astyochus, seeing that the allies were zealous in the cause,
although he had fully meant to carry out his threat, now
determined to relieve the Chians.

But in the meantime he received a message from Caunus, 41
informing him that the twenty-seven   *But he hears of*
ships and his Lacedaemonian advisers   *the twenty-seven ships*
had arrived. He thought that every-   *bringing the commis-*
thing should give way to the importance   *sioners from Lacedae-*
of convoying so large a reinforcement   *mon, and coasts south-*
which would secure to the Lacedae-   *ward to meet them. He*
monians greater command of the sea,   *is persuaded by the*
and that he must first of all provide   *Cnidians to sail against*
for the safe passage of the commis-   *twenty Athenian ships*
which are watching for
them.
sioners who were to report on his conduct. So he at once
gave up his intended expedition to Chios and sailed for

---

[a] Cp. vii. 27 fin.

Caunus. As he coasted along he made a descent on the island of Cos Meropis. The city was unfortified and had been overthrown by an earthquake, the greatest which has ever happened within our memory. The citizens had fled into the mountains ; so he sacked the town and overran and despoiled the country, but let go the free inhabitants whom he found. From Cos he came by night to Cnidus, and was prevailed upon by the importunity of the Cnidians, instead of disembarking his men, to sail at once, just as he was, against twenty Athenian ships with which Charminus (one of the generals at Samos) was watching for the twenty-seven ships expected from Peloponnesus, being those which Astyochus was going to escort. The Athenians at Samos had heard from Melos of their coming, and Charminus was cruising off the islands of Symè, Chalcè, and Rhodes, and on the coast of Lycia ; he had by this time discovered that they were at Caunus.

42   So Astyochus sailed at once to Symè before his arrival

His ships lose their way in the fog, and his left wing is attacked and defeated by the Athenians, who in their turn fly at the sudden appearance of the rest of the fleet.

was reported, in the hope that he might come upon the Athenian squadron in the open sea. The rain and cloudy state of the atmosphere caused confusion among his ships, which lost their way in the dark. When dawn broke, the fleet was dispersed and the left wing alone was visible to the Athenians, while the other ships were still straggling off the shore of the island. Charminus and the Athenians put out to sea with part of their twenty ships, supposing that these were only the squadron from Caunus for which they were watching. They at once attacked them, sank three of them, disabled others, and were gaining the victory, when to their surprise there appeared the larger part of the Lacedaemonian fleet threatening to surround them. Whereupon they fled, and in their flight lost six ships, but with the rest gained the island of Teutlussa, and thence Halicarnassus. The Peloponnesians touched at Cnidus, and there uniting with the twenty-seven ships from Caunus, they all sailed to Symè and raised a trophy; they then returned and put into port again at Cnidus.

As soon as the Athenians heard the result of the sea- 43 fight they sailed from Samos to Symè with their whole fleet. They did not attack the Peloponnesians at Cnidus, nor the Peloponnesians them; but they carried away the heavy tackle of their own ships which had been left at Symè, and touching at Loryma, a place on the mainland, returned to Samos. *The Peloponnesians, who are now at Cnidus, confer with Tissaphernes. Lichas points out the consequences involved in the two treaties. Tissaphernes goes away in a rage.* The Peloponnesians were now all together at Cnidus, and were making the repairs necessary after the battle, while the Lacedaemonian commissioners conferred with Tissaphernes (who was himself on the spot) as to any matters in his past dealings with them at which they were displeased, and as to the best manner of securing their common interests in the future conduct of the war. Lichas entered into the enquiry with great energy; he took exception to both the treaties; that of Chalcideus and that of Theramenes were equally objectionable. For the King at that time of day to claim power over all the countries which his ancestors had formerly held was monstrous. If either treaty were carried out, the inhabitants of all the islands, of Thessaly, of Locris, and of all Hellas, as far as Boeotia, would again be reduced to slavery; instead of giving the Hellenes freedom, the Lacedaemonians would be imposing upon them the yoke of Persia. So he desired them to conclude some more satisfactory treaty, for he would have nothing to say to these; he did not want to have the fleet maintained upon any such terms. Tissaphernes was indignant, and without settling anything went away in a rage.

Meanwhile the Peloponnesians had been receiving 44 communications from the chief men of Rhodes, and resolved to sail thither. They hoped to gain over an island

which was strong alike in sailors and in infantry ; if successful, they might henceforward main-

The Peloponnesians persuade (11) Rhodes to revolt; there they draw up their ships and do nothing for eleven weeks. The Athenians, who arrive too late to hinder the revolt, make descents upon the island.

tain their navy by the help of their
own allies without asking Tissaphernes for money. So in the same
winter they sailed from Cnidus against
Rhodes, and first attacked Camirus
with ninety-four ships. The inhabitants,
who were in ignorance of the plot and
dwelt in an unfortified city, were alarmed and began to fly.
The Lacedaemonians re-assured them, and assembling the
people not only of Camirus, but of Lindus and Ialysus,
the two other cities of Rhodes, persuaded all of them to
revolt from the Athenians. Thus Rhodes went over to the
Peloponnesians. Nearly at the same time the Athenians,
who had heard of their intentions, brought up the fleet
from Samos, hoping to forestall them ; they appeared in
the offing, but finding that they were just too late, sailed to
Chalcè for the present, and thence back to Samos. They
then fought against Rhodes, making descents upon it from
Chalcè, Cos, and Samos, while the Peloponnesians, having
collected thirty-two talents [a] from the Rhodians, drew up
their ships, and did nothing for eleven weeks.

45   Before the Peloponnesians had removed to Rhodes
affairs took a new turn. After the

Alcibiades, in fear of his life from the Spartans, retires to Tissaphernes, whom he supplies with arguments against the Peloponnesians and instructs in various ways. By his advice the pay is curtailed, and the revolted cities who beg for money are refused.

death of Chalcideus and the engagement at Miletus [b], Alcibiades fell under
suspicion at Sparta, and orders came
from home to Astyochus that he should
be put to death. Agis hated him, and
he was generally distrusted. In fear
he retired to Tissaphernes, and soon,
by working upon him, did all he could
to injure the Peloponnesian cause. He
was his constant adviser, and induced him to cut down the

---

[a] £64,000.   [b] Cp. viii. 24 init., 25.

pay of the sailors from an Attic drachma to half a drachma [a],
and this was only to be given at irregular intervals. Tissaphernes was instructed by him to tell the Peloponnesians
that the Athenians, with their long experience of naval
affairs, gave half a drachma only, not from poverty, but
lest their sailors should be demoralised by high pay, and
spend their money on pleasures which injured their health,
and thereby impaired their efficiency; [b] the payment too
was made irregularly, that the arrears, which they would
forfeit by desertion, might be a pledge of their continuance
in the service [b]. He also recommended him to bribe the
trierarchs and the generals of the allied cities into consenting. They all yielded with the exception of the Syracusans: Hermocrates alone stood firm on behalf of the
whole alliance. When the allies who had revolted came
asking for money, Alcibiades drove them away himself,
saying on behalf of Tissaphernes that the Chians must
have lost all sense of shame; they were the richest people
in Hellas, and now, when they were being saved by foreign
aid, they wanted other men, not only to risk life, but to
expend money in their cause. To the other cities he
replied that, having paid such large sums to the Athenians
before they revolted, they would be inexcusable if they were
not willing to contribute as much and even more for their
own benefit. He represented further that Tissaphernes
was now carrying on the war at his own expense, and
must be expected to be careful. But if supplies should
come from the King he would restore the full pay, and do
whatever was reasonable for the cities.

Alcibiades also advised Tissaphernes not to be in a 46
hurry about putting an end to the war, and neither to
bring up the Phoenician fleet which he was preparing,
nor to give pay to more Hellenic sailors; he should not
be so anxious to put the whole power both by sea and

---

[a] About 4*d*.   [b] Others translate (omitting 'the payment too was
made irregularly'), 'also lest they should get away from their ships too
freely, leaving the pay still owing them as a pledge.'

land into the same hands.   Let the dominion only remain divided, and then, whichever of the two rivals was

*Tissaphernes should
balance the contending
powers against one
another and finally get
rid of both. The Athen-
ians are the more
natural allies of the
King because they only
desire empire at sea, and
do not profess to be
the liberators of Hellas.
Tissaphernes approves,
and at once begins to
pursue the policy indi-
cated to him.*
troublesome, the King might always
use the other against him.   But if one
defeated the other and became supreme
on both elements, who would help
Tissaphernes to overthrow the conqueror?   He would have to take the
field in person and fight, which he
might not like, at great risk and expense.   The danger would be easily
averted at a fraction of the cost, and
at no risk to himself, if he wore out
the Hellenes in internal strife.   Alcib-
iades also said that the Athenians would be more suitable
partners of empire, because they were less likely to encroach
by land, and both their principles and their practice in carrying on the war accorded better with the King's interest.
For if he helped them to subject the element of the sea to
themselves, they would gladly help him in the subjugation
of the Hellenes who were in his country, whereas the Lacedaemonians came to be their liberators.   But a power
which was at that very moment emancipating the Hellenes
from the dominion of another Hellenic power like themselves would not be satisfied to leave them under the yoke
of the Barbarian [a] if they once succeeded in crushing the
Athenians [a].   So he advised him first to wear them both
out, and when he had clipped the Athenians as close as he
could, then to get the Peloponnesians out of his country.
To this course Tissaphernes was strongly inclined, if we
may judge from his acts.   For he gave his full confidence
to Alcibiades, whose advice he approved, and kept the
Peloponnesians ill-provided, at the same time refusing to

---

[a] More literally : 'unless they failed at some time or other to crush
the Athenians'; or 'unless the Persians got the Lacedaemonians out of
the way': see note.

let them fight at sea, and insisting that they must wait until the Phoenician ships arrived; they would then fight at an advantage. In this manner he ruined their affairs and impaired the efficiency of their navy, which had once been in first-rate condition. There were many other ways in which he showed openly and unmistakeably that he was not in earnest in the cause of his allies.

In giving this advice to Tissaphernes and the King, now that he had passed under their protection, Alcibiades said what he really thought to be most for their interests[a]. But he had another motive; he was preparing the way for his own return from exile. He knew that, if he did not destroy his country altogether, the time would come when he would per-suade his countrymen to recall him; and he thought that his arguments would be most effectual if he were seen to be on intimate terms with Tissaphernes. And the result proved that he was right. The Athenian soldiers at Samos soon perceived that he had great influence with him, and he sent messages to the chief persons among them, whom he begged to remember him to all good men and true, and to let them know that he would be glad to return to his country and cast in his lot with them. He would at the same time make Tissaphernes their friend; but they must establish an oligarchy, and abolish the villainous demo-cracy which had driven him out. Partly moved by these messages, but still more of their own inclination, the trier-archs and leading Athenians at Samos were now eager to overthrow the democracy.

Alcibiades intrigues with the leading men at Samos for his own restoration. He would make Tissaphernes the friend of Athens. But there was one condition: —Abolish the demo-cracy.

The matter was stirred in the camp first of all, and introduced into the city afterwards. A few persons went over from Samos to Alcibiades, and conferred with him: to them he held out the hope that he would make, first

47

48

---

[a] Cp. v. 43 init.

of all Tissaphernes, and secondly the King himself, their friend, if they would put down demo-

A few of the oligarchs confer with Alcibiades. They form a conspiracy in the camp. The King's pay proves a telling argument. Phrynichus alone sees the drift of their policy. What does Alcibiades care about oligarchy? What do the allied cities care? And why should the King suddenly make friends of his old enemies the Athenians ?

cracy; the King would then be better able to trust them. And so the aristocracy, on whom the heaviest burdens are apt to fall[a], conceived great hopes of getting the government into their own hands, and overcoming their enemies. Returning to Samos, the envoys drew all such as seemed desirable accomplices into a conspiracy, while the language held in public to the main body of the army was that the King would be their friend and would supply them with money if Alcibiades was restored and democracy given up. Now the multitude were at first dissatisfied with the scheme, but the prospect of the King's pay was so grateful to them that they offered no opposition; and the authors of the movement, after they had broached the idea to the people, once more considered the proposals of Alcibiades among themselves and the members of their clubs. Most of them thought the matter safe and straightforward enough. Phrynichus, who was still general, was of another mind. He maintained, and rightly, that Alcibiades cared no more for oligarchy than he did for democracy, and in seeking to change the existing form of government was only considering how he might be recalled and restored to his country at the invitation of the clubs; whereas their one care should be to avoid disunion. Why should the King go out of his way to join the Athenians whom he did not trust, when he would only get into trouble with the Peloponnesians, who were now as great a naval power, and held some of the most important cities in his dominion ?—it would be much easier for him to make friends with them, who had never done him any harm. As to the allies, to whom they had promised the blessings of oligarchy which they were now

---

[a] Cp. viii. 63 fin.

about to enjoy themselves, he would be bound that the
revolted cities would not return to them, and that their old
allies would be not a whit more loyal in consequence. The
form of government was indifferent to them if they could
only be free, but they did not want to be in subjection either
to an oligarchy or to a democracy. And as for the so-
called nobility, the allies thought that they would be quite
as troublesome as the people ; they were the persons who
suggested crimes to the popular mind ; who provided the
means for their execution ; and who reaped the fruits
themselves. As far as it rested with the oligarchy the
punishment of death would be inflicted unscrupulously,
and without trial, whereas the people brought the oligarchs
to their senses, and were a refuge to which the oppressed
might always have recourse. Experience had taught the
cities this lesson, and he was well aware of their feelings.
He was therefore himself utterly dissatisfied with the
proposals of Alcibiades, and disapproved of the whole
affair.

But the conspirators who were present were not at all **49**
shaken in their opinion. They accepted *The conspirators are*
the plan and prepared to send Peisander *unshaken. Peisander*
and other envoys to Athens, that they *sent to Athens.*
might manage the recall of Alcibiades and the overthrow
of the democracy, and finally make Tissaphernes a friend
of the Athenians.

Phrynichus now knew that a proposal would be made **50**
for the restoration of Alcibiades, which *Phrynichus, thinking*
the Athenians would certainly accept ; *to betray Alcibiades to*
and having opposed his return he feared *Astyochus, is himself*
that Alcibiades, if he were recalled, *betrayed by them both.*
He continues to make
would do him a mischief, because he *treasonable proposals to*
had stood in his way. So he had re- *them ;*
course to the following device. He secretly sent a letter
to Astyochus, the Lacedaemonian admiral, who was still
at Miletus, informing him that Alcibiades was gaining over
Tissaphernes to the Athenians and ruining the Pelopon-

nesian interests. He gave full particulars, adding that Astyochus must excuse him if he sought to harm an enemy even at some cost to his country [a]. Now Astyochus had no idea of punishing Alcibiades, who moreover no longer came within his reach. On the contrary, he went to him and to Tissaphernes at Magnesia, and, turning informer, told them of the letter which he had received from Samos. (He was believed to have sold himself to Tissaphernes, to whom he now betrayed everything; and this was the reason why he was so unwilling to bestir himself about the reduction of the pay [b].) Alcibiades immediately sent a despatch denouncing to the leaders of the army at Samos the treason of Phrynichus, and demanding that he should be put to death. Phrynichus was confounded [c], and in fact the revelation placed him in the greatest danger. However he sent again to Astyochus, blaming him for having violated his former confidence. He then proceeded to say that he was ready to give the Peloponnesians the opportunity of destroying the whole Athenian army, and he explained in detail how Samos, which was unfortified, might best be attacked; adding that he was in danger of his life for their sakes, and that he need no longer apologise if by this or any other means he could save himself from destruction at the hands of his worst enemies. Again the message was communicated by Astyochus to Alcibiades.

51 Now Phrynichus was well aware of his treachery, and he knew that another letter from Alcibiades giving further information was on the point of arriving. Before its arrival he himself warned the army that, Samos being unwalled and some of the ships not anchoring within the harbour, the enemy were going to attack the fleet; of this he had certain knowledge. They

of which he also gives information to the Athenians. Thus he is purged of his treason, and outwits Alcibiades, who is thought to have acted from spite.

---

[a] Cp. vi. 92 for a similar excuse. [b] Cp. viii. 45 med. [c] Placing the comma after Φρύνιχος.

ought therefore to fortify the place as quickly as they could, and to take every precaution. As he was a general he could execute his proposals by his own authority. So they set to work, and in consequence Samos, which would have been fortified in any case, was fortified all the sooner. Not long afterwards the expected letter came from Alcibiades warning the Athenians that the army was being betrayed by Phrynichus, and that the enemy were going to make an attack. But Alcibiades was not trusted; he was thought to have attributed to Phrynichus out of personal animosity complicity in the enemy's designs, with which he was himself acquainted. Thus he did him no harm, but rather strengthened his position by telling the same tale.

Alcibiades still continued his practices with Tissaphernes, **52** whom he now sought to draw over to the Athenian interest. But Tissaphernes was afraid of the Peloponnesians, who had more ships on the spot than the Athenians. And yet he would have liked, if he could, to have been persuaded; especially when he saw the opposition which the Peloponnesians raised at Cnidus to the treaty of Theramenes[a]. For his quarrel with *Tissaphernes under the influence of Alcibiades would have liked to join the Athenians. For he had quarrelled with the Peloponnesians before the protest of Lichas at Cnidus, and it confirmed the warning which he had received from Alcibiades. But he is afraid.* them had broken out before the Peloponnesians went to Rhodes, where they were at present stationed[b]; and the words of Alcibiades, who had previously warned Tissaphernes that the Lacedaemonians were the liberators of all the cities of Hellas, were verified by the protest of Lichas, who declared that 'for the King to hold all the cities which he or his ancestors had held was a stipulation not to be endured.' So Alcibiades, who was playing for a great stake, was very assiduous in paying his court to Tissaphernes.

---

[a] Cp. viii. 43.   [b] Cp. viii. 45 init.

53   Meanwhile Peisander and the other envoys who had been sent from Samos arrived at Athens and made their proposals to the people.

Peisander and his colleagues arrive at Athens and insist on the recall of Alcibiades and the modification of the democracy. Violent indignation is aroused.

They said much in few words, insisting above all that if the Athenians restored Alcibiades and modified their democracy they might secure the alliance of the King and gain the victory over the Peloponnesians. There was great opposition to any change in the democracy, and the enemies of Alcibiades were loud in protesting that it would be a dreadful thing if he were permitted to return in defiance of the law. The Eumolpidae and Ceryces called heaven and earth to witness that the city must never restore a man who had been banished for profaning the mysteries. Amid violent expressions of indignation Peisander came forward, and having up the objectors one by one he pointed out to them that the Peloponnesians had a fleet ready for action as large as their own, that they numbered more cities among their allies, and that they were furnished with money by Tissaphernes and the King; whereas the Athenians had spent everything : he then asked them whether there was the least hope of saving the country unless the King could be won over. They all acknowledged that there was none. He then said to them plainly :—

‘But this alliance is impossible unless we are governed in a wiser manner, and office is confined to a smaller number : then the King will trust us. Do not let us be dwelling on the form of the constitution [a], which we may hereafter change as we please, when the very existence of Athens is at stake. And we must restore Alcibiades, who is the only man living capable of saving us.’

54   The people were very angry at the first suggestion of an oligarchy; but when Peisander proved to them that they had no other resource, partly in fear, and partly in hope

---

[a] Reading βουλεύωμεν with most MSS.

that it might be hereafter changed, they gave way.   So
a decree was passed that Peisander
himself and ten others should go *But is there any*
out and negotiate to the best of their *alternative? It is at*
judgment with Tissaphernes and Al- *ander shall go and*
cibiades.   Peisander also denounced *negotiate with Alcib-*
Phrynichus, and therefore the people *iades.*
dismissed him and his colleague Scironides from their
commands, and appointed Diomedon and Leon to be
admirals in their room.   Peisander thought that Phrynichus would stand in the way of the negotiations with
Alcibiades, and for this reason he calumniated him,
alleging that he had betrayed Iasus and Amorges.   Then
he went, one after another, to all the clubs which already
existed in Athens for the management of trials and elec-
tions, and exhorted them to unite, and by concerted action
put down the democracy.   When he had completed all
the necessary preparations and the plot was ripe, he and
his colleagues proceeded on their voyage to Tissaphernes.

During the same winter Leon and Diomedon, who had 55
now entered upon their command, *The Athenians com-*
made a descent upon Rhodes. They *mand Rhodes from*
found the Peloponnesian fleet drawn *Chalcè. The blockade*
up out of their reach, but they landed, *of Chios. The Chians*
and defeated the Rhodians who came *make a sally, in which*
out to meet them.   From Rhodes they *after a partial success*
retired to Chalcè[a], which henceforth *they are defeated and*
Pedaritus is slain.
they made their base of operations rather than Cos, because
they could there better command any movement which
might be made by the Peloponnesian fleet.   About this
time Xenophantidas, a Lacedaemonian, brought word to
Rhodes from Pedaritus, the governor of Chios, that the
Athenian fortification was now completed[b], and that if the
Peloponnesians with their whole fleet did not at once come
to the rescue Chios would be lost.   So they began to think

---

[a] Cp. viii. 44 fin., 60 fin.   [b] Cp. viii. 40 fin.

of sending help. Meanwhile Pedaritus in person with his
mercenaries [a] and the whole Chian army attacked the lines
which protected the Athenian fleet ; he took a part of the
wall and obtained possession of certain ships which were
drawn up on shore. But the Athenians rushed out upon
them, and first putting to flight the Chians, soon defeated
the rest of his forces. Pedaritus himself was slain, together
with many of the Chians, and a great quantity of arms was
taken.

56   The Chians were now blockaded more closely than ever

*Peisander goes to
Tissaphernes, who does
not want to be persuaded,
and to Alcibiades, who
does not want to be
thought incapable of
persuading him. So
they demand too much,
and the Athenian en-
voys leave in a rage at
the tricks of Alcibiades.*

both by sea and land, and there was
a great famine in the place. Meanwhile Peisander and his colleagues
came to Tissaphernes and proposed an
agreement. But Alcibiades was not as
yet quite sure of Tissaphernes, who
was more afraid of the Peloponnesians
than of the Athenians, and was still
desirous, in accordance with the lesson
which he had been taught by Alcibiades himself, to wear
them both out. So he had recourse to the device of making
Tissaphernes ask too much, that the negotiations might be
broken off. And I imagine that Tissaphernes himself
equally wanted them to fail ; he was moved by his fears,
while Alcibiades, seeing that his reluctance was insuperable, did not wish the Athenians to think that he was
unable to persuade him —he wanted them to believe that
Tissaphernes was already persuaded and anxious to make
terms but could not, because they themselves would not
grant enough. And so, speaking on behalf of Tissaphernes
who was himself present, he made such exorbitant demands that, although for a time the Athenians were willing
to grant anything which he asked, at length the responsibility of breaking off the conference was thrown upon them.
He and Tissaphernes demanded, first the cession of all

---

[a] Cp. viii. 28 fin., 38 med.

Ionia to the King, then that of the neighbouring islands; and there were some other conditions. Thus far the Athenians offered no opposition. But at last, fearing that his utter inability to fulfil his promise would be exposed, at the third interview he demanded permission for the King to build ships, and sail along his own coast wherever and with as many vessels as he pleased. This was too much; the Athenians now perceived that matters were hopeless, and that they had been duped by Alcibiades. So they departed in anger to Samos.

Immediately afterwards, and during the same winter, 57 Tissaphernes came down to Caunus wishing to bring back the Peloponnesians to Miletus, and once more to make a treaty with them on such terms as he could get; he was willing to maintain them, for he did not want to become wholly their enemy, and was afraid that if their large fleet were at a loss for supplies they might be compelled to fight and be defeated, or their crews might desert; in either case the Athenians would gain their ends without his assistance. Above all he feared lest they should ravage the adjoining mainland in search of food. Taking into account all these possibilities, and true to his policy, which was to hold the balance evenly between the two contending powers, he sent for the Lacedaemonians, furnished them with supplies, and made a third treaty with them, which ran as follows:—

Tissaphernes, holding the balance, now thinks that the time has come to make another treaty with the Lacedaemonians.

'In the thirteenth year of the reign of Darius the King, 58 when Alexippidas was Ephor at Lacedaemon, a treaty was made in the plain of the Maeander between the Lacedaemonians and their allies on the one hand, and Tissaphernes, Hieramenes, and the sons of Pharnaces on the other, touching the interests of the King, and of the Lacedaemonians and their allies.

This treaty, made in the name of Tissaphernes on the King's behalf, does not extend the recognition of the King's rights beyond Asia. The obnoxious clause is omitted.

' I. All the King's country which is in Asia shall continue to be the King's, and the King shall act as he pleases in respect of his own country.

' II. The Lacedaemonians and their allies shall not go against the King's country to do hurt, and the King shall not go against the country of the Lacedaemonians and their allies to do hurt. If any of the Lacedaemonians or their allies go against the King's country and do hurt, the Lacedaemonians and their allies shall interfere : and if any of the dwellers in the King's country shall go against the country of the Lacedaemonians and their allies and do hurt, the King shall interfere.

' III. Tissaphernes shall provide maintenance for the number of ships which the Lacedaemonians have at present, according to the agreement, until the King's ships arrive. When they have arrived, the Lacedaemonians and their allies may either maintain their own ships, or they may receive the maintenance of their ships from Tissaphernes. But in this case the Lacedaemonians and their allies shall at the end of the war repay to Tissaphernes the money which they have received.

' IV. When the King's ships have arrived, the ships of the Lacedaemonians and of their allies and of the King shall carry on the war in common, as may seem best to Tissaphernes and to the Lacedaemonians and their allies : and if they wish to make peace with the Athenians both parties shall make peace on the same terms.'

59   Such was the treaty. Tissaphernes now prepared to bring up the Phoenician ships, as he had promised, and to fulfil his other pledges. He was anxious at all events to be seen making a beginning.

60   Towards the end of the winter, Oropus, which was occupied by an Athenian garrison, was betrayed to the Boeotians. Certain of the Eretrians and of the Oropians themselves, both having an eye to the revolt of Euboea, were concerned in the enterprise. For Oropos, facing Eretria, while held by the Athenians could not be other

than a serious annoyance, both to Eretria and to the whole of Euboea. Having now possession of Oropus the Eretrians came to Rhodes, and invited the Peloponnesians to Euboea. They were however more disposed to relieve the distress of Chios, and thither they sailed from Rhodes with their whole fleet. Near Triopium they descried the Athenian ships in the open sea sailing from Chalcè : neither fleet attacked the other, but both

Oropus, by the help of certain Eretrians, is betrayed to the Boeotians. Instead of going to Euboea, the Peloponnesians determine to relieve Chios, but are hindered by the appearance of the Athenian fleet. Both fleets return to their original stations at Samos and at Miletus.

arrived safely, the one at Samos, and the other at Miletus. The Lacedaemonians now saw that they could no longer relieve Chios without a battle at sea. So the winter ended, and with it the twentieth year in the Peloponnesian War of which Thucydides wrote the history.

At the beginning of the following spring, Dercyllidas, 61 a Spartan, was sent at the head of a small army along the coast to the Hellespont. He was to effect the revolt of Abydos, a Milesian colony. The Chians, while Astyochus was doubting whether he could assist them, were compelled by the pressure of the

The Chians, assisted by their new governor, Leon the Spartan, with twelve ships, make a sally with thirty-six ships and gain an advantage over thirty-two Athenian ships.

blockade to fight at sea. While he was still at Rhodes they had obtained from Miletus, after the death of Pedaritus, a new governor, Leon, a Spartan, who had come out as a marine with Antisthenes[a]; he brought with him twelve ships, five Thurian, four Syracusan, one from Anaea, one Milesian, and one which was Leon's own; they had been employed in guarding Miletus. The Chians made a sally with their whole force, and seized a strong position; their ships at the same time, to the number of thirty-six, sailed out and fought with the thirty-two of the Athenians. The engagement was severe; the Chians and

---

[a] Cp. viii. 39 init.

their allies had rather the advantage, but evening had come on; so they retired to the city.

62   Soon afterwards Dercyllidas arrived at the Hellespont

Dercyllidas arrives at the Hellespont and in-duces (12) Abydos and (13) Lampsacus to re-volt. Strombichides pursues him and re-covers Lampsacus, but not Abydos.

from Miletus; Abydos, and two days later Lampsacus, revolted to him and Pharnabazus. Strombichides, having intelligence, hastened thither from Chios with twenty-four Athenian ships, of which some were transports con-veying hoplites. Defeating the Lamps-acenes who came out against him, he took Lampsacus, which was unfortified, at the first onset. He made plunder of the slaves and property which he found there, and, reinstating the free inhabitants, went on to Abydos. But the people of Abydos would not yield, and though he attempted to take the place by assault, he failed; so he crossed over to Sestos, a city of the Chersonese opposite Abydos, which the Persians had formerly held. There he placed a garrison to keep watch over the entire Hellespont.

63   Meanwhile the Chians gained more command of the sea,

In the absence of Strombichides, the Chians get more con-trol of the sea, and Astyochus offers battle to the Athenians.

and Astyochus and the Peloponnesians at Miletus, hearing of the naval engage-ment and of the withdrawal of Strom-bichides and his ships, took courage. Sailing to Chios with two ships, Asty-ochus fetched away the fleet [a] which was there, and with his united forces made a demonstration against Samos. But the Athenian crews, who were in a state of mutual distrust, did not go out to meet him; so he sailed back to Miletus.

For about this time, or rather sooner, the democracy

The conspirators at Samos give up Alcib-iades, but, with the help of some of the Samians, resolve to persevere in their plan.

at Athens had been subverted. Peis-ander and his fellow envoys, on their return to Samos after their visit to Tissaphernes, had strengthened their interest in the army, and had even

---

[a] i. e. the allied fleet, not the Chian: cp. 61 med.

persuaded the chief men of Samos to join them in setting up an oligarchy, [a] although they had lately risen against their own countrymen [a] in order to put down oligarchy [b]. At the same time conferring among themselves, the Athenian leaders at Samos came to the conclusion that since Alcibiades would not join they had better leave him alone; for indeed he was not the sort of person who was suited to an oligarchy. But they determined, as they were already compromised, to proceed by themselves, and to take measures for carrying the movement through; they meant also to persevere in the war, and were willing enough to contribute money or anything else which might be wanted out of their own houses, since they would now be toiling, not for others, but for themselves [c].

Having thus encouraged one another in their purpose **64** they sent Peisander and one half of the envoys back to Athens. They were to carry out the scheme at home, and had directions to set up an oligarchy in the subject-cities at which they touched on their voyage. The other half were despatched different ways to other subject-cities.

They want to put down democracy in the subject-cities. But the allies, especially the Thasians, having gained a better government, do not care to retain their connexion with Athens.

Diotrephes, who was then at Chios, was sent to assume the command in Chalcidicè and on the coast of Thrace, to which he had been previously appointed. On arriving at Thasos he put down the democracy. But within about two months of his departure the Thasians began to fortify their city; they did not want to have an aristocracy dependent on Athens when they were daily expecting to obtain their liberty from Lacedaemon. For there were Thasian exiles who had been driven out by the Athenians dwelling in Peloponnesus, and they, with the assistance of their friends at home, were exerting themselves vigorously to obtain ships and

---

[a] Or, 'although there had just been an insurrection in Samos itself.'
[b] Cp. viii. 21, 73 init.   [c] Cp. viii. 48 init.

effect the revolt of Thasos. The recent change was exactly what they desired ; for the government had been reformed without danger to themselves, and the democracy, who would have opposed them, had been overthrown. Thus the result in the case of Thasos, and also, as I imagine, of many other states, was the opposite of what the oligarchical conspirators had intended. For the subject-cities, having secured a moderate form of government, and having no fear of being called to account for their proceedings, aimed at absolute freedom ; they scorned the n sham independence a proffered to them by the Athenians.

65   Peisander and his colleagues pursued their voyage and,

Peisander returns to Athens, where he finds the work already half done. Assassination of Androcles, the enemy of Alcibiades. Programme of the new party.

as they had agreed, put down the democracies in the different states. From some places they obtained the assistance of heavy-armed troops, which they took with them to Athens b. There they found the revolution more than half accomplished by the oligarchical clubs. Some of the younger citizens had conspired and secretly assassinated one Androcles, one of the chief leaders of the people, who had been foremost in procuring the banishment of Alcibiades c. Their motives were twofold : they killed him because he was a demagogue ; but more because they hoped to gratify Alcibiades, whom they were still expecting to return, and to make Tissaphernes their friend. A few others who were inconvenient to them they made away with in a like secret manner. Meanwhile they declared in their public programme that no one ought to receive pay who was not on military service ; and that not more than five thousand should have a share in the government ; those, namely, who were best able to serve the state in person and with their money.

---

a Or, 'pretence of law and order,' reading τῆς ὑπούλου εὐνομίας with Dionysius, supported by Schol., and two good MSS. ; see note.

b Cp. viii. 69 med.   c Cp. vi. 89 fin.

These were only pretences intended to look well in the **66** eyes of the people; for the authors of the revolution fully meant to retain the new government in their own hands. The popular assembly and the council of five hundred were still convoked; but nothing was brought before them of which the conspirators had not approved; the speakers were of their

The conspirators for a time reign supreme; they put out of the way secretly any inconvenient persons; the people, from mutual fear and mistrust, cannot combine and retaliate.

party and the things to be said had been all arranged by them beforehand. No one any longer raised his voice against them; for the citizens were afraid when they saw the strength of the conspiracy, and if any one did utter a word, he was put out of the way in some convenient manner. No search was made for the assassins; and though there might be suspicion, no one was brought to trial; the people were so depressed and afraid to move that he who escaped violence thought himself fortunate, even though he had never said a word. Their minds were cowed by the supposed number of the conspirators, which they greatly exaggerated, having no means of discovering the truth, since the size of the city prevented them from knowing one another. For the same reason a man [a] could not conspire and retaliate [a], because he was unable to express his sorrow or indignation to another; he could not make a confidant of a stranger, and he would not trust his acquaintance. The members of the popular party all approached one another with suspicion; every one was supposed to have a hand in what was going on. Some were concerned whom no one would ever have thought likely to turn oligarchs; their adhesion created the worst mistrust among the multitude, and by making it impossible for them to rely upon one another, greatly contributed to the security of the few.

---

[a] Or, taking ἐπιβουλεύσαντα as the object: 'could not defend himself against the wiles of an enemy.'

67   Such was the state of affairs when Peisander and his
colleagues arrived at Athens. They
immediately set to work and prepared
to strike the final blow. First, they
called an assembly and proposed the
election of ten commissioners, who
should be empowered to frame for the
city the best constitution which they
could devise ; this was to be laid before
the people on a fixed day. When the
day arrived they ⁿ summoned an assembly to meet in the
temple ⁿ of Poseidon at Colonus without the walls, and
distant rather more than a mile. But the commissioners
only moved that any Athenian should be allowed to
propose whatever resolution he pleased—nothing more ;
threatening at the same time with severe penalties anybody who indicted the proposer for unconstitutional
action, or otherwise offered injury to him. The whole
scheme now came to light. A motion was made to abolish
all the existing magistracies and the payment of magistrates, and to choose a presiding board of five ; these five
were to choose a hundred, and each of the hundred was
to co-opt three others. The Four Hundred thus selected
were to meet in the council-chamber ; they were to have
absolute authority, and might govern as they deemed best ;
the Five Thousand were to be summoned by them whenever they chose.

*The final stroke.
First the 'graphè pa-
ranomon' is repealed ;
then, on the proposal of
Peisander, all existing
magistracies are abol-
ished and replaced by
a board of five, which
creates another of four
hundred.*

68   The mover of this proposal, and to outward appearance
the most active partisan of the revolution, was Peisander,
but the real author and maturer of the whole scheme, who
had been longest interested in it, was Antiphon, a man
inferior in virtue to none of his contemporaries, and possessed of remarkable powers of thought and gifts of speech.
He did not like to come forward in the assembly, or in

ⁿ Reading ξυνέλεξαν. Or, 'called an assembly to meet within the
narrow bounds of the temple' (ʹυνέκλησαν); see note.

any other public arena. To the multitude, who were suspicious of his great abilities, he was an object of dislike ; but there was no man who could do more for any who consulted him, whether their business lay in the courts of justice or in the assembly. And when the government of the Four Hundred was overthrown and became exposed to the vengeance of the people, and he being accused of taking part in the plot had to speak in his own case, his defence was undoubtedly the best ever made by any

The leading intellect of the revolution was Antiphon, who had hitherto led a retired life; he was the best adviser of clients, and when his own turn came made the best defence of himself. Phrynichus and Theramenes were also men of great ability, and fit instruments to accomplish the arduous task.

man tried on a capital charge down to my time. Phrynichus also showed extraordinary zeal in the interests of the oligarchy. He was afraid of Alcibiades, whom he knew to be cognisant of the intrigue which when at Samos he had carried on with Astyochus [a], and he thought that no oligarchy would ever be likely to restore him. Having once set his hand to the work he was deemed by the others to be the man upon whom they could best depend in the hour of danger. Another chief leader of the revolutionary party was Theramenes the son of Hagnon, a good speaker and a sagacious man. No wonder then that, in the hands of all these able men, the attempt, however arduous, succeeded. For an easy thing it certainly was not, about one hundred years after the fall of the tyrants, to destroy the liberties of the Athenians, who not only were a free, but during more than one half of this time had been an imperial people.

The assembly passed all these measures without a dissentient voice, and was then dissolved. And now the Four Hundred were introduced into the council-chamber. The manner was as follows :—The whole population were always on ser-   69

The old council of the five hundred is broken up. The members depart as they are bidden, taking their pay with them.

---

[a] Cp. viii. 50, 51.

vice, either manning the walls or drawn up at their places of arms, for the enemy were at Decelea[a].   On the day of the assembly those who were not in the conspiracy were allowed to go home as usual, while the conspirators were quietly told to remain, not actually by their arms, but at a short distance; if anybody opposed what was doing they were to arm and interfere.   There were also on the spot some Andrians and Tenians, three hundred Carystians, and some of the Athenian colonists from Aegina[b], who received similar instructions; they had all been told to bring with them from their homes their own arms for this especial purpose[c].   Having disposed their forces the Four Hundred arrived, every one with a dagger concealed about his person, and with them a bodyguard of a hundred and twenty Hellenic youths whose services they used for any act of violence which they had in hand.   They broke in upon the council of five hundred as they sat in the council-chamber, and told them to take their pay and begone. They had brought with them the pay of the senators for the remainder of their yearly term of office, which they handed to them as they went out.

70   In this manner the council retired without offering any remonstrance; and the rest of the citizens kept perfectly quiet and made no counter-movement. The Four Hundred then installed themselves in the council-chamber; for the present they elected by lot Prytanes of their own number, and did all that was customary in the way of prayers and sacrifices to the Gods at their entrance into office.   Soon however they wholly changed the democratic system; and although they did not recall the exiles, because Alcibiades was one of them, they governed the city with a high hand.   Some few whom they thought would be better out of the way were put to death by them, others imprisoned, others again

They are replaced by the Four Hundred, who govern despotically and try to make peace with Lacedaemon.

---

[a] Cp. vii. 28 init.   [b] Cp. ii 27.   [c] Cp. viii. 65 init.

exiled. They also sent heralds to Agis, the Lacedaemonian king, who was at Decelea, saying that they desired to conclude a peace with him; and that they expected him to be more ready to treat with them than with the perfidious democracy.

But he, thinking that the city must be in an unsettled 71 state and that the people would not so quickly yield up their ancient liberty, thinking too that the appearance of a great Lacedaemonian army would increase their excitement, and far from convinced that civil strife was not at that very moment raging among them, gave unfavourable answers to the envoys of the Four Hundred. He

Agis, thinking that the city is now at his mercy, refuses to treat with them. But approaching too near the wall, he is undeceived. The Four Hundred at his suggestion send an embassy to Lacedaemon.

sent to Peloponnesus for large reinforcements, and then, with the garrison at Decelea and the newly arrived troops, came down in person to the very walls of Athens. He expected that the Athenians, distracted by civil strife, would be quite at his mercy; there would be such a panic created by the presence of enemies both within and without the walls, that he might even succeed in taking the city at the first onset; for the Long Walls would be deserted, and he could not fail of capturing them. But when he drew near there was no sign of the slightest disorder within; the Athenians, sending out their cavalry and a force of heavy and light-armed troops and archers, struck down a few of his soldiers who had ventured too far, and retained possession of some arms and dead bodies; whereupon, having found out his mistake, he withdrew to Decelea. There he and the garrison remained at their posts; but he ordered the newly arrived troops, after they had continued a few days in Attica, to return home. The Four Hundred resumed negotiations, and Agis was now more ready to listen to them. At his suggestion they sent envoys to Lacedaemon in the hope of coming to terms.

72   They also sent ten commissioners to Samos, who were

They also send an   to pacify the army, and to explain that
embassy to Samos, who   the oligarchy was not established with
are to make an apology   any design of injuring Athens or her
for them.   citizens, but for the preservation of the
whole state. The promoters of the change, they said, were
five thousand, not four hundred; but never hitherto, owing
to the pressure of war and of business abroad, had so many
as five thousand assembled to deliberate even on the most
important questions. They instructed them to say anything else which would have a good effect, and sent them
on their mission as soon as they themselves were installed
in the government. For they were afraid, and not without
reason as the event showed, that the Athenian sailors
would be impatient of the oligarchical system, and that
disaffection would begin at Samos and end in their own
overthrow.

73   At the very time when the Four Hundred were estab-

But a reaction has   lishing themselves at Athens, a reaction
set in at Samos. The   had set in against the oligarchical
Samian oligarchs, who   movement at Samos. Some Samians of
had themselves changed   the popular party, which had originally
sides, begin to use   risen up against the nobles, had changed
violence. Hyperbolus,   sides again when Peisander came to the
a low demagogue, is   island [a] and, persuaded by him and his
assassinated by them   Athenian accomplices at Samos, had
and their Athenian ac-   formed a body of three hundred con-
complices. The sailors   spirators and prepared to attack the
of the fleet rise and put   rest of the popular party who had previously been their
them down.
comrades. There was a certain Hyperbolus, an Athenian
of no character, who, not for any fear of his power and
influence, but for his villany, and because the city was
ashamed of him, had been ostracised. This man was
assassinated by them, and they were abetted in the act by
Charminus, one of the generals, and by certain of the

---

[a] Cp. viii. 21, 63 med.

Athenians at Samos, to whom they pledged their faith. They also joined these Athenians in other deeds of violence, and were eager to fall upon the popular party. But the people, discovering their intention, gave information to the generals Leon and Diomedon, who were impatient of the attempted oligarchy because they were respected by the multitude, to Thrasybulus and Thrasyllus, one of whom was a trierarch and the other a private soldier, and to others who were thought to be the steadiest opponents of the oligarchical movement. They entreated them not to allow the Samian people to be destroyed, and the island of Samos, without which the Athenian empire would never have lasted until then, to be estranged. Thereupon the generals went to the soldiers one by one, and begged them to interfere, addressing themselves especially to the Parali, or crew of the ship Paralus, all freeborn Athenians, who were at any time ready to attack oligarchy, real or imaginary. Leon and Diomedon, whenever they sailed to any other place, left some ships for the protection of the Samians. And so, when the three hundred began the attack, all the crews, especially the Parali, hastened to the rescue, and the popular party gained the victory. Of the three hundred they slew about thirty, and the three most guilty were banished; the rest they forgave, and henceforward all lived together under a democracy.

Chaereas the son of Archestratus, an Athenian, who had 74 been active in the movement, was quickly despatched in the ship Paralus by the Samians and the army to Athens, there to report the defeat of the Samian oligarchy, for as yet they did not know that the government was in the hands of the Four Hundred. No sooner had *The Parali, who convey the report of the revolution to Athens, are very coldly received. Chaereas their leader escapes to Samos, and tells all manner of lies about the oligarchs.* he arrived than the Four Hundred imprisoned two or three of the Parali, and taking away their ship transferred the rest of the crew to a troop-ship which was ordered to keep guard about Euboea. Chaereas, seeing promptly how matters stood, had contrived to steal away and get back to Samos, where he told the soldiers with much aggravation the news from Athens, how they were punishing everybody with stripes, and how no one might speak a word against the government; he declared that their wives and children were being outraged, and that the oligarchy were going to take the relations of all the men serving at Samos who were not of their faction and shut them up, intending, if the fleet did not submit, to put them to death. And he added a great many other falsehoods.

75   When the army heard his report they instantly rushed upon the chief authors of the recent oligarchy who were present, and their confederates, and tried to stone them. But they were deterred by the warnings of the moderate party, who begged them not to ruin everything by violence while the enemy were lying close to them, prow threatening prow. Thrasybulus the son of Lycus, and Thrasyllus, who were the chief leaders of the reaction, now thought that the time had come for the open proclamation of democracy among the Athenians at Samos, and they bound the soldiers, more especially those of the oligarchical party, by the most solemn oaths to maintain a democracy and be of one mind, to prosecute vigorously the war with Peloponnesus, to be enemies to the Four Hundred, and to hold no parley with them by heralds. All the Samians who were of full age took the same oath, and the Athenian soldiers determined to make common cause with the Samians in their troubles and dangers, and invited them to share their fortunes. They considered that neither the Samians nor themselves had any place of refuge to which they could turn, but that, whether the Four Hundred or their enemies at Miletus gained the day, they were doomed.

The army at Samos are beside themselves. But instead of taking violent measures they are persuaded by Thrasyllus and Thrasybulus to proclaim, and swear allegiance to, the democracy. The Samians unite with them in the oath.

There was now an obstinate struggle; the one party 76
determined to force democracy upon
the city, the other to force oligarchy
upon the fleet. The soldiers proceeded
to summon an assembly, at which they
deposed their former generals, and any
trierarchs whom they suspected, and
chose others. Among the new generals
Thrasybulus and Thrasyllus naturally
found a place. One after another the
men rose and encouraged their comrades by various arguments. 'We
ought not to despond,' they said, ' because the city has revolted from us, for
they are few and we are many; they

Thrasyllus and Thrasybulus are elected generals. The sailors encourage one another. They are few, we are many. They have revolted from us, not we from them. We receive the tribute; we hold Samos; we guard Piraeus; we can drive them off the sea. They are no loss; they have neither money nor sense nor virtue. And Alcibiades will gain over the King.

have lost us and not we them, and our resources are
far greater.   Having the whole navy with us we can
compel the subject-states to pay us tribute as well as if we
sailed forth from the Piraeus ; Samos is our own—no weak
city, but one which in the Samian war all but wrested from
Athens the dominion of the sea; and the position which
we hold against our Peloponnesian enemies is as strong as
heretofore.   And again, with the help of the fleet we are
better able to obtain supplies than the Athenians at home.
Indeed the only reason why the citizens have so long
retained the command of the Piraeus is that we who are
stationed at Samos are the advanced guard of the Piraeus
itself.   And now if they will not agree to give us back the
constitution, it will come to this—that we shall be better
able to drive them off the sea than they us.   The help
which the city gives us against our enemies is poor and
worthless ; and we have lost nothing in losing them. They
have no longer any money to send' (the soldiers were
supplying themselves).   'They cannot aid us by good
counsel ; and yet for what other reason do states exercise
authority over armies ?   But in this respect too they are
useless.   They have gone altogether astray, and over-

thrown the constitution of their country, which we maintain and will endeavour to make the oligarchy maintain likewise. Our advisers in the camp then are at least as good as theirs in the city. Alcibiades, if we procure his recall and pardon, will be delighted to obtain for us the alliance of the King. And above all, if these hopes fail entirely, yet, while we have our great navy, there are many places of refuge open to us in which we shall find city and lands.'

77   Having met and encouraged one another by these and similar appeals, they displayed a cor-

The oligarchic envoys remain at Delos.

responding energy in their preparations for war. And the ten commissioners whom the Four Hundred had sent out to Samos, hearing when they reached Delos how matters stood, went no further.

78   Meanwhile the Peloponnesians in the fleet at Miletus had likewise troubles among themselves.

The Peloponnesian sailors complain bitterly of Astyochus and Tissaphernes.

The sailors complained loudly to one another that their cause was ruined by Astyochus and Tissaphernes. 'Asty-ochus,' they said, 'refused to fight before [a], while we were strong and the Athenian navy weak, and will not fight now when they are reported to be in a state of anarchy, and their fleet is not as yet united. We are kept waiting for Tissaphernes and the Phoenician ships, which are a mere pretence and nothing more, and we shall soon be utterly exhausted. Tissaphernes never brings up the promised reinforcement, and he destroys our navy by his scanty and irregular payments: the time has come when we must fight.' The Syracusans were especially vehement in the matter.

79   Astyochus and the allies became aware of the outcry, and had resolved in council to fight a decisive battle. This resolution was confirmed when they heard of the confusion at Samos. So they put to sea with all their ships, in number a hundred and twelve, and ordering the

---

[a] Cp. viii. 38 fin., 44 fin., 55 init , 60 fin.

Milesians to march along the coast towards Mycalè, sailed thither themselves. But the Athenians with their fleet of eighty-two ships, which had come out of Samos and were just then moored at Glaucè on the promontory of Mycalè, a point of the mainland not far off, saw the Peloponnesians bearing down upon them, and returned, thinking that with their inferior numbers they were not justified in risking their all. Besides,

Astyochus with a hundred and twelve ships offers battle to the Athenians. They prefer to await the return of Strombichides, whose ships arriving raise their number to a hundred and eight. They in their turn offer battle to the Peloponnesians, who decline it.

having previous information from Miletus that the Peloponnesians were anxious to fight, they had sent a messenger to Strombichides at the Hellespont, and were waiting for him to come to their aid with the ships from Chios which had gone to Abydos [a]. So they retreated to Samos, and the Peloponnesians sailed for Mycalè and there established themselves, together with the land-forces of Miletus and of the neighbouring cities. On the following day they were on the point of attacking Samos, when news came that Strombichides had arrived with the fleet from the Hellespont; whereupon the Peloponnesians immediately retired towards Miletus, and the Athenians themselves, thus reinforced, sailed against Miletus with a hundred and eight ships. They had hoped to fight a decisive battle, but no one came out to meet them, and they returned to Samos.

The Peloponnesians had not gone out because they 80 thought [b]that even with their united force they could not risk a battle[b]. But not knowing how to maintain so large a fleet, especially since Tissaphernes never paid them properly, they at once while the summer lasted sent Clearchus the son of Rhamphias with forty ships to Pharnabazus, this being the commission which he had

---

[a] Cp. viii. 62.   [b] Or, 'that they were not a match for the now united forces of the enemy.'

originally received from Peloponnesus [a]. Pharnabazus had been inviting them to come, and promised to maintain them; the Byzantians likewise had been sending envoys to them proposing to revolt. The Peloponnesian squadron put out into the open sea that they might not be seen on their voyage by the Athenians. They were caught in a storm; Clearchus and most of his ships found refuge at Delos, and thence returned to Miletus. He himself proceeded later by land to the Hellespont and assumed his command. But ten ships under Helixus of Megara arrived safely, and effected the revolt of Byzantium. The Athenians at Samos, receiving information of these movements, sent a naval force to guard the Hellespont; and off Byzantium a small engagement was fought by eight ships against eight.

The Peloponnesians, disgusted with Tissaphernes, accept the invitation of Pharnabazus and the Byzantians, and send forty ships to the Hellespont. Ten of them arrive and effect the revolt of (14) Byzantium.

81   Ever since Thrasybulus restored the democracy at Samos he had strongly insisted that Alcibiades should be recalled; the other Athenian leaders were of the same mind, and at last the consent of the army was obtained at an assembly which voted his return and full pardon. Thrasybulus then sailed to Tissaphernes, and brought Alcibiades to Samos, convinced that there was no help for the Athenians unless by his means Tissaphernes could be drawn away from the Peloponnesians. An assembly was called, at which Alcibiades lamented the cruel and unjust fate which had banished him; he then spoke at length of their political prospects; and bright indeed were the hopes of future victory with which he inspired them, while he magnified to excess his present influence over Tissaphernes. He meant thereby first to frighten

Alcibiades laments to the Athenians at Samos the sad misunderstanding which has arisen about himself, and inspires the whole fleet with hopes of victory. Tissaphernes will do anything for them.

---

[a] Cp viii. 8 med.

the oligarchy at home, and effect the dissolution of their clubs; and secondly, to exalt himself in the eyes of the army at Samos and fortify their resolution; thirdly, to widen the breach between Tissaphernes and the enemy, and blast the hopes of the Lacedaemonians. Having these objects in view, Alcibiades carried his fulsome assurances to the utmost. Tissaphernes, he said, had promised him that if he could only trust the Athenians they should not want for food while he had anything to give, no not if he were driven at last to turn his own bed into money; that he would bring up the Phoenician ships (which were already at Aspendus) to assist the Athenians instead of the Peloponnesians; but that he could not trust the Athenians unless Alcibiades were restored and became surety for them.

Hearing all this, and a great deal more, the Athenians 82 immediately appointed him a colleague *They want to sail to* of their other generals, and placed *the Piraeus, but are* everything in his hands; no man *restrained by Alcibiades.* among them would have given up for all the world the hope of deliverance and of vengeance on the Four Hundred which was now aroused in them; so excited were they that under the influence of his words they despised the Peloponnesians, and were ready to sail at once for the Piraeus. But in spite of the eagerness of the multitude he absolutely forbade them to go thither and leave behind them enemies nearer at hand. Having been elected general, he said, he would make the conduct of the war his first care, and go at once to Tissaphernes. And he went straight from the assembly, in order that he might be thought to do nothing without Tissaphernes; at the same time he wished to be honoured in the eyes of Tissaphernes himself, and to show him that he had now been chosen general, and that a time had come when he could do him a good or a bad turn. Thus Alcibiades frightened the Athenians with Tissaphernes, and Tissaphernes with the Athenians.

83   The Peloponnesians at Miletus, who had already con-

The dislike of the Peloponnesians to Tissaphernes increases more and more. The sailors are ready to mutiny.

ceived a mistrust of Tissaphernes, when they heard of the restoration of Alcibiades were still more exasperated against him. About the time of the advance in force of the Athenians on Miletus, Tissaphernes, observing that the Peloponnesians would not put out to sea and fight with them, had become much more remiss in paying the fleet; and previously to this a dislike of him, arising out of his connexion with Alcibiades, had gained ground. He was now more hated than ever. As before, the soldiers began to gather in knots and to express discontent; and not only the soldiers, but some men of position complained that they had never yet received their full pay, and that the sum given was too small, while even this was irregularly paid; if nobody would fight, or go where food could be got, the men would desert. All these grievances they laid to the charge of Astyochus, who humoured Tissaphernes for his own gain.

84   While these thoughts were passing in their minds the

Their discontent breaks out into open violence against Astyochus. The Milesians in a like spirit drive out the garrison of Tissaphernes. They are rebuked by Lichas, whose reproof they deeply resent.

behaviour of Astyochus gave occasion to an outbreak. The Syracusan and Thurian sailors were for the most part free men, and therefore bolder than the rest in assailing him with demands for pay. Astyochus answered them roughly and threatened them; he even raised his stick against Dorieus of Thurii who was pleading the cause of

his own sailors. When the men saw the action they, sailor-like, lost all control of themselves, and rushed upon him, intending to stone him; but he, perceiving what was coming, ran to an altar, where taking refuge he escaped unhurt, and they were parted. The Milesians, who were likewise discontented, captured by a sudden assault a fort which had been built in Miletus by Tissaphernes, and drove out the garrison which he had placed there. Of this proceeding the allies approved, especially the Syracusans; Lichas, however, was displeased, and said that the Milesians and the inhabitants of the King's country should submit to the necessary humiliation, and manage to keep on good terms with Tissaphernes until the war was well over. His conduct on this and on other occasions excited a strong feeling against him among the Milesians; and afterwards, when he fell sick and died, they would not let him be buried where his Lacedaemonian comrades would have laid him.

While the Lacedaemonians were quarrelling in this manner with Astyochus and Tissaphernes, Mindarus arrived from Lacedaemon; he had been appointed to succeed Astyochus, who surrendered to him the command of the fleet and sailed home. Tissaphernes sent with him an envoy, one of his own attendants, a Carian named Gaulites, who spoke both Greek and Persian[a]. He was instructed to complain of the destruction of the fort by the Milesians, and also to defend Tissaphernes against their charges. For he knew that Milesian envoys were going to Sparta chiefly to accuse him, and Hermocrates with them, who would explain how he, aided by Alcibiades, was playing a double game and ruining the Peloponnesian cause. Now Tissaphernes owed Hermocrates a grudge ever since they quarrelled about the payment of the sailors[b]. And when afterwards he had been exiled from Syracuse, and other generals, Potamis, Myscon, and Demarchus, came to take the command of the Syracusan ships at Miletus[c], Tissaphernes attacked him with still greater violence in his exile, declaring among other things that Hermocrates had asked him for money and had been refused, and that this

85

Mindarus succeeds Astyochus. Tissaphernes sends an envoy to Sparta, who is to defend him against Hermocrates and the Milesians. Malignity of Tissaphernes towards Hermocrates.

---

[a] Cp. iv. 109 med.   [b] Cp. viii. 45 med.   [c] Cp. Xen Hell. i. 1. 27 foll.

was the reason of the enmity which he conceived [a] against him.   And so Astyochus, the Milesians, and Hermocrates sailed away to Lacedaemon.   Alcibiades had by this time returned from Tissaphernes to Samos.

86   The envoys whom the Four Hundred had sent to pacify the army and give explanations left

The envoys of the Four Hundred come to Samos after the return of Alcibiades.   They are roughly received by the multitude, who want to sail at once to the Piraeus.   But they are prevented by Alcibiades, who dismisses the envoys with smooth words. A greater service never done to Athens.

Delos [b] and came to Samos after the return of Alcibiades, and an assembly was held at which they endeavoured to speak.   At first the soldiers would not listen to them, but shouted 'Death to the subverters of the democracy.' When quiet had been with difficulty restored, the envoys told them that the change was not meant for the destruction but for the preservation of the state, and that there was no intention of betraying Athens to the enemy, which might have been effected by the new government already if they had pleased during the recent invasion.   They declared that all the Five Thousand were in turn to have a share in the administration [c]; and that the families of the sailors were not being outraged, as Chaereas slanderously reported, or in any way molested; they were living quietly in their several homes.   They defended themselves at length, but the more they said, the more furious and unwilling to listen grew the multitude. Various proposals were made; above all they wanted to sail to the Piraeus.   Then Alcibiades appears to have done as eminent [d] a service to the state as any man ever did.   For if the Athenians at Samos in their excitement had been allowed to sail against their fellow-citizens, the enemy would instantly have obtained possession of Ionia and the Hellespont.   This he prevented, and at that moment no one else could have restrained the multitude: but he did restrain them, and with sharp words protected

---

[a] Or, 'displayed.'   [b] Cp. viii. 77.   [c] Cp. viii. 93 med.
[d] Reading πρῶτος.

the envoys against the fury of individuals in the crowd. He then dismissed them himself with the reply that he had nothing to say against the rule of the Five Thousand, but that the Four Hundred must be got rid of, and the old council of Five Hundred restored. If they had reduced the expenditure in order that the soldiers on service might be better off for supplies, he highly approved. For the rest he entreated them to stand firm, and not give way to the enemy; if the city was preserved, there was good hope that they might be reconciled amongst themselves, but if once anything happened either to the army at Samos or to their fellow-citizens at home, there would be no one left to be reconciled with.

There were also present envoys from Argos, who proffered their aid ' to the Athenian people at Samos.' Alcibiades complimented them, and requested them to come with their forces when they were summoned; he then dismissed them. These Argives came with the Parali who had been ordered by the Four Hundred to cruise off Euboea in a troop-ship[a]; they were afterwards employed in conveying to Lacedaemon certain envoys sent by the Four Hundred, Laespodias, Aristophon, and Melesias. But when they were near Argos on their voyage the crews seized the envoys, and, as they were among the chief authors of the revolution, delivered them over to the Argives; while they, instead of returning to Athens, went from Argos to Samos, and brought with them in their trireme the Argive ambassadors.

The Parali who have escaped from Athens bring envoys from Argos, offering aid.

During the same summer, and just at the time when the 87 Peloponnesians were most offended with Tissaphernes on various grounds, and above all on account of the restoration of Alcibiades, which finally proved him to be a partisan of the Athenians, he, as if he were wanting to clear himself of these suspicions, prepared to go to

---

[a] Cp. viii. 74 med.

Aspendus and fetch the Phoenician ships; and he desired

Tissaphernes goes to fetch the Phoenician ships. What was his real intention? There were various answers. Thucydides is convinced that he was only pursuing his neutralising policy.

Lichas to go with him. He also said that he would assign the charge of the army to his lieutenant Tamos, who would provide for them during his absence. Why he went to Aspendus, and having gone there never brought the ships, is a question not easy to answer, and which has been answered in various ways. For the Phoenician fleet of a hundred and forty-seven ships came as far as Aspendus—there is no doubt about this; but why they never came further is matter of conjecture. Some think that, in going to Aspendus, Tissaphernes was still pursuing his policy of wearing out the Peloponnesians; at any rate Tamos, who was in charge, supplied them no better, but rather worse. Others are of opinion that he brought up the Phoenician fleet to Aspendus in order to make money by selling the crews their discharge; for he certainly had no idea of using them in actual service. Others think that he was influenced by the outcry against him which had reached Lacedaemon; and that he wanted to create an impression of his honesty: 'Now at any rate he has gone to fetch the ships, and they are really manned.' I believe beyond all question that he wanted to wear out and to neutralise the Hellenic forces; his object was to damage them both while he was losing time in going to Aspendus, and to paralyse their action, and not strengthen either of them by his alliance. For if he had chosen to finish the war, finished it might have been once for all, as any one may see: he would have brought up the ships, and would in all probability have given the victory to the Lacedae-monians, who lay opposite to the Athenians and were fully a match for them already. The excuse which he gave for not bringing them is the most conclusive evidence against him; he said that there was not as many collected as the King had commanded. But if so, the King would have been all the better pleased, for his money would have been saved and Tissaphernes would have accomplished the same result at less expense. Whatever may have been his intention, Tissaphernes came to Aspendus and conferred with the Phoenicians, and the Peloponnesians at his request sent Philip, a Lacedaemonian, with two triremes to fetch the ships.

Alcibiades, when he learned that Tissaphernes was going 88 to Aspendus, sailed thitherward himself with thirteen ships, promising the army at Samos that he would not fail to do them a great service. He would either bring the Phoenician ships to *Alcibiades, knowing that Tissaphernes never intended to bring up the Phoenician fleet, promises to keep it back.* the Athenians, or, at any rate, make sure that they did not join the Peloponnesians. He had probably known all along the real mind of Tissaphernes, and that he never meant to bring them at all. He wanted further to injure him as much as possible in the opinion of the Peloponnesians when they observed how friendly Tissaphernes was towards himself and the Athenians; their distrust would compel him to change sides. So he set sail and went on his voyage eastward, making directly for Phaselis and Caunus.

The commissioners sent by the Four Hundred returned 89 from Samos to Athens and reported the words of Alcibiades—how he bade them stand firm and not give way to the enemy, and what great hopes he entertained of reconciling the army to the city, and of overcoming the Peloponnesians. The greater number of the oligarchs, who were already dissatisfied, and would have gladly got out of the whole affair if they safely could, were *The conciliatory language of Alcibiades indicates to the more moderate of the oligarchs a path of escape. Theramenes and Aristocrates begin to talk about the Five Thousand. They see another revolution coming, and each man wants to take the lead in it.* now much encouraged. They began to come together and to criticise the conduct of affairs. Their leaders were some of the oligarchical generals and actually in office at the time, for example, Theramenes the son of Hagnon and

Aristocrates the son of Scellius. They had been among
the chief authors of the revolution, ª but now, fearing, as
they urged, the army at Samos, and being in good earnest
afraid of Alcibiades, fearing also lest their colleagues, who
were sending envoys to Lacedaemon ᵇ, might, unauthorised
by the majority, betray the city, they did not indeed openly
profess ª that they meant to get rid of extreme oligarchy,
but they maintained that the Five Thousand should be
established in reality and not in name, and the constitution
made more equal. This was the political phrase of which
they availed themselves, but the truth was that most of
them were given up to private ambition of that sort which
is more fatal than anything to an oligarchy succeeding
a democracy. For the instant an oligarchy is established
the promoters of it disdain mere equality, and everybody
thinks that he ought to be far above everybody else.
Whereas in a democracy, when an election is made, a man
is less disappointed at a failure because he has not been
competing with his equals. The influence which most
sensibly affected them were the great power of Alcibiades
at Samos, and an impression that the oligarchy was not
likely to be permanent. Accordingly every one was
struggling hard to be the first champion of the people
himself.

90   The leading men among the Four Hundred most violently
opposed to the restoration of democracy were Phrynichus,
who had been general at Samos, and had there come into
antagonism with Alcibiades ᶜ, Aristarchus, a man who had
always been the most thorough-going enemy of the
people, Peisander, and Antiphon. These and the other
leaders, both at the first establishment of the oligarchy ᵈ,
and again later when the army at Samos declared for the

ª Or, retaining ἔπεμπον : 'and now fearing, as they urged, the army
at Samos, and being in good earnest afraid of Alcibiades, they joined in
sending envoys to Lacedaemon, but only lest, if left to themselves, the
envoys should betray the city. They did not openly profess' etc.

ᵇ Cp. viii. 90 init.   ᶜ Cp. viii. 48.   ᵈ Cp. viii. 71 fin.

democracy [a], sent envoys of their own number to Lacedaemon, and were always anxious to make peace; meanwhile they continued the fortification which they had begun to build at Eetionea. They were confirmed in their purposes after the return of their own ambassadors from Samos; for they saw that not only the people, but even those who had appeared steadfast adherents of their own party, were now changing their minds. So, fearing what might happen both at Athens and Samos, they sent Antiphon, Phrynichus, and ten

Phrynichus, Aristarchus, Peisander, and Antiphon, the thoroughgoing oligarchs, are ready to betray Athens to the enemy if they can save their own power. They send, for the third time, an embassy to Sparta, and carry on with increased vigour the fortification of Eetionea.

others, in great haste, authorising them to make peace with Lacedaemon upon anything like tolerable terms; at the same time they proceeded more diligently than ever with the fortification of Eetionea. The design was (so Theramenes and his party averred) not to bar the Piraeus against the fleet at Samos should they sail thither with hostile intentions, but rather to admit the enemy with his sea and land forces whenever they pleased. This Eetionea is the mole of the Piraeus and forms one side of the entrance; the new fortification was to be so connected with the previously existing wall, which looked towards the land, that a handful of men stationed between the two walls might command the approach from the sea. For the old wall looking towards the land, and the new inner wall in process of construction facing the water, ended at the same point in one of the two forts which protected the narrow mouth of the harbour. A cross-wall was added, taking in the largest storehouse in the Piraeus and the nearest to the new fortification, which it joined; this the authorities held themselves, and commanded every one to deposit their corn there, not only what came in by sea but what they had on the spot, and to take from thence all that they wanted to sell.

---

[a] Cp. viii. 86 fin.

91   For some time Theramenes had been circulating whispers

The envoys are un- of their designs, and when the envoys
successful : but a Lace- returned from Lacedaemon without
daemonian squadron having effected anything in the nature
hovering about the
coast seems to be acting of a treaty for the Athenian people, he
in concert with the declared that this fort was likely to
ruling party. prove the ruin of Athens. Now the
Euboeans had requested the Peloponnesians to send them
a fleet [a], and just at this time two and forty ships, including
Italian vessels from Tarentum and Locri and a few from
Sicily, were stationed at Las in Laconia, and were making
ready to sail to Euboea under the command of Agesandridas the son of Agesander, a Spartan. Theramenes insisted
that these ships were intended, not for Euboea, but for the
party who were fortifying Eetionea, and that, if the people
were not on the alert, they would be undone before they
knew where they were. The charge was not a mere
calumny, but had some foundation in the disposition of
the ruling party. For what would have best pleased them
would have been, retaining the oligarchy in any case, to
have preserved the Athenian empire over the allies; failing this, to keep merely their ships and walls, and to be
independent; if this too proved impracticable, at any rate
they would not see democracy restored, and themselves
fall the first victims, but would rather bring in the enemy
and come to terms with them, not caring if thereby the
city lost walls and ships and everything else, provided that
they could save their own lives.

92   So they worked diligently at the fort, which had entrances
and postern-gates and every facility for introducing the
enemy, and did their best to finish the building in time.
As yet the murmurs of discontent had been secret and confined to a few; when suddenly Phrynichus, after his return
from the embassy to Lacedaemon, in a full market-place,
having just quitted the council-chamber, was struck by an
assassin, one of the force employed in guarding the frontier,

[a] Cp. viii. 60 med.

and fell dead.   The man who dealt the blow escaped;
his accomplice, an Argive, was seized
and put to the torture by order of the
Four Hundred, but did not disclose any
name or say who had instigated the
deed.   All he would confess was that
a number of persons used to assemble
at the house of the commander of the
frontier guard, and in other houses.
No further measures followed; and
so Theramenes and Aristocrates, and
the other citizens, whether members of
the Four Hundred or not, who were
of the same mind, were emboldened to
take decided steps.   For the Peloponnesians had already sailed round from
Las, and having overrun Aegina had
cast anchor at Epidaurus; and Thera-

*Phrynichus is assas-
sinated.   The enemies
of the oligarchy, secretly
instigated by Thera-
menes, now grow bolder.
The soldiers who were
building the fort seize
the oligarch Alexicles.
Theramenes promises
the Four Hundred to
go and release him.
He pretends to rate the
soldiers, but in reality
connives at their con-
duct.   After a scene of
tumult, in which the
two parties nearly come
to blows, the fort is
demolished to the cry of
' Let the Five Thousand
rule.'*

menes insisted that if they had been on their way to Euboea
they would never have gone up the Saronic gulf to Aegina
and then returned and anchored at Epidaurus, but that
some one had invited them for the purposes which he had
always alleged; it was impossible therefore to be any
longer indifferent.   After many insinuations and inflam-
matory harangues, the people began to take active measures.
The hoplites who were at work on the fortification of
Eetionea in the Piraeus, among whom was Aristocrates
with his own tribe, which, as taxiarch, he commanded,
seized Alexicles, an oligarchical general who had been
most concerned with the clubs, and shut him up in a
house.   Others joined in the act, including one Hermon,
who commanded the Peripoli stationed at Munychia;
above all, the rank and file of the hoplites heartily approved.
The Four Hundred, who were assembled in the council-
house when the news was brought to them, were ready in
a moment to take up arms, except Theramenes and his
associates, who disapproved of their proceedings; to these

they began to use threats. Theramenes protested, and offered to go with them at once and rescue Alexicles. So, taking one of the generals who was of his own faction, he went down to the Piraeus. Aristarchus and certain young knights came also to the scene of action. Great and bewildering was the tumult, for in the city the people fancied that the Piraeus was in the hands of the insurgents, and that their prisoner had been killed, and the inhabitants of the Piraeus that they were on the point of being attacked from the city. The elder men with difficulty restrained the citizens, who were running up and down and flying to arms. Thucydides of Pharsalus, the proxenus of Athens in that city, happening to be on the spot, kept throwing himself in every man's way and loudly entreating the people, when the enemy was lying in wait so near, not to destroy their country. At length they were pacified, and refrained from laying hands on one another. Theramenes, who was himself a general, came to the Piraeus, and in an angry voice pretended to rate the soldiers, while Aristarchus and the party opposed to the people were furious. No effect was produced on the mass of the hoplites, who were for going to work at once. They began asking Theramenes if he thought that the fort was being built to any good end, and whether it would not be better demolished. He answered that, if they thought so, he thought so too. And immediately the hoplites and a crowd of men from the Piraeus got on the walls and began to pull them down. The cry addressed to the people was, 'Whoever wishes the Five Thousand to rule and not the Four Hundred, let him come and help us.' For they still veiled their real minds under the name of the Five Thousand, and did not venture to say outright 'Whoever wishes the people to rule': they feared that the Five Thousand might actually exist, and that a man speaking in ignorance to his neighbour might get into trouble. The Four Hundred therefore did not wish the Five Thousand either to exist or to be known not to exist, thinking that to give so many a share in the government would be downright democracy, while at the same time the mystery tended to make the people afraid of one another.

The next day the Four Hundred, although much dis-93 turbed, met in the council-chamber. *The soldiers march* Meanwhile the hoplites in the Piraeus *from the Piraeus to the* let go Alexicles whom they had seized, *city. The Four Hun-* and having demolished the fort went *dred send deputies to* to the theatre of Dionysus near Muny-*them and try negotia-* chia; there piling arms they held an *tion. They promise to* assembly, and resolved to march at *publish the names of* once to the city, which they accordingly *the Five Thousand;* did, and again piled arms in the temple *out of whom the Four* of the Dioscuri. Presently deputies appeared sent by the *Hundred are to be* *elected.* Four Hundred. These conversed with them singly, and tried to persuade the more reasonable part of them to keep quiet and restrain their comrades, promising that they would publish the names of the Five Thousand, and that out of these the Four Hundred should be in turn elected in such a manner as the Five Thousand might think fit. In the meantime they begged them not to ruin everything, or to drive the city upon the enemy. The discussion became general on both sides, and at length the whole body of soldiers grew calmer, and turned their thoughts to the danger which threatened the commonwealth. They finally agreed that an assembly should be held on a fixed day in the theatre of Dionysus to deliberate on the restor‧ ation of harmony.

When the day arrived and the assembly was on the 94 point of meeting in the theatre of Dionysus, news came that Agesandri-*But meanwhile the* das and his forty-two ships had crossed *Lacedaemonian squad-* over from Megara, and were sailing *ron approaches nearer,* along the coast of Salamis. Every *and there is general* *consternation.* man of the popular party thought that this was what they had been so often told by Theramenes and his friends, and that the ships were sailing to the fort, happily now demolished. Nor is it impossible that Agesandridas may have been hovering about Epidaurus and the neighbourhood by agreement; but it is equally likely that he lingered there of his own accord, with an eye to the agitation which prevailed at Athens, hoping to be on the spot at the critical moment. Instantly upon the arrival of the news the whole city rushed down to the Piraeus, [a] thinking that a conflict with their enemies more serious than their domestic strife [a] was now awaiting them, not at a distance, but at the very mouth of the harbour. Some embarked in the ships which were lying ready; others launched fresh ships; others manned the walls and prepared to defend the entrance of the Piraeus.

95   The Peloponnesian squadron, however, sailed onward,

The ships pass onward to Euboea and put in at Oropus. A small Athenian fleet follows them, but being constrained to fight hurriedly, are utterly defeated, and the Peloponnesians obtain possession of the whole island, which revolts (15).

doubled the promontory of Sunium, and then, after putting in between Thoricus and Prasiae, finally proceeded to Oropus. The Athenians in their haste were compelled to employ crews not yet trained to work together, for the city was in a state of revolution, and the matter was vital and urgent; Euboea was all in all to them now that they were shut out from Attica [b]. They despatched a fleet under the command of Thymochares to Eretria; these ships, added to those which were at Euboea before, made up thirty-six. No sooner had they arrived than they were constrained to fight; for Agesandridas, after his men had taken their midday meal, brought out his own ships from Oropus, which is distant by sea about seven miles from the city of Eretria, and bore down upon them. The Athenians at once began to man their

---

[a] Omitting ἤ with one MS. Otherwise, retaining ἤ with a great majority of MSS.: 'thinking that a conflict among themselves more serious than the attack of their enemies' etc.   [b] Cp. vii. 27 fin., 28 init.

ships, fancying that their crews were close at hand; but
it had been so contrived that they were getting their provisions from houses at the end of the town, and not in the
market, for the Eretrians intentionally sold nothing there
that the men might lose time in embarking; the enemy
would then come upon them before they were ready, and
they would be compelled to put out as best they could.
A signal was also raised at Eretria telling the fleet at
Oropus when to attack. The Athenians putting out in
this hurried manner, and fighting off the harbour of
Eretria, nevertheless resisted for a little while, but before
long they fled and were pursued to the shore. Those of
them who took refuge in the city of Eretria, relying on
the friendship of the inhabitants, fared worst, for they
were butchered by them; but such as gained the fortified
position which the Athenians held in the Eretrian territory
escaped, and also the crews of the vessels which reached
Chalcis. The Peloponnesians, who had taken twenty-two
Athenian ships and had killed or made prisoners of the
men, erected a trophy. Not long afterwards they induced
all Euboea to revolt, except Oreus of which the Athenians
still maintained possession. They then set in order the
affairs of the island.

When the news of the battle and of the defection of 96
Euboea was brought to Athens, the
Athenians were panic-stricken. Nothing *The Athenians have*
which had happened before, not even *reason to despair; for*
the ruin of the Sicilian expedition, how- *they see the army re-*
volting, Euboea lost, no
ever overwhelming at the time, had so *more ships, the enemy*
terrified them. The army at Samos *all but in the Piraeus.*
was in insurrection; they had no ships *But they are saved by*
in reserve or crews to man them; there *the supineness of the*
Lacedaemonians.
was revolution at home—civil war might break out at any
moment: and by this new and terrible misfortune they
had lost, not only their ships, but what was worse, Euboea,
on which they were more dependent for supplies than on
Attica itself. Had they not reason to despair? But what

touched them nearest, and most agitated their minds, was the fear lest their enemies, emboldened by victory, should at once attack the Piraeus, in which no ships were left; indeed they fancied that they were all but there. And had the Peloponnesians been a little more enterprising they could easily have executed such a plan. Either they might have cruised near, and would then have aggravated the divisions in the city; or by remaining and carrying on a blockade they might have compelled the fleet in Ionia, although hostile to the oligarchy, to come and assist their kindred and their native city; and then the Hellespont, Ionia, all the islands between Ionia and Euboea, in a word, the whole Athenian empire, would have fallen into their hands. But on this as on so many other occasions the Lacedaemonians proved themselves to be the most convenient enemies whom the Athenians could possibly have had. For the two peoples were of very different tempers; the one quick, the other slow; the one adventurous, the other timorous [a]; and the Lacedaemonian character was of great service to the Athenians, the more so because the empire for which they were fighting was maritime. And this view is confirmed by the defeat of the Athenians at Syracuse; for the Syracusans, who were most like them [b], fought best against them.

97   When the news came the Athenians in their extremity

They immediately depose the Four Hundred, and establish a new government (the best which Thucydides had known) of Five Thousand, being the citizens who supplied themselves with arms. Pay for offices abolished. Alcibiades recalled.

still contrived to man twenty ships, and immediately summoned an assembly (the first of many) in the place called the Pnyx, where they had always been in the habit of meeting; at which assembly they deposed the Four Hundred, and voted that the government should be in the hands of the Five Thousand; this number was to include all who could furnish themselves with arms. No one was

----

[a] Cp. i. 70.   [b] Cp. i. 141 med.; vii. 55.

to receive pay for holding any office, on pain of falling under a curse. In the numerous other assemblies which were afterwards held they appointed Nomothetae, and by a series of decrees established a constitution. This government during its early days was the best which the Athenians ever enjoyed within my memory. Oligarchy and Democracy were duly attempered. And thus after the miserable state into which she had fallen, the city was again able to raise her head. The people also passed a vote recalling Alcibiades and others from exile, and sending to him and to the army in Samos exhorted them to act vigorously.

When this new revolution began, Peisander, Alexicles, 98 and the other leaders of the oligarchy   *Betrayal of Oenoè to* stole away to Decelea; all except *the Peloponnesians by* Aristarchus, who, being one of the   *Aristarchus.* generals at the time, gathered round him hastily a few archers of the most barbarous sort and made his way to Oenoè. This was an Athenian fort on the borders of Boeotia which the Corinthians [a], having called the Boeotians to their aid, were now besieging on their own account, in order to revenge an overthrow inflicted by the garrison of Oenoè upon a party of them who were going home from Decelea. Aristarchus entered into communication with the besiegers, and deceived the garrison by telling them that the Athenian government had come to terms with the Lacedaemonians, and that by one of the conditions of the peace they were required to give up the place to the Boeotians. They, trusting him, whom they knew to be a general, and being in entire ignorance of what had happened because they were closely invested, capitulated and came out. Thus Oenoè was taken and occupied by the Boeotians; and the oligarchical revolution at Athens came to an end.

---

[a] Or, 'which Corinthian volunteers,' omitting 'on their own account.'

99   During this summer and about the same time Mindarus

No sign of the Phoe-nician ships. The Pelo-ponnesians now become aware that Tissaphernes is thoroughly dishonest, and transfer their fleet to Pharnabazus at the Hellespont. They are detained at Chios.

transferred the fleet of the Pelopon-nesians to the Hellespont. They had been waiting at Miletus. But none of the commissioners whom Tissaphernes on going to Aspendus appointed to supply the fleet gave them anything; and neither the Phoenician ships nor Tissaphernes himself had as yet made their appearance; Philip, who had been sent with Tissa-phernes, and Hippocrates, a Spartan then in Phaselis, had informed the admiral Mindarus that the ships would never come, and that Tissaphernes was thoroughly dishonest in his dealings with them. All this time Pharnabazus was inviting them and was eager to secure the assistance of the fleet; he wanted, like Tissaphernes, to raise a revolt, whereby he hoped to profit, among the cities in his own dominion which still remained faithful to Athens. So at length Mindarus, in good order and giving the signal sud-denly, lest he should be discovered by the Athenians at Samos, put to sea from Miletus with seventy-three ships, and set sail for the Hellespont, whither in this same summer a Peloponnesian force had already gone in sixteen ships, and had overrun a portion of the Chersonese. But meeting with a storm Mindarus was driven into Icarus, and being detained there five or six days by stress of weather, he put in at Chios.

100   When Thrasyllus at Samos heard that he had started

The Athenians pur-sue them. Observing that they are at Chios, they stop at Lesbos to watch them, and during their stay besiege Eresus (16), which has revolted.

from Miletus he sailed away in all haste with fifty-five ships, fearing that the enemy might get into the Hellespont before him. Observing that Mindarus was at Chios, and thinking that he could keep him there, he placed scouts at Lesbos and on the mainland opposite, that he might be informed if the ships made any attempt to sail away. He himself coasted along the island to Methymna and ordered a supply of barley-meal and other provisions, intending, if he were long detained, to make Lesbos his head-quarters while attacking Chios. He wanted also to sail against the Lesbian town of Eresus, which had revolted, and, if possible, to destroy the place. Now certain of the chief citizens of Methymna who had been driven into exile had conveyed to the island about fifty hoplites, partisans of theirs, from Cymè, besides others whom they hired on the mainland, to the number of three hundred in all. They were commanded by Anaxander, a Theban, who was chosen leader because the Lesbians were of Theban descent[a]. They first of all attacked Methymna. In this attempt they were foiled by the timely arrival of the Athenian garrison from Mytilenè, and being a second time repulsed outside the walls, had marched over the mountains and induced Eresus to revolt. Thither Thrasyllus sailed, having determined to attack them with all his ships. He found that Thrasybulus had already reached the place, having started from Samos with five ships as soon as he heard that the exiles had landed. But he had come too late to prevent the revolt, and was lying off Eresus. There Thrasyllus was also joined by two ships which were on their way home from the Hellespont, and by a squadron from Methymna. The whole fleet now consisted of sixty-seven ships, from the crews of which the generals formed an army, and prepared by the help of engines and by every possible means to take Eresus.

Meanwhile Mindarus and the Peloponnesian fleet at 101 Chios, having spent two days in provisioning, and having received from the Chians three Chian tesseracosts[b] for each man, on the third day sailed hastily from Chios, not going through

The Peloponnesian fleet, stealing away before dawn from Chios, on the evening of the second day arrives at the Hellespont.

---

[a] Cp. iii. 2 fin., 5 med., 13 init. ; viii. 5 init.   [b] A small Chian coin of which the exact value is unknown : if it amounted to $\frac{1}{40}$th of the gold stater (20 drachmae) it would be worth 3 obols, 4*d*.

the open sea [a], lest they should fall in with the ships
blockading Eresus, but making directly for the mainland
and keeping Lesbos on the left. They touched at the
harbour of the island Carteria, which belongs to Phocaea,
and there taking their midday meal, sailed past the Cymaean
territory, and supped at Argennusae on the mainland over
against Mytilenè. They sailed away some time before
dawn, and at Harmatus, which is opposite Methymna on
the mainland, they again took their midday meal; they
quickly passed by the promontory of Lectum, Larissa,
Hamaxitus, and the neighbouring towns, and finally
arrived at Rhoeteum in the Hellespont before midnight.
Some of the ships also put into Sigeum and other places
in the neighbourhood.

102   The Athenians, who lay with eighteen ships at Sestos [b],

The Athenian squad-
ron at Sestos escapes
from them with some
loss,

knew from the beacons which their
scouts kindled, and from the sudden
blaze of many watch-fires which appeared in the enemy's country, that the
Peloponnesians were on the point of sailing into the strait.
That very night, getting close under the Chersonese, they
moved towards Elaeus, in the hope of reaching the open
sea before the enemy's ships arrived. They passed unseen the sixteen Peloponnesian ships [c] which were at
Abydos, and had been told by [d] their now approaching
friends to keep a sharp look-out if the Athenians tried to
get away. At dawn of day they sighted the fleet of
Mindarus, which immediately gave chase; most of them
escaped in the direction of Imbros and Lemnos, but the
four which were hindermost were caught off Elaeus. One
which ran ashore near the temple of Protesilaus the Peloponnesians took, together with the crew; two others
without the crews; a fourth they burnt on the shore of
Imbros; the crew escaped.

---

[a] Inserting οὐ before πελάγιαι with Haacke, and most editors.   [b] Cp.
viii. 80 fin.   [c] Cp. viii. 99 fin.   [d] Or 'had told.'

For the rest of that day they blockaded Elaeus with 103
the ships from Abydos which had now *and rejoins the rest of*
joined them; the united fleet number- *the Athenian fleet,*
ing eighty-six; but as the town would *which, on finding that*
not yield they sailed away to Abydos. *the Peloponnesians had*
gone northward, had
The Athenians, whose scouts had *immediately pursued*
failed them, and who had never ima- *them.*
gined that the enemy's fleet could pass them undetected,
were quietly besieging Eresus; but on finding out their
mistake they instantly set sail and followed the enemy to
the Hellespont. They fell in with and took two Peloponnesian ships, which during the pursuit had ventured
too far into the open sea. On the following day they
came to Elaeus, where they remained at anchor, and the
ships which had taken refuge at Imbros joined them; the
next five days were spent in making preparations for
the impending engagement.

After this they fought, and the manner of the battle was 104
as follows. The Athenians began to *Battle of Cynossema*
sail in column close along the shore *between   eighty-eight*
towards Sestos, when the Pelopon- *Peloponnesian   and*
nesians, observing them, likewise put *seventy-six   Athenian*
to sea from Abydos. Perceiving that *ships. The Pelopon-*
nesians try to shut up
a battle was imminent, the Athenians, *their enemies in the*
numbering seventy-six ships, extended *strait.   A   counter-*
their line along the Chersonese from *movement of Thrasy-*
bulus, which weakens
Idacus to Arrhiani, and the Pelopon- *the centre of the Athen-*
nesians, numbering eighty-eight ships, *ians, nearly proves fatal*
from Abydos to Dardanus. The Syra- *to them.*
cusans held the right wing of the Peloponnesians; the
other wing, on which were the swiftest ships, was led by
Mindarus himself. Thrasyllus commanded the left wing
of the Athenians, and Thrasybulus the right; the other
generals had their several posts. The Peloponnesians
were eager to begin the engagement, intending, as their
left wing extended beyond the right of the Athenians, to
prevent them, if possible, from sailing out of the straits

again, and also to thrust their centre back on the land which was near. The Athenians, seeing their intention, advanced from the land the wing on which the enemy wanted to cut them off, and succeeded in getting beyond them. But their left wing by this time had passed the promontory of Cynossema, and the result was that the centre of their line was thinned and weakened—all the more since their numbers were inferior and the sharp projection of the shore about Cynossema hindered those who were on one side from seeing what was taking place on the other.

105   So the Peloponnesians, falling upon the centre of the

But in the moment of victory the Peloponnesians fall into confusion and are defeated by a sudden turn of Thrasybulus.
Athenian fleet, forced their enemies' ships back on the beach, and having gained a decisive advantage, disembarked to follow up their victory. Neither Thrasybulus on the right wing, who was pressed hard by superior numbers, nor Thrasyllus on the left, was able to assist them. The promontory of Cynossema hindered the left wing from seeing the action, and the ships of the Syracusans and others, equal in number to their own, kept them fully engaged. But at last, while the victorious Peloponnesians were incautiously pursuing, some one ship, some another, a part of their line began to fall into disorder. Thrasybulus remarked their confusion, and at once left off extending his wing; then turning upon the ships which were opposed to him, he repulsed and put them to flight; he next faced[a] the conquering and now scattered ships of the Peloponnesian centre, struck at them, and threw them into such a panic that hardly any of them resisted. The Syracusans too had by this time given way to Thrasyllus, and were still more inclined to fly when they saw the others flying.

---

[a] Or, 'intercepted.'

After the rout the Peloponnesians effected their escape, 106 most of them to the river Midius first, and then to Abydos. Not many ships were taken by the Athenians; for the Hellespont, being narrow, afforded a retreat to the enemy within a short distance. Nevertheless nothing could have been more opportune for them

Effect of the battle on the mind of the Athenians: hope of final victory. Twenty - one ships of the enemy were taken and fifteen of their own lost.

than this victory at sea ; for some time past they had feared the Peloponnesian navy on account of their disaster in Sicily, as well as of the various smaller defeats which they had sustained[a]. But now they ceased to depreciate themselves or to think much of their enemies' seamanship. They had taken eight Chian vessels, five Corinthian, two Ambracian, two Boeotian, and of the Leucadians, Lacedaemonians, Syracusans, and Pellenians one each. Their own loss amounted to fifteen ships. They raised a trophy on the promontory of Cynossema, and then collecting the wrecks, and giving up to the enemy his dead under a flag of truce, sent a trireme carrying intelligence of the victory to Athens. On the arrival of the ship and the news of a success so incredible after the calamities which had befallen them in Euboea and during the revolution, the Athenians were greatly encouraged. They thought that their affairs were no longer hopeless, and that if they were energetic they might still win.

The Athenians at Sestos promptly repaired their ships, 107 and on the fourth day were proceeding against Cyzicus, which had revolted, when, seeing the eight Peloponnesian ships[b] from Byzantium anchored at Harpagium and Priapus, they bore

Eight more Peloponnesian ships captured by the Athenians. They recover Cyzicus (17) which has revolted.

down upon them, and defeating the land-forces which were acting with them, took the ships. They then went and recovered Cyzicus, which was unwalled, and exacted a

---

[a] Cp. viii. 95, 102.   [b] Cp. viii. 80 fin.

contribution from the inhabitants. Meanwhile the Peloponnesians sailed from Abydos to Elaeus, and recovered as many of their own captured vessels as were still seaworthy; the rest had been burnt by the Elaeusians. They then sent Hippocrates and Epicles to Euboea to bring up the ships which were there.

108   About the same time Alcibiades sailed back with his thirteen ships[a] from Caunus and Phaselis to Samos, announcing that he had prevented the Phoenician fleet from coming to the assistance of the enemy, and that he had made Tissaphernes a greater friend of the Athenians than ever. He then manned nine additional ships, and exacted large sums of money from the Halicarnassians. He also fortified Cos[b], where he left a governor, and towards the autumn returned to Samos.

Alcibiades returns from Tissaphernes, whom he professes to have made a fast friend of the Athenians.

When Tissaphernes heard that the Peloponnesian fleet had sailed from Miletus to the Hellespont, he broke up his camp at Aspendus and marched away towards Ionia. Now after the arrival of the Peloponnesians at the Hellespont, the Antandrians, who are Aeolians, had procured from them at Abydos a force of infantry, which they led through Mount Ida and introduced into their city. They were oppressed by Arsaces the Persian, a lieutenant of Tissaphernes. This Arsaces, when the Athenians, wishing to purify Delos, expelled the inhabitants and they settled in Adramyttium[c], professing to have a quarrel which he did not wish to declare openly, asked their best soldiers to form an army for him. He then led them out of the town as friends and allies, and, taking advantage of their midday meal, surrounded them with his own troops, and shot them down. This deed alarmed

Tissaphernes marches away to Ionia. The cruelty and treachery of his lieutenant Arsaces induce the Antandrians to obtain a garrison from the Peloponnesians.

---

[a] Cp. viii. 88 init.   [b] Cp. viii. 41 med.   [c] Cp. v. 1.

the Antandrians, who thought that they might meet· with some similar violence at his hands ; and as he was imposing upon them burdens which were too heavy for them, they expelled his garrison from their citadel.

Tissaphernes, who was already offended at the expul- 109 sion of his garrison from Miletus [a], and from Cnidus [b], where the same thing had happened, perceived that this new injury was the work of the Pelopon- nesians. He felt that they were now

Tissaphernes deter- mines to follow the Peloponnesians and accuse them, while ex- cusing himself.

his determined enemies, and was apprehensive of some further injury. He was also disgusted at discovering that Pharnabazus had induced the Peloponnesians to join him, and was likely in less time and at less expense to be more successful in the war with the Athenians than himself. He therefore determined to go to the Hellespont, and complain of their con- duct in the affair of Antandrus, offer-

He stops on his way at Ephesus, and sacri- fices to Artemis.

ing at the same time the most plausible defence which he could concerning the non-arrival of the Phoenician fleet and their other grievances. He first went to Ephesus, and there offered sacrifice to Artemis. . . .

[With the end of the winter which follows this summer the twenty-first year of the Peloponnesian War is com- pleted.]

[a] Cp. viii. 84 med.   [b] Cp. viii. 35 init.

INDEX

A.

Abdera, situation of, ii. 97 init. ; Nymphodorus of Abdera, ii. 29.

Abydos, a Milesian colony, viii. 61 init. ; revolts to the Lacedaemonians, *ib.* 62 ; Strombichides recalled from, *ib.* 79 med. ; the Peloponnesian head-quarters, *ib.* 102-108.

Acamantis, an Athenian tribe, iv. 118 fin.

Acanthus, an Andrian colony, iv. 84 init. ; revolts from Athens, *ib.* 84-88 ; provision respecting, in the treaty between Lacedaemon and Athens, v. 18, § vi ; speech of Brasidas at, iv. 85-87, 114 med., 120 med. ; Acanthian troops with Brasidas, *ib.* 124 init.

Acanthus, a Lacedaemonian, swears to the Treaty of Peace and the Alliance, v. 19 med., *ib.* 24 init.

Acarnan, eponymous hero of Acarnania, ii. 102 fin.

Acarnania, named after Acarnan, ii. 102 fin. ; opposite to Cephallenia, ii. 30 fin. ; invaded by the Ambraciots, *ib.* 80-82 ; the Acarnanians always carry arms, i. 5 fin. ; skilful slingers, ii. 81 fin., vii. 31 fin. ; their common council, iii. 105 init. ; allies of Athens [except Oeniadae, ii. 102 init.], ii. 7 fin., 9 med., 68 fin., iii. 95 med., 102 med., iv. 77 med., 89, 101 med., vii. 57 fin., 60 fin., 67 med. ; expedition of Phormio against Oeniadae, ii. 102 ; request as their commander a relation of Phormio, iii. 7 ; attack Leucas, iii 94 init. med. ; defeat the Ambraciots, *ib.* 105-113 ; conclude a treaty with Ambracia, *ib.* 114 med. ; colonise Anactorium, iv. 49.

Acesines, a river in Sicily, iv. 25 med.

Achaea [in Peloponnesus], restored by the Athenians, i. 115 init. [cp. i. 111 fin.] ; redemanded from the Lacedaemonians by Cleon, iv. 21 med. ; resettled by the Lacedaemonians, v. 82 init. ; [Achaeans, early name of Hellenes, i. 3 med.] ; [found Scionè on return from Troy, iv. 120 init.] ; [not allowed to join in the foundation of Heraclea, iii. 92 fin.] ; founders of Zacynthus, ii. 66 ; allies of the Athenians, i. 111 fin.; at first neutral, except the Pellenes, ii. 9 init. ; support the Peloponnesians in the engagement off Erineus, vii. 34 init.

Achaea [Pthiotis], iv. 78 init.; subject to the Thessalians, viii. 3 med.

Acharnae, the largest of the Athenian demes, ii. 19 fin., *ib.* 21 fin., 23 init.; ravaged by the Peloponnesians, *ib.* 19 fin.

Achelous, ii. 102 med., iii. 7 med., 106 init.; description of its Delta, ii. 102 med.

Acheron, a river in Thesprotis, i. 46 fin.

Acherusian lake, in Thesprotis, i. 46 med.

Achilles, followers of, the original Hellenes, i. 3 med.

Acrae, founded by the Syracusans, vi. 5 init.

Acraean height, in Sicily, vii. 78 fin.

Acragas, a river in Sicily, vi. 4 med.

Acragas, *see* Agrigentum.

Acropolis of Athens : ii. 13 med., 15 med.; taken by Cylon, i. 126 ; anciently called *Polis*, ii. 15 fin.; preserved from occupation in the plague, ii. 17 init.; treaties of peace recorded on tablets there, v. 18, § xi; 23, § iv; 47 fin.; inscription in, commemorating the oppression of the tyrants, vi. 55 init.

Acrothous, in Actè, iv. 109 med.

Actè, the peninsula of, iv. 109.

Actium, the Corinthian fleet met by a Corcyraean herald at, i. 29 med.; the Corinthians encamp near, *ib.* 30 fin.

Adeimantus, father of Aristeus, a Corinthian, i. 60 med.

Admetus, king of Molossians, protects Themistocles, i. 136, 137.

Adramyttium, settled by the Delians, v. 1 fin., viii. 108 fin.

Aeantides, son-in-law of Hippias the tyrant, vi. 59 fin.

Aegaleos, Mount, in Attica, ii. 19 fin.

Aegean Sea, i. 98 med., iv. 109 med.

Aegina, on the direct route from Athens to Argos, v. 53 fin.; colonised from Athens, ii. 27, vii. 57 init., viii. 69 med.; Corcyraean envoys deposited in, iii. 72 init.; the settlers in Aegina at Mantinea, v. 74 fin.; at Syracuse, vii. 57 init.; aid in the oligarchical conspiracy at Athens, viii. 69 med.; the Sicilian expedition races as far as, vi. 32 med.; the reinforcements stay at, vii. 20 fin., 26 init.; ravaged by the Peloponnesians, viii. 92 med.; former naval power of the Aeginetans, i. 14 fin.; first war between the Aeginetans and Athenians, *ib.* 14 fin., *ib.* 41 init.; second, *ib.* 105; come to terms with the Athenians, *ib.* 108 fin.; the Aeginetans secretly urge on the war, *ib.* 67 med.; the Lacedaemonians demand their independence, *ib.* 139 init., 140 med.; expelled by the Athenians, ii. 27 init.; settled by the Lacedaemonians at Thyrea, *ib.* med.; assist the Lacedaemonians in the war of Ithomè, *ib.* fin.; attacked by the Athenians in Thyrea, iv. 56 fin., 57 init.; the survivors put to death, *ib.* fin.

Aegitium, in Aetolia, iii. 97 med.

Aeimnestus, a Plataean, father of Lacon, iii. 52 fin.

Aeneas, a Corinthian, iv. 119 med.

Aenesias, Ephor at Sparta, ii. 2 init.

Aenianians, in Malis, v. 51 init.

Aenus, in Thrace, iv. 28 med.; founded from Boeotia, vii. 57 med.; tributary to Athens, *ib.*

Aeoladas, a Theban, father of Pagondas, iv. 91 med.

Aeolian countries and cities, Boeotia, vii. 57 med.; Lesbos, *ib.* [cp. iii. 2 fin., 5 med., 13 init., viii. 4 med., 100 med.]; Tenedos, vii. 57; Aenus, *ib.*; Cymè, iii. 31 init.; Antandros, viii. 108 med.

Aeolian islands, *see* **Liparaean** islands.

Aeolian subjects of the Athenians before Syracuse, vii. 57 med.

Aeolians, ancient occupants of Corinth, iv. 42 med.

Aeolis, former name of Calydon and Pleuron, iii. 102 med.

Aesimides, a Corcyraean commander, i. 47 init.

Aeson, an Argive envoy to Lacedaemon, v. 40 fin.

Aethaea, Lacedaemonian Perioeci of, i. 101 init.

Aethiopia, plague said to have begun in, ii. 48 init.

Aetna, eruption of, iii. 116; the third since the Hellenic settlements of Sicily, *ib.*

Aetolia, customs of the Aetolians, i. 5 fin., iii. 94 fin.; disastrous campaign of the Athenians in, *ib.* 94 med.–98 [cp. iv. 30 init.]; the Aetolians persuade the Lacedaemonians to send an expedition against Naupactus, *ib.* 100; join in the expedition, *ib.* 102 init.; Aetolians before Syracuse, vii. 57 fin.

Agamemnon, power of, i. 9; possessed a great navy, *ib.*

Agatharchidas, a Corinthian commander, ii. 83 fin.

Agatharchus, a Sicilian commander, vii. 25 init., 70 init.

Agesander, father of Agesandridas, a *Spartan, viii. 91 med.

Agesandridas, a Spartan commander, viii. 91 med., 94, 95.

Agesippidas, a Lacedaemonian commander, v. 56 init.

Agis, king of Lacedaemon, iii. 89 init., iv. 2 init.; invades Attica, *ib.* 2 init., 6; swears to the Treaty of Alliance, v. 24 init.; marches towards Argos, but retires, *ib.* 54; attacks Argos, *ib.* 57; surrounds the Argives, *ib.* 58, 59; makes a truce with the Argives, *ib.* 60 init.; blamed for his conduct, and threatened with punishment, *ib.* 60 med., 63;

nearly commits a second error, *ib.* 65 init.; draws the Argives into the plain, before Mantinea, *ib.* fin.; surprised by the enemy, *ib.* 66 init.; defeats the enemy, *ib.* 70–74; leads a new expedition to Argos, *ib.* 83 init.; invades Attica, and fortifies Decelea, vii. 19 init., 27 med.; raises money for a navy, viii. 3 init.; his great powers, viii. 4 fin.; rejects the peace proposals of the Athenian oligarchs, *ib.* 70 fin.; repulsed from the walls of Athens, *ib.* 71; advises the Four Hundred to send ambassadors to Sparta, *ib.* fin.; an enemy of Alcibiades, viii. 12 fin., 45 init.

Agraeans, in Aetolia, ii. 102 med., iii. 106 med.; *ib.* 111 fin., 114 med.; forced into the Athenian alliance, iv. 77 fin.; employed in a descent upon Sicyon, *ib.* 101 med.

Agrianians, in Paeonia, ii. 96 med.

Agrigentum, founded from Gela, vi. 4 med.; gained over by Phaeax to the Athenian alliance, v. 4 fin.; remains neutral in the war between Syracuse and Athens, vii. 32 med., *ib.* 33 init., *ib.* 58 init.; falls into revolution, vii. 46; victory of the anti-Syracusan party, *ib.* 50 init.

Alcaeus, Archon at Athens, v. 19 init., *ib.* 25 init.

Alcamenes, a Lacedaemonian commander, viii. 4; ordered to Lesbos by Agis, *ib.* 8 med.; driven into Piraeum by the Athenians and slain, *ib.* 10 fin.

Alcibiades, the name Lacedaemonian, viii. 6 med.; his extravagant character, vi. 12 fin.; his unpopularity helped to ruin Athens, *ib.* 15; his victories at Olympia, *ib.* 16 init.; head of the war party at Athens, v. 43 init., vi. 15 init.; irritated by the contempt of the Lacedaemonians, v. 43 med.; negotiates an alliance with Argos,

Alcibiades (*cont.*)—

Mantinea and Elis, *ib.* 44, 46; deceives the Lacedaemonian envoys, *ib.* 45; his activity in Peloponnesus, *ib.* 52 fin., 53, 55 [cp. vi. 16 fin.]; persuades the Athenians to declare the treaty broken and resettle the Helots at Pylos, *ib.* 56 med.; ambassador at Argos, *ib.* 61 med., 76 med.; seizes a number of suspected Argives, *ib.* 84 init.; appointed one of the generals in Sicily, vi. 8 med.; speech of, *ib.* 16–18; accused of mutilating the Hermae and celebrating the mysteries in private houses, *ib.* 28 init.; begs in vain to be tried before sailing, *ib.* 29; opinion of, in a council of war, *ib.* 48; summoned home, *ib.* 53 init., 61; escapes at Thurii, *ib.* fin.; condemned to death, *ib.*; causes the failure of a plot to betray Messina, *ib.* 74 init.; goes to Lacedaemon, *ib.* 88 fin.; his speech there, *ib.* 89–92; persuades the Lacedaemonians to fortify Decelea, vii. 18 init.; supports the Chians at Sparta, viii. 6 med.; persuades the Spartan government not to give up the Chian expedition, viii. 12; sent to Ionia with Chalcideus, *ib.* 12 fin.; induces the revolt of Chios, Erythrae, Clazomenae, *ib.* 14; chases Strombichides into Samos, *ib.* 16; causes the revolt of Teos, *ib.* fin.; and of Miletus, *ib.* 17; present at an engagement before Miletus, *ib.* 26 fin.; falls into disfavour with the Lacedaemonians, *ib.* 45 init.; retires to Tissaphernes, and endeavours to ruin the Peloponnesian cause, *ib.* med.; repulses the revolted cities when they beg money, *ib.* fin.; instructs Tissaphernes to balance the Athenians and Lacedaemonians against each other, *ib.* 46; conspires with some Athenians at Samos to overthrow the democracy, *ib.* 47–49; opposed by Phrynichus, *ib.* 48 fin.; whom he endeavours unsuccessfully to ruin, *ib.* 50, 51; seeks to draw Tissaphernes over to the Athenian cause, *ib.* 52 init.; persuades Tissaphernes to demand impossible terms from Peisander, *ib.* 56; recalled by the Athenians at Samos, *ib.* 81 init.; encourages them with extravagant hopes, *ib.* 81; restrains them from sailing to the Piraeus, *ib.* 82; made commander-in-chief, *ib.*; goes to Tissaphernes, *ib.*; again restrains the people from sailing to the Piraeus, and thus performs an eminent service, *ib.* 86 med.; sails to Aspendus, promising to keep the Phoenician fleet back, *ib.* 88; recalled by the Athenians at home, *ib.* 97 fin.; returns from Caunus, professing to have secured Tissaphernes' friendship for Athens, *ib.* 108 init.; returns to Samos, *ib.* med.

Alcidas, takes command of the Peloponnesian fleet sent to Lesbos, iii. 16 fin., 26 init.; arrives too late, *ib.* 29; determines to return, *ib.* 31; slaughters his captives, *ib.* 32; is chased to Patmos by the Athenians, *ib.* 33, 69 init.; sails to Corcyra, *ib.* 69, 76; engages the Athenians, *ib.* 77, 78; retires, *ib.* 79–81; helps in the foundation of Heraclea, *ib.* 92 fin.

Alcinadas, a Lacedaemonian, swears to the Treaty of Peace and the Alliance, v. 19 med.; *ib.* 24 init.

Alcinous, temple of Zeus and Alcinous at Corcyra, iii. 70 med.

Alciphron, an Argive, makes terms with Agis, v. 59 fin., 60 init.

Alcisthenes, an Athenian, father of Demosthenes, iii. 91 init., iv. 66 med., vii. 16 fin.

Alcmaeon, the story of, ii. 102 fin.

Alcmaeonidae, aid in the deposition of Hippias, vi. 59 fin.

Alexander, the father of Perdiccas, king of Macedonia, i. 57 init., *ib.* 137 init.; of Argive descent, ii. 99 init.

Alexarchus, a Corinthian commander, vii. 19 med.

Alexicles, an Athenian general of the oligarchical party, seized by the popular party, viii. 92 med.; released, 93 init.; flees to Decelea, 98 init.

Alexippidas, Ephor at Lacedaemon, viii. 58 init.

Alicyaei, in Sicily, vii. 32 med.

Allies [of the Athenians], ii. 9 fin.; character of the league, i. 19; used to meet at Delos, i. 96 fin.; formerly independent, *ib.* 97 init.; their gradual subjugation, *ib.* 99 [cp. iii. 10, 11, vi. 76]; those present before Syracuse, vii. 57; admired in Hellas for their adoption of Athenian language and manners, vii. 63 med.

Allies [of the Lacedaemonians], ii. 9 init.; formation of the league, i. 18; its character, *ib.* 19; allies summoned to Sparta, i. 67; again summoned, *ib.* 119; vote for war, *ib.* 125.

Almopia, in Macedonia, ii. 99 fin.

Alopè, in Locris, ii. 26 fin.

Altar, of Apollo the Founder, at Naxos, vi. 3 init.; the Pythian Apollo, erected by Pisistratus at Athens, *ib.* 54 fin.; [Athenè] in the Acropolis, i. 126 med.; the awful Goddesses at Athens, *ib.*; the Twelve Gods at Athens, vi. 54 fin.; Olympian Zeus, v. 50 init.

Altars, a sanctuary and refuge, iv. 98 fin., v. 60 fin., viii. 84 med.

Alyzia, in Acarnania, vii. 31 init.

Ambracia, a Corinthian colony, ii. 80 med., vii. 58 med.; an ally of the Lacedaemonians, ii. 9 init.; the Ambraciots the most warlike of the Epirots, iii. 108 med.; they send troops to Epidamnus, i. 26 init.; furnish ships to Corinth, *ib.* 27 fin., *ib.* 46 init., 48 fin.; defeated in the engagement off Sybota, *ib.* 49 med.; attack the Amphilochian Argives, ii. 68; invade Acarnania, *ib.* 80; retire, *ib.* 82; send reinforcements to Alcidas, iii. 69; persuade the Lacedaemonians to attack the Amphilochian Argos, *ib.* 102 fin.; join the Lacedaemonians in the expedition, *ib.* 105, 106; defeated by the Acarnanians, under Demosthenes, *ib.* 107, 108; deserted by the Peloponnesians, *ib.* 109, 111; total destruction of their reinforcements, *ib.* 112, 113; greatness of the calamity, *ib.* 113 fin.; conclude a treaty with the Acarnanians, *ib.* 114 med.; receive a garrison from Corinth, *ib.* fin.; assist Gylippus with ships, vi. 104 med., vii. 4 fin., 7 init., 58 med.; present at Cynossema, viii. 106 med.; Ambraciot envoys sent by the Syracusans to the Sicilian cities after the capture of Plemmyrium, vii. 25 fin.; slain by the Sicels, *ib.* 32.

Ambracian gulf, i. 29 med., 55 init.

Ameiniades, Athenian ambassador to Seuthes, ii. 67 med.

Ameinias, a Lacedaemonian envoy, iv. 132 fin.

Ameinocles, the Corinthian shipbuilder, i. 13 init.

Ammeas, a Plataean commander, iii. 22 med.

Amorges, the bastard son of Pissuthnes, revolts in Caria, viii. 5 fin., 19 init.; captured by the Peloponnesians, and handed over to Tissaphernes, *ib.* 28 med.; said

Amorges (*cont.*)—
by Peisander to have been betrayed by Phrynichus, *ib.* 54 med.

Ampelidas, a Lacedaemonian envoy to Argos, v. 22 med.

Amphiaraus, father of Amphilochus, ii. 68 init. ; of Alcmaeon, ii. 102 med.

Amphias, an Epidaurian, iv. 119 med.

Amphidorus, a Megarian, iv. 119 med.

Amphilochia, colonised by Amphilochus, ii. 68 init. ; the Amphilochians barbarians, *ib.* med., iii. 112 fin. ; learnt Greek from the Ambraciots, ii. 68 med. ; expelled by the Ambraciots, ii. 68 med. ; reinstated by Athenian aid, *ib.* fin. ; attacked by the Ambraciots and Lacedaemonians, iii. 105 ; join Demosthenes at Olpae, *ib.* 107 init. ; defeated, 108 med. ; destroy the Ambraciot fugitives from Idomenè, *ib.* 112 ; make a treaty with Ambracia, *ib.* 114 med.

Amphilochian Hills, iii. 112 init.

Amphipolis, formerly called 'The Nine Ways,' i. 100 fin., iv. 102 med. ; origin of the name, iv. 102 fin. ; attempted colonisation of, by Aristagoras, iv. 102 init. ; unsuccessful settlement of, by the Athenians, i. 100 fin., iv. 102 init. ; colonised by Hagnon, iv. 102 med., v. 11 init. ; 'Thracian gates' of, v. 10 init., med. ; temple of Athenè at, *ib.* ; captured by Brasidas, iv. 102–106 ; battle of, v. 6–11, 12 fin. ; ordered to be surrendered under treaty, iv. 18, § v ; not surrendered, *ib.* 21, 35, 46 ; abandonment of an Athenian expedition against, v. 83 fin. ; unsuccessfully attacked by the Athenians, vii. 9 ; the Amphipolitans make Brasidas their founder, v. 11 init.

Amphissa, in Ozolian Locris, iii. 101 init.

Amyclae, temple of Apollo at, v. 18, § xi : *ib.* 23, § iv.

Amyntas, son of Philip, ii. 95 fin., *ib.* 100 med.

Amyrtaeus, the Egyptian king in the fens, i. 110 init., *ib.* 112 med.

Anactorium, i. 29 med. ; sends aid to Corinth, *ib.* 46 init., ii. 9 init. ; hostile to the Acarnanians, iii. 114 fin. ; held by the Corinthians and Corcyraeans in common, i. 55 init. ; captured by the Corinthians, *ib.* ; betrayed to the Athenians, iv. 49 init. ; colonised by the Acarnanians, *ib.* fin. ; occupied by the Athenians, vii. 31 init. ; not surrendered in the Treaty of Peace, v. 30 med. ; Anactorians assist in the invasion of Acarnania, ii. 80 med., 81 med.

Anaea, viii. 19 init. ; occupied by Samian refugees, iii. 19 fin., iv. 75 med. ; the Anaeans destroy an Athenian army under Lysicles, iii. 19 fin. ; remonstrate with Alcidas for the slaughter of his captives, *ib.* 32 ; aid the Chians, viii. 61 med.

Anapus, river in Acarnania, ii. 82 init.

Anapus, river in Sicily, vi. 96 fin., vii. 42 fin., 78 init. ; bridge over, vi. 66 med.

Anaxander, a Theban commander, viii. 100 med.

Anaxilas, tyrant of Rhegium, vi. 4 fin. ; founder of Messenè, *ib.*

Andocides, commands the reinforcements sent to Corcyra after Sybota, i. 51 med.

Androcles, an Athenian popular leader, viii. 65 init. ; active in procuring the banishment of Alcibiades, *ib.* ; murdered by the oligarchical conspirators, *ib.*

Androcrates, the shrine of, at Plataea, iii. 24 init.

Andromedes, a Lacedaemonian envoy, v. 42 init.

Andros, island of, ii. 55 ; the Andrians subjects and tributaries of the Athenians, iv. 42 init., vii. 57 init. ; Andrians employed by the oligarchs at Athens, viii. 69 med. ;—Andrian colonies: Acanthus, iv. 84 init. ; Argilus, *ib.* 103 med. ; Sanè, iv. 109 med. ; Stagirus, *ib.* 88 fin.

Androsthenes, Olympic victor, v. 49 init.

Aneristus, Lacedaemonian ambassador to Persia, ii. 67 init.

Antandrus, an Aeolian town, viii. 108 med. ; captured by the Lesbian refugees, iv. 52 fin. ; recaptured by the Athenians, *ib.* 75 med. ; introduces a Lacedaemonian garrison, expelling the Persians, viii. 108 med.

Anthemus, in Macedonia, ii. 99 fin., 100 med.

Anthenè, on the borders of Argos and Lacedaemon, v. 41 init.

Anthesterion, the Attic month, ii. 15 fin.

Anticles, an Athenian commander, i. 117 med.

Antigenes, father of Socrates, an Athenian, ii. 23 med.

Antimenidas, a Lacedaemonian envoy, v. 42 init.

Antimnestus, father of Hierophon, an Athenian, iii. 105 fin.

Antiochus, king of the Orestians, ii. 80 fin.

Antiphemus, joint founder, with Entimus, of Gela, vi. 4 med.

Antiphon, the soul of the oligarchical conspiracy at Athens, viii. 68 init., 90 init.; his abilities and virtue, *ib.* ; disliked by the people, *ib.* ; afterwards tried for his share in the plot, *ib.*; sent to make peace with Lacedaemon, *ib.* 90 med.

Antippus, a Lacedaemonian, swears to the Treaty of Peace and the Alliance, v. 19 med. ; *ib.* 24 init.

Antiquity, inferiority of, i. 1 fin.; poverty of, i. 11 fin.

Antissa, in Lesbos, viii. 23 med.; the Antissaeans defeat the Methymnaeans, iii. 18 init.; Antissa taken by the Athenians, *ib.* 28 fin.

Antisthenes, a Spartan, viii. 39 med., 61 med.

Aphrodisia, in Laconia, iv. 56 init.

Aphroditè, temple of, at Eryx, vi. 46 med.

Aphytis, in Pallenè, i. 64 fin.

Apidanus, river in Thessaly, iv. 78 fin.

Apodotians, in Aetolia, iii. 94 fin.

Apollo, Polycrates dedicates Rhenea to, i. 13 fin., iii. 104 init.; temple of, at Actium, i. 29 med. ; at Amyclae, v. 18, § xi ; 23, § iv ; at Argos, *ib.* 47 fin.; opposite Cythera, vii. 26 med. ; at Deli̇um, iv. 76 med., 90 init., 97 init. ; at Leucas, iii. 94 med.; at Naupactus, ii. 91 init. ; on Triopium, viii. 35 med. ; of the Pythian Apollo, at Athens, ii. 15 med. ; at Delphi, iv. 118, § i ; v. 18, § ii ; of Apollo Pythaeus, at Argos [?], v. 53 init.; altar of, Apollo 'the Founder' at Naxos, in Sicily, vi. 3 init. ; of the Pythian Apollo in the Athenian Agora, vi. 54 fin.; festival of Apollo Maloeis, iii. 3 med. ; shrine of Apollo Temenites at Syracuse, vi. 75 init., 99 fin., 100 fin. ; ancient oracle of Apollo to Alcmaeon, ii. 102 fin. ; Homeric Hymn to Apollo quoted, iii. 104 med.

Apollodorus, father of Charicles, an Athenian, vii. 20 init.

Apollonia, a colony of Corinth, i. 26 init.

Arcadia, did not change its inhabitants anciently, i. 2 med.; portion of, subjected by the Mantineans, v. 29 init.; Arcadians supplied

Arcadia (*cont.*)—

by Agamemnon with ships for the Trojan War, i. 9 fin.; Arcadian mercenaries at Notium, iii. 34; in the Athenian service before Syracuse, vii. 57 med.; on the Syracusan side, vii. 19 fin., 58 med.; Arcadian allies of the Lacedaemonians join them in invading Argos, *ib.* 57 med., 58 fin., 60 med.; summoned by the Lacedaemonians to Tegea, *ib.* 64; present at Mantinea, *ib.* 67 med., 73 init.; furnish ships to the Lacedaemonians, viii. 3 fin.; war between some Arcadian tribes and the Lepreans, v. 31. [*See* also Heraeans, Maenalia, Mantinea, Orchomenus, Parrhasians, Tegea.]

Arcesilaus, father of Lichas, a Lacedaemonian, v. 50 med., 76 med., viii. 39 init.

Archedicè, daughter of Hippias the tyrant, vi. 59 med.; her epitaph, *ib.*

Archelaus, son of Perdiccas, king of Macedonia, ii. 100 init.

Archers, at Athens, numbers of the horse and foot archers, ii. 13 fin.; horse archers sent to Melos, v. 84 med.; to Sicily, vi. 94 fin.; barbarian archers, viii. 98 init.

Archestratus, an Athenian commander, i. 57 fin.; father of Chaereas, viii. 74 init.

Archetimus, a Corinthian commander, i. 29 init.

Archias, the founder of Syracuse, vi. 3 med.; [of Camarina] betrays Camarina to the Syracusans, iv. 25 med.

Archidamus, king of Lacedaemon, i. 79 fin.; father of Agis, iii. 89 init.; his prudent character, *ib.* fin.; friend of Pericles, ii. 13 init.; speech of, i. 80–85; leader of the first expedition into Attica, ii. 10 fin.; second speech, *ib.* 11;

sends a herald to Athens, *ib.* 12; leads the army to Oenoè, *ib.* 18 init.; blamed for delay, *ib.* med.; enters Attica, *ib.* 19 init.; halts at Acharnae, *ib.* 20; retires, *ib.* 23 fin.; invades Attica a second time, *ib.* 47 init., 55–57; attacks Plataea, *ib.* 71 init.; offers terms to the Plataeans, *ib.* 71–74; invades Attica a third time, iii. 1.

Archippus, father of Aristides, an Athenian, iv. 50 init.

Archonides, a Sicel king, friend of the Athenians, vii. 1 fin.

Archons, their former power at Athens, i. 126 med.; Pisistratus, vi. 54 fin.; Themistocles, i. 93 init.; Pythodorus, ii. 2 init.; Alcaeus, v. 19 init., 25 init.; Archonship kept by the Pisistratidae in their own family, vi. 54 fin.

Arcturus, rising of, ii. 78 init.

Ares, temple of, at Megara, iv. 67 init.

Argennusae, a town opposite Mytilenè, viii. 101 med.

Argilus, a colony from Andros, iv. 103 init.; provision respecting, in the treaty of peace, v. 18, § vi; the Argilians assist Brasidas in his attempt on Amphipolis, iv. 103 med.; the Argilian servant of Pausanias, i. 132, 133; Cerdylium in Argilian territory, v. 6 med.

Arginus, Mount, opposite Chios, viii. 34 init.

Argos [the Amphilochian], iii. 102 fin., 105 init., 107 init.; founded by Amphilochus, ii. 68 init. [*See* also Amphilochia.]

Argos [in Peloponnesus], residence of Themistocles there, after his ostracism, i. 135 med., 137 med.; forms alliance with the Athenians, i. 102 fin.; the Corinthians warned from Argos of the intended Athenian invasion, iv. 42

Argos (*cont.*)—

med.; hostile to Lacedaemon, i. 102 fin., v. 22 med.; truce for 30 years between Lacedaemon and Argos, v. 14 fin.; magistrates of Argos, *ib.* 47 fin.; its democratical constitution, v. 29 med., 44 med.; temple of Here at Argos, iv. 133 init.; time reckoned by the succession of high priestesses there, ii. 2 init.; kings of Macedonia originally from Argos, ii. 99 init.; Argives used as a general name for the Hellenes by Homer, i. 3 med.; Argives assist the Athenians at Tanagra, i. 107 fin.; neutral at the beginning of the war, ii. 9 init.; refuse to renew the peace with Lacedaemon, v. 14 fin., 22 med.; head a confederacy against the Lacedaemonians, *ib.* 27, 28 foll.; aspire to lead Peloponnesus, *ib.* 28 med. [cp. 69 med.]; ally themselves with the Mantineans, *ib.* 29; Eleans, *ib.* 31; Corinthians and Chalcidians, *ib.* 31 fin.; the Lacedaemonians seek their alliance, *ib.* 36; the Argives fail in attempting an alliance with the Boeotians, *ib.* 37, 38; are compelled to make terms with Sparta, *ib.* 40, 41; send envoys to Athens at Alcibiades' invitation, *ib.* 43, 44; ally themselves to Athens, *ib.* 46 fin., 47; aid the Eleans to exclude the Lacedaemonians from the Olympic games, *ib.* 50 med.; aid Alcibiades in organising the affairs of the confederacy, *ib.* 52 med.; make war on Epidaurus, *ib.* 53, 54 fin., 55 fin., 56 fin.; take the field against the Lacedaemonians, *ib.* 51 init.; surrounded by the Lacedaemonians, *ib.* 59 med.; unaware of their danger, *ib.*; obtain through Thrasyllus and Alciphron a truce, *ib.* 59 fin., 60 init.; blame them for their conduct, 60 fin., 61 init.; capture Orchomenus, *ib.* 61 fin.; prepare against Tegea, *ib.* 62 fin.; again attacked by the Lacedaemonians, *ib.* 64; dissatisfied with their generals, *ib.* 65; found by the Lacedaemonians unexpectedly in battle array, *ib.* 66, 67; defeated by the Lacedaemonians at Mantinea, *ib.* 70-74; make peace and alliance with the Lacedaemonians, *ib.* 76-80; renounce their allies, *ib.* 78; have their government changed by the Lacedaemonians and the oligarchical party, *ib.* 81 fin.; the popular party defeat the oligarchs and renew the Athenian alliance, *ib.* 82; the Thousand select Argives trained by the city, *ib.* 67 fin., 72 med., 73 fin.; begin the Long Walls, 82 fin.; ravage Phliasia, *ib.* 83 med., again, *ib.* 115 init.; three hundred Argives of the Lacedaemonian party deported by Alcibiades, *ib.* 84 init.; given up to the Argives for execution, vi. 61 med.; the Argives suspect some of their citizens of instigating a Lacedaemonian invasion, v. 116 init.; treacherously attack and capture Orneae, vi. 7 med.; induced by Alcibiades to join the Sicilian expedition, vi. 29 med., 43 fin., vii. 57 med.; present in the various engagements before Syracuse, vi. 67 init., 70 med., 100 fin., vii. 44 fin.; cause confusion in the night attack on Epipolae by their Doric Paean, vii. 44 fin.; invade the Thyraean territory, vi. 95 med.; have their lands wasted by the Lacedaemonians, *ib.* 105 init.; aid the Athenians in ravaging the Lacedaemonian coast, *ib.* med.; ravage Phliasia, *ib.* fin.; reinforce the Athenians

Argos (*cont.*)—

before Miletus, viii. 25 init. ; defeated by the Milesians, *ib.* med. ; go home in a rage, *ib.* 27 fin. ; send envoys to the Athenians at Samos, *ib.* 86 fin. ; an Argive one of the murderers of Phrynichus, *ib.* 92 init.

Arianthidas, a Theban Boeotarch at Delium, iv. 91 med.

Ariphron, father of Hippocrates, an Athenian, iv. 66 med.

Aristagoras, of Miletus, attempts to found a colony at Ennea Hodoi, iv. 102 init.

Aristarchus, a conspicuous leader of the oligarchical party, viii. 90 init. ; endeavours vainly to prevent the destruction of the fort Eetionea, *ib.* 92 fin. ; betrays Oenoè to Boeotia, *ib.* 98.

Aristeus, son of Adeimantus, a Corinthian, takes command of the forces sent from Corinth to Potidaea, i. 60 ; made general of the Chalcidian forces, *ib.* 62 init. ; engages the Athenians, *ib.* fin. ; fights his way into Potidaea, *ib.* 63 init. ; sails out of Potidaea, *ib.* 65 med. ; defeats the Sermylians, *ib.* fin. ; sent as ambassador to the King, ii. 67 init. ; given up by the Thracians to the Athenians, *ib.* med. ; put to death, *ib.* fin.

Aristeus, son of Pellichus, a Corinthian commander, i. 29 init.

Aristeus, a Lacedaemonian envoy, iv. 132 fin.

Aristides, son of Archippus, an Athenian general, captures Artaphernes at Eion, iv. 50 init. ; recovers Antandrus, *ib.* 75 init.

Aristides, son of Lysimachus, goes on an embassy to Sparta, i. 91 init. ; settlement of Athenian tribute in his time, v. 18, § vi.

Aristocleides, father of Hestiodorus, an Athenian, ii. 70 init.

Aristocles, brother of Pleistoanax, accused of bribing the Delphian priestess, v. 16 med.

Aristocles, a Spartan polemarch, v. 71 fin. ; banished for cowardice at Mantinea, *ib.* 72 init.

Aristocrates, an Athenian, swears to the Treaty of Peace and the Alliance, v. 19 fin., 24 med.; sent to enquire into the suspected treachery of the Chians, viii. 9 med.

Aristocrates, son of Scellius, a chief author in the oligarchical revolution, viii. 89 init. ; heads a moderate party in the oligarchy, *ib.* 89; aids in the destruction of Eetionea, *ib.* 92 med.

Aristogiton, slays Hipparchus, i. 20 med., vi. 54 init., *ib.* 56–58.

Ariston, a Corinthian, the ablest pilot in the Syracusan fleet, vii. 39 med.

Aristonous, joint founder, with Pystilus, of Agrigentum, vi. 4 med.

Aristonous, of Larissa, a Thessalian commander, ii. 22 fin.

Aristonymus, an Athenian, one of the ambassadors sent to proclaim the one year's truce, iv. 122 ; refuses to admit Scionè, *ib.*

Aristonymus, father of Euphamidas, a Corinthian, ii. 33 med., iv. 119 med.

Aristophon, an envoy from the Four Hundred to Sparta, viii. 86 fin.

Aristoteles, an Athenian commander, iii. 105 med.

Arms, custom of carrying arms once common to all Hellenes, i. 5 fin., 6 init. ; the custom first abandoned by the Athenians, *ib.* 6 init.

Arnae, in Chalcidicè, iv. 103 init.

Arnè, Boeotians expelled from, i. 12 med.

Arnissa, in Macedonia, iv. 128 med.

Arrhiani, in the Thracian Chersonese, viii. 104 init.

Arrhibaeus, king of the Lyncestians, iv. 79 fin. ; attacked by Perdiccas, *ib.* 83; defeated, *ib.* 124; Perdiccas' Illyrian troops desert to him, *ib.* 125 init. ; the pass into his country, *ib.* 127 fin.

Arsaces, a lieutenant of Tissaphernes, viii. 108 med. ; massacres the Delians, *ib.* fin.

Artabazus, son of Pharnaces, sent by Xerxes with letters to Pausanias, i. 129 init., 132 fin.

Artaphernes, a Persian ambassador to Sparta, intercepted by the Athenians, iv. 50.

Artas, an Iapygian prince, furnishes javelin-men to the Athenians, vii. 33 med.

Artaxerxes, son of Xerxes, king of Persia, i. 104 init. ; succeeds to the throne, *ib.* 137 med. ; his reception of Themistocles, *ib.* 138 ; his death, iv. 50 fin. ; the father of Darius Nothus, viii. 5 init.

Artemis, temple of, at Rhegium, vi. 44 fin.; at Ephesus, viii. 109 fin.

Artemisium, a month at Sparta, v. 19 init.

Artemisium, battle of, iii. 54 med.

Arts : in the arts, as in politics, the new must prevail over the old, i. 71 init.

Artynae, the magistrates at Argos, v. 47 fin.

Asia : the Barbarians of Asia wear girdles in wrestling and boxing matches, i. 6 fin. ; Pelops brought his wealth from Asia, *ib.* 9 init. ; no single nation, even in Asia, could compare with the Scythians if united, ii. 97 fin. ; Magnesia in Asia, i. 138 fin. ; the Thracians of Asia, iv. 75 fin.: ' the King's country in Asia,' viii. 58.

Asinè, a city in Laconia, iv. 13 init., 54 fin., vi. 93 med.

Asopius, father of Phormio, an Athenian, i. 64 med.

Asopius, son of Phormio, ravages the Laconian coast, iii. 7 init. ; attacks Oeniadae, *ib.* med. ; falls in a descent upon Leucas, *ib.* fin.

Asopolaus, father of Astymachus, a Plataean, iii. 52 fin.

Asopus, river in Boeotia, ii. 5 init.

Aspendus, viii. 81 fin., 87 med., 88 init., 99 init., 108 med.

Assembly, the Athenian, summoned by Pericles as general, ii. 59 fin. ; forms of, iv. 118 fin. ; usually held in the Pnyx, viii. 97 init. ; Peisander summons an assembly at Colonus, *ib.* 67 med. ; the assembly summoned to the temple of Dionysus in Munychia for ' the restoration of harmony,' *ib.* 93 fin., 94 init. ; the oligarchs pretend that so many as 5,000 citizens never met in one assembly, *ib.* 72 med.

Assembly, the Lacedaemonian, mode of voting at, i. 87 init.

Assinarus, river in Sicily, capture of Nicias' division at, vii. 84.

Assyrian character, used by the Persians, iv. 50 med.

Astacus, in Acarnania, captured by the Athenians, who expel the tyrant Evarchus, ii. 30 med. ; the town is retaken and Evarchus restored by the Corinthians, *ib.* 33 init. ; landing of Phormio near Astacus, *ib.* 102 init.

Astymachus, a Plataean, one of those chosen to plead before the Lacedaemonians, iii. 52 fin.

Astyochus, a Lacedaemonian admiral, viii. 20 med. ; entrusted with the command of the whole navy in Asia, *ib.* ; arrives at Lesbos, *ib.* 23 init. ; fails to save Lesbos from the Athenians, *ib.* med., fin. ; summoned to Chios to avert a revolution, *ib.* 24 fin., *ib.* 31 init. ; fails to recover Clazomenae and Pteleum, *ib.* 31 med. ; enraged with the Chians for refusing to assist in the revolt of Lesbos, *ib.* 32 fin.,

Astyochus (*cont.*)—

33 init., 38 fin., 39 med.; narrowly escapes the Athenians, 33 med.; he is complained of to Sparta by Pedaritus, *ib.* 38; the Spartans send out commissioners to him, *ib.* 39 fin.; at last determines to aid the Chians, *ib.* 40 fin.; hearing that reinforcements are coming, goes to meet them, *ib.* 41; defeats an Athenian squadron, *ib.* 42; receives orders from Sparta to put Alcibiades to death, *ib.* 45 init.; betrays Phrynichus to Alcibiades, *ib.* 50; believed to have sold himself to Tissaphernes, *ib.* 50 med., *ib.* 83 fin.; sails to Miletus with a view to relieve Chios, *ib.* 60 fin.; offers battle to the Athenians, *ib.* 63 init.; excites by his conduct great dissatisfaction in the fleet, *ib.* 78; offers battle to the Athenians, but declines when they offer battle afterwards, *ib.* 79; stoned by the sailors for offering to strike Dorieus, *ib.* 84 init.; superseded by Mindarus, *ib.* 85 init.

Atalantè, island off Locris, fortified by the Athenians, ii. 32; inundation of the sea there, iii. 89 med.; ordered to be surrendered by the treaty, v. 18, § viii.

Atalantè, in Macedonia, ii. 100 med.

Athenaeus, a Lacedaemonian, iv. 119 init., *ib.* 122.

Athenagoras, a popular leader at Syracuse, vi. 35 fin.; speech of, *ib.* 36–40.

Athenagoras, father of Timagoras of Cyzicus, viii. 6 init.

Athenè of the Brazen House, curse of, i. 128; temple of, at Lecythus, iv.116; at Amphipolis, v. 10 init.; at Athens, v. 23 fin.; image of, in the Acropolis at Athens, ii. 13 med.

Athenian Empire, foundation of, i. 14 fin., *ib.* 18 med., *ib.* 74 med., *ib.*

93; rise of, *ib.* 19, 89–118, *ib.* 118; character of, *ib.* 19; justification of, *ib.* 75, vi. 82, 83.

Athens, once inhabited by Tyrrhenians, iv. 109 fin. [cp. ii. 17 med.]; formed by Theseus from the ancient communes, ii. 15 init.; small extent of ancient Athens, *ib.* 15 med.; largeness of the population, i. 80 med.; appearance of, compared to Sparta, i. 10 init.; destruction of, in the Persian war, i. 89 fin.; building of the City Walls, i. 90, 91, 93; of the Long Walls, *ib.* 107 init., 108 med.; plague of Athens, ii. 47–54, 58, iii. 87; resources of Athens, ii. 13; the revolution at Athens, viii. 47–72; restoration of the democracy, *ib.* 73–77, 86, 89–93, 97; the government immediately after the restoration the best within Thucydides' recollection, viii. 97 fin.; 'the school of Hellas,' ii. 41 init.; freedom of life in, ii. 37, vii. 69 med. [*See also* Attica.]

Athenians, of Ionian race, vi. 82 init., vii. 57 init.; have always inhabited the same land, i. 2 fin.; their colonies to Ionia and the islands, i. 2 fin., 12 fin.; the first Hellenes to adopt refined habits, i. 6 med.; their ignorance of their own history, *ib.* 20 init., vi. 53 fin., 54, 55; their activity and restlessness, especially in contrast with the Lacedaemonian character, i. 69, 70, 102 med., iv. 55 med., vi. 87 med., viii. 96 fin.; treatment of their allies, i. 19, 76, 99, iii. 10, vi. 76, 84, 85; general detestation of them in Hellas, i. 119 med., ii. 8 fin., 11 init., 63 init.; their wealth and military resources, ii. 13 med.; their fondness for a country life, *ib.* 15 init.; become sailors, i. 18 med., 93 fin. [cp. iv. 12 fin., vii. 21 med.]; assured of empire by their naval

Athenians (*cont.*)—

superiority, ii. 62; willing to face any odds at sea, *ib.* 88 fin.; perfection of their navy, iii. 17; mode of burying the dead in the war, ii. 34; their greatness and glory, ii. 37-41, 63, 64; for half a century an imperial people, viii. 68 fin.; maintain the children of the fallen at the public expense, ii. 46; their mistakes in the war, *ib.* 65; their love of rhetoric, iii. 38 med., 40 init.; their over cleverness and suspiciousness, *ib.* 43; their fickle temperament, vii. 48 med.; their elation at success, iv. 65 fin.; their impatience of discipline, vii. 14 init., fin.; 'never retired from a siege through fear of another foe,' v. 111 init.; the most experienced soldiers in Hellas, vi. 72 med., vii. 61 fin. [B.C. 510]; the Athenians governed by tyrants, i. 18 init., vi. 53 fin.-59; the tyrants put down by the Lacedaemonians, i. 18 init., vi. 53 fin.; the Athenians make war on the Aeginetans [B.C. 491], i. 14 fin., their services in the Persian war, *ib.* 73, 74, ii. 36 med.; the Athenians build their walls and the Piraeus, i. 91, 93 [B.C. 480-B.C. 479]; the Athenians join in the capture of Byzantium and Cyprus, *ib.* 94; obtain the leadership of the allies, *ib.* 95, 96, 99 [cp. *ib.* 18, 19]; subject Eion, Scyros, Carystus, Naxos, *ib.* 98; conquer the Persians at the Eurymedon, *ib.* 100 init.; subdue the revolted Thasians, *ib.* 100, 101; fail in an attempt to colonise Amphipolis, *ib.* 100 fin.; called in by the Lacedaemonians during the siege of Ithomè, *ib.* 101, 102; dismissed by the Lacedaemonians, *ib.* 102 med.; offended at the Lacedaemonians and form alliance with Argos, *ib.* fin.; settle the Helots at Naupac-

tus, *ib.* 103 med.; make alliance with the Megarians, *ib.* 103 fin.; occupy Nisaea, *ib.*; aid the revolted Egyptians, *ib.* 104; defeated by the Corinthians and Epidaurians at Halieis, *ib.* 105 init.; defeat the Peloponnesians off Cecryphaleia, *ib.*; go to war again with the Aeginetans [B.C. 459], *ib.* 105; defeat the Aeginetans at sea, *ib.* init.; gain a slight advantage over the Corinthians, *ib.* fin.; inflict a severe defeat on them, *ib.* 106; build their Long Walls, *ib.* 107 init., 108 med.; are defeated by the Lacedaemonians at Tanagra, *ib.* 107 fin., 108 init.; defeat the Boeotians at Oenophyta, *ib.* 108 med.; compel Aegina to surrender, *ib.* 108 fin.; take Chalcis and defeat the Sicyonians, *ib.* fin.; driven out of Memphis, *ib.* 109; their reinforcements destroyed, *ib.* 110; unsuccessfully attack Pharsalus, *ib.* 111 init.; defeat the Sicyonians and make an attempt on Oeniadae, *ib.* fin.; send ships to Egypt, *ib.* 112 init.; fight in Cyprus, *ib.* med.; take Chaeronea but are defeated at Coronea, *ib.* 113; their garrison in Megara is slaughtered, *ib.* 114 init.; first invasion of Attica, *ib.* med.; Euboea revolts, *ib.* init.; is reduced, *ib.* fin.; the Athenians make peace with the Lacedaemonians, *ib.* 115 init.; establish a democracy at Samos, *ib.* med.; the Samians and Byzantines revolt, *ib.* the Athenians defeat the Samians, *ib.* 116 med.; blockade Samos, *ib.* fin.; send reinforcements to Samos, *ib.* 117; capture Samos, *ib.* fin. [cp. i. 40 fin., 41 init.] [The Peloponnesian War]; the Athenians enter into alliance with Corcyra, *ib.* 44; send assistance to Corcyra, *ib.* 45; fight with the Corcyraeans at sea against the

Athenians (*cont.*)—

Corinthians, *ib.* 49 fin.; send reinforcements, *ib.* 50 fin., 51; order the Potidaeans to raze their walls, *ib.* 56 med.; quarrel with Perdiccas, *ib.* 57 init.; despatch troops to Potidaea, *ib.* 57 fin., 61 init., 64 med.; come to terms with Perdiccas, *ib.* 61 med.; defeat the Chalcidians, *ib.* 62, 63; invest Potidaea, *ib.* 64; ill-feeling of, against the Corinthians, *ib.* 66, 103 fin.; exclude the Megarians from their harbours, *ib.* 67 fin., 139 init. [cp. iv. 66 init.]; speech of at Sparta, *ib.* 72–78; desire the Lacedaemonians to drive away the curse of Taenarus and of Athenè, *ib.* 128, 135 init.; discuss the demands of the Lacedaemonians, *ib.* 139; make a final offer of arbitration to the Lacedaemonians, *ib.* 145; seize the Boeotians in Attica and garrison Plataea, ii. 6; meditate sending an embassy to the king, *ib.* 7 init.; send ambassadors to places adjacent to Peloponnesus, *ib.* fin.; their allies, *ib.* 9 med.; refuse to hear a messenger from Archidamus, *ib.* 12 init.; collect into the city by Pericles' advice, *ib.* 14–16; send an expedition round the Peloponnese, *ib.* 17 fin., 23, 25, 30; are angry with Pericles for not leading them out, *ib.* 21; defeated at Phrygia, *ib.* med.; receive aid from the Thessalians, *ib.* 22 fin.; set apart a reserve for the war, *ib.* 24 [cp. viii. 15 med.]; send a fleet to Locris, *ib.* 26; expel the Aeginetans, *ib.* 27 init.; make Nymphodorus their Proxenus, and become allies of Sitalces, *ib.* 29; invade Megara, *ib.* 31; fortify Atalantè, *ib.* 32; celebrate the funeral of the fallen, *ib.* 34; suffer from the plague, *ib.* 47–54, 58; again restrained by Pericles from

sallying out against the Lacedaemonians, *ib.* 55 fin.; send an expedition round Peloponnese, *ib.* 56; unsuccessfully attack Potidaea, *ib.* 58; send envoys to Sparta, *ib.* 59 med.; turn upon and fine Pericles, *ib.* 59–65 init.; elect him general, *ib.* 65 init.; capture Aristeus of Corinth and other envoys to Persia, and put them to death, *ib.* 67; send Phormio to aid the Amphilochians, *ib.* 68; send Phormio with a fleet round Peloponnese, *ib.* 69 init.; despatch ships to collect money in Asia, *ib.* fin.; capture Potidaea, *ib.* 70 init.; blame the generals there, *ib.* med.; send colonists to Potidaea, *ib.* fin.; encourage the Plataeans to resist, *ib.* 73; send an expedition to Chalcidicè, *ib.* 79; are defeated, *ib.*; defeat the Peloponnesians at sea, *ib.* 83, 84; gain a second victory, *ib.* 86, 92; thrown into a panic by the news of Brasidas' landing in Salamis, *ib.* 93, 94; make an expedition into Acarnania, *ib.* 102; receive warning of the Lesbian revolt, iii. 2; attempt to surprise Mytilenè, *ib.* 3; successfully engage the Lesbians, *ib.* 4; blockade Mytilenè by sea, *ib.* 6; send an expedition round Peloponnese, *ib.* 7, 16 med.; send another expedition, *ib.* 16; their great expenditure on the war, *ib.* 17; the perfection of their navy, *ib.*; despatch reinforcements to Mytilenè, *ib.* 18 fin.; complete the blockade, *ib.*; raise a property tax, *ib.* 19 init.; attempt to collect money from the allies, *ib.* fin.; gain possession of Mytilenè, *ib.* 27, 28; take Notium, *ib.* 34; reduce Pyrrha and Eresus, *ib.* 35; put Salaethus to death and order the slaughter of all the grown-up citizens of Mytilenè, *ib.* 36 init.; repent, *ib.*

Athenians (*cont.*)—

med.; summon a second assembly, *ib.* fin.; send a ship in time to save Mytilenè, *ib.* 49; put to death the Lesbians judged most guilty, *ib.* 50 init.; divide the island among Athenian colonists, *ib.* med.; occupy Minoa, *ib.* 51; arrest envoys from Corcyra, *ib.* 72 init.; send a fleet to Corcyra, *ib.* 75; engage at sea with the Peloponnesians, *ib.* 77, 78; send twenty ships to Sicily, *ib.* 86 init.; the plague reappears, *ib.* 87; the Athenians ravage the Aeolian islands, *ib.* 88; proceedings in Sicily, *ib.* 90, 99, 103, 115, iv. 24, 25; send a fleet round the Peloponnese, iii. 91 init.; land at Oropus, and win a battle at Tanagra, *ib.* med., fin.; alarmed by the founding of Heraclea, *ib.* 93 init.; attack Leucas, *ib.* 94 init., med.; disastrous expedition into Aetolia, *ib* 95-98; purify Delos and restore the festival, *ib.* 104; send reinforcements to Sicily, *ib.* 115; fortify Pylos, iv. 4; take and lose again Eion, *ib.* 7; repulse the Lacedaemonians, *ib.* 11, 12; defeat the Lacedaemonians in the harbour, *ib.* 14; cut off the Spartans in Sphacteria, *ib.* 15; grant a truce to the Lacedaemonians, *ib.* 16; demand impossible terms, *ib.* 21, 22; renew the blockade, *ib.* 23; find the blockade difficult, *ib.* 26; despatch Cleon with reinforcements, *ib.* 27, 28; attack Sphacteria and compel the surrender of the Spartans, *ib.* 31-38; again reject the peace proposals of the Lacedaemonians, *ib.* 41 fin.; invade the Corinthian territory, &c., *ib.* 42-45; aid the Corcyraeans to capture Istonè, *ib.* 46; deliver the prisoners to the Corcyraeans, *ib.* 47; proceed

to Sicily, *ib.* 48 fin.; aid the Acarnanians to capture Anactorium, *ib.* 49; capture a Persian ambassador to Sparta, *ib.* 50 init.; send him back with an embassy of their own, *ib.* fin.; order the Chians to dismantle their walls, *ib.* 51; capture Cythera, *ib.* 53, 54; ravage the Lacedaemonian coast, *ib.* 54 fin., 55; capture Thyrea, *ib.* 57; quit Sicily, *ib.* 65 med.; punish their generals, *ib.*; unsuccessfully attempt Megara, *ib.* 66-68; capture Nisaea, *ib.* 69; engage the Boeotian cavalry, *ib.* 72; unwilling to fight with Brasidas, *ib.* 73; recapture Antandrus, *ib.* 75 med.; plan an invasion of Boeotia, *ib.* 76, 77; declare Perdiccas an enemy, *ib.* 82; defeated at Delium, *ib.* 90-96; the Boeotians refuse to give up the dead, *ib.* 97-99; the Athenian garrison in Delium is captured by the Boeotians, and the dead are then given up, *ib.* 100, 101 init.; repulsed by the Sicyonians, *ib.* 101 med.; lose Amphipolis, *ib.* 102-106; Thucydides saves Eion, *ib.* 105; driven from the long walls of Megara, *ib.* 109 init.; lose Actè, *ib.* med., fin.; Toronè, *ib.* 110-113; Lecythus, *ib.* 114-116; make a truce for a year with the Lacedaemonians, *ib.* 117-119; Scionè revolts, and the Athenians exclude it from the treaty, *ib.* 120, 122 init.; they decree its total destruction, *ib.* fin.; defeated by the Mendaeans, who also revolt, *ib.* 129; capture Mendè, *ib.* 130 fin.; invest Scionè, *ib.* 131; come to an understanding with Perdiccas, *ib.* 132 init.; again purify Delos, v. 1; send Cleon to Chalcidicè, *ib.* 2; capture Toronè, *ib.* 3; send an embassy under Phaeax to

Athenians (*cont.*)—

Sicily, *ib*. 4, 5 ; defeated at Amphipolis, *ib*. 6–12 ; become eager for peace, *ib*. 14 init. ; make a treaty with the Lacedaemonians, *ib*. 17–19 ; conclude an alliance with the Lacedaemonians, *ib*. 22 fin.–24 ; release the prisoners from the island, *ib*. 24 fin. ; take and destroy Scionè, *ib*. 32 init. ; replace the Delians in Delos, *ib*. ; refuse a ten days' armistice to the Corinthians, *ib*. med. ; begin to mistrust the Lacedaemonians, *ib*. 35 ; withdraw the Helots from Pylos, *ib*. 35 fin. ; send ambassadors to Sparta, *ib*. 36 init. ; negotiate uselessly with the Lacedaemonians, *ib*. 39 init. ; indignant at the destruction of Panactum, *ib*. 42 fin. ; the war party at Athens intrigue for the abrogation of the treaty, *ib*. 43 ; the Athenians make alliance with the Argives, *ib*. 46 fin., 47 ; replace the Helots at Pylos, *ib*. 56 med. ; solemnly record that the Lacedaemonians have broken their oaths, *ib*. ; send a force to Argos, *ib*. 61 init. ; share in the battle of Mantinea, *ib*. 69, 72–74 ; invest Epidaurus, *ib*. 75 fin. ; their alliance is renounced by the Argives, *ib*. 78 ; withdraw their troops from Epidaurus, *ib*. 80 fin. the Dians revolt, *ib*. 82 init. ; the Argives renew their alliance, and, with Athenian help, build their Long Walls, *ib*. fin. ; the Athenians blockade Perdiccas, *ib*. 83 fin. ; carry off 300 Argives whom they suspect, *ib*. 84 init. ; attack Melos, *ib*. med. ; hold a conference with the Melian authorities, *ib*. 85–113 ; blockade Melos, *ib*. 114, 115 fin., 116 med. ; capture Melos, destroy or enslave the inhabitants, and colonise the island, *ib*. ; spoil, from Pylos, the Lacedaemonians, *ib*. 115 init. ; the Corinthians declare war upon them, *ib*. ; the Athenians determine to send an expedition to Sicily, vi, 1, 6 init. ; send envoys to Egesta, *ib*. 6 fin. ; decide on war, *ib*. 8 ; assist the Argives in the capture of Orneae, *ib*. 7 med. ; ravage Macedonia, *ib*. fin. ; the envoys return from Sicily, *ib*. 8 init. ; debate in the Assembly, *ib*. 9–23 ; seized with enthusiasm for the expedition, *ib*. 24 ; greatly disturbed by the mutilation of the Hermae, *ib*. 27 fin. ; Alcibiades is accused, of profaning the mysteries, but sent to Sicily untried, *ib*. 28, 29 ; the expedition starts for Sicily, *ib*. 30–32 ; review of the troops at Corcyra, *ib*. 42 ; the Athenians arrive at Rhegium, *ib*. 43, 44 ; deceived by the Egesteans, *ib*. 46 ; the generals hold a council of war, *ib*. 47–49 ; Alcibiades' opinion prevails, *ib*. 50 ; the Athenians sail to Syracuse, *ib*. 50 ; obtain possession of Catana, *ib*. 51 ; not received at Camarina, *ib*. 52 ; the excitement about the mutilation of the Hermae continues, *ib*. 53, 60 ; the Athenians send to arrest Alcibiades, *ib*. 53, 61 init. ; condemn him to death, *ib*. 61 fin. ; proceedings of, in Sicily, *ib*. 62, 63 ; capture Hyccara, *ib*. 62 init. ; sail to Syracuse, *ib*. 64, 65 ; defeat the Syracusans, *ib*. 66–71 ; fail in an attempt on Messenè, which Alcibiades betrays, *ib*. 74 ; send home for money and cavalry, *ib*. fin. [cp. 93 fin., 94 fin.] ; send an embassy to Camarina, *ib*. fin., 75 ; Euphemus' speech, *ib*. 81–87 ; fail to win over the Camarinaeans, *ib*. 88 init. ; negotiate with the Sicels, *ib*. med. ; winter

Athenians (*cont.*)—

at Catana and prepare for a spring campaign, *ib*. fin.; receive aid from home, *ib*. 93 fin., 94 fin.; prosecute the campaign, *ib*. 94; capture Epipolae and fortify Labdalum, *ib*. 96, 97; receive Sicilian reinforcements, *ib*. 98 init.; begin to build a wall of circumvallation, and defeat the Syracusans in various engagements, *ib*. 98-101; repulse the Syracusans from Epipolae, *ib*. 102; begin a double wall from Epipolae to the sea, *ib*. 103 init., vii. 2 fin.; openly violate the peace with the Lacedaemonians, vi. 105; Athenian ships arrive at Rhegium too late to stop Gylippus, vii. 1 init.; return no answer to Gylippus' demand that they shall quit Sicily, *ib*. 3 init.; are driven out of Labdalum, *ib*. fin.; repulse an attack on their lines, *ib*. 4 init.; fortify Plemmyrium, *ib*.; defeat the Syracusans, *ib*. 5 med.; defeated by the Syracusans, *ib*. 6; the Athenians, aided by Perdiccas, make an attempt upon Amphipolis, *ib*. 9; the Athenians at home receive the despatch of Nicias, *ib*. 10–15; send a second expedition to Sicily under Demosthenes, *ib*. 16; send a fleet round Peloponnese, *ib*. 20; conquer the Syracusans at sea, but lose Plemmyrium, *ib*. 22, 23; skirmish with the Syracusans in the harbour, *ib*. 25 med.; ravage the Laconian coast, and fortify an isthmus there, *ib*. 26; resolve to send back some Thracians who have come too late to join the reinforcements to Sicily, *ib*. 27 init. [who sack Mycalessus on their way, 29, 30]; suffer terribly from the occupation of Decelea by the Lacedaemonians, *ib*. 27, 28; Demosthenes meets Eury-

medon with news from Sicily, *ib*. 31 init.; Demosthenes and Eurymedon collect troops in Acarnania and Corcyra, *ib*. fin.; the Athenians in Sicily induce the Sicels to destroy reinforcements on their way to Syracuse, *ib*. 32; Demosthenes arrives at Thurii, *ib*. 33; the Athenians at Naupactus fight an indecisive engagement at sea with the Corinthians, *ib*. 34; consider themselves defeated because not signally the victors, *ib*. fin.; defeated at sea by the Syracusans, *ib*. 37–41; repulsed in a night attack on Epipolae, *ib*. 43–45; the Athenian generals hold a council, *ib*. 47–49 init.; Nicias wishes to delay and Demosthenes yields, *ib*. 49 fin.; Nicias at last consents to move, but terrified by an eclipse remains another 27 days, *ib*. 50; the Athenians are again defeated at sea by the Syracusans, *ib*. 52; gain a slight advantage by land, *ib*. 53; why they failed to conquer Syracuse, *ib*. 55; the list of their allies before Syracuse, *ib*. 57; determine to fight their way out, *ib*. 60; Nicias addresses the troops, *ib*. 61–64; and the trierarchs, *ib*. 69; the Athenians are completly defeated at sea, *ib*. 70, 71; overwhelmed by misery refuse to renew the struggle, *ib*. 72; are misled by false information and delay their retreat three days, *ib*. 73, 74; their misery and terror when commencing the retreat, *ib*. 75; encouraged and consoled by Nicias, *ib*. 76, 77; during four days are harassed and at length confronted by the enemy, *ib*. 78, 79; fall back, *ib*. 79 fin.; recommence retreat, changing their route, *ib*. 80 init.; seized with a panic, *ib*. med.; the second division is

Athenians (*cont.*)—

overtaken and compelled to surrender, *ib.* 81, 82; the first meets the same fate on the Assinarus, *ib.* 83–85; three hundred escape, *ib.* 83 fin.; but are captured, *ib.* 85 med.; Nicias and Demosthenes are put to death, *ib.* 86; the prisoners are cruelly treated by the Syracusans, *ib.* 87; the Athenians at home in fury and terror, but determined not to yield, viii. 1; suspect the Chians of treason, *ib.* 9, 10 init.; defeat a Peloponnesian squadron and blockade them in Piraeum, *ib.* 10, 11 init.; intercept, but do not succeed in capturing, a Peloponnesian fleet, *ib.* 13; on the news of the revolt of Chios pass a decree allowing the use of their reserve fund and ships, *ib.* 15 init.; prepare a great fleet for Asia under Strombichides and Thrasycles, *ib.* fin.; Strombichides is chased from Teos, *ib.* 16; arrives at Miletus too late to stop a revolt, *ib.* 17; captures four Chian ships, *ib.* 19; the Athenians at Piraeum lose four ships in a sally of the Peloponnesian fleet, *ib.* 20 init.; Diomedon recovers Teos, but fails to take Erae, *ib.* fin; the Athenians grant the Samians independence after a democratic revolution, *ib.* 21; reconquer Lesbos which had revolted, and Clazomenae, *ib.* 23; win a slight advantage at Miletus, *ib.* 24 init.; fight three successful battles against the Chians, *ib.* med.; win a victory before Miletus, *ib.* 25; withdraw to Samos on the approach of a Peloponnesian fleet, *ib.* 27 fin.; receive reinforcements from home, *ib.* 25 init., 30 init.; prepare to attack Miletus, *ib.* 30 fin.; lose three ships in a storm, *ib.* 34 init.; fail to take Cnidus which had revolted, *ib.* 35; blockade Chios, *ib.* 38 init., 40; cannot induce the Peloponnesians at Miletus to fight, *ib.* 38 fin.; defeated at sea, *ib.* 41, 42, 43 init.; Rhodes revolts, the Athenians attack it from Chalcè, Cos, and Samos, *ib.* 44; the oligarchical party at Samos, by Alcibiades' instigation, prepares the way for a revolution, *ib.* 47, 48 init.; Phrynichus resists, *ib.* 48 med.; Peisander is sent to Tissaphernes, *ib.* 49; Phrynichus out-manœuvres Alcibiades, who seeks to ruin him, *ib.* 50, 51; those at home agree to change the government, *ib.* 53, 54; send Peisander to negotiate with Alcibiades, *ib.* 54 init.; remove Phrynichus and appoint Leon and Diomedon generals, *ib.* med.; Leon and Diomedon make a descent upon Rhodes, *ib.* 55 init.; the Athenians at Chios defeat the Chians and press on the blockade, *ib.* 55 fin., 56 init.; Peisander's embassy fails through Alcibiades' unreasonable demands, *ib.* 56 med.; Oropus is betrayed to the Boeotians, *ib.* 60 init.; the Athenian fleet retire to Samos for the winter, passing in sight of the Peloponnesians, *ib.* fin.; they are worsted at sea by the Chians, *ib.* 61 fin.; Lampsacus and Abydos revolt, *ib.* 62 init.; Strombichides retakes Lampsacus but fails at Abydos, *ib.* med.; the Athenians at Samos decline Astyochus' offer of battle, *ib.* 63 init.; the conspirators at Samos give up Alcibiades, but prosecute their plan, *ib.* 63 fin.; order Pisander to put down democracy in the cities, *ib.* 64; the conspirators at home declare for a (pretended) government of 5,000, *ib.* 65; crush opposition by terrorism, *ib.* 66; repeal the graphè paranomon, *ib.* 67

Athenians (*cont.*)—

init.; propose a government of 400, *ib.* 67 fin.; description of the leaders of the conspiracy, *ib.* 68; they instal the 400 in the place of the senate, *ib.* 69, 70; send heralds to Agis at Decelea, *ib.* 70 fin.; despatch envoys to Sparta, *ib.* 71 fin.; and to Samos, *ib.* 72; the Athenians at Samos defeat an oligarchical conspiracy. *ib.* 73; send Chaereas in the Paralus to Athens, *ib.* 74; on his return with an unfavourable report the army and the Samians swear allegiance to the democracy, *ib.* 75; the army appoints Thrasyllus and Thrasybulus generals, *ib.* 76 init.; the men encourage each other, *ib.* med.; the commissioners sent by the 400 do not venture beyond Delos, *ib.* 77; the Athenians at Samos refuse battle with Astyochus, but afterwards offer it, *ib.* 79; recall Alcibiades, *ib.* 81 init.; the army eager to sail to the Piraeus, Alcibiades restrains them, *ib.* 82 init.; the envoys of the Four Hundred now come to Samos, *ib.* 86 [cp. 72 init., 77]; they are roughly received by the army, *ib.* 86 init.; Alcibiades again dissuades the army from sailing to Athens, *ib.* med.; the Argives offer assistance, *ib.* fin.; the Four Hundred in alarm send envoys to Lacedaemon for peace on any terms, *ib.* 90 med.; fortify Eetionea, *ib.* fin.; the envoys return unsuccessful, *ib.* 91 init.; Theramenes begins to withdraw from the oligarchs, *ib.* passim; the hoplites under his instigation destroy Eetionea, *ib.* 92; panic in the city, *ib.* med.; the Four Hundred induce the people to fix a day for an assembly 'to restore harmony,' *ib.* 93; a Lacedaemonian squadron approaches and the Athenians hurriedly equip a fleet, *ib.* 94; utterly defeated at sea and lose Euboea, *ib.* 95; panic-stricken by their defeat, *ib.* 96 init.; depose the 400, *ib.* 97; recall Alcibiades, *ib.* fin.; the leaders of the oligarchs retire to Decelea, *ib.* 98; the Athenian fleet sails to the Hellespont, *ib.* 100; attacks Eresus on the way, *ib.* fin.; the Athenian squadron at Sestos is chased by the Lacedaemonian fleet, *ib.* 102; the fleet at Lesbos at once sails from Eresus to Elaeus, *ib.* 103; they defeat the Lacedaemonians at sea off Cynossema, *ib.* 104, 105; encouraged by their good fortune, *ib.* 106; capture eight Peloponnesian ships, *ib.* 107; recover Cyzicus, which had revolted, *ib.* 107 med.; Alcibiades returns to Samos, professing to have secured Tissaphernes' friendship for them, *ib.* 108 init.

Athletes, used to wear girdles in gymnastic contests, i. 6 fin.; honours paid to, iv. 121 med.

Athos, Mount, iv. 109 med, v. 3 fin., 35 init., 82 init.

Atintanians, a people in Epirus, ii. 80 fin.

Atreus, son of Pelops, i. 9 passim.

Attica, early history of, i. 2 fin.; Ionia colonised from, *ib.*, *ib.* 12 fin.; ii. 15 fin.; anciently divided into Communes, ii. 15 init.; invaded by the Lacedaemonians, i. 114 med.; ii. 21 init.; invasion in first year of the War, ii. 18–23; in the second, *ib.* 47, 55, 56; in the third, Plataea attacked instead, ii. 71 init.; in the fourth, iii. 1; in the fifth, *ib.* 26; in the sixth averted by an earthquake, *ib.* 89 init.; in the seventh, iv. 2 init., 6; in the nineteenth, vii. 19 init.

Aulon, in Chalcidicè, iv. 103 init.

Autocharidas, a Lacedaemonian general, v. 12.

Autocles, son of Tolmaeus, an Athenian general, iv. 53 init., 119 fin.

Axius, river in Macedonia, ii. 99 med.

B.

Barbarians, term not used in Homer, i. 3 med.; carry arms in daily life, *ib.* 6 init.; various barbarous races : the Aetolians, iii. 94 fin.; the Amphilochians, ii. 68 init.; in Athos, iv. 109; the Epirots, ii. 80 82; the Illyrians, iv. 126 med.; in Sicily, vi. 2; *ib.* 11 fin.; the Taulantians, i. 24 init.: the Thracians, ii. 96-98, 101; iv. 75 fin.; vii. 27; Xerxes called 'the Barbarian,' i. 14 fin., 18.

Battus, a Corinthian commander, iv. 43 init.

Bells, use of by sentinels, iv. 135 med.

Beroea, in Macedonia, i. 61 med.

Bisaltia, in Macedonia, ii. 99 fin.

Bisaltians [in Athos], iv. 109 fin.

Bithynian Thracians, iv. 75 fin.

Boeotarchs, Pythangelus, ii. 2 med.; Diemporus, *ib.*; Pagondas, iv. 91 med.; Arianthidas, *ib.*; Scirphondas, vii. 30 fin.; their powers, v. 37, 38.

Boeotia, early history, i. 2 med., iii. 61 med.; formerly called Cadmeis, i. 12 med.; fertility of, *ib.* 2 med.; bordered on one side by Phocis, iii. 95 init.; the Four Councils of Boeotia, v. 38; earthquakes in Boeotia, iii. 87 fin.

Boeotians, the, expelled from Arnè by the Thessalians, i. 12 med.; all but the Plataeans joined the Persians, iii. 62 init. [cp. viii. 43 fin.]; subdued by the Athenians after Oenophyta, i. 108 med.; become allies of the Athenians, *ib.* 111 init.; regain their freedom at Coronea, *ib.* 113 fin., iii.

62 fin., 67 med., iv. 92 fin.; the Boeotians in Attica seized after the attempt on Plataea, ii. 6 med.; furnish cavalry to the Lacedaemonians at the opening of the War, *ib.* 9 med., 12 fin.; ravage Plataea, *ib.* 12 fin.; worst the Athenians in a cavalry skirmish at Phrygia in Attica, *ib.* 22 med.; supply half the besieging force at Plataea, *ib.* 78 med.; invaded by the Athenians, iii. 91; assist Brasidas to save Megara from the Athenians, iv. 70, 72; the democratic party in Boeotia concert an Athenian invasion, *ib.* 76, 77; the plot is betrayed, *ib.* 89; the Athenians under Hippocrates arrive and fortify Delium, *ib.* 90; the Boeotians defeat the Athenians at Delium, *ib.* 91-96; quibble with the Athenians about giving up the dead, *ib.* 97-99; capture Delium, *ib.* 100; the Lacedaemonians promise to invite the Boeotians to join in the Truce, *ib.* 118 init.; Panactum is betrayed to the Boeotians, v. 3 fin.; refuse to join in the fifty years' Peace, *ib.* 17 fin.; had only a ten days' armistice with the Athenians, *ib.* 26 med., 32 med.; refuse to join the Argive alliance, *ib.* 31 fin.; 32 med.; fail to gain from the Athenians a ten days' armistice for the Corinthians, *ib.* fin.; the Lacedaemonians promise to try to bring the Boeotians into the Treaty, *ib.* 35 fin.; the new Lacedaemonian ephors propose to the Boeotians that they should enter the Argive alliance, *ib.* 36; the Boeotians at first agree, *ib.* 37; the Boeotian Councils reject the offer, *ib.* 38; the Boeotians form a separate alliance with Lacedaemon, surrendering Panactum and their Athenian prisoners to them, *ib.*

Boeotians (*cont.*)—

39; take possession of Heraclea, *ib.* 52 init.; take part in the Lacedaemonian invasion of Argos, *ib.* 57 fin.–60; summoned by the Lacedaemonians to Mantinea, *ib.* 64 med; invite a small body of Lacedaemonian troops to the Isthmus, and thus raise suspicion at Athens against Alcibiades, vi. 61 init.; send aid to Sicily, vii. 19 med., 58 med.; these engaged against their Plataean countrymen, *ib.* 57 init.; make the first stand against the Athenians on Epipolae, *ib.* 43 fin.; sack of Mycalessus by the Thracians, *ib.* 29, 30; the Boeotians furnish the Lacedaemonians with ships, viii. 3 fin.; aid the revolt of Lesbos, *ib.* 4 fin.; Oropus is betrayed to the Boeotians, *ib.* 60 init.; Oenoe is betrayed to the Boeotians, *ib.* 98; the Boeotians lose two ships at Cynossema, *ib.* 106 med.

Boeum, in Doris, i. 107 init.

Bolbè, Lake, in Macedonia, i. 58 fin., iv. 103 init.

Bolissus, in Chios, viii. 24 med.

Bomieans, in Aetolia, iii. 96 fin.

Boriades, an Aetolian envoy, iii. 100 init.

Bottiaea, ii. 100 med.; the Bottiaeans expelled from, by the Macedonians, ii. 99 med.

Botticè, revolts from Athens, i. 56–58; devastated by Phormio, *ib.* 65 fin.; ravaged by Sitalces, ii. 101; the Bottiaeans there defeat the Athenians, *ib.* 79; aid the Chalcidians to expel the Athenians from Eion, iv. 7.

Brasidas, saves Methonè, ii. 25 med.; the first Spartan to gain distinction in the War, *ib.*; sent out as adviser of Cnemus, *ib.* 85 init.; concerts with the other commanders an attack on the Piraeus, *ib.* 93; sent as adviser of Alcidas, iii. 69 med., *ib.* 76 med.; advises Alcidas to attack Corcyra, *ib.* 79 fin.; distinguishes himself at Pylos, iv. 11 med.; wounded, *ib.* 12 init.; saves Megara, *ib.* 70-73; marches through Thessaly to Chalcidicè, *ib.* 78; favourable impression produced by him, *ib.* 81, 108 med.; a good speaker, *ib.* 84 fin.; his army, Peloponnesian mercenaries and Helots, *ib.* 80 fin. [cp. *ib.* 70 med.]; allies himself with Perdiccas, *ib.* 83 init.; quarrels with him, *ib.* fin.; gains over Acanthus and Stagirus, *ib.* 84-88; speech of, at Acanthus, *ib.* 85-87; captures Amphipolis, *ib.* 103-106; repulsed from Eion, *ib.* 107 init.; brings over Myrcinus, Galepsus, and Oesymè, *ib.* fin.; takes Toronè and Lecythus, *ib.* 110-116; receives honours from the Scionaeans, *ib.* 121; refuses to surrender Scionè under the Truce, *ib.* 122; receives the Mendaeans in defiance of the Truce, *ib.* 123 init.; garrisons Mendè and Scionè, *ib.* fin.; defeats the Lyncestians, *ib.* 124; deserted by the Macedonians, *ib.* 125; his speech to his soldiers, *ib.* 126; defeats the Illyrians, *ib.* 127, 128; receives commissioners from Lacedaemon, *ib.* 132 fin.; attempts Potidaea, *ib.* 135; defeats the Athenians at Amphipolis, v. 6-10; speech of, *ib.* 9; his death, *ib.* 10 fin.; buried in the Agora of Amphipolis, *ib.* 11 init.; receives the honours of a founder from the Amphipolitans, *ib.* 11 med.; a great enemy to peace, *ib.* 16 init.; his Helot soldiers settled at Lepreum, *ib.* 34 med.; his old soldiers present at Mantinea, *ib.* 67 init., 71 fin., 72 med.

Brauro, helps in the assassination of her husband, Pittacus, king of the Edonians, iv. 107 fin.

Bricinniae, in Leontine territory, v. 4 med.

Bridge over the Strymon, iv. 103 fin.; over the Anapus, vi. 66 med.

Brilessus, Mount, in Attica, ii. 23 init.

Bromerus, father of Arrhibaeus the king of the Lyncestians, iv. 83 init.

Bromiscus, in Chalcidicè, iv. 103 init.

Bucolium, in Arcadia, iv. 134 fin.

Budorum, a station in Salamis from which the Athenians used to watch Megara, ii. 94 fin., iii. 51 med.

Buphras, in Laconia, iv. 118 med.

Burial, Carian mode of, i. 8 init.

Byzantium, captured by Pausanias, and entrusted to Gongylus, i. 94, 128 med., 129 med.; expulsion of Pausanias from Byzantium, *ib.* 131 init.; insignificant engagement at sea off Byzantium, viii. 80 fin. [cp. *ib.* 107 init.]; the Byzantines revolt from Athens, i. 115 fin.; submit, *ib.* 117 fin.; revolt again, viii. 80.

C.

Cacyparis, river in Sicily, vii. 80 fin.

Cadmeis, old name of Boeotia, i. 12 med.

Caeadas, a chasm into which malefactors were flung at Sparta, i. 134 med.

Caecinus, a river of Locris in Italy, iii. 103 fin.

Calex, a river near Heraclea on the Pontus, iv. 75 fin.

Callias, father of Callicrates, a Corinthian, i. 29 init. [Athenians] (I) son of Hyperechides, father-

in-law of Hippias the tyrant, vi. 55 init.; (II) father of Hipponicus, iii. 91 med.; (III) son of Calliades, an Athenian commander, i. 61 init., *ib.* 62 med.; killed at Potidaea, *ib.* 63 fin.

Callicrates, a Corinthian commander, i. 29 init.

Callieans, an Aetolian tribe, iii. 96 fin.

Calligitus, a Megarian exile at the Court of Pharnabazus, viii. 6 init.; goes as envoy to Sparta, *ib.*, *ib.* 8 init., 39 init.

Callimachus, father of Learchus, an Athenian, ii. 67 med.; father of Phanomachus, an Athenian, ii. 70 init.

Callirrhoè, ancient name of the fountain Enneacrounos at Athens, ii. 15 fin.

Calydon, name given to the ancient Aeolis, iii. 102 med.

Camarina, founded from Syracuse, vi. 5 med.; recolonised by Hippocrates, *ib.* fin.; by Gela, *ib.*; in alliance with Leontini, iii. 86 init.; plan to betray it to Syracuse, iv. 25 med.; Camarinaeans make a truce with Gela, *ib.* 58 init.; receive Morgantinè from the Syracusans, *ib.* 65 init.; refuse to receive the Athenian expedition, vi. 52; send a small force to the Syracusans, *ib.* 67 fin.; receive and hear embassies both from Athens and Syracuse, *ib.* 75-87; resolve on neutrality, *ib.* 88 init.; send aid to Syracuse after the capture of Plemmyrium, vii. 33 init., 58 init.

Cambyses, son of Cyrus, king of Persia, the Ionians in his time masters of the sea about their own coast, i. 13 fin.

Camirus, in Rhodes, revolts from Athens, viii. 44 med.

Canal, cut by the Persians across the Isthmus of Athos, iv. 109 init.

Canastraeum, promontory of, in Pallenè, iv. 110 fin.

Capaton, father of Proxenus, an Italian Locrian, iii. 103 fin.

Carcinus, an Athenian commander, ii. 23 med.

Cardamylè, in Chios, viii. 24 med.

Caria, Carians expelled by Minos from the Cyclades, i. 4; addicted to piracy, *ib.* 8 init.; their mode of burial, *ib.* init.; the Athenians send look-out ships to the Carian coast in the Samian insurrection, *ib.* 116 init.; maritime Caria subject to the Athenians, ii.9 fin.; the Athenians send a squadron to the Carian coast to protect their Phoenician trade, *ib.* 69 med.; Carians destroy an Athenian expedition, iii. 19 fin.; Amorges in Caria revolts from the King, viii. 5 fin.; Gaulites, a Carian speaking Greek and Persian, *ib.* 85 init.

Carnea, feast at Lacedaemon, v. 75, 76 init.

Carneus, sacred month among the Dorians, v. 54 med.

Carteria, a Phocaean island, viii. 101 med.

Carthage, ambitious plans of Alcibiades for attacking Carthage, vi. 15 med., 90 init.; always in fear of an Athenian invasion, *ib.* 34 init.; relations of the Phoenician colonies in Sicily to Carthage, *ib.* 2 fin.; Carthaginians defeated at sea by the Phocaeans, i. 13 fin.

Caryae, in Laconia, v. 55 med.

Carystus, in Euboea, of Dryopian origin, vii. 57 med.; subjected by the Athenians, i. 98 med.; the Carystians become allies of the Athenians, iv. 42 init., vii. 57 med.

Casmenae, founded by the Syracusans, vi. 5 med.

Castle, the White, a portion of Memphis, i. 104 fin.

Catana, founded by Thucles and Evarchus, vi. 3 fin.; lies under mount Aetna, iii. 116 init.; at first refuses to receive the Athenian expedition, vi. 50 med.; after the entry of some Athenian soldiers votes an alliance with Athens, *ib.* 51 fin., vii. 57 fin., 85 fin.; becomes the Athenian station, vi. 51 fin., 52 fin., 62 fin.; the Syracusans eager to attack Catana, *ib.* 63 fin.; the Athenians by a false message draw the Syracusans to Catana while they sail to Syracuse, *ib.* 64, 65; the Athenians retire to Catana at the beginning of winter, *ib.* 72 init.; start from Catana on an expedition against Messenè, *ib.* 74; the Syracusans destroy the Athenian encampment at Catana, *ib.* 75 med.; the Athenians rebuild their camp, *ib.* 88 med.; start from thence on various expeditions, *ib.* 94; abandon Catana, *ib.* 97 init.; are supplied with horses from Catana, *ib.* 98 init.; Catana and Naxos mentioned by Nicias as unable to support the Athenian forces, vii. 14 med.; Demosthenes on his arrival thinks the winter spent at Catana a mistake, *ib.* 42 med.; after Epipolae wishes to retire to Catana, *ib.* 49 med.; the Athenian army at Syracuse fed from Catana, *ib.* 60 init.; at first wish to retreat by sea to Catana, *ib.* med., 72; the Athenian line of retreat in the opposite direction to Catana, *ib.* 80 init.; the Athenian fugitives find a refuge at Catana, *ib.* 85 fin.

Caulonia, in Italy, vii. 25 init.

Caunus, in Caria, called 'Caunus in Asia,' viii. 39 fin.; Pericles

Caunus (*cont.*)—
sails towards Caunus in the Samian revolt, i. 116 fin. ; the Lacedaemonian commissioners to Astyochus put in at Caunus, viii. 39 fin. [cp. 42 med.] ; Astyochus sails for Caunus, *ib.* 41 init. ; Tissaphernes comes to Caunus, *ib.* 57 init. ; Alcibiades sails for Caunus, *ib.* 88 fin. [cp. 108 init.]

Cecalus, father of Nicasus, a Megarian, iv. 119 med.

Cecrops, state of Attica in his time, ii. 15 init.

Cecryphaleia, victory of the Athenians off, i. 105 init.

Cenaeum, in Euboea, iii. 93 init.

Cenchreae, the port of Corinth, the Corinthians leave half their troops at Cenchreae to guard Crommyon, iv. 42 fin., 44 med. ; a Lacedaemonian fleet starting for Chios from Cenchreae is driven into Piraeum, viii. 10 init. ; escapes and returns to Cenchreae, *ib.* 20 init. ; Astyochus starts from Cenchreae, *ib.* 23 init.

Centoripa, a Sicel town, captured by the Athenians, vi. 94 med. ; allied to Athens, vii. 32 med.

Ceos, the Ceans subjects of the Athenians, vii. 57 init.

Cephallenia, repulse of the Corinthians in a descent upon Cephallenia, ii, 33 fin. ; an important station to the Athenians, *ib.* 80 init. [cp. 7 fin.] ; the Cephallenians [of Palè] furnish a convoy to the Corinthians, i. 27 fin. ; become allies of the Athenians, ii. 7 fin., 30 fin., iii. 94 init., 95 med., vi. 85 med., vii. 31 init., 57 med. ; the Messenians from Pylos settled by the Athenians at Cranii in Cephallenia, v. 35 fin. ; withdrawn, *ib.* 56 med.

Ceramicus, the, at Athens, vi. 57 init., 58 init. [ii. 34 med.]

Cercinè, Mount, in Macedonia, ii. 98 init.

Cerdylium, Mount, near Amphipolis, v. 6-10.

Ceryces, the, at Athens, protest against the return of Alcibiades, viii. 53 med.

Cestrinè, in Epirus, i. 46 fin.

Chaereas, an Athenian, sent as envoy from the army at Samos, viii. 74 init. ; escapes from Athens and brings an exaggerated report to Samos, *ib.* fin., 86 init.

Chaeronea, in Boeotia, its situation, iv. 76 med. ; a dependency of the Boeotian Orchomenus, *ib.* ; taken by the Athenians under Tolmides, i. 113 ; Orchomenian exiles plot its betrayal to the Athenians, iv. 76 med. ; the plot fails, *ib.* 89.

Chalaeans, a tribe of Ozolian Locrians, iii. 101 fin.

Chalcè, island of, near Rhodes, viii. 41 fin., 44 fin., 55 init., 60 fin.

Chalcedon, a Megarian colony, iv. 75 fin.

Chalcideus, a Spartan admiral, viii. 6 fin., 8 init. ; sent to Ionia with Alcibiades, *ib.* 11 fin., 12 fin. ; is pursued by the Athenians on his way. *ib.* 15 med. ; induces the revolt of Chios, Erythrae, Clazomenae, *ib.* 14 ; chases Strombichides into Samos, *ib.* 16 ; causes the revolt of Teos, *ib.* fin. ; and of Miletus, *ib.* 17 ; garrisons Chios, *ib.* 17 init. [cp. 32 med.] ; negotiates a treaty between the King and Sparta, *ib.* 18, 36, 43 med. ; falls in a skirmish at Panormus, *ib.* 24 init. ; his forces afterwards engaged before Miletus, *ib.* 25 med.

Chalcidian cities, the, of Sicily, founded from Chalcis in Euboea, vi. 3-5 ; akin to the Athenians,

Chalcidian cities *(cont.)*

iv. 61 med., 64 med. ; the Chalcidian dialect, vi. 5 init. ; invite the Athenians to Sicily, iii. 86 med., iv. 61 med.

Chalcidicè [on the coast of Thrace], revolts from Athens, i. 56–58; devastated by Phormio, *ib.* 65 fin.; by Sitalces, ii. 95 init., 101; Cleon's expedition against Chalcidicè, v. 2–11; Thucydides in command there, iv. 104 fin.; the Chalcidians pull down their cities and retire to Olynthus, i. 58 fin.; defeat the Athenians, ii. 79; retake Eion from the Athenians, iv. 7; invite Brasidas, *ib.* 79, 80 init.; Chalcidian ambassadors accompany Brasidas in his Macedonian campaign, *ib.* 83 med.; the Chalcidians instigate the revolt of Amphipolis, *ib.* 103 med.; aid in garrisoning Mendè and Scionè, *ib.* 123 fin.; supply Brasidas with troops against Arrhibaeus, *ib.* 124 init.; the Chalcidian prisoners taken in Toronè are sent to Athens, and afterwards exchanged, v. 3 fin.; Chalcidian forces at the battle of Amphipolis, *ib.* 6 fin.; pursue the retreating Athenians, *ib.* 10 fin.; provisions respecting the Chalcidian cities in the Treaty of Peace, *ib.* 18, §§ v–vii, ix, x; the Chalcidians refuse to accept the Treaty, *ib.* 21 med.; join the Argive alliance, *ib.* 31 fin.; renew the alliance with Lacedaemon, *ib.* 80 med.; receive the Dians who had revolted from the Athenians, *ib.* 82 init.; maintain a ten days' armistice with the Athenians, vi. 7 fin.

Chalcis, in Aetolia, taken by the Athenians, i. 108 fin., ii. 83 med.

Chalcis, in Euboea, vii. 29 init.; the mother city of the Chalcidian cities in Sicily, vi. 3–5; of Cymè in Italy, *ib.* 4 fin.; war between Chalcis and Eretria, i. 15 fin.; Chalcis subject to the Athenians, vi. 76 init., vii. 57 init.; the Athenians retreat to Chalcis after the sea-fight off Eretria, viii. 95 fin.

Chance, to chance men ascribe whatever belies their calculation, i. 140 init.

Chaones, a people in Epirus, are barbarians, ii. 68 fin.; have no king, *ib.* 80 fin.; their military reputation, *ib.* 81 med.; assist in the invasion of Acarnania, *ib.* 80 fin.; defeated by the Stratians, *ib.* 81.

Charadrus, scene of military trials at Argos, v. 60 fin.

Charicles, an Athenian commander, vii. 20, 26.

Charminus, an Athenian commander, viii. 30 init., 41 fin.; defeated by the Lacedaemonians, *ib.* 42; abets the murder of Hyperbolus, *ib.* 73 med.

Charoeades, an Athenian commander in Sicily, iii. 86 init.; killed in action, *ib.* 90 init.

Charybdis, the whirlpool of, iv. 24 fin.

Cheimerium, in Thesprotia, i. 30 fin.; situation of, *ib.* 46 med.; Corinthian fleet anchors there, *ib.*

Chersonesus, in Corinthian territory, iv. 42 init., 43 init.

Chersonese, the Thracian, cultivated by the Greek armament at Troy, i. 11 med.; ravaged by the Lacedaemonians, viii. 99 fin.; naval operations off its coast, *ib.* 102–105.

Children, a man without children has no stake in the country, ii. 44 fin.

Children of the fallen, maintained at the public charge in Athens, ii. 46 fin.

Chionis, a Lacedaemonian, swears to the Treaty of Peace and the Alliance, v. 19 med., 24 init.

Chios, its moderate and stable government, viii. 24 med. ; its naval power, *ib.* 6 fin. [cp. i. 19 init., ii. 9 fin., 56 med.]; its riches, viii. 24 med. ; great number of slaves there, *ib.* 40 med.; Chios and Lesbos the only free allies of Athens, iii. 10 med., vi. 85 med., vii. 57 init. ; Homer at Chios, iii. 104 fin.; the Chians assist the Athenians against the Samians, i. 116, 117; furnish ships in the siege of Potidaea, ii. 56 med., vi. 31 init.; Alcidas puts some Chian prisoners to death, iii. 32 init.; releases the remainder on a remonstrance from the Samian exiles, *ib.* fin. ; Chians aid the Athenians at Pylos, iv. 13 med. ; ordered by the Athenians to dismantle their walls, *ib.* 51 ; furnish ships against Mendè and Scionè, *ib.* 129 init.; against Melos, v. 84 init.; aid the Athenians at Syracuse, vi. 43 init., 85 med., vii. 20 med., 57 init.; negotiate with the Lacedaemonians about revolting, viii. 5 init.; received into alliance, *ib.* 6; send the Athenians ships as a pledge of fidelity, *ib.* 9 med. ; revolt, *ib.* 14 med.; employed by Alcibiades to raise revolt in Ionia, beginning with Miletus, *ib.* 17; four of their ships are taken by the Athenians, *ib.* 19 init.; induce Lebedus and Erae to revolt, *ib.* fin.; then Methymna and Mytilenè, *ib.* 22 ; lose a few ships off Lesbos, *ib.* 23 med.; defeated in three battles by the Athenians, *ib.* 24 med. ; their sufferings lead some to negotiate with the Athenians, *ib.* 24 fin., 31 init., 38 med. ; aid in the capture of Iasus, *ib.* 28 init.;

the Athenians prepare to attack them, *ib.* 30; the Chians refuse to assist Astyochus in procuring the revolt of Lesbos, *ib.* 32 fin. ; three Chian ships are chased by the Athenians into Chios, *ib.* 34 init.; have their government changed by the Lacedaemonians, *ib.* 38 med. ; completely blockaded, *ib.* 40 ; implore the aid of Astyochus, *ib.* 38 fin., 40 init. ; defeated by the Athenians and more closely blockaded, *ib.* 55 fin., 56 init.; gain an advantage at sea over the Athenians, *ib.* 61 fin. ; regain the command of the sea, on the withdrawal of a part of the Athenian fleet, *ib.* 62 init., 63 init.; the Athenians plan a fresh attack on Chios, on the arrival of a Lacedaemonian fleet under Mindarus, *ib.* 100 ; the Lacedaemonians slip away, *ib.* 101 ; the Chians lose eight ships at Cynossema, *ib.* 106 med. ; Chian tesseracosts, viii. 101 init.

Choenix, an Athenian measure, iv. 16 med. [See note.]

Choerades, Iapygian islands, vii. 33 med.

Choruses, once sent by the Athenians to the festival at Delos, iii. 104 fin.

Chromon, Demosthenes' Messenian guide in Aetolia, iii. 98 med.

Chrysippus, murdered by Atreus, i. 9 med.

Chrysis, priestess of Herè at Argos, ii. 2 init., iv. 133 med.; causes the conflagration of the temple, iv. 133 med. ; flees to Phlius, *ib.*

Chrysis, father of Eumachus, a Corinthian, ii. 33 med.

Cilicians : the Cilicians and Phoenicians defeated at Salamis [in Cyprus] by the Athenians, i. 112 med.

Cimon, son of Miltiades, captures Eion, i. 98 init. ; conquers the Persians at the Eurymedon, *ib.* 100 init. ; commands the Athenian reinforcements at the siege of Ithomè, *ib.* 102 init. ; dies in Cyprus, *ib.* 112 med.

Cimon, father of Lacedaemonius, an Athenian, i. 45.

Cithaeron, Mt., ii. 75 init., iii. 24 init.

Cities, ancient cities small, i. 2 med.; resembled scattered villages, *ib.* 10 init.; at first built inland, afterwards on the seashore, *ib.* 7 ; the cities of Ionia unfortified, iii. 33 med. ; ' The City,' name for Acropolis at Athens, ii. 15 fin.

Citium, in Cyprus, i. 112 med.

Citizen, the citizen must be sacrificed to the state, ii. 60 init., 61 fin.

Citizenship, the Lacedaemonians deprive those who had been prisoners at Sphacteria of citizenship, v. 34 fin.

Clarus, in Ionia, iii. 33 init.

Classes of the citizens at Athens, iii. 16 init., vi. 43 med.

Clazomenae, built on an island, viii. 14 fin. ; the Clazomenians revolt from Athens, *ib.*; fortify Polichnè, *ib.*; aid in the revolt of Teos, *ib.* 16; the Peloponnesian infantry march towards Clazomenae, *ib.* 22 fin. ; they are subdued by the Athenians, *ib.* 23 fin. ; repulse a Peloponnesian attack, *ib.* 31 med.

Cleaenetus, father of Cleon, an Athenian, iii. 36 fin.

Cleandridas, father of Gylippus, a Spartan, vi. 93 med.

Clearchus, a Lacedaemonian commander, viii. 8 med. ; appointed to the Hellespont, *ib.* 39 med., 80.

Clearidas, a Lacedaemonian, made governor of Amphipolis, iv. 132 fin. ; commands with Brasidas at the battle of Amphipolis, v. 6–11 ; refuses to surrender Amphipolis, *ib.* 21 med. ; brings home the troops of Brasidas, *ib.* 34 init.

Cleinias, the father of Alcibiades, an Athenian, v. 43 init. ; another, father of Theopompus [?], ii. 26 ; another, father of Cleopompus, *ib.* 58.

Cleïppides, an Athenian commander, iii. 3 med.

Cleobulus, ephor at Sparta, v. 36 init. ; favours the war party, *ib.*; negotiates with the Boeotians and Corinthians, *ib.* 36–38.

Cleombrotus, father of Pausanias, a Lacedaemonian, i. 94 init. ; of Nicomedes, *ib.* 107 init.

Cleomedes, an Athenian general in the attack on Melos, v. 84 fin.

Cleomenes, king of Sparta, expels the ' accursed persons' from Athens, i. 126 fin.

Cleomenes, the uncle of king Pausanias, iii. 26 med.

Cleon, a great popular leader, iii. 36 fin., iv. 21 med. ; hostile to Nicias, iv. 27 fin. ; a great enemy to peace, v. 16 init.; his arrogance, *ib.* 7 med. ; carries the decree condemning the Mytilenaeans to death, iii. 36 fin. ; his speech against its repeal, *ib.* 37-40 ; moves and carries the slaughter of 1000 Mytilenaean captives at Athens, *ib.* 50 init. ; causes the breaking off of negotiations with Sparta, iv. 21, 22 ; is sent in place of Nicias to Pylos, *ib.* 27, 28 ; selects Demosthenes as his colleague, *ib.* 29 init. ; makes with Demosthenes an attack on Sphacteria, *ib.* 31–37 ; compels the surrender of the Lacedaemonians, *ib.* 36 ; carries a decree for the destruc-

Cleon (*cont.*)—

tion of Scionè, *ib.* 122 fin.; captures Toronè, v. 2, 3; takes Galepsus, and attempts Stagirus, *ib.* 6 init.; defeated and slain at Amphipolis, *ib.* 6–11.

Cleonae, in Actè, iv. 109 med.

Cleonae, in Argolis, in alliance with Argos, v. 67 fin.; sends troops to Mantinea, *ib.* 72 fin., 74 med.; a Lacedaemonian army invading Argos turns back at Cleonae in consequence of an earthquake, vi. 95 init.

Cleonymus, father of Clearidas, a Lacedaemonian, iv. 132 fin.

Cleopompus, an Athenian commander, ii. 26 init., 58 init.

Cleruchi, in Lesbos, iii. 50 med.

Clubs, the, at Athens, viii. 48 med., 54 fin., 81 med. [cp. iii. 82 med.]

Cnemus, a Lacedaemonian commander, ravages Zacynthus, ii. 66; invades Acarnania, *ib.* 80–82; defeated by Phormio, *ib.* 83, 84; receives Brasidas and two other commissioners from Lacedaemon, *ib.* 85 init.; second defeat of, *ib.* 86–92; concerts with Brasidas an attack upon the Piraeus, *ib.* 93, 94.

Cnidis, father of Xenares, a Lacedaemonian, v. 51 fin.

Cnidus, revolts from Athens, viii. 35 init.; attacked by the Athenians, *ib.* fin.; the Cnidians persuade Astyochus to attack the Athenians under Charminus, *ib.* 41 fin.; fleet of the Lacedaemonians assembles at; their commissioners confer with Tissaphernes, *ib.* 42-44 init. [cp. 52 init.]; Tissaphernes' garrison expelled from, *ib.* 109 init.; Lipara a Cnidian colony, iii. 88 init.; Triopium in Cnidian territory, viii 35 med.

Colonae, in the Troad, i. 131 init.

Colonies, how anciently founded, i. 4 init., 24 init.; honours given by colonies to their mother city, *ib.* 25 fin. [cp. *ib.* 34, 38]; shares in a colony secured by a deposit, without immediately quitting home, *ib.* 27 init.; magistrates sent by the mother city, *ib.* 56 fin.; laws given by the mother city, iii. 34 fin. [cp. vi. 4, 5]; foundation of the Lacedaemonian colony, Heraclea, iii. 92, 93; the honours of the foundation of Amphipolis transferred to Brasidas, v. 11 init.; leaders chosen from the mother city, viii. 100 med.; the Hellenic colonies of Sicily, vi. 3–5.

Colonus, near Athens, Temple of Poseidon at, viii. 67 med.

Colophon, taken by Paches, iii. 34 init.; made an Athenian colony, *ib.* fin.

Colophonian Port, near Toronè, v. 2 med.

Columns, an inscription recording the oppression of the tyrants inscribed on a column at Athens, vi. 55 init.; treaties ordered to be inscribed on columns, v. 18, xi; 23, iv; 47 fin.; the infraction of the treaty inscribed on the same column by the Athenians, *ib.* 56 med.

Commanders, speech of the Peloponnesian, ii. 87.

Commissioners, sent by the Lacedaemonians as advisers to their officers, ii. 85 init., iii. 69 med., 76; v. 63 fin.; viii. 39 init.

Common-places, of speeches at critical moments, vii. 69 med.

Confederacy, a confederacy lacks a central power, i. 141 fin.

Conon, an Athenian, governor of Naupactus, vii. 31 med.

Controversy, Melian, v. 85–113.

Copae, on Lake Copais, in Boeotia, iv. 93 fin.

Corcyra, mother city of Epidamnus, i. 24 init. ; formerly inhabited by the Phaeacians, *ib.* 25 fin. ; under obligation to Themistocles, but afraid to shelter him, *ib.* 136 init. ; its importance, i. 36 fin., 44 fin., 68 fin., ii. 7 fin. ; the Sicilian expedition musters at Corcyra, vi. 30 init., 32 med., 34 med., 42, 43 init. ; Demosthenes sails to Corcyra with the reinforcements for Sicily, vii. 26 fin. ; collects troops there, *ib.* 31, 33 med. ; naval engagement between the Corinthians and Corcyraeans [B.C. 664], *ib.* 13 med.; the Corcyraeans colonists of the Corinthians, i. 25 med.; their detestation and disrespect to their mother city, *ib.*, *ib.* 38 [cp. vii. 57 med.] ; they refuse aid to the Epidamnians, i. 24 fin. ; besiege Epidamnus, *ib.* 26; send an embassy to Corinth, *ib.* 28 ; conquer the Corinthians at sea, *ib.* 29 ; slaughter their prisoners [except the Corinthians] after the battle, *ib.* 30 init.; send an embassy to Athens, *ib.* 31 ; their speech, *ib.* 32–36; obtain alliance with the Athenians, *ib.* 44 ; fight at sea with the aid of the Athenians against the Corinthians, *ib.* 48–51 ; offer the Corinthians battle, *ib.* 52 ; want to kill the Corinthian messengers, *ib.* 53 med.; set up a trophy on Sybota, *ib.* 54 init. ; claim the victory, *ib.* fin. ; driven from Anactorium by the Corinthians, *ib.* 55 init. ; the Corinthians intrigue with their Corcyraean prisoners, *ib.* med. ; the Corcyraeans receive an embassy from Athens, ii. 7 fin. ; furnish the Athenians with ships, *ib.* 9 med., 25 init.; fall into sedition, iii. 69 fin., 70 init.; the prisoners return and promote a revolt from Athens, *ib.* 70 init. ; oligarchs

worsted in a law suit by Peithias, *ib.* med. ; they murder him and his partisans, *ib.* fin. ; try to win over the people, *ib.* 71 ; on the arrival of a Corinthian trireme they attack and defeat the people, *ib.* 72; receive aid from the mainland but cannot induce the slaves to join them by offers of freedom, *ib.* 73 ; the people defeat the oligarchs, *ib.* 74 ; Nicostratus the Athenian commander tries to effect a reconciliation, *ib.* 75 ; on the proposal of the popular leaders five ships are manned from the opposite party, but the crews take sanctuary, *ib.* med. ; the people disarm and remove the others from the temple of Herè to an island, *ib.* fin. ; the Corcyraeans and Athenians engage the Lacedaemonians, and are defeated, *ib.* 77, 78 ; replace the prisoners in the temple of Herè, *ib.* 79 init. ; persuade some of the aristocratic party to help to man a fleet, *ib.* 80 ; the Lacedaemonian fleet retires on the approach of the Athenians, and the people massacre their opponents, *ib.* 81 ; this massacre the first example of the horrors of revolutionary warfare in Hellas, *ib.* 85 init. ; the surviving oligarchs occupy Mount Istonè, *ib.* 85, iv. 2 med., *ib.* 46 ; the people capture Istonè, *ib.* 46 med. ; treacherously massacre their prisoners, *ib.* 46 fin.–48 ; send aid to the Athenians against Syracuse, vii. 31 fin., 44 fin., 57 med.; alarm the Athenians at Epipolae by their Dorian Paean, *ib.* 44 fin.

Corinth, once inhabited by Aeolians, iv. 42 med.; triremes first built at Corinth, i. 13 init.; an early centre of commerce, *ib.* med.; ἀφνειόν, *ib.* ; its naval power, *ib.* 36 fin.; influence of Corinth among the

Corinth (cont.)—

barbarous races of Epirus, *ib.* 47 fin. ; naval engagement between the Corcyraeans and Corinthians [B.C. 664], *ib.* 13 med. ; [B.C. 491] the Corinthians lend ships for the Aeginetan war to Athens, *ib.* 41 init.; [B.C. 461–445] make war upon the Megarians, *ib.* 103 med. ; defeat the Athenians at Halieis, *ib.* 105 init.; invade Megara, *ib.* 105 med. ; are defeated, *ib.* 105 fin.; suffer great loss, *ib.* 106 ; assist the Megarians to revolt, *ib.* 114 med. ; [the Peloponnesian war] the Corinthians take the Epidamnians under their protection, *ib.* 25 med. ; hatred of, to the Corcyraeans, *ib.* ; send aid to Epidamnus, *ib.* 26 init. ; and a colony, *ib.* 27 init. ; receive an embassy from Corcyra, *ib.* 28 ; conquered at sea by the Corcyraeans, *ib.* 29 ; send an embassy to Athens, *ib.* 31 fin. ; speech of, *ib.* 37–43 ; sail against Corcyra, *ib.* 46 init. ; fight at sea with the Corcyraeans, *ib.* 48–50 ; retire before the Athenian reinforcements, *ib.* 51 ; hold a parley with the Athenians, *ib.* 53 ; return home, *ib.* 54 ; set up a trophy at Sybota, *ib.* init. ; claim the victory, *ib.* med. ; on the road capture Anactorium, *ib.* 55 init.; their alliance is sought by Perdiccas, *ib.* 57 med. ; they send troops to Potidaea, *ib.* 60 [cp. ii. 70 med.]; had a bitter hatred of the Athenians, i. 66, of old, 103 fin.; invite the allies to Sparta, *ib.* 67 init. ; speech of their ambassadors, *ib.* 68–71 ; urge on the war, *ib.* 119 fin.; second speech of, *ib.* 120–124; furnish the Lacedaemonians with ships, ii. 9 med. ; lose Sollium, *ib.* 30 init. ; restore Evarchus, *ib.* 33 init. ; are defeated in Cephallenia, *ib.* fin.; prepare with others a fleet to assist the Lacedaemonian expedition against Acarnania, *ib.* 80 med. ; arriving too late they are attacked and defeated by Phormio, *ib.* 83, 84 ; suffer a second defeat, *ib.* 90–92 ; share in the projected surprise of the Piraeus, *ib.* 93–95 ; induce their Corcyraean prisoners [see i. 55] to attempt an oligarchical revolution at Corcyra, iii. 70 init.; send back an embassy with them, *ib.*, *ib.* 74 fin. ; refuse to aid the oligarchs in Istonè, *ib.* 85 med. ; garrison Ambracia, *ib.* 114 fin., iv. 42 fin. ; repulse an Athenian invasion, iv. 43, 44 ; driven out of Anactorium by the Athenians and Acarnanians, *ib.* 49 ; receive and aid Brasidas, *ib.* 70 med., 74 init. ; join in the one year's Truce, *ib.* 119 med. ; dissatisfied with the treaty between the Lacedaemonians and Athenians, v. 17 fin., 25 init., 35 init. ; send envoys to Argos, *ib.* 27 ; the Lacedaemonians remonstrate with them, *ib.* 30 ; they join the Argive alliance, *ib.* 31 fin. ; apply to the Boeotians, *ib.* 32 med.; the new Spartan ephors wish them in concert with the Boeotians to bring the Argives into the Lacedaemonian alliance, *ib.* 36 ; the negotiation fails, *ib.* 38 ; the Corinthians refuse to join the Athenian and Argive alliance, *ib.* 48, 50 fin. ; prevent the construction of a fort at Rhium by Alcibiades, *ib.* 52 fin.; the Argives attack Epidaurus, hoping by its capture to check the Corinthians, *ib.* 53 ; a Corinthian envoy attends a conference at Mantinea, *ib.* 55 ; the Corinthians send a contingent to meet the Lacedaemonians at Phlius, *ib.* 57 fin. ; engage the Argives, *ib.* 59 init. ; are too late for Mantinea, *ib.* 64 med., 75 init.;

Corinth (*cont.*)—

do not join the Lacedaemonians in an expedition against Argos, *ib.* 83 init. ; declare war against the Athenians, *ib.* 115 med. ; again withhold support from a Lacedaemonian attack on Argos, vi. 7 init. ; receive an embassy from Syracuse, *ib.* 73, 88 med. ; vote the Syracusans aid, *ib.* 88 fin. ; send envoys with them to Sparta, *ib.* ; send ships and troops to Sicily, *ib.* 93 med., 104 init., vii. 2 init., 4 fin., 7 init., 17 med., 19 med , 31 init. ; Corinthian ambassadors go from Syracuse to the Sicilian states, vii. 25 fin. ; fight at sea with the Athenians, after preparing their fleet in a special manner, *ib.* 34 ; claim the victory because not severely defeated, *ib.* fin. ; their forces before Syracuse, *ib.* 58 med. ; one of their pilots, Ariston, the ablest in the whole fleet, *ib.* 39 ; their ships fight in the last battle in the harbour, *ib.* 70 init. ; the Corinthians said to have instigated the execution of Nicias and Demosthenes, *ib.* 86 fin. ; Agis deposits Phthiote Achaean hostages with them, viii. 3 med.; the Corinthians contribute ships to the Lacedaemonian fleet, *ib.* fin. ; the allies meet in conference at Corinth, *ib.* 8 ; the Corinthians refuse to join the Chian expedition until after the Isthmian Games, *ib.* 9 init. ; the fleet is chased into Piraeum by the Athenians, *ib.* 10 ; the Corinthians come to assist them, *ib.* 11 init. ; the fleet breaks the blockade, *ib.* 20 init. ; the Corinthians discourage a second Lesbian revolt, *ib.* 32 init. ; send out five ships to Astyochus, *ib.* 33 init. [cp. 23 fin.] ; besiege Oenoè, *ib.*

98 ; lose five ships at Cynossema, *ib.* 106 med.

Coroebus, father of Ammeas, a Plataean, iii. 22 med.

Coronea, in Boeotia, iv. 93 fin. ; defeat of the Athenians there, i. 113, iii. 62 fin., 67 med., iv. 92 fin.

Coronta, in Acarnania, ii. 102 init.

Corycus, promontory in Erythraea, viii. 14 init., 33 init. 34 init.

Coryphasium, the Lacedaemonian name of Pylos, iv. 3 med., *ib.* 118, iii ; ordered to be restored under treaty, v. 18, § viii.

Cos Meropis, devastated by an earthquake, viii. 41 med.; ravaged by the Peloponnesians, *ib.* ; fortified by the Athenians, *ib.* 108 init. [cp. 44 fin., 55 init.]

Cotylè, a measure, solid or liquid, iv. 16 med. [cp. vii. 87 med.]

Cotyrta, in Laconia, iv. 56 init.

Councils : Council of 80 at Argos, v. 47 fin. ; the Four Councils of the Boeotians, *ib.* 38 ;—the Council at Athens, viii. 66 init. ; formed into one body by Theseus from the Communes, ii. 15 init.; expelled by the oligarchs, viii. 69 ; Alcibiades demands its restoration, *ib.* 86 med. ;—Council of Elders appointed at Athens, after the defeat before Syracuse, viii. 1 fin.

Counsel, the two things most adverse to good counsel, iii. 42 init ; wise counsel more formidable to an enemy than over-severity, *ib.* 48 fin.

Courts, profits derived by the Athenians from, vi. 91 fin.

Cranii, in Cephallenia, settlement of the Helots at, v. 35 fin. ; their removal to Pylos, *ib.* 56 med. ; Cranians, ii. 30 fin., *ib.* 33 fin.

Cranonians, of Thessaly, ii. 22 fin.

Crataemenes, one of the founders of Zanclè, vi. 4 fin.

Cratesicles, father of Thrasymelidas, a Lacedaemonian, iv. 11 init.

Crestonians, in Actè, iv. 109 fin.

Cretan Sea, the, iv. 53 fin., v. 110 init.

Crete, campaign of the Athenians in, ii. 85 fin.; Alcidas caught in a storm off, iii. 69 init.; Cretan and Rhodian origin of Gela, vi. 4 med., vii. 57 med.; Cretan archers, vi. 25 fin., 43 fin.; Cretan mercenaries in the Athenian army before Syracuse, vii. 57 med.

Crisaean Gulf, the, i. 107 med., ii. 69 init., 83 init.; its mouth, ii. 86 init.; Siphae on the Crisaean Gulf, iv. 76 init.

Crocyleium, in Aetolia, iii. 96 med.

Croesus, conquered by Cyrus, i. 16.

Crommyon, near Corinth, iv. 42 fin., 44 med., 45 init.

Crotona, refuses passage to an Athenian army, vii. 35 med.

Crusis, in Mygdonia, ii. 79 med.

Cyclades, colonised by Minos, i. 4; all subject to Athens, except Melos and Cythera, ii. 9 fin.

Cyclopes, the, oldest inhabitants of Sicily, vi. 2 init.

Cydonia, in Crete, ii. 85 fin.

Cyllenè, the Elean dockyard, i. 30 med., ii. 84 fin., 86 init., iii. 69 init., 76 init., vi. 88 fin.; burnt by the Corcyraeans, i. 30 med.

Cylon, the story of, i. 126 init.

Cymè, in Aeolis, iii. 31 init., viii. 22 fin., 31 fin., 100 med.; the territory of, viii. 101 med.

Cymè, in Italy, a colony from Chalcis in Euboea, vi. 4 fin.

Cynes, an Acarnanian, ii. 102 init.

Cynossema, a promontory in the Hellespont, viii. 104 fin., 106 fin.; battle of, *ib.* 104–106.

Cynuria, on the border of Argos and Laconia, iv. 56 med.; quarrel between the Lacedaemonians and the Argives respecting, v. 14 fin.; stipulation about, in the treaty between the Lacedaemonians and Argives, *ib.* 41.

Cyprus subdued by Pausanias, i. 94, 128 med.; attacked by the Athenians, *ib.* 104 med., 112 med.

Cypsela, in Arcadia, v. 33 med.

Cyrenè, i. 110 init.; Cyrenaeans assist Lacedaemonian ships on the way to Syracuse, vii. 50 init.

Cyrrhus, in Macedonia, ii. 100 med.

Cyrus, king of Persia [father of Cambyses], i. 16; [son of Darius], ii. 65 fin.

Cythera, inhabited by Lacedaemonian Perioeci, iv. 53 med.; the 'Judge of Cythera,' *ib.*; importance of the island, *ib.* fin.; captured by the Athenians, *ib.* 54; the Athenians plunder Laconia from, v. 14 med.; ordered to be restored under treaty, *ib.* 18, viii.; the Cytherians in the Athenian service before Syracuse, vii. 57 med.

Cytinium, in Doris, i. 107 init., iii. 95 init., 102 init.

Cyzicus revolts from Athens, viii. 107 init.; retaken, *ib.* med.; Timagoras, a Cyzicene exile in Pharnabazus' service, *ib.* 6 init., 8 init., 39 init.

D.

Daïmachus, father of Eupompidas, a Plataean, iii. 20 init.

Daïthus, a Lacedaemonian, swears to the Treaty of Peace and the Alliance, v. 19 med., *ib* 24 init.

Damagetus, a Lacedaemonian, swears to the Treaty of Peace and the Alliance, v. 19 med., 24 init.

Damagon, a Lacedaemonian, one of the founders of Heraclea, iii. 92 fin.

Damotimus, a Sicyonian, iv. 119 med.

Danaäns, a name for the Hellenes in Homer, i. 3 med.

Daphnus, near Clazomenae, viii. 23 fin., 31 med.

Dardanus, on the Hellespont, viii. 104 init.

Daric Staters, viii. 28 fin.

Darius, king of Persia, succeeds Cambyses, i. 14 med.; reduces the islands, *ib.* 16; Aristagoras of Miletus and Darius, iv. 102 init.; influence of the tyrants of Lampsacus with him, v. 59 med.; Hippias takes refuge with him, *ib.* fin.

Darius II, son of Artaxerxes, king of Persia, viii. 5 init., 37, 58 init.

Dascon, joint founder with Menecolus of Camarina, vi. 5 med.

Dascon, near Syracuse, vi. 66 med.

Dascylium, satrapy of, in Asia Minor, i. 129 init.

Daulia, an ancient name of a part of Phocis, ii. 29 med; the 'Daulian bird,' *ib.*

Death, the penalty of, proved by experience to be no deterrent, iii. 45.

Decelea, fortification of, suggested by Alcibiades, vi. 91 med.; vii. 18 init.; determined on and carried out by the Lacedaemonians, vi. 93 init., vii. 18 fin., 19 init.; terrible mischief thus occasioned to the Athenians, *ib.* 27, 28; Agis at Decelea, viii. 4 fin.; the occupation of Decelea causes the whole Athenian population to be on service, *ib.* 69 init.; the 400 send heralds to Agis there, *ib.* 70 fin.; Agis marches from Decelea to Athens, *ib.* 71 init.; returns, *ib.* fin.; the 400 resume negotiations

with Agis there, *ib.*; Corinthian troops in the garrison, *ib.* 98 med.

Deiniadas, a Chian commander, viii. 22 fin.

Deinias, father of Cleïppides, an Athenian, iii. 3 med.

Delium, a temple of Apollo, near Tanagra, iv. 76 med.; fortified by the Athenians, *ib.* 90; captured by the Boeotians, *ib.* 100; battle of, *ib.* 93–96; effect of their defeat upon the Athenians, v. 14 init., 15 fin.; the Boeotians charge the Athenians with sacrilege for occupying it, *ib.* 97, 98.

Delos, iii. 29, viii. 77, 80 med., 86 init.; purified by Pisistratus, iii. 104 init.; purified by the Athenians, i. 8 init., iii. 104 init.; second purification of, v. 1; the first treasury of the Athenian Alliance, i. 96 fin.; earthquake in, ii. 8 med.; ancient games at, iii. 104 med.: restored by the Athenians, *ib.* fin.; the Delians settled at Adramyttium, v. 1 fin., viii. 108 fin.; restored by the Athenians, v. 32 init.; treacherous massacre of those at Adramyttium by the Persians, viii. 108 fin.

Delphi, temple of, v, 18, xi; handed over by the Lacedaemonians to the Delphians, i. 112 fin.; by the Athenians to the Phocians, *ib.*; provision respecting, in the treaty between the Lacedaemonians and Athenians, v. 18, ii.; spoils sent to, iv. 134 med.; alleged corruption of the priestess by Pleistoanax, v. 16 med.; treasury of, i. 121 med., *ib.* 143 init.; tripod of, i. 132 init., iii. 57 med.

Delphic Oracle, *see* Oracle.

Delphinium, in Chios, fortified by the Athenians, viii. 38 init., 40 fin.

Demaratus, an Athenian commander, vi. 105 fin.

Demarchus, a Syracusan general, viii. 85 fin.

Demeas, father of Philocrates, an Athenian, v. 116 fin.

Demiurgi, the, a magistracy at Mantinea, v. 47 fin.; at Elis, *ib*.

Democracy, the democracy everywhere the friend of Athens, iii. 47 init., 82 init.; Pericles' description of the Athenian democracy, ii. 37-40; Cleon's, iii. 37 foll.; Diodotus', iii. 42 foll.; the people the best judges of a matter, ii. 40 init., vi. 39; democracies manageable enough when under the influence of terror, viii. 1 fin.; the weaknesses of a democracy, ii. 65 init., iii. 37., vi. 89 med.; democracy more stable than oligarchy, viii. 89 fin.

Demodocus, an Athenian general, iv. 75 init.

Demosthenes, commands an expedition round Peloponnese, iii. 91 init.; ravages Leucas, *ib*. 94 init.; invades Aetolia, *ib*. fin.-98; retires to Naupactus after his failure, *ib*. 98 fin.; saves Naupactus, *ib*. 102 med.; takes command of the Acarnanians against the Ambraciots, *ib*. 105 med. [cp. vii. 57 fin.]; defeats the Ambraciots, iii. 107-111; destroys the Ambraciot reinforcements, *ib*. 112, 113; returns to Athens, *ib*. 114 init.; sent on a special commission, iv. 2 fin.; fortifies Pylos, *ib*. 3-5; prepares to meet the Lacedaemonians, *ib*. 9; speech of, *ib*. 10; repulses the Lacedaemonians, *ib*. 11, 12; selected by Cleon as his colleague, *ib*. 29 init.; plans and executes an attack on Sphacteria, *ib*. 29-37; forces the Lacedaemonians to surrender, *ib*. 38; attempts Megara, *ib*. 66-68; captures Nisaea, *ib*. 69; plans an invasion of Boeotia, *ib*. 76, 77;

failure of the attempt, *ib*. 89 init.; invades Sicyonia, *ib*. 101 med.; swears to the Treaty of Peace and the Alliance, v. 19 fin., 24 med.; sent to Epidaurus, *ib*. 80 fin.; chosen as a colleague of Nicias, vii. 16 fin., 20; ravages the Laconian coast and fortifies an isthmus there on his way, *ib*. 26; meets Eurymedon at Corcyra and sends reinforcements to Naupactus, *ib*. 31; holds a review at Thurii, *ib*. 33 fin.; arrives at Syracuse, *ib*. 42 init.; resolves to strike a blow at once, *ib*. 42 med.; fails in a night attack on Epipolae, *ib*. 43-45; votes in a council of war for immediate departure, *ib*. 47; when Nicias resists, proposes moving the camp, *ib*. 49; commands in the last sea fight, *ib*. 69-71 fin.; anxious to renew the engagement, *ib*. 72; commands one division in the retreat, vii. 78 foll.; overtaken and compelled to surrender, *ib*. 81, 82; put to death by the Syracusans, *ib*. 86.

Demoteles, a Locrian commander, iv. 25 fin.

Dercyllidas, a Spartan, sent to the Hellespont, viii. 61 init.; effects the revolt of Abydos and Lampsacus, *ib*. 62.

Derdas, a Macedonian, i. 57 init., 59 fin.

Dersaeans, a Thracian tribe, ii. 101 med.

Desertion of slaves, injury caused by, vii. 27 fin., viii. 40 med.

Deucalion, father of Helen, i. 3 init.

Diacritus, father of Melesippus, a Spartan, ii. 12 init.

Diagoras, father of Dorieus, a Thurian, viii. 35 init.

Diasia, the festival of Zeus the Gracious, at Athens, i. 126 med.

Dictidians, in Mt. Athos, v. 35 init.

Didymè, one of the Liparaean islands, iii. 88 med.

Diemporus, a Theban Boeotarch, ii. 2 med.

Dii, a Thracian tribe, ii. 96 med., 98 fin.; come too late to Athens to join Demosthenes' expedition to Sicily, vii. 27 init.; on their way back sack Mycalessus, *ib.* 29, 30.

Diitrephes, father of Nicostratus, an Athenian, iii. 75 init., iv. 53 init., 119; another leads a number of Thracian mercenaries home, vii. 29, 30.

Diodotus, an Athenian, opposes the slaughter of the Mytilenaeans, iii. 41; his speech, *ib.* 42-48.

Diomedon, an Athenian commander, viii. 19 med.; popular with the people, *ib.* 73 med.; makes agreement with the Teans, *ib.* 20 fin.; fails to capture Erae, *ib.*; regains Lesbos which had revolted, *ib.* 23; carries on war successfully against Chios, *ib.* 24 med.; appointed with Leon to the chief command at Samos, *ib.* 54 med.; makes a descent upon Rhodes, *ib.* 55 init.; aids the democratic reaction at Samos, *ib.* 73 fin.

Diomilus, an Andrian exile, vi. 96 fin.; made commander of a chosen body of Syracusan troops, *ib.*; slain in battle, *ib.* 97 fin.

Dionysia, the ancient, ii. 15 med.; the City Dionysia, v. 20 init., 23, § iv.

Dionysus, temple of, 'in the Marshes,' ii. 15 med.; temple of, at Corcyra, iii. 81 fin.; theatre of, near Munychia, viii. 93 init., fin., 94 init.

Dioscuri, temple of the, at Athens, viii. 93 init.; at Corcyra, iii. 75 med.; at Toronè, iv. 110 init.

Diotimus, son of Strombichus, an Athenian commander, i. 45; father of Strombichides, viii. 15 med.

Diotrephes, an Athenian commander, sent to take command in Chalcidicè, viii 64 init.; puts down the democracy in Thasos, *ib.*

Diphilus, an Athenian commander, vii. 34 med.

Dium, in Macedonia, iv. 78 fin.

Dium, in Mount Athos, iv. 109; revolts from the Athenians, v. 82 init.

Divers, employed at Sphacteria, iv. 26 fin.; and at Syracuse, vii. 25 med.

Doberus, in Paeonia, ii. 98 med., 99 init., 100 init.

Dockyard, the Lacedaemonian [Gythium], burnt by the Athenians, i. 108 fin.

Dolopes, in Thessaly, v. 51 init.

Dolopes, the old inhabitants of Scyros, i. 98 init.

Dolopians, in Epirus, ii. 102 init.

Dolphins, leaden, i.e. heavy weights used to sink an enemy's ship, vii. 41 init.

Dorcis, a Lacedaemonian, sent out to succeed Pausanias in his command, i. 95 fin.

Dorians, attack Corinth, iv. 42 med.; conquer the Peloponnesus, i. 12 med.; colonise Lacedaemon, *ib.* 18 init., 107 init., iii. 92 init. [v. 16 fin.]; attacked by the Phocians, i. 107 init.; contrasted with Ionians, *ib.* 124 init., v. 9 init., vi. 77 med., 80 fin., 82 init., vii. 5 fin., 57 init. and med., viii. 25 med.; hold the month Carneus sacred, v. 54 med.; opposed to Dorians in the siege of Syracuse, vii. 57 med.; Dorians in Asia, Athenian subjects, ii. 9 fin.; Dorians in Sicily, iv. 64 med., vi. 4, 5, 77 med.; allies of the Syracusans, iii. 86 init., iv. 61 med., 64 med., vi. 6 med., 80

Dorians *(cont.)*—

fin., vii. 58 init.; Dorian dialect spoken by the Messenians, iii. 112 med., iv. 41 med.; mixed with Chalcidian at Himera, vi. 5 init.; Dorian Paean, alarm caused by the Paean of their Dorian allies to the Athenians at the attack on Epipolae, vii. 44 fin.

Dorieus, of Rhodes, twice conqueror at Olympia, iii. 8.

Dorieus, sent out in command of ten Thurian ships, viii. 35 init.; threatened with violence by Astyochus, *ib.* 84 init.

Dorus, a Thessalian, iv. 78 init.

Drabescus, in Thrace, Athenian colonists slaughtered there by the Thracians, i. 100 fin., iv. 102 med.

Drachmae, Aeginetan, v. 47, § iv; Attic, one Attic drachma paid each day per man by Tissaphernes, viij. 29 init.; the Athenians paid but half a drachma, *ib.* 45 init.; Corinthian, i. 27 init.

Droans, a Thracian tribe, ii. 101 med.

Droughts during the Peloponnesian War, i. 23 med.

Drymussa, an island off Clazomenae, viii. 31 fin.

Dryopes, Carystius in Euboea inhabited by, vii. 57 init.

Dryoscephalae, in Boeotia, iii. 24 init.

Dymè, in Achaia, ii. 84 med. and fin.

E.

Earth, 'the whole earth is the sepulchre of famous men,' ii. 43 med.

Earth, Temple of, at Athens, ii. 15 med.

Earthquakes, frequency of, during the Peloponnesian War, i. 23 med.; great earthquake before the siege of Ithomè, i. 101 init., 128 init., iii. 54 fin.; at Delos, ii.

8 med.; in the fifth year of the war, iii. 87 fin., 89 init.; the probable cause of an extraordinary ebb and flow of the sea, *ib.* 89; Lacedaemonian expeditions stopped by, *ib.* 89 init., vi. 95 init.; at the beginning of the eighth year of the War, iv. 52 init.; assemblies interrupted by, v. 45 fin., 50 fin; earthquakes at Athens, *ib.* 45 fin.; at Corinth, *ib.* 50 fin.; at Cleonae, vi. 95 init.; at Sparta, viii. 6 fin.; at Cos, *ib.* 41 med.; the Lacedaemonians supersede an admiral because of an earthquake, *ib.* 6 fin.

Eccritus, a Spartan commander, vii. 19 med.

Echecratides, king of Thessaly, i. 111 init.

Echetimidas, father of Taurus, a Lacedaemonian, iv. 119 init.

Echinades, islands at the mouth of the Achelous, ii. 102 med.

Eclipses of the sun, ii. 28, iv. 52 init.; great number of, during the Peloponnesian War, i. 23 med.; only occur at the new moon, ii. 28 [cp. iv. 52]; eclipse of the moon, vii. 50 fin.

Edoni, iv. 109 fin.; old inhabitants of Amphipolis, i. 100 fin., iv. 102 med.; drive out Aristagoras of Miletus, iv. 102 init.; destroy the Athenian settlers, *ib.*; expelled by the Macedonians from Mygdonia, ii. 99 med.; Myrcinus, an Edonian town, iv. 107 fin.; Pittacus, king of the Edonians, *ib.*; Brasidas summons their whole forces, v. 6 med.

Eetionea, part of the Piraeus, fortified by the oligarchs, viii. 90 med., 91 med., 92 init.; destroyed by the soldiers at the instigation of Theramenes, *ib.* 92.

Egesta, Trojan origin of, vi. 2 init., vii. 57 fin.; Egesteans at war with

Egesta (*cont.*)—

Selinus, vi. 6 med.; send envoys to Athens, *ib.*; deceive the Athenians about their wealth, *ib.* 8 init., 46; their cavalry aid the Athenians to capture Hyccara, *ib.* 62 med.; they supply the Athenians with thirty talents, *ib.*; the Athenians send to them for horses, *ib.* 88 med. [cp. 98 init.]; the Egestaeans furnish the Athenians with cavalry, *ib.* 98 init.

Egypt revolts from the King, i. 104 init.; subdued by the Persians, *ib.* 109, 110; destruction of the Athenian reinforcements in, *ib.* 110 fin.; third Athenian fleet sent to Egypt without results, *ib.* 112 med.; visited by the plague, ii. 48 init.; Egyptians in the fens most warlike, i. 110 med.; Egyptian body-guard of Pausanias, *ib.* 130 init.; Egyptian vessels at Cythera, iv. 53 fin.; at Triopium, viii. 35 med.

Eidomenè, in Macedonia, ii. 100 med.

Eighty, Council of, at Argos, v. 47 fin.

Eion, in Chalcidicè, a colony of Mendè, iv. 7.

Eion, upon the Strymon, iv. 50 init., 108 init., v. 6–12; taken by the Athenians, i. 98 init., iv. 102 fin.; saved by Thucydides, iv. 106 fin., 107 init.; Artaphernes, a Persian envoy to Sparta, captured by the Athenians there, *ib.* 50 init.

Elaeus, in the Thracian Chersonese, viii. 102, 103, 107 fin.

Elaphebolion, a month at Athens, iv. 118 fin., v. 19 init.

Eleatis, part of Thesprotia, i. 46 med.

Eleus [*al.* Leros], viii. 27 init.

Eleusinium, a temple at Athens, ii. 17 init.

Eleusis, in Attica, i. 114 fin., ii. 19 med., 20 init., 21 init., iv. 68 med.; war of the Eleusinians with Erechtheus, ii. 15 init.

Elimiots, a Macedonian tribe, ii. 99 init.

Elis, ii. 25 med., 66 init.; Eleans furnish the Corinthians with ships, i. 27 fin., 46 init.; the Corcyraeans burn their dockyard at Cyllene, *ib.* 30 med.; supply a naval contingent to the Lacedaemonian confederacy, ii. 9 med.; defeated by the Athenians, *ib.* 25 med.; dissatisfied with the treaty between the Lacedaemonians and Athenians, v. 17 fin.; join the Argive alliance, *ib.* 31 init.; quarrel with the Lacedaemonians about Lepreum, *ib.* med.; make an alliance with Athens, *ib.* 43 fin., 44 med., 46 fin, 47; exclude the Lacedaemonians from the Olympic games, v. 49, 50; aid the Argives, *ib.* 58 init.; go home, on the other allies refusing to attack Lepreum, *ib.* 62; aid the Mantineans against Epidaurus, *ib.* 75 fin.; the Argives desert them, *ib.* 78; Teutiaplus, an Elean in Alcidas' army, iii. 29 fin.

Ellomenus, in Leucadia, iii. 94 init.

Elymi, a partly Trojan race in Sicily, vi. 2 med.

Embatum, near Erythrae, iii. 29 fin., 32 init.

Empedias, a Lacedaemonian, swears to the Treaty of Peace and the Alliance, v. 19 med., 24 init.

Empire, the three things most fatal to, iii. 40 init.; an empire cannot be cut down like a household, vi. 18 med.; an empire once gained cannot be abandoned, i. 75, ii. 63; those who seek empire always arouse hatred, i. 76, ii. 64 fin., iii. 37 init.

Endius, envoy to Athens, v. 44 fin.;
Ephor at Sparta, viii. 6 med.; an
hereditary friend of Alcibiades,
ib.; persuaded by Alcibiades not
to give up the expedition to
Chios, *ib.* 12.

Enemies, great enemies more readily forgiven than small ones, iv.
19 fin. [cp. v. 91 init.]; complaisance to an enemy a mistake, i.
34 fin. ; men neglect their own
interests when attacking an enemy, *ib.* 41 fin.

Engines, battering, used at the
siege of Plataea, ii. 76 med.;
engine to fire a wooden wall
used at Delium, iv. 100 ; at Lecythus, *ib.* 115 med. ; engine at
Minoa, iii. 51 med.

Enipeus, a river of Thessaly, iv. 78
med.

Ennea Hodoi, *see* Amphipolis and
Nine Ways.

Enneacrounos, a fountain at Athens,
ii. 15 fin.

Enomoties, the smallest divisions
in the Lacedaemonian army, v.
68.

Entimus, joint founder, with Antiphemus, of Gela, vi. 4 med.

Envy, does not follow the dead, ii.
45 med.

Eordia, a region of Macedonia, ii.
99 fin.

Ephesus, Themistocles reaches
Ephesus in his flight, i. 137 med.;
Alcidas at Ephesus, iii. 32 init.,
33 init.; Athenian ambassadors
to the King return thence, iv.
50 fin.; a Chian ship chased by
the Athenians escapes to Ephesus, viii. 19 med. ; Tissaphernes
sacrifices to Artemis at Ephesus,
ib. 109 fin. ; Ionian festival at
Ephesus, iii. 104 med.

Ephors, at Sparta ; their powers, i.
87 init., 131 fin. ; Sthenelaidas,
ib. 85 fin.; Aenesias, ii. 2 init. ;
Pleistolas, v. 19 init ; Cleobulus,
ib. 36 init., 37 init.; Xenares, *ib.*;
Endius, viii. 6 med. ; Alexippidas, *ib.* 58 init.

Ephyrè, in Thesprotia, i. 46
med.

Epicles, father of Proteas, an Athenian, i. 45 med., ii. 23 med.

Epicles, a Lacedaemonian general,
viii. 107 fin.

Epicurus, father of Paches, an
Athenian, iii. 18 fin.

Epicydidas, a Lacedaemonian
general, v. 12.

Epidamnus, a colony of the Corcyraeans, i. 24 init. ; situation of,
ib. 26 fin. ; the Epidamnians seek
aid from Corcyra, *ib.* 24 fin.; are
refused, *ib.*; ordered by the Oracle
to apply to Corinth, *ib.* 25 init.;
receive colonists from Corinth,
ib. 26 init. ; are besieged by the
Corcyraeans, *ib.* fin. ; surrender
their city, *ib.* 29 fin. ; the affair
of Epidamnus one of the avowed
causes of the Peloponnesian War,
ib. 23 fin., 146; the Corcyraean
prisoners taken in it won over
by the Corinthians, iii. 70.

Epidaurus, its territory ravaged by
the Athenians, ii. 56 med. [cp. vi.
31 init.]; again, iv. 45; adjoins the
Corinthian, viii. 10 fin. ; attacked
by Argos, v. 53, 54 fin., 55 fin., 56
fin.; garrisoned by the Lacedaemonians, *ib.* 56 init.; a Peloponnesian fleet anchors there, viii.
92 med., 94 med. ; besieged by
the Argive allies, *ib.* 75 fin.; the
Argives agree by treaty to evacuate Epidaurus, *ib.* 76, ii. iv; the
Athenians evacuate Epidaurus,
ib. 80 ; Epidaurians defeated by
the Athenians at Halieis, i. 105 ;
assist the Megarians to revolt, *ib.*
114 med. ; furnish a convoy to
Corinth, *ib.* 27 fin.; invade Argos,
v. 75 med. ; supply ships to the
Lacedaemonian navy, viii. 3
fin.

Epidaurus Limera, in Laconia, iv. 56 med., vi. 105 fin., vii. 18 med., 26 init.

Epipolae, situation and importance of, vi. 96, vii. 2 ; captured by the Athenians, vi. 97; fortified, *ib.* 101 init.; unsuccessfully attacked by the Syracusans, *ib.* 102; Gylippus enters Syracuse by way of, vii. 1, 2 ; the Syracusans defeated there, *ib.* 5 ; the Syracusans defeat the Athenians and carry their cross-wall past the Athenian wall on Epipolae, *ib.* 6 ; night engagement upon, *ib.* 43–45.

Epirus, Epirot tribes join the expedition of Cnemus, ii. 80 fin.

Epitadas, the Spartan commander in Sphacteria, iv. 8 fin., 31 med., 33 init., 39 med.; death of, *ib.* 38 init.

Erae, in the territory of Teos, revolts from Athens, viii. 19 fin. ; unsuccessfully attacked by the Athenians, *ib.* 20 fin.

Erasinides, a Corinthian commander, vii. 7 init.

Erasistratus, father of Phaeax, an Athenian, v. 4 init.

Eratocleides, father of Phalius, a Corinthian, i. 24 init.

Erechtheus, king of Athens, ii. 15 init.

Eresus, strengthened by the revolted Lesbians, iii. 18 init.; captured by Paches, *ib.* 35 init.; Astyochus goes there and raises a revolt, viii. 23 med. [cp. fin.] ; again revolts, *ib.* 100 med. ; besieged by the Athenians, *ib.* fin., 101 init., 103 med.

Eretria, war of the Eretrians with the Chalcidians, i. 15 fin.; subject to Athens, vii. 57 init. ; betray Oropus to the Boeotians, vii. 60 init. ; the Eretrians go to Rhodes and ask assistance from the Lacedaemonians, *ib.* med. ; aid

Peloponnesians to defeat the Athenians at Oropus, *ib.* 95 ; Mendè, an Eretrian colony, iv. 123 init.

Erineum, in Doris, i. 107 init.

Erineus, in Achaia, vii. 34 init., fin.

Erineus, river in Sicily, vii. 80 fin., 82 fin.

Eruption of Aetna, iii. 116; of Hiera, in the Lipari islands, *ib.* 88 med.

Erythrae, in Boeotia, iii. 24 med.

Erythrae, in Ionia, iii. 33 med. ; revolts from Athens, viii. 5, 6, 14 med. ; the Erythraeans assist in the revolt of Teos, *ib.* 16 med. ; the Athenians hold two forts in the Erythraean territory, *ib.* 24 init.; Pedaritus sails from Erythrae for Chios, *ib.* 28 fin., 32 med.; Astyochus, narrowly escaping the Athenians, returns thither from Corycus, *ib.* 33 ; trick of certain Erythraean prisoners, *ib.*

Eryx, in Sicily, vi. 2 med. ; temple of Aphroditè there, *ib.* 46 med.

Eryxidaïdas, father of Philocharidas, a Lacedaemonian, iv. 119 med.

Eteonicus, a Lacedaemonian commander, viii. 23 med.

Euboea, Carystus revolts from Athens, the other Euboeans remain quiet, i. 98; Euboea revolts, *ib.* 114 init.; is subdued, *ib.* fin. [cp. 23 fin.], iv. 92 med., vi. 76, 84 ; the Athenians remove their flocks to Euboea before the Peloponnesian invasion, ii. 14 ; the Athenians take precautions for the safety of Euboea, *ib.* 26 [cp. iii. 17 init.], viii. 1 fin. ; plundered by Locrian pirates, ii. 32 fin. ; the Lacedaemonians form designs upon Euboea, iii. 92, 93 ; the Euboeans negotiate with Agis about a fresh revolt, viii. 4 [cp. 60 init.] ; all Euboea, except Oreus revolts, *ib.* 95 fin.; Athens

Euboea (*cont.*)—

supplied from, vii. 28 init., viii. 96 init. ; effect of its loss on the Athenians, viii. 95 init., 96 init. ; Hestiaea colonised by the Athenians, vii. 57 init. ; the thirty years' peace after the taking of Euboea, i. 23 fin., 146 ; earthquakes in Euboea, iii. 87, 89 init.

Eubulus, a Chian (?) commander, viii. 23 med.

Eucles, an Athenian general, iv. 104 med.

Eucles, a Syracusan general, vi. 103 fin.

Euclides, one of the founders of Himera, vi. 5 init.

Eucrates, father of Diodotus, an Athenian, iii. 41.

Euctemon, an Athenian commander, viii. 30.

Euetion, an Athenian commander, unsuccessfully attacks Amphipolis, vii. 9.

Eumachus, a Corinthian commander, ii. 33 med.

Eumolpidae, their protest against the return of Alcibiades, viii. 53 med.

Eupaïdas, father of Amphias, an Epidaurian, iv. 119 fin.

Eupalium, a town in Ozolian Locris, iii. 96 med., 102 init.

Euphamidas, a Corinthian, ii. 33 init., iv. 119 med., v. 55 init.

Euphemus, an Athenian envoy, vi. 75 fin. ; speech of, at Camarina, *ib.* 82–88.

Euphiletus, father of Charoeades, an Athenian, iii. 86 init.

Eupompidas, a Plataean, iii. 20 init.

Euripides, father of Xenophon, an Athenian, ii. 70 init., 79 init.

Euripus, the, strait between Euboea and the mainland, vii. 29 init.

Europus, in Macedonia, ii. 100 med.

Eurybatus, a Corcyraean commander, i. 47 init.

Euryelus, the highest point of Epipolae, vi. 97 med., vii. 2 med., 43 med.

Eurylochus, commands a Lacedaemonian expedition against Naupactus, iii. 100 ; subdues Locris, *ib.* 101 ; fails to take Naupactus, *ib.* 102 init. ; retires to Aeolis, *ib.* med. ; joins the Ambraciots at Olpae, *ib.* 106 ; defeated, *ib.* 107, 108 ; his death, *ib.* 109 init.

Eurymachus, a Theban, the chief agent in planning the surprise of Plataea, ii. 2 med. ; killed by the Plataeans, *ib.* 5 fin.

Eurymedon, river in Pamphylia, defeat of the Persians there, i. 100 init.

Eurymedon, an Athenian commander, brings an Athenian fleet to Corcyra, iii. 80 fin. ; commands in Boeotia, *ib.* 91 med. ; sent with a fleet to Sicily, *ib.* 115 fin., iv. 2 med., 46 init., 47 ; summoned by Demosthenes to his aid at Pylos, iv. 8 init. ; conduct of, at Corcyra, *ib.* 46 ; fined by the Athenians, *ib.* 65 med. ; sent to Sicily as a colleague of Nicias, vii. 16 fin. ; meets Demosthenes at Corcyra, *ib.* 31 med. ; commands under Demosthenes in the attack on Epipolae, *ib.* 43 med. ; supports Demosthenes against Nicias in the council of war, *ib.* 49 fin. ; falls in a sea fight, *ib.* 52.

Eurystheus, slain in Attica by the Heraclidae, i. 9 med.

Eurytanians, an Aetolian tribe, iii. 94 fin.

Eurytimus, father of Archetimus, a Corinthian, i. 29 init.

Eustrophus, an Argive envoy, v. 40 fin.

Euthycles, father of Xenocleides, a Corinthian, i. 46 init., iii. 114 fin.

Euthydemus, an Athenian, swears to the Treaty of Peace and the

Euthydemus (*cont.*)—

Alliance, v. 19 fin., 24 med. ; joined with Nicias in command before Syracuse, vii. 16 init. ; commands under Demosthenes in the last sea fight, *ib.* 69 fin.

Euxine, the, ii. 96 init., 97 fin.

Evalas, a Spartan commander, viii. 22 fin.

Evarchus, driven from Astacus by the Athenians, ii. 30 med. ; restored by the Corinthians, *ib.* 33 init.

Evarchus, founder of Catana, vi. 3 fin.

Evenus, river in Aetolia, ii. 83 med.

Evesperitae, in Libya, vii. 50 init.

Execestus, father of Sicanus, a Syracusan, vi. 73.

Exiles, the faults of, vi. 12 init., 92 init.

Expediency and justice, i. 36, 42 init., 76, iii. 40 med., 44, 56, 82 fin., v. 90, 98, 107.

F.

Famines, famine in Cyprus, i. 112 med.; during the war, i. 23 med.; in Potidaea during the siege, ii. 70 init. ; in Corcyra, iv. 2 fin. ; in Plataea, iii. 52 init., med. ; famine, the most miserable of deaths, iii. 59 fin.

Fear, renders skill useless, ii. 87 med. ; the only solid basis of alliance, iii. 11 init. [cp. 12 init.]

Festivals, of Zeus 'the Gracious,' i. 126 med. ; the Synoecia at Athens, ii. 15 med.; the Dionysia at Athens, *ib.* v. 23, § iv; of Apollo Maloeis at Mytilenè, iii. 3 med. ; the Hyacinthia at Sparta, v. 23, § iv; *ib.* 41 fin.; the Great Panathenaea at Athens, *ib.* 47 fin., vi. 56 med.; the Gymnopaediae at Sparta, v. 82 init.; the Carnea at Sparta, *ib.* 54 med., 75 med., 76 init.; Heracles at Syracuse, vii.

73 med.; rigid observance of festivals by the Lacedaemonians, iv. 5 init., v. 54, 82 init.; festivals at Athens, i. 70 fin., ii. 38 init.

Fines, Pericles fined, ii. 65 init.; fines imposed on members of the oligarchical party at Corcyra, iii. 70 med. ; on Eurymedon by the Athenians, iv. 65 ; on the Lacedaemonians by the Eleans, v. 49; on Agis by the Lacedaemonians, *ib.* 63.

Five Hundred, council of, or Senate, at Athens, viii. 66 init. ; broken up by the oligarchs, *ib.* 69 ; its restoration demanded by Alcibiades, *ib.* 86 med.

Five Thousand, the sham government of, offered by the oligarchical conspirators, viii. 65 fin., 67 fin., 72 med., 86 med.; used as a cloak for restoration of democracy, *ib.* 89 med., 92 fin.; the oligarchs promise to publish the names of the 5000, *ib.* 93; established by the people, *ib.* 97 ; excellence of the constitution, *ib.*

Flute-players, employed in the Lacedaemonian army, v. 70.

Fortune, uncertainty of, i. 140 med., iii. 59 init. ; man not the master of fortune, iv. 64 init., vi. 23 med., 78 med.; from the Gods, v. 112 med.

Fortune, good, the nemesis which follows upon, iv. 17 med.; ordinary good fortune better than extraordinary, iii. 39 med.

Four Hundred, government of, introduced by the oligarchical conspirators at Athens, viii. 67–70; despatch heralds to Agis and afterwards to Sparta, *ib.* 70 fin., 71 fin.; send commissioners to Samos, *ib.* 72 init.; detain the crew of the Paralus, who bring news of the revolution, *ib.* 74 ; reception of their envoys at Sa-

Four Hundred (*cont.*)—

mos, *ib.* 86 init., med.; their envoys to Sparta captured by the Parali who had escaped, *ib.* fin.; dissensions arise, *ib.* 89; the leaders willing to betray Athens to the enemy to save their own power, *ib.* 90 init., 91 fin.; fortify Eetionea, *ib.* 90 med., 91 med.; enter into negotiations with the popular party after the destruction of Eetionea, *ib.* 93; deposed, *ib.* 97 init.

Funeral, public, of those who first fell in the war, ii. 34; of Brasidas, v. 11 init.

G.

Galepsus, in Thrace, a Thasian colony, iv. 107 fin.; revolts from Athens, *ib.*; stormed by the Athenians, v. 6 init.

Games, Delian, iii. 104 med.; Ephesian, *ib.*; Pythian, v. 1 init.; Olympian, iii. 8, v. 47 fin., 49, 50; Isthmian, viii. 9, 10 init.

Garments, offered at sepulchres, iii. 58 med.

Gates, the Thracian, at Amphipolis, v. 10 init.

Gaulites, a Carian, viii. 85 init.

Gela, a river in Sicily, vi. 4 med.

Gela, founded from Rhodes by Antiphemus and Entimus, vi. 4 med., vii. 57 med.; Agrigentum founded from, vi. 4 med.; borders on Camarina, vii. 58 init.; conference at, iv. 58; receives and assists Gylippus, vii. 1 fin.; sends aid to Syracuse, *ib.* 33 init., 57 med.

Gelo, tyrant of Syracuse, vi. 4 init.; expels the Megareans, *ib.*, *ib.* 94 init.; colonises Camarina a third time, *ib.* 5 fin.

General, speech of a Syracusan, vi. 41.

Geraestus, in Euboea, iii. 3 fin.

Geraneia, Mount, in Megaris, i. 105

med., 107 med., 108 init., iv. 70 med.

Gerastius, a Spartan month, iv. 119 init.

Geta, a Sicel fort, vii. 2 med.

Getae, a people bordering on the Scythians, ii. 96 init, 98 fin.

Gigonus, in Chalcidicè, i. 61 fin.

Glaucè, in the territory of Mycalè, viii. 79 init.

Glaucon, an Athenian commander, i. 51 med.

Goaxis, sons of, kill Pittacus, king of the Edonians, iv. 107 fin.

Goddess, curse of the, i. 126.

Gods, the, portions of land dedicated to, in the confiscation of Lesbos, iii. 50 med.; the, worshipped at common altars, *ib.* 59 init.; altar of the Twelve Gods at Athens, v. 54 fin.

Gods, the, protect the right, i. 86 fin., v. 104; approve the principle, 'That they should rule who can,' v. 105 init.; their jealousy, vii. 77 med.

Gold mines in Thrace; workings owned by Thucydides, iv. 105 init.

Gongylus, an Eretrian, an envoy of Pausanias, i. 128 med.

Gongylus, a Corinthian commander, vii. 2 init.

Gortynia, in Macedonia, ii. 100 med.

Gortys, in Crete, ii. 85 med.

Graaeans, a Paeonian tribe, ii. 96 med.

Graphè paranomon, at Athens, repealed by the oligarchy, viii. 67.

Grappling irons, *see* Ships.

Grasshoppers, ornaments in the form of, once worn at Athens, i. 6 med.

Greatness exposed to the attacks both of envy and of fear, vi. 78 med.

Grestonia, a district of Macedonia, ii. 99 fin., 100 med.

Guardians of the Law, a magistracy at Elis, v. 47 fin.

Gulf, the Ambracian, i. 55 init., ii. 68 init., iii. 107 init. ; Crisaean, i. 107 med., ii. 69 med., 83 init., 84 init., 90-92 fin., iv. 76 init. ; Iasian, viii. 26 med. ; Ionian, i. 24 init , ii. 97 fin., vi. 13 med., 30 init., 34 med., 44 in.t., 104 init., vii. 33 med., 57 fin. ; Malian, iii. 96 fin., iv. 100 init., viii. 3 init. ; Saronic, iii. 15, viii. 92 init. ; Terinaean, vi. 104 med. ; Tyrrhenian, vi. 62 init., vii. 58 init.

Gylippus appointed commander of the Syracusan forces by the Lacedaemonians, vi. 93 med. ; arrives at Tarentum, *ib.* 104 init.; fails in a mission to Thurii, *ib.* med. ; makes his way into Syracuse, vii. 1, 2 ; offers battle on Epipolae, *ib.* 3 init. ; captures Labdalum, *ib.* fin. ; fails in an attack on the Athenian lines, *ib.* 4 init. ; is defeated, *ib.* 5 ; defeats the Athenians, *ib.* 6 ; goes into Sicily to collect allies, *ib.* 7 med. [cp. 12 init.] ; returning, he urges the Syracusans to try their fortune at sea, *ib.* 21 ; captures Plemmyrium, *ib.* 23 ; makes a diversion by land while the Syracusan fleet attacks the Athenians, *ib.* 37 ; goes to collect reinforcements, *ib.* 46 fin., 50 init. ; sustains a slight defeat, *ib.* 53 ; exhorts the Syracusans before the battle in the harbour, *ib.* 66-68 ; blocks the roads against the Athenian retreat, *ib.* 74 ; compels the surrender first of Demosthenes', and then of Nicias' division, *ib.* 78-85 ; opposes the putting to death of Nicias and Demosthenes, *ib.* 86 init.

Gymnopaediae, festival of, at Lacedaemon, v. 82 init.

Gyrtonians, a Thessalian people, ii. 22 fin.

Habronichus, Athenian ambassador to Sparta with Themistocles, i. 91 init.

Haemus, Mount, in Thrace, ii. 96 init.

Hagnon, an Athenian commander, son of Nicias, ii. 58 ; colleague of Pericles at Samos [B.C. 439], i. 117 med. ; the coloniser of Amphipolis, iv. 102, v. 11 init. ; brings reinforcements to Potidaea, ii. 58, vi. 31 init. ; commander in Chalcidicè, ii. 95 fin. ; swears to the Treaty of Peace and the Alliance, v. 19 fin., 24 med.

Hagnon, father of Theramenes, viii. 68 fin., 89 init.

Halex, a river of Locris in Italy, iii. 99.

Haliartus, in Boeotia, iv. 93 fin.

Halicarnassus, an Athenian fleet escapes thither, viii. 42 fin. ; the Athenians exact money from them, *ib.* 108 init.

Halieis, defeat of the Athenians there, i. 105 init. ; ravaged by the Athenians, ii. 56 fin. ; again, iv. 45.

Halys, river in Asia Minor, i. 16.

Hamaxitus, in the Troad, viii. 101 fin.

Harbour, the Great, of Syracuse, vi. 101 med., vii. 4 med., 22 fin. ; defeat of the Syracusans at the mouth of, *ib.* 23 ; second sea fight there, *ib.* 37–41 ; third sea fight, *ib.* 52 ; fourth and greatest, *ib.* 70, 71 ; the lesser harbour, *ib.* 22 init.

Harmatus, opposite Methymna, viii. 101 fin.

Harmodius and Aristogiton, conspiracy of, against Hipparchus, i. 20 med., vi. 54 init., 56-58.

Harpagium, on the Propontis, viii. 107 init.

Hebrus, the river, in Thrace, ii. 96 fin.

Hegesander, ambassador from Sparta to Athens, i. 139 med. ; father of Pasitelidas, a Lacedaemonian, iv. 132 fin.

Hegesander, a Thespian commander, vii. 19 med.

Hegesippidas, Lacedaemonian governor of Heraclea, v. 52 init. ; dismissed by the Boeotians, *ib.*

Helen, the suitors of, i. 9 init.

Helixus, a Megarian commander, viii. 80 fin.

Hellanicus, inaccuracy of, i. 97 fin.

Hellas, early condition of, i. 2 ; Trojan War first common action of, *ib.* 3 init. and fin. ; name derived from Hellen, and not given at first to the whole country, *ib.* 3 med. ; Minos first possessor of a navy in, *ib.* 4 init. ; piracy, honourable in, *ib.* 4, 5 ; ancient custom of carrying arms in, *ib.* 6 init. ; its older towns built inland, *ib.* 7 ; rise of tyrannies in, *ib.* 13 init. ; sends out colonies, *ib.* 12 ; the headship of Hellas transferred from Lacedaemon to Athens, i. 18, 95, 96 ; the war between Chalcis and Eretria the first in which Hellas was divided into parties, *ib.* 15 fin. ; agitation in Hellas before the War, i. 1 med., ii. 8, 11 init. ; after the failure of the Syracusan expedition, viii. 2 init. ; astonishment in Hellas at the surrender of the Spartans in Sphacteria, iv. 40 init. ; popular delusion about the number of heavy infantry in Hellas, vi. 17 med. ; Hellenes, word not used by Homer, i. 3 med. ; in ancient times always carried arms, *ib.* 6 init. ; once had many Barbarian customs, *ib.* 5 and 6 ; their ignorance of

their own history, i. 20, vi. 54 init. ; generally under-estimated the Athenian power, iv. 108 med., vii. 28 fin., viii. 2 med., 24 fin.

Hellen, gave name to Hellas, i. 3 med.

Hellenotamiae, the officers who received the tribute of the Allies at Athens, i. 96.

Hellespont, the allies in the Persian War at the Hellespont, i. 89 med. ; Pausanias in command there, *ib.* 95 med., 128 med. ; Athenian allies at the Hellespont, ii. 9 fin. [cp. vi. 77 med.] ; Athenian tribute ships in the Hellespont, iv. 75 init. ; Pharnabazus, satrap at the Hellespont, seeks aid of Lacedaemon, viii. 6 ; the Lacedaemonians determine to send a fleet there under Clearchus, *ib.* 8 med. ; the land forces intended for the Hellespont disperse, *ib.* 23 fin. ; Dercyllidas is sent thither overland, *ib.* 61, 62 ; the Athenian fleet leaves the Hellespont for Samos, *ib.* 79 ; Clearchus proceeds thither, Byzantium revolts, viii. 80 ; the Hellespont saved to Athens by Alcibiades' resolution in preventing the fleet sailing to the Piraeus, *ib.* 86 med. [cp. 96 med.] ; the Peloponnesian fleet sets sail for the Hellespont, *ib.* 99 ; the Athenians follow, *ib.* 100 ; operations in the Hellespont and battle of Cynossema, *ib.* 102-107 ; Tissaphernes is annoyed on hearing that the Peloponnesians had gone to the Hellespont, *ib.* 108 med., 109 init.

Helorine road, near Syracuse, vi. 66 fin., 70 fin., vii. 80 fin.

Helos, in Laconia, iv. 54 fin.

Helots, murder of, at Taenarus, i. 128 init. ; massacre of, iv. 80

Helots (*cont.*)—

med. ; intrigue with Pausanias, i. 132 med. ; revolt from the Lacedaemonians, *ib.* 101, ii. 27 fin., iii. 54 fin., iv. 56 fin. ; surrender, i. 103 init. ; settled at Naupactus by the Athenians, *ib.* 11, 9 med. ; carry supplies into Sphacteria, iv. 26 med. ; desert to the Messenians in Pylos, iv. 41 init. ; withdrawn from Pylos, v. 35 fin. ; replaced, *ib.* 56 med.; taken by the Athenians to Syracuse, vii. 57 med. [cp. *ib.* 31 init.]; Demosthenes fortifies an isthmus in Laconia in order that the Helots may desert thither, *ib.* 26 med. ; seven hundred sent with Brasidas, iv. 80 fin. ; afterwards settled at Lepreum, v. 34 med. ; the Lacedaemonians send a body of Helots and Neodamodes to Sicily, *ib.* 19 med., 58 med. [Compare Messenians.]

Hephaestus, the forge of, believed to be in Hiera, iii. 88 med.

Heraclea, in Trachis, iv. 78 init.; founded by the Lacedaemonians, iii. 92, 100 fin. ; failure of the colony, *ib.* 93 ; regulated by the Lacedaemonians, v. 12 fin. ; the Heracleans are defeated by the neighbouring tribes, *ib.* 51 ; Heraclea taken over by the Boeotians, *ib.* 52.

Heraclea, in Pontus, iv. 75 fin.

Heracles, temple of, at Mantinea, v. 64 fin., 66 init. ; festival of, at Syracuse, vii. 73 med.

Heraclidae, slay Eurystheus in Attica, i. 9 med. ; conquer the Peloponnesus, *ib.* 12 med. ; Phalius, a Corinthian of the Heraclid race, *ib.* 24 init.; Archias, founder of Syracuse, a Heraclid, vi. 3 med.

Heraclides, one of the Syracusan generals, vi. 73 ; deposed on a charge of treachery, *ib.* 103 fin.

Heraeans, of Arcadia, v. 67 init.

Herè, temple of, at Argos, iv. 133; at Corcyra, i. 24 fin., iii. 75 fin., 79 init., 81 med. ; at Epidaurus, v. 75 fin. ; at Plataea, iii. 68 fin.

Hermae, mutilation of the, vi. 27, 28 ; excitement at Athens about, *ib.* 53, 60; confession of one of the prisoners, *ib.* 60 med.

Hermaeondas, a Theban, iii. 5 med.

Hermes, temple of, near Mycalessus, vii. 29 med.

Hermionè, i. 128 med., 131 init. ; its territory ravaged by the Athenians, ii. 56 med. ; the Hermionians furnish a convoy to Corinth, i. 27 fin. ; supply ships to the Lacedaemonian navy, viii. 3 fin. [cp. *ib.* 33 init.]

Hermocrates, speech of, iv. 59–64; second speech of, vi. 33, 34 ; encourages the Syracusans after defeat, *ib.* 72 ; made general with two others, *ib.* 73 init., 96 med., 99 init. ; speech at Camarina, *ib.* 76–80; deposed, *ib.* 103 fin.; encourages the Syracusans to prepare a fleet, vii. 21 fin.; contrives by a stratagem to delay the Athenian retreat, *ib.* 73; brings a fleet to Asia, viii. 26 init.; remonstrates with Tissaphernes for reducing the ships' pay, *ib.* 29 med. ; again, *ib.* 45 med. ; incurs the hatred of Tissaphernes, *ib.* 85 ; goes to Sparta to expose him, *ib* ; exiled, *ib.* fin.

Hermon, an Athenian, commander of the Peripoli, viii. 92 med.

Hermon, father of Hermocrates, a Syracusan, iv. 58 fin., vi. 32 fin.

Hesiod, said to have been killed at Nemea, iii. 96 init.

Hessians, an Ozolian Locrian tribe, iii. 101 fin.

Hestiaea, in Euboea, expulsion of the Hestiaeans by the Athenians, i. 114 fin.; colonised from Athens, vii. 57 init.

Hestiodorus, an Athenian commander, ii. 70 init.

Hiera, one of the Liparaean islands, iii. 88 med.

Hieramenes, mentioned with Tissaphernes in the third treaty with the Lacedaemonians, viii. 58 init.

Hiereans, a Malian tribe, iii. 92 init.

Hierophon, an Athenian commander, iii. 105 med.

Himera, colonised from Zanclè, vi. 5 init.; the only Hellenic city on the north coast, *ib.* 69 init.; the Athenians and Sicels invade its territory, iii. 115; the Himeraeans aid Gylippus, vii. 1, 58 init.

Himeraeum, in Thrace, vii. 9 fin.

Hippagretas, one of the Spartan commanders at Sphacteria, iv. 38 init.

Hipparchus, son of Pisistratus, never actually tyrant, i. 20 init., vi. 54 init., 55 fin.; slain by Harmodius and Aristogiton, i. 20, vi. 54, 56–58; left no children, vi. 55 init.

Hippias, commander of the garrison at Notium, treacherously seized by Paches, iii. 34 med.

Hippias, eldest son of Pisistratus, i. 20 init., vi. 54 init., 55 init.; his children, vi. 55; becomes more oppressive, *ib.* 59 init.; deposed by the Lacedaemonians, *ib.* fin.; goes to Persia and returns to take part at Marathon, *ib.*

Hippias, father of Pisistratus, vi. 54 fin.

Hippocles, an Athenian commander, viii. 13.

Hippoclus, tyrant of Lampsacus, vi. 59 med.

Hippocrates, an Athenian general, fellow commander with Demo-sthenes, iv. 66 med.; attempts Megara and captures Nisaea, *ib.* 66–69; plans with Demosthenes an invasion of Boeotia, *ib.* 76, 77; fortifies Delium, *ib.* 90; speech of, *ib.* 95; defeated and slain, *ib.* 96, 101 init.

Hippocrates, a Lacedaemonian commander, loses part of his fleet off Triopium by an Athenian attack, viii. 35; informs Mindarus of the treachery of Tissaphernes, *ib.* 99 med.; sent to Euboea, *ib.* 107 fin.

Hippocrates, tyrant of Gela, vi. 5 fin.; refounds Camarina, *ib.*

Hippolochidas, a Thessalian, aids Brasidas in his march through Thessaly, iv. 78 init.

Hipponicus, an Athenian general, iii. 91 med.

Hipponoïdas, a Spartan polemarch, v. 71 fin.; banished for cowardice at Mantinea, *ib.* 72 init.

Homer quoted, (Il. ii. 108), i. 9 fin.; (ii. 570), *ib.* 13 med.; (from the Hymn to Apollo), iii. 104 med.; the testimony of, shows the comparative smallness of the Trojan War, i. 10 med.; his use of the name Hellenes, *ib.* 3 med. [*See* Poets.]

Honour, the love of, is ever young, ii. 44 fin.; often lures men to destruction, v. 111 med.

Hope, the deceitfulness of, iii. 39 med., 45, iv. 108 med., v. 103; the higher the hope, the greater the courage, vii. 67 init.

Hyacinthia, festival of, at Lacedaemon, v. 23, § iv; 41 fin.

Hyaeans, an Ozolian Locrian tribe, iii. 101 fin.

Hybla Geleatis, in Sicily, unsuccessfully attacked by the Athenians, vi. 62 fin., 63 med.; the Hyblaeans have their corn burnt by the Athenians, *ib.* 94 fin.

Hyblon, a Sicel king, vi. 4 init.

Hyccara, in Sicily, captured by the Athenians, vi. 62 med. [cp. vii. 13 fin.]

Hylias, a river in Italy, vii. 35 med.

Hyllaic harbour at Corcyra, iii. 72 fin., 81 init.

Hyperbolus, an Athenian, ostracised, viii. 73 init. ; murdered by the oligarchical conspirators, *ib.* med.

Hyperechides, father of Callias, an Athenian, vi. 55 init.

Hysiae, in Argos, captured by the Lacedaemonians, v. 83 med.

Hysiae, in Boeotia, iii. 24 med.

Hystaspes, father of Pissuthnes, a Persian, i. 115 med.

I.

Ialysus, in Rhodes, viii. 44 med.

Iapygia, promontory of, vi. 30 init., 34 med., vii. 33 med. ; Iapygian mercenaries hired by the Athenians against Syracuse, vii. 33 med., 57 fin.

Iasian Gulf, viii. 26 med.

Iasus, in Ionia, its wealth, viii. 28 med. ; captured by the Peloponnesians, *ib.* ; Peisander accuses Phrynichus of having betrayed it, *ib.* 54.

Iberians, the Sicanians originally Iberians, vi. 2 init. ; the most warlike of barbarians, *ib.* 90 med.

Icarus, an island in the Aegean, iii. 29 init., viii. 99 fin.

Ichthys, promontory of, in Elis, ii. 25 fin.

Ida, Mount, in the Troad, iv. 52 fin., viii. 108 med.

Idacus, in the Thracian Chersonese, viii. 104 init.

Idomenè, a hill in Amphilochia, iii. 112, 113.

Ilium, *see* Troy.

Illyrians hired by Perdiccas, iv. 124 fin. ; desert, *ib.* 125 init. ; attack and are defeated by Brasidas, *ib.* 127, 128 ; the Taulantians, an Illyrian tribe, make war upon Epidamnus, i. 24 init. ; aid the Corcyraeans to besiege Epidamnus, *ib.* 26 fin.

Imbros, colonised from Athens, vii. 57 init. ; Imbrian settlers at Athens ; serve under Cleon at Sphacteria, iv. 28 med. ; at Amphipolis, v. 8 init. ; support the Athenians in the Lesbian revolt, iii. 5 init. ; an Athenian squadron escapes to Imbros, viii. 102, 103.

Imperial powers acquire empire by assisting all who invoke their aid, vi. 18 init. ; to imperial powers nothing is inconsistent which is expedient, *ib.* 85.

Inarus, king of the Libyans, revolts from the King, i. 104 init. ; calls in the Athenians, *ib* ; is betrayed and impaled, *ib.* 110 med.

Inessa, a Sicel town, attacked by the Athenians, iii. 103 init. ; the Inessians have their crops burnt by the Athenians, vi. 94 fin.

Inexperience, in war, no excuse for misbehaviour, ii. 87 med.

Injustice, more resented than violence, i. 76 med., iv. 86 med. ; not those who suffer, but those who do injustice, should take time to think, i. 86 fin.

Intelligence, folly of over-, i. 84 fin., iii. 43 med., 83 fin.

Iolaus, the lieutenant of Perdiccas, i. 62 med.

Iolcius, an Athenian, swears to the Treaty of Peace and the Alliance, v. 19 fin., 24 med.

Ion, father of Tydeus, a Chian, viii. 38 med.

Ionia, colonised from Attica, i. 2 fin., 12 fin, 95 init., ii. 15 med., iii. 86 med., iv. 61 med., vii. 57

Ionia (*cont.*)—

init. ; habits of life common to the older Athenians and Ionians, i. 6 med. ; Ionians possessed a great fleet in the time of Cyrus, *ib*. 13 fin. ; subdued by Cyrus and Darius, *ib*. 16; the Ionians fleeing from the Persians found colonies in Sicily, vi. 4 fin. ; the Ionians put themselves under the headship of Athens, i. 95 init., vi. 76 med. ; Ionian exiles urge the Lacedaemonians to raise a revolt in Ionia, iii. 31 ; the Lacedaemonians exclude Ionians from their colony of Heraclea, *ib*. 92 fin.; the Ionians and Tissaphernes beg aid at Sparta for a revolt, viii. 5, 6 ; Ionia revolts, *ib*. 14–22 ; Tissaphernes demands all Ionia for the king, *ib*. 56 fin.

Ionians contrasted with Dorians, i. 124 init., v. 9 init., vi. 77 med., 80 fin., 82 init., vii. 5 fin., 57 init. and med., viii. 25 med.

Ionian Gulf, the, i. 24 init., ii. 97 fin., vi. 13 med., 30 init., 34 med., 44 init., 104 init., vii. 33 med., 57 fin.

Ionian festival of the Dionysia, ii. 15 med. ; at Delos, iii. 104 med. ; at Ephesus, *ib*. med.

Ipneans, an Ozolian Locrian tribe, iii. 101 fin.

Isarchidas, a Corinthian commander, i. 29 init.

Isarchus, father of Isarchidas, a Corinthian, i. 29 init.

Ischagoras, a Lacedaemonian commander, iv. 132 ; swears to the Treaty of Peace and the Alliance, v. 19 init., 24 init. ; goes as envoy to Chalcidicè, *ib*. 21.

Isocrates, a Corinthian commander, ii. 83 fin.

Isolochus, father of Pythodorus, an Athenian, iii. 115 init.

Ister, the river, ii. 96 init., 97 init.

Isthmian Games, viii. 9 init., 10 init.

Isthmionicus, an Athenian, swears to the Treaty of Peace and the Alliance, v. 19 fin., 24 med.

Isthmus, of Corinth, advantageously situated for trade, i. 13 med. ; its situation, iv. 42 med. ; the Lacedaemonians summon the allies to the Isthmus, ii. 10, 13 init., 18 med. ; again, iii. 15 ; earthquakes stop the Lacedaemonian army at the Isthmus, *ib*. 89 init. ; the Treaty of Peace ordered to be inscribed on a pillar at the Isthmus, v. 18, xi ; a small Lacedaemonian force comes to the Isthmus during the excitement about the Hermae at Athens, vi. 61 init.

Isthmus, of Leucas, iii. 81 init., iv. 8 init.

Isthmus, of Pallenè, i. 56 init., 62 init., 64 init.

Istonè, Mount, occupied by the Corcyraean oligarchs, iii. 85, iv. 2 med., 46 init. ; capture of, *ib*. 46 med.

Italus, a Sicel king who gave his name to Italy, vi. 2 med.

Italy, named from King Italus, vi. 2 med.; the mother country of the Sicels, *ib*. ; most of the Hellenic colonies in, founded from Peloponnesus, i. 12 fin. ; the Lacedaemonians order their Italian allies to furnish a naval contingent, ii. 7 med. ; the Locrians side with the Syracusans, the Rhegians with the Leontines, iii. 86 med. [cp. iv. 1 med., 24]; the Athenians send an embassy to, v. 4, 5 ; Hermocrates advises the Syracusans to seek allies in, vi. 34 ; the Italian cities refuse to receive the Athenian expedition to Syracuse, *ib*. 44 ; the Syracusans send envoys to the Italian cities, *ib*. 88 fin. ; the Athenians obtain supplies from them, *ib*. 103 init. [cp. vii. 14 med., 25 init.]; Gylippus

Italy (*cont.*)—

goes to Thurii and Tarentum, vi. 104 ; the second Athenian expedition reaches Italy, vii. 33 ; Italian allies of the Athenians before Syracuse, *ib.* 57 fin. ; the Syracusans retain their Italian, Sicilian, and Athenian prisoners after the others are sold, *ib.* 87 fin. ; Italian vessels join the Lacedaemonians, viii. 91 init.

Itamenes, a Persian commander, iii. 34 init.

Ithomè, mount, seized by the Helots, i. 101 init., iii. 54 fin. ; besieged by the Lacedaemonians, i. 102 init. ; surrendered, *ib.* 103.

Itonaeans, colonists of the Italian Locrians, v. 5 fin.

Itys, the legend of, ii. 29 init.

J.

Justice, an idle word to the strong, i. 76 fin., v. 89 fin. ; justice and expediency, i. 36, 42 init., 76, iii. 40 med., 44, 56, 82 fin., v. 90, 98, 107 ; the Lacedaemonian conception of, a 'do-nothing' policy, i. 71 init.

K.

Kindness, a little, done in season may cancel a greater previous wrong, i. 42 fin.

Kings of Lacedaemon, common mistake that they have two votes in council, i. 20 fin. ; could be imprisoned by the Ephors, *ib.* 131 fin. ; the government carried on by regents in their minority, i. 107 init., 132 init. ; give all orders in the field, v. 66 med.

Kings of Persia : Cyrus, i. 13 fin. ; Cambyses, *ib.* ; Darius, *ib.* 14 med. ; Xerxes, *ib.*, 129 ; Artaxerxes, *ib.* 104 init., 137 med., iv.

50 fin ; Darius Nothus, viii. 5 init., 18, 37, 58.

Kings in ancient Hellas, their constitutional character, i. 13 init.

Knights, the, at Athens, iii. 16 init ; the Three Hundred (so called) at Sparta, v. 72 fin.

Kropeia (in Attica), ii. 19 fin.

L.

Labdalum, a fort built by the Athenians on Epipolae, vi. 97 fin., 98 med. ; captured by Gylippus, vii. 3.

Lacedaemon contrasted with Athens, i. 10 init. ; founded by the Dorians, *ib.* 18 init., 107 init. ; long unsettled, *ib.* 18 init. ; never subject to tyrants, *ib.* ; its excellent constitution, *ib.* ; common mistakes about, *ib.* 20 fin. ; the Lacedaemonians a pattern of nobility in Hellas, iii. 53 fin., 57 init. ; 'liberators of Hellas,' i. 69 init., ii. 8 fin., iii. 59 fin., iv. 85 init., 108 init., v. 9 fin., viii. 43 fin., 46 med., 52 fin. ; their slothful character, especially in contrast with the Athenians, i. 69, 70, 84 init., 102 med., iv. 55 med., viii. 96 fin. ; their freedom from passion, v. 63 med. ; force strict oligarchies on their subjects, i. 19 init. [cp. 76 init., 144 med., iv. 132 fin.], v. 81 fin., viii. 38 med. ; bad administration of colony by Heraclea, iii. 93 fin., v. 52 init. ; different character of, at home and abroad, v. 105 fin. ; their bad conduct abroad, i. 77 fin. [cp. *ib.* 95 fin.] ; their slaughter of traders, ii. 67 fin., iii. 32 ; their treatment of the Helots, i. 128 init., iv. 80 med. ; the great number of their slaves, viii. 40 med. ; simplicity of Lacedaemonian life, i. 6 med. ; the Lacedaemonians first to strip

Lacedaemon (*cont.*)—

naked in the games, *ib.* ; decide by cries, not by voting, *ib.* 87 init. ; observance of omens, &c., iii. 89 init., v. 54 med., 55 med., 116 init., vi. 95 init., viii. 6 fin. ; importance attached by them to religious observances, iv. 5 init., v. 54 med., 75 init., 82 init. ; their brevity of speech, iv. 17 init. ; their military prowess, *ib.* 12 fin. ; their prestige, *ib.* 18 init. ; the common belief that they would never surrender, *ib.* 40 init. ; secrecy of their government, v. 54 init., 68 init., 74 fin. ; its moderation and stability, viii. 24 med. ; their exclusion of foreigners, i. 144 init. [cp. ii. 39 init.] ; powers of their kings, v. 66 med., viii. 4 fin. ; organisation of their army, iii. 109 init., iv. 8 fin., 38 init., v. 66 fin., 68 fin. ; sometimes send out commissioners to advise a general, ii. 85 init., iii. 69 med., 76, v. 63 fin., viii. 39 init. ; march to the sound of music, v. 70 ; do not pursue a defeated enemy far, *ib.* 73 fin. ; recovery of their influence after Mantinea, *ib.* 77 med. Lacedaemonians, the, put down the tyrants, i. 18 init., vi. 53 fin., 59 fin. ; become one of the leading powers of Hellas, *ib.* 18 fin. [cp. *ib.* 10 init.] ; endeavour to prevent the Athenians from building their walls, *ib.* 90 init. ; deceived by Themistocles, *ib.* 90-92 ; their friendly feeling toward the Athenians after the Persian War, *ib.* 92 ; summon Pausanias to Lacedaemon, *ib.* 95 init., 131 init. ; the Helots revolt, *ib.* 101 init. ; the Lacedaemonians call in the Athenians, *ib.* 102 init. ; dismiss them and so cause the first open quarrel between themselves and the Athenians, *ib.* med. ; assist the Dorians against the Phocians, *ib.* 107 init. ; defeat the Athenians at Tanagra, *ib.* fin., 108 init.; engage in the 'Sacred War,' *ib.* 112 fin. ; invade Attica, *ib.* 114 med. ; conclude a thirty years' truce with the Athenians, *ib.* 115 init. ; take alarm at the growth of the Athenian empire, *ib.* 118 ; promise aid to the Potidaeans, *ib.* 58 med. ; summon the allies, *ib.* 67 med. ; vote that the treaty was broken, *ib.* 79, 87 ; their reasons, *ib.* 88, 118 ; consult the oracle, *ib.* 118 fin. ; summon the allies a second time, *ib.* 119 init. ; vote for war, *ib.* 125 ; send embassies to Athens, *ib.* 126 init. ; make a final demand from the Athenians, *ib.* 139 ; meditate sending embassies to the King, ii. 7 init. ; the list of their allies, *ib.* 9 init. ; summon the allies to the Isthmus, before invading Attica, *ib.* 10 ; unsuccessfully attack Oenoè, *ib.* 18 ; enter and ravage Attica, *ib.* 19-22 ; defeat the Athenians at Phrygia, *ib.* 22 med. ; retire, *ib.* 23 fin. ; settle the Aeginetans at Thyrea, *ib.* 27 ; (2nd year) again invade Attica, *ib.* 47 init. ; reach Laurium, *ib.* 55 ; quit Attica, *ib.* 57 ; reject offers of peace, *ib.* 59 med. ; attack Zacynthus, *ib.* 66 ; send ambassadors to the King, *ib.* 67 ; (3rd year) attack and finally blockade Plataea, *ib.* 71-78 ; invade Acarnania, *ib.* 80 ; defeated at sea by the Athenians, *ib.* 83, 84 ; send commissioners to assist their admiral, *ib.* 85 init. ; again defeated, *ib.* 86-92 ; meditate an attack on Piraeus, *ib.* 93 init. ; ravage Salamis, *ib.* fin. ; (4th year) invade Attica, iii. 1 ; send the Mytilenaean envoys to Olympia, *ib.* 8 ; receive the Myti-

Lacedaemon (*cont.*)—

lenaeans into alliance, *ib.* 15 init.; summon the allies to the Isthmus, *ib.* med. ; send a fleet to Lesbos, *ib.* 16 fin. ; send Salaethus to Mytilenè, *ib.* 25 init. ; (5th year) invade Attica, *ib.* 26 ; arrive too late to save Lesbos, *ib.* 29 ; compel Plataea to surrender, *ib.* 52 init. ; put the Plataeans to death, *ib.* 68; raze Plataea, *ib.* ; prepare an expedition to Corcyra, *ib.* 69 ; engage the Athenians and Corcyraeans, *ib.* 76-78 ; retire, *ib.* 79-81 init. ; (6th year) deterred by earthquakes from the invasion of Attica, *ib.* 89 init. ; colonise Heraclea, *ib.* 92, 93, 100 ; send an army against Naupactus, *ib.* 100-102 ; invade Amphilochia, *ib.* 105, 106; defeated, *ib.* 107, 108; desert the Ambraciots, *ib.* 109, 111 ; (7th year) invade Attica, iv. 2 init. ; return on the news of the capture of Pylos, *ib.* 6 ; occupy Sphacteria, *ib.* 8 fin.; unsuccessfully assault Pylos, *ib.* 11, 12 ; defeated in the harbour, *ib.* 14 ; make a truce with the Athenians, and send ambassadors to Athens, *ib.* 15, 16 ; their speech, *ib.* 17-20 ; the Lacedaemonians break off negotiations, *ib.* 21, 22 ; their troops in Sphacteria attacked and forced to surrender, *ib.* 31-38 ; they sue for peace, *ib.* 41 ; negotiate with the King, *ib.* 50 med. ; (8th year) the Athenians take Cythera, *ib.* 53, 54 ; the Lacedaemonians are panic-stricken at their ill success in the war, *ib.* 55 ; their garrison in Nisaea surrenders to the Athenians, *ib.* 69 fin. ; they encourage the expedition of Brasidas into Chalcidicè, *ib.* 80 init. ; capture Amphipolis, *ib.* 103-106 ; (9th year) make a truce for a year with the Athenians, *ib.* 117-119,;

Brasidas attempts Potidaea, *ib.* 135; (10th year) defeats the Athenians and falls at Amphipolis, v. 6-11 ; (11th year) the Lacedaemonians become eager for peace, *ib.* 14 ; bring back Pleistoanax from exile, *ib.* 16 fin. ; make a treaty with the Athenians, *ib.* 17-19 ; conclude an alliance with the Athenians, *ib.* 22 fin.-24 ; fall into contempt with and displease the Peloponnesians, *ib.* 28 fin., 29 fin. ; send envoys to Corinth, *ib.* 30 ; support the Lepreans against Elis, *ib.* 31 med.; make war upon the Parrhasians, *ib.* 33 ; emancipate the Helot soldiers of Brasidas, and disfranchise the prisoners from Pylos, *ib.* 34 ; conclude an alliance with the Boeotians in order to gain Panactum, *ib.* 39 ; (12th year) receive Argive envoys and prepare to conclude a treaty with them, *ib.* 40, 41 ; announce the destruction of Panactum at Athens, *ib.* 42 ; their envoys at Athens are tricked by Alcibiades, *ib.* 43-45 ; refuse to give up the Boeotian alliance at the demand of the Athenians, *ib.* 46 med.; excluded by the Eleans from the Olympic games, *ib.* 49 ; (13th year) expelled from Heraclea by the Boeotians, *ib.* 51, 52; start on an expedition against Argos but turn back, *ib.* 54 init.; again start and return, *ib.* 55 med.; garrison Epidaurus, *ib.* 56 init. ; (14th year) march against Argos, *ib.* 57 ; surround the Argives, *ib.* 58, 59; furious with Agis for making a truce with the Argives, *ib.* 60 med., 63 ; march to the support of Tegea, *ib.* 64 init. ; surprised by the Argives before Mantinea, *ib.* 66 init. ; gain a great victory, *ib.* 70-74 ; make alliance with Argos, *ib.* 76-

Lacedaemon (*cont.*)—

79; (15th year) send an expedition to Argos, but retire, *ib.* 82 med. ; send another, *ib.* 83 init. ; (16th year) again start against Argos, but are turned back by unfavourable sacrifices, *ib.* 116 init. ; ravage Argos, vi. 7 init. ; settle the Argive exiles at Orneae, *ib.* ; order the Chalcidians to assist Perdiccas, *ib.* fin. ; they refuse, *ib.* ; (17th year) send a force to the Isthmus, which increases the panic at Athens after the mutilation of the Hermae, *ib.* 61 init. ; receive Corinthian and Syracusan ambassadors, *ib.* 73 init., 88 fin. ; Alcibiades speaks in their behalf, *ib.* 89-92 ; the Lacedaemonians appoint Gylippus commander of the Syracusan army, *ib.* 93 med. ; (18th year) invade Argos, but are stopped by an earthquake, *ib.* 95 ; consider the Athenians guilty of first breaking the treaty [cp. vi. 105 init.] and prepare for war with a good spirit, vii. 18 ; (19th year) invade Attica and fortify Decelea, *ib.* 19 init. ; send troops to Sicily, *ib.* 17 fin., 19 med., 58 med. ; Nicias surrenders himself to them, trusting to their friendly feeling for him, *ib.* 85 init., 86 med. ; the Lacedaemonians derive hope from the failure of the Sicilian expedition, viii. 2 fin. ; raise money and order ships to be built, *ib.* 3 ; Agis at Decelea negotiates with the Lesbians and Euboeans who desire to revolt, *ib.* 4 ; the Lacedaemonians send a commissioner to Chios, *ib.* 6 fin. ; ally themselves to Chios and Erythrae, *ib.* ; (20th year) order a fleet to Chios, *ib.* 7, 8 ; defeated at sea and driven into Piraeum, *ib.* 10, 11 ; discouraged by this unfortunate beginning, *ib.* 11 fin. ; persuaded by Alcibiades not to

give way, *ib.* 12 ; cause the revolt of Chios, Erythrae, Clazomenae, Teos, Miletus, *ib.* 14-17 ; make an alliance with the King, *ib.* 18 ; break out of Piraeum, *ib.* 20 init. ; induce Mytilenè and Methymna to revolt, *ib.* 22 ; baffled in their plans on Lesbos, *ib.* 23 ; defeated by the Athenians before Miletus, *ib.* 25 ; capture Iasos, *ib.* 28 ; fail to retake Clazomenae, *ib.* 31 ; surprised and lose six ships off Triopium, *ib.* 35 med. ; make a new treaty with the King, *ib.* 36, 37 ; alter the government of Chios, *ib.* 38 med. ; send aid to Pharnabazus, *ib.* 39 init., 80 ; send advisers to Astyochus, *ib.* 39 init. ; defeat an Athenian squadron, *ib.* 42 ; distrust Alcibiades and order his death, *ib.* 45 init. ; Astyochus is believed to have sold himself to Tissaphernes, *ib.* 50 med. ; Pedaritus, their governor at Chios, is killed in battle, *ib.* 55 fin. ; they make a third treaty with the Persians, *ib.* 57, 58 ; are invited by the Eretrians to Euboea, *ib.* 60 med. ; (21st year) send Dercyllidas to the Hellespont, *ib.* 61 init., 62 init. ; offer the Athenians battle off Samos, *ib.* 63 init. ; Agis at Decelea receives heralds from the Four Hundred, *ib.* 70 fin. ; he sends them to Sparta, *ib.* 71 fin. ; the sailors at Miletus complain of Astyochus and Tissaphernes, *ib.* 78 ; Astyochus again offers battle to the Athenians, *ib.* 79 init. ; but declines to engage the Athenians when they offer, *ib.* fin. ; the Lacedaemonians send aid to Pharnabazus, and cause the revolt of Byzantium, *ib.* 80 ; the sailors at Miletus break out into open violence against Astyochus, *ib.* 84 init. ; the Lacedaemonians send Mindarus to succeed As-

Lacedaemon (*cont.*)—

tyochus, *ib.* 85 init. ; receive twelve ambassadors from the oligarchs at Athens, *ib.* 90 med. ; do not come to terms with them, *ib.* 91 init. ; despatch a fleet to Euboea, *ib.* 91 init. ; defeat the Athenians at sea, *ib.* 95 ; do not follow up their success, *ib.* 96 ; leave Tissaphernes in disgust and sail to the Hellespont, *ib.* 99; arrive at Rhoeteum, *ib.* 101 fin. ; chase the Athenian squadron at Sestos, and capture a few vessels, *ib.* 102 ; defeated at sea by the Athenians off Cynossema, *ib.* 104, 105 ; lose eight more ships, *ib.* 107 init. ; aid in expelling the Persian garrison from Antandros, *ib.* 108 med., and from Cnidus, *ib.* 109 init. [See also for the latter part, Astyochus, Alcibiades, Lichas, Pedaritus, Tissaphernes, &c.]

Lacedaemonius, son of Cimon, an Athenian commander, i. 45.

Laches, an Athenian, commands an expedition to Sicily, iii. 86 init., vi. 8 init., 6 med., 75 med. ; his proceedings in Sicily, *ib.* 90, 99, 103, 115 init. ; superseded by Pythodorus, *ib.* 115 init. ; moves the conclusion of the one year's Truce, iv. 118 fin.; swears to the Treaty of Peace and the Alliance, v. 19 fin., 24 med. [cp. 43 med.] ; brings an Athenian force to Argos, *ib.* 61 ; reduces Orchomenus, *ib.* fin. ; slain at Mantinea, *ib.* 74 fin.

Lacon, a Plataean, iii. 52 fin.

Ladè, an island opposite Miletus, viii. 17 fin., 24 init.

Laeaeans, a Paeonian tribe, ii. 96 med.

Laespodias, an Athenian general, vi. 105 fin. ; goes as an envoy from the Four Hundred to Sparta, viii. 86 fin.

Laestrygones, oldest inhabitants of Sicily, vi. 2 init.

Lamachus, an Athenian commander, leads an expedition into the Pontus, iv. 75 ; swears to the Treaty of Peace and the Alliance, v. 19 fin., 24 med. ; made one of the generals in Sicily, vi. 8 med. ; advocates in a council of war an immediate attack on Syracuse, *ib.* 49; votes however with Alcibiades, *ib.* 50 init. ; falls in battle, *ib.* 101 fin., 103 init., med.

Lamis, founder of Trotilus and Thapsus, vi. 4 init.

Lampon, an Athenian, swears to the Treaty of Peace and the Alliance, v. 19 fin , 24 med.

Lampsacus, given to Themistocles by the King, i. 138 fin. ; famous for wine, *ib.* ; becomes the refuge of Hippias, vi. 59 ; its tyrants, *ib.*; revolts from Athens, viii. 62 init.; retaken, *ib.* med.

Laodicium, in Arcadia, battle of, iv. 134.

Laophon, father of Calligitus, a Megarian, viii. 6 init.

Laphilus, a Lacedaemonian, swears to the Treaty of Peace and the Alliance, v. 19 med , 24 init.

Larissa, on the Hellespont, viii. 101 fin.

Larissa, in Thessaly, iv. 78 init. ; the Larissaeans assist the Athenians in the first invasion of Attica, ii. 22 fin. ; their two factions, *ib.*

Las, in Laconia, viii. 91 med., 92 init.

Laurium, silver mines of, ii. 55 init., vi. 91 fin.

Laws, not lightly to be set aside, iii. 37 med. (cp. vi. 14) ; Athenian respect for, especially the unwritten law of society, ii. 37 fin.

Lawsuits, between the Athenians and their allies decided by Athenian law, i. 77 init.

Leagrus, father of Glaucon, an Athenian, i. 51 med.

Learchus, an Athenian ambassador to Sitalces, ii. 67 med.

Lebedus, in Ionia, revolts from Athens, viii. 19 fin.

Lectum, promontory of, viii. 101 fin.

Lecythus, a high point of Toronè, iv. 113 fin.; captured by Brasidas, *ib.* 114–116; dedicated by Brasidas to Athenè, *ib.* 116.

Lemnos, viii. 102 fin.; once inhabited by Tyrrhenians, iv. 109 init.; colonised from Athens, iv. 28 fin., vii. 57 init.; visited by the plague, ii. 47 med.; the Athenians deposit Samian hostages there, i. 115 med.; the Lemnians support the Athenians in the Lesbian revolt, iii. 5 init.; fight under Cleon at Sphacteria, iv. 28 fin.; at Amphipolis, v. 8 init. (cp. Imbros); present before Syracuse, vii. 57 init.

Leocorium, a temple at Athens, i. 20 med., vi. 57 fin.

Leocrates, an Athenian commander, i. 105 init.

Leogoras, father of Andocides, an Athenian, i. 51 med.

Leon, a Lacedaemonian, one of the founders of Heraclea, iii. 92 fin ; another, goes as envoy to Athens, v. 44 fin.; another, father of Pedaritus, viii. 28 fin.; another, succeeds Pedaritus at Chios, *ib.* 61 med ; gains an advantage over the Athenians at sea, *ib.* fin.

Leon, an Athenian, swears to the Treaty of Peace and the Alliance, v. 19 fin., 24 med.; an Athenian general [?the same], viii. 23 init.; popular with the multitude, *ib.* 73 med.; comes with reinforcements to Diomedon, *ib.* 23 init.; regains Lesbos which had revolted, *ib.* 23 med.; carries on war successfully against Chios, *ib.* 24 med.; appointed with Diomedon to the chief command

at Samos, *ib.* 54 med.; makes a descent upon Rhodes, *ib.* 55 init.; aids the democratic reaction at Samos, *ib.* 73 fin.

Leon, near Syracuse, vi. 97 init.

Leonidas, father of Pleistarchus king of Sparta, i. 132 init.

Leontiades, father of Eurymachus a Theban, ii. 2 med.

Leontini, founded from Chalcis in Euboea by Thucles, vi. 3 fin.; the Leontines of Ionian descent, iii. 86 med., vi. 44 fin., 46 init., 50 fin., 76 med., 77 init., 79 med.; at war with Syracuse, *ib.* 86 init.; obtain assistance from Athens, *ib.* fin.; unsuccessfully attack Messenè, iv. 25 fin.; revolution in, v. 4 init.; the Athenians espouse their cause as an excuse for the conquest of Sicily, *ib.* fin., vi. 8 med., 19 init., 33 init., 47 fin., 48 fin., 63 fin., 76 init., 77 init., 84 med.

Leotychides, king of Sparta, i. 89 init.

Lepreum, assisted by the Lacedaemonians in a quarrel with the Eleans, v. 31; the Lacedaemonians settle the Helots and Neodamodes there, *ib.* 34 med.; they break the Olympic Truce by bringing a garrison into Lepreum, *ib.* 49 init.; the Lepreans do not attend the Olympic festival, *ib.* 50 init.; the Eleans are angry with their allies for not attacking Lepreum, *ib.* 62.

Leros [*al.* Eleus], viii. 26 init., 27 init.

Lesbos : the Lesbians kindred of the Boeotians, iii. 2 fin., vii. 57 med., viii. 4 med., 100 med. [cp. iii. 5 med., 13 init.]; with the Chians, the only independent allies of Athens, i. 19, vi. 85 med., vii. 57 init.; furnish ships to the Athenians, ii. 9 fin., 56 med., vi. 31 init.; the Lesbians

Lesbos (*cont.*)—

aid the Athenians against the Samians, i. 116, 117 ; revolt from Athens, iii. 2 [*see* Mytilenè] ; are received into the Lacedaemonian confederacy, *ib.* 15 init.; the affairs of Lesbos set in order by Paches, *ib.* 35 ; the land divided among Athenian citizens, *ib.* 50 ; the Lesbian refugees capture Antandrus, iv. 52 med. [which the Athenians recover, *ib.* 75 med.] ; the Lesbians negotiate with Agis about a fresh revolt, viii. 4 med.; revolt and are again subdued, *ib.* 22, 23 ; renew negotiations with Astyochus, *ib.* 32 init. ; Pedaritus refuses them aid from Chios, *ib.* fin.; the Athenian fleet on the way to the Hellespont puts in at Lesbos, and prepares to attack Eresus, *ib.* 100.

Leucas, a Corinthian colony, i. 30 init. ; devastated by the Corcyraeans, *ib.* ; attacked by the Athenians, iii. 94 init., 95 med., 102 med.

Leucadian Isthmus, iii. 81 init, 94 med., iv. 8 init. ; garrisoned by the Corinthians, iv. 42 fin. ; naval engagement between the Peloponnesians returning from Sicily, and the Athenians, off Leucadia, viii. 13 ; the Leucadians send troops to Epidamnus, i. 26 init. ; furnish ships to Corinth, *ib.* 27 fin., 46 init. ; Corinthian fleet sails from Leucas, *ib.* 46 med. ; the Leucadians supply the Lacedaemonians with ships, ii. 9 med. ; assist in the invasion of Acarnania, *ib.* 80 fin., 81 med. ; a Leucadian vessel is sunk by an Athenian off Naupactus, *ib.* 91 med., 92 med. ; the Leucadians repulse an Athenian descent, iii. 7 ; send a squadron to Cyllenè to reinforce Alcidas, *ib.* 69 med. ; aid

Gylippus with a fleet, vi. 104 init., vii. 4 fin., 7 init. ; present before Syracuse, vii. 58 med. ; lose one ship in the battle of Cynossema, viii. 106 med.

Leucimnè, Corcyraeans raise a trophy on, i. 30 init. ; Corcyraean station at, *ib.* fin., 47 med., 51 fin. ; the Peloponnesians land there, iii. 79 fin.

Leuconium, in Chios, viii. 24 med.

Leuctra, in Laconia, v. 54 init.

Libya, visited by the plague, ii. 48 init. ; trade between Libya and Laconia, iv. 53 fin. ; Phocians returning from Troy are driven to Libya, vi. 2 med. ; a Peloponnesian fleet on the way to Syracuse is driven to Libya, vii. 50 init. ; the Libyans besiege the Evesperitae, *ib.* ; Inaros, king of the Libyans, i. 104 init., 110 med.

Lichas, a Lacedaemonian, victor at Olympia, v. 50 med. ; struck by the officers, *ib.* ; envoy to Argos, *ib.* 22 med. ; again, *ib.* 76 med. ; goes with ten others as adviser to Astyochus, viii. 39 init.; objects to the treaties made with the king, *ib.* 43, 52 fin. ; goes with Tissaphernes to Aspendus, *ib.* 87 init. ; rebukes the Milesians for driving out a Persian garrison, *ib.* 84 med. ; his unpopularity at Miletus, *ib.* fin. ; dies there, *ib.*

Ligurians, the, drove the Sicanians out of Iberia, vi. 2 init.

Limnaea, in Acarnania, ii. 80 fin., iii. 106 med.

Lindii, the Acropolis of Gela, vi. 4 med.

Lindus, in Rhodes, viii. 44.

Liparaean [or Aeolian] islands : the Liparaeans colonists of the Cnidians, iii. 88 ; invaded by the Athenians, *ib.* ; again, *ib.* 115 init.

Locrians [Opuntian], subjected by the Persians, viii. 43 fin. ; allies

Locrians (*cont.*)—

of the Lacedaemonians, v. 64 med.; give hostages to the Athenians, i. 108 med.; present at the battle of Coronea, *ib.* 113; furnish the Lacedaemonians with cavalry, ii. 9 med.; Atalantè, islet off Locris, seized by the Athenians to prevent privateering, *ib.* 32 init. [cp. v. 18, § viii]; the Locrians defeated by the Athenians, ii. 26; inundation of the sea on the Locrian coast, iii. 89 med.; the Locrian coast ravaged by the Athenians, *ib.* 91 fin.; Locrian cavalry pursue the Athenians after Delium, iv. 96 fin.; the Locrians supply the Lacedaemonians with ships, viii. 3 fin.

Locrians [Ozolian], always carry arms, i. 5 fin.; old inhabitants of Naupactus, *ib.* 103 med.; allied to the Athenians, iii. 95 fin., 97 med.; subdued by the Lacedaemonians, *ib.* 101; go to war with the Phocians, v. 32 init.

Locris, in Italy: the Locrians in alliance with the Syracusans, iii. 86 med.; defeated by the Athenians, *ib.* 99; again, *ib.* 103 fin.; cause Messenè to revolt, iv. 1 init.; join the Syracusans in attacking the Rhegians, *ib.* 24, 25; invited to Messenè during a revolution, v. 5 init.; expelled, *ib.*; make a treaty with Athens, *ib.* fin.; hostile to the Athenian expedition to Sicily, vi. 44 med. [cp. vii. 35 fin.]; send ships to the Lacedaemonians, viii. 91 init.

Loryma, in Caria, viii. 43 init.

Lot, use of the lot to determine which side should first execute a treaty, v. 21 init.; in the distribution of an army between a number of generals, viii. 30 init.

Lycaeum, Mount, in Arcadia, v. 16 fin., 54 init.

Lycia, ii. 69 med., viii. 41 fin.

Lycomedes, father of Archestratus, an Athenian, i. 57 fin.; another, father of Cleomedes, v. 84 fin.

Lycophron, a Lacedaemonian, sent out as adviser to Cnemus, ii. 85 init.

Lycophron, a Corinthian general, iv. 43; death of, *ib.* 44 init.

Lycus, father of Thrasybulus, an Athenian, viii. 75 init.

Lyncus, in Upper Macedonia, ii. 99 init.; under the rule of Arrhibaeus, iv. 83 init.; invaded by Perdiccas and Brasidas, *ib.*; invaded a second time by them, *ib.* 124 init.; Brasidas retreats through Lyncus, *ib.* 125-128, 129 init.

Lysicles, father of Habronichus, an Athenian, i. 91 init.; another, sent to exact money in Caria and Lycia, iii. 19 init.; falls in battle, *ib.* fin.

Lysimachidas, father of Arianthidas, a Theban, iv. 91 med.

Lysimachus, father of Aristides, an Athenian, i. 91 init.

Lysimachus, father of Heraclides, a Syracusan, vi. 73 init.

Lysimelea, a marsh near Syracuse, vii. 53 med.

Lysistratus, an Olynthian, iv. 110 fin.

M.

Macarius, a Spartan commander, iii. 100 fin.; falls at the battle of Olpae, *ib.* 109 init.

Macedonia, its early history, ii. 99; kings of Macedonia originally from Argos, *ib.* init., v. 80 med.; the Athenians send an expedition against Macedonia, i. 57-61; Macedonian troops sent by Perdiccas too late for the Lacedaemonian expedition into Acarnania, ii. 80 fin.; the Thracians invade Macedonia under Sital-

Macedonia (*cont.*)—

ces, *ib.* 95–101 ; the military strength of Macedonia much increased by Archelaus, *ib.* 100 init. ; Brasidas in Macedonia, iv. 78 fin., 82, 83 ; second expedition of Brasidas into Macedonia, *ib.* 124–128 ; the Athenians blockade Macedonia, v. 83 fin. ; Macedonia ravaged from Methonè by the Athenians, vi. 7 fin.

Machaon, a Corinthian commander, ii. 83 fin.

Maeander, plain of the, iii. 19 fin., viii. 58 init.

Maedi, a Thracian tribe, ii. 98 med.

Maenalia, part of Arcadia, v. 64 init. ; Maenalians at Mantinea, *ib.* 67 med. ; hostages taken from the Maenalians by the Argives to be given up under treaty, *ib.* 77, I.

Magistrates, the good magistrate is not always bound by the letter of the law, vi. 14.

Magnesia, in Asia, given to Themistocles by the king, i. 138 fin. ; Astyochus goes to Tissaphernes and Alcibiades at Magnesia, viii. 50 med.

Magnesians, dependents of Thessalians, ii. 101 med.

Malea, Cape, in Lesbos, iii. 4 fin., 6 fin.

Malea, Cape, in Laconia, iv. 53 med., 54 init., viii. 39 med.

Malian Gulf, the, iii. 96 fin., viii. 3 init. ; darters and slingers from the Malian Gulf, iv. 100 init.

Malians, iii. 92 init., v. 51 init.

Maloeis, Apollo, festival of, at Mytilenè, iii. 3 med.

Mantinea, defeat of Mantinean troops sent by the Lacedaemonians into Acarnania, iii. 107, 108 ; they escape by a secret treaty with Demosthenes, *ib.* 109, 111 ; the Mantineans fight with the Tegeans, iv. 134 [cp. v. 65 med.] ; conquer a part of Arcadia, v. 29 init. ; secede from the Lacedaemonian to the Argive alliance, *ib.*; driven from Parrhasia by the Lacedaemonians, *ib.* 33 ; send, at Alcibiades' bidding, an embassy to Athens, *ib.* 43 fin., 44 ; make an alliance with Athens, *ib.* 46, 47 [cp. *ib.* 105 med.] ; send a guard to the Olympic games, *ib.* 50 med. ; conference between the Argive allies at Mantinea, *ib.* 55 init. ; the Mantineans aid the Argives when invaded by the Lacedaemonians, *ib.* 58 init. ; compel the Argives to break their truce with the Lacedaemonians, *ib.* 61, 62 ; their territory invaded by the Lacedaemonians, *ib.* 64 fin., 65 ; battle of Mantinea, *ib.* 66–74 ; one of the greatest of Hellenic battles, *ib.* 74 init. ; its moral effect, *ib.* 75 init. ; the Mantineans invade Epidaurus with their allies, *ib.* fin. ; frequent violations of the Treaty of Peace in the Mantinean and Epidaurian wars, *ib.* 26 med. ; the Mantinean alliance renounced by the Argives, *ib.* 78 ; the Mantineans are compelled to come to terms with the Lacedaemonians, *ib.* 81 init. ; induced by Alcibiades, join the Athenian expedition against Syracuse, vi. 29 med., 43 fin., 61 med., 67 init., 68 init. ; the Mantinean troops before Syracuse mercenaries, vii. 57 fin.

Marathon, battle of, i. 18 med. ; the Athenians boast that they fought alone there, *ib.* 73 fin. ; the dead buried on the field, ii. 34 med. ; Hippias at Marathon, vi. 59 fin.

Marathussa, an island off Clazomenae, viii. 31 fin.

Mareia, in Egypt, i. 104 init.

Marriage, questions about marriage occasion a war between Selinus and Egesta, vi. 6 init. ; marriages between the nobles and the people forbidden at Samos, viii. 21 fin. ; the water of the fountain Callirrhoè used at Athens in marriage rites, ii. 15 fin.

Massalia, colonised by the Phocaeans, i. 13 fin.

Mecyberna, in Chalcidicè, provision respecting, in the Treaty of Peace, v. 18, § vii ; captured by the Olynthians, *ib.* 39 init.

Medeon, in Acarnania, iii. 106 med.

Medes, part of the garrison of the White Castle in Memphis, i. 104 fin. ; in Pausanias' body guard, *ib.* 130 med. [*See* Persia, and War, The Persian.]

Megabates, Persian satrap of Dascylium, i. 129 init.

Megabazus, a Persian, ambassador to Lacedaemon, i. 109 init.

Megabyzus, son of Zopyrus, a Persian, reconquers Egypt, i. 109 med., 110.

Megacles, father of Onasimus, a Sicyonian, iv. 119 med.

Megara, Theagenes, tyrant of [before B.C. 632 ?], i. 126 init. ; the Megarians, pressed in war by the Corinthians, revolt from Lacedaemon to Athens, *ib.* 103 fin., see Forbes, Bk. i. p. 133 ; the Athenians build the Long Walls of Megara, *ib.* ; Megara is invaded by the Corinthians, *ib.* 105 med. ; the Megarian territory ravaged by the Lacedaemonians, *ib.* 108 init. ; the Megarians revolt from Athens, *ib.* 114 init. ; furnish aid to Corinth against Corcyra, *ib.* 27 med., 46 init., 48 fin. ; are excluded by the Athenians from their harbours, *ib.* 67 fin. [cp. i. 42 fin. (?)] ; complain against the Athenians at Sparta, *ib.* ; the

Lacedaemonians require the Athenians to remove this restriction, *ib.* 139 init. ; the Athenians bring counter charges against the Megarians, *ib.* med. ; the Megarians furnish the Lacedaemonians with ships, ii. 9 init.; the Athenians invade Megara, *ib.* 31 ; do so twice yearly until the capture of Nisaea, *ib.* [cp. iv. 66 init.] ; some Megarians suggest to Brasidas an attack on the Piraeus, ii. 93, 94 ; Minoa, the island in front of Megara, is captured by the Athenians, iii. 51 ; the Megarian exiles sheltered for a year by the Thebans at Plataea, *ib.* 68 med.; the popular leaders at Megara attempt to bring in the Athenians, iv. 66, 67 ; the Athenians capture the Long Walls and Nisaea, *ib.* 68, 69; Megara saved by Brasidas, *ib.* 70-73 ; he is received into the city, *ib.* 73 fin.; the exiles recalled, *ib.* 74 ; their cruel revenge, *ib.* ; long duration of the oligarchical government at Megara, *ib.* fin. ; Megarians reinforce the Boeotians after Delium, *ib.* 100 init. ; assent to the one year's truce, *ib.* 119 med.; dissatisfied with the treaty between the Lacedaemonians and Athenians, v. 17 fin. ; refuse to join the Argive alliance, *ib.* 31 fin.; act with the Boeotians, *ib.* 38 init.; aid the Lacedaemonians in the invasion of Argos, *ib.* 58 fin. 59 med., 60 med. ; Megarian exiles accompany the Athenians to Sicily, vi. 43 fin., vii. 57 med. ; the Megarians furnish ships to the Lacedaemonians, viii. 3 fin., 33 init.

Megara, in Sicily, founded from Thapsus, mother city of Selinus, vi. 4 init. ; depopulated by Gelo, *ib.*, *ib.* 94 init.; Lamachus wishes to make Megara the Athenian

Megara (*cont.*)—

naval station, *ib.* 49 fin.; fortified by the Syracusans, *ib.* 75 init.; its lands ravaged by the Athenians, *ib.* 94 init.; the Athenians capture a Syracusan ship off Megara, vii. 25 init.;—Megarian colonies in Sicily, vi. 4 init.; Chalcedon, a Megarian colony, iv. 75 fin.

Meiciades, a Corcyraean commander, i. 47 init.

Melaeans, a people in Italy, colonists of the Locrians, v. 5 fin.

Melancridas, a Spartan admiral, viii. 6 fin.

Melanopus, father of Laches, an Athenian, iii. 86 init.

Melanthus, a Lacedaemonian commander, viii. 4 med.

Meleas, a Lacedaemonian commander, iii. 5 med.

Melesander, an Athenian commander, sent to levy money in Lycia and Caria, ii. 69 med.

Melesias, an envoy from the Four Hundred to Sparta, viii. 86 fin.

Melesippus, a Lacedaemonian, sent to Athens with the final demands of the Lacedaemonians, i. 139 med.; sent by Archidamus to Athens, ii. 12; words of, on quitting Attica, *ib.* fin.

Melitia, in Achaea Phthiotis, iv. 78 init. and fin.

Melos, one of the Cyclades, ii. 9 fin.; a colony of the Lacedaemonians, v. 84 med.; hostile to the Athenians, ii. 9 fin., iii. 91 init.; ravaged by the Athenians, *ib.*; again attacked by the Athenians, v. 84 fin.; conference of the Melians with the Athenians, *ib.* 85–113. Melos blockaded by the Athenians, *ib.* 114, 115 fin., 116 med.; captured, *ib.* 116 fin.; fate of the citizens, *ib.*; capture of three Athenian ships off Melos, viii. 39 fin., 41 fin.

Memphis, attacked by the Athenians, i. 104 med.; captured by the Persians, *ib.* 109 fin.

Menander, an Athenian commander in Sicily, vii. 16 init.; commands under Demosthenes in the attack on Epipolae, *ib.* 43 med.; and in the last sea fight, *ib.* 69 fin.

Menas, a Lacedaemonian, swears to the Treaty of Peace and the Alliance, v. 19 med., 24 init.; goes as envoy to Chalcidicè, *ib.* 21.

Mendè, an Eretrian colony, iv. 123 init.; mother city of Eion in Chalcidicè, *ib.* 7; revolts to Brasidas, *ib.* 121 fin., 123 init.; the Mendaeans repulse the Athenians, *ib.* 129; the city is taken by the Athenians, *ib.* 130; the Peloponnesian garrison escapes to Scionè, *ib.* 131 fin.

Mendesian mouth of the Nile, i. 110 fin.

Menecolus, joint founder with Dascon of Camarina, vi. 5 med.

Menecrates, a Megarian, swears to the one year's Truce, iv. 119 med.

Menedaeus, a Spartan commander, iii. 100 fin.; deserts his Ambraciot allies, *ib.* 109, 111.

Menippus, father of Hippocles, an Athenian, viii. 13.

Meno, a Thessalian of Pharsalus, ii. 22 fin.

Mercenaries, Arcadian, iii. 34 init., vii. 19 med., 58 med. [cp. *ib.* 48 fin.], [Mantineans], iii. 109 med., vii. 57 fin.; Aetolian, vii. 57 fin.; Cretan, vii. 57 fin.; Iapygian, vii. 33 med., 57 fin.; Peloponnesian, i. 60, iv. 52 init., 76 med., viii. 28 fin.; Thracian, iv. 129 med., v. 6 fin., vii. 27 init., 29, 30; under Tissaphernes, viii. 25 init.

— foreign sailors in the Athenian service, i. 121 med., 141 init., vii. 13 med.

Messapians, an Ozolian Locrian tribe, iii. 101 fin.; an Iapygian tribe, vii. 33 med.

Messenè, in Sicily, originally named Zanclè, vi. 4 fin.; re-peopled by Anaxilas, *ib.*; geographical importance of, iv. 1 init., vi. 48 fin.; the Messenians come to terms with the Athenians, iii. 90 fin.; revolt from Athens, iv. 1 init.; Messenè becomes the headquarters of the Syracusans in the war with Rhegium, *ib.* 24; the Messenians attack and are defeated by the Naxians, *ib.* 25 med.; quarrels in Messenè, v. 5 init.; the Messenians refuse to receive Alcibiades, vi. 50 init.; attempt to betray Messenè to the Athenians frustrated by Alcibiades, *ib.* 74.

Messenians in Peloponnesus, old inhabitants of Laconia, i. 101 med., iv. 41 init.; use the Doric dialect, iii. 112 med., iv. 3 fin., 41 init.; settled by the Athenians at Naupactus, i. 103, ii. 9 med.; accompany the Athenians on an expedition round Peloponnesus, ii. 25 fin.; aid Phormio at Naupactus, *ib.* 90; serve under Phormio in Acarnania, *ib.* 102 init.; under Nicostratus at Corcyra, iii. 75 init., 81 init.; persuade Demosthenes to attack Aetolia, *ib.* 94-98; serve under Demosthenes at Olpae, *ib.* 107 init., 108 med., 112 med.; Demosthenes wishes to settle them at Pylos, iv. 3 fin.; a Messenian privateer joins him there, *ib.* 9 med.; the Messenians assist in the capture of Sphacteria, *ib.* 32 med.; stratagem of their general, *ib.* 36; garrison Pylos, *ib* 41 init.; withdrawn, v. 35 fin.; replaced, *ib.* 56; taken by the Athenians to Syracuse, vii. 57 med. [cp. *ib.* 31.] [Compare Helots.]

Metagenes, a Lacedaemonian, swears to the Fifty Years' Peace and the Alliance, v. 19 med.; *ib.* 24 init.

Metapontium, in Italy, allied to the Athenians, vii. 33 med.; lends aid against Syracuse, *ib.*, *ib.* 57 fin.

Methonè, between Epidaurus and Troezen, iv. 45; ordered to be restored under treaty, v. 18, § viii.

Methonè, in Macedonia, vi. 7 fin.; Methonaean light-armed troops under Nicias at Mendè, iv. 129 fin.

Methonè, in Laconia, ii. 25 init.

Methydrium, in Arcadia, v. 58 init.

Methymna, colonised from Boeotia, vii. 57 med.; opposite Harmatus, viii. 101 fin.; the Methymnaeans independent allies of Athens, iii. 50 med., vi. 85 med., vii. 57 med.; refuse to join in the revolt of Lesbos, iii. 2 init., 5 init.; defeated in an attack on Antissa, *ib.* 18 med.; revolt from Athens, viii. 22 fin.; re-conquered by the Athenians, *ib.* 23 fin.; Methymnaean exiles attempt Methymna, viii. 100 med.; induce Eresus to revolt, *ib.* fin.

Metics, metic hoplites at Athens, ii. 13 fin., 31 fin., iv. 90 init.; serve in the fleet, i. 143 init., iii. 16 init. [cp. vii. 63 med.]

Metropolis, in Acarnania, iii. 107 init.

Midius, a river near Abydos, viii. 106 init.

Might before right, i. 77, iii. 39 med., v 85 ff.

Migrations in ancient Hellas, i. 2, 12.

Miletus, situated on a peninsula, viii. 25 fin.; the Milesians, Ionians, and tributaries of the Athenians, vii. 57 init.; quarrel with the Samians, i. 115 init.; the Athenians defeat the Samians sailing from Miletus, *ib.* 116 med.;

Miletus (*cont.*)—

Milesian hoplites accompany the Athenians in the expedition against Corinth, iv. 42 init.; aid in the capture of Cythera, *ib.* 53, 54; the Milesians, at Alcibiades' persuasion, revolt from Athens, viii. 17; defeated by the Athenians, *ib.* 24 init.; conquer the Argive allies of the Athenians, but forced to retreat by the Athenians, *ib.* 25 [this defeat causes Alcibiades to fall into suspicion at Sparta, *ib.* 45 init.]; Alcibiades urges the Peloponnesian fleet to relieve Miletus, *ib.* 26 fin.; the Athenians retire from Miletus, *ib.* 27 fin.; Philip is put in command of Miletus, *ib.* 28 fin.; Tissaphernes comes there, *ib.* 29 init.; a division of the Athenian army watches Miletus, *ib.* 30 med.; Astyochus assumes command of the fleet at Miletus, *ib.* 33 init.; the Peloponnesians at Miletus, *ib.* 35, 36, 39; Astyochus leaves Miletus, *ib.* 41; Tissaphernes invites the Peloponnesians to Miletus, *ib.* 57 init., 60 fin.; the fleet at Miletus offers battle to the Athenians, *ib.* 63 init.; discontent of the Peloponnesian sailors at Miletus, *ib.* 78; the Milesians, acting in concert with the fleet, offer the Athenians battle, *ib.* 79; the Peloponnesians at Miletus send a fleet to the Hellespont, *ib.* 80; the sailors at Miletus break out into open violence against Astyochus, *ib.* 83, 84 init.; the Milesians expel the Persian garrison, *ib.* 84 med.; resent the reproof which they receive from Lichas, *ib.* fin.; send envoys to Sparta to complain of Astyochus, *ib.* 85 init., fin.; the Peloponnesian fleet leaves Miletus for the Hellespont, *ib.* 99, 100 init., 108 med.

Miltiades, the great, father of Cimon, i. 98 init., 100 init.

Mimas, Mount, viii. 34 fin.

Mindarus, sent from Lacedaemon to succeed Astyochus, viii. 85 init.; sails to the Hellespont, *ib.* 99; escapes the Athenian watch, *ib.* 101; captures four of the Athenian squadron in the Hellespont, *ib.* 102; defeated by the Athenians off Cynossema, *ib.* 104, 105.

Mines, gold, on the coast opposite Thasos, i. 100 med., iv. 105 init.; silver, at Laurium, ii. 55, vi. 91 fin.

Minoa, an island off Megara, captured by Nicias, iii. 51, iv. 67 init.; retained by the Athenians under the truce for a year, *ib.* 118, iii.

Minos, first possessor of a navy in Hellas, i. 4; conquers the Cyclades, *ib.*; expels the Carians, *ib.*; puts down piracy, *ib.*, *ib.* 8 med.

Minyans, the Minyan Orchomenus, iv. 76 med.

Molobrus, father of Epitadas, a Lacedaemonian, iv. 8 fin.

Molossians, Admetus, king of the Molossians, shelters Themistocles, i. 136, 137; the Molossians assist in the Lacedaemonian invasion of Acarnania, ii. 80 fin.

Molycrium, a Corinthian colony, subject to Athens, ii. 84 fin., iii. 102 init.; taken by the Peloponnesians, iii. 102 init.; the Molycrian Rhium, ii. 86 init.

Morgantinè, handed over to the Camarinaeans, iv. 65 init.

Motyè, a Phoenician settlement in Sicily, vi. 2 fin.

Munychia, a harbour of Athens, ii. 13 fin.; Peripoli stationed at Munychia, viii. 92 med.; a Dionysiac Theatre near, *ib.* 93 init.

Mycalè, battle of, i. 89 init.; Athenian and Peloponnesian fleets at Mycalè, viii. 79.

Mycalessus, in Boeotia, vii. 29 init.; sacked by Thracians in Athenian service, *ib.* 29, 30.

Mycenae, kingdom of, i. 9; the small remains of Mycenae do not disprove its former greatness, *ib.* 10.

Myconus, one of the Cyclades, iii. 29 med.

Mygdonia, part of, assigned to the Chalcidians by Perdiccas, i. 58 fin.; once inhabited by the Edonians, ii. 99 med.; ravaged by Sitalces, 100 med.

Mylae, a town of the Messenians in Sicily, iii. 90 med.; captured by the Athenians, *ib.* fin.

Myletidae, Syracusan exiles, take part in colonising Himera, vi. 5 init.

Myoneans, an Ozolian Locrian tribe, iii. 101 med.

Myonnesus, near Teos, iii. 32 init.

Myrcinus, an Edonian town, joins Brasidas, iv. 107 fin.; Myrcinian targeteers at the battle of Amphipolis, v. 6 fin.; Myrcinian cavalry there, *ib.* 10 fin.; Cleon killed by a Myrcinian targeteer, *ib.*

Myronides, an Athenian, defeats the Corinthians in Megaris, i. 105 fin.; defeats the Boeotians at Oenophyta, *ib.* 108 med. [cp. iv. 95 fin.]

Myrrhinè, wife of Hippias, the tyrant of Athens, vi. 55 med.

Myrtilus, an Athenian, swears to the Treaty of Peace and the Alliance, v. 19 fin., 24 med.

Myscon, a Syracusan general, viii. 85 fin.

Mysteries, profanation of the mysteries at Athens, vi. 28 med.; Alcibiades accused, *ib.*; supposed to be part of a plot against the democracy, *ib.* fin., 60 init., 61 init.; Alcibiades and some of his comrades summoned home from Sicily, *ib.* 53 init., 61 med.

Mytilenè, the Mytilenaeans revolt from Athens, iii. 2; send envoys to Lacedaemon and Athens, *ib.* 4; to Lacedaemon again, *ib.* 5 fin.; the Athenians blockade Mytilenè by sea, *ib.* 6; the envoys attend the Olympic festival at the bidding of the Lacedaemonians, *ib.* 8; their speech, *ib.* 9–14; the Mytilenaeans are taken into alliance by the Lacedaemonians, *ib.* 15 init.; unsuccessfully attack Methymna, *ib.* 18 init.; Mytilenè is blockaded by land, *ib.* fin.; Salaethus is sent from Lacedaemon to Mytilenè, *ib.* 25; Salaethus arms the people, who insist on surrendering the city, *ib.* 27, 28; the news reaching the Peloponnesian fleet, Teutiaplus advises an immediate attack on Mytilenè, *ib.* 29, 30; Paches sends Salaethus, and the most guilty of the Mytilenaeans to Athens, *ib.* 35; all the grown up citizens condemned to death by the Athenians, *ib.* 36 init.; feeling at Athens changes, *ib.* fin.; speech of Cleon against the recall of the decree, *ib.* 37–40; of Diodotus in favour of recalling it, *ib.* 41-48; the decree is recalled, *ib.* 49 init.; the second ship sent to stay the slaughter arrives in time by great exertions, *ib.* fin.; the captives at Athens put to death, their fleet and dependencies taken away, the walls of Mytilenè razed, *ib.* 50; Lesbian refugees take Rhoeteum and Antandrus, iv. 52; driven out again by the Athenians, *ib.* 75 med.; Mytilenè revolts a second time, viii. 22 fin.; recaptured by the Athenians, *ib.* 23 med.; garrisoned by the Athenians, viii. 100 med.

Myus, a city in Caria (Ionia), iii. 19 fin.; given by the King to Themistocles, i. 138 fin.

N.

Nature, human, 'always ready to transgress the laws,' iii. 84 med.; 'prone to domineer over the subservient,' iv. 61 med., v. 105 init.; prompts men to accept a proffered empire, i. 76 med.; ever credulous, *ib.* 20; jealous, ii. 35 fin.; changes with the changes of fortune, i. 84 init., 140 init., ii. 61, iii. 39 med., iv. 17 fin.; prone to error, iii. 45 init., iv. 18 init.; misled in its judgments by hope, iii. 39 med., iv. 108 med.; yields when met in a yielding spirit, iv. 19 fin.; inherent vanity of, v. 68 init.; sameness of, i. 21 fin., 76 med., iii. 45 fin., 82 init.

Naucleides, a Plataean, invites the Thebans to Plataea, ii. 2 med.

Naucrates, father of Damotimus, a Sicyonian, iv. 119 med.

Naupactus, settled by the Helots from Ithomè, i. 103 med.; allied to the Athenians, ii. 9 med.; becomes the head-quarters of an Athenian fleet, *ib.* 69, 84 fin., 92 fin., iii. 114 init., iv. 13 med.; the Peloponnesians hope to take it, ii. 80 med.; victory of the Athenians off Naupactus, *ib.* 83, 84 [cp. iii. 78]; feigned attack of the Peloponnesians upon, ii. 90 init.; second victory of the Athenians off, *ib.* 91, 92; Phormio makes an expedition from Naupactus into Acarnania, *ib.* 102, 103; Phormio's son, Asopius, succeeds him at Naupactus, iii. 7; Nicostratus sails to Corcyra from Naupactus, *ib.* 75 init.; the Messenians of Naupactus persuade Demosthenes to attack Aetolia, *ib.* 94 fin.–98; Demosthenes remains at Naupactus after his defeat, *ib.* 98 fin.; the Aetolians persuade the Lacedaemonians to make an expedition against Naupactus, *ib.* 100; Demosthenes, by the aid of the Acarnanians, saves the place, *ib.* 102; Athenian ships from Naupactus come to Pylos, iv. 13 med.; the Messenians of Naupactus send a garrison to Pylos, *ib.* 41 init.; the Athenian forces at Naupactus capture Anactorium, *ib.* 49; Demosthenes comes to Naupactus to aid Hippocrates in the invasion of Boeotia, *ib.* 76, 77; the Corinthians prepare a fleet to attack the Athenians at Naupactus, vii. 17 fin., 19 fin.; Demosthenes and Eurymedon send reinforcements, *ib.* 31 med.; indecisive action off Naupactus, *ib.* 34; the Messenians of Naupactus send a force to Sicily, *ib.* 31 init., 57 med.

Naval tactics: unskilfulness of earlier tactics, i. 49 init. [cp. vii. 62]; Athenian naval tactics, ii. 83, 84, 89 med., 91, iii. 78, vii. 36, 49 med.

Navy: Minos the first possessor of a navy, i. 4; the fleet which carried the Hellenes to Troy, *ib.* 9 fin., 10 med.; the early Hellenic navies, *ib.* 13, 14 [cp. iii. 104 init.]; progress of naval invention, *ib.* 13 init., 14 fin. [*see* Ships]; importance of its navy to Athens, *ib.* 93, ii. 13 init., vii. 66 init., viii. 66 [*see* Athens]; the greatest number reached by the Athenian navy, iii. 17 init.; composition and number of the Lacedaemonian fleet, ii. 7 fin., viii. 3 fin.; quick deterioration of navies, vii. 14 init.

Naxos, subjugated by the Athenians, i. 98 fin.; Themistocles is

Naxos *(cont.)*—

carried to Naxos in his flight, and narrowly escapes the Athenians there, *ib.* 137 init.

Naxos [in Sicily], founded from Chalcis by Thucles, vi. 3 init. ; altar of Apollo the Founder at, *ib.* ; the Naxians kinsmen of the Leontines, vi. 20 med. ; defeat the Messenians, iv. 25 ; receive the Athenian expedition, vi. 50 med. ; become allies of Athens, vii. 14 med., *ib.* 57 fin. ; Naxos is made the winter quarters of the Athenians, vi. 72 init., 74 fin , 75 med. ; they abandon it for Catana, *ib.* 88 med. ; the Naxians furnish the Athenians with cavalry, *ib.* 98 init.

Neapolis, a Carthaginian factory in Libya, vii. 50 init.

Neighbours ever enemies, iv. 95 med. [cp. v. 69 med., vi. 88 init.]

Nemea, in Locris, death of Hesiod at, iii. 96 init. ; temple of Nemean Zeus, *ib.*

Nemea, in Argolis, v. 58-60.

Neodamodes, meaning of the word, vii. 58 med. ; settled with the Helots at Lepreum, v. 34 med. ; Neodamodes at Mantinea, *ib.* 67 init. ; sent to Syracuse with the Helots by the Lacedaemonians, vii. 19 med., 58 med.; three hundred Neodamodes sent out to Agis, viii. 4 med.

Nericus, in Leucas, iii. 7 fin.

Nestus, a river in Thrace, ii. 96 fin.

Nicanor, a Chaonian leader, ii. 80 fin.

Nicasus, a Megarian, swears to the one year's Truce, iv. 119 med.

Niceratus, father of Nicias, an Athenian, iii. 51 init., 91 init., iv. 27 fin., 42 init., 53 init., 119 fin., 129 med., v. 16 init., 83 fin., vi. 8 med.

Niciades, an Athenian, epistates at the passing of the one year's Truce, iv. 118 fin.

Nicias, of Gortys, ii. 85 fin.

Nicias, father of Hagnon, an Athenian, ii. 58 init., iv. 102 med.

Nicias, his religiousness, vii. 77 med., 86 fin. ; his superstitious temper, *ib.* 50 fin. ; his dilatoriness, *ib.* 42 med. ; his ill health, vi. 102 med., vii. 15 fin., 77 init.; captures Minoa, iii. 51 init. ; ravages Melos, *ib.* 91 init. ; defeats the Tanagraeans, *ib.* fin.; ravages Locris, *ib.* ; yields his command at Pylos to Cleon, iv. 27, 28 ; leads an expedition into the Corinthian territory, *ib.* 42-45; captures Cythera, *ib.* 53, 54 ; swears to the one year's Truce, *ib.* 119 fin. ; wounded in an attempt to take Mendè, *ib.* 129 ; his anxiety for peace, v. 16 init., 43 med. [cp. vii. 86 med.] ; swears to the Treaty of Peace and the Alliance, v. 19 fin., 24 med. ; goes on an unsuccessful embassy to Sparta, *ib.* 46 ; designed for the command of an expedition to Chalcidicè, which Perdiccas frustrates, *ib.* 83 fin.; appointed one of the generals in Sicily, vi. 8 med. ; speech of, *ib.* 9-14 ; second speech of, *ib.* 20-23 ; gives an estimate of the forces required, *ib.* 25 ; argues in a council of war for an attack on Selinus, *ib.* 47 ; goes to Egesta, *ib.* 62 ; defeats the Syracusans, *ib.* 67-70; saves Epipolae, *ib.* 102; becomes sole commander after the death of Lamachus, *ib.* 103 fin. ; negotiates with the Syracusans, *ib.* [cp. vii. 48 init., *ib.* 49 init., *ib.* 73 fin., *ib.* 86 fin.] ; fails to prevent the coming of Gylippus, vii. 1, 2 ; fortifies Plemmyrium, *ib.* 4 med. ; defeated by the Syracusans, *ib.* 6 ; sends a dispatch to Athens, *ib.* 8, 10, 11-15 ; destroys by an

Nicias (*cont.*)—

ambush the Syracusan reinforcements, *ib.* 32 ; left in the Athenian lines while Demosthenes attacks Epipolae, *ib.* 43 med.; swayed by information from Syracuse and fear of public opinion at home, he refuses to abandon the siege, *ib.* 48, 49 ; yields at last, *ib.* 50 med.; but, an eclipse of the moon occurring, decides in accordance with the general feeling to remain thrice nine days, *ib.* 50 fin. ; exhorts the army before the last battle, *ib.* 61–64 ; addresses the trierarchs, *ib.* 69 ; encourages his retreating soldiers, *ib.* 76, 77 ; commands one division in the retreat, *ib.* 78 init. foll. ; overtaken and compelled to surrender, *ib.* 83–85 ; put to death by the Syracusans, *ib.* 86.

Nicolaus, a Lacedaemonian ambassador to Persia, ii. 67 init.

Nicomachus, a Phocian, betrays to the Lacedaemonians the Athenian plan for the conquest of Boeotia, iv. 89 init.

Nicomedes, a Lacedaemonian, general in place of King Pleistoanax, i. 107 init.

Nicon, a Boeotian, commands the reinforcements to Syracuse, vii. 19 med.

Niconidas, a Thessalian, escorts Brasidas through Thessaly, iv. 78 init.

Nicostratus, an Athenian general, sails to Corcyra ; his humane conduct there, iii. 75 ; colleague of Nicias, iv. 53 init. ; assists in the capture of Cythera, *ib.* 53, 54 ; of Mendè, *ib.* 129, 130 ; and in the blockade of Scionè, *ib.* 131 ; swears to the one year's Truce, *ib.* 119 fin. ; brings with Laches an expedition to Argos, v. 61 init. ; falls at Mantinea, *ib.* 74 fin.

Nightingale, called by the poets the 'Daulian Bird,' ii. 29 init.

Nile, i. 104 med., 110 fin.

Nine Ways, old name of Amphipolis, i. 100 fin., iv. 102 med.

Nisaea, the harbour of Megara, ii. 93 init., iv. 66 fin ; connected with the city by the Long Walls, i. 103 fin. ; occupied by the Athenians, *ib.*, *ib.* 114 init. ; restored under the thirty years' Peace, *ib.* 115 init. ; Cleon demands its surrender with other places after the blockade of Sphacteria, iv. 21 fin.; garrisoned by Peloponnesian forces, *ib.* 66 fin. ; captured by the Athenians, *ib.* 69 ; Brasidas arrives too late to save it, *ib.* 70 fin.; cavalry engagement before Nisaea, *ib.* 72 fin. ; the Athenians at Nisaea refuse battle with Brasidas, *ib.* 73 [cp. Brasidas' account, *ib.* 85 fin., 108 med.] ; not given up under the treaty, v. 17 med.

Nisus, Temple of, at Nisaea, iv. 118, iii.

Nomothetae, appointed at Athens after the deposition of the Four Hundred, viii. 97 med.

Notium, seditions there, Paches gains the city by a trick, iii. 34 ; handed over to the Colophonians by the Athenians, *ib.* fin.

Nymphodorus, of Abdera, negotiates an alliance between his brother-in-law Sitalces and the Athenians, ii. 29.

O.

Obols, Aeginetan, v. 47, iv.

Ocytus, father of Aeneas, a Corinthian, iv. 119 med.

Odomantians, a people in Thrace, ii. 101 med. ; Polles, their king, v. 6 init.

Odrysians, a people in Thrace, their empire founded by Teres,

Odrysians (*cont.*)—

ii. 29 init. ; Sitalces, their king, becomes the ally of the Athenians, *ib.* fin. ; his campaign against Perdiccas, *ib.* 95, 98–101 ; the greatness and wealth of his kingdom, *ib.* 96, 97.

Odysseus, his passage through Charybdis, iv. 24 fin.

Oeantheans, an Ozolian Locrian tribe, iii. 101 fin.

Oeneon, a town in Ozolian Locris, iii. 95 fin., 68 fin., 102 init.

Oeniadae, in Acarnania, its situation, ii. 102 init. ; hostile to the Athenians, *ib.* 82, 102 init., iii. 94 init. ; besieged by Pericles, i. 111 fin. ; attacked by Asopius, iii. 7 med. ; the fugitives from Olpae find refuge there, *ib.* 114 med. ; compelled to enter the Athenian alliance, iv. 77 fin.

Oenoè, an Athenian fort on the Boeotian frontier, ii. 18 init. ; unsuccessfully attacked by the Lacedaemonians, *ib.* 19 init. ; besieged by the Corinthians, viii. 98 ; betrayed to the Boeotians by Aristarchus, *ib.*

Oenophyta, battle of, i. 108 med. [cp. iv. 95 fin.]

Oenussae, islands before Chios, viii. 24 init.

Oesymè, in Thrace, a Thasian colony, revolts from Athens, iv. 107 fin.

Oetaeans, a people in Thessaly, iii. 92 init., viii. 3 init.

Oligarchy, oligarchies quickly fall a victim to private ambition, viii. 89 fin. ; their cruelty and unscrupulousness, *ib.* 48 fin. ; their selfishness, vi. 39 fin. ; the oligarchies everywhere hostile to Athens, i. 19 init., 76 init., 144 med., iii. 47 med., 82 init.

Olophyxus, in Actè, iv. 109 med.

Olorus, father of Thucydides, iv. 104 fin.

Olpae, a hill fort in Acarnania, iii. 105 init. ; battle of Olpae, *ib.* 106-109 ; the Peloponnesians steal away from Olpae under truce with Demosthenes, *ib.* 111 ; destruction of the Ambraciot reinforcements on the way to Olpae, *ib.* 110, 112, 113.

Olpaeans, a people in Orolian Locris, iii. 101 fin.

Olympia, treasury at, i. 121 med., 143 init. ;—the Mytilenaean envoys meet the allies in council at Olympia, iii. 8 ; treaties inscribed on pillars there, v. 18, xi ; 47 fin. ;—games at Olympia, i. 126 init., iii. 8, v. 49, 50 ; the treaty between Athens and Argos ordered to be renewed thirty days before the festival, v. 47 fin. ; exclusion of the Lacedaemonians by the Eleans, *ib.* 49 ;—Olympic victors : Cylon, i. 126 init. ; Dorieus, iii. 8 ; Androsthenes, v. 49 init. ; Lichas, *ib.* 50 med. ;—Olympic Truce, *ib.* 49 med. ;—Olympian Zeus, *ib.* 31 med., 50 init.

Olympieum, temple near Syracuse, vi. 64 med., 65 fin., 70 fin., 75 init., vii. 4 fin., 37, 42 fin.

Olympus, Mount, between Thessaly and Macedonia, iv. 78 fin.

Olynthus, in Chalcidicè, its situation, i. 63 med. ; the Chalcidians leave their towns on the coast and settle at, *ib.* 58 fin. ; battle of, *ib.* 62, 63 ; Olynthian reinforcements decide an engagement before Spartolus, ii. 79 ; Brasidas sends the women and children from Mendè and Scionè to Olynthus, iv. 123 fin. ; the Olynthians exchange prisoners with the Athenians, v. 3 fin. ; provision respecting Olynthus in the Treaty of Peace, *ib.* 18, § vi ; the Olynthians capture Mecyberna, *ib.* 39 init.

Omens eagerly sought for at the commencement of the War, ii. 8 med.

Onasimus, a Sicyonian, swears to the one year's Truce, iv. 119 med.

Onetorides, father of Diemporus, a Theban, ii. 2 med.

Oneum, Mount, in Corinthian territory, iv. 44 med.

Onomacles, an Athenian commander, viii. 25 init., 30 med.

Ophioneans, an Aetolian tribe, iii. 94 fin., 96 med. ; Tolophus, an Ophionean, *ib.* 100 init.

Opici, drove the Sicels out of Italy, vi. 2 med. ; Opicia, vi. 4 med.

Opus, in Locris, ii. 32.

Oracle, Delphian, consulted by Cylon, i. 126 init. ; by the Epidamnians, *ib.* 25 init. ; by the Lacedaemonians before beginning the war, *ib.* 118 fin., 123 med., ii. 54 med. ; before colonising Heraclea, iii. 92 fin. ; orders Pausanias to be buried in the temple of Athenè, i. 134 fin.; provision respecting, in the one year's Truce, iv. 118, i. ; — ancient oracle about the suppliant of Ithomaean Zeus, current among the Lacedaemonians, i. 103 med.; about Alcmaeon, ii. 102 fin. ; about Hesiod, iii. 96 init. ; about the Pelasgian ground, ii. 17 med.; current at Athens during the plague, *ib.* 54 init. ; about the restoration of Pleistoanax, v. 16 med. ; about the restoration of the Delians, *ib.* 32 init. ; about the thrice nine years, current at the beginning of the War, *ib.* 26 fin. ; the only one justified by events, *ib.*; — oracles recited at the beginning of the War, ii. 8 med., 21 fin. ;—the oracles helpless in the plague, *ib.* 47 fin. ; often ruin those who trust them, v. 103 fin.; unpopularity of oracle-mongers after Sicilian expedition, viii. 1.

Orchomenus, in Arcadia, besieged by the Argives and Athenians, v. 61 med. ; surrenders, *ib.* fin.

Orchomenus, in Boeotia, i. 113 init. ; earthquakes at, iii. 87 fin. ; formerly called the 'Minyan,' iv. 76 init. ; conspiracy to betray the city to the Athenians, *ib.*

Orestes, exiled son of a Thessalian king, i. 111 init.

Orestheum, in Maenalia, iv. 134 med., v. 64 init.

Orestians, a people in Epirus, ii 80 fin.

Oreus (= Hestiaea), the only city retained by Athens in Euboea after the second revolt, viii. 95 fin.

Orneae, in Argolis, the Orneatae on the Argive side at Mantinea, v. 67 fin., 72 fin., 74 med. ; the Argive exiles settled at Orneae, vi. 7 init. ; the town treacherously captured by the Argives, *ib.* med.

Orobiae, in Euboea, iii. 89 init.

Oroedus, king of the Paravaeans, ii. 80 fin.

Oropus, subject to the Athenians, ii. 23 fin , iii. 91 med., iv. 96 fin.; on the Athenian border, iv. 91 med., 99 med.; provisions brought from Euboea to Athens through Oropus, vii. 28 init. ; betrayed to the Boeotians, viii. 60 init. ; a Peloponnesian squadron puts in at Oropus, *ib.* 95.

Ortygia, the original site of Syracuse, vi. 3 med.

Oscius, a river in Thrace, ii. 96 fin.

Ostracism of Themistocles, i. 135 ; of Hyperbolus, viii. 73 init.

P.

Paches, an Athenian commander, sent with reinforcements to Mytilenè, iii. 18 fin. ; obtains possession of the city, *ib.* 27, 28; cha˞es Alcidas to Patmos, *ib.*

Paches (*cont.*)—

33 med.; captures Notium by treachery, *ib.* 34; reduces Pyrrha and Eresus, *ib.* 35 init.; sends Salaethus captive to Athens with the most guilty of the Mytilenaeans, *ib.*, *ib.* 50 init.; receives orders to put to death all the grown up citizens of Mytilenè, *ib.* 36; a countermand reaches him in time to save the city, *ib.* 49 fin.

Paean, confusion occasioned at Epipolae by the Doric Paeans of the Athenian allies, vii. 44 fin.

Paeonians, subjects of Sitalces, ii. 96 med., 98 med.

Pagondas, one of the Boeotarchs from Thebes, iv. 91 med.; his speech to his soldiers, *ib.* 92; defeats the Athenians at Delium, *ib.* 93, 96.

Palaereans, in Acarnania, Sollium given to them by the Athenians, ii. 30 init.

Palè, in Cephallenia, ii. 30 fin.; the Paleans furnish four ships to the Corinthians, i. 27 fin.

Pallenè, peninsula in Chalcidicè, i. 56 init., 64, iv. 116 init., 120 init., 123 init., 129 init.; its isthmus, i. 64 init., iv. 120 med.

Pamillus colonises Selinus from Megara in Sicily, vi. 4 init.

Pamphylia, i. 100 init.

Panactum, an Athenian fortress on the Boeotian border, betrayed to the Boeotians, v. 3 fin.; ordered to be restored under the Treaty of Peace, *ib.* 18, § viii; the Lacedaemonians promise to get it back for the Athenians, *ib.* 35 fin.; they entreat the Boeotians to give it up to them, *ib.* 36 fin.; the Boeotians demolish it, *ib.* 39 fin., 42 init.; rage of the Athenians at its destruction, *ib.* 42 fin.; the Lacedaemonians demand Pylos in return for Panactum, *ib.*

44 fin.; the Athenians request the Lacedaemonians to rebuild and restore it, *ib.* 46 med.

Panaeans, in Thrace, ii. 101 med.

Panaerus, a friend of Brasidas in Thessaly, iv. 78 init.

Panathenaea, the Great, at Athens, v. 47 fin., vi. 56 med.; the Panathenaic procession, i. 20 fin., vi. 57 init.

Pancratium, Androsthenes victor in the, at Olympia, v. 49 init.

Pandion, king of Athens, ii. 29 init.

Pangaeus, Mount, in Thrace, ii. 99 med.

Panic, liability of great armies to panics, iv. 125 init., vii. 80 med.

Panormus, in Achaia, ii. 86 med., 92 init.

Panormus, in Milesian territory, viii. 24 init.

Panormus, in Sicily, a Phoenician settlement, vi. 2 fin.

Pantacyas, a river in Sicily, vi. 4 init.

Paralians, part of the Malians, iii. 92 init.

Paralus, a district in Attica, ii. 55 init.

Paralus, the Athenian sacred vessel, iii. 33, 77 fin.; the crew all freemen and ardent enemies of oligarchy, viii. 73 fin.; assist the democratic revolution at Samos, *ib.*; go to Athens, and are ill received by the oligarchs, *ib.* 74; sent to cruise off Euboea, *ib.*, *ib.* 86 fin.; ordered to convey ambassadors to Sparta, *ib.* 86 fin.; mutiny and give up the ambassadors to the Argives, *ib.*; come to Samos with Argive envoys, *ib.*

Paravaeans, a people in Epirus, ii. 80 fin.

Parnassus, Mount, in Phocis, iii. 95 init.

Parnes, Mount, in Attica, ii. 23 init.

Paros, Thasos a Parian colony, iv. 104 fin.

Parrhasians, in Arcadia, campaign of the Lacedaemonians against, v. 33.

Party associations, evil of, iii. 82 med. ; party spirit, growth of, in Hellas, *ib.* fin.

Pasitelidas, a Lacedaemonian, made governor of Toronè, iv. 132 fin. ; defeated and captured by the Athenians, v. 3 med.

Patmos, iii. 33 med.

Patrae, in Achaia, ii. 83 med., 84 fin., v. 52 fin.

Patrocles, father of Tantalus, a Lacedaemonian, iv. 57 med.

Pausanias, guardian of Pleistarchus, i. 132 init. ; the victor of Plataea, ii. 71 med., iii. 54 fin., 58 med., 68 init. ; takes command of the Hellenic forces, i. 94 ; captures Byzantium, *ib., ib.* 129 med. ; becomes unpopular, *ib.* 95 init. ; summoned to Sparta, *ib.* ; acquitted of conspiracy with Persia, *ib., ib.* 128 init ; negotiates with Xerxes, *ib.* 128-130 ; recalled to Sparta and imprisoned, *ib.* 131 ; intrigues with the Helots, 132 med. ; betrayed by his servant, *ib.* fin , 133 ; escapes to the temple of Athenè, *ib.* 134 init ; is starved to death, *ib.* med. ; ordered by the Delphian oracle to be buried in the temple, *ib.* fin.

Pausanias, son of Pleistoanax, king of Sparta, iii. 26 med.

Pausanias, a Macedonian, brother of Derdas, i. 61 fin., cp. *ib.* 59 fin.

Pay for holding office abolished by the oligarchs at Athens, viii. 65 fin., 67 fin. ; the same provision adopted in the new constitution, *ib.* 97 med. ; pay of the Athenian senate, *ib.* 69 fin. ;—pay of sailors usually half a drachma, viii. 29 init., 45 init. ; Tissaphernes pays a drachma for a month, *ib.* 29 init. ; the double rate paid to the sailors in the fleet at Potidaea and to those engaged in the Sicilian expedition, iii. 17 fin., vi. 31 med. ;—pay of Athenian heavy-armed, iii. 17 med. ; rates of pay fixed by the treaty between Athens and Argos for various troops, v. 47, iv. ; pay of Thracian mercenaries, vii. 27 init.

Peace of five years between Peloponnesians and Athenians, i. 112 init. ; of thirty years after the recovery of Euboea, *ib.* 67 med., 87 fin., 115 init. 146, ii. 2 init. ; violated by the attack on Plataea, *ib.* 7 init. ; treaty of peace and alliance for fifty years at the end of the first ten years of the War, v. 18 ; this peace only nominal, *ib.* 26 ; peace and alliance for one hundred years between the Acarnanians and Ambraciots, iii. 114 med.; treaty of peace between Argos and Lacedaemon, v. 77 ; treaty of alliance, *ib.* 79 ; the three treaties between Lacedaemon and Persia, viii. 17 fin., 18, 36, 37, 57 fin., 58 ; treaties inscribed on columns, v. 18, xi ; 23, iv ; 47 fin., 56 med.

Peace, not always preferable to war, i. 120 med. ; 'has honours and glories of her own,' iv. 62 init.

Pedaritus, a Lacedaemonian, sent from Lacedaemon as governor of Chios, viii. 28 fin. ; arrives there, *ib.* 32 med. ; refuses to aid Astyochus in the revolt of Lesbos, *ib.* fin. ; deceived by a trick of certain Erythraean prisoners, *ib.* 33 fin. ; alters the government of Chios, *ib.* 38 med. ; requests the aid of Astyochus, *ib.* 38 fin., 40 init. ; complains to Sparta of Astyochus, 38 fin. ;

Pedaritus (*cont.*)—

falls in an engagement before Chios, *ib.* 55 fin.

Pegae, in Megaris, commands the pass over Mount Geraneia, i. 107 med.; becomes subject to the Athenians, *ib.* 103 fin., 111 med.; restored under the thirty years' Peace, *ib.* 115 init.; demanded with other places by the Athenians after the blockade of Sphacteria, iv. 21 fin.; occupied by Megarian exiles, *ib.* 66 init., 74 init. (cp. iii. 68 med.).

Peiraïkè, ii. 23 fin.

Peisander, one of the leading oligarchs at Athens, viii. 90 init.; sent to Athens to forward the oligarchical conspiracy, *ib.* 49; gains the consent of the people, *ib.* 53, 54; is sent to negotiate with Alcibiades and Tissaphernes, *ib.* 54 init.; baffled by Alcibiades, *ib.* 56; sent home with orders to put down democracy in the cities, *ib.* 64, 65 init.; proposes to substitute a government of Four Hundred for the democracy, *ib.* 67; breaks up the old senate and installs the Four Hundred, *ib.* 69, 70; stirs up an oligarchical revolution at Samos, *ib.* 73 init.; retreats to Decelea on the dissolution of the Four Hundred, *ib.* 98 init.

Peithias, a Corcyraean popular leader murdered by the oligarchs, iii. 70.

Pelasgians, most widely spread of ancient tribes in Greece, i. 3 init.; the Pelasgians of Actè, iv. 109 fin.; the 'Pelasgian Ground' at Athens, ii. 17 med.

Pelè, an island off Clazomenae, viii. 31 fin.

Pella, in Macedonia, ii. 99 med., 100 med.

Pellenè, in Achaea, said by the Scionaeans to be their mother

city, iv. 120 init.; the Pellenaeans allies of Lacedaemonians, ii. 9 init.; join Lacedaemonians in the invasion of Argos, v. 58 fin., 59 med., 60 med.; furnish Lacedaemonians with ships, viii. 3 fin.; lose one ship in the battle of Cynossema, *ib.* 106 med.

Pellichus, father of Aristeus, a Corinthian, i. 29 init.

Peloponnesus, its name derived from Pelops, i. 9 init.; frequent changes of its ancient inhabitants, *ib.* 2 med.; its conquest by the Heraclidae, *ib.* 12 med.; divided into five parts, *ib.* 10 init.; the greater part of Sicily and Italy colonised from Peloponnesus, *ib.* 12 fin. [cp. vi. 77 med.]; all, except Argos and Achaea, included in the Lacedaemonian alliance, ii. 9 init.; the plague little felt in Peloponnesus, *ib.* 54 fin.; provisions respecting the Peloponnesian cities in the treaties between Lacedaemon and Argos, v. 77, §§ v, vi; 76, §§ ii, iv, v, vi; employment of Peloponnesian mercenaries, i. 60, iii. 34 init., 109 med., iv. 52 init., 76 med., vii. 19 med., 57 fin., 58 med. [cp. *ib.* 48 fin.], viii. 28 fin.; Pericles' account of the Peloponnesian character, i. 141, 142 [For actions performed under Lacedaemonian leadership, *see* Lacedaemon.]

Pelops, gave his name to the Peloponnesus, i. 9 init.

Pelorus, promontory near Messenè in Sicily, iv. 25 init.

Penalties, increased severity of penalties does not add to their effectiveness, iii. 45.

entecosties, a division of the Lacedaemonian army, v. 68.

Politics, in politics, as in the arts, the new must prevail over the old, i. 71 init.; general interest in politics at Athens, ii. 40 init.

Peparethus, island of, earthquake there, iii. 89 fin.

Perdiccas, king of Macedonia, quarrels with the Athenians, i. 56, 57; sends envoys to Sparta, *ib.* 57 med.; persuades the Chalcidians to revolt, *ib.* 57, 58; assigns the Chalcidians part of Mygdonia, *ib.* 58 fin.; reconciled to the Athenians, *ib.* 61 med.; deserts them, *ib.* 62 init., 63; again reconciled to the Athenians, ii. 29 fin.; sends assistance to the Ambraciots, *ib.* 80 fin.; his perfidy to Sitalces, *ib.* 95 med.; attacked by Sitalces, *ib.* 95–101; gains over Seuthes, *ib.* 101 fin.; marries his sister to Seuthes, *ib.*; invites Brasidas, iv. 79; declared an enemy by the Athenians, *ib.* 82; in concert with Brasidas makes war upon Arrhibaeus, *ib.* 83; assists Brasidas at Amphipolis, *ib.* 103 med., 107 fin.; Perdiccas and Brasidas defeat the Lyncestians, *ib.* 124; Perdiccas loses his army by a panic, *ib.* 125 init.; quarrels with Brasidas, *ib.* 128 fin.; joins the Athenians, *ib.* 132 init.; Cleon demands reinforcements from him, v. 6 init.; joins the Lacedaemonian and Argive alliance, *ib.* 80 med.; blockaded by the Athenians, *ib.* 83 fin.; has his territory ravaged by the Athenians, vi. 7 fin.; aids the Athenians to attack Amphipolis, vii. 9.

Pericles, the Athenian statesman, leads an expedition to Sicyon and to Oeniadae, i. 111 fin.; subdues Euboea, *ib.* 114; conquers Samos, *ib.* 116, 117; under the 'curse of the Goddess,' *ib.* 127 init.; leader of the Athenian state, *ib.* fin.; opposed to the Lacedaemonians, *ib.*; his speech, *ib.* 140–144; the Athenians

follow his counsel, *ib.* 145, ii. 12 init.; he promises his lands to the public if spared by the enemy, ii. 13 init.; his advice to the Athenians, *ib.*, *ib.* 22 init.; the Athenians grow angry with him when the Lacedaemonians appear in Attica, *ib.* 21, 22; he commands in the invasion of Megara, *ib.* 31 init.; his funeral speech, *ib.* 35–46; commands an expedition round Peloponnese, *ib.* 56 [cp. vi. 31 init.]; blamed and fined by the Athenians, ii. 59, 65; his defence, *ib.* 60–64; elected general, *ib.* 65 init.; his death and eulogy, *ib.* 65 med.

Periclidas, father of Athenaeus, a Lacedaemonian, iv. 119 init.

Perieres, one of the founders of Zanclè, vi. 4 fin.

Perioeci, the, of Thuria and Aethaea aid the Helots to revolt, i. 101 init.; the Perioeci of Elis defeated by the Athenians, ii. 25 fin.; the Lacedaemonian Perioeci assist in the foundation of Heraclea, iii. 92 fin.; present at the attack on Pylos, iv. 8 init.; the Perioeci of Cythera, *ib.* 53 med.; Phrynis, one of the Perioeci, sent as commissioner to Chios, viii. 6 fin.; Chian Perioeci, *ib.* 22 fin.

Peripoli, at Athens, or 'frontier guard,' iv. 67 init., viii. 92 med.; Phrynichus assassinated by one of them, viii. 92 init.

Perrhaebia, in Thessaly, iv. 78 fin.

Persia, visited by the plague, ii. 48 init.; Persians prefer giving to receiving, *ib.* 97 med.; Persian apparel and luxury affected by Pausanias, i. 130; Persian language learned by Themistocles, *ib.* 138 init.; Persian dispatches written in the Assyrian cha-

Persia (*cont.*)—

racter, iv. 50 init. ; Persian nobles quartered at Athens, i. 89 fin. ; Persians form part of the garrison in Memphis, *ib.* 104 fin. ; Persian spoil in the Acropolis at Athens, ii. 13 med. [*See* Kings, Persian, Medes, and War, The Persian.]

Perseus, i. 9 med.

Petra, promontory near Rhegium, vii. 35 fin.

Phacium, in Thessaly, iv. 78 fin.

Phaeacians, their ancient naval renown, i. 25 fin.

Phaeax, an Athenian envoy in Sicily, v. 4, 5.

Phaedimus, a Lacedaemonian envoy, v. 42 init.

Phaeinis, priestess of Herè at Argos, iv. 133 fin.

Phaenippus, an Athenian, registrar at the conclusion of the one year's Truce, iv. 118 fin.

Phagres, in Thrace, ii. 99 med.

Phalerum, one of the harbours at Athens, i. 107 init., ii. 13 fin.; Phaleric Wall, *ib., ib.*

Phalius, a Corinthian, the founder of Epidamnus, i. 24 init.

Phanae, in Chios, viii. 24 med.

Phanomachus, an Athenian, commander at Potidaea, ii. 70 init.

Phanoteus, in Phocis, iv. 76 med., 89 med.

Pharax, father of Styphon, a Lacedaemonian, iv. 38 init.

Pharnabazus, (i) satrap of the Hellespont, viii. 6 init., 62 init. ; begs aid from Lacedaemon, *ib.* 8 init., 39 init., 80 med., 99 med., 108 med., 109 init. ; (ii) father of Pharnaces, ii. 67 med.

Pharnaces, three Persians,(i) father of Artabazus, i. 129 init. ; (ii) son of Pharnabazus, ii. 67 med. ; settles the Delians at Adramyttium, v. 1 fin. [cp. viii. 108 med.]; (iii) father of Pharnabazus, satrap

of the Hellespont, viii. 6 init. [? same as ii].

Pharnaces, the sons of, viii. 58 init.

Pharos, in Egypt, i. 104 init.

Pharsalus, in Thessaly, attacked by the Athenians, i. 111 init. ; sends aid to the Athenians, ii. 22 fin. ; friends of Brasidas there, iv. 78 init. ; Thucydides of Pharsalus, proxenus of Athens, viii. 92 med.

Phaselis, in Lycia, ii. 69 fin., viii. 88 fin., 99 med., 108 init.

Phea, in Elis, vii. 31 init. ; captured by the Messenians, ii. 25 med. ; given up, *ib.* fin.

Pheraeans, in Thessaly, ii. 22 fin.

Philemon, father of Ameiniades, an Athenian, ii. 67 med.

Philip, a Lacedaemonian, governor of Miletus, viii. 28 fin. ; goes to fetch the Phoenician fleet from Aspendus, *ib.* 87 fin., 99 med.

Philip, a Macedonian, brother of Perdiccas, i. 57 init., ii. 95 med. ; father of Amyntas, ii. 95 fin., 100 med. ; joins with the Athenians, i. 57 init., 59, 61 fin.

Philocharidas, a Lacedaemonian, swears to the one year's Truce, iv. 119 init. ; swears to the Treaty of Peace and the Alliance, v. 19 med., 24 init.; commissioner in Chalcidicè, *ib.* 21 ; ambassador at Athens, *ib.* 44 fin.

Philocrates, an Athenian commander, brings reinforcements to Melos, v. 116 fin.

Philoctetes, his ships the smallest that went to Troy, i. 10 med.

Philomela, story of, ii. 29 init.

Phlius, in Peloponnesus, the Corinthians request money for the expedition against Epidamnus from the Phliasians, i. 27 fin. ; Phliasian troops with Brasidas at Megara, iv. 70 med. ; the priestess Chrysis flies for refuge to Phlius, *ib.* 133 fin. ; the Lace-

Phlius (*cont.*)—

daemonian alliance meets at Phlius for the invasion of Argos, v. 57 ; the whole Phliasian force takes part in the campaign, *ib.* fin., 58 med., 59 med., 60 med. ; Phlius three times invaded by the Argives, *ib.* 83 med., 115 init., vi. 105 fin.

Phocaea, in Ionia, viii. 31 fin. ; the Phocaeans found Massalia, i. 13 fin. ; conquer the Carthaginians at sea, *ib.* ; Carteria, in Phocaean territory, viii. 101 med.; Phocaean staters, iv. 52 med.

Phocaeae, part of Leontini, v. 4 med.

Phocis, formerly inhabited by Thracians, ii. 29 init. ; some of the Phocians settle in Sicily after the Trojan War, vi. 2 init. ; the Phocians attack the Dorians, i. 107 init. ; are defeated, *ib.* med. ; become the allies of the Athenians, *ib.* 111 init. ; receive the temple of Delphi from the Athenians, *ib.* 112 fin. ; in the Lacedaemonian alliance at the beginning of the War, ii. 9 med., Demosthenes intends to gain them over, iii. 95 med. ; the Phocians at enmity with the Locrians of Amphissa, *ib.* 101 init. ; certain Phocians engage in the Athenian plan for the subjugation of Boeotia, iv. 76 med. ; a Phocian, Nicomachus, betrays the plan, *ib.* 89 med. ; the Phocians go to war with the Locrians, v. 32 init. ; are summoned by the Lacedaemonians to Mantinea, *ib.* 64 med. ; furnish the Lacedaemonians with ships, viii. 3 fin. (with cavalry in ii. 9).

Phoenicians, the, addicted to piracy, i. 8 init. ; their colonisation of Sicily, vi. 2 fin. [cp. *ib.* 46 med.] ; services of their fleet under the Persian kings, i. 16 fin., 100 init., 112 med., 116 init.;

trade between Attica and Phoenicia, ii. 69 ; Tissaphernes prepares a Phoenician fleet, viii. 46 init., 59 [cp. *ib.* 58, §§ iii, iv.] ; keeps the Peloponnesians waiting for the ships, *ib.* 46 fin.; the Peloponnesians grow impatient, *ib.* 78 ; Alcibiades pretends that he will secure the Phoenician ships for the Athenians, *ib.* 81, 88, 108 ; Tissaphernes goes to Aspendus to fetch the Phoenician ships : why did he not bring them ? *ib.* 87 ; the Peloponnesians abandon all hope of the Phoenician fleet, *ib.* 99 init.; Tissaphernes determines to excuse himself to the Peloponnesians for not bringing up the ships, *ib.* 109.

Phoenicus, an harbour under Mount Mimas, viii. 34 fin.

Phormio, an Athenian commander, brings reinforcements to Samos, i. 117 med. ; sent to Potidaea, *ib.* 64 med., ii. 29 fin. ; ravages Chalcidicè, i. 65 fin. ; aids the Acarnanians, ii. 68 fin. ; stations himself at Naupactus, *ib.* 69 init., 80 med., 81 init. ; defeats the Lacedaemonians, *ib.* 83, 84 ; asks for reinforcements, *ib.* 85 med. ; his second victory, *ib.* 86-92 ; his speech, *ib.* 89 ; leads an expedition into Acarnania, ii. 102 ; sails back to Athens, *ib.* 103.

Photius, a Chaonian leader, ii. 80 fin.

Phrygia, in Attica, ii. 22 med.

Phrynichus, an Athenian commander, brings reinforcements from Athens, viii. 25 init. ; overrules his colleagues, and declines a battle, *ib.* 27 ; opposes the proposals of Alcibiades to overthrow the democracy, *ib.* 48 med. ; outwits him when he attempts his ruin, *ib.* 50, 51 ; deposed from his command, *ib.*

Phrynichus (*cont.*)—
54 med. ; takes a great part in the oligarchical conspiracy, *ib.* 68 med., 90 init. ; sent to make peace with Lacedaemon, *ib.* 90 med.; returns unsuccessful, *ib.* 91 init.; assassinated, *ib.* 92 init.; his sagacious temper, *ib.* 27 fin., 68 med.

Phrynis, one of the Lacedaemonian Perioeci, goes as commissioner to Chios, viii. 6 med.

Phthiotis, *see* Achaea (Phthiotis).

Phyleides, father of Pythangelus, a Theban, ii. 2 med.

Phyrcus, fortress in Elis, v. 49 init.

Physca, in Macedonia, ii. 99 fin.

Phytia, in Acarnania, iii. 106 med.

Pieria, in Macedonia, ii. 99 med , 100 med.; 'the Pierian vale,' *ib.* 99 med.

Pierium, in Thessaly, v. 13 init.

Pindus, Mount, in Thessaly, ii. 102 init.

Piracy, honourable in ancient Hellas, i. 5 ; put down by Minos, *ib.* 4 fin.; by the Corinthians, *ib.* 13 fin.

Piraeum, a harbour in the Corinthian territory, viii. 10 fin., 11 init., 14 med., 15 fin., 20 init.

Piraeus, fortified by Themistocles, i. 93 ; the circuit of Piraeus and Munychia not quite seven miles, ii. 13 fin. ; Piraeus inhabited by the refugees from Attica, *ib.* 17 fin. ; visited by the plague, *ib.* 48 init. ; the Lacedaemonian commanders plan an attack on the Piraeus, but do not carry it out, *ib.* 93, 94 ; the Athenians expect the enemy at the Piraeus after the disaster in Sicily, viii. 1 med.; Piraeus protected from attack by the army at Samos, *ib.* 76 med. ; the army at Samos want to sail to the Piraeus, *ib.* 82 init., 86 med. ; the oligarchs fortify Eetionea in order to secure the Piraeus, *ib.* 90; tumult in Piraeus,

the people destroy the fort, *ib.* 92 ; the hoplites in Piraeus march to Athens, *ib.* 93 init. ; a Lacedaemonian fleet appearing off Salamis, the citizens rush down to the Piraeus, *ib.* 94 ; the Athenians expect an attack upon the Piraeus after their defeat off Euboea, *ib.* 96 med. ; its final capture by the Lacedaemonians, v. 26 init.

Pisistratidae, moderate character of their government, vi. 54 med ; overthrown by the Lacedaemonians, *ib.* 53 fin., 59 fin.

Pisistratus, tyrant of Athens, i. 20, vi. 53 fin., 54 ; his purification of Delos, iii. 104 init.

Pisistratus [grandson of the tyrant], vi. 54 fin.

Pissuthnes, a Persian, satrap of Lower Asia, iii. 31 fin. ; aids the Samians to revolt, i. 115 med. ; sends assistance to the Persian party at Notium, iii. 34 init.

Pitanate Division, never existed at Lacedaemon, i. 20 fin.

Pittacus, king of Edonia, his assassination, iv. 107 fin.

Plague, the, at Athens, i. 23 med., ii. 47–52; first appeared at Lemnos, ii. 47 med. ; lawlessness caused by the plague, *ib.* 53 ; not serious in the Peloponnese, *ib.* 54 fin. ; in the fleet, *ib.* 57 ; breaks out in the army at Potidaea, *ib.* 58 ; second outbreak at Athens, iii. 87.

Plataea, the city small, ii. 77 init. ; eight miles from Thebes, *ib.* 5 init. ; conduct of the Plataeans during the Persian War, iii. 54, 55 ; their care of the sepulchres of the fallen at Plataea, *ib.* 58 med. ; they receive their independence from Pausanias, ii. 71 med. ; send assistance to Sparta during the Helot revolt, iii. 54 fin. ; their hostility to Thebes,

Plataea *(cont.)*—
ii. 71 fin., iii. 55 init., 57 med.,
58 init., 59 med., 61; allied to
Athens, ii. 73 fin., iii. 3 init.,
55 init, 62, 63, 68 fin.; attacked
at night by the Thebans in time
of peace, ii. 2, iii. 65 [cp. vii.
18 med.]; surrender, ii. 3 init.;
rally, attack and defeat them, *ib.*;
kill their prisoners, *ib.* 5 fin., 6;
receive a garrison from Athens,
ib. 6 fin.; their territory ravaged
by the Boeotians, *ib.* 12 fin.;
Plataea is attacked by the Lacedaemonians, *ib.* 70 init.; the
Plataeans protest, *ib.* med.; vainly
negotiate with Archidamus, *ib.*
72–74; baffle the enemy by
various stratagems, *ib.* 75–77;
are blockaded, *ib.* 78; part of
them break out of the town, iii.
20-24; reason why the Lacedaemonians did not storm Plataea, *ib.* 52 init.; the Plataeans
surrender, *ib.* med.; their speech
to the Lacedaemonian judges, *ib.*
53–59; they are put to death,
and Plataea razed, *ib.* 68; the
Lacedaemonians do this in order
to gratify the Thebans, *ib.* fin.;
light-armed Plataeans serve with
the Athenians at Megara, iv.
67; the Boeotians collect at
Plataea, intending to relieve
Megara, *ib.* 72 init.; Plataea not
given up under the Treaty of
Peace, v. 17 med. [cp. iii. 52
init.]; the Athenians give Scionè
to the Plataeans, v. 32 init.; the
Plataeans serve against their
Boeotian countrymen at Syracuse, vii. 57 med.
Plataea, battle of, i. 130 init., iii.
54 med., 58 med.
Pleistarchus, king of Sparta, Pausanias his guardian, i. 132 init.
Pleistoanax, king of Lacedaemon,
Nicomedes his guardian, i. 107
init.; brother of Cleomenes,
father of king Pausanias, iii. 26
med.; invades Attica, *ib.* 114
med.; accused of having been
bribed to retreat, ii. 21 init., v.
16 fin.; said to have tampered
with the Delphian oracle, v. 16
med.; restored, *ib.*; anxious for
peace, *ib.*; swears to the Alliance,
ib. 24 init.; leads an expedition
against the Parrhasians, *ib.* 33;
leads reinforcements to Agis, but
returns when the victory of Mantinea is reported, *ib.* 75 init.
Pleistolas, Ephor at Lacedaemon,
swears to the Treaty of Peace
and the Alliance, v. 19 med., 24
init., 25 init.
Plemmyrium, a promontory opposite Syracuse, fortified by Nicias,
vii. 4 med.; captured by Gylippus, *ib.* 22 init., 23 init.; garrisoned by the Syracusans, *ib.* 24
init.; disastrous consequences to
the Athenians from its loss, *ib.*
24, 36 fin.; Eurymedon, meeting Demosthenes on his way,
reports its capture, *ib.* 31 med.
Pleuron, in Aetolia, iii. 102 fin.
Pnyx, place where the Athenian
assembly met, viii. 97 init.
Poets, untrustworthy witnesses to
history, i. 10 med., 21 init., ii. 41
med.
Polemarchs, magistrates at Mantinea, v. 47 fin.; officers in the
Lacedaemonian army, *ib.* 66 med.
Polichnè, near Clazomenae, fortified by the Clazomenians, viii.
14 fin.; retaken by the Athenians, *ib.* 23 fin.
Polichnitae, inhabitants of Polichnè
in Crete, ii. 85 fin.
Polis, in Locris, iii. 101 fin.
Polles, king of the Odomantians,
v. 6 init.
Pollis, an Argive who went un-
officially to the King, ii. 67 init.
Polyanthes, a Corinthian commander, vii. 34 init.

Polycrates, tyrant of Samos, had a large navy, i. 13 fin., iii. 104 init.; dedicates Rhenea to Apollo, i. 13 fin., iii. 104 init.

Polydamidas, a Lacedaemonian, iv. 123 fin. ; defeats the Athenians at Mendè, *ib.* 129 med. ; attacked by the Mendaeans, *ib.* 130 med.

Polymedes, of Larissa, ii. 22 fin.

Pontus, the Lesbians send to the Pontus for troops and supplies, iii. 2 init. ; Lamachus sails into the Pontus, iv. 75 ; Chalcedon situated at its mouth, *ib.* fin.

Poseidon, Temple of, at Colonus, viii. 67 med. ; at Nisaea, iv. 118, § iii; on coast of Pallenè, *ib.* 129 med. ; at Taenarus, i. 128 init., 133 init. ; ships dedicated to him after a victory, ii. 84 fin., 92 fin.

Potamis, a Syracusan general, succeeds Hermocrates at Miletus, viii. 85 med.

Potidaea, a Corinthian colony, i. 56 init. ; a tributary of Athens, *ib.* ; importance of its situation, iv. 120 fin. ; the Potidaeans ordered by the Athenians to pull down their walls, i. 56 med., 57 fin. ; send embassies to Athens and Sparta ; they are encouraged by the Lacedaemonians and revolt, *ib.* 58, 118 init. ; receive aid from Corinth, *ib.* 60 ; the Athenians send an expedition against Potidaea, *ib.* 57 fin., 61 ; battle of Potidaea, *ib.* 62, 63 ; Aristeus retreats into Potidaea, *ib.* 63 init.; Potidaea invested, *ib.* 64 ; Aristeus leaves Potidaea, *ib.* 65 ; the affair causes great ill-feeling between Corinth and Athens, *ib.* 66 ; the Corinthians complain at Sparta, *ib.* 67 ; beg assistance, *ib.* 71 med. ; Archidamus urges moderation, *ib.* 85 ; the Corinthians, anxious to save Potidaea,

press on the war, *ib.* 119, 124 init. ; the Lacedaemonians bid the Athenians quit Potidaea, *ib.* 139 init., 140 med. ; Hagnon brings fresh troops to Potidaea ; the plague conveyed by them to the forces there, ii. 58; Aristeus endeavours to gain Sitalces' assistance for Potidaea, *ib.* 67; Potidaea surrenders, *ib.* 70 ; is colonised by the Athenians, *ib.* fin. ; expense of the siege, ii. 13 med., 70 med., iii. 17 med., vi. 31 init.; three thousand Athenian troops engaged in the siege, ii. 31 med.; Athenians escape to Potidaea after the battle of Spartolus, ii. 79 fin. ; Brasidas plans an attack on Potidaea, iv. 121 fin. ; Nicias starts from Potidaea against Mendè, *ib.* 129 med. ; Brasidas unsuccessfully attempts Potidaea, *ib.* 135.

Potidania, in Aetolia, iii. 96 med.

Poverty, no bar to success and no disgrace at Athens, ii. 37 med., 40 init. ; the hope natural to poverty of one day becoming rich, *ib.* 42 med. ;—poverty of antiquity, i. 11.

Prasiae, in Attica, viii. 95 init.

Prasiae, in Laconia, destroyed by the Athenians, ii. 56 fin. ; they ravage its territory, vi. 105 fin., vii. 18 med.

Priapus, on the Propontis, viii. 107 init.

Prienè, in Ionia, i. 115 init.

Prisoners of War, provision respecting, in the Treaty of Peace, v. 18, § ix (cp. *ib.* 3 fin.).

Procles, (i) an Athenian commander, iii. 91 init.; falls in the Aetolian expedition, *ib.* 98 fin. ; (ii) another, swears to the Treaty of Peace and the Alliance, v. 19 fin., *ib.* 24 med.

Procnè, wife of Tereus, the Thracian king, ii. 29 init.

Pronnaeans, in Cephallenia, ii. 30 fin.

Prophecies, current before the War, ii. 8 init.

Prophets, present with armies, vi. 69 med. ; the Athenians indignant with the prophets who had encouraged the Sicilian expedition, viii. 1 init. [*See* Oracles.]

Propylaea of the Acropolis at Athens, ii. 13 med.

Proschium, in Aetolia, iii. 102 fin., 106 init.

Prosopitis, an island in the Nile, i. 109 fin.

Protè, an island near Pylus, iv. 13 med.

Proteas, an Athenian commander, sent to Corcyra, i. 45 ; and to cruise round Peloponnesus, ii. 23 med.

Protesilaus, temple of, near Elaeus, viii. 102 fin.

Proxenus, a Locrian commander, iii. 103 fin.

Prytanes, at Athens, iv. 118 fin., v. 47 fin., vi. 14 init., viii. 70 init.

Psammetichus, father of Inarus, i. 104 init.

Pteleum [of uncertain locality], ordered to be restored under the Peace, v. 18, viii.

Pteleum, a fort in Erythraean territory, viii. 24 init., 31 med.

Ptoeodorus, a Theban exile, iv. 76 init.

Ptychia, a small island near Corcyra, iv. 46 med.

Punishment of death does not prevent crime, iii. 45 ; too severe punishment of rebels inexpedient, *ib.* 46.

Pydna, in Macedonia, i. 137 init. ; besieged by the Athenians, i. 61 med.

Pylos, in Messenia, called Coryphasium by the Lacedaemonians, iv. 3 med., v. 18, viii ; forty-six miles from Sparta, iv. 3 med. ; fortified by the Athenians, *ib.* 3-5 ; the news recalls the Lacedaemonians from Attica, *ib.* 6 ; unsuccessfully assaulted by the Lacedaemonians, *ib.* 11, 12 ; the Athenian fleet defeats the Lacedaemonian, and cuts off the troops in Sphacteria, *ib.* 13, 14 ; the Lacedaemonians make a truce with the Athenians at Pylos, and send ambassadors to Athens, *ib.* 15, 16 ; the truce ends, the Athenians retain the Peloponnesian ships, *ib.* 23 ; sufferings of the Athenians at Pylos while blockading Sphacteria, *ib.* 26 ; garrisoned by the Messenians, *ib.* 41 init. ; the Lacedaemonians in dread of a Helot revolt, while the Athenians were at Pylos, *ib.* 80 init. ; Cleon's success at Pylos increases his confidence at Amphipolis, v. 7 med. ; the Athenians repent that they did not make peace after Pylos ; the Lacedaemonians disheartened by its capture, *ib.* 14 ; the Athenians replace the Messenians at Pylos by a garrison of their own, *ib.* 35 fin. ; the Lacedaemonians negotiate at Athens with a view to the exchange of Pylos for Panactum, *ib.* 36 fin., 39 med., 44-46 ; the Athenians put the Helots back in Pylos, *ib.* 56 med. ; marauding expeditions of the Athenians from Pylos, *ib.* 115 init., vi. 105, vii. 18 med., 26 med.; Alcibiades pretends to have done the Lacedaemonians service after loss of Pylos, vi. 89 init. ; the Lacedaemonians consider their misfortune at Pylos deserved, because they began the war, vii. 18 ; the Messenians from Pylos serve with the Athenians before Syracuse, *ib.* 57 med. ; compa-

Pylos (*cont.*)—

rison between the naval engagement at Pylos and the last battle in the Great Harbour at Syracuse, *ib.* 71 fin.; Demosthenes the greatest foe of the Lacedaemonians, Nicias their greatest friend, in the matter of Pylos, *ib.* 86 med. [*See* Sphacteria.]

Pyrasians, people of Pyrasus in Thessaly, ii. 22 fin.

Pyrrha, in Lesbos, iii. 18 init., 25 init., viii. 23 init.; taken by Paches, iii. 35 init.

Pyrrhichus, father of Ariston, a Corinthian, vii. 39 init.

Pystilus, joint founder with Aristonous of Agrigentum, vi. 4 med.

Pythangelus, a Theban Boeotarch, ii. 2 med.

Pythen, a Corinthian, sails with Gylippus to Sicily, vi. 104, vii. 1 init.; in command at the last fight in the harbour, vii. 70 init.

Pythes, of Abdera, father of Nymphodorus, ii. 29 init.

Pythian Games, v. 1 init. [*See* Apollo, Delphi, Oracle.]

Pythodorus, an Athenian, archon at the commencement of the War, ii. 2 init.; supersedes Laches in Sicily, iii. 115 med., iv. 2 med.; sent into exile, iv. 65 med.; swears to the Treaty of Peace and the Alliance, v. 19 fin., 24 med.; has a command in an expedition to Laconia, which violates the Treaty, vi. 105.

Q.

Quarries, at Syracuse, used as a prison for the Athenian captives, vii. 86, 87.

R.

Religion, is lost amid party strife, iii. 82 fin.; all religious restraint disappears during the plague, ii. 53.

Reserve fund and ships set apart by the Athenians, ii. 24, viii. 15 init.

Revenge not always successful because just, iv. 62 fin.; sweetness of revenge, ii. 42 fin., iii. 40 fin., vii. 68 init.

Revenue, the Athenian, raised by tribute from the allies, i. 122 init., ii. 13 med., 69, iii. 13 fin., 19, 39 fin., 46 init., iv. 87 fin., vi. 91 fin.; from mines at Laurium, ii. 55, vi. 91 fin.; by a property tax, iii. 19; by profits made from the land, and the law courts, vi. 91 fin.; the tribute commuted for a duty of 5 per cent. on imports and exports, vii. 28 fin.

Revolutions, horrors of the revolution at Corcyra, iii. 81, 84, iv. 46-48; growth of the revolutionary spirit in Hellas, iii. 82, 83 [cp. vii. 57 fin.]; the oligarchical revolution at Megara, iv. 74.

Rhamphias, (i) a Lacedaemonian, brings with others the last demands of the Lacedaemonians to Athens, i. 139 med.; sets out to Chalcidicè, but returns on news of Brasidas' death, v. 12, 13: (ii) another [?], father of Clearchus, viii. 8 med., 39 med., 80 init.

Rhegium, its important position, iv. 24 med.; Anaxilaus, tyrant of, vi. 4 fin.; the Rhegians, Ionians and kindred of the Leontines, iii. 86 med., vi. 44 fin., 46 init., 79 med.; the Athenians aid them, iii. 86 fin.; they sail with the Athenians against the Lipari islands, *ib.* 88; Athenian reinforcements arrive at Rhegium, *ib.* 115; the Rhegians fall into sedition and are attacked by the Locrians, iv. 1 med., 24, 25; refuse to receive the Athenian expedition to Sicily, vi. 44; the Athenians disappointed at this refusal, *ib.* 46 init.; part of the

Rhegium (*cont.*)—
Athenians stay at Rhegium till assured of a reception at Catana, *ib.* 50, 51 ; Gylippus puts in there, on his way to Syracuse, vii. 1 med. ; the Athenians lie in wait for a Corinthian fleet off Rhegium, *ib.* 4 fin.

Rheiti, in Attica, ii. 19 med.

Rhenea, the island near Delos, dedicated to Apollo by Polycrates, i. 13 fin., iii. 104 init.

Rhetus, in Corinthian territory, iv. 42 init.

Rhium, in Achaia, ii. 86 init., 92 fin., v. 52 fin. ; – the Molycrian, ii. 84 fin., 86 init.

Rhodes, viii. 41 fin.; colonised from Argos, vii. 57 med. ; assists in the colonisation of Gela, vi. 4 med., vii. 57 fin.; Rhodian troops serve in the expedition to Sicily, vi. 43, vii. 57 med.; Rhodes revolts from Athens, viii. 44 ; the Peloponnesians take up their station there, *ib.*, *ib.* 52 med.; the Athenians make descents upon Rhodes, *ib.* 44 fin., 55 init. ; the Peloponnesians quit Rhodes, *ib.* 60.

Rhodopè, Mount, in Thessaly, ii. 96 init.

Rhoeteum, in the Troad, viii. 101 fin. ; captured by the Lesbian refugees, iv. 52 init.

Rhypae, in Achaia, vii. 34 init.

Roll [κατάλογος] of persons liable to military service at Athens, iii. 87, vi. 31 med., 43 init., vii. 20 med., viii. 24 init.

Ruling states not cruel to the vanquished, v. 91 init.

S.

Sabylinthus, a Molossian, guardian of the king Tharypas, ii. 80 fin.

Sacon, one of the founders of Himera, vi. 5 init.

Sacrilege, committed, by the slaughter of Cylon's adherents, i. 126 ; by the murder of the Helots at Taenarus, *ib.* 128 init. ; by the starving to death of Pausanias, *ib.* 134 ; in the Corcyraean sedition, iii. 81 ; provision against, in the one year's Truce, ii. 118, § ii ; the Athenians charged with, by the Boeotians, on account of the occupation of Delium, *ib.* 97-99.

Sadocus, son of Sitalces king of the Odrysians, made an Athenian citizen, ii. 29 fin.; gives up Aristeus and the Lacedaemonian ambassadors to the Athenians, *ib.* 67.

Salaethus, a Lacedaemonian, sent to Mytilenè, iii. 25 init. ; arms the people, *ib.* 27 ; captured by the Athenians, *ib.* 35 init. ; put to death by them, *ib.* 36 init.

Salaminia, the Athenian sacred vessel, iii. 33 med., 77 fin., vi. 53 init., 61.

Salamis, battle of, i. 73 fin., 137 fin.; the island ravaged by the Lacedaemonians, ii. 93, 94 ; Attic ships guard it, iii. 17 init. ; the Athenians blockade Megara from Salamis, ii. 93 fin., 94 fin., iii. 51 init. ; the appearance of a Peloponnesian fleet off Salamis causes a panic at Athens, viii. 94.

Salamis, in Cyprus, victory of the Athenians there, i. 112 med.

Salynthius, king of the Agraeans, iii. 111 fin., 114 med. ; subdued by the Athenians, iv. 77 fin.

Samaeans, in Cephallenia, ii. 30 fin.

Saminthus, in Argolis, v. 58 fin.

Samos, 'no small city,' viii. 76 med. ; one of the first Hellenic States to possess a navy, i. 13 init., fin.; Polycrates tyrant of, *ib.* 13 fin., iii. 104 init. ; Samians expel the Chalcidians from Zanclè, and are themselves driven out by Anaxilas, vi. 4 fin. ; the Samians quarrel with the Mile-

Samos (*cont.*)—

sians, i. 115 init.; revolt from Athens, i. 40 fin., 41 med., 115, viii. 76 med.; are defeated, i. 116 init.; defeat the Athenians, *ib.* 117 init.; surrender, *ib.* fin.; Samian exiles settle at Anaea, iii. 19 fin., 32 init., iv. 75 med.; Strombichides with an Athenian fleet sails to Samos, viii. 16, 17 init., 19 fin.; the Samians revolt and establish a democracy, the Athenians grant them independence, *ib.* 21; Samos becomes the headquarters of the Athenian fleet, *ib.* 25 init., 27 fin., 30 init., 33 med., 35 med., 39 fin., 41 fin., 44 fin., 60 fin., 63 init., 79; the leading Athenians at Samos, instigated by Alcibiades, begin to plot the overthrow of the democracy, *ib.* 47–54, 63 fin.; the Samians, with the aid of Athenian sailors, crush the revolution attempted by the oligarchs at Samos, *ib.* 73; the Samians unite with the Athenians against the Four Hundred, *ib.* 75–77; part of the Athenian fleet leaves Samos for the Hellespont, *ib.* 80 fin.; the Athenians at Samos recall Alcibiades, *ib.* 81 init.; Alcibiades at Samos, *ib.* 81, 82; envoys from the Four Hundred comè to Samos, *ib.* 86 init.; the Argives offer aid, *ib.* fin.; Alcibiades leaves Samos to join Tissaphernes, *ib.* 88; the Peloponnesians sailing for the Hellespont try to evade the Athenians at Samos, *ib.* 99; the Athenians pursue them from Samos, *ib.* 100; Alcibiades returns to Samos, *ib.* 108.

Sandius, a hill in Caria, iii. 19 fin.

Sanè, an Andrian colony in Athos, iv. 109 med.; provision respecting Sanè, in the Treaty of Peace, v. 18, § vii.

Sardis, i. 115 med.

Sargeus, a Sicyonian commander at Syracuse, vii. 19 fin.

Saronic Gulf, iii. 15 med., viii. 92 init.

Scandea, in Cythera, iv. 54.

Scellias, father òf Aristocrates, an Athenian, viii. 89 med.

Scionè, founded by Pellenians returning from Troy, iv. 120 init.; revolts froṃ Athens, *ib.*; the Scionaeans crown Brasidas, *ib.* 121 init.; the Athenians and Lacedaemonians disagree about Scionè, *ib.* 122; the Athenians decree its destruction, *ib.* fin.; the Athenians prepare to attack Scionè, *ib.* 129 init.; the Scionaeans aid the Mendaeans, *ib.* med., 130 init.; the Peloponnesian garrison of Mendè flees to Scionè, *ib.* 131 fin.; Scionè is invested, *ib.* 132 init., 133 fin.; provisions respecting Scionè in the Treaty of Peace, v. 18, §§ ix, x; captured by the Athenians, the citizens slain, and the city given to the Plataeans, *ib.* 32 init.

Sciritis, a district of Laconia, v. 33 med.; the Sciritae form the left wing of the Lacedaemonian army, *ib.* 67 init.; present at the battle of Mantinea, *ib.* 68 med., 71 med., 72 med.

Scironides, an Athenian commander, viii. 25 init.; dismissed, 54 med.

Scirphondas, a Theban Boeotarch, vii. 30 fin.

Scolus, in Chalcidicè, provision respecting, in the Treaty of Peace, v. 18, § vi.

Scombrus, mountain in Thrace from which the Strymon rises, ii. 96 fin.

Scyllaeum, promontory near Troezen, v. 53 fin.

Scyros, island of, subdued and colonised by the Athenians, i. 98 init.

Scytalè, use of, at Lacedaemon, i. 131 med.

Scythians, ii. 96 med., 97 fin.

Sea, Aegaean, i. 98, iv. 109 init. ; Cretan, iv. 53 fin., v. 110 init. ; Hellenic, i. 4 init.; Sicilian, iv. 24 fin., 53 fin.,vi. 13 med.; Tyrrhenian, iv. 24 fin. [*See* Gulf.]

Sea, mastery of the, gained by Minos, i. 4, 8 med. ; by the Corinthians, the Ionians, and by Polycrates, *ib.* 13 ; by the Athenians, *see* Athenians (v. 56 init.).

Selinus, founded by Pamillus from Megara, vi. 4 init. [cp. vii. 57 med.] ; the Selinuntians make war on Egesta, vi. 6 init., 13 fin.; a large and powerful city, *ib.* 20 fin. ; Nicias in a council of war urges attack on Selinus instead of Syracuse, *ib.* 47 ; the Athenian generals sail towards Selinus, *ib.* 62 init. ; the Selinuntians join the Syracusans, *ib.* 65 med., 67 med. ; they receive and assist Gylippus, vii. 1 fin., 58 init. ; contribute to the Sicilian fleet which is despatched to Asia, viii. 26 init.

Sermylè, in Sithonia, provision respecting, in the Treaty of Peace, v. 18, § x ; defeat of the Sermylians by Aristeus, i. 65 fin.

Sestos, siege and capture of (in the Persian War), i. 89 med., viii. 62 fin.; becomes the Athenian headquarters in the Hellespont, viii. 62 fin., 102 init., 104 init., 107 init.

Seuthes, king of the Odrysians, the successor of Sitalces, ii. 97 med., iv. 101 fin. ; gained over by Perdiccas, ii. 101 fin. ; marries Perdiccas' sister, *ib.*

Ships in ancient times had no decks, i. 10 fin. ; the ships in the fleet at Salamis not completely decked, *ib.* 14 fin.; invention of triremes, *ib.* 13 init. ; the prows of ships built thicker, in order to disable the lighter Athenian vessels, vii. 34 med., 36, 62 med. ; use of grappling irons to catch an enemy's ship, iv. 25 init., vii. 62 fin. ; ships covered with hides in order to prevent the grapnels holding, vii. 65 ;—ships, dedicated to Poseidon as trophies of a victory, ii. 84 fin., 92 fin.

Sicania, an old name of Sicily, vi. 2 init. ; the Sicanians Iberian by descent, *ib.*; Hyccara of Sicanian origin, *ib.* 62 med.

Sicanus, river in Iberia, vi. 2 init.

Sicanus, a Syracusan general, vi. 73, 96 ; deposed, *ib.* 103 fin. ; sent to Agrigentum, vii. 46 ; fails in his mission, *ib.* 50 init. ; commands a division of the Syracusan fleet in the last sea fight, *ib.* 70 init.

Sicels, their occupation of Sicily, vi. 2 med., 3 fin.; gave name to the island, *ib.* 2 med. ; district inhabited by them, v. 4 fin., vi. 62 med., 94 med. ; those in the interior independent, vi. 88 med. ; Zanclè named from the Sicel word for a sickle, *ib.* 4 fin. ; Hyblon, Archonides, Sicel kings, *ib.* 4 init., vii. 1 fin. ; the greater part of the Sicels join the Athenians, iii. 103 init., 115 init., iv. 25 med., vi. 65 med., 88 med., 98 init., 103 med., vii. 57 fin. ; the Syracusans try to gain them over, vi. 45 [cp. *ib.* 34 init., 88 med.] ; Alcibiades wishes to secure their friendship before attacking Syracuse, *ib.* 48 init.; some of them aid Gylippus, vii. 1 fin., 58 init. ; he captures Getae, a Sicel fort, *ib.* 2 med.; the Sicel allies of the Athenians destroy the reinforcements sent by the Sicilian cities to Syracuse, *ib.* 32 ; the Athenians expect aid from the Sicels on their retreat, *ib.* 77 fin., 80 fin.

Sicily, its original settlement, vi. 2 ; Hellenic colonies there, *ib.* 3-5 [cp. i. 12 fin.] ; anciently called Trinacria and Sicania, vi. 2 init.; the Sicilian tyrants, i. 14 med., 17, 18 init. ; populousness and democratic character of the Sicilian states, vi. 17 init., 20, vii. 28 med., 55, viii. 96 fin. ; the Lacedaemonians order their Sicilian allies to furnish a fleet, ii. 7 med. [cp. iii. 86 init.] ; the Athenians send an expedition under Laches to Sicily, iii. 86, 88, 90, 99, 103 ; reinforcements under Pythodorus arrive in Sicily, *ib.* 115 ; eruption of Aetna, *ib.* 116 ; proceedings of the second Athenian expedition in Sicily, iv. 2, 24, 25, 65 fin.; conference of the Sicilian states at Gela, *ib.* 58-65 init.; embassy of Phaeax from Athens to Sicily, v. 4, 5 ; third and great expedition against Sicily ; the preparation, vi. 1, 6, 8-29 ; the armament leaves Piraeus, *ib.* 30, 32 ; its magnitude, *ib.* 31, 43, vii. 76 fin.; reception of the news in Sicily, vi. 33-41 ; the Athenian fleet reaches Catana, *ib.* 42-52 ; course of the campaign until the almost complete investment of Syracuse, *ib.* 62-104 ; Gylippus arrives in Sicily and enters Syracuse, vii. 1, 2 ; the good fortune of the Athenians begins to decline, *ib.* 3-16 ; the Athenians determine to send Demosthenes with reinforcements, *ib.* 17, 18 init., 20 ; the Athenians at Syracuse lose command of the sea, *ib.* 21-25, 36-41 ; Demosthenes proceeds to Sicily, *ib.* 26, 31, 33. 35 ; the attack on Epipolae, *ib.* 42-45 ; the Syracusans gain a fresh victory at sea, *ib.* 46 56 ; enumeration of the hostile forces in Sicily, *ib.* 57, 58 ; the last battle in the harbour, *ib.* 59-71 ; the retreat and final surrender, *ib.* 72-87 ; a Sicilian contingent is sent to the Lacedaemonian fleet in Asia, viii. 2 fin., 26 init., 28 med., 29, 35 init., 45 med., 78 fin., 84 init., 85 fin., 106 med. ; Sicilian ships in the fleet destined for Euboea, *ib.* 91 init.

Sicyon, the Sicyonians defeated by the Athenians, i. 108 fin., 111 fin.; aid the Megarians to revolt, *ib.* 114 med. ; furnish the Lacedaemonians with ships, ii. 9 med. ; prepare ships for the Lacedaemonian expedition against Acarnania, *ib.* 80 med. ; with Brasidas at Megara, iv. 70 med. ; defeat the Athenians, *ib.* 101 med. ; aid in preventing Alcibiades' plan for fortifying Rhium, v. 52 fin. ; join the Lacedaemonians in the invasion of Argolis, *ib.* 58-60 ; have their government changed by the Lacedaemonians, *ib.* 81 fin.; send troops to Sicily, vii. 19 fin., 58 med. ; contribute ships to the Lacedaemonian fleet, viii. 3 fin.

Sidussa, a fort in the Erythraean territory, viii. 24 init.

Sigeum, in the Hellespont, viii. 101 fin.

Simonides, an Athenian general, iv. 7.

Simplicity, a large element in a noble nature, iii. 83 init.

Simus, one of the founders of Himera, vi. 5 init.

Singaeans, inhabitants of Singè in Sithonia, provision respecting, in the Treaty of Peace, v. 18, § vii.

Sinti, a people on the borders of Macedonia, ii. 98 init.

Siphae, port of Thespiae, in Boeotia, plan to betray the city, iv. 76 init., 77 med.; failure of the plot, *ib.* 89 init., 101 med.

Sitalces, king of the Odrysians, becomes the ally of Athens, ii. 29 fin., 95 med. ; makes war upon

Sitalces (*cont.*)—

Perdiccas, *ib.* 95-101; dies and is succeeded by Seuthes, iv. 101 fin.

Six Hundred, the, the Council at Elis, v. 47 fin.

Skill only to be acquired by incessant application, i. 142 fin., vi. 18 fin.; inspires confidence, vi. 72 fin., vii. 67 init.; without courage useless, ii. 87 med.

Slaves, more than twenty thousand Athenian slaves desert during the occupation of Decelea, vii. 27 fin.; great numbers of the Chian slaves, viii. 40 init.; they desert to the Athenians, *ib.* med.

Socrates, an Athenian commander, ii. 23 med.

Sollium, belonging to Corinth, in Acarnania, taken by the Athenians, ii. 30 init.; Demosthenes comes to Sollium on his way to Aetolia, iii. 95 med.; the Corinthians complain that the Lacedaemonians did not recover Sollium for them, v. 30 med.

Soloeis, a Phoenician settlement in Sicily, vi. 2 fin.

Solygea, a village in the Corinthian territory, iv. 42, 43; Solygean ridge, a position once occupied by the Dorian invaders of Corinth, iv. 42 init.

Soothsayers, *see* Prophets, Oracles.

Sophocles, an Athenian commander, sent with reinforcements to Sicily, iii. 115 fin., iv. 2 med., 46 init.; his conduct at Corcyra, iv. 47; condemned to exile, *ib.* 65 med.

Sostratides, father of Sophocles, an Athenian, iii. 115 fin.

Sparadocus, father of Seuthes, a Thracian, ii. 101 fin., iv. 101 fin.

Sparta, *see* Lacedaemon.

Spartolus, in Bottice, defeat of the Athenians there, ii. 79; provision respecting, in the Treaty of Peace, v. 18, § vi.

Speeches, Thucydides only vouches for their general accuracy, i. 22 init.; speech of Alcibiades at Athens, vi. 16-18; at Sparta, *ib.* 89-92; Archidamus (1), i. 80-85, (2) ii. 11; the Athenians at Sparta, i. 73-78; Athenagoras, vi. 36-40; Brasidas at Acanthus, iv. 85-87; to his soldiers in Macedonia, *ib.* 126; at Amphipolis, v. 9; Cleon, iii. 37-40; Corinthians at Athens, i. 37-43; at Sparta (1), *ib.* 68-71, (2) *ib.* 120-124; Corcyraeans, i. 32-36; Demosthenes, iv. 10; Diodotus, iii. 42-48; Euphemus, vi. 82-87; Gylippus, vii. 66-68; Hermocrates at Gela, iv. 59-64; at Syracuse, vi. 33, 34; at Camarina, vi. 76-80; Hippocrates, iv. 95; the Lacedaemonian ambassadors, iv. 17-20; Mytilenaeans, iii. 9-14; Nicias at Athens (1), vi. 9-14, (2) *ib.* 20-23; at Syracuse (1), *ib.* 68, (2) vii. 61-64, (3) *ib.* 77; Pagondas, iv. 92; Peloponnesian commanders, ii. 87; Pericles (1), i. 140-144, (2) [funeral speech], ii. 35-46, (3) *ib.* 60-64; Phormio, ii. 89; Plataeans, iii. 53-59; Sthenelaidas, i. 86; Thebans, iii. 61-67; Teutiaplus, iii. 30.

Sphacteria, the island off Messenia, iv. 8 med.; occupied by the Lacedaemonians, *ib.*; blockaded by the Athenians, *ib.* 14 fin., 26; successful attack upon, *ib.* 31-39; restoration of the prisoners taken in, v. 24 fin.; their treatment at Sparta, *ib.* 34 fin.; the surrender of Sphacteria the severest blow Sparta had ever experienced, *ib.* 14 med.

Stages, a lieutenant of Tissaphernes, viii. 16 fin.

Stagirus, in Chalcidice, an Andrian colony, iv. 88 fin.; revolts from Athens, *ib.*; unsuccessfully attacked by the Athenians, v. 6

Stagirus (*cont.*)—

init.; provision respecting, in the Treaty of Peace, *ib.* 18, § vi.

State, a, is composed not of walls or ships, but of men, vii. 77 fin. [cp. i. 143 fin.].

Stesagoras, a Samian commander, i. 116 fin.

Sthenelaidas, a Lacedaemonian Ephor, his speech, i. 85 fin., 86; [? the same] father of Alcamenes, viii. 5 init.

Stratodemus, a Lacedaemonian, ambassador to the King, ii. 67 init.

Stratonicè, sister of Perdiccas, wife of Seuthes, ii. 101 fin.

Stratus, in Acarnania, ii. 80 fin.; the Stratians defeat the Chaonians, *ib.* 81 med.; certain Stratians expelled by the Athenians, *ib.* 102 init.; the Peloponnesians on their way to Olpae pass by Stratus, iii. 106.

Stroebus, father of Leocrates, an Athenian, i. 105 init.

Strombichides, an Athenian, sent in command of an expedition against Chios, viii. 15 med.; pursues Chalcideus, *ib.*; is chased into Samos, *ib.* 16; arrives too late to prevent the revolt of Miletus, *ib.* 17 fin.; sent to Chios, *ib.* 30 fin.; fails to recover Abydos, which had revolted, *ib.* 62 fin.; returns to Samos, *ib.* 79 fin.

Strombichus, father of Diotimus, an Athenian, i. 45.

Strongylè, one of the Aeolian islands, iii. 88 med.

Strophacus, a friend of Brasidas in Thessaly, iv. 78 init.

Strymon, the river, in Thrace, i. 100 fin., ii. 99 med., iv. 102, 108 init., vii. 9 fin.; rises in Mount Scombrus, ii. 96 fin.; lake formed by it, v. 7 fin.

Styphon, one of the Lacedaemonian commanders at Sphacteria, iv. 38 init.

Styreans, people of Styra in Euboea, subjects of the Athenians, vii. 57 init.

Sunium, promontory of, in Attica, vii. 28 init., viii. 95 init.; fortified by the Athenians, viii. 4 init.

Superstition, earthquakes cause expeditions to be abandoned, iii. 89 init., vi. 95 init.; a commander changed, viii. 6 fin.; assemblies broken up, v. 45 fin., 50 fin.; an eclipse of the moon causes the fatal delay at Syracuse, vii. 50 fin.; unpropitious sacrifices lead to the abandonment of an expedition, v. 54 med., 55 med., 116 init.; superstitious observance of festivals by the Lacedaemonians, iv. 5 init., v. 54 med., 75 init., 82 init.

Sybaris, a river in Italy, vii. 35 med.

Sybota, (1) islands off Thesprotia, i. 47, 54 init.: (2) a harbour in Thesprotia, *ib.* 50 med., 52 init., 54 init., iii. 76 fin.

Sycè, near Syracuse, vi. 98 med.

Symaethus, a river in Sicily, vi. 65 med.

Symè, island of, viii. 41 fin., 42 fin., 43 init.

Synoecia, a festival at Athens, ii. 15 med.

Syracuse, founded from Corinth by Archias, vi. 3 med.; mother city of various states in Sicily, *ib.* 5; equal in size and resources to Athens, *ib.* 20, vii. 28 [cp. vi. 17 init.]; fought the best of all Hellenic States against the Athenians, viii. 96 fin. [cp. vii. 55 init.]; constantly in revolution, vi. 38 med.; the Syracusans go to war with Leontini, iii. 86 init.; defeat the Athenians, *ib.* 103 med.; cause Messenè to revolt, iv. 1 init.; attack the Rhegians, *ib.* 24, 25; hand over Morgantinè to Camarina, *ib.* 65 init.; aid the olig-

Syracuse (*cont.*)—

archical party at Leontini, v. 4; the news of the Athenian expedition arrives, the Syracusans first doubt, then prepare, *ib.* 32 fin.-41, 45; the Athenians sail to Syracuse, and return to Catana, *ib.* 50-52; the Syracusans repulse an Athenian landing with loss, *ib.* 52 fin. ; they are encouraged by the inactivity of the Athenians, *ib.* 63 ; the Athenians entice them to Catana in order to cover their landing, *ib.* 64, 65 ; the Syracusans are defeated by the Athenians, *ib.* 66-71 ; encouraged by Hermocrates, *ib.* 72 ; send envoys to Peloponnesus, *ib.* 73 ; extend their walls and send an embassy to Camarina, *ib.* 75 ; promised aid by the Corinthians, *ib.* 88 fin. ; the Lacedaemonians appoint Gylippus to command the Syracusan forces, *ib.* 93 med. ; the Syracusans resist the Athenians near Megara and on the Terias, *ib.* 94 ; defeated on Epipolae, *ib.* 96, 97 ; receive another check and raise a counter wall, which the Athenians destroy, *ib.* 98-100; again suffer a defeat, *ib.* 101 ; repulsed in an attack on Epipolae, *ib.* 102 ; fall into despair and negotiate unsuccessfully with Nicias, *ib.* 103 ; change their commanders, *ib.* fin.; on the point of surrendering, vii. 2 init.; hearing of the coming of Gylippus go out to meet him, *ib.* 2 fin. ; take Labdalum, *ib.* 3 fin.; build a counter wall, *ib.* 4 init. ; fail in an attack on the Athenian lines, *ib.*; defeated by the Athenians, *ib.* 5 ; defeat the Athenians and carry their cross wall past the Athenian wall, *ib.* 6 ; begin to form a navy, *ib.* 7 fin., 12, 21 ; Gylippus brings in reinforcements from the Sicil-

ian cities, *ib.* 21 init. ; the Syracusans capture Plemmyrium, but are defeated at sea, *ib.* 22, 23 ; send a third embassy to Peloponnese, and despatch a fleet to intercept the Athenian convoys, *ib.* 25 init. ; skirmish with the Athenians in the harbour, *ib.* med.; send envoys to the Sicilian cities, *ib.* fin.; more Sicilian reinforcements arrive, *ib.* 33 init. ; the Syracusans rebuild their fleet, adopting the Corinthian invention of flatter and stronger prows, *ib.* 36 ; fight an indecisive engagement, *ib.* 38 ; renew the attack suddenly the next day, and gain a complete victory, *ib.* 39-41 ; become filled with confidence, *ib.* 41 fin.; their spirits are dashed by the arrival of Demosthenes, *ib.* 42 init. ; defeat the Athenians in a night engagement on Epipolae, *ib.* 43-45 ; a party among them willing to surrender, *ib.* 48 init., 49 init., 73 fin., 86 med.; the Syracusans attack the Athenians by sea and land, *ib.* 51-54 ; encouraged by their success, *ib.* 56; the Syracusan allies enumerated, *ib.* 58; close the mouth of the harbour, *ib.* 59; prepare for a final struggle at sea, *ib.* 65 ; win a complete victory, *ib.* 70-71 ; prevent the retreat of the Athenians and force them to surrender, *ib.* 78-85 ; kill Nicias and Demosthenes, *ib.* 86 init. ; cruelly treat their prisoners, *ib.* 87 ; send a fleet under Hermocrates to Asia, viii. 26 init., 35 init.; distinguish themselves in the capture of Iasos, *ib.* 28 med. ; their sailors mostly freemen, *ib.* 84 init. ; their boldness in demanding full pay of Tissaphernes, *ib.* 45 med., 78 fin., 84 init. ; change their commanders and banish Hermo-

Syracuse (*cont.*)—
crates, *ib.* 85 fin.; take part in the battle of Cynossema, *ib.* 104-106.

T.

Taenarus, promontory of, vii. 19 med. ; temple of Poseidon at, i. 128 init., 133 init. ; the ' curse of Taenarus,' *ib.* 128 init.

Tamos, a Persian, lieutenant of Tissaphernes, viii. 31 med., 87.

Tanagra, defeat of the Athenians there, 107 fin., 108 init.; its walls razed by the Athenians, *ib.* 108 med.; the Tanagraeans are defeated by the Athenians, iii. 91 fin. ; the Boeotians gather at Tanagra before the battle of Delium, iv. 91 init.; the Tanagraeans on the left wing at Delium, *ib.* 93 fin. ; the Boeotians retire to Tanagra after Delium, *ib.* 97 init.; the territory of Tanagra ravaged by Thracians under Diitrephes, vii. 29 init.

Tantalus, a Lacedaemonian, governor of Thyrea, iv. 57.

Tarentum, vi. 34 med., 104 med., vii. 1 init.; hostile to the Athenian expedition to Sicily, vi. 44 med. ; ships from Tarentum join the Lacedaemonian fleet intended for Euboea, viii. 91 med.

Taulantians, an Illyrian race, near Epidamnus, i. 24 init.

Taurus, a Lacedaemonian, swears to the one year's Truce, iv. 119 init.

Tax, property, of two hundred talents at Athens, iii. 19 ; of 5 per cent. on the produce of the soil imposed by the Pisistratidae, vi. 54 med. ; on imports by the Athenians, vii. 28 fin.

Tegea, in Arcadia, constantly at war with Mantinea, v. 65 med. ; the Tegeans fight with the Mantineans, iv. 134 ; refuse to join the Argive alliance, v. 32 init.; take part in the Lacedaemonian expedition against Argos, *ib.* 57 med. ; the Argive confederacy prepare to attack Tegea, *ib.* 62 ; the Lacedaemonians occupy Tegea, *ib.* 64 med. ; the Tegeans fight on the right wing at Mantinea, *ib.* 67-74 ; the Lacedaemonian dead buried at Tegea, *ib.* 74 med. ; the Lacedaemonian reinforcements do not proceed beyond Tegea, *ib.* 75 init. ; the Lacedaemonians march thither in order to make terms with the Argives, *ib.* 76 init., 78; the Lacedaemonians march to support the oligarchy at Argos, but turn back at Tegea, *ib.* 82 init.

Teichium, in Aetolia, iii. 96 med.

Teichiussa, in Milesian territory, viii. 26 med., 28 init.

Tellias, a Syracusan general, vi. 103 fin.

Tellis, a Lacedaemonian, father of Brasidas, ii. 25 init., iii. 69 med.; iv. 70 init. ; swears to the Treaty of Peace and the Alliance, v. 19 med., 24 init.

Temenidae, ancestors of the Macedonian kings, ii. 99 init.

Temenites, part of Syracuse, vii. 3 med. ; shrine of Apollo Temenites, vi. 75 init., 99 fin., 100 fin.

Temple, *see* under the various deities.

Temple of Zeus, a place between Lebedus and Colophon, viii. 19 med.

Tenedos, founded from Boeotia, vii. 57 med. ; tributary to Athens, *ib.*; the inhabitants warn the Athenians of the Lesbian revolt, iii. 2 init. ; the Athenians place their Mytilenaean prisoners there for a time, *ib.* 28 fin., 35.

Tenos, one of the Cyclades ; the Tenians tributary to Athens, vii. 57 init. ; Tenians in the service

Tenos (*cont.*)—
of the oligarchs at Athens, viii. 69 med.

Teos, iii. 32 init. ; revolts from Athens, viii. 16, 19 fin. ; the Teians agree with the Athenians, and promise neutrality, *ib.* 20 fin.

Teres, the great Odrysian king, father of Sitalces, ii. 29 init., 67 init., 95 init. ; not the same as the Tereus of mythology, *ib.* 29 init.

Tereus, the ancient Thracian king, ii. 29 init.

Terias, a river in Sicily, vi. 50 med., 94 init.

Terinaean Gulf, in southern Italy, vi. 104 med.

Terror, the reign of, at Athens, viii. 66.

Tesseracosts, a Chian coin, viii. 101 init.

Teutiaplus, an Elean, his speech, iii. 30.

Teutlussa, an island near Rhodes, viii. 42 fin.

Thapsus, near Syracuse, founded from Megara by Lamis, vi. 4 init. ; peninsula of, *ib.* 97 init., 99 fin., 101 med., 102 fin., vii. 49 med.

Tharypas, king of the Molossians, ii. 80 fin.

Thasos, a Parian colony, iv. 104 fin. ; mother city of Galepsus and Oesymè, *ib.* 107 fin., v. 6 init.; revolts from the Athenians, i. 100 med. [cp. viii. 64 med.] ; asks the Lacedaemonians to invade Attica, i. 101 init. ; surrenders, *ib.* fin. ; Thucydides at Thasos, iv. 104 fin., 105 init. ; the Thasians have their government changed by the oligarchical conspirators at Samos, *ib.* 64 init. ; prepare to revolt, *ib.*

Theaenetus, a Plataean diviner, suggests the plan for breaking out of Plataea, iii. 20 init.

Theagenes, tyrant of Megara, father-in-law of Cylon, i. 126 init.

Theagenes, an Athenian, chosen with Cleon as Commissioner to Sphacteria, iv. 27 med. ; swears to the Treaty of Peace and the Alliance, v. 19 fin., 24 med.

Theatre of Dionysus, near Munychia, viii. 93 init.

Thebes, once allied to Persia, i. 90 med., iii. 56 med., 58 fin., 59, 62 ; its hostility to Plataea, ii. 71 med., 72 med., iii. 55 init., 57 med., 58 init., 59 med. ; Theban Boeotarchs, iv. 91 med. ; the Thebans furnish the Corinthians with money for the expedition against Epidamnus, i. 27 fin. ; surprise Plataea in time of peace, ii. 2, iii. 56 init., vii. 18 med. ; are defeated, ii. 3 ; surrender, *ib.* 4 ; send reinforcements, *ib.* 5 init. ; come to terms, *ib.* fin. ; their speech against the Plataeans, iii. 61–67 ; their treatment of Plataea, *ib.* 68 fin. ; defeated by the Athenians at Tanagra, *ib.* 91 fin. ; a Theban exile, Ptoeodorus, plots with the Athenians to betray Boeotia, iv. 76 init. ; the Thebans on the right wing at Delium, *ib.* 93 fin.; their formation there, *ib.*; they dismantle the walls of Thespiae, *ib.* 133 init. ; suppress a rising at Thespiae, vi. 95 fin. ; send aid to Syracuse, vii. 19 med. ; drive the Thracians to their ships after the sack of Mycalessus, *ib.* 30.

Themistocles, founder of the naval power of Athens, i. 14 fin., 93 ; the victor at Salamis, *ib.* 74 init. [cp. *ib.* 137 fin.]; honours paid to him by the Lacedaemonians, *ib.* 74 init., 91 init. ; outwits the Lacedaemonians, *ib.* 90, 91 ; builds the Piraeus, *ib.* 93 ; ostra-

Themistocles (*cont.*)—
cised, *ib.* 135 init. ; implicated in the plot of Pausanias, *ib.* ; takes refuge with Admetus, *ib.* 136; flees to Ephesus, *ib.* 137 init. ; goes to the Persian court, *ib.* 138; dies, *ib.* fin. ; said to have been buried in Attica, *ib.* ; his character, *ib.* med.

Theodorus, father of Procles, an Athenian, iii. 91 init.

Theolytus, father of Cynes[tyrant?] of Coronta, ii. 102 init.

Theori, a magistracy at Mantinea, v. 47 fin. ; Alcibiades as Θεωρός of Athens at Olympia, vi. 16 init.; the Athenians send Theori to the Isthmian Games, viii. 10 init. ; Sicilian Theori before sailing sacrifice to Apollo at Naxos, vi. 3 init.

Thera, one of the Cyclades, not allied to the Athenians, ii. 9 fin.

Theramenes, an Athenian, a chief leader in the oligarchical revolution at Athens, viii. 68 fin. ; begins with others to form a moderate party within the oligarchy, *ib.* 89, 90 med., 91 ; instigates the soldiers to destroy the fort Eetionea, *ib.* 92, 94 init.

Theramenes, a Lacedaemonian commander, brings reinforcements to Astyochus, viii. 26 init., 29 med. ; persuaded by Alcibiades to go to the relief of Miletus, *ib.* 26 fin., 27 init., 28 init. ; negotiates a treaty with the King, *ib.* 36, 37, 43 med.; lost at sea, *ib.* 38 init.

Thermè, in Macedonia, taken by the Athenians, i. 61 med. ; restored to Perdiccas, ii. 29 fin.

Thermon, a Spartan, sent by Agis to Piraeum, viii. 11 med.

Thermopylae, ii. 101 init., iii. 92 fin. ; battle of Thermopylae compared to that of Sphacteria, iv. 36 fin.

Theseus, unites the Attic communes into one city, ii. 15 init. ; temple of, at Athens, vi. 61 med.

Thespiae, in Boeotia, iv. 76 init. ; the Thespians on the left wing at Delium, *ib.* 93 fin. ; suffer severe loss, *ib.* 96 med., 133 init. ; have their walls dismantled by the Thebans, *ib.* 133 init. ; popular revolution there, quelled by the Thebans, vi. 95 fin. ; the Thespians send aid to Syracuse, vii. 19 init., 25 med.

Thesprotia, i 30 fin., 46 med., 50 med. ; the Thesprotians have no king, ii. 80 fin.

Thessaly, its early history, i. 12 med. ; once held by the Persians, viii. 43 fin. ; forms alliance with the Athenians, i. 102 fin. [cp. *ib.* 107 fin., iv. 78 med.]; the Thessalians desert from the Athenians at Tanagra, i. 107 fin. ; assist the Athenians in the first invasion of Attica, ii. 22 med.; take alarm at the expedition of Sitalces, *ib.* 101 med. ; make war on Heraclea, iii. 93 med. ; some of the leading Thessalians escort Brasidas through Thessaly, iv. 78; the Thessalians refuse Rhamphias and the Peloponnesians passage, v. 13 ; certain Thessalians aid in a defeat of the Heracleans, *ib.* 51 init.; the Thessalians angry with Agis for extorting money from the Achaeans of Phthia, viii. 3 med.

Thessalus, brother of Hippias, i. 20 med., vi. 55 init.

Thoricus, in Attica, viii. 95 init.

Thousand Argives, the, a select force trained at the expense of the state, v. 67 fin., 72 med., 73 fin.

Thrace, European, divided among various tribes : Agrianians, ii. 96 med. ; Dersaeans, *b.* 101 med. ;

Thrace (*cont.*)—

Dii, *ib.* 96 med., 98 fin., vii. 27 init. ; Droans, ii. 101 med. ; Edonians, i. 100 fin., ii. 99 med., iv. 102 med., 107 fin., 109 fin , v. 6 fin. ; Getae, ii. 96 init., 98 fin.; Graaeans, *ib.* 96 fin. ; Laeaeans, *ib.* 96 med. ; Maedi, *ib.* 98 med.; Odomantians,*ib.*101 med.; Odrysians, *ib.* 29, 96 init., 97, 98 fin., 101 med. ; Paeonians, *ib.* 96 fin., 98 med. ; Panaeans, *ib.* 101 med.; Sinti, *ib.* 98 med. ; Tilataeans, *ib.* 96 fin. ; Treres, *ib.* 96 fin. ; Triballi, *ib.* 96 fin , iv. 101 fin. ; — gold mines in Thrace, i. 100 med., iv. 105 init. ;—the Thracians prefer receiving to giving, ii. 97 med. ; uncivilized, *ib.* fin. ; their ferocity, vii. 30 fin.; once inhabited Phocis, ii. 29 init. ; destroy the Athenian colonists at Ennea Hodoi, i. 100 fin., iv. 102 med. ; march, under the leadership of Sitalces, against Perdiccas, ii. 95-101. [*See* Odrysians, Perdiccas, Sitalces.] Thracian mercenaries in Athenian service at Mendè, iv. 129 init. ; the Thracians are asked for aid by Cleon at Amphipolis, v. 6 init. ; the Edonian and Myrcinian Thracians serve under Brasidas, *ib.* fin., 10 fin.; Thracian mercenaries sent home from Athens sack Mycalessus, vii. 27 init., 30.

Thracians, the Bithynian, in Asia, iv. 75 fin.

Thrasybulus, an Athenian, one of the steadiest opponents of the oligarchs at Athens, viii. 73 med.; persuades the army and the Samians to swear allegiance to the democracy, *ib.* 75 ; appointed general with Thrasyllus, *ib.* 76 init. ; procures the restoration of Alcibiades, *ib.* 81 init. ; sails to Eresus which had revolted, *ib.*

100 fin. ; aids Thrasyllus at Cynossema, *ib.* 104, 105.

Thrasycles, an Athenian, swears to the Treaty of Peace and the Alliance, v. 19 fin., 24 med. ; sent with twelve ships to Chios, viii. 15 med., 17 fin., 19 med.

Thrasyllus, one of the steadiest opponents of the oligarchs at Athens, viii. 73 med. ; persuades the army and the Samians to swear allegiance to the democracy, *ib.* 75 ; appointed general with Thrasybulus, *ib.* 76 init.; follows Mindarus to Chios, *ib.* 100 init. ; sets about besieging Eresus, *ib.* 100 fin., 103 init. ; pursues Mindarus to the Hellespont, *ib.* med. ; defeats him off Cynossema, *ib.* 104, 105.

Thrasyllus, an Argive general, makes terms with Agis, v. 59 fin., 60 init. ; attacked by the Argives, *ib.* 60 fin.

Thrasymelidas, a Spartan, admiral in command at Pylos, iv. 11 init.

Thria, in Attica, i. 114 fin., ii. 19 med., 20 init., 21 init.

Thronium, in Locris, ii. 26.

Thucles, the founder of Naxos in Sicily, vi. 3 init. ; of Leontini and Catana, *ib.* fin.

Thucles, father of Eurymedon, an Athenian, iii. 80 fin., 91 med., vii. 16 fin.

Thucydides, motives for writing his history, i. 1 ; its truthfulness, *ib.* 21-23, v. 26 fin. ; the speeches only generally accurate, i. 22 init.; his reasons for describing the period between the Persian and Peloponnesian Wars, *ib.* 97 ; reason for reckoning his history by summers and winters, v. 20 ; attacked by the plague, ii. 48 fin. ; appointed general on coast of Thrace, iv. 104 fin. ; a leading man in Thrace, *ib.* 105 init. ;

Thucydides (*cont.*)—

fails to save Amphipolis, *ib.* 106 fin. ; repulses Brasidas from Eion, *ib.* 107 init. ; exiled, v. 26 fin. ; lived throughout the war,*ib.*

Thucydides, an Athenian commander at Samos, i. 117 med.

Thucydides, of Pharsalus, proxenus of Athens, viii. 92 med. ; helps to prevent the panic after the destruction of Eetionea, *ib.*

Thunder-storm, effect of, on armies, vi. 70 init., vii. 79 med.

Thuria, in Laconia, Perioeci of, i. 101 init.

Thurii, in Italy, Alcibiades conceals himself there, vi. 61 fin., 88 fin., the Thurians refuse to receive Gylippus, *ib.* 104 med. ; expel an anti-Athenian party, vii. 33 fin., 35 init., 57 fin. ; send ships to the Peloponnesians in Asia, viii. 35 init., 61 med. ; the sailors mostly freemen, *ib.* 84 init. ; their boldness in demanding full pay from Tissaphernes, *ib.* 78 fin., 84 init.

Thyamis, a river on the borders of Thesprotia, i. 46 fin.

Thyamus, Mount, in Aetolia, iii. 106 fin.

Thymochares, an Athenian commander, viii. 95 init.

Thyrea, in Laconia, given to the Aeginetans by the Lacedaemonians, ii. 27 med., iv. 56 fin.; captured by the Athenians, iv. 57 ; the Argives in their treaty with Lacedaemon insert a stipulation that they and the Lacedaemonians should fight for Thyrea, v. 41 med. ; the district of Thyrea invaded by the Argives, vi. 95.

Thyssus, in Athos, iv. 109 med. ; allied with the Athenians, v. 35 init. ; captured by the Dictidians, *ib.*

Tilataeans, a Thracian tribe, ii. 96 fin.

Timagoras, a Cyzicene exile at the court of Pharnabazus, viii. 6 init.; goes as envoy to Sparta, *ib.*, *ib.* 8 init., 39 init.

Timagoras, a Tegean ambassador to Persia, ii. 67.

Timanor, a Corinthian commander, i. 29 init.

Timanthes, father of Timanor, a Corinthian, i. 29 init.

Timocrates, an Athenian, father of Aristoteles, iii. 105 fin. ; swears to the Treaty of Peace and the Alliance, v. 19 fin., 24 med.

Timocrates, a Spartan, sent out as adviser to Cnemus, ii. 85 init. ; kills himself, *ib.* 93 med.

Timocrates, father of Timoxenus, a Corinthian, ii. 33 init.

Timoxenus, a Corinthian commander, ii 33 init.

Tisamenus, a Trachinian, envoy to Sparta, iii. 92 init.

Tisander, an Aetolian, envoy to Sparta, iii. 100 init.

Tisias, an Athenian general at Melos, v. 84 fin.

Tisimachus, father of Tisias, an Athenian, v. 84 fin.

Tissaphernes, governor of the provinces on the coast of Asia, viii. 5 init. ; sends an envoy to ask the aid of Sparta, *ib.*; negotiates a treaty between Sparta and the King, *ib.* 17 fin., 18 ; demolishes a fort at Teos, *ib.* 20 fin. ; present at an engagement before Miletus, *ib.* 25 init. ; persuades the Peloponnesians to attack Iasus, *ib.* 28 init. ; reduces the pay of the Peloponnesian fleet, *ib.* 29 ; causes Cnidus to revolt, *ib.* 35 init. (cp. *ib.* 109) ; makes a second treaty with the Lacedaemonians, *ib.* 37 ; enraged at Lichas for objecting to the treaties with the King, *ib.* 43 fin. ; instructed by Alcibiades to balance the contending parties,

Tissaphernes (*cont.*)—
ib. 45 46 [cp. *ib.* 87] ; persuaded by Alcibiades to offer impossible terms to Peisander, *ib.* 56; makes a third treaty with the Lacedaemonians, *ib.* 57, 58 ; now shows himself more ready to fulfil his engagements, *ib.* 59 ; his dilatory conduct, *ib.* 78, 80 init.; becomes more and more hateful to the Lacedaemonian fleet, *ib.* 83 ; puts a garrison in Miletus, which the Milesians drive out, *ib.* 84 med. ; sends an envoy to Sparta, *ib.* 85 init.; his malignity against Hermocrates, *ib.* fin. ; goes to fetch the Phoenician ships, *ib.* 87; why he did not bring them, *ib.* ; marches towards Ionia, viii. 108 med. ; starts for the Hellespont to remonstrate with the Lacedaemonians, *ib.* 109; goes to Ephesus and offers sacrifice to Artemis, *ib.* fin.

Tlepolemus, an Athenian commander at Samos, i. 117 med.

Tolmaeus, (i) father of Tolmides, an Athenian, i. 108 fin., 113 init.; (ii) another, father of Autocles, iv. 53 init., 119 fin.

Tolmides, an Athenian, commands an expedition round Peloponnesus, i. 108 fin. ; defeated at Coronea, *ib.* 113.

Tolmides, father of Theaenetus, a Plataean, iii. 20 init.

Tolophonians, an Ozolian Locrian tribe, iii. 101 fin.

Tolophus, an Aetolian, ambassador to Corinth, iii. 100 init.

Tomeus, Mount, near Pylos, iv. 118, § iii.

Toronè, in Chalcidicè, iv. 120 med., 122 init., 129 init. ; captured by Brasidas, iv. 110–114 ; entrusted by him to Pasitelidas, *ib.* 132 fin.; retaken by the Athenians, v. 2, 3 ; provision respecting, in the

treaty between Athens and Lacedaemon, *ib.* 18, § x.

Torylaus, a friend of Brasidas in Thessaly, iv. 78 init.

Trachinians, one of the Malian tribes, iii. 92 init. [*See* Heraclea.]

Trade, no trade in ancient Hellas, i. 2 init. ; ancient trade chiefly by land, *ib.* 13 med. ; trade between maritime and inland places, i. 120 med. ; trade in corn at Athens, viii. 4 init. [cp. vi. 20 fin.] ; trade between Egypt and Athens, viii. 35 med. ; between Africa and Peloponnesus, iv. 53 fin.

Tradition, Peloponnesian traditions, i. 9 init. ; ancient traditions too readily received, *ib.* 20 init.

Tragia, an island off Samos, Athenian victory there, i. 116 med.

Treasury of the Athenian confederacy originally at Delos, i. 96 ; contents of the Athenian treasury in the Acropolis, ii. 13 med. ; treasuries of Delphi and Olympia, i. 121 med., 143 init.

Treaties, *see* Peace.

Treres, a Thracian tribe, ii. 96 fin.

Triballi, a Thracian tribe, ii. 96 fin., iv. 101 fin.

Tribute of the Athenian allies, its amount, i. 96 fin., ii. 13 med. ; its first imposition, i. 96 init. ; its amount as fixed in the time of Aristides, v. 18, § vi ; changed to a duty of 5 per cent., vii. 28 fin. ;—tribute collected in the Odrysian Empire, ii. 97 med.

Trierarchs, at Athens, vi. 31 init., vii. 69 init., 70 fin.

Trinacria, the ancient name of Sicily, vi. 2 init.

Triopium, promontory near Cnidus, viii. 35, 60 fin. ; temple of Apollo there, *ib.* 35 med.

Tripod, at Delphi, dedicated as a memorial of the Persian War, i. 132 med., iii. 57 med.

Tripodiscus, in Megara, iv. 70.

Triremes, first built at Corinth, i. 13 init. [*See* Ships.]

Tritaeans, an Ozolian Locrian tribe, iii. 101 fin.

Troezen, in Peloponnesus, restored by the Athenians under the Thirty Years' Peace, i. 115 init.; the Troezenians furnish a convoy to Corinth, *ib.* 27 fin. ; the territory of Troezen ravaged by the Athenians, ii. 56 fin. ; Cleon persuades the Athenians to demand the restitution of Troezen, iv. 21 fin. ; the Athenians seize Methone and ravage the territory of Troezen, *ib.* 45 [cp. *ib.* 118, § iii] ; the Troezenians furnish the Lacedaemonians with ships, viii. 3 fin.

Trogilus, near Syracuse, vi. 99 init., vii. 2 fin.

Trojan, colonists in Sicily, vi. 2 med. ; took, together with the Sicanians, the name of Elymi, *ib.*

Trotilus, founded from Megara by Lamis, vi. 4 init.

Troy, *see* War, Trojan.

Truce, for a year between the Lacedaemonians and Athenians, iv. 117–119 ; with ten days' notice, between the Athenians and the Boeotians, v. 26 med., 32 med. ; between the Athenians and the Chalcidians, vi. 7 fin. [cp. *ib.* 10 med.]

Truth, little sought after by mankind, i. 20 fin. [cp. vi. 54 init.]; pains taken by Thucydides to ascertain the truth, i. 22, v. 25 fin.

Twelve Gods, altar of the, in the Athenian Agora, vi. 54 fin.

Tydeus, a Chian, executed on a charge of conspiracy with the Athenians, viii. 38 med.

Tyndareus, the oath of the suitors of Helen to him, i. 9 init.

Tyrannies, rise of, in Hellas, i. 13 init. ; the Sicilian tyrants, *ib.* 14 med., 17, 18 init. ; policy of the early tyrants, *ib.* 17 ; the tyrants overthrown by the Lacedaemonians, *ib.* 18 init., vi. 53 fin., 59 fin.

Tyrants, Anaxilas of Rhegium, vi. 4 fin. ; Evarchus of Astacus, ii. 30 med., 33 init. ; Hippocles of Lampsacus, vi. 59 med. ; Hippocrates of Gela, *ib.* 5 fin. ; the Pisistratidae at Athens, i. 20, vi. 53 fin.–59 ; Polycrates of Samos, i. 13 fin., iii. 104 med.

Tyrrhenia [Etruria], the Tyrrhenians friendly to Athens, vi. 88 med. ; send the Athenians aid, *ib.* 103 med., vii. 53, 54, 57 fin.

Tyrrhenian Gulf, vi. 62 init., vii. 58 init. ;—Sea, iv. 24 fin.

Tyrrhenians, the old Pelasgian inhabitants of Lemnos and Athens, iv. 109 fin.

V.

Vengeance, the vengeance which follows closest upon a wrong the most adequate, iii. 38 init. ; sweetness of vengeance, ii. 42 fin., iii. 40 fin., vii. 68 init.

Vote, vulgar error that the kings of Lacedaemon have two votes, i. 20 fin.

W.

Walls, the Long Walls [of Athens], i. 69 init., 107 init., 108 med., ii. 13 fin. ; [of Megara], built by the Athenians, i. 103 fin. ; razed by the Megarians, iv. 109 init. ; [of Patrae], v. 52 fin. ; [of Argos], *ib.* 82 ; destroyed by the Lacedaemonians, *ib.* 83 init. ; the Walls of Athens, *ib.* 90–93 ; of the Piraeus, *ib.* 93, ii. 13 fin. ; of Phalerum, ii. 13 fin.

War, Peloponnesian, continues, without a break, ten years to the Treaty of Peace, v. 20 ; its length and greatness, i. 23 ; its causes, *ib.* fin., 55 fin., 56-66, 146 ; state of feeling before, *ib.* 66 med., ii. 8, 11 init., vii. 28 med. ; reasons of the Lacedaemonians for entering upon, i. 23 fin., 88 ; preparations and allies of either side, ii. 7-9 ; actual commencement of the War, i. 118 init., ii. 1 ; cp. v. 20 init. ; lasted 27 years, as foretold by an oracle, v. 26.

> End of 1st year, ii. 47 init.
> ,,   2nd ,, ,, 70 fin.
> ,,   3rd ,, ,, 103 fin.
> ,,   4th ,, iii. 25 fin.
> ,,   5th ,, ,, 88 fin.
> ,,   6th ,, ,, 116 fin.
> ,,   7th ,. iv. 51 fin.
> ,,   8th ,, ,, 116 fin.
> ,,   9th ,, ,, 135.
> ,,   10th ,, v. 20 init.
> ,,   11th ,, ,, 39 fin.
> ,,   12th ,, ,, 51 fin.
> ,,   13th ,, ,, 56 fin.
> ,,   14th ,, ,, 81 fin.
> ,,   15th ,, ,, 83 fin.
> ,,   16th ,, vi. 7 fin.
> ,,   17th ,, ,, 93 fin.
> ,,   18th ,, vii. 18 fin.
> ,,   19th ,, viii. 6 fin.
> ,,   20th ,, ,, 60 fin.
> ,,   21st ,, ,, 109 fin.

War, the Persian, i. 14 med., 18 fin., 23 init., 41 init., 69 med., 73, 74, 89, 90 init., 93 fin., 95 fin., 97, 142 med., vi. 82 init., viii. 24 med. ; events of—Marathon, i. 18 med., vi. 59 fin. ; Thermopylae, iv. 36 fin. ; Artemisium, iii. 54 med. ; Salamis, i. 73 fin., 137 fin. ; Mycalè, i. 89 init. ; Plataea, *ib.* 130 init., iii. 54 med., 58 med. ; capture of Byzantium, i. 128 med. ; of Eion, Scyros, Naxos, *ib.* 98 ; battle of the Eurymedon, *ib.* 100 init. ; Persian occupation of Sestos alluded to in viii. 62 fin. ; dedication of the tripod at Delphi, i. 132 med., iii. 57 med. ; its object principally the destruction of Athens, vi. 33 fin.

War, the Sacred, i. 112 fin.

War, Trojan, first common action of Hellas, i. 3 init. and fin. ; not equal to more modern wars, *ib.* 9-11 ; reason of its length, *ib.* 11 ; changes in Hellas after the return from Troy, *ib.* 12 [cp. ii. 68 init.]

War, maxims of, 'war a matter of money,' i. 83 ; 'war waits for no man,' *ib.* 142 init. ; 'the battle not always to the strong,' ii. 11 med., 89 med., v. 102 ; necessity of discipline, ii. 11 fin. ; courage is fortified by justifiable contempt, *ib.* 62 fin.; 'victory on the side of the greatest battalions,' *ib.* 87 fin. ; much to be learned from mistakes, *ib.* ; a good general is never off his guard, iii. 30 fin., v. 9 init. ; when danger has to be faced reflection is useless, iv. 10 init. ; war much a matter of chance, i. 78 init., 120 fin., iv. 18 med., vii. 61 fin. ; importance of reinforcements brought up at the right time, v. 9 med. ; 'find out an enemy's weak points,' iv. 126 med., vi. 91 fin. ;—deterioration of character caused by war, iii. 82 init. ; its inscrutable nature, i. 78 init. ; no experienced man believes that war is a good or safe thing, *ib.* 80 init. ; wars are supported out of accumulated wealth, not out of forced contributions, *ib.* 141 med. ; misery of war, iv. 59 init.

Weak, the, must go to the wall, v. 89 fin.

'Wells,' the, in Acarnania, iii. 105 init., 106 fin.

Women, the glory of woman to restrain her weakness, and avoid both praise and blame, ii. 45 fin. ; take part in war, ii. 4 init. med., iii. 74 init.

X.

Xanthippus, father of Pericles, an Athenian, i. 111 med., i. 127 init.

Xenares, (1) Ephor at Sparta, v. 36 init., 46 fin. ; favours the war party, *ib.* 36 med. ; negotiates with the Boeotians and Corinthians, *ib.* 36-38 : (ii) another, the Lacedaemonian governor of Heraclea, v. 51 fin. ; slain in battle, *ib.*

Xenocleides, a Corinthian commander, i. 46 init., iii. 114 fin.

Xenon, a Theban commander at Syracuse, vii. 19 med.

Xenophanes, father of Lamachus, an Athenian, vi. 8 med.

Xenophantidas, a Lacedaemonian, viii. 55 med.

Xenophon, an Athenian commander at Potidaea, ii. 70 init. ; in Chalcidicè, *ib.* 79.

Xenotimus, father of Carcinus, an Athenian, ii. 23 med.

Xerxes, king of Persia, father of Artaxerxes, i. 137 med., iv. 50 fin. ; his expedition against Hellas, i. 14 med., 118 init., iii. 56 med. ; warned by Themistocles after Salamis, i. 137 fin. ; his letter to Pausanias, *ib.* 129.

Z.

Zacynthus, an island opposite Elis, an Achaean colony, ii. 66 ; its importance to the Athenians, *ib.* 7 fin., 80 init. ; the Zacynthians assist the Corcyraeans, i. 47 ; become the allies of Athens, ii. 7 fin., 9 med., 66, iv. 8 init., 13 med., vii. 57 med. ; Zacynthus is ravaged by the Lacedaemonians, ii. 66 ; the Zacynthians furnish Demosthenes with troops for service in Sicily, vii. 31 init., 57 med.

Zanclè : Messenè in Sicily originally so called from the Sicel word for a sickle, vi. 4 fin. [*See* Messenè.]

Zeus, Ithomean, i. 103 med. ; 'the Gracious,' *ib.* 126 med. ; the 'God of Freedom,' ii. 71 init. ; Olympian, iii. 14 init., v. 31 init. ; Nemean, iii. 96 init. ; Lycaean, v. 16 fin. ; temples of Zeus, at Athens, ii. 15 med. ; Corcyra, iii. 70 med. ; Mount Lycaeum, v. 16 fin. ; between Lebedus and Colophon, viii. 19 med. ; Mantinea, v. 47 fin. ; Olympia, iii. 14 init., v. 50 init. ; Syracuse, vi. 64 med., 65 fin., 70 init., 70 fin., 75 init., vii. 4 fin., 37 fin., 42 fin.

Zeuxidamus, father of Archidamus the Lacedaemonian king, ii. 19 med., 47 init., iii. 1 init.

Zeuxidas, a Lacedaemonian, swears to the Treaty of Peace and the Alliance, v. 19 med., 24 init.

Zopyrus, father of Megabyzus, a Persian, i. 109 med.

GREAT BOOKS IN PHILOSOPHY PAPERBACK SERIES

ETHICS

Aristotle—*The Nicomachean Ethics*	$8.95
Marcus Aurelius—*Meditations*	5.95
Jeremy Bentham—*The Principles of Morals and Legislation*	8.95
John Dewey—*The Moral Writings of John Dewey, Revised Edition* (edited by James Gouinlock)	11.95
Epictetus—*Enchiridion*	4.95
Immanuel Kant—*Fundamental Principles of the Metaphysic of Morals*	5.95
John Stuart Mill—*Utilitarianism*	5.95
George Edward Moore—*Principia Ethica*	8.95
Friedrich Nietzsche—*Beyond Good and Evil*	8.95
Plato—*Protagoras, Philebus,* and *Gorgias*	7.95
Bertrand Russell—*Bertrand Russell On Ethics, Sex, and Marriage* (edited by Al Seckel)	19.95
Arthur Schopenhauer—*The Wisdom of Life* and *Counsels and Maxims*	7.95
Benedict de Spinoza—*Ethics* and *The Improvement of the Understanding*	9.95

SOCIAL AND POLITICAL PHILOSOPHY

Aristotle—*The Politics*	7.95
Francis Bacon—*Essays*	6.95
Mikhail Bakunin—*The Basic Bakunin: Writings, 1869–1871* (translated and edited by Robert M. Cutler)	11.95
Edmund Burke—*Reflections on the Revolution in France*	7.95
John Dewey—*Freedom and Culture*	10.95
G. W. F. Hegel—*The Philosophy of History*	9.95
G. W. F. Hegel—*Philosophy of Right*	9.95
Thomas Hobbes—*The Leviathan*	7.95
Sidney Hook—*Paradoxes of Freedom*	9.95
Sidney Hook—*Reason, Social Myths, and Democracy*	11.95
John Locke—*Second Treatise on Civil Government*	5.95
Niccolo Machiavelli—*The Prince*	5.95
Karl Marx—*The Poverty of Philosophy*	7.95
Karl Marx/Frederick Engels—*The Economic and Philosophic Manuscripts of 1844* and *The Communist Manifesto*	6.95
John Stuart Mill—*Considerations on Representative Government*	6.95
John Stuart Mill—*On Liberty*	5.95
John Stuart Mill—*On Socialism*	7.95
John Stuart Mill—*The Subjection of Women*	5.95
Friedrich Nietzsche—*Thus Spake Zarathustra*	9.95
Thomas Paine—*Common Sense*	6.95
Thomas Paine—*Rights of Man*	7.95
Plato—*Lysis, Phaedrus,* and *Symposium*	6.95
Plato—*The Republic*	9.95
Jean-Jacques Rousseau—*The Social Contract*	5.95
Mary Wollstonecraft—*A Vindication of the Rights of Men*	5.95
Mary Wollstonecraft—*A Vindication of the Rights of Women*	6.95

METAPHYSICS/EPISTEMOLOGY

Aristotle—*De Anima*	6.95
Aristotle—*The Metaphysics*	9.95
George Berkeley—*Three Dialogues Between Hylas and Philonous*	5.95
René Descartes—*Discourse on Method* and *The Meditations*	6.95
John Dewey—*How We Think*	10.95
John Dewey—*The Influence of Darwin on Philosophy and Other Essays*	11.95
Epicurus—*The Essential Epicurus: Letters, Principal Doctrines,*	
Vatican Sayings, and Fragments	
(translated, and with an introduction, by Eugene O'Connor)	5.95
Sidney Hook—*The Quest for Being*	11.95
David Hume—*An Enquiry Concerning Human Understanding*	6.95
David Hume—*Treatise of Human Nature*	9.95
William James—*The Meaning of Truth*	11.95
William James—*Pragmatism*	7.95
Immanuel Kant—*Critique of Practical Reason*	7.95
Immanuel Kant—*Critique of Pure Reason*	9.95
Gottfried Wilhelm Leibniz—*Discourse on Method* and the *Monadology*	6.95
John Locke—*An Essay Concerning Human Understanding*	9.95
Plato—*The Euthyphro, Apology, Crito, and Phaedo*	5.95
Bertrand Russell—*The Problems of Philosophy*	8.95
George Santayana—*The Life of Reason*	9.95
Sextus Empiricus—*Outlines of Pyrrhonism*	8.95

PHILOSOPHY OF RELIGION

Marcus Tullius Cicero—*The Nature of the Gods* and *On Divination*	6.95
Ludwig Feuerbach—*The Essence of Christianity*	8.95
David Hume—*Dialogues Concerning Natural Religion*	5.95
John Locke—*A Letter Concerning Toleration*	5.95
Lucretius—*On the Nature of Things*	7.95
John Stuart Mill—*Three Essays on Religion*	7.95
Thomas Paine—*The Age of Reason*	13.95
Bertrand Russell—*Bertrand Russell On God and Religion* (edited by Al Seckel)	19.95

ESTHETICS

Aristotle—*The Poetics*	5.95
Aristotle—*Treatise on Rhetoric*	7.95

GREAT MINDS PAPERBACK SERIES

ECONOMICS

Charlotte Perkins Gilman—*Women and Economics: A Study of the*	
Economic Relation between Women and Men	11.95
John Maynard Keynes—*The General Theory of Employment, Interest, and Money*	11.95
Alfred Marshall—*Principles of Economics*	11.95
David Ricardo—*Principles of Political Economy and Taxation*	10.95
Adam Smith—*Wealth of Nations*	9.95
Thorstein Veblen—*The Theory of the Leisure Class*	11.95

RELIGION

Thomas Henry Huxley—*Agnosticism and Christianity and Other Essays*	10.95
Ernest Renan—*The Life of Jesus*	11.95
Voltaire—*A Treatise on Toleration and Other Essays*	8.95

4811

SCIENCE

Nicolaus Copernicus—*On the Revolutions of Heavenly Spheres*	8.95
Charles Darwin—*The Descent of Man*	18.95
Charles Darwin—*The Origin of Species*	10.95
Albert Einstein—*Relativity*	8.95
Michael Faraday—*The Forces of Matter*	8.95
Galileo Galilei—*Dialogues Concerning Two New Sciences*	9.95
Ernst Haeckel—*The Riddle of the Universe*	11.95
William Harvey—*On the Motion of the Heart and Blood in Animals*	9.95
Julian Huxley—*Evolutionary Humanism*	10.95
Edward Jenner—*Vaccination against Smallpox*	5.95
Johannes Kepler—*Epitome of Copernican Astronomy* and *Harmonies of the World*	8.95
Isaac Newton—*The Principia*	14.95
Louis Pasteur and Joseph Lister—*Germ Theory and Its Application to Medicine* and *On the Antiseptic Principle of the Practice of Surgery*	7.95
Alfred Russel Wallace—*Island Life*	16.95

HISTORY

Edward Gibbon—*On Christianity*	9.95
Herodotus—*The History*	13.95
Thucydides—*History of the Peloponnesian War*	15.95
Andrew D. White—*A History of the Warfare of Science with Theology in Christendom*	19.95

SOCIOLOGY

Emile Durkheim—*Ethics and the Sociology of Morals* (translated with an introduction by Robert T. Hall)	8.95

CRITICAL ESSAYS

Desiderius Erasmus—*The Praise of Folly*	9.95
Jonathan Swift—*A Modest Proposal and Other Satires* (with an introduction by George R. Levine)	8.95
H. G. Wells—*The Conquest of Tme* (with an introduction by Martin Gardner)	8.95

(Prices subject to change without notice.)

ORDER FORM

Prometheus Books
59 John Glenn Drive • Amherst, New York 14228–2197
Telephone: (716) 691–0133

Phone Orders (24 hours):
Toll free (800) 421–0351 • FAX (716) 691–0137
Email: PBooks6205@aol.com

Ship to: _____

Address _____

_____

City _____

County (*N.Y. State Only*) _____

Telephone _____

Prometheus Acct. # _____

❑ Payment enclosed (or)

Charge to ❑ VISA ❑ MasterCard

A/C: ⬜⬜⬜⬜⬜⬜⬜⬜⬜⬜⬜⬜⬜⬜⬜⬜⬜⬜⬜

Exp. Date _____ / _____

Signature _____